Praise for Sigmund Freud's
The Interpretation of Dreams

"Freud's classic. Freud has been a dominant force in Western thinking and here's the book that started it all."
—*Psychology Today*

"[An] epoch-making book."
—*The Economist*

"Today, those practicing quicker therapies and psychopharmacology outnumber psychoanalysts, but Dr. Freud is indisputably with us, informing the very way we think about being human."
—*Life* magazine

"Freud's achievement was to give a name to the fears of his age."
—*New Statesman*

"At the beginning of our century, the publication of *The Interpretation of Dreams* changed our everyday perception of that essential component of human existence."
—*The Daily Mail*

"Sigmund Freud's *The Interpretation of Dreams* sold fewer than 400 copies in its first six years, but the fires it lit are still blazing."
—Brooke Gladstone, co-host and managing editor, NPR's *On the Media*

SIGMUND
FREUD
THE INTERPRETATION
OF DREAMS

SIGMUND
FREUD
THE INTERPRETATION
OF DREAMS

Translated from the German and edited by

James Strachey

Flectere si nequeo superos, Acheronta movebo

BASIC
BOOKS

A Member of the Perseus Books Group
New York

This complete and definitive text, translated and edited by James Strachey, was first published in the United States in 1955 by Basic Books, Inc. by arrangement with George Allen & Unwin Ltd. and The Hogarth Press, Ltd.

Translation copyright © 1955 by James Strachey.

This edition published by Basic Books in 2010.

Books published by Basic Books are available at special discounts for bulk purchases in the United States by corporations, institutions, and other organizations. For more information, please contact the Special Markets Department at the Perseus Books Group, 2300 Chestnut Street, Suite 200, Philadelphia, PA 19103, or call (800) 255-1514, or e-mail special.markets @perseusbooks.com.

Set in 10 point Adobe Garamond

Library of Congress Cataloging-in-Publication Data

Freud, Sigmund, 1856–1939.
    [Traumdeutung. English]
    The interpretation of dreams / Sigmund Freud ; translated from the German and edited by James Strachey.
        p. cm.
    "This complete and definitive text, translated and edited by James Strachey, was first published in the United States in 1955 by Basic Books."
    Includes bibliographical references and index.
    ISBN 978-0-465-01977-9 (alk. paper)
    1. Dreams. 2. Psychoanalysis. I. Strachey, James. II. Title.
BF1078.F72 2010
154.6'3—dc22   2009034599

LSC-C

Printing 12, 2021

CONTENTS

NOTE

The present edition is a reprint of that included in Vols. IV and V of the *Standard Edition*, London, 1953 (The Hogarth Press and The Institute of Psycho-Analysis). A few additional notes will be found on p. 623. The editor is deeply indebted to Miss Anna Freud for her unfailing help and criticism at every stage of the work.

EDITOR'S INTRODUCTION

(1)

BIBLIOGRAPHICAL

(a) GERMAN EDITIONS:

1900 *Die Traumdeutung.* Leipzig and Vienna: Franz Deuticke. Pp. iv + 375.

1909 2nd ed. (Enlarged and revised.) Same publishers. Pp. vi + 389.

1911 3rd ed. (Enlarged and revised.) Same publishers. Pp. x + 418.

1914 4th ed. (Enlarged and revised.) Same publishers. Pp. x + 498.

1919 5th ed. (Enlarged and revised.) Same publishers. Pp. ix + 474.

1921 6th ed. ⎱ (Reprints of 5th ed. except for new preface and revised
1922 7th ed. ⎰ bibliography.) Pp. vii + 478.

1925 Vol. II and part of Vol. III of Freud, *Gesammelte Schriften.* (Enlarged and revised.) Leipzig, Vienna and Zurich: Internationaler Psychoanalytischer Verlag. Pp. 543 and 1–185.

1930 8th ed. (Enlarged and revised.) Leipzig and Vienna: Franz Deuticke. Pp. x + 435.

1942 In Double Volume II & III of Freud, *Gesammelte Werke.* (Reprint of 8th ed.) London: Imago Publishing Co. Pp. xv and 1–642.

(b) ENGLISH TRANSLATIONS:

1913 By A. A. Brill. London: George Allen & Co.; New York: The Macmillan Co. Pp. xiii + 510.

1915 2nd ed. London: George Allen & Unwin; New York: The Macmillan Co. Pp. xiii + 510.

1932 3rd ed. (Completely revised and largely rewritten by various unspecified hands.) London: George Allen & Unwin; New York: The Macmillan Co. Pp. 600.

1938   In *The Basic Writings of Sigmund Freud*. Pp. 181–549. (Reprint of 3rd ed. with almost the whole of Chapter _ omitted.) New York: Random House.

The present, entirely new, translation is by James Strachey.

ACTUALLY *Die Traumdeutung* made its first appearance in 1899. The fact is mentioned by Freud at the beginning of his second paper on Josef Popper (1932*c*): 'It was in the winter of 1899 that my book on the interpretation of dreams (though its title-page was post-dated into the new century) at length lay before me. But we now have more precise information from his correspondence with Wilhelm Fliess (Freud, 1950*a*). In his letter of November 5, 1899 (Letter 123), Freud announces that 'yesterday at length the book appeared'; and from the preceding letter it seems that Freud himself had received two advance copies about a fortnight earlier, one of which he had sent to Fliess as a birthday present.

The Interpretation of Dreams was one of the two books—the *Three Essays on the Theory of Sexuality* (1905*d*) was the other—which Freud kept more or less systematically 'up to date' as they passed through their series of editions. After the third edition of the present work, the changes in it were not indicated in any way; and this produced a somewhat confusing effect on the reader of the later editions, since the new material sometimes implied a knowledge of modifications in Freud's views dating from times long subsequent to the period at which the book was originally written. In an attempt to get over this difficulty, the editors of the first collected edition of Freud's works (the *Gesammelte Schriften*) reprinted the first edition of *The Interpretation of Dreams* in its original form in one volume, and put into a second volume all the material that had been added subsequently. Unfortunately, however, the work was not carried out very systematically, for the additions themselves were not dated and thereby much of the advantage of the plan was sacrificed. In subsequent editions a return was made to the old, undifferentiated single volume.

By far the greater number of additions dealing with any single subject are those concerned with symbolism in dreams. Freud explains in his 'History of the Psycho-Analytic Movement' (1914*d*), as well as at the beginning of Chapter VI, Section E (p. 363), of the present work, that he arrived late at a full realization of the importance of this side of the subject. In the first edition, the discussion of symbolism was limited to a few pages and a single specimen dream (giving instances of sexual symbolism) at the end of the Section on 'Considerations of Representability' in Chapter VI. In the second edition (1909), nothing was added to this Section; but, on the other hand, several pages on sexual symbolism were inserted at the end of the Section on 'Typical Dreams' in Chapter V. These were very considerably expanded in the third edition (1911), while the original passage in Chapter VI still remained unaltered. A reorganization was evidently overdue, and in the fourth edition (1914) an entirely new Section on Symbolism was introduced into Chapter VI, and into this the material on the subject that had accumulated in Chapter V was now transplanted, together with a quantity of entirely fresh material. No changes in the *structure* of the book were made in later editions, though much further matter was added. After the two-volume version (1925)—that is, in the eighth edition (1930)—some passages in the Section on 'Typical Dreams' in Chapter V, which had been altogether dropped at an earlier stage, were re-inserted.

In the fourth, fifth, sixth and seventh editions (that is from 1914 to 1922), two essays by Otto Rank (on 'Dreams and Creative Writing' and 'Dreams and Myths') were printed at the end of Chapter V_, but were subsequently omitted.

There remain the bibliographies. The first edition contained a list of some eighty books, to the great majority of which Freud refers in the text. This was left unchanged in the second and third editions, but in the third a second list was added, of some forty books written since 1900. Thereafter both lists began to increase rapidly, till in the eighth edition the first list contained some 260 works and the second over 200. At this stage only a minority of the titles in the first (pre-1900) list were of books actually mentioned in Freud's text; while, on the other hand, the second (post-1900) list (as may be gathered from Freud's own remarks in his various prefaces) could not really keep pace with the production of analytic or quasi-analytic writings on the subject. Furthermore, quite a number of works quoted by Freud in the text were not to be found in *either* list. It seems probable that, from the third edition onwards, Otto Rank became chiefly responsible for these bibliographies.

(2)

HISTORICAL

The publication of Freud's correspondence with Fliess enables us to follow the composition of *The Interpretation of Dreams* in some detail. In his 'History of the Psycho-Analytic Movement' (1914*d*), Freud wrote, looking back upon his leisurely rate of publication in earlier days: '*The Interpretation of Dreams*, for instance, was finished in all essentials at the beginning of 1896 but was not written down until the summer of 1899.' Again, in the introductory remarks to his paper on the psychological consequences of the anatomical distinction between the sexes (1925*j*), he wrote: 'My *Interpretation of Dreams* and my "Fragment of an Analysis of a Case of Hysteria" [1905*e*] . . . were suppressed by me—if not for the nine years enjoined by Horace—at all events for four or five years before I allowed them to be published.' We are now in a position to amplify and in certain respects to correct these later recollections, on the basis of the author's contemporary evidence.

Apart from a number of scattered references to the subject—which, in his correspondence, go back at least as early as 1882—the first important published evidence of Freud's interest in dreams occurs in the course of a long footnote to the first of his case histories (that of Frau Emmy von N., under the date of May 15) in Breuer and Freud's *Studies on Hysteria* (1895). He is discussing the fact that neurotic patients seem to be under a necessity to bring into association with one another any ideas that happen to be simultaneously present in their minds. He goes on: 'Not long ago I was able to convince myself of the strength of this compulsion towards association from some observations made in a different field. For several weeks I found myself obliged to exchange my usual bed for a harder one, in which I had more numerous or more vivid dreams, or in which, it may be, I was unable to reach the normal depth of sleep. In the first quarter of an hour after waking I remembered all the dreams I had had during the night, and I took the trouble to write them down and try to solve them. I succeeded in tracing all these dreams back to two factors: (1) to the necessity for working out any ideas which I had only dwelt upon cursorily during the day—which had only been touched upon and not finally dealt with; and (2) to the compulsion to link together any ideas that might be present in the same state of consciousness. The senseless and contradictory character of the dreams could be traced back to the uncontrolled ascendancy of this latter factor.'

This passage cannot unfortunately be exactly dated. The preface to the volume was written in April 1895. A letter of June 22, 1894 (Letter 19), seems to imply that the case histories were already finished then, and this was quite certainly so by March 4, 1895. Freud's letter of that date (Letter 22) is of particular interest, as giving the first hint of the theory of wish-fulfilment: in the course of it he quotes the story of the medical student's 'dream of convenience' which is included on p. 150 of the present volume. It was not, however, until July 24, 1895, that the analysis of his own dream of Irma's injection—the specimen dream of Chapter II—established that theory definitely in Freud's mind. (See Letter 137 of June, 1900.) In September of this same year (1895) Freud wrote the first part of his 'Project for a Scientific Psychology' (published as an Appendix to the Fliess correspondence) and Sections 19, 20 and 21 of this 'Project' constitute a first approach to a coherent theory of dreams. It already includes many important elements which re-appear in the present work, such as (1) the wish-fulfilling character of dreams, (2) their hallucinatory character, (3) the regressive functioning of the mind in hallucinations and dreams (this had already been indicated by Breuer in his theoretical contribution to *Studies on Hysteria*), (4) the fact that the state of sleep involves motor paralysis, (5) the nature of the mechanism of displacement in dreams and (6) the similarity between the mechanisms of dreams and of neurotic symptoms. More than all this, however, the 'Project' gives a clear indication of what is probably the most momentous of the discoveries given to the world in *The Interpretation of Dreams*—the distinction between the two different modes of mental functioning, the Primary and Secondary Processes.

This, however, is far from exhausting the importance of the 'Project' and of the letters to Fliess written in connection with it towards the end of 1895. It is no exaggeration to say that much of the seventh chapter of *The Interpretation of Dreams*, and, indeed, of Freud's later 'metapsychological' studies, has only become fully intelligible since the publication of the 'Project.'

Students of Freud's theoretical writings have been aware that even in his profoundest psychological speculations little or no discussion is to be found upon some of the *most* fundamental of the concepts of which he makes use: such concepts, for instance, as 'mental energy,' 'sums of excitation,' 'cathexis,' 'quantity,' 'quality,' 'intensity,' and so on. Almost the only explicit approach to a discussion of these concepts among Freud's published works is the penultimate sentence of his first paper on the 'Neuro-Psychoses of Defence' (1894*a*), in which he lays down a hypothesis that 'in mental functions something is to be distinguished—a charge of affect or sum of excitation—which possesses all the characteristics of a quantity (though we have no means of measuring it), which is capable of increase, diminution, displacement and discharge, and which is spread over the memory-traces of ideas somewhat as an electric charge is spread over the surface of a body.' The paucity of explanation of such basic notions in Freud's later writings suggests that he was taking it for granted that they were as much a matter of course to his readers as they were to himself; and we owe it as a debt of gratitude to the posthumously published correspondence with Fliess that it throws so much light precisely upon these obscurities.

It is, of course, impossible to enter here into any detailed discussion of the subject, and the reader must be referred to the volume itself (Freud, 1950*a*) and to Dr. Kris's illuminating introduction to it.[1] The crux of the position can, however, be indicated quite simply. The essence of Freud's 'Project' lay in the notion of combining into a single whole two theories of different origin. The first of these was derived ultimately from the physiological school of Helmholtz, of which Freud's teacher, the physiologist Brücke, was a principal member. According to this theory, neurophysiology, and consequently psychology, was governed by purely chemico-physical laws. Such, for instance, was the 'law of constancy,' frequently mentioned both by Freud and Breuer and expressed in these terms in 1892 (in a posthumously published draft, Breuer and Freud, 1940): 'The nervous system endeavours to keep constant something in its functional condition that may be described as the "sum of excitation."' The greater part of the theoretical contribution made by Breuer (another disciple of the Helmholtz school) to the *Studies on Hysteria* was an elaborate construction along these lines. The second main theory called into play by Freud in his 'Project' was the anatomical doctrine of the neurone, which was becoming accepted by neuro-anatomists at the end of the eighties. (The term 'neurone' was only introduced, by Waldeyer, in 1891.) This doctrine laid it down that the functional unit of the central nervous system was a distinct cell, having no direct anatomical continuity with adjacent cells. The opening sentences of the 'Project' show clearly how its basis lay in a combination of these two theories. Its aim, wrote Freud, was 'to represent psychical processes as quantitatively determined states of specifiable material particles.' He went on to postulate that these 'material particles' were the neurones and that what distinguished their being in a state of activity from their being in a state of rest was a 'quantity' which was 'subject to the general laws of motion.' Thus a neurone

---

[1] Bernfeld's paper on 'Freud's Earliest Theories' (1944) is also of great interest in this connection.

might either be 'empty' or 'filled with a certain quantity,' that is 'cathected.'[1] 'Nervous excitation' was to be interpreted as a 'quantity' flowing through a system of neurones, and such a current might either be resisted or facilitated according to the state of the 'contact-barriers' between the neurones. (It was only later, in 1897, that the term 'synapse' was introduced by Foster and Sherrington.) The functioning of the whole nervous system was subject to a general principle of 'inertia,' according to which neurones always tend to get rid of any 'quantity' with which they may be filled—a principle correlative with the principle of 'constancy.' Using these and similar concepts as his bricks, Freud constructed a highly complicated and extraordinarily ingenious working model of the mind as a piece of neurological machinery.

A principal part was played in Freud's scheme by a hypothetical division of the neurones into three classes or systems, differentiated according to their modes of functioning. Of these the first two were concerned respectively with *external* stimuli and *internal* excitations. Both of these operated on a purely *quantitative* basis; that is to say, their actions were wholly determined by the magnitude of the nervous excitations impinging on them. The third system was correlated with the *qualitative* differences which distinguish conscious sensations and feelings. This division of the neurones into three systems was the basis of elaborate physiological explanations of such things as the working of memory, the perception of reality, the process of thought, and also the phenomena of dreaming and of neurotic disorder.

But obscurities and difficulties began to accumulate and, during the months after writing the 'Project,' Freud was continually emending his theories. As time passed, his interest was gradually diverted from neurological and theoretical on to psychological and clinical problems, and he eventually abandoned the entire scheme. And when some years later, in the seventh chapter of the present book, he took the theoretical problem up once more—though he certainly never gave up his belief that ultimately a physical groundwork for psychology would be established—the neuro-physiological basis was ostensibly dropped. Nevertheless—and this is why the 'Project' is of importance to readers of *The Interpretation of*

---

[1] It must be emphasized that these speculations of Freud's date from a period many years before any systematic investigations had been made into the nature of nervous impulses and the conditions governing their transmission.

Dreams—much of the general pattern of the earlier scheme, and many of its elements, were carried over into the new one. The systems of neurones were replaced by *psychical* systems or agencies; a hypothetical 'cathexis' of psychical energy took the place of the physical 'quantity'; the principle of inertia became the basis of the pleasure (or, as Freud here called it, the unpleasure) principle. Moreover, some of the detailed accounts of psychical processes given in the seventh chapter owe much to their physiological forerunners and can be more easily understood by reference to them. This applies, for instance, to the description of the laying down of memory-traces in the 'mnemic systems,' to the discussion of the nature of wishes and of the different ways of satisfying them, and to the stress laid upon the part played by verbal thought-processes in the making of adjustments to the demands of reality.

All of this is enough largely to justify Freud's assertion that *The Interpretation of Dreams* 'was finished in all essentials at the beginning of 1896.' Nevertheless, we are now in a position to add some qualifications. Thus, the existence of the Oedipus complex was only established during the summer and autumn of 1897 (Letters 64 to 71); and though this was not in itself a direct contribution to the theory of dreams, it nevertheless played a large part in emphasizing the *infantile* roots of the unconscious wishes underlying dreams. Of more obvious theoretical importance was the discovery of the omnipresence in dreams of the wish to sleep. This was announced by Freud as late as on June 9, 1899 (Letter 108). Again, the first hint at the process of 'secondary revision' seems to be given in a letter of July 7, 1897 (Letter 66). The similarity in structure between dreams and neurotic symptoms had, as we have seen, already been remarked on in the 'Project' in 1895, and was alluded to at intervals up to the autumn of 1897. Curiously enough, however, it seems thereafter to have been forgotten; for it is announced on January 3, 1899 (Letter 101), as a new discovery and as an explanation of why the book had so long remained unfinished.

The Fliess correspondence enables us to follow the actual process of composition in some detail. The idea of writing the book is first mentioned by Freud in May 1897, but quickly put on one side, probably because his interest began to be centred at that time on his self-analysis, which was to lead during the summer to his discovery of the Oedipus complex. At the end of the year the book was taken up once more, and in the early months of 1898 a first draft of the whole work seems to have been completed, with the exception of the first chapter.[1] Work upon it came to a standstill in June of that year and was not resumed after the summer vacation. On October 23, 1898 (Letter 99), Freud writes that the book 'remains stationary, unchanged; I have no motive for preparing it for publication, and the gap in the psychology [i.e., Chapter VII] as well as the gap left by removing the completely analysed sample dream are obstacles to my finishing it which I have not yet overcome.' There was a pause of many months, till suddenly, and, as Freud himself writes, 'for no particular reason,' the book began to stir again towards the end of May 1899. Thereafter it proceeded rapidly. The first chapter, dealing with the literature, which had always been a bug-bear to Freud, was finished in June and the first pages sent to the printer. The revision of the middle chapters was completed by the end of August, and the last, psychological, chapter was entirely re-written and the final pages despatched early in September.

Both the manuscript and the proofs were regularly submitted by Freud to Fliess for his criticism. He seems to have had considerable influence on the final shape of the book, and to have been responsible for the omission (evidently on grounds of discretion) of an analysis of one important dream of Freud's own (cf. p. xviii). But the severest criticisms came from the author himself, and these were directed principally against the style and literary form. 'I think,' he wrote on September 21, 1899 (Letter 119), when the book was finished, 'my self-criticism was not entirely unjustified. Somewhere hidden within me I too have some fragmentary sense of form, some appreciation of beauty as a species of perfection; and the involved sentences of my book on dreams, bolstered up on indirect phrases and with sidelong glances at their subject-matter, have gravely affronted some ideal within me. And I am scarcely wrong in regarding this lack of form as a sign of an incomplete mastery of the material.'

But in spite of these self-criticisms, and in spite of the depression which followed the almost total neglect of the book by the outside world—only 351 copies were sold in the first six years after publication—*The Interpretation of Dreams* was always regarded by Freud as his most important work: 'Insight such as this,' as he wrote in his preface to the third English edition, 'falls to one's lot but once in a lifetime.'

---

[1] This must be what is alluded to in a passage on p. 483 of the present work, in which Freud remarks that he had 'postponed the printing of the finished manuscript for more than a year.' Actually the first chapter had still to be written.

(3)

THE PRESENT ENGLISH EDITION

The present translation is based on the eighth (1930) German edition, the last published during its author's life. At the same time, it differs from all previous editions (both German and English) in an important respect, for it is in the nature of a 'Variorum' edition. An effort has been made to indicate, with dates, every alteration of substance introduced into the book since its first issue. Wherever material has been dropped or greatly modified in later editions, the cancelled passage or earlier version is given in a footnote. The only exception is that Rank's two appendices to Chapter VI have been omitted. The question of their inclusion was seriously considered; but it was decided against doing so. The essays are entirely self-contained and have no direct connections with Freud's book; they would have filled another fifty pages or so; and they would be particularly unenlightening to English readers, since they deal in the main with German literature and German mythology.

The bibliographies have been entirely recast. The first of these contains a list of every work actually referred to in the text or footnotes. This bibliography is also arranged to serve as an Author Index. The second bibliography contains all the works in the German pre-1900 list *not* actually quoted by Freud. It has seemed worth while to print this, since no other comparably full bibliography of the older literature on dreams is easily accessible. Writings *after* 1900, apart from those actually quoted and consequently included in the first bibliography, have been disregarded. A warning must, however, be issued in regard to both my lists. Investigation has shown a very high proportion of errors in the German bibliographies. These have been corrected wherever possible; but quite a number of the entries have proved to be untraceable in London, and these (which are distinguished by an asterisk) must be regarded as suspect.

Editorial additions are printed in square brackets. Many readers will no doubt be irritated by the number of references and other explanatory notes. The references, however, are essentially to Freud's own writings, and very few will be found to other authors (apart, of course, from references made by Freud himself). In any case, the fact must be faced that *The Interpretation of Dreams* is one of the major classics of scientific literature and that the time has come to treat it as such. It is the editor's hope and belief that actually the references, and more particularly the cross-references to other parts of the work itself, will make it easier for serious students to follow the intricacies of the material. Readers in search of mere entertainment—if there are any such—must steel themselves to disregard these parentheses.

A word must be added upon the translation itself. Great attention has had, of course, to be paid to the details of the wording of the text of dreams. Where the English rendering strikes the reader as unusually stiff, he may assume that the stiffness has been imposed by some verbal necessity determined by the interpretation that is to follow. Where there are inconsistencies between different versions of the text of the same dream, he may assume that there are parallel inconsistencies in the original. These verbal difficulties culminate in the fairly frequent instances in which an interpretation depends entirely upon a pun. There are three methods of dealing with such situations. The translator can omit the dream entirely, or he can replace it by another parallel dream, whether derived from his own experience or fabricated *ad hoc*. These two methods have been the ones adopted in the main in the earlier translations of the book. But there are serious objections to them. We must once more remember that we are dealing with a scientific classic. What we want to hear about are the examples chosen by Freud—not by someone else. Accordingly the present translator has adopted the pedantic and tiresome third alternative of keeping the original German pun and laboriously explaining it in a square bracket or footnote. Any amusement that might be got out of it completely evaporates in the process. But that, unfortunately, is a sacrifice that has to be made.

Help in the laborious task of proof-reading has been generously given (among others) by Mrs. R. S. Partridge and Dr. C. F. Rycroft. Mrs. Partridge is also largely responsible for the index. The revision of the bibliographies has in the main been carried out by Mr. G. Talland.

Finally, the editor's thanks are due to Dr. Ernest Jones for his constant advice and encouragement. The first volume of his Freud biography will be found to throw invaluable light on the background of this work as a whole, as well as on many of its details.

Preface to the First Edition

I HAVE attempted in this volume to give an account of the interpretation of dreams; and in doing so I have not, I believe, trespassed beyond the sphere of interest covered by neuro-pathology. For psychological investigation shows that the dream is the first member of a class of abnormal psychical phenomena of which further members, such as hysterical pho bias, obsessions and delusions, are bound for practical reasons to be a matter of concern to physicians. As will be seen in the sequel, dreams can make no such claim to practical importance; but their theoretical value as a paradigm is on the other hand proportionately greater. Anyone who has failed to explain the origin of dream-images can scarcely hope to understand phobias, obsessions or delusions or to bring a therapeutic influence to bear on them.

But the same correlation that is responsible for the importance of the subject must also bear the blame for the deficiencies of the present work. The broken threads which so frequently interrupt my presentation are nothing less than the many points of contact between the problem of the formation of dreams and the more comprehensive problems of psychopathology. These cannot be treated here, but, if time and strength allow and further material comes to hand, will form the subject of later communications.

The difficulties of presentation have been further increased by the peculiarities of the material which I have had to use to illustrate the interpreting of dreams. It will become plain in the course of the work itself why it is that none of the dreams already reported in the literature of the subject or collected from unknown sources could be of any use for my purposes. The only dreams open to my choice were my own and those of my patients undergoing psychoanalytic treatment. But I was precluded from using the latter material by the fact that in its case the dream-processes were subject to an undesirable complication owing to the added presence of neurotic features. But if I was to report my own dreams, it inevitably followed that I should have to reveal to the public gaze more of the intimacies of my mental life than I liked, or than is normally necessary for any writer who is a man of science and not a poet. Such was the painful but unavoidable necessity; and I have submitted to it rather than totally abandon the possibility of giving the evidence for my psychological findings. Naturally, however, I have been unable to resist the temptation of taking the edge off some of my indiscretions by omissions and substitutions. But whenever this has happened, the value of my instances has been very definitely diminished. I can only express a hope that readers of this book will put themselves in my difficult situation and treat me with indulgence, and further, that anyone who finds any sort of reference to himself in my dreams may be willing to grant me the right of freedom of thought—in my dream-life, if nowhere else.

Preface to the Second Edition

IF within ten years of the publication of this book (which is very far from being an easy one to read) a second edition is called for, this is not due to the interest taken in it by the professional circles to whom my original preface was addressed. My psychiatric colleagues seem to have taken no trouble to overcome the initial bewilderment created by my new approach to dreams. The professional philosophers have become accustomed to polishing off the problems of dream-life (which they treat as a mere appendix to conscious states) in a few sentences—and usually in the same ones; and they have evidently failed to notice that we have something here from which a number of inferences can be drawn that are bound to transform our psychological theories. The attitude adopted by reviewers in the scientific periodicals could only lead one to suppose that my work was doomed to be sunk into complete silence; while the small group or gallant supporters, who practise medical psycho-analysis under my guidance and who follow my example in interpreting dreams and make use of their interpretations in treating neurotics, would never have exhausted the first edition of the book. Thus it is that I feel indebted to a wider circle of educated and curious-minded readers, whose interest has led me to take up once more after nine years this difficult, but in many respects fundamental, work.

I am glad to say that I have found little to change in it. Here and there I have inserted some new material, added some fresh points of detail derived from my increased experience, and at some few points recast my statements. But the essence of what I have written about dreams and their interpretation, as well as about the psychological theorems to be deduced from them—all this remains unaltered: subjectively at all events, it has stood the test of time. Anyone who is acquainted with my other writings (on the aetiology and mechanism of the psycho-neuroses) will know that I have never put forward inconclusive opinions as though they were established facts, and that I have always sought to modify my statements so that they may keep in step with my advancing knowledge. In the sphere of my dream-life I have been able to leave my original assertions unchanged. During the long years in which I have been working at the problems of the neuroses I have often been in doubt and sometimes been shaken in my convictions. At such times it has always been the *Interpretation of Dreams* that has given me back my certainty. It is thus a sure instinct which has led my many scientific opponents to refuse to follow me more especially in my researches upon dreams.

An equal durability and power to withstand any far-reaching alterations during the process of revision has been shown by the *material* of the book, consisting as it does of dreams of my own which have for the most part been overtaken or made valueless by the march of events and by which I illustrated the rules of dream-interpretation. For this book has a further subjective significance for me personally—a significance which I only grasped after I had completed it. It was, I found, a portion of my own self-analysis, my reaction to my father's death—that is to say, to the most important event, the most poignant loss, of a man's life. Having discovered that this was so, I felt unable to obliterate the traces of the experience.[1] To my readers, however, it will be a matter of indifference upon what particular material they learn to appreciate the importance of dreams and how to interpret them.

Wherever I have found it impossible to incorporate some essential addition into the original context, I have indicated its more recent date by enclosing it in square brackets.[2]

BERCHTESGADEN, *Summer* 1908

---

[1] [Freud's father had died in 1896. Some account of his feelings at the time will be found in his letter to Fliess of November 2, 1896. (Freud 1950*a*, Letter 50.)]

[2] [*Footnote added* 1914.] In later editions [from the fourth onwards] these were omitted.

Preface to the Third Edition

NINE years elapsed between the first and second editions of this book, but after scarcely more than a single year a third edition has become necessary. This new turn of events may please me; but just as formerly I was unwilling to regard the neglect of my book by readers as evidence of its worthlessness, so I cannot claim that the interest which is now being taken in it is a proof of its excellence.

Even the *Interpretation of Dreams* has not been left untouched by the advance of scientific knowledge. When I wrote it in 1899, my theory of sexuality was not yet in existence and the analysis of the more complicated forms of psycho-neurosis was only just beginning. It was my hope that dream-interpretation would help to make possible the psychological analysis of neuroses; since then a deeper understanding of neuroses has reacted in turn upon our view of dreams. The theory of dream-interpretation has itself developed further in a direction on which insufficient stress had been laid in the first edition of this book. My own experience, as well as the works of Wilhelm Stekel and others, have since taught me to form a truer estimate of the extent and importance of symbolism in dreams (or rather in unconscious thinking). Thus in the course of these years much has accumulated which demands attention. I have endeavoured to take these innovations into account by making numerous interpolations in the text and by additional footnotes. If these additions threaten at times to burst the whole framework of the book or if I have not everywhere succeeded in bringing the original text up to the level of our present knowledge, I must ask the reader's indulgence for these deficiencies: they are the results and signs of the present increasingly rapid development of our science. I may even venture to prophesy in what other directions later editions of this book—if any should be needed—will differ from the present one. They will have on the one hand to afford closer contact with the copious material presented in imaginative writing, in myths, in linguistic usage and in folklore; while on the other hand they will have to deal in greater detail than has here been possible with the relations of dreams to neuroses and mental diseases.

Herr Otto Rank has given me valuable assistance in selecting the additional matter and has been entirely responsible for correcting the proofs. I owe my thanks to him and to many others for their contributions and corrections.

VIENNA, *Spring* 1911

Preface to the Fourth Edition

LAST year (1913) Dr. A. A. Brill of New York produced an English translation of this book (*The Interpretation of Dreams*, G. Allen & Co., London).

On this occasion Dr. Otto Rank has not only corrected the proofs but has also contributed two self-contained chapters to the text—the appendices to Chapter VI.

VIENNA, *June* 1914

Preface to the Fifth Edition

INTEREST in the *Interpretation of Dreams* has not flagged even during the World War, and while it is still in progress a new edition has become necessary. It has not been possible, however, to notice fully publications since 1914; neither Dr. Rank nor I have any knowledge of foreign works since that date.

A Hungarian translation, prepared by Dr. Hollós and Dr. Ferenczi, is on the point of appearing. In 1916–17 my *Introductory Lectures on Psycho-Analysis* were published in Vienna by Hugo Heller. The central section of these, comprising eleven lectures, is devoted to an account of dreams which aims at being more elementary and at being in closer contact with the theory of the neuroses than the present work. On the whole it is in the nature of an epitome of the *Interpretation of Dreams*, though at certain points it enters into greater detail.

I have not been able to bring myself to embark upon any fundamental revision of this book, which might bring it up to the level of our present psycho-analytic views but would on the other hand destroy its historic character. I think, however, that after an existence of nearly twenty years it has accomplished its task.

BUDAPEST-STEINBRUCH, *July* 1918

Preface to the Sixth Edition

OWING to the difficulties in which the book trade is placed at present, this new edition has long been in demand, and the preceding edition has, for the first time, been reprinted without any alterations. Only the bibliography at the end of the volume has been completed and brought up to date by Dr. Otto Rank.

Thus my assumption that after an existence of nearly twenty years this book had accomplished its task has not been confirmed. On the contrary, I might say that it has a new task to perform. If its earlier function was to offer some information on the nature of dreams, now it has the no less important duty of dealing with the obstinate misunderstandings to which that information is subject.

Vienna, *April* 1921

Preface to the Eighth Edition

DURING the interval between the publication of the last (seventh) edition of this book in 1922 and the present one, my *Gesammelte Schriften* [Collected Writings] have been issued in Vienna by the Internationaler Psychoanalytischer Verlag. The second volume of that collection consists of an exact reprint of the first edition of the *Interpretation of Dreams*, while the third volume contains all the additions that have since been made to it. The translations of the book which have appeared during the same interval are based upon the usual, single-volume, form of the work: a French one by I. Meyerson published under the title of *La science des rêves* in the 'Bibliothèque de Philosophie Contemporaine' in 1926; a Swedish one by John Landquist, *Drömtydning* (1927); and a Spanish one by Luis López-Ballesteros y de Torres [1922], which occupies Volumes VI and VII of the *Obras Completas*. The Hungarian translation, which I thought was on the point of completion as long ago as in 1918, has even now not appeared.[1]

In the present revised edition of the work I have again treated it essentially as an historic document and I have only made such alterations in it as were suggested by the clarification and deepening of my own opinions. In accordance with this, I have finally given up the idea of including a list of works on the problems of dreams published since the book's first appearance, and that section has now been dropped. The two essays which Otto Rank contributed to earlier editions, on 'Dreams and Creative Writing' and 'Dreams and Myths', have also been omitted. [See p. xx.]

VIENNA, *December* 1929

---

[1] [It was published in 1934.—During Freud's lifetime, in addition to the translations mentioned in these prefaces, a Russian version appeared in 1913, a Japanese one in 1930 and a Czech one in 1938.]

Preface to the Third (Revised) English Edition[1]

In 1909 G. Stanley Hall invited me to Clark University, in Worcester, to give the first lectures on psycho-analysis. In the same year Dr. Brill published the first of his translations of my writings, which were soon followed by further ones. If psycho-analysis now plays a role in American intellectual life, or if it does so in the future, a large part of this result will have to be attributed to this and other activities of Dr. Brill's.

His first translation of *The Interpretation of Dreams* appeared in 1913. Since then much has taken place in the world, and much has been changed in our views about the neuroses. This book, with the new contribution to psychology which surprised the world when it was published (1900), remains essentially unaltered. It contains, even according to my present-day judgment, the most valuable of all the discoveries it has been my good fortune to make. Insight such as this falls to one's lot but once in a lifetime.

FREUD

Vienna, *March* 15, 1931

---

[1] [This is not included in the German editions and no German text is extant. It is here reprinted exactly from the 1932 English edition.]

THE INTERPRETATION
OF DREAMS

CHAPTER I

THE SCIENTIFIC LITERATURE DEALING WITH THE PROBLEMS OF DREAMS[1]

IN the pages that follow I shall bring forward proof that there is a psychological technique which makes it possible to interpret dreams, and that, if that procedure is employed, every dream reveals itself as a psychical structure which has a meaning and which can be inserted at an assignable point in the mental activities of waking life. I shall further endeavour to elucidate the processes to which the strangeness and obscurity of dreams are due and to deduce from those processes the nature of the psychical forces by whose concurrent or mutually opposing action dreams are generated. Having gone thus far, my description will break off, for it will have reached a point at which the problem of dreams merges into more comprehensive problems, the solution of which must be approached upon the basis of material of another kind.

I shall give by way of preface a review of the work done by earlier writers on the subject as well as of the present position of the problems of dreams in the world of science, since in the course of my discussion I shall not often have occasion to revert to those topics. For, in spite of many thousands of years of effort, the scientific understanding of dreams has made very little advance—a fact so generally admitted in the literature that it seems unnecessary to quote instances in support of it. In these writings,

---

[1] [*Footnote added* in second to seventh editions:] Up to the date of the first publication of this book (1900).

of which a list appears at the end of my work, many stimulating observations are to be found and a quantity of interesting material bearing upon our theme, but little or nothing that touches upon the essential nature of dreams or that offers a final solution of any of their enigmas. And still less, of course, has passed into the knowledge of educated laymen.

It may be asked[1] what view was taken of dreams in prehistoric times by primitive races of men and what effect dreams may have had upon the formation of their conceptions of the world and of the soul; and this is a subject of such great interest that it is only with much reluctance that I refrain from dealing with it in this connection. I must refer my readers to the standard works of Sir John Lubbock, Herbert Spencer, E. B. Tylor and others, and I will only add that we shall not be able to appreciate the wide range of these problems and speculations until we have dealt with the task that lies before us here—the interpretation of dreams.

The prehistoric view of dreams is no doubt echoed in the attitude adopted towards dreams by the peoples of classical antiquity.[2] They took it as axiomatic that dreams were connected with the world of superhuman beings in whom they believed and that they were revelations from gods and daemons. There could be no question, moreover, that for the dreamer dreams had an important purpose, which was as a rule to foretell the future. The extraordinary variety in the content of dreams and in the impression they produced made it difficult, however, to have any uniform view of them and made it necessary to classify dreams into numerous groups and subdivisions according to their importance and trustworthiness. The position adopted towards dreams by individual philosophers in antiquity was naturally dependent to some extent upon their attitude towards divination in general.

In the two works of Aristotle which deal with dreams, they have already become a subject for psychological study. We are told that dreams are not sent by the gods and are not of a divine character, but that they are 'daemonic,' since nature is 'daemonic' and not divine. Dreams, that is, do not arise from supernatural manifestations but follow the laws of the human

---

[1] [This paragraph and the next were added in 1914.]
[2] [*Footnote added* 1914:] What follows is based on Büchsen-schütz's scholarly study (1868).

spirit, though the latter, it is true, is akin to the divine. Dreams are defined as the mental activity of the sleeper in so far as he is asleep.[1]

Aristotle was aware of some of the characteristics of dream-life. He knew, for instance, that dreams give a magnified construction to small stimuli arising during sleep. 'Men think that they are walking through fire and are tremendously hot, when there is only a slight heating about certain parts.'[2] And from this circumstance he draws the conclusion that dreams may very well betray to a physician the first signs of some bodily change which has not been observed in waking.[3]

Before the time of Aristotle, as we know, the ancients regarded dreams not as a product of the dreaming mind but as something introduced by a divine agency; and already the two opposing currents, which we shall find influencing opinions of dream-life at every period of history, were making themselves felt. The distinction was drawn between truthful and valuable dreams, sent to the sleeper to warn him or foretell the future, and vain, deceitful and worthless dreams, whose purpose it was to mislead or destroy him.

Gruppe (1906, **2**, 930)[4] quotes a classification of dreams on these lines made by Macrobius and Artemidorus [of Daldis (see p. 130 n. 2)]: 'Dreams were divided into two classes. One class was supposed to be influenced by the present or past, but to have no future significance. It included the ἐνύπνια

---

[1] [*De divinatione per somnum*, II (*Trans.*, 1935, 377) and *De somnus*, III (*Trans.*, 1935, 365).—In the first edition (1900) this paragraph ran: 'The first work in which dreams were treated as a subject for psychological study seems to be that of Aristotle (*On Dreams and Their Interpretation*). Aristotle declares that dreams are of a "daemonic" but not of a "divine" nature; no doubt this distinction has some great significance if we knew how to translate it correctly.' The next paragraph ended with the sentence: 'My own insufficient knowledge and my lack of specialist assistance prevent my entering more deeply into Aristotle's treatise.' These passages were altered into their present form in 1914; and a note in *Gesammelte Schriften*, 3 (1925), 4, points out that in fact Aristotle wrote not one but two works on the subject.]

[2] [*De divinatione*, I (*Trans.*, 1935, 375)].

[3] [*Footnote added* 1914:] The Greek physician Hippocrates deals with the relation of dreams to illnesses in one of the chapters of his famous work [*Ancient Medicine*, X (*Trans.*, 1923, 31). See also *Regimen*, IV, 88, passim. (*Trans.*, 1931, 425, etc.)].

[4] [This paragraph was added as a footnote in 1911 and included in the text in 1914.]

or *insomnia*, which gave a direct representation of a given idea or of its opposite—e.g. of hunger or of its satiation—and the φαντάσματα, which lent a fantastic extension to the given idea—e.g. the nightmare or *ephialtes*. The other class, on the contrary, was supposed to determine the future. It included (1) direct prophecies received in a dream (the χρηματισμός or *oraculum*), (2) previsions of some future event (the ὄραμα or *visio*) and (3) symbolic dreams, which needed interpretation (the ὄνειρος or *somnium*). This theory persisted for many centuries.'

This variation in the value that was to be assigned to dreams[1] was closely related to the problem of 'interpreting' them. Important consequences were in general to be expected from dreams. But dreams were not all immediately comprehensible and it was impossible to tell whether a particular unintelligible dream might not be making some important announcement. This provided an incentive for elaborating a method by which the unintelligible content of a dream might be replaced by one that was comprehensible and significant. In the later years of antiquity Artemidorus of Daldis was regarded as the greatest authority on the interpretation of dreams, and the survival of his exhaustive work [*Oneirocritica*] must compensate us for the loss of the other writings on the same subject.[2]

The pre-scientific view of dreams adopted by the peoples of antiquity was certainly in complete harmony with their view of the universe in general, which led them to project into the external world as though they were realities things which in fact enjoyed reality only within their own minds. Moreover, their view of dreams took into account the principal impression produced upon the waking mind in the morning by what is left of a dream in the memory: an impression of something alien, arising from another world and contrasting with the remaining contents of the

---

[1] [This paragraph was added in 1914.]

[2] [*Footnote added* 1914:] For the further history of dream-interpretation in the Middle Ages see Diepgen (1912) and the monographs of Förster (1910 and 1911), Gotthard (1912), etc. Dream-interpretation among the Jews has been discussed by Almoli (1848), Amram (1901), and Löwinger (1908); also, quite recently and taking account of psychoanalytic findings, by Lauer (1913). Information upon dream-interpretation among the Arabs has been given by Drexl (1909), Schwarz (1913) and the missionary Tfinkdji (1913); among the Japanese by Miura (1906) and Iwaya (1902); among the Chinese by Secker (1909–10); and among the people of India by Negelein (1912).

mind. Incidentally, it would be a mistake to suppose that the theory of the supernatural origin of dreams is without its supporters in our own days. We may leave on one side pietistic and mystical writers, who, indeed, are perfectly justified in remaining in occupation of what is left of the once wide domain of the supernatural so long as that field is not conquered by scientific explanation. But apart from them, one comes across clear-headed men, without any extravagant ideas, who seek to support their religious faith in the existence and activity of superhuman spiritual forces precisely by the inexplicable nature of the phenomena of dreaming. (Cf. Haffner, 1887.) The high esteem in which dream-life is held by some schools of philosophy (by the followers of Schelling,[1] for instance) is clearly an echo of the divine nature of dreams which was undisputed in antiquity. Nor are discussions of the premonitory character of dreams and their power to foretell the future at an end. For attempts at giving a psychological explanation have been inadequate to cover the material collected, however decidedly the sympathies of those of a scientific cast of mind may incline against accepting any such beliefs.

It is difficult to write a history of the scientific study of the problems of dreams because, however valuable that study may have been at a few points, no line of advance in any particular direction can be traced. No foundation has been laid of secure findings upon which a later investigator might build; but each new writer examines the same problems afresh and begins again, as it were, from the beginning. If I attempted to take those who have written on the question in chronological order and to give a summary of their views upon the problems of dreams, I should have to abandon any hope of giving a comprehensive general picture of the present state of knowledge of the subject. I have therefore chosen to frame my account according to topics rather than authors and, as I raise each dream-problem in turn, I shall bring forward whatever material the literature contains for its solution.

---

[1] [The chief exponent of the pantheistic 'Philosophy of Nature,' popular in Germany during the early part of the nineteenth century.—Freud often recurred to the question of the occult significance of dreams. Cf. Freud 1922a, 1925i (Part 3) and 1933a (Lecture 30). An allegedly premonitory dream is discussed in Freud 1941c [1899], printed as an Appendix to this work, p. 617. See also pp. 93 and 615 below.]

Since, however, it has been impossible for me to cover the whole of the literature of the subject, widely scattered as it is and trenching upon many other fields, I must ask my readers to be satisfied so long as no fundamental fact and no important point of view is overlooked in my description.

Until recently most writers on the subject have felt obliged to treat sleep and dreams as a single topic, and as a rule they have dealt in addition with analogous conditions on the fringe of pathology, and dream-like states, such as hallucinations, visions and so on. The latest works, on the contrary, show a preference for a restricted theme and take as their subject, perhaps, some isolated question in the field of dream-life. I should be glad to see in this change of attitude the expression of a conviction that in such obscure matters it will only be possible to arrive at explanations and agreed results by a series of detailed investigations. A piece of detailed research of that kind, predominantly psychological in character, is all I have to offer in these pages. I have had little occasion to deal with the problem of sleep, for that is essentially a problem of physiology, even though one of the characteristics of the state of sleep must be that it brings about modifications in the conditions of functioning of the mental apparatus. The literature on the subject of sleep is accordingly disregarded in what follows.

The questions raised by a scientific enquiry into the phenomena of dreams as such may be grouped under the headings which follow, though a certain amount of overlapping cannot be avoided.

(A)

THE RELATION OF DREAMS TO WAKING LIFE

The unsophisticated waking judgement of someone who has just woken from sleep assumes that his dreams, even if they did not themselves come from another world, had at all events carried him off into another world. The old physiologist Burdach (1838, 499), to whom we owe a careful and shrewd account of the phenomena of dreams, has given expression to this conviction in a much-quoted passage: 'In dreams, daily life, with its labours and pleasures, its joys and pains, is never repeated. On the contrary, dreams have as their very aim to free us from it. Even when our whole mind has been filled with something, when we are torn by some deep sorrow or when all our intellectual power is absorbed in some problem, a dream will do no more than enter into the tone of our mood and represent reality in symbols.' I. H. Fichte (1864, 1, 541), in the same sense, actually speaks of 'complementary dreams' and describes them as one of the secret benefactions of the self-healing nature of the spirit.[1] Strümpell (1877, 16) writes to similar effect in his study on the nature and origin of dreams—a work which is widely and deservedly held in high esteem: 'A man who dreams is removed from the world of waking consciousness.' So too (ibid., 17): 'In dreams our memory of the ordered contents of waking consciousness and of its normal behaviour is as good as completely lost.' And again (ibid., 19) he writes that 'the mind is cut off in dreams, almost without memory, from the ordinary content and affairs of waking life.'

The preponderant majority of writers, however, take a contrary view of the relation of dreams to waking life. Thus Haffner (1887, 245): 'In the first place, dreams carry on waking life. Our dreams regularly attach themselves to the ideas that have been in our consciousness shortly before. Accurate observation will almost always find a thread which connects a dream with the experiences of the previous day.' Weygandt (1893,

---

[1] [This sentence was added in 1914.]

6) specifically contradicts Burdach's statement which I have just quoted: 'For it may often, and apparently in the majority of dreams, be observed that they actually lead us back to ordinary life instead of freeing us from it.' Maury (1878, 51) advances a concise formula: 'Nous rêvons de ce que nous avons vu, dit, désiré ou fait';[1] while Jessen, in his book on psychology (1855, 530), remarks at somewhat greater length: 'The content of a dream is invariably more or less determined by the individual personality of the dreamer, by his age, sex, class, standard of education and habitual way of living, and by the events and experiences of his whole previous life.'

The most uncompromising attitude on this question[2] is adopted by J. G. E. Maass, the philosopher (1805, [1, 168 and 173]), quoted by Winterstein (1912): 'Experience confirms our view that we dream most frequently of the things on which our warmest passions are centred. And this shows that our passions must have an influence on the production of our dreams. The ambitious man dreams of the laurels he has won (or imagines he has won) or of those he has still to win; while the lover is busied in his dreams with the object of his sweet hopes. . . . All the sensual desires and repulsions that slumber in the heart can, if anything sets them in motion, cause a dream to arise from the ideas that are associated with them or cause those ideas to intervene in a dream that is already present.'

The same view was taken in antiquity on the dependence of the content of dreams upon waking life. Radestock (1879, 134) tells us how before Xerxes started on his expedition against Greece, he was given sound advice of a discouraging kind but was always urged on again by his dreams; whereupon Artabanus, the sensible old Persian interpreter of dreams, observed to him pertinently that as a rule dream-pictures contain what the waking man already thinks.

Lucretius' didactic poem *De rerum natura* contains the following passage (IV, 962):

> Et quo quisque fere studio devinctus adhaeret
> aut quibus in rebus multum sumus ante morati
> atque in ea ratione fuit
> contenta magis mens, in somnis eadem plerumque videmur

---

[1] ['We dream of what we have seen, said, desired or done.']
[2] [This paragraph was added in 1914.]

cbire; causidici causas agere et componere leges, indupera-
tores pugnare ac proelia obire . . . [1]

Cicero (*De divinatione*, II, lxvii, 140) writes to exactly the same effect as
Maury so many years later: 'Maximeque reliquiae rerum earum moventur
in animis et agitantur de quibus vigilantes aut cogitavimus aut egimus.'[2]

The contradiction between these two views upon the relation between
dream-life and waking life seems in fact insoluble. It is therefore relevant
at this point to recall the discussion of the subject by Hildebrandt (1875,
8 ff.), who believes that it is impossible to describe the characteristics of
dreams at all except by means of 'a series of [three] contrasts which seem
to sharpen into contradictions.' The first of these contrasts,' he writes, 'is
afforded on the one hand by the completeness with which dreams are se-
cluded and separated from real and actual life and on the other hand by
their constant encroachment upon each other and their constant mutual
dependence. A dream is something completely severed from the reality
experienced in waking life, something, as one might say, with an hermet-
ically sealed existence of its own, and separated from real life by an impassable gulf. It sets us free from reality, extinguishes our normal memory
of it and places us in another world and in a quite other life-story which
in essentials has nothing to do with our real one. . . . ' Hildebrandt goes
on to show how when we fall asleep our whole being with all its forms of
existence 'disappears, as it were, through an invisible trap-door.' Then,
perhaps, the dreamer may make a sea-voyage to St. Helena in order to offer Napoleon, who is a prisoner there, a choice bargain in Moselle wines.
He is received most affably by the ex-Emperor and feels almost sorry
when he wakes and the interesting illusion is destroyed. But let us compare the situation in the dream, proceeds Hildebrandt, with reality. The

---

[1] ['And whatever be the pursuit to which one clings with devotion, whatever the
things on which we have been occupied much in the past, the mind being thus
more intent upon that pursuit, it is generally the same things that we seem to
encounter in dreams: pleaders to plead their cause and collate laws, generals to
contend and engage battle . . . ' (Rouse's translation in the Loeb Classical Library, 1924, 317.)]

[2] ['Then especially do the remnants of our waking thoughts and deeds move and
stir within the soul.' (Falconer's translation in the Loeb Classical Library, 1922,
527.)]

dreamer has never been a wine-merchant and has never wished to be. He has never gone on a sea-voyage, and if he did, St. Helena would be the last place he would choose to go to. He nourishes no sympathetic feelings whatever towards Napoleon, but on the contrary a fierce patriotic hatred. And, on top of all the rest, the dreamer was not even born when Napoleon died on the island; so that to have any personal relations with him was beyond the bounds of possibility. Thus the dream-experience appears as something alien inserted between two sections of life which are perfectly continuous and consistent with each other.

'And yet,' continues Hildebrandt [ibid., 10], 'What appears to be the contrary of this is equally true and correct. In spite of everything, the most intimate relationship goes hand in hand, I believe, with the seclusion and separation. We may even go so far as to say that whatever dreams may offer, they derive their material from reality and from the intellectual life that revolves around that reality. . . . Whatever strange results they may achieve, they can never in fact get free from the real world; and their most sublime as well as their most ridiculous structures must always borrow their basic material either from what has passed before our eyes in the world of the senses or from what has already found a place somewhere in the course of our waking thoughts—in other words from what we have already experienced either externally or internally.'

(B)

THE MATERIAL OF DREAMS—MEMORY IN DREAMS

All the material making up the content of a dream is in some way derived from experience, that is to say, has been reproduced or remembered in the dream—so much at least we may regard as an undisputed fact. But it would be a mistake to suppose that a connection of this kind between the content of a dream and reality is bound to come to light easily, as an immediate result of comparing them. The connection requires, on the contrary, to be looked for diligently, and in a whole quantity of cases it may long remain hidden. The reason for this lies in a number of peculiarities which are exhibited by the faculty of memory in dreams and which, though generally remarked upon, have hitherto resisted explanation. It will be worth while to examine these characteristics more closely.

It may happen that a piece of material occurs in the content of a dream which in the waking state we do not recognize as forming a part of our knowledge or experience. We remember, of course, having dreamt the thing in question, but we cannot remember whether or when we experienced it in real life. We are thus left in doubt as to the source which has been drawn upon by the dream and are tempted to believe that dreams have a power of independent production. Then at last, often after a long interval, some fresh experience recalls the lost memory of the other event and at the same time reveals the source of the dream. We are thus driven to admit that in the dream we knew and remembered something which was beyond the reach of our waking memory.[1]

A particularly striking example of this is given by Delboeuf [1885, 107 ff.] from his own experience. He saw in a dream the courtyard of his house covered with snow and found two small lizards half-frozen and buried under it. Being an animal-lover, he picked them up, warmed them, and carried them back to the little hole in the masonry where they belonged. He further gave them a few leaves of a small fern which grew on the wall and of which, as he knew, they were very fond. In the dream he knew the name of the plant: *Asplenium ruta muralis*. The dream proceeded and, after a digression, came back to the lizards. Delboeuf then saw to his astonishment two new ones which were busy on the remains of the fern. He then looked round him and saw a fifth and then a sixth lizard making their way to the hole in the wall, until the whole roadway was filled with a procession of lizards, all moving in the same direction . . . and so on.

When he was awake, Delboeuf knew the Latin names of very few plants and an *Asplenium* was not among them. To his great surprise he was able to confirm the fact that a fern of this name actually exists. Its correct name is *Asplenium ruta muraria*, which had been slightly distorted in the dream. It was hardly possible that this could be a coincidence; and it remained a mystery to Delboeuf how he had acquired his knowledge of the name '*Asplenium*' in his dream.

The dream occurred in 1862. Sixteen years later, while the philosopher was on a visit to one of his friends, he saw a little album of pressed flowers of the sort that are sold to foreigners as mementos in some parts of Switzerland.

---

[1] [*Footnote added* 1914:] Vaschide (1911) remarks that it has often been observed that in dreams people speak foreign languages more fluently and correctly than in waking life.

A recollection began to dawn on him—he opened the herbarium, found the *Asplenium* of his dream and saw its Latin name written underneath it in his own handwriting. The facts could now be established. In 1860 (two years before the lizard dream) a sister of this same friend had visited Delboeuf on her honeymoon. She had with her the album, which was to be a gift to her brother, and Delboeuf took the trouble to write its Latin name under each dried plant, at the dictation of a botanist.

Good luck, which made this example so well worth recording, enabled Delboeuf to trace yet another part of the content of the dream to its forgotten source. One day in 1877 he happened to take up an old volume of an illustrated periodical and in it he found a picture of the whole procession of lizards which he had dreamed of in 1862. The volume was dated 1861 and Delboeuf remembered having been a subscriber to the paper from its first number.

The fact that dreams have at their command memories which are inaccessible in waking life is so remarkable and of such theoretical importance that I should like to draw still more attention to it by relating some further 'hypermnesic' dreams. Maury [1878, 142] tells us how for some time the word 'Mussidan' kept coming into his head during the day. He knew nothing about it except that it was the name of a town in France. One night he dreamt that he was talking to someone who told him he came from Mussidan, and who, on being asked where that was, replied that it was a small town in the Department of Dordogne. When he woke up, Maury had no belief in the information given him in the dream; he learnt from a gazetteer, however, that it was perfectly correct. In this case the fact of the dream's superior knowledge was confirmed, but the forgotten source of that knowledge was not discovered.

Jessen (1855, 551) reports a very similar event in a dream dating from remoter times: 'To this class belongs among others a dream of the elder Scaliger (quoted by Hennings, 1784, 300) who wrote a poem in praise of the famous men of Verona. A man who called himself Brugnolus appeared to him in a dream and complained that he had been overlooked. Although Scaliger could not remember having ever heard of him, he wrote some verses on him. His son learnt later in Verona that someone named Brugnolus had in fact been celebrated there as a critic.'

The Marquis d'Hervey de St. Denys [1867, 305],[1] quoted by Vaschide (1911, 232 f.), describes a hypermnesic dream which has a special pecu-

---

[1][This paragraph and the next were added in 1914.]

liarity, for it was followed by another dream which completed the recognition of what was at first an unidentified memory: 'I once dreamt of a young woman with golden hair, whom I saw talking to my sister while showing her some embroidery. She seemed very familiar to me in the dream and I thought I had seen her very often before. After I woke up, I still had her face very clearly before me but I was totally unable to recognize it. I then went to sleep once more and the dream-picture was repeated. . . . But in this second dream I spoke to the fair-haired lady and asked her if I had not had the pleasure of meeting her before somewhere. "Of course," she replied, "don't you remember the plage at Pornic?" I immediately woke up again and I was then able to recollect clearly all the details associated with the attractive vision in the dream.'

The same author [ibid., 306] (quoted again by Vaschide, ibid., 233–4) tells how a musician of his acquaintance once heard in a dream a tune which seemed to him entirely new. It was not until several years later that he found the same tune in an old collected volume of musical pieces, though he still could not remember ever having looked through it before.

I understand that Myers [1892] has published a whole collection of hypermnesic dreams of this kind in the *Proceedings* of the Society for Psychical Research; but these are unluckily inaccessible to me.

No one who occupies himself with dreams can, I believe, fail to discover that it is a very common event for a dream to give evidence of knowledge and memories which the waking subject is unaware of possessing. In my psycho-analytic work with nervous patients, of which I shall speak later, I am in a position several times a week to prove to patients from their dreams that they are really quite familiar with quotations, obscene words and so on, and make use of them in their dreams, though they have forgotten them in their waking life. I will add one more innocent case of hypermnesia in a dream, because of the great ease with which it was possible to trace the source of the knowledge that was accessible only in the dream.

One of my patients dreamt in the course of a fairly lengthy dream that he had ordered a 'Kontuszówka' while he was in a café. After telling me this, he asked me what a 'Kontuszówka' was, as he had never heard the name. I was able to tell him in reply that it was a Polish liqueur, and that he could not have invented the name as it had long been familiar to me from advertisements on the hoardings. At first he would not believe me; but some days later, after making his dream come true in a café, he noticed the name on a hoarding at a street corner which he must have gone past at least twice a day for several months.

I have noticed myself[1] from my own dreams how much it is a matter of chance whether one discovers the source of particular elements of a dream. Thus, for several years before completing this book, I was pursued by the picture of a church tower of very simple design, which I could not remember ever having seen. Then I suddenly recognized it, with absolute certainty, at a small station on the line between Salzburg and Reichenhall. That was during the second half of the eighteen-nineties and I had travelled over the line for the first time in 1886. During later years, when I was already deeply absorbed in the study of dreams, the frequent recurrence in my dreams of the picture of a particular unusual-looking place became a positive nuisance to me. In a specific spatial relation to myself, on my left-hand side, I saw a dark space out of which there glimmered a number of grotesque sandstone figures. A faint recollection, which I was unwilling to credit, told me it was the entrance to a beer-cellar. But I failed to discover either the meaning of the dream-picture or its origin. In 1907 I happened to be in Padua, which, to my regret, I had not been able to visit since 1895. My first visit to that lovely University town had been a disappointment, as I had not been able to see Giotto's frescoes in the Madonna dell' Arena. I had turned back halfway along the street leading there, on being told that the chapel was closed on that particular day. On my second visit, twelve years later, I decided to make up for this and the first thing I did was to set off towards the Arena chapel. In the street leading to it, on my left-hand side as I walked along and in all probability at the point at which I had turned back in 1895, I came upon the place I had seen so often in my dreams, with the sandstone figures that formed part of it. It was in fact the entrance to the garden of a restaurant.

One of the sources from which dreams derive material for reproduction—material which is in part neither remembered nor used in the activities of waking thought—is childhood experience. I will quote only a few of the authors who have noticed and stressed this fact.

Hildebrandt (1875, 23): 'I have already expressly admitted that dreams sometimes bring back to our minds, with a wonderful power of reproduction, very remote and even forgotten events from our earliest years.'

Strümpell (1877, 40): 'The position is even more remarkable when we observe how dreams sometimes bring to light, as it were, from beneath

---

[1] [This paragraph was added in 1909.]

the deepest piles of débris under which the earliest experiences of youth are buried in later times, pictures of particular localities, things or people, completely intact and with all their original freshness. This is not limited to experiences which created a lively impression when they occurred or enjoy a high degree of psychical importance and return later in a dream as genuine recollections at which waking consciousness will rejoice. On the contrary, the depths of memory in dreams also include pictures of people, things, localities and events dating from the earliest times, which either never possessed any psychical importance or more than a slight degree of vividness, or which have long since lost what they may have possessed of either, and which consequently seem completely alien and unknown alike to the dreaming and waking mind till their earlier origin has been discovered.'

Volkelt (1875, 119): 'It is especially remarkable how readily memories of childhood and youth make their way into dreams. Dreams are continually reminding us of things which we have ceased to think of and which have long ceased to be important to us.'

Since dreams have material from childhood at their command, and since, as we all know, that material is for the most part blotted out by gaps in our conscious faculty of memory, these circumstances give rise to interesting hypermnesic dreams, of which I will once more give a few examples.

Maury (1878, 92) relates how when he was a child he used often to go from Meaux, which was his birthplace, to the neighbouring village of Trilport, where his father was superintending the building of a bridge. One night in a dream he found himself in Trilport and was once more playing in the village street. A man came up to him who was wearing a sort of uniform. Maury asked him his name and he replied that he was called C. and was a watchman at the bridge. Maury awoke feeling sceptical as to the correctness of the memory, and asked an old maid-servant, who had been with him since his childhood, whether she could remember a man of that name. 'Why, yes,' was the reply, 'he was the watchman at the bridge when your father was building it.'

Maury (ibid., 143–4) gives another equally well corroborated example of the accuracy of a memory of childhood emerging in a dream. It was dreamt by a Monsieur F., who as a child had lived at Montbrison. Twenty-five years after leaving it, he decided to revisit his home and some friends of the family whom he had not since met. During the night before his departure he dreamt that he was already at Montbrison and, near the town, met a gentleman whom he did not know by sight but who told him he was Monsieur T., a friend of his father's. The dreamer was aware that when he was a child he had known someone of that name, but in his waking state no longer remembered what he looked like. A few days later he actually reached Montbrison, found the locality which in his dream had seemed unknown to him, and there met a gentleman whom he at once recognized as the Monsieur T. in the dream. The real person, however, looked much older than he had appeared in the dream.

At this point I may mention a dream of my own, in which what had to be traced was not an impression but a connection. I had a dream of someone who I knew in my dream was the doctor in my native town. His face was indistinct, but was confused with a picture of one of the masters at my secondary school, whom I still meet occasionally. When I woke up I could not discover what connection there was between these two men. I made some enquiries from my mother, however, about this doctor who dated back to the earliest years of my childhood, and learnt that he had only one eye. The schoolmaster whose figure had covered that of the doctor in the dream, was also one-eyed. It was thirty-eight years since I had seen the doctor, and so far as I know I had never thought of him in my waking life, though a scar on my chin might have reminded me of his attentions.[1]

A number of writers, on the other hand, assert that elements are to be found in most dreams, which are derived from the very last few days before they were dreamt; and this sounds like an attempt to counterbalance the laying of too much weight upon the part played in dream-life by experiences in childhood. Thus Robert (1886, 46) actually declares that normal dreams are as a rule concerned only with the impressions of the past few days. We shall find, however, that the theory of dreams constructed by Robert makes it essential for him to bring forward the most recent impressions and leave the oldest out of sight. None the less the fact

---

[1] [The last clause of this sentence was added in 1909, appears in all later editions up to 1922, but was afterwards omitted. The reference to this same man on p. 292 below only makes sense if it alludes to this omitted clause. The accident that caused the scar is mentioned in the disguised autobiographical case history in Freud (1899*a*), and the event itself is probably described below on p. 560. This dream plays an important part in a letter to Fliess of October 15, 1897 (Freud, 1950*a*, Letter 71); it is also described in Freud, 1916–17, Lecture 13.]

stated by him remains correct, as I am able to confirm from my own investigations. An American writer, Nelson [1888, 380 f.], is of the opinion that the impressions most frequently employed in a dream arise from the day next but one before the dream occurs, or from the day preceding that one—as though the impressions of the day *immediately* before the dream were not sufficiently attenuated or remote.

Several writers who are anxious not to cast doubts on the intimate connection between the content of dreams and waking life have been struck by the fact that impressions with which waking thoughts are intensely occupied only appear in dreams after they have been pushed somewhat aside by the workings of daytime thought. Thus, after the death of someone dear to them, people do not as a rule dream of him to begin with, while they are overwhelmed by grief (Delage, 1891, [40]). On the other hand one of the most recent observers, Miss Hallam (Hallam and Weed, 1896, 410–11), has collected instances to the contrary, thus asserting the right of each of us to psychological individualism in this respect.

The third, most striking and least comprehensible characteristic of memory in dreams is shown in the *choice* of material reproduced. For what is found worth remembering is not, as in waking life, only what is most important, but on the contrary what is most indifferent and insignificant as well. On this point I will quote those writers who have given the strongest expression to their astonishment.

Hildebrandt (1875, 11): 'For the remarkable thing is that dreams derive their elements not from major and stirring events nor the powerful and compelling interests of the preceding day, but from incidental details, from the worthless fragments, one might say, of what has been recently experienced or of the remoter past. A family bereavement, which has moved us deeply and under whose immediate shadow we have fallen asleep late at night, is blotted out of our memory till with our first waking moment it returns to it again with disturbing violence. On the other hand, a wart on the forehead of a stranger whom we met in the street and to whom we gave no second thought after passing him *has* a part to play in our dream. . . . '

Strümpell (1877, 39): 'There are cases in which the analysis of a dream shows that some of its components are indeed derived from experiences of the previous day or its predecessor, but experiences so unimportant and trivial from the point of view of waking consciousness that they were forgotten soon after they occurred. Experiences of this kind include, for instance, remarks accidentally overheard, or another person's actions inattentively observed, or passing glimpses of people or things, or odd fragments of what one has read, and so on.'

Havelock Ellis (1899, 727): 'The profound emotions of waking life, the questions and problems on which we spread our chief voluntary mental energy, are not those which usually present themselves at once to dream consciousness. It is, so far as the immediate past is concerned, mostly the trifling, the incidental, the "forgotten" impressions of daily life which reappear in our dreams. The psychic activities that are awake most intensely are those that sleep most profoundly.'

Binz (1878, 44-5) actually makes this particular peculiarity of memory in dreams the occasion for expressing his dissatisfaction with the explanations of dreams which he himself has supported: 'And the natural dream raises similar problems. Why do we not always dream of the mnemic impressions of the day we have just lived through? Why do we often, without any apparent motive, plunge instead into the remote and almost extinct past? Why does consciousness so often in dreams receive the impression of *indifferent* memory-images, while the brain cells, just where they carry the most sensitive marks of what has been experienced, lie for the most part silent and still, unless they have been stirred into fresh activity shortly before, during waking life?'

It is easy to see how the remarkable preference shown by the memory in dreams for indifferent, and consequently unnoticed, elements in waking experience is bound to lead people to overlook in general the dependence of dreams upon waking life and at all events to make it difficult in any particular instance to prove that dependence. Thus Miss Whiton Calkins (1893, 315), in her statistical study of her own and her collaborator's dreams, found that in eleven per cent of the total there was no visible connection with waking life. Hildebrandt (1875, [12 f.]) is unquestionably right in asserting that we should be able to explain the genesis of every dream-image if we devoted enough time and trouble to tracing its origin. He speaks of this as 'an exceedingly laborious and thankless task. For as a rule it ends in hunting out every kind of utterly worthless psychical event from the remotest corners of the chambers of one's memory, and in dragging to light once again every kind of completely indifferent moment of the past from the oblivion in which it was buried in the very hour, perhaps, after it occurred.' I can only regret that this keen-sighted author allowed himself to be deterred from following the path which had this inauspicious beginning; if he had followed it, it would have led him to the very heart of the explanation of dreams.

The way in which the memory behaves in dreams is undoubtedly of the greatest importance for any theory of memory in general. It teaches us that 'nothing which we have once mentally possessed can be entirely lost' (Scholz, 1893, 59); or, as Delboeuf [1885, 115] puts it, 'que toute impression même la plus insignifiante, laisse une trace inaltérable, indéfiniment susceptible de reparaître au jour.'[1] This is a conclusion to which we are also driven by many pathological phenomena of mental life. Certain theories about dreams which we shall mention later seek to account for their absurdity and incoherence by a partial forgetting of what we know during the day. When we bear in mind the extraordinary efficiency that we have just seen exhibited by memory in dreams we shall have a lively sense of the contradiction which these theories involve.

It might perhaps occur to us that the phenomenon of dreaming could be reduced entirely to that of memory: dreams, it might be supposed, are a manifestation of a reproductive activity which is at work even in the night and which is an end in itself. This would tally with statements such as those made by Pilcz (1899), according to which there is a fixed relation observable between the time at which a dream occurs and its content— impressions from the remotest past being reproduced in dreams during deep sleep, while more recent impressions appear towards morning. But views of this sort are inherently improbable owing to the manner in which dreams deal with the material that is to be remembered. Strümpell [1877, 18] rightly points out that dreams do not reproduce experiences. They take one step forward, but the next step in the chain is omitted, or appears in an altered form, or is replaced by something entirely extraneous. Dreams yield no more than *fragments* of reproductions; and this is so general a rule that theoretical conclusions may be based on it. It is true that there are exceptional cases in which a dream repeats an experience with as much completeness as is attainable by our waking memory. Delboeuf [1885, 239 f.] tells how one of his university colleagues[2] had a dream which reproduced

---

[1] ['That even the most insignificant impression leaves an unalterable trace, which is indefinitely capable of revival.']

[2] [In the first edition the words 'who is now teaching in Vienna' appeared here but they were cut out in 1909. In *Ges. Schr.* **3** (1925), 8, Freud remarks that 'the words were no doubt rightly omitted, especially as the man in question had died.']

in all its details a dangerous carriage-accident he had had, with an almost miraculous escape. Miss Calkins (1893) mentions two dreams whose content was an exact reproduction of an event of the previous day, and I shall myself have occasion later to report an example I came across of a childhood experience re-appearing in a dream without modification. [See pp. 212 and 219.][1]

(C)

THE STIMULI AND SOURCES OF DREAMS

There is a popular saying that 'dreams come from indigestion' and this helps us to see what is meant by the stimuli and sources of dreams. Behind these concepts lies a theory according to which dreams are a result of a disturbance of sleep: we should not have had a dream unless something disturbing had happened during our sleep, and the dream was a reaction to that disturbance.

Discussions upon the exciting causes of dreams occupy a very large space in the literature of the subject. The problem could obviously only arise after dreams had become a subject of biological investigation. The ancients, who believed that dreams were inspired by the gods, had no need to look around for their stimulus: dreams emanated from the will of divine or daemonic powers and their content arose from the knowledge or purpose of those powers. Science was immediately faced by the question of whether the stimulus to dreaming was always the same or whether there could be many kinds of such stimuli; and this involved the consideration of whether the explanation of the causation of dreams fell within the province of psychology or rather of physiology. Most authorities seem

---

[1] [*Footnote added* 1909:] Subsequent experience leads me to add that it by no means rarely happens that innocent and unimportant actions of the previous day are repeated in a dream: such, for instance, as packing a trunk, preparing food in the kitchen, and so on. What the dreamer is himself stressing in dreams of this kind is not, however, the content of the memory but the fact of its being 'real': 'I really *did* do all that yesterday.' [Cf. below pp. 210 and 383 f. The topics discussed in this and the preceding section are taken up again in the first two sections of Chapter V (pp. 187 ff.)

to agree in assuming that the causes that disturb sleep—that is, the sources of dreaming—may be of many kinds and that somatic stimuli and mental excitations alike may come to act as instigators of dreams. Opinions differ widely, however, in the preference they show for one or the other source of dreams and in the order of importance which they assign to them as factors in the production of dreams.

Any complete enumeration of the sources of dreams leads to a recognition of four kinds of source; and these have also been used for the classification of dreams themselves. They are: (1) external (objective) sensory excitations; (2) internal (subjective) sensory excitations; (3) internal (organic) somatic stimuli; and (4) purely psychical sources of stimulation.

1. External Sensory Stimuli

The younger Strümpell [1883–4; Engl. trans. (1912), 2, 160], the son of the philosopher whose book on dreams has already given us several hints upon their problems, published a well-known account of his observations upon one of his patients who was afflicted with general anaesthesia of the surface of his body and paralysis of several of his higher sense organs. If the few of this man's sensory channels which remained open to the external world were closed, he would fall asleep. Now when we ourselves wish to go to sleep we are in the habit of trying to produce a situation similar to that of Strümpell's experiment. We close our most important sensory channels, our eyes, and try to protect the other senses from all stimuli or from any modification of the stimuli acting on them. We then fall asleep, even though our plan is never completely realized. We cannot keep stimuli completely away from our sense organs nor can we completely suspend the excitability of our sense organs. The fact that a fairly powerful stimulus will awaken us at any time is evidence that 'even in sleep the soul is in constant contact with the extracorporeal world.'[1] The sensory stimuli that reach us during sleep may very well become sources of dreams.

Now there are a great number of such stimuli, ranging from the unavoidable ones which the state of sleep itself necessarily involves or must tolerate from time to time, to the accidental, rousing stimuli which may or do put an end to sleep. A bright light may force its way into our eyes,

---

[1] [Cf. Burdach's remarks on p. 82 f.]

or a noise may make itself heard, or some strong-smelling substance may stimulate the mucous membrane of our nose. By unintentional movements during our sleep we may uncover some part of our body and expose it to sensations of chill, or by a change in posture we may ourselves bring about sensations of pressure or contact. We may be stung by a gnat, or some small mishap during the night may impinge upon several of our senses at once. Attentive observers have collected a whole series of dreams in which there has been such a far-reaching correspondence between a stimulus noticed on waking and a portion of the content of the dream that it has been possible to identify the stimulus as the source of the dream.

I will quote from Jessen (1855, 527 f.) a collection of dreams of this kind which may be traced back to objective, and more or less accidental, sensory stimulation.

'Every noise that is indistinctly perceived arouses corresponding dream-images. A peal of thunder will set us in the midst of a battle; the crowing of a cock may turn into a man's cry of terror; the creaking of a door may produce a dream of burglars. If our bedclothes fall off in the night, we may dream, perhaps, of walking about naked or of falling into water. If we are lying crosswise in bed and push our feet over the edge, we may dream that we are standing on the brink of a frightful precipice or that we are falling over a cliff. If our head happens to get under the pillow, we dream of being beneath a huge overhanging rock which is on the point of burying us under its weight. Accumulations of semen lead to lascivious dreams, local pains produce ideas of being ill-treated, attacked or injured. . . .

'Meier (1758, 33) once dreamt that he was overpowered by some men who stretched him out on his back on the ground and drove a stake into the earth between his big toe and the next one. While he was imagining this in the dream he woke up and found that a straw was sticking between his toes. On another occasion, according to Hennings (1784, 258), when Meier had fastened his shirt rather tight round his neck, he dreamt that he was being hanged. Hoffbauer [(1796, 146)] dreamt when he was a young man of falling down from a high wall, and when he woke up found that his bedstead had collapsed and that he had really fallen on to the floor. . . . Gregory reports that once, when he was lying with his feet on a hot-water bottle, he dreamt he had climbed to the top of Mount Etna and that the ground there was intolerably hot. Another man, who was sleeping with a hot poultice on his head, dreamt that he was being scalped by a band of Red Indians; while a third, who was wearing a damp nightshirt, imagined that he was being dragged through a stream. An attack of gout that came on suddenly during sleep caused the patient to believe he was in the hands of the Inquisition and being tortured on the rack. (Macnish [1835, 40].)'

The argument based on the similarity between the stimulus and the content of the dream gains in strength if it is possible deliberately to convey a sensory stimulus to the sleeper and produce in him a dream corresponding to that stimulus. According to Macnish (loc. Cit.), quoted by Jessen (1855, 529), experiments of this sort had already been made by Girou de Buzareingues [1848, 55]. 'He left his knee uncovered and dreamt that he was travelling at night in a mail coach. He remarks upon this that travellers will no doubt be aware how cold one's knees become at night in a coach. Another time he left his head uncovered at the back and dreamt that he was taking part in a religious ceremony in the open air. It must be explained that in the country in which he lived it was the custom always to keep the head covered except in circumstances such as these.'

Maury (1878, [154–6]) brings forward some new observations of dreams produced in himself. (A number of other experiments were unsuccessful.)

(1) His lips and the tip of his nose were tickled with a feather.—He dreamt of a frightful form of torture: a mask made of pitch was placed on his face and then pulled off, so that it took his skin off with it.

(2) A pair of scissors was sharpened on a pair of pliers.—He heard bells pealing, followed by alarm-bells, and he was back in the June days of 1848.

(3) He was given some eau-de-cologne to smell.—He was in Cairo, in Johann Maria Farina's shop. Some absurd adventures followed, which he could not reproduce.

(4) He was pinched lightly on the neck.—He dreamt he was being given a mustard plaster and thought of the doctor who had treated him as a child.

(5) A hot iron was brought close to his face.—He dreamt that the 'chauffeurs'[1] had made their way into the house and were forcing its inhabitants to give up their money by sticking their feet into braziers of hot coal. The Duchess of Abrantès, whose secretary he was in the dream, then appeared.

---

[1] The 'chauffeurs' [heaters] were bands of robbers in La Vendée [at the time of the French Revolution], who made use of the method of torture described above.

(8) A drop of water was dropped on his forehead.—He was in Italy, was sweating violently and was drinking white Orvieto wine.

(9) Light from a candle was repeatedly shone upon him through a sheet of red paper.—He dreamt of the weather and of the heat, and was once again in a storm he had experienced in the English Channel.

Other attempts at producing dreams experimentally have been reported by Hervey de Saint-Denys [1867, 268 f. and 376 f.], Weygandt (1893) and others.

Many writers have commented upon 'the striking facility with which dreams are able to weave a sudden impression from the world of the senses into their own structure so that it comes as what appears to be a pre-arranged catastrophe that has been gradually led up to.' (Hildebrandt, 1875, [36].) 'In my youth,' this author goes on, 'I used to make use of an alarm-clock in order to be up regularly at a fixed hour. It must have happened hundreds of times that the noise produced by this instrument fitted into an ostensibly lengthy and connected dream as though the whole dream had been leading up to that one event and had reached its appointed end in what was a logically indispensable climax.' [Ibid., 37.]

I shall quote three of these alarm-clock dreams presently in another connection. [Pp. 60.]

Volkelt (1875, 108 f.) writes: 'A composer once dreamt that he was giving a class and was trying to make a point clear to his pupils. When he had done, he turned to one of the boys and asked him if he had followed. The boy shouted back like a lunatic: "Oh ja! [Oh yes!]" He began to reprove the boy angrily for shouting, but the whole class broke out into cries first of "Orja!," then of "Eurjo!" and finally of "Feuerjo!"[1] At this point he was woken up by actual cries of "Feuerjo!" in the street.'

Garnier (1865, [1, 476]) tells how Napoleon I was woken by a bomb explosion while he was asleep in his carriage. He had a dream that he was once more crossing the Tagliamento under the Austrian bombardment, and at last started up with a cry: 'We are undermined!'[2]

A dream dreamt by Maury (1878, 161) has become famous. He was ill and lying in his room in bed, with his mother sitting beside him, and dreamt that it was during the Reign of Terror. After witnessing a number of frightful scenes of murder, he was finally himself brought before the

---

[1] [The first two of these last three exclamations are meaningless; the third is the conventional cry for an alarm of fire.]

[2] [Further considered below on pp. 252 f. and 501 f.]

revolutionary tribunal. There he saw Robespierre, Marat, Fouquier-Tinville and the rest of the grim heroes of those terrible days. He was questioned by them, and, after a number of incidents which were not retained in his memory, was condemned, and led to the place of execution surrounded by an immense mob. He climbed on to the scaffold and was bound to the plank by the executioner. It was tipped up. The blade of the guillotine fell. He felt his head being separated from his body, woke up in extreme anxiety—and found that the top of the bed had fallen down and had struck his cervical vertebrae just in the way in which the blade of the guillotine would actually have struck them.

This dream was the basis of an interesting discussion between Le Lorrain (1894) and Egger (1895) in the *Revue philosophique*. The question raised was whether and how it was possible for a dreamer to compress such an apparently superabundant quantity of material into the short period elapsing between his perceiving the rousing stimulus and his waking.[1]

Examples of this kind leave an impression that of all the sources of dreams the best confirmed are objective sensory stimuli during sleep. Moreover they are the only sources whatever taken into account by laymen. If an educated man, who is unacquainted with the literature of dreams, is asked how dreams arise, he will infallibly answer with a reference to some instance he has come across in which a dream was explained by an objective sensory stimulus discovered after waking. Scientific enquiry, however, cannot stop there. It finds an occasion for further questions in the observed fact that the stimulus which impinges on the senses during sleep does not appear in the dream in its real shape but is replaced by another image in some way related to it. But the relation connecting the stimulus of the dream to the dream which is its result is, to quote Maury's words (1854, 72), 'une affinité quelconque, mais qui n'est pas unique et exclusive.'[2] Let us consider in this connection three of Hildebrandt's alarm-clock dreams (1875, 37 f.). The question they raise is why the same stimulus should have provoked three such different dreams and why it should have provoked these rather than any other.

'I dreamt, then, that one spring morning I was going for a walk and was strolling through the green fields till I came to a neighbouring village, where I saw the villagers in their best clothes, with hymn-books under

---

[1] [Further discussed below, pp. 93 and 500 f.]

[2] ['An affinity of some kind, but one which is not unique and exclusive.']

their arms, flocking to the church. Of course! It was Sunday, and early morning service would soon be beginning. I decided I would attend it; but first, as I was rather hot from walking, I went into the churchyard which surrounded the church, to cool down. While I was reading some of the tombstones, I heard the bell-ringer climbing up the church tower and at the top of it I now saw the little village bell which would presently give the signal for the beginning of devotions. For quite a while it hung there motionless, then it began to swing, and suddenly its peal began to ring out clear and piercing—so clear and piercing that it put an end to my sleep. But what was ringing was the alarm-clock.

'Here is another instance. It was a bright winter's day and the streets were covered with deep snow. I had agreed to join a party for a sleigh-ride; but I had to wait a long time before news came that the sleigh was at the door. Now followed the preparations for getting in—the fur rug spread out, the foot-muff put ready—and at last I was sitting in my seat. But even then the moment of departure was delayed till a pull at the reins gave the waiting horses the signal. Then off they started, and, with a violent shake, the sleigh bells broke into their familiar jingle—with such violence, in fact, that in a moment the cobweb of my dream was torn through. And once again it was only the shrill sound of the alarm-clock.

'And now yet a third example. I saw a kitchen-maid, carrying several dozen plates piled on one another, walking along the passage to the dining-room. The column of china in her arms seemed to me in danger of losing its balance. "Take care," I exclaimed, "or you'll drop the whole load." The inevitable rejoinder duly followed: she was quite accustomed to that kind of job, and so on. And meanwhile my anxious looks followed the advancing figure. Then—just as I expected—she stumbled at the threshold and the fragile crockery slipped and rattled and clattered in a hundred pieces on the floor. But the noise continued without ceasing, and soon it seemed no longer to be a clattering; it was turning into a ringing—and the ringing, as my waking self now became aware, was only the alarm-clock doing its duty.'

The question of why the mind mistakes the nature of objective sensory stimuli in dreams receives almost the same answer from Strümpell (1877, [103]) as from Wundt (1874, [659 f.]): the mind receives stimuli that reach it during sleep under conditions favourable to the formation of illusions. A sense-impression is recognized by us and correctly interpreted—that is, it is placed in the group of memories to which, in accordance with all our previous experiences, it belongs—provided the impression is sufficiently strong, clear and lasting and provided we have sufficient time at our disposal for considering the matter. If these conditions are not fulfilled, we mistake the object which is the source of the impression: we form an illusion about it. 'If someone goes for a walk in the open country and has an indeterminate perception of a distant object, he may at first believe it to be a horse.' On a closer view he may be led to interpret it as a cow lying down, and the image may finally resolve itself definitely into a group of people sitting on the ground. The impressions received by the mind from external stimuli during sleep are of a similarly indeterminate nature; and on their basis the mind forms illusions, since a greater or smaller number of memory-images are aroused by the impression and it is through them that it acquires its psychical value. From *which* of the many groups of memories concerned the related images shall be aroused and *which* of the possible associative connections shall accordingly be put into action—these questions too, on Strümpell's theory, are indeterminable and are, as it were, left open to the arbitrary decision of the mind.

At this point we are faced with a choice between two alternatives. We may admit it as a fact that it is impossible to follow the laws governing the formation of dreams any further; and we may accordingly refrain from enquiring whether there may not be other determinants governing the interpretation put by the dreamer upon the illusion called up by the sense-impression. Or, on the other hand, we may have a suspicion that the sensory stimulus which impinges on the sleeper plays only a modest part in generating his dream and that other factors determine the choice of the memory-images which are to be aroused in him. In fact, if we examine Maury's experimentally produced dreams (which I have related in such detail for this very reason), we shall be tempted to say that the experiment in fact accounts for the origin of only one element of the dreams; the rest of their content seems too self-contained, too definite in its details, to be explicable solely by the necessity for fitting in with the element experimentally introduced from outside. Indeed, one begins to have doubts about the illusion theory and about the power of objective impressions to give a shape to dreams when one finds that those impressions are sometimes subjected in dreams to the most peculiar and far-fetched interpretations. Thus Simon (1888) tells us of a dream in which he saw some gigantic figures seated at table and clearly heard the frightful snapping noise made by their jaws coming together as they chewed.

When he awoke he heard the beat of a horse's hooves galloping past his window. The noise made by the horse's hooves may have suggested ideas from a group of memories connected with *Gulliver's Travels*—the giants of Brobdingnag and the virtuous Houyhnhnms—if I may venture on an interpretation without the dreamer's assistance. Is it not probable, then, that the choice of such an unusual group of memories as these was facilitated by motives other than the objective stimulus alone?[1]

2. INTERNAL (SUBJECTIVE) SENSORY EXCITATIONS

In spite of any objections to the contrary, it has to be admitted that the part played by objective sensory excitations during sleep in provoking dreams remains indisputable. And if such stimuli may appear, from their nature and frequency, insufficient to explain *every* dream-image, we shall be encouraged to seek for other sources of dreams analogous to them in their operation. I cannot say when the idea first cropped up of taking *internal* (subjective) excitations of the sense organs into account alongside of the *external* sensory stimuli. It is, however, the case that this is done, more or less explicitly, in all the more recent discussions of the aetiology of dreams. 'An essential part is also played, I believe,' writes Wundt (1874, 657), 'in the production of the illusions that occur in dreams by the subjective visual and auditory sensations which are familiar to us in the waking state as the formless areas of luminosity which become visible to us when our field of vision is darkened, as ringing or buzzing in the ears, and so on. Especially important among these are the subjective excitations of the retina. It is in this way that is to be explained the remarkable tendency of dreams to conjure up before the eyes similar or identical objects in large numbers. We see before us innumerable birds or butterflies or fishes or coloured beads or flowers, etc. Here the luminous dust in the darkened field of vision has taken on a fantastic shape, and the numerous specks of which it consists are incorporated into the dream as an

---

[1] [*Footnote added* 1911:] The appearance of gigantic figures in a dream gives grounds for supposing that some scene from the dreamer's childhood is involved [Cf. p. 417.]—[*Added* 1925:] Incidentally, the interpretation given in the text, pointing to a reminiscence of *Gulliver's Travels*, is a good example of what an interpretation ought not to be. The interpreter of a dream should not give free play to his own ingenuity and neglect the dreamer's associations.

equal number of separate images; and these, on account of their mobility, are regarded as *moving* objects.—This is no doubt also the basis of the great fondness shown by dreams for animal figures of every sort; for the immense variety of such forms can adjust itself easily to the particular form assumed by the subjective luminous images.'

As sources of dream-images, subjective sensory excitations have the obvious advantage of not being dependent, like objective ones, upon external chance. They are ready to hand, as one might say, whenever they are needed as an explanation. But they are at a disadvantage compared with objective sensory stimuli in that the part they play in instigating a dream is scarcely or not at all open to confirmation, as is the case with objective stimuli, by observation and experiment. The chief evidence in favour of the power of subjective sensory excitations to instigate dreams is provided by what are known as 'hypnagogic hallucinations,' or, to use Johannes Müller's term (1826), 'imaginative visual phenomena.' These are images, often very vivid and rapidly changing, which are apt to appear—quite habitually in some people—during the period of falling asleep; and they may also persist for a time after the eyes have been opened. Maury, who was subject to them in a high degree, has made an exhaustive examination of them and maintains (as did Müller [ibid., 49 f.] before him) their connection and indeed their identity with dream-images. In order to produce them, he says (Maury, 1878, 59 f.), a certain amount of mental passivity, a relaxation of the strain of attention, is necessary. It is enough, however, to fall into a lethargic state of this kind for no more than a second (provided that one has the necessary predisposition) in order to have a hypnagogic hallucination. After this one may perhaps wake up again and the process may be repeated several times until one finally falls asleep. Maury found that if he then woke up once more after not too long an interval, he was able to detect in his dream the same images that had floated before his eyes as hypnagogic hallucinations before he fell asleep. (Ibid., 134 f.) This was the case on one occasion with a number of grotesque figures with distorted faces and strange *coiffures* which pestered him with extreme pertinacity while he was going to sleep and which he remembered having dreamt about after he woke. Another time, when he was suffering from hunger owing to having put himself on a light diet, he had a hypnagogic vision of a plate and a hand armed with a fork which was helping itself to some of the food from the plate. In the dream which followed he was sitting at a well-spread table and heard the noise made by the diners with their forks. Yet another time, when he went to sleep with his eyes in an irritated and painful state, he had a hypnagogic hallucination of some microscopically small signs which he could only decipher one by one with the greatest difficulty, he was woken from his sleep an hour later and remembered a dream in which there was an open book printed in very small type which he was reading painfully.

Auditory hallucinations of words, names, and so on can also occur hypnagogically in the same way as visual images, and may then be repeated in a dream—just as an overture announces the principal themes which are to be heard in the opera that is to follow.

A more recent observer of hypnagogic hallucinations, G. Trumbull Ladd (1892), has followed the same lines as Müller and Maury. After some practice he succeeded in being able to wake himself suddenly without opening his eyes, from two to five minutes after gradually falling asleep. He thus had an opportunity of comparing the retinal sensations which were just disappearing with the dream-images persisting in his memory. He declares that it was possible in every case to recognize an internal relation between the two, for the luminous points and lines of the idioretinal light provided, as it were, an outline drawing or diagram of the figures mentally perceived in the dream. For instance, an arrangement of the luminous points in the retina in parallel lines corresponded to a dream in which he had been seeing, clearly spread out in front of him, some lines of print which he was engaged in reading. Or, to use his own words, 'the clearly printed page which I was reading in my dream faded away into an object that appeared to my waking consciousness like a section of an actual page of print when seen through an oval hole in a piece of paper at too great a distance to distinguish more than an occasional fragment of a word, and even that dimly.' Ladd is of the opinion (though he does not underestimate the part played in the phenomenon by central [cerebral] factors) that scarcely a single visual dream occurs without the participation of material provided by intraocular retinal excitation. This applies especially to dreams occurring soon after falling asleep in a dark room, while the source of stimulus for dreams occurring in the morning shortly before waking is the objective light which penetrates the eyes in a room that is growing light. The changing, perpetually shifting character of the excitation of the idioretinal light corresponds precisely to the constantly moving succession of images shown us by our dreams. No one who attaches importance to these observations of Ladd's will underestimate the part played in dreams by these subjective sources of stimulation, for, as we know, visual images constitute the principal component of our dreams. The contributions from the other senses, except for that of hearing, are intermittent and of less importance.

3. Internal Organic Somatic Stimuli

Since we are now engaged in looking for sources of dreams inside the organism instead of outside it, we must bear in mind that almost all our internal organs, though they give us scarcely any news of their working so long as they are in a healthy state, become a source of what are mainly distressing sensations when they are in what we describe as states of excitation, or during illnesses. These sensations must be equated with the sensory or painful stimuli reaching us from the outside. The experience of ages is reflected in—to take an example—Strümpell's remarks on the subject (1877, 107): 'During sleep the mind attains a far deeper and wider sensory consciousness of somatic events than during the waking state. It is obliged to receive and be affected by impressions of stimuli from parts of the body and from changes in the body of which it knows nothing when awake.' So early a writer as Aristotle regarded it as quite possible that the beginnings of an illness might make themselves felt in dreams before anything could be noticed of it in waking life, owing to the magnifying effect produced upon impressions by dreams. (See above, p. 37.) Medical writers, too, who were certainly far from believing in the prophetic power of dreams, have not disputed their significance as premonitors of illness. (Cf. Simon, 1888, 31, and many earlier writers.[1])

---

[1] [*Footnote added* 1914:] Apart from the diagnostic value ascribed to dreams (e.g. in the works of Hippocrates [see above p. 37 n. 2]), their *therapeutic* importance in antiquity must also be borne in mind. In Greece there were dream oracles, which were regularly visited by patients in search of recovery. A sick man would enter the temple of Apollo or Aesculapius, would perform various ceremonies there, would be purified by lustration, massage and incense, and then, in a state of exaltation, would be stretched on the skin of a ram that had been sacrificed. He would then fall asleep and would dream of the remedies for his illness. These would be revealed to him either in their natural form or in symbols and pictures which would afterwards be interpreted by the priests. For further information upon therapeutic dreams among the Greeks see Lehmann (1908, **1**, 74), Bouché-Leclercq (1879–1882), Hermann (1858, §41, 262 ff., and 1882, §38, 356), Böttinger (1795, 163 ff.), Lloyd (1877), Döllinger (1857, 130).—[A comment on the 'diagnostic' value of dreams will be found near the beginning of Freud, 1917d.]

Instances of the diagnostic power of dreams seem to be vouched for in more recent times. Thus Tissié (1898, 62 f.) quotes from Artigues (1884, 43) the story of a forty-three-year-old woman, who, while apparently in perfect health, was for some years tormented by anxiety-dreams. She was then medically examined and found to be in the early stages of an affection of the heart, to which she eventually succumbed.

Pronounced disorders of the internal organs obviously act as instigators of dreams in a whole number of cases. The frequency of anxiety-dreams in diseases of the heart and lungs is generally recognized. Indeed, this side of dream-life is placed in the foreground by so many authorities that I am content with a mere reference to the literature: Radestock [1879, 70], Spitta [1882, 241 f.], Maury [1878, 33 f.], Simon (1888), Tissié [1898, 60 ff.]. Tissié is even of the opinion that the particular organ affected gives a characteristic impress to the content of the dream. Thus the dreams of those suffering from diseases of the heart are usually short and come to a terrifying end at the moment of waking; their content almost always includes a situation involving a horrible death. Sufferers from diseases of the lungs dream of suffocation, crowding and fleeing, and are remarkably subject to the familiar nightmare. (It may be remarked, incidentally, that Börner (1855) has succeeded in provoking the latter experimentally by lying on his face or covering the respiratory apertures.) In the case of digestive disorders dreams contain ideas connected with enjoyment of food or disgust. Finally, the influence of sexual excitement on the content of dreams can be adequately appreciated by everyone from his own experience and provides the theory that dreams are instigated by organic stimuli with its most powerful support.

No one, moreover, who goes through the literature of the subject can fail to notice that some writers, such as Maury [1878, 451 f.] and Weygandt (1893), were led to the study of dream problems by the effect of their own illnesses upon the content of their dreams.

Nevertheless, though these facts are established beyond a doubt, their importance for the study of the sources of dreams is not so great as might have been hoped. Dreams are phenomena which occur in healthy people—perhaps in everyone, perhaps every night—and it is obvious that organic illness cannot be counted among its indispensable conditions. And what we are concerned with is not the origin of certain special dreams but the source that instigates the ordinary dreams of normal people.

We need only go a step further, however, in order to come upon a source of dreams more copious than any we have so far considered, one indeed which seems as though it could never run dry. If it is established that the interior of the body when it is in a diseased state becomes a source of stimuli for dreams, and if we admit that during sleep the mind, being diverted from the external world, is able to pay more attention to the interior of the body, then it seems plausible to suppose that the internal organs do not need to be diseased before they can cause excitations to reach the sleeping mind—excitations which are somehow turned into dream-images. While we are awake we are aware of a diffuse general sensibility or coenaesthesia, but only as a vague quality of our mood; to this feeling, according to medical opinion, all the organic systems contribute a share. At night, however, it would seem that this same feeling, grown into a powerful influence and acting through its various components, becomes the strongest and at the same time the commonest source for instigating dream-images. If this is so, it would only remain to investigate the laws according to which the organic stimuli turn into dream-images.

We have here reached the theory of the origin of dreams which is preferred by all the medical authorities. The obscurity in which the centre of our being (the '*moi splanchnique*,' as Tissié [1898, 23] calls it) is veiled from our knowledge and the obscurity surrounding the origin of dreams tally too well not to be brought into relation to each other. The line of thought which regards vegetative organic sensation as the constructor of dreams has, moreover, a particular attraction for medical men since it allows of a single aetiology for dreams and mental diseases, whose manifestations have so much in common; for coenaesthetic changes and stimuli arising from the internal organs are also held largely responsible for the origin of the psychoses. It is not surprising, therefore, that the origin of the theory of somatic stimulation may be traced back to more than one independent source.

The line of argument developed by the philosopher Schopenhauer in 1851 has had a decisive influence on a number of writers. Our picture of the universe, in his view, is arrived at by our intellect taking the impressions that impinge on it from outside and remoulding them into the forms of time, space and causality. During the daytime the stimuli from the interior of the organism, from the sympathetic nervous system, exercise at the most an unconscious effect upon our mood. But at night, when we are no longer deafened by the impressions of the day, those which arise from within are able to attract attention—just as at night we can hear the murmuring of a brook which is drowned by daytime noises. But how is the intellect to react to these stimuli otherwise than by carrying out its own peculiar function on them? The stimuli are accordingly remodelled into forms occupying space and time and obeying the rules of causality, and thus dreams arise [cf. Schopenhauer, 1862, 1, 249 ff.]. Scherner (1861) and after him Volkelt (1875) endeavoured subsequently to investigate in more detail the relation between somatic stimuli and dream-images, but I shall postpone my consideration of these attempts till we reach the section dealing with the various theories about dreams. [See below, pp. 109 ff.]

Krauss [1859, 255], the psychiatrist, in an investigation carried through with remarkable consistency, traces the origin alike of dreams and of deliria[1] and delusions to the same factor, namely to organically determined sensations. It is scarcely possible to think of any part of the organism which might not be the starting point of a dream or of a delusion. Organically determined sensations 'may be divided into two classes: (1) those constituting the general mood (coenaesthesia) and (2) the specific sensations immanent in the principal systems of the vegetative organism. Of these latter five groups are to be distinguished: (a) muscular, (b) respiratory, (c) gastric, (d) sexual and (e) peripheral sensations.' Krauss supposes that the process by which dream-images arise on the basis of somatic stimuli is as follows. The sensation that has been aroused evokes a cognate image, in accordance with some law of association. It combines with the image into an organic structure, to which, however, consciousness reacts abnormally. For it pays no attention to the *sensation*, but directs the whole of it to the accompanying *images*—which explains why the true facts were for so long misunderstood. Krauss has a special term for describing this process: the 'trans-substantiation' of sensations into dream-images.

The influence of organic somatic stimuli upon the formation of dreams is almost universally accepted today; but the question of the laws that govern the relation between them is answered in very various ways, and often by obscure pronouncements. On the basis of the theory of somatic stimulation, dream-interpretation is thus faced with the special problem of tracing back the content of a dream to the organic stimuli which caused it; and, if the rules for interpretation laid down by Scherner (1861) are not accepted, one is often faced with the awkward fact that the

---

[1] [Perhaps 'hallucinations'; see p. 87 n.]

only thing that reveals the existence of the organic stimulus is precisely the content of the dream itself.

There is a fair amount of agreement, however, over the interpretation of various forms of dreams that are described as 'typical,' because they occur in large numbers of people and with very similar content. Such are the familiar dreams of falling from a height, of teeth falling out, of flying and of embarrassment at being naked or insufficiently clad. This last dream is attributed simply to the sleeper's perceiving that he has thrown off his bedclothes in his sleep and is lying exposed to the air. The dream of teeth falling out is traced back to a 'dental stimulus,' though this does not necessarily imply that the excitation of the teeth is a pathological one. According to Strümpel [1877, 119] the flying dream is the image which is found appropriate by the mind as an interpretation of the stimulus produced by the rising and sinking of the lobes of the lungs at times when cutaneous sensations in the thorax have ceased to be conscious: it is this latter circumstance that leads to the feeling which is attached to the idea of floating. The dream of falling from a height is said to be due to an arm falling away from the body or a flexed knee being suddenly extended at a time when the sense of cutaneous pressure is beginning to be no longer conscious; the movements in question cause the tactile sensations to become conscious once more, and the transition to consciousness is represented psychically by the dream of falling (ibid., 118). The obvious weakness of these attempted explanations, plausible though they are, lies in the fact that, without any other evidence, they can make successive hypotheses that this or that group of organic sensations enters or disappears from mental perception, till a constellation has been reached which affords an explanation of the dream. I shall later have occasion to return to the question of typical dreams and their origin. [Cf. pp. 259 ff. and 395 ff.]

Simon (1888, 34 f.) has attempted to deduce some of the rules governing the way in which organic stimuli determine the resultant dreams by comparing a series of similar dreams. He asserts that if an organic apparatus which normally plays a part in the expression of an emotion is brought by some extraneous cause during sleep into the state of excitation which is usually produced by the emotion, then a dream will arise which will contain images appropriate to the emotion in question. Another rule lays it down that if during sleep an organ is in a state of activity, excitation or disturbance, the dream will produce images related to the performance of the function which is discharged by the organ concerned.

Mourly Vold (1896) has set out to prove experimentally in one particular field the effect on the production of dreams which is asserted by the theory of somatic stimulation. His experiments consisted in altering the position of a sleeper's limbs and comparing the resultant dreams with the alterations made. He states his findings as follows:

(1) The position of a limb in the dream corresponds approximately to its position in reality. Thus, we dream of the limb being in a static condition when it is so actually.

(2) If we dream of a limb moving, then one of the positions passed through in the course of completing the movement invariably corresponds to the limb's actual position.

(3) The position of the dreamer's own limb may be ascribed in the dream to some other person.

(4) The dream may be of the movement in question being *hindered.*

(5) The limb which is in the position in question may appear in the dream as an animal or monster, in which case a certain analogy is established between them.

(6) The position of a limb may give rise in the dream to thoughts which have some connection with the limb. Thus, if the fingers are concerned, we dream of numbers.

I should be inclined to conclude from findings such as these that even the theory of somatic stimulation has not succeeded in completely doing away with the apparent absence of determination in the choice of what dream-images are to be produced.[1]

4. Psychical Sources of Stimulation

When we were dealing with the relations of dreams to waking life and with the material of dreams, we found that the most ancient and the most recent students of dreams were united in believing that men dream of what they do during the daytime and of what interests them while they are awake [pp. 41 f.]. Such an interest, carried over from waking life into sleep, would not only be a mental bond, a link between dreams and life, but would also provide us with a further source of dreams and one not to be

---

[1] [*Footnote added* 1914:] This author has since produced a two-volume report on his experiments (1910 and 1912), which is referred to below. [See p. 243 n. 2.]

despised. Indeed, taken in conjunction with the interests that develop during sleep—the stimuli that impinge on the sleeper—it might be enough to explain the origin of all dream-images. But we have also heard the opposite asserted, namely that dreams withdraw the sleeper from the interests of daytime and that, as a rule, we only start dreaming of the things that have most struck us during the day, after they have lost the spice of actuality in waking life. [Pp. 41 and 51.] Thus at every step we take in our analysis of dream-life we come to feel that it is impossible to make generalizations without covering ourselves by such qualifying phrases as 'frequently,' 'as a rule' or 'in most cases,' and without being prepared to admit the validity of exceptions.

If it were a fact that waking interests, along with internal and external stimuli during sleep, sufficed to exhaust the aetiology of dreams, we ought to be in a position to give a satisfactory account of the origin of every element of a dream: the riddle of the sources of dreams would be solved, and it would only remain to define the share taken respectively by psychical and somatic stimuli in any particular dream. Actually no such complete explanation of a dream has ever yet been achieved, and anyone who has attempted it has found portions (and usually very numerous portions) of the dream regarding whose origin he could find nothing to say. Daytime interests are clearly not such far-reaching psychical sources of dreams as might have been expected from the categorical assertions that everyone continues to carry on his daily business in his dreams.

No other psychical sources of dreams are known. So it comes about that all the explanations of dreams given in the literature of the subject—with the possible exception of Scherner's, which will be dealt with later [see p. 109]—leave a great gap when it comes to assigning an origin for the ideational images which constitute the most characteristic material of dreams. In this embarrassing situation, a majority of the writers on the subject have tended to reduce to a minimum the part played by psychical factors in instigating dreams, since those factors are so hard to come at. It is true that they divide dreams into two main classes—those 'due to nervous stimulation' and those 'due to association,' of which the latter have their source exclusively in reproduction [of material already experienced] (cf. Wundt, 1874, 657 f.). Nevertheless they cannot escape a doubt 'whether any dream can take place without being given an impetus by some somatic stimulus' (Volkelt, 1875, 127). It is difficult even to give a description of purely associative dreams. 'In associative dreams proper, there can be no question of any such solid core [derived from somatic stimulation]. Even the very centre of the dream is only loosely put together. The ideational processes, which in any dream are ungoverned by reason or common sense, are here no longer even held together by any relatively important somatic or mental excitations, and are thus abandoned to their own kaleidoscopic changes and to their own jumbled confusion.' (Ibid., 118.) Wundt (1874, 656–7), too, seeks to minimize the psychical factor in the instigation of dreams. He declares that there seems to be no justification for regarding the phantasms of dreams as pure hallucinations; most dream-images are probably in fact illusions, since they arise from faint sense-impressions, which never cease during sleep. Weygandt (1893, 17) has adopted this same view and made its application general. He asserts of *all* dream-images 'that their primary causes are sensory stimuli and that only later do reproductive associations become attached to them.' Tissié (1898, 183) goes even further in putting a limit to the psychical sources of stimulation: 'Les rêves d'origine absolument psychique n'existent pas'; and (ibid., 6) 'les pensées de nos rêves nous viennent du dehors. . . .'[1]

Those writers who, like that eminent philosopher Wundt, take up a middle position do not fail to remark that in most dreams somatic stimuli and the psychical instigators (whether unknown or recognized as daytime interests) work in cooperation.

We shall find later that the enigma of the formation of dreams can be solved by the revelation of an unsuspected psychical source of stimulation. Meanwhile we shall feel no surprise at the over-estimation of the part played in forming dreams by stimuli which do not arise from mental life. Not only are they easy to discover and even open to experimental confirmation; but the somatic view of the origin of dreams is completely in line with the prevailing trend of thought in psychiatry today. It is true that the dominance of the brain over the organism is asserted with apparent confidence. Nevertheless, anything that might indicate that mental life is in any way independent of demonstrable organic changes or that its manifestations are in any way spontaneous alarms the modern psychiatrist, as though a recognition of such things would inevitably bring back the days of the Philosophy of Nature [see p. 39 n.], and of the metaphysical view of the nature of mind. The suspicions of the psychiatrists have

---

[1] ['Dreams of purely psychical origin do not exist.' 'The thoughts in our dreams reach us from outside.']

put the mind, as it were, under tutelage, and they now insist that none of its impulses shall be allowed to suggest that it has any means of its own. This behaviour of theirs only shows how little trust they really have in the validity of a causal connection between the somatic and the mental. Even when investigation shows that the primary exciting cause of a phenomenon is psychical, deeper research will one day trace the path further and discover an organic basis for the mental event. But if at the moment we cannot see beyond the mental, that is no reason for denying its existence.[1]

(D)

WHY DREAMS ARE FORGOTTEN AFTER WAKING

It is a proverbial fact that dreams melt away in the morning. They can, of course, be remembered; for we only know dreams from our memory of them after we are awake. But we very often have a feeling that we have only remembered a dream in part and that there was more of it during the night; we can observe, too, how the recollection of a dream, which was still lively in the morning, will melt away, except for a few small fragments, in the course of the day; we often know we have dreamt, without knowing what we have dreamt; and we are so familiar with the fact of dreams being liable to be forgotten, that we see no absurdity in the possibility of someone having had a dream in the night and of his not being aware in the morning either of what he has dreamt or even of the fact that he has dreamt at all. On the other hand, it sometimes happens that dreams show an extraordinary persistence in the memory. I have analysed dreams in my patients which occurred twenty-five and more years earlier; and I can remember a dream of my own separated by at least thirty-seven years from today and yet as fresh as ever in my memory. All of this is very remarkable and not immediately intelligible.

The most detailed account of the forgetting of dreams is the one given by Strümpell [1877, 79 f.]. It is evidently a complex phenomenon, for Strümpell traces it back not to a single cause but to a whole number of them.

---

[1] [The topics in this section are taken up again in Section C of Chapter V (pp. 240 ff.).]

In the first place, all the causes that lead to forgetting in waking life are operative for dreams as well. When we are awake we regularly forget countless sensations and perceptions at once, because they were too weak or because the mental excitation attaching to them was too slight. The same holds good of many dream-images: they are forgotten because they are too weak, while stronger images adjacent to them are remembered. The factor of intensity, however, is certainly not in itself enough to determine whether a dream-image shall be recollected. Strümpell [1877, 82] admits, as well as other writers (e.g. Calkins, 1893, 312), that we often forget dream-images which we know were very vivid, while a very large number which are shadowy and lacking in sensory force are among those retained in the memory. Moreover when we are awake we tend easily to forget an event which occurs only once and more readily to notice what can be perceived repeatedly. Now most dream-images are unique experiences;[1] and that fact will contribute impartially towards making us forget all dreams. Far more importance attaches to a third cause of forgetting. If sensations, ideas, thoughts, and so on, are to attain a certain degree of susceptibility to being remembered, it is essential that they should not remain isolated but should be arranged in appropriate concatenations and groupings. If a short line of verse is divided up into its component words and these are mixed up, it becomes very hard to remember. 'If words are properly arranged and put into the relevant order, one word will help another, and the whole, being charged with meaning, will be easily taken up by the memory and retained for a long time. It is in general as difficult and unusual to retain what is nonsensical as it is to retain what is confused and disordered.' [Strümpell, 1877, 83.] Now dreams are in most cases lacking in intelligibility and orderliness. The compositions which constitute dreams are barren of the qualities which would make it possible to remember them, and they are forgotten because as a rule they fall to pieces a moment later. Radestock (1879, 168), however, claims to have observed that it is the most peculiar dreams that are best remembered, and this, it must be admitted, would scarcely tally with what has just been said.

Strümpell [1877, 82 f.] believes that certain other factors derived from the relation between dreaming and waking life are of still greater importance in causing dreams to be forgotten. The liability of dreams to be forgotten by waking consciousness is evidently only the counterpart of the

---

[1] Dreams that recur periodically have often been observed. Cf. the collection given by Chabaneix (1897). [Cf. pp. 212 f.]

fact which has been mentioned earlier [p. 53] that dreams scarcely ever take over ordered recollections from waking life, but only details selected from them, which they tear from the psychical context in which they are usually remembered in the waking state. Thus dream-compositions find no place in the company of the psychical sequences with which the mind is filled. There is nothing that can help us to remember them. 'In this way dream-structures are, as it were, lifted above the floor of our mental life and float in psychical space like clouds in the sky, scattered by the first breath of wind.' (Strümpell, 1877, 87.) After waking, moreover, the world of the senses presses forward and at once takes possession of the attention with a force which very few dream-images can resist; so that here too we have another factor tending in the same direction. Dreams give way before the impressions of a new day just as the brilliance of the stars yields to the light of the sun.

Finally, there is another fact to be borne in mind as likely to lead to dreams being forgotten, namely that most people take very little interest in their dreams. Anyone, such as a scientific investigator, who pays attention to his dreams over a period of time will have more dreams than usual—which no doubt means that he remembers his dreams with greater ease and frequency.

Two further reasons why dreams should be forgotten, which Benini [1898, 155–6] quotes as having been brought forward by Bonatelli [1880] as additions to those mentioned by Strümpell, seem in fact to be already covered by the latter. They are (1) that the alteration in coenaesthesia between the sleeping and waking states is unfavourable to reciprocal reproduction between them; and (2) that the different arrangement of the ideational material in dreams makes them untranslatable, as it were, for waking consciousness.

In view of all these reasons in favour of dreams being forgotten, it is in fact (as Strümpell himself insists [1877, 6]) very remarkable that so many of them are retained in the memory. The repeated attempts by writers on the subject to lay down the rules governing the recollection of dreams amount to an admission that here too we are faced by something puzzling and unexplained. Certain particular characteristics of the recollection of dreams have been rightly emphasized recently (cf. Radestock, 1879, [169], and Tissié, 1898, [148 f.]), such as the fact that when a dream seems in the morning to have been forgotten, it may nevertheless be recollected during the course of the day, if its content, forgotten though it is, is touched upon by some chance perception.

But the recollection of dreams in general is open to an objection which is bound to reduce their value very completely in critical opinion. Since so great a proportion of dreams is lost altogether, we may well doubt whether our memory of what is left of them may not be falsified.

These doubts as to the accuracy of the reproduction of dreams are also expressed by Strümpell (1877, [119]): 'Thus it may easily happen that waking consciousness unwittingly makes interpolations in the memory of a dream: we persuade ourselves that we have dreamt all kinds of things that were not contained in the actual dreams.'

Jessen (1855, 547) writes with special emphasis on this point: 'More-over, in investigating and interpreting coherent and consistent dreams a particular circumstance must be borne in mind which, as it seems to me, has hitherto received too little attention. In such cases the truth is almost always obscured by the fact that when we recall dreams of this kind to our memory we almost always—unintentionally and without noticing the fact—fill in the gaps in the dream-images. It is seldom or never that a co-herent dream was in fact as coherent as it seems to us in memory. Even the most truth-loving of men is scarcely able to relate a noteworthy dream without some additions or embellishments. The tendency of the human mind to see everything connectedly is so strong that in memory it unwit-tingly fills in any lack of coherence there may be in an incoherent dream.'

Some remarks made by Egger [1895, 41], though they were no doubt arrived at independently, read almost like a translation of this passage from Jessen: '. . . L'observation des rêves a ses difficultés spéciales et le seul moyen d'éviter tout erreur en pareille matière est de confier au papier sans le moindre retard ce que l'on vient d'éprouver et de remarquer; sinon, l'oubli vient vite ou total ou partiel; l'oubli total est sans gravité; mais l'oubli partiel est perfide; car si l'on se met ensuite à raconter ce que l'on n'a pas oublié, on est exposé à compléter par imagination les frag-ments incohérents et disjoints fournis par la mémoire . . . ; on devient artiste à son insu, et le récit périodiquement répété s'impose à la créance de son auteur, qui, de bonne foi, le présente comme un fait authentique, dûment établi selon les bonnes méthodes. . . .'[1]

---

[1] ['There are peculiar difficulties in observing dreams, and the only way of escap-ing all errors in such matters is to put down upon paper with the least possible delay what we have just experienced or observed. Otherwise forgetfulness, whether total or partial, quickly supervenes. Total forgetfulness is not serious; but partial forgetfulness is treacherous. For if we then proceed to give an account

Very similar ideas are expressed by Spitta (1882, 338), who seems to believe that it is not until we try to reproduce a dream that we introduce order of any kind into its loosely associated elements: we 'change things that are merely juxtaposed into sequences or causal chains, that is to say, we introduce a process of logical connection which is lacking in the dream.'

Since the only check that we have upon the validity of our memory is objective confirmation, and since that is unobtainable for dreams, which are our own personal experience and of which the only source we have is our recollection, what value can we still attach to our memory of dreams?[1]

(E)
THE DISTINGUISHING PSYCHOLOGICAL CHARACTERISTICS OF DREAMS

Our scientific consideration of dreams starts off from the assumption that they are products of our own mental activity. Nevertheless the finished dream strikes us as something alien to us. We are so little obliged to acknowledge our responsibility for it that [in German] we are just as ready to say 'mir hat geträumt' ['I had a dream,' literally 'a dream came to me'] as 'ich habe geträumt' ['I dreamt']. What is the origin of this feeling that dreams are extraneous to our minds? In view of our discussion upon the sources of dreams, we must conclude that the strangeness cannot be due to the material that finds its way into their content, since that material is for the most part common to dreaming and waking life. The question arises whether in dreams there may not be modifications in the processes of the mind which produce the impression we are discussing; and we shall therefore make an attempt at drawing a picture of the psychological attributes of dreams.

---

of what we have not forgotten, we are liable to fill in from our imagination the incoherent and disjointed fragments furnished by memory. . . . We unwittingly become creative artists; and the tale, if it is repeated from time to time, imposes itself on its author's own belief, and he ends by offering it in good faith as an authentic fact duly and legitimately established.']

[1] [The questions raised in this section are taken up in Chapter VII, Section A (pp. 516 ff.).]

No one has emphasized more sharply the essential difference between dreaming and waking life or drawn more far-reaching conclusions from it than G. T. Fechner in a passage in his *Elemente der Psychophysik* (1889, **2**, 520–1). In his opinion, 'neither the mere lowering of conscious mental life below the main threshold,' nor the withdrawal of attention from the influences of the external world, are enough to explain the characteristics of dream-life as contrasted with waking life. He suspects, rather, that *the scene of action of dreams is different from that of waking ideational life.* 'If the scene of action of psychophysical activity were the same in sleeping and waking, dreams could, in my view, only be a prolongation at a lower degree of intensity of waking ideational life and, moreover, would necessarily be of the same material and form. But the facts are quite otherwise.'

It is not clear what Fechner had in mind in speaking of this change of location of mental activity; nor, so far as I know, has anyone else pursued the path indicated by his words. We may, I think, dismiss the possibility of giving the phrase an anatomical interpretation and supposing it to refer to physiological cerebral localization or even to the histological layers of the cerebral cortex. It may be, however, that the suggestion will eventually prove to be sagacious and fertile, if it can be applied to a *mental* apparatus built up of a number of agencies arranged in a series one behind the other.[1]

Other writers have contented themselves with drawing attention to the more tangible of the distinguishing characteristics of dream-life and with taking them as a starting-point for attempts at more far-reaching explanations.

It has justly been remarked that one of the principal peculiarities of dream-life makes its appearance during the very process of falling asleep and may be described as a phenomenon heralding sleep. According to Schleiermacher (1862, 351), what characterizes the waking state is the fact that thought-activity takes place in *concepts* and not in *images*. Now dreams think essentially in images; and with the approach of sleep it is possible to observe how, in proportion as voluntary activities become more difficult, involuntary ideas arise, all of which fall into the class of images. Incapacity for ideational work of the kind which we feel as intentionally willed and the emergence (habitually associated with such states

---

[1] [This idea is taken up and developed in Chapter VII, Section B, of the present work (pp. 535 ff.).]

of abstraction) of images—these are two characteristics which persevere in dreams and which the psychological analysis of dreams forces us to recognize as essential features of dream-life. We have already seen [pp. 63 ff.] that these images—hypnagogic hallucinations—are themselves identical in their content with dream-images.[1]

Dreams, then, think predominantly in visual images—but not exclusively. They make use of auditory images as well, and, to a lesser extent, of impressions belonging to the other senses. Many things, too, occur in dreams (just as they normally do in waking life) simply as thoughts or ideas—probably, that is to say, in the form of residues of verbal presentations. Nevertheless, what are truly characteristic of dreams are only those elements of their content which behave like images, which are more like perceptions, that is, than they are like mnemic presentations. Leaving on one side all the arguments, so familiar to psychiatrists, on the nature of hallucinations, we shall be in agreement with every authority on the subject in asserting that dreams *hallucinate*—that they replace thoughts by hallucinations. In this respect there is no distinction between visual and acoustic presentations: it has been observed that if one falls asleep with the memory of a series of musical notes in one's mind, the memory becomes transformed into an hallucination of the same melody; while, if one then wakes up again—and the two states may alternate more than once during the process of dropping asleep—the hallucination gives way in turn to the mnemic presentation, which is at once fainter and qualitatively different from it.

The transformation of ideas into hallucinations is not the only respect in which dreams differ from corresponding thoughts in waking life. Dreams construct a *situation* out of these images; they represent an event which is actually happening; as Spitta (1882, 145) puts it, they 'dramatize' an idea. But this feature of dream-life can only be fully understood if we further recognize that in dreams—as a rule, for there are exceptions which require special examination—we appear not to *think* but to *experience*; that is to say, we attach complete belief to the hallucinations. Not

---

[1] [*Footnote added* 1911:] Silberer (1909) has given some nice examples of the way in which, in a drowsy state, even abstract thoughts become converted into pictorial plastic images which seek to express the same meaning. [*Added* 1925:] I shall have occasion to return to this discovery in another connection. [See pp. 358 ff. and 507 ff.]

until we wake up does the critical comment arise that we have not experienced anything but have merely been thinking in a peculiar way, or in other words dreaming. It is this characteristic that distinguishes true dreams from daydreaming, which is never confused with reality.

Burdach (1838, 502 f.) summarizes the features of dream-life which we have so far discussed in the following words: 'These are among the essential features of dreams: (a) In dreams the subjective activity of our minds appears in an objective form, for our perceptive faculties regard the products of our imagination as though they were sense impressions. . . . (b) Sleep signifies an end of the authority of the self. Hence falling asleep brings a certain degree of passivity along with it. . . . The images that accompany sleep can occur only on condition that the authority of the self is reduced.'

The next thing is to try to explain the belief which the mind accords to dream-hallucinations, a belief which can only arise after some kind of 'authoritative' activity of the self has ceased. Strümpell (1877) argues that in this respect the mind is carrying out its function correctly and in conformity with its own mechanism. Far from being mere presentations, the elements of dreams are true and real mental experiences of the same kind as arise in a waking state through the agency of the senses. (Ibid., 34.) The waking mind produces ideas and thoughts in verbal images and in speech; but in dreams it does so in true sensory images. (Ibid., 35.) Moreover, there is a spatial consciousness in dreams, since sensations and images are assigned to an external space, just as they are in waking. (Ibid., 36.) It must therefore be allowed that in dreams the mind is in the same relation to its images and perceptions as it is in waking. (Ibid., 43.) If it is nevertheless in error in so doing, that is because in the state of sleep it lacks the criterion which alone makes it possible to distinguish between sense-perceptions arising from without and from within. It is unable to submit its dream-images to the only tests which could prove their objective reality. In addition to this, it disregards the distinction between images which are only interchangeable *arbitrarily* and cases where the element of arbitrariness is absent. It is in error because it is unable to apply the law of causality to the content of its dreams. (Ibid., 50–1.) In short, the fact of its having turned away from the external world is also the reason for its belief in the subjective world of dreams.

Delboeuf (1885, 84) arrives at the same conclusion after somewhat different psychological arguments. We believe in the reality of dream-images, he says, because in our sleep we have no other impressions with which to compare them, because we are detached from the external world. But the reason why we believe in the truth of these hallucinations is not because it is impossible to put them to the test *within* the dream. A dream can seem to offer us such tests: it can let us touch the rose that we see—and yet we are dreaming. In Delboeuf's opinion there is only one valid criterion of whether we are dreaming or awake, and that is the purely empirical one of the fact of waking up. I conclude that everything I experienced between falling asleep and waking up was illusory, when, on awaking, I find that I am lying undressed in bed. During sleep I took the dream-images as real owing to my mental habit (which cannot be put to sleep) of assuming the existence of an external world with which I contrast my own ego.[1]

---

[1] Haffner (1887, 243) attempts, like Delboeuf, to explain the activity of dreaming by the modification which the introduction of an abnormal condition must inevitably produce in the otherwise correct functioning of an intact mental apparatus; but he gives a somewhat different account of that condition. According to him the first mark of a dream is its independence of space and time, i.e. the fact of a presentation being emancipated from the position occupied by the subject in the spatial and temporal order of events. The second basic feature of dreams is connected with this—namely, the fact that hallucinations, phantasies and imaginary combinations are confused with external perceptions. 'All the higher powers of the mind—in particular the formation of concepts and the powers of judgement and inference on the one hand and free self-determination on the other hand—are attached to sensory images and have at all times a background of such images. It follows, therefore, that these higher activities too take their part in the disorderliness of the dream-images. I say "take their part," since in themselves our powers of judgement and of will are in no way altered in sleep. Our activities are just as clear-sighted and just as free as in waking life. Even in his dreams a man cannot violate the laws of thought as such—he cannot, for instance, regard as identical things that appear to him as contraries, and so on. So too in dreams he can only desire what he looks upon as a good (*sub ratione boni*). But the human spirit is led astray in dreams in its *application* of the laws of thought and of will through confusing one idea with another. Thus it comes about that we are guilty of the grossest contradictions in dreams, while at the same time we can make the clearest judgements, draw the most logical inferences and come to the most virtuous and saintly decisions. . . . Lack of orientation is the whole secret of the flights taken by our imagination in dreams, and lack of critical reflection and of communication with other people is the main source of the unbridled extravagance exhibited in dreams by our judgements as well as by our hopes and wishes.' (Ibid., 18.) [The problem of 'reality-testing' is considered later, on p. 566.]

Detachment from the external world seems thus to be regarded as the factor determining the most marked features of dream-life. It is therefore worth while quoting some penetrating remarks made long ago by Burdach which throw light on the relations between the sleeping mind and the external world and which are calculated to prevent our setting too great store by the conclusions drawn in the last few pages. 'Sleep,' he writes, 'can occur only on condition that the mind is not irritated by sensory stimuli. . . . But the actual precondition of sleep is not so much absence of sensory stimuli as absence of interest in them.[1] Some sense impressions may actually be necessary in order to calm the mind. Thus the miller can only sleep so long as he hears the clacking of his mill; and anyone who feels that burning a night-light is a necessary precaution, finds it impossible to get to sleep in the dark.' (Burdach, 1838, 482.)

'In sleep the mind isolates itself from the external world and withdraws from its own periphery. . . . Nevertheless connection is not broken off entirely. If we could not hear or feel while we were actually asleep, but only after we had woken up, it would be impossible to wake us at all. . . . The persistence of sensation is proved even more clearly by the fact that what rouses us is not always the mere sensory strength of an impression but its psychical context: a sleeping man is not aroused by an indifferent word, but if he is called by name he wakes. . . . Thus the mind in sleep distinguishes between sensations. . . . It is for that reason that the absence of a sensory stimulus can wake a man if it is related to something of ideational importance to him; so it is that the man with the night-light wakes if it is extinguished and the miller is roused if his mill comes to a stop. He is awakened, that is, by the cessation of a sensory activity; and this implies that that activity was perceived by him, but, since it was indifferent, or rather satisfying, did not disturb his mind.' (Ibid., 485–6.)

Even if we disregard these objections—and they are by no means trifling ones—we shall have to confess that the features of dream-life which we have considered hitherto, and which have been ascribed to its detachment from the external world, do not account completely for its strange character. For it should be possible otherwise to turn the hallucinations in a dream back into ideas, and its situations into thoughts, and in that way to solve the problem of dream-interpretation. And that in fact is

---

[1] [*Footnote added* 1914:] Cf. the 'désintérêt' which Claparède (1905, 306 f.) regards as the mechanism of falling asleep.

what we are doing when, after waking, we reproduce a dream from memory; but, whether we succeed in making this re-translation wholly or only in part, the dream remains no less enigmatic than before.

And indeed all the authorities unhesitatingly assume that yet other and more deep-going modifications of the ideational material of waking life take place in dreams. Strümpell (1877, 27–8) has endeavoured to put his finger on one such modification in the following passage: 'With the cessation of sensory functioning and of normal vital consciousness, the mind loses the soil in which its feelings, desires, interests and activities are rooted. The psychical states, too—feelings, interests, judgements of value—which are linked to mnemic images in waking life, are subjected to . . . an obscuring pressure, as a result of which their connection with those images is broken; perceptual images of things, persons, places, events and actions in waking life are reproduced separately in great numbers, but none of them carries its psychical value along with it. That value is detached from them and they thus float about in the mind at their own sweet will. . . . ' According to Strümpell, the fact of images being denuded of their *psychical value* (which in turn goes back to detachment from the external world) plays a principal part in creating the impression of strangeness which distinguishes dreams from actual life in our memory.

We have seen [cf. p. 79] that falling asleep at once involves the loss of one of our mental activities, namely our power of giving intentional guidance to the sequence of our ideas. We are now faced by the suggestion, which is in any case a plausible one, that the effects of the state of sleep may extend over all the faculties of the mind. Some of these seem to be entirely suspended; but the question now arises whether the rest continue to operate normally and whether under such conditions they are *capable* of normal work. And here it may be asked whether the distinguishing features of dreams cannot be explained by the lowering of psychical efficiency in the sleeping state—a notion which finds support in the impression made by dreams on our waking judgement. Dreams are disconnected, they accept the most violent contradictions without the least objection, they admit impossibilities, they disregard knowledge which carries great weight with us in the day-time, they reveal us as ethical and moral imbeciles. Anyone who when he was awake behaved in the sort of way that is shown in situations in dreams would be considered insane. Anyone who when he was awake talked in the sort of way that people talk in dreams or described the sort of thing that happens in dreams would give us the impression of being muddle-headed or feeble-minded. It seems to be no more than putting the truth into words when we express our very low opinion of mental activity in dreams and assert that in dreams the higher intellectual faculties in particular are suspended or at all events gravely impaired.

The authorities display unusual unanimity—exceptions will be treated later [pp. 88 ff.]—in expressing opinions of this kind on dreams; and these judgements lead directly to a particular theory or explanation of dream-life. But it is time for me to leave generalities and to give instead a series of quotations from various writers—philosophers and physicians—upon the psychological characteristics of dreams.

According to Lemoine (1855), the 'incoherence' of dream-images is the one essential characteristic of dreams.

Maury (1878, 163) agrees with him: 'Il n'y a pas de rêves absolument raisonnables et qui ne contiennent quelque incohérence, quelque anachronisme, quelque absurdité.'[1]

Spitta [1882, 193] quotes Hegel as saying that dreams are devoid of all objectives and reasonable coherence.

Dugas [1897a, 417] writes: 'Le rêve c'est l'anarchie psychique affective et mentale, c'est le jeu des fonctions livrées à ellesmêmes et s'exerçant sans contrôle et sans but; dans le rêve l'esprit est un automate spirituel.'[2]

Even Volkelt (1875, 14), whose theory is far from regarding psychical activity during sleep as purposeless, speaks of 'the relaxing, disconnecting and confusing of ideational life, which in the waking state is held together by the logical force of the central ego.'

The *absurdity* of the associations of ideas that occur in dreams could scarcely be criticized more sharply than it was by Cicero (*De divinatione*, II, [lxxi, 146]): 'Nihil tam praepostere, tam incondite, tam monstruose cogitari potest, quod non possimus somniare.'[3]

Fechner (1889, **2,** 522) writes: 'It is as though psychological activity had been transported from the brain of a reasonable man into that of a fool.'

---

[1] ['There are no dreams that are *absolutely* reasonable and that do not contain some incoherence, anachronism or absurdity.']

[2] ['A dream is psychical, emotional and mental anarchy; it is the play of functions left to their own devices and acting without control or purpose; in dreams the spirit becomes a spiritual automaton.']

[3] ['There is no imaginable thing too absurd, too involved, or too abnormal for us to dream about it.' (Falconer's translation in the Loeb Classical Library, 1922, 533.)]

Radestock (1879, 145): 'In fact it seems impossible to detect any fixed laws in this crazy activity. After withdrawing from the strict policing exercised over the course of waking ideas by the rational will and the attention, dreams melt into a mad whirl of kaleidoscopic confusion.'

Hildebrandt (1875, 45): 'What astonishing leaps a dreamer may make, for instance, in drawing inferences! How calmly he is prepared to see the most familiar lessons of experience turned upside down. What laughable contradictions he is ready to accept in the laws of nature and society before, as we say, things get beyond a joke and the excessive strain of nonsense wakes him up. We calculate without a qualm that three times three make twenty; we are not in the least surprised when a dog quotes a line of poetry, or when a dead man walks to his grave on his own legs, or when we see a rock floating on the water; we proceed gravely on an important mission to the Duchy of Bernburg or to the Principality of Liechtenstein to inspect their naval forces; or we are persuaded to enlist under Charles XII shortly before the battle of Poltava.'

Binz (1878, 33), having in mind the theory of dreams which is based upon such impressions as these, writes: 'The content of at least nine out of ten dreams is nonsensical. We bring together in them people and things that have no connection whatever with one another. Next moment there is a shift in the kaleidoscope and we are faced by a new grouping, more senseless and crazy, if possible, than the last. And so the changing play of the incompletely sleeping brain goes on, till we awake and clasp our forehead and wonder whether we still possess the capacity for rational ideas and thoughts.'

Maury (1878, 50) finds a parallel to the relation between dream-images and waking thoughts which will be highly significant to physicians: 'La production de ces images que chez l'homme éveillé fait le plus souvent naître la volonté, correspond, pour l'intelligence, à ce que sont pour la motilité certains mouvements que nous offre la chorée et les affections paralytiques . . . '[1] He further regards dreams as 'toute une série de dégradations de la faculté pensante et raisonnante.' (Ibid., 27.)[2]

---

[1] ['The production of these images (which in a waking person are usually provoked by the will) corresponds in the sphere of intelligence to the place taken in the sphere of motion by some of the movements observable in chorea and paralytic disorders.']

[2] ['A whole series of degradations of the thinking and reasoning faculty.']

It is scarcely necessary to quote the writers who repeat Maury's opinion in relation to the various higher mental functions. Strümpell (1877, 26), for instance, remarks that in dreams—even, of course, where there is no manifest nonsense—there is an eclipse of all the logical operations of the mind which are based on relations and connections. Spitta (1882, 148) declares that ideas that occur in dreams seem to be completely withdrawn from the law of causality. Radestock (1879, [153–4]) and other writers insist upon the weakness of judgement and inference characteristic of dreams. According to Jodl (1896, 123), there is no critical faculty in dreams, no power of correcting one set of perceptions by reference to the general content of consciousness. The same author remarks that 'every kind of conscious activity occurs in dreams, but only in an incomplete, inhibited and isolated fashion.' The contradictions with our waking knowledge in which dreams are involved are explained by Stricker (1879, 98) and many others as being due to facts being forgotten in dreams or to logical relations between ideas having disappeared. And so on, and so on.

Nevertheless, the writers who in general take so unfavourable a view of psychical functioning in dreams allow that a certain remnant of mental activity still remains in them. This is explictly admitted by Wundt, whose theories have had a determining influence on so many other workers in this field. What, it may be asked, is the nature of the remnant of normal mental activity which persists in dreams? There is fairly general agreement that the reproductive faculty, the memory, seems to have suffered least, and indeed that it shows a certain superiority to the same function in waking life (see Section B above), though some part of the absurdities of dreaming seems to be explicable by its forgetfulness. In the opinion of Spitta (1882, 84 f.) the part of the mind which is not affected by sleep is the life of the sentiments and it is this which directs dreams. By 'sentiment' ['Gemüt'] he means 'the stable assemblage of feelings which constitutes the innermost subjective essence of a human being.'

Scholz (1893, 64) believes that one of the mental activities operating in dreams is a tendency to subject the dream-material to 're-interpretation in allegorical terms.' Siebeck too (1877, 11) sees in dreams a faculty of the mind for 'wider interpretation,' which is exercised upon all sensations and perceptions. There is particular difficulty in assessing the position in dreams of what is ostensibly the highest of the psychical functions, that of consciousness. Since all that we know of dreams is derived from consciousness, there can be no doubt of its persisting in them; yet Spitta (1882, 84–5) believes that what persists in dreams is only consciousness and not *self*-consciousness. Delboeuf (1885, 19), however, confesses that he is unable to follow the distinction.

The laws of association governing the sequence of ideas hold good of dream-images, and indeed their dominance is even more clearly and strongly expressed in dreams. 'Dreams,' says Strümpell (1877, 70), 'run their course, as it seems, according to the laws either of bare ideas or of organic stimuli accompanying such ideas—that is, without being in any way affected by reflection or commonsense or aesthetic taste or moral judgement.' [See pp. 83 f. and 242.]

The authors whose views I am now giving picture the process of forming dreams in some such way as this. The totality of the sensory stimuli generated during sleep from the various sources which I have already enumerated [see Section C above] arouse in the mind in the first place a number of ideas, which are represented in the form of hallucinations or more properly, according to Wundt [see p. 71], of illusions, in view of their derivation from external and internal stimuli. These ideas become linked together according to the familiar laws of association and, according to the same laws, call up a further series of ideas (or images). The whole of this material is then worked over, so far as it will allow, by what still remain in operation of the organizing and thinking faculties of the mind. (See, for instance, Wundt [1874, 658] and Weygandt [1893].) All that remain undiscovered are the motives which decide whether the calling-up of images arising from non-external sources shall proceed along one chain of associations or another.

It has often been remarked, however, that the associations connecting dream-images with one another are of a quite special kind and differ from those which operate in waking thought. Thus Volkelt (1875, 15) writes: 'In dreams the associations seem to play at catch-as-catch-can in accordance with chance similarities and connections that are barely perceptible. Every dream is stuffed full of slovenly and perfunctory associations of this kind.' Maury (1878, 126) attaches very great importance to this feature of the way in which ideas are linked in dreams, since it enables him to draw a close analogy between dream-life and certain mental disorders. He specifies two main features of a '*délire*': '(1) une action spontanée et comme automatique de l'esprit; (2) une association vicieuse et irrégulière des idées.'[1]

---

[1] ['(1) A mental act which is spontaneous and as it were automatic; (2) an invalid and irregular association of ideas.'—N.B. In French (and similarly in German) psychiatry '*délire*' has the meaning of a delusional state.]

Maury himself gives two excellent instances of dreams of his own in which dream-images were linked together merely through a similarity in the sound of words. He once dreamt that he was on a pilgrimage (*pélerinage*) to Jerusalem or Mecca; after many adventures he found himself visiting *Pell*etier, the chemist, who, after some conversation, gave him a zinc shovel (*pelle*); in the next part of the dream this turned into a great broad-sword. (Ibid., 137.) In another dream he was walking along a highway and reading the number of *kilo*metres on the milestones; then he was in a grocer's shop where there was a big pair of scales, and a man was putting kilogramme weights into the scale in order to weigh Maury; the grocer then said to him: 'You're not in Paris but on the island of *Gilolo*.' Several other scenes followed, in which he saw a *Lo*belia flower, and then General *Lo*pez, of whose death he had read shortly before. Finally, while he was playing a game of *lo*tto, he woke up. (Ibid., 126.)[1]

We shall no doubt be prepared to find, however, that this low estimate of psychical functioning in dreams has not been allowed to pass without contradiction—though contradiction on this point would seem to be no easy matter. For instance, Spitta (1882, 118), one of the disparagers of dream-life, insists that the same psychological laws which regulate waking life also hold good in dreams; and another, Dugas (1897*a*), declares that 'le rêve n'est pas déraison ni même irraison pure.'[2] But such assertions carry little weight so long as their authors make no attempt to reconcile them with their own descriptions of the psychical anarchy and disruption of every function that prevail in dreams. It seems, however, to have dawned upon some other writers that the madness of dreams may not be without method and may even be simulated, like that of the Danish prince on whom this shrewd judgement was passed. These latter writers cannot have judged by appearances; or the appearance presented to them by dreams must have been a different one.

Thus Havelock Ellis (1899, 721), without dwelling on the apparent absurdity of dreams, speaks of them as 'an archaic world of vast emotions and imperfect thoughts,' the study of which might reveal to us primitive stages in the evolution of mental life.

---

[1] [*Footnote added* 1909:] At a later stage [p. 534 n. 1] we shall come to understand the meaning of dreams such as this which are filled with alliterations and similar-sounding first syllables.

[2] ['Dreams are not contrary to reason or even entirely lacking in reason.']

The same view[1] is expressed by James Sully (1893, 362) in a manner that is both more sweeping and more penetrating. His words deserve all the more attention when we bear in mind that he was more firmly convinced, perhaps, than any other psychologist that dreams have a disguised meaning. 'Now our dreams are a means of conserving these successive [earlier] personalities. *When asleep we go back to the old ways of looking at things and of feeling about them, to impulses and activities which long ago dominated us.*'

The sagacious Delboeuf (1885, 222) declares (though he puts himself in the wrong by not giving any refutation of the material which contradicts his thesis): 'Dans le sommeil, hormis la perception, toutes les facultés de l'esprit, intelligence, imagination, mémoire, volonté, moralité, restent intactes dans leur essence; seulement elles s'appliquent à des objets imaginaires et mobiles. Le songeur est un acteur qui joue à volonté les fous et les sages, les bourreaux et les victimes, les nains et les géants, les démons et les anges.'[2]

The most energetic opponent of those who seek to depreciate psychical functioning in dreams seems to be the Marquis d'Hervey de Saint-Denys [1867], with whom Maury carried on a lively controversy, and whose book, in spite of all my efforts, I have not succeeded in procuring.[3] Maury (1878, 19) writes of him: 'M. le Marquis d'Hervey prête à l'intelligence durant le sommeil, toute sa liberté d'action et d'attention et il ne semble faire consister le sommeil que dans l'occlusion des sens, dans leur fermeture au monde extérieur; en sorte que l'homme qui dort ne se distingue guère, selon sa manière de voir, de l'homme qui laisse vaguer sa pensée en se bouchant les sens; toute la différence qui sépare alors la pensée ordinaire de celle du dormeur c'est que, chez celui-ci, l'idée prend une forme visible, objective et ressemble, à s'y méprendre, à la sensation déterminée par les objets extérieurs; le souvenir revêt l'apparence du fait

---

[1] [This paragraph was added in 1914.]

[2] ['In sleep, all the mental faculties (except for perception)—intelligence, imagination, memory, will and morality—remain essentially intact; they are merely applied to imaginary and unstable objects. A dreamer is an actor who at his own will plays the parts of madmen and philosophers, of executioners and their victims, of dwarfs and giants, of demons and angels.']

[3] [This work, by a famous sinologist, was published anonymously.]

présent.'[1] To this Maury adds 'qu'il y a une différence de plus et capitale à savoir que les facultés intellectuelles de l'homme endormi n'offrent pas l'équilibre qu'elles gardent chez l'homme éveillé.'[2]

Vaschide (1911, 146 f.)[3] gives us a clearer account of Hervey de Saint-Denys' book and quotes a passage from it [1867, 35] upon the apparent incoherence of dreams: 'L'image du rêve est la copie de l'idée. Le principal est l'idée; la vision n'est qu'accessoire. Ceci établi, il faut savoir suivre la marche des idées, il faut savoir analyser le tissu des rêves; l'incohérence devient alors compréhensible, les conceptions les plus fantasques deviennent des faits simples et parfaitement logiques. . . . Les rêves les plus bizarres trouvent même une explication des plus logiques quand on sait les analyser.'[4]

Johan Stärcke (1913, 243) has pointed out that a similar explanation of the incoherence of dreams was put forward by an earlier writer, Wolf Davidson (1799, 136), whose work was unknown to me: 'The remarkable leaps taken by our ideas in dreams all have their basis in the law of association; sometimes, however, these connections occur in the mind very obscurely, so that our ideas often seem to have taken a leap when in fact there has been none.'

---

[1] ['The Marquis d'Hervey attributes complete liberty of action and attention to the intelligence during sleep, and he seems to think that sleep consists merely in the blocking of the senses, in their being closed to the external world. So that on his view a sleeping man would hardly be different from a man who shut off his senses and allowed his thoughts to wander; the only distinction between ordinary thoughts and those of a sleeper would be that, in the latter, ideas assume a visible and objective shape and are indistinguishable from sensations determined by external objects, while memories take on the appearance of present events.']

[2] ['There is a further distinction and one of capital importance: namely, that the intellectual faculties of a sleeping man do not exhibit the balance maintained in a man who is awake.']

[3] [This paragraph and the next were added in 1914.]

[4] ['Dream-images are copies of ideas. The essential thing is the idea, the vision is a mere accessory. When this is once established, we must know how to follow the sequence of the ideas, we must know how to analyse the texture of dreams; their incoherence then becomes intelligible, and the most fantastic notions become simple and perfectly logical facts. . . . We can even find a most logical explanation for the strangest dreams if we know how to analyse them.'—This is not in fact a verbatim quotation from Hervey de Saint-Denys, but a paraphrase by Vaschide.]

The literature of the subject thus shows a very wide range of variation in the value which it assigns to dreams as psychical products. This range extends from the deepest disparagement, of the kind with which we have become familiar, through hints at a yet undisclosed worth, to an overvaluation which ranks dreams far higher than any of the functions of waking life. Hildebrandt (1875, 19 f.), who, as we have heard [see above, p. 43], has summed up the whole of the psychological features of dream-life in three antinomies, makes use of the two extreme ends of this range of values for his third paradox: 'it is a contrast between an intensification of mental life, an enhancement of it that not infrequently amounts to virtuosity, and, on the other hand, a deterioration and enfeeblement which often sinks below the level of humanity. As regards the former, there are few of us who could not affirm, from our own experience, that there emerges from time to time in the creations and fabrics of the genius of dreams a depth and intimacy of emotion, a tenderness of feeling, a clarity of vision, a subtlety of observation, and a brilliance of wit such as we should never claim to have at our permanent command in our waking lives. There lies in dreams a marvellous poetry, an apt allegory, an incomparable humour, a rare irony. A dream looks upon the world in a light of strange idealism and often enhances the effects of what it sees by its deep understanding of their essential nature. It pictures earthly beauty to our eyes in a truly heavenly splendour and clothes dignity with the highest majesty, it shows us our everyday fears in the ghastliest shape and turns our amusement into jokes of indescribable pungency. And sometimes, when we are awake and still under the full impact of an experience like one of these, we cannot but feel that never in our life has the real world offered us its equal.'

We may well ask whether the disparaging remarks quoted on earlier pages and this enthusiastic eulogy can possibly relate to the same thing. Is it that some of our authorities have overlooked the nonsensical dreams and others the profound and subtle ones? And if dreams of both kinds occur, dreams that justify both estimates, may it not be a waste of time to look for any distinguishing psychological feature of dreams? Will it not be enough to say that in dreams *anything* is possible—from the deepest degradation of mental life to an exaltation of it which is rare in waking hours? However convenient a solution of this kind might be, what lies against it is the fact that all of the efforts at research into the problem of dreams seem to be based on a conviction that some distinguishing feature does exist, which is universally valid in its essential outline and which would clear these apparent contradictions out of the way.

There can be no doubt that the psychical achievements of dreams received readier and warmer recognition during the intellectual period
which has now been left behind, when the human mind was dominated
by philosophy and not by the exact natural sciences. Pronouncements
such as that by Schubert (1814, 20 f.) that dreams are a liberation of the
spirit from the power of external nature, a freeing of the soul from the
bonds of the senses, and similar remarks by the younger Fichte (1864, **1**,
143 f.)[1] and others, all of which represent dreams as an elevation of mental life to a higher level, seem to us now to be scarcely intelligible; today
they are repeated only by mystics and pietists.[2] The introduction of the
scientific mode of thought has brought along with it a reaction in the es-
timation of dreams. Medical writers in especial tend to regard psychical
activity in dreams as trivial and valueless; while philosophers and non-
professional observers—amateur psychologists—whose contributions to
this particular subject are not to be despised, have (in closer alignment
with popular feeling) retained a belief in the psychical value of dreams.
Anyone who is inclined to take a low view of psychical functioning in
dreams will naturally prefer to assign their source to somatic stimulation;
whereas those who believe that the dreaming mind retains the greater part
of its waking capacities have of course no reason for denying that the
stimulus to dreaming can arise within the dreaming mind itself.

Of the superior faculties which even a sober comparison may be inclined to attribute to dream-life, the most marked is that of memory; we
have already [in Section B above] discussed at length the not uncommon
evidence in favour of this view. Another point of superiority in dream-
life, often praised by earlier writers—that it rises superior to distance in
time and space—may easily be shown to have no basis in fact. As Hildebrandt (1875, [25]) points out, this advantage is an illusory one; for
dreaming rises superior to time and space in precisely the same way as
does waking thought, and for the very reason that it is merely a form of
thought. It has been claimed for dreams that they enjoy yet another advantage over waking life in relation to time—that they are independent
of the passage of time in yet another respect. Dreams such as the one

---

[1] Cf. Haffner (1887) and Spitta (1882, 11 f.).

[2] [*Footnote added* 1914:] That brilliant mystic Du Prel, one of the few authors for
whose neglect in earlier editions of this book I should wish to express my regret,
declares that the gateway to metaphysics, so far as men are concerned, lies not
in waking life but in the dream. (Du Prel, 1885, 59.)

dreamt by Maury of his own guillotining (see above, p. 58) seem to show that a dream is able to compress into a very short space of time an amount of perceptual matter far greater than the amount of ideational matter that can be dealt with by our waking mind. This conclusion has however been countered by various arguments; since the papers by Le Lorrain (1894) and Egger (1895) on the apparent duration of dreams, a long and interesting discussion on the subject has developed, but it seems unlikely that the last word has yet been said on this subtle question and the deep implications which it involves.[1]

Reports of numerous cases as well as the collection of instances made by Chabaneix (1897) seem to put it beyond dispute that dreams can carry on the intellectual work of daytime and bring it to conclusions which had not been reached during the day, and that they can resolve doubts and problems and be the source of new inspiration for poets and musical composers. But though the fact may be beyond dispute, its implications are open to many doubts, which raise matters of principle.[2]

Lastly, dreams are reputed to have the power of divining the future. Here we have a conflict in which almost insuperable scepticism is met by obstinately repeated assertions. No doubt we shall be acting rightly in not insisting that this view has no basis at all in fact, since it is possible that before long a number of the instances cited may find an explanation within the bounds of natural psychology.[3]

(F)

THE MORAL SENSE IN DREAMS

For reasons which will only become apparent after my own investigations into dreams have been taken into account, I have isolated from the subject of the psychology of dreams the special problem of whether and

---

[1] [*Footnote added* 1914:] A further bibliography and a critical discussion of these problems will be found in Tobowolska (1900). [Cf. also pp. 500 f.]

[2] [*Footnote added* 1914:] Cf. the criticism in Havelock Ellis (1911, 265). [See also below, p. 563 f.]

[3] [Cf. the posthumously published paper by Freud (1941c) printed as an Appendix at the end of this work (p. 617).]

to what extent moral dispositions and feelings extend into dream-life. Here too we are met by the same contradictory views which, curiously enough, we have found adopted by different authors in regard to all the other functions of the mind during dreams. Some assert that the dictates of morality have no place in dreams, while others maintain no less positively that the moral character of man persists in his dream-life.

Appeal to the common experience of dreams seems to establish beyond any doubt the correctness of the former of these views. Jessen (1855, 553) writes: 'Nor do we become better or more virtuous in sleep. On the contrary, conscience seems to be silent in dreams, for we feel no pity in them and may commit the worst crimes—theft, violence and murder—with complete indifference and with no subsequent feelings of remorse.'

Radestock (1879, 164): 'It should be borne in mind that associations occur and ideas are linked together in dreams without any regard for reflection, common sense, aesthetic taste or moral judgement. Judgement is extremely weak and ethical indifference reigns supreme.'

Volkelt (1875, 23): 'In dreams, as we are all aware, proceedings are especially unbridled in sexual matters. The dreamer himself is utterly shameless and devoid of any moral feeling or judgement; moreover, he sees everyone else, including those for whom he has the deepest respect, engaged in acts with which he would be horrified to associate them while he was awake, even in his thoughts.'

In diametrical opposition to these, we find statements such as Schopenhauer's [1862, 1, 245] that everyone who figures in a dream acts and speaks in complete accordance with his character. K. P. Fischer (1850, 72 f.), quoted by Spitta (1882, 188), declares that subjective feelings and longings, or affects and passions, reveal themselves in the freedom of dream-life, and that people's moral characteristics are reflected in their dreams.

Haffner (1884, 251): 'With rare exceptions . . . a virtuous man will be virtuous in his dreams as well; he will resist temptations and will keep himself aloof from hatred, envy, anger and all other vices. But a sinful man will as a rule find in his dreams the same images that he had before his eyes while he was awake.'

Scholz [Jewett's translation, 1893, 62]: 'In dreams is truth: in dreams we learn to know ourselves as we are in spite of all the disguises we wear to the world, [whether they be ennobling or humiliating]. . . . The honourable man cannot commit a crime in dreams, or if he does he is horrified over it as over something contrary to his nature. The Roman Emperor who put a man to death who had dreamt that he had assassinated the ruler, was justified in so doing if he reasoned that the thoughts one has in dreams, one has, too, when awake. The common expression "I wouldn't dream of such a thing" has a doubly correct significance when it refers to something which can have no lodgement in our hearts or mind.' (Plato, on the contrary, thought that the best men are those who only *dream* what other men *do* in their waking life.)[1]

Pfaff (1868, [9]), quoted by Spitta (1882, 192), alters the wording of a familiar saying: 'Tell me some of your dreams, and I will tell you about your inner self.'

The problem of morality in dreams is taken as the centre of interest by Hildebrandt, from whose small volume I have already quoted so much— for, of all the contributions to the study of dreams which I have come across, it is the most perfect in form and the richest in ideas. Hildebrandt [1875, 54] too lays it down as a rule that the purer the life the purer the dream, and the more impure the one the more impure the other. He believes that man's moral nature persists in dreams. 'Whereas,' he writes, 'even the grossest mistake in arithmetic, even the most romantic reversal of scientific laws, even the most ridiculous anachronism fails to upset us or even to arouse our suspicions, yet we never lose sight of the distinction between good and evil, between right and wrong or between virtue and vice. However much of what accompanies us in the daytime may drop away in our sleeping hours, Kant's categorical imperative is a companion who follows so close at our heels that we cannot be free of it even in sleep. . . . But this can only be explained by the fact that what is fundamental in man's nature, his moral being, is too firmly fixed to be affected by the kaleidoscopic shuffling to which the imagination, the reason, the memory and other such faculties must submit in dreams.' (Ibid., 45 f.)

As the discussion of this subject proceeds, however, both groups of writers begin to exhibit remarkable shifts and inconsistencies in their opinions. Those who maintain that the moral personality of man ceases to operate in dreams should, in strict logic, lose all interest in immoral dreams. They could rule out any attempt at holding a dreamer responsible for his dreams, or at deducing from the wickedness of his dreams that he had an

---

[1] [This sentence was added in 1914. Cf. also p. 614. The reference is no doubt to the opening sections of Book IX of the *Republic*. (*Trans.*, 1871, 409 f.)]

evil streak in his character, just as confidently as they would reject a similar attempt at deducing from the absurdity of his dreams that his intellectual activities in waking life were worthless. The other group, who believe that the 'categorical imperative' extends to dreams, should logically accept unqualified responsibility for immoral dreams. We could only hope for their sake that they would have no such reprehensible dreams of their own to upset their firm belief in their own moral character.

It appears, however, that no one is as confident as all that of how far he is good or bad, and that no one can deny the recollection of immoral dreams of his own. For writers in both groups, irrespective of the opposition between their opinions on dream-morality, make efforts at explaining the origin of immoral dreams; and a fresh difference of opinion develops, according as their origin is sought in the functions of the mind or in deleterious effects produced on the mind by somatic causes. Thus the compelling logic of facts forces the supporters of both the responsibility and the irresponsibility of dream-life to unite in recognizing that the immorality of dreams has a specific psychical source.

Those who believe that morality extends to dreams are, however, all careful to avoid assuming *complete* responsibility for their dreams. Thus Haffner (1887, 250) writes: 'We are not responsible for our dreams, since our thought and will have been deprived in them of the basis upon which alone our life possesses truth and reality . . . For that reason no dream-wishes or dream-actions can be virtuous or sinful.' Nevertheless, he goes on, men are responsible for their sinful dreams in so far as they cause them indirectly. They have the duty of morally cleansing their minds not only in their waking life but more especially before going to sleep.

Hildebrandt [1875, 48 f.] presents us with a far deeper analysis of this mingled rejection and acceptance of responsibility for the moral content of dreams. He argues that in considering the immoral appearance of dreams allowance must be made for the dramatic form in which they are couched, for their compression of the most complicated processes of reflection into the briefest periods of time, as well as for the way in which, as even he admits, the ideational elements of dreams become confused and deprived of their significance. He confesses that he has the greatest hesitation, nevertheless, in thinking that all responsibility for sins and faults in dreams can be repudiated.

'When we are anxious to disown some unjust accusation, especially one that relates to our aims and intentions, we often use the phrase "I should never dream of such a thing." We are in that way expressing, on the one hand, our feeling that the region of dreams is the most remote and furthest in which we are answerable for our thoughts, since thoughts in that region are so loosely connected with our essential self that they are scarcely to be regarded as ours; but nevertheless, since we feel obliged expressly to deny the existence of these thoughts in this region, we are at the same time admitting indirectly that our self-justification would not be complete unless it extended so far. And I think that in this we are speaking, although unconsciously, the language of truth.' (Ibid., 49.)

'It is impossible to think of any action in a dream for which the original motive has not in some way or other—whether as a wish, or desire or impulse—passed through the waking mind.' We must admit, Hildebrandt proceeds, that this original impulse was not invented by the dream; the dream merely copied it and spun it out, it merely elaborated in dramatic form a scrap of historical material which it had found in us; it merely dramatized the Apostle's words: 'Whosoever hateth his brother is a murderer.' [1 John iii, 15.] And although after we have awoken, conscious of our moral strength, we may smile at the whole elaborate structure of the sinful dream, yet the original material from which the structure was derived will fail to raise a smile. We feel responsible for the dreamer's errors—not for the whole amount of them, but for a certain percentage. 'In short, if we understand in this scarcely disputable sense Christ's saying that "out of the heart proceed evil thoughts" [Matt. xv, 19], we can hardly escape the conviction that a sin committed in a dream bears with it at least an obscure minimum of guilt.' (Hildebrandt, 1875, 51 ff.)

Thus Hildebrandt finds the source of immorality in dreams in the germs and hints of evil impulses which, in the form of temptations, pass through our minds during the day; and he does not hesitate to include these immoral elements in his estimate of a person's moral value. These same thoughts, as we know, and this same estimate of them, are what have led the pious and saintly in every age to confess themselves miserable sinners.[1]

There can of course be no doubt as to the general existence of such incompatible ideas; they occur in most people and in spheres other than

---

[1] [*Footnote added* 1914:] It is of some interest to learn the attitude of the Inquisition to our problem. In Caesar Careña's *Tractatus de Officio sanctissimae Inquisitionis*, 1659, the following passage occurs: 'If anyone speaks heresies in a dream, the inquisitors should take occasion to enquire into his way of life, for what occupies a man during the day is wont to come again in his sleep.' (Communicated by Dr. Ehniger, St. Urban, Switzerland.)

that of ethics. Sometimes, however, they have been judged less seriously. Spitta (1882, 194) quotes some remarks by Zeller [1818, 120–1], which are relevant in this connection: 'A mind is seldom so happily organized as to possess complete power at every moment and not to have the regular and clear course of its thoughts constantly interrupted not only by inessential but by positively grotesque and nonsensical ideas. Indeed, the greatest thinkers have had to complain of this dreamlike, teasing and tormenting rabble of ideas, which have disturbed their deepest reflections and their most solemn and earnest thoughts.'

A more revealing light is thrown upon the psychological position of these incompatible thoughts by another remark of Hildebrandt's (1875, 55), to the effect that dreams give us an occasional glimpse into depths and recesses of our nature to which we usually have no access in our waking state. Kant expresses the same idea in a passage in his *Anthropologie* [1798][1] in which he declares that dreams seem to exist in order to show us our hidden natures and to reveal to us, not what we are, but what we might have been if we had been brought up differently. Radestock (1879, 84), too, says that dreams often do no more than reveal to us what we would not admit to ourselves and that it is therefore unfair of us to stigmatize them as liars and deceivers. Erdmann [1852, 115] writes: 'Dreams have never shown me what I ought to think of a man; but I have occasionally learnt from a dream, greatly to my own astonishment, what I *do* think of a man and how I feel towards him.' Similarly I. H. Fichte (1864, **1**, 539) remarks: 'The nature of our dreams gives a far more truthful reflection of our whole disposition than we are able to learn of it from self-observation in waking life.'[2]

It will be seen that the emergence of impulses which are foreign to our moral consciousness is merely analogous to what we have already learnt—the fact that dreams have access to ideational material which is absent in our waking state or plays but a small part in it. Thus Benini (1898) writes: 'Certe nostre inclinazioni che si credevano soffocate e spente da un pezzo, si ridestano; passioni vecchie e sepolte rivivono; cose e persone a cui non pensiamo mai, ci vengono dinanzi.'[3] And Volkelt (1875, 105): 'Ideas, too, which have entered waking consciousness almost unnoticed and have per-

---

[1] [Not traceable.]

[2] [The last two sentences were added in 1914.]

[3] ['Certain of our desires which have seemed for a time to be stifled and extinguished are re-awakened; old and buried passions come to life again; things and persons of whom we never think appear before us.']

haps never again been called to memory, very frequently announce their presence in the mind through dreams.' At this point, finally, we may recall Schleiermacher's assertion [see above, p. 78] that the act of falling asleep is accompanied by the appearance of 'involuntary ideas' or images.

We may, then, class together under the heading of 'involuntary ideas' the whole of the ideational material the emergence of which, alike in immoral and in absurd dreams, causes us so much bewilderment. There is, however, one important point of difference: involuntary ideas in the moral sphere contradict our usual attitude of mind, whereas the others merely strike us as strange. No step has yet been taken towards a deeper knowledge which would resolve this distinction.

The question next arises as to the *significance* of the appearance of involuntary ideas in dreams, as to the light which the emergence during the night of these morally incompatible impulses throws upon the psychology of the waking and dreaming mind. And here we find a fresh division of opinion and yet another different grouping of the authorities. The line of thought adopted by Hildebrandt and others who share his fundamental position inevitably leads to the view that immoral impulses possess a certain degree of power even in waking life, though it is an inhibited power, unable to force its way into action, and that in sleep something is put out of action which acts like an inhibition in the daytime and has prevented us from being aware of the existence of such impulses. Thus dreams would reveal the true nature of man, though not his whole nature, and they would constitute one means of rendering the hidden interior of the mind accessible to our knowledge. Only upon some such premises as these can Hildebrandt [1875, 56] base his attribution to dreams of warning powers, which draw our attention to moral infirmities in our mind, just as physicians admit that dreams can bring unobserved physical illnesses to our conscious notice. So, too, Spitta must be adopting this view when, in speaking [1882, 193 f.] of the sources of excitation which impinge upon the mind (at puberty, for instance), he consoles the dreamer with the assurance that he will have done all that lies within his power if he leads a strictly virtuous life in his waking hours, and if he takes care to suppress sinful thoughts whenever they arise and to prevent their maturing and turning into acts. According to this view we might define the 'involuntary ideas' as ideas which had been 'suppressed' during the day, and we should have to regard their emergence as a genuine mental phenomenon.

Other writers, however, regard this last conclusion as unjustifiable. Thus Jessen (1855) believes that involuntary ideas, both in dreams and in waking, and in feverish and other delirious conditions, 'have the character of a volitional activity that has been put to rest and of a more or less mechanical succession of images and ideas provoked by internal impulses.' All that an immoral dream proves as to the dreamer's mental life is, in Jessen's view, that on some occasion he had cognizance of the ideational content in question; it is certainly no evidence of a mental impulse of the dreamer's own.

As regards another writer, Maury, it would almost seem as though he too attributes to the dreaming condition a capacity, not for the arbitrary destruction of mental activity, but for analysing it into its components. He writes as follows of dreams which transgress the bounds of morality: 'Ce sont nos penchants qui parlent et qui nous font agir, sans que la conscience nous retienne, bien que parfois elle nous avertisse. J'ai mes défauts et mes penchants vicieux; à l'état de veille je tâche de lutter contre eux, et il m'arrive assez souvent de n'y pas succomber. Mais dans mes songes j'y succombe toujours ou pour mieux dire j'agis par leur impulsion, sans crainte et sans remords. . . . Evidemment les visions qui se déroulent devant ma pensée et qui constituent le rêve, me sont suggérées par les incitations que je ressens et que ma volonté absente ne cherche pas à refouler.' (Maury, 1878, 113.)[1]

No one who believes in the capacity of dreams to reveal an immoral tendency of the dreamer's which is really present though suppressed or concealed, could express his view more precisely than in Maury's words: 'En rêve l'homme se révèle donc tout entier à soi-même dans sa nudité et sa misère natives. Dès qu'il suspend l'exercice de sa volonté, il devient le jouet de toutes les passions contres lesquelles, à l'état de veille, la conscience, le sentiment de l'honneur, la crainte nous défendent.' (Ibid., 165.)[2] In another passage we find these pertinent sentences: 'Dans le

---

[1] ['It is our impulses that are speaking and making us act, while our conscience does not hold us back, though it sometimes warns us. I have my faults and my vicious impulses; while I am awake I try to resist them, and quite often I succeed in not yielding to them. But in my dreams I *always* yield to them, or rather I act under their pressure without fear or remorse. . . . The visions which unroll before my mind and which constitute a dream are clearly suggested by the urges which I feel and which my absent will does not attempt to repress.']

[2] ['Thus in dreams a man stands self-revealed in all his native nakedness and poverty. As soon as he suspends the exercise of his will, he becomes the plaything of all the passions against which he is defended while he is awake by his conscience, his sense of honour and his fears.']

songe, c'est surtout l'homme instinctif qui se révèle. . . . L'homme revient pour ainsi dire à l'état de nature quand il rêve; mais moins les idées acquises ont pénétré dans son esprit, plus les penchants en désaccord avec elles conservent encore sur lui l'influence dans le rêve.' (Ibid., 462.)[1] He goes on to relate by way of example how in his dreams he is not infrequently the victim of the very superstition which he has been attacking in his writings with particular vehemence.

These penetrating reflections of Maury's, however, lose their value in the investigation of dream-life owing to the fact that he regards the phenomena which he has observed with such accuracy as no more than proofs of an '*automatisme psychologique*' which, in his view, dominates dreams and which he looks upon as the exact opposite of mental activity.

Stricker (1879, [51]) writes: 'Dreams do not consist solely of illusions. If, for instance, one is afraid of robbers in a dream, the robbers, it is true, are imaginary—but the fear is real.' This calls our attention to the fact that *affects* in dreams cannot be judged in the same way as the remainder of their content; and we are faced by the problem of what part of the psychical processes occurring in dreams is to be regarded as real, that is to say, has a claim to be classed among the psychical processes of waking life.[2]

(G)
THEORIES OF DREAMING AND ITS FUNCTION

Any disquisition upon dreams which seeks to explain as many as possible of their observed characteristics from a particular point of view, and which at the same time defines the position occupied by dreams in a wider sphere of phenomena, deserves to be called a theory of dreams. The various theories will be found to differ in that they select one or the other

---

[1] ['What is revealed in dreams is primarily the man of instinct. . . . Man may be said to return in his dreams to a state of nature. But the less his mind has been penetrated by acquired ideas, the more it remains influenced in dreams by impulses of a contrary nature.']

[2] [The question of affects in dreams is discussed in Section H of Chapter VI (pp. 466 ff.). The whole topic of moral responsibility for dreams is touched upon below on pp. 613 f. and considered at greater length in Section B of Freud 1925*i*.]

characteristic of dreams as the essential one and take it as the point of departure for their explanations and correlations. It need not necessarily be possible to infer a *function* of dreaming (whether utilitarian or otherwise) from the theory. Nevertheless, since we have a habit of looking for teleological explanations, we shall be more ready to accept theories which are bound up with the attribution of a function to dreaming.

We have already made the acquaintance of several sets of views which deserve more or less to be called theories of dreams in this sense of the term. The belief held in antiquity that dreams were sent by the gods in order to guide the actions of men was a complete theory of dreams, giving information on everything worth knowing about them. Since dreams have become an object of scientific research a considerable number of theories have been developed, including some that are extremely incomplete.

Without attempting any exhaustive enumeration, we may try to divide theories of dreams into the following three rough groups, according to their underlying assumptions as to the amount and nature of psychical activity in dreams.

(1) There are the theories, such as that of Delboeuf [1885, 221 f.], according to which the whole of psychical activity continues in dreams. The mind, they assume, does not sleep and its apparatus remains intact; but, since it falls under the conditions of the state of sleep, which differ from those of waking life, its normal functioning necessarily produces different results during sleep. The question arises in regard to these theories whether they are capable of deriving all the distinctions between dreams and waking thought from the conditions of the state of sleep. Moreover, there is no possibility of their being able to suggest any *function* for dreaming; they offer no reason why we should dream, why the complicated mechanism of the mental apparatus should continue to operate even when set in circumstances for which it appears undesigned. Either dreamless sleep or, if disturbing stimuli intervene, awakening, would seem to be the only expedient reactions—rather than the third alternative of dreaming.

(2) There are the theories which, on the contrary, presuppose that dreams imply a lowering of psychical activity, a loosening of connections, and an impoverishment of the material accessible. These theories must imply the attribution to sleep of characteristics quite different from those suggested, for instance, by Delboeuf. Sleep, according to such theories, has a far-reaching influence upon the mind; it does not consist merely in

the mind being shut off from the external world; it forces its way, rather, into the mental mechanism and throws it temporarily out of use. If I may venture on a simile from the sphere of psychiatry, the first group of theories construct dreams on the model of paranoia, while the second group make them resemble mental deficiency or confusional states.

The theory according to which only a fragment of mental activity finds expression in dreams, since it has been paralysed by sleep, is by far the most popular with medical writers and in the scientific world generally. In so far as any general interest may be supposed to exist in the explanation of dreams, this may be described as the ruling theory. It is to be remarked how easily this theory avoids the worst stumbling-block in the way of any explanation of dreams—the difficulty of dealing with the contradictions involved in them. It regards dreams as a result of a partial awakening—'a gradual, partial and at the same time highly abnormal awakening,' to quote a remark of Herbart's upon dreams (1892, 307). Thus, this theory can make use of a series of conditions of ever-increasing wakefulness, culminating in the completely waking state, in order to account for the series of variations in efficiency of mental functioning in dreams, ranging from the inefficiency revealed by their occasional absurdity up to fully concentrated intellectual functioning. [See p. 203.]

Those who find that they cannot dispense with a statement in terms of physiology, or to whom a statement in such terms seems more scientific, will find what they want in the account given by Binz (1878, 43): 'This condition' (of torpor) 'comes to an end in the early hours of the morning, but only by degrees. The products of fatigue which have accumulated in the albumen of the brain gradually diminish; more and more of them are decomposed or eliminated by the unceasing flow of the blood-stream. Here and there separate groups of cells begin to emerge into wakefulness, while the torpid state still persists all around them. The isolated work of these separate groups now appears before our clouded consciousness, unchecked by other portions of the brain which govern the process of association. For that reason the images produced, which correspond for the most part to material impressions of the more recent past, are strung together in a wild and irregular manner. The number of the liberated brain cells constantly grows and the senselessness of the dreams correspondingly diminishes.'

This view of dreaming as an incomplete, partial waking state is no doubt to be found in the writings of every modern physiologist and philosopher. The most elaborate exposition of it is given by Maury (1878, 6 f.).

It often appears as though that author imagined that the waking or sleeping state could be shifted from one anatomical region to another, each particular anatomical region being linked to one particular psychical function. I will merely remark at this point that, even if the theory of partial waking were confirmed, its details would still remain very much open to discussion.

This view naturally leaves no room for assigning any function to dreaming. The logical conclusion that follows from it as to the position and significance of dreams is correctly stated by Binz (1878, 35): 'Every observed fact forces us to conclude that dreams must be characterized as *somatic* processes, which are in every case useless and in many cases positively pathological. . . .'

The application to dreams of the term 'somatic,' which is italicized by Binz himself, has more than one bearing. It alludes, in the first place, to the *aetiology* of dreams which seemed particularly plausible to Binz when he studied the experimental production of dreams by the use of toxic substances. For theories of this kind involve a tendency to limit the instigation of dreams so far as possible to somatic causes. Put in its most extreme form the view is as follows. Once we have put ourselves to sleep by excluding all stimuli, there is no need and no occasion for dreaming until the morning, when the process of being gradually awakened by the impact of fresh stimuli might be reflected in the phenomenon of dreaming. It is impracticable, however, to keep our sleep free from stimuli; they impinge upon the sleeper from all sides—like the germs of life of which Mephistopheles complained[1]—from without and from within and even from parts of his body which are quite unnoticed in waking life. Thus sleep is disturbed; first one corner of the mind is shaken into wakefulness and then another; the mind functions for a brief moment with its awakened portion and is then glad to fall asleep once more. Dreams are a reaction to the disturbance of sleep brought about by a stimulus—a reaction, incidentally, which is quite superfluous.

But the description of dreaming—which, after all is said and done, remains a function of the mind—as a somatic process implies another meaning as well. It is intended to show that dreams are unworthy to rank

---

[1] [In his first conversation with Faust (Part I, [Scene 3]), Mephistopheles complained bitterly that his destructive efforts were perpetually frustrated by the emergence of thousands of fresh germs of life. The whole passage is quoted by Freud in a footnote to Section VI of *Civilization and Its Discontents* (1930a).]

as psychical processes. Dreaming has often been compared with 'the ten fingers of a man who knows nothing of music wandering over the keys of a piano' [Strümpell, 1877, 84; cf. p. 242 below]; and this simile shows as well as anything the sort of opinion that is usually held of dreaming by representatives of the exact sciences. On this view a dream is something wholly and completely incapable of interpretation; for how could the ten fingers of an unmusical player produce a piece of music?

Even in the distant past there was no lack of critics of the theory of partial waking. Thus Burdach (1838, 508 f.) wrote: 'When it is said that dreams are a partial waking, in the first place this throws no light either on waking or on sleeping, and in the second place it says no more than that some mental forces are active in dreams while others are at rest. But variability of this kind occurs throughout life.'

This ruling theory, which regards dreams as a somatic process, underlies a most interesting hypothesis put forward for the first time by Robert in 1886. It is particularly attractive since it is able to suggest a function, a utilitarian purpose, for dreaming. Robert takes as the groundwork of his theory two facts of observation which we have already considered in the course of our examination of the material of dreams (see above, pp. 51 ff.), namely that we dream so frequently of the most trivial daily impressions and that we so rarely carry over into our dreams our important daily interests. Robert (1886, 10) asserts that it is universally true that things which we have thoroughly thought out never become instigators of dreams but only things which are in our minds in an uncompleted shape or which have merely been touched upon by our thoughts in passing: 'The reason why it is usually impossible to explain dreams is precisely because they are caused by sensory impressions of the preceding day which failed to attract enough of the dreamer's attention.' [Ibid., 19–20.] Thus the condition which determines whether an impression shall find its way into a dream is whether the process of working over the impression was interrupted or whether the impression was too unimportant to have a right to be worked over at all.

Robert describes dreams as 'a somatic process of excretion of which we become aware in our mental reaction to it.' [Ibid., 9.] Dreams are excretions of thoughts that have been stifled at birth. 'A man deprived of the capacity for dreaming would in course of time become mentally deranged, because a great mass of uncompleted, unworked-out thoughts and superficial impressions would accumulate in his brain and would be bound by their bulk to smother the thoughts which should be assimilated into his memory as completed wholes.' [Ibid., 10.] Dreams serve as a safety-valve for the over-burdened brain. They possess the power to heal and relieve. (Ibid., 32.)

We should be misunderstanding Robert if we were to ask him how it can come about that the mind is relieved through the presentation of ideas in dreams. What Robert is clearly doing is to infer from these two features of the material of dreams that by some means or other an expulsion of worthless impressions is accomplished during sleep as a somatic process, and that dreaming is not a special sort of psychical process but merely the information we receive of that expulsion. Moreover, excretion is not the only event which occurs in the mind at night. Robert himself adds that, besides this, the suggestions arising during the previous day are worked out and that 'whatever parts of the undigested thoughts are not excreted are bound together into a rounded whole by threads of thought borrowed from the imagination and thus inserted in the memory as a harmless imaginative picture.' (Ibid., 23.)

But Robert's theory is diametrically opposed to the ruling one in its estimate of the nature of the *sources* of dreams. According to the latter, there would be no dreaming at all if the mind were not being constantly wakened by external and internal sensory stimuli. But in Robert's view the impulsion to dreaming arises in the mind itself—in the fact of its becoming overloaded and requiring relief; and he concludes with perfect logic that causes derived from somatic conditions play a subordinate part as determinants of dreams, and that such causes would be quite incapable of provoking dreams in a mind in which there was no material for the construction of dreams derived from waking consciousness. The only qualification he makes is to admit that the phantasy-images arising in dreams out of the depths of the mind may be affected by nervous stimuli. (Ibid., 48.) After all, therefore, Robert does not regard dreams as so completely dependent upon somatic events. Nevertheless, in his view dreams are not psychical processes, they have no place among the psychical processes of waking life; they are somatic processes occurring every night in the apparatus that is concerned with mental activity, and they have as their function the task of protecting that apparatus from excessive tension—or, to change the metaphor—of acting as scavengers of the mind.[1]

---

[1] [Robert's theory is further discussed on pp. 200 f. and 577.—In the course of a footnote to *Studies on Hysteria* (Breuer and Freud, 1895), quoted in the Editor's Introduction, p. xiii f., Freud accepted this theory of Robert's as describing one of the two main factors in the production of dreams.]

Another writer, Yves Delage, bases his theory on the same features of dreams, as revealed in the choice of their material; and it is instructive to notice the way in which a slight variation in his view of the same things leads him to conclusions of a very different bearing.

Delage (1891, 41) tells us that he experienced in his own person, on the occasion of the death of someone of whom he was fond, the fact that we do *not* dream of what has occupied all our thoughts during the day, or not until it has begun to give place to other daytime concerns. His investigations among other people confirmed him in the general truth of this fact. He makes what would be an interesting observation of this kind, if it should prove to have general validity, on the dreams of young married couples: 'S'ils ont été fortement épris, presque jamais ils n'ont rêvé l'un de l'autre avant le mariage ou pendant la lune de miel; et s'ils ont rêvé d'amour c'est pour être infidèles avec quelque personne indifférente ou odieuse.'[1] [Ibid., 41.] What, then, do we dream of? Delage identifies the material that occurs in our dreams as consisting of fragments and residues of the preceding days and of earlier times. Everything that appears in our dreams, even though we are inclined at first to regard it as a creation of our dream-life, turns out, when we have examined it more closely, to be unrecognized reproduction [of material already experienced]—'souvenir inconscient.'[2] But this ideational material possesses a common characteristic: it originates from impressions which probably affected our senses more strongly than our intelligence or from which our attention was diverted very soon after they emerged. The less conscious and at the same time the more powerful an impression has been, the more chance it has of playing a part in the next dream.

Here we have what are essentially the same two categories of impressions as are stressed by Robert: the trivial ones and those that have not been dealt with. Delage, however, gives the situation a different turn, for he holds that it is because these impressions have not been dealt with that they are capable of producing dreams, not because they are trivial. It is true in a certain sense that trivial impressions, too, have not been dealt with completely; being in the nature of fresh impressions, they are 'autant de ressorts tendus'[3] which are released during sleep. A powerful impression

---

[1] ['If they were deeply in love, they almost never dreamt of each other before marriage or during their honeymoon; and if they had erotic dreams they were unfaithful in them with some indifferent or repellent person.']

[2] ['Unconscious memory.']

[3] ['They are so many springs under tension.']

which happens to have met with some check in the process of being worked over or which has been purposely held under restraint has more claim to play a part in dreams than an impression which is weak and almost unnoticed. The psychical energy which has been stored up during the daytime by being inhibited and suppressed becomes the motive force for dreams at night. Psychical material that has been suppressed comes to light in dreams. [Ibid., 1891, 43 .][1]

At this point, unluckily, Delage interrupts his train of thought. He can attribute only the smallest share in dreams to any independent psychical activity; and thus he brings his theory into line with the ruling theory of the partial awakening of the brain: 'En somme le rêve est le produit de la pensée errante, sans but et sans direction, se fixant successivement sur les souvenirs, qui ont gardé assez d'intensité pour se placer sur sa route et l'arrêter au passage, établissant entre eux un lien tantôt faible et indécis, tantôt plus fort et plus serré, selon que l'activité actuelle du cerveau est plus ou moins abolie par le sommeil.' [Ibid., 46.][2]

(3) We may place in a third group those theories which ascribe to the dreaming mind a capacity and inclination for carrying out special psychical activities of which it is largely or totally incapable in waking life. The putting of these faculties into force usually provides dreaming with a utilitarian function. Most of the estimates formed of dreaming by earlier writers on psychology fall into this class. It will be enough, however, for me to quote a sentence from Burdach (1838, 512). Dreaming, he writes, 'is a natural activity of the mind which is not limited by the power of individuality, which is not interrupted by self-consciousness and which is

---

[1] [*Footnote added* 1909:] Anatole France expresses exactly the same idea in *Le lys rouge*: 'Ce que nous voyons la nuit, ce sont les restes malheureux de ce que nous avons négligé dans la veille. Le rêve est souvent la revanche des choses qu'on méprise ou le reproche des êtres abandonnés.' ['What we see during the night are the miserable remnants of what we have neglected during the previous day. A dream is often a retaliation on the part of what we despise or a reproach on the part of those we have deserted.']

[2] ['In short, dreams are the product of thought wandering without purpose or direction, attaching itself in turn to memories which have retained enough intensity to stand in its way and interrupt its course, and linking them together by a bond which is sometimes weak and vague and sometimes stronger and closer, according as the brain's activity at the moment is abolished by sleep to a greater or less extent.']

not directed by self-determination, but which is the freely operating vitality of the sensory centres.'

This revelling of the mind in the free use of its own forces is evidently regarded by Burdach and the rest as a condition in which the mind is refreshed and collects new strength for the day's work—in which, in fact, it enjoys a sort of holiday. Thus Burdach [ibid., 514] quotes with approval the charming words in which the poet Novalis praises the reign of dreams: 'Dreams are a shield against the humdrum monotony of life; they set imagination free from its chains so that it may throw into confusion all the pictures of everyday existence and break into the unceasing gravity of grown men with the joyful play of a child. Without dreams we should surely grow sooner old; so we may look on them—not, perhaps as a gift from on high—but as a precious recreation, as friendly companions on our pilgrimage to the grave.' [*Heinrich von Ofterdingen* (1802), Part I, Chap. 1.]

The reviving and healing function of dreams is described with still more insistence by Purkinje (1846, 456): 'These functions are performed especially by productive dreams. They are the easy play of the imagination and have no connection with the affairs of daytime. The mind has no wish to prolong the tensions of waking life; it seeks to relax them and to recover from them. It produces above all conditions contrary to the waking ones. It cures sorrow by joy, cares by hopes and pictures of happy distraction, hatred by love and friendliness, fear by courage and foresight; it allays doubt by conviction and firm faith, and vain expectation by fulfilment. Many of the spirit's wounds which are being constantly re-opened during the day are healed by sleep, which covers them and shields them from fresh injury. The healing action of time is based partly on this.' We all have a feeling that sleep has a beneficial effect upon mental activities, and the obscure working of the popular mind refuses to let itself be robbed of its belief that dreaming is one of the ways in which sleep dispenses its benefits.

The most original and far-reaching attempt to explain dreaming as a special activity of the mind, capable of free expansion only during the state of sleep, was that undertaken by Scherner in 1861. His book is written in a turgid and high-flown style and is inspired by an almost intoxicated enthusiasm for his subject which is bound to repel anyone who cannot share in his fervour. It puts such difficulties in the way of an analysis of its contents that we turn with relief to the clearer and briefer exposition of Scherner's doctrines given by the philosopher Volkelt. 'Suggestive gleams

of meaning proceed like lightning-flashes out of these mystical agglomer-
ations, these clouds of glory and splendour—but they do not illuminate a
philosopher's path.' It is in these terms that Scherner's writings are judged
even by his disciple. [Volkelt, 1875, 29.]

Scherner is not one of those who believe that the capacities of the mind
continue undiminished in dream-life. He himself [in Volkelt's words
(ibid., 30)] shows how the centralized core of the ego—its spontaneous
energy—is deprived of its nervous force in dreams, how as a result of this
decentralization the processes of cognition, feeling, willing and ideation
are modified, and how the remnants of these psychical functions no longer
possess a truly mental character but become nothing more than mechanisms. But by way of contrast, the mental activity which may be described
as 'imagination,' liberated from the domination of reason and from any
moderating control, leaps into a position of unlimited sovereignty.
Though dream-imagination makes use of recent waking memories for its
building material, it erects them into structures bearing not the remotest
resemblance to those of waking life; it reveals itself in dreams as possessing
not merely reproductive but *productive* powers. [Ibid., 31.] Its characteristics are what lend their peculiar features to dreams. It shows a preference
for what is immoderate, exaggerated and monstrous. But at the same time,
being freed from the hindrances of the categories of thought, it gains in
pliancy, agility and versatility. It is susceptible in the subtlest manner to the
shades of the tender feelings and to passionate emotions, and promptly in-
corporates our inner life into external plastic pictures. Imagination in
dreams is without the power of conceptual speech. It is obliged to paint
what it has to say pictorially, and, since there are no concepts to exercise
an attenuating influence, it makes full and powerful use of the pictorial
form. Thus, however clear its speech may be, it is diffuse, clumsy and awkward. The clarity of its speech suffers particularly from the fact that it has
a dislike of representing an object by its proper image, and prefers some
extraneous image which will express only that particular one of the object's
attributes which it is seeking to represent. Here we have the 'symbolizing
activity' of the imagination. . . . [Ibid., 32.] Another very important point
is that dream-imagination never depicts things completely, but only in
outline and even so only in the roughest fashion. For this reason its paintings seem like inspired sketches. It does not halt, however, at the mere representation of an object; it is under an internal necessity to involve the
dream-ego to a greater or less extent with the object and thus produce an
event. For instance, a dream caused by a visual stimulus may represent gold

coins in the street; the dreamer will pick them up delightedly and carry them off. [Ibid., 33.]

The material with which dream-imagination accomplishes its artistic work is principally, according to Scherner, provided by the organic somatic stimuli which are so obscure during the daytime. (See above, pp. 65 ff.) Thus the excessively fantastic hypothesis put forward by Scherner and the perhaps unduly sober doctrines of Wundt and other physiologists, which are poles asunder in other respects, are entirely at one in regard to their theory of the sources and instigators of dreams. According to the physiological view, however, the mental reaction to the internal somatic stimuli is exhausted with the provoking of certain ideas appropriate to the stimuli; these ideas give rise to others along associative lines and at this point the course of psychical events in dreams seems to be at an end. According to Scherner, on the other hand, the somatic stimuli do no more than provide the mind with material of which it can make use for its imaginative purposes. The formation of dreams only begins, in Scherner's eyes, at the point which the other writers regard as its end.

What dream-imagination does to the somatic stimuli cannot, of course, be regarded as serving any useful purpose. It plays about with them, and pictures the organic sources, from which the stimuli of the dream in question have arisen, in some kind of plastic symbolism. Scherner is of the opinion—though here Volkelt [1875, 37] and others refuse to follow him—that dream-imagination has one particular favourite way of representing the organism as a whole: namely as a house. Fortunately, however, it does not seem to be restricted to this one method of representation. On the other hand, it may make use of a whole row of houses to indicate a single organ; for instance, a very long street of houses may represent a stimulus from the intestines. Again, separate portions of a house may stand for separate portions of the body; thus, in a dream caused by a headache, the head may be represented by the ceiling of a room covered with disgusting, toad-like spiders. [Ibid., 33 f.]

Leaving this house-symbolism on one side, any number of other kinds of things may be used to represent the parts of the body from which the stimulus to the dream has arisen. 'Thus the breathing lung will be symbolically represented by a blazing furnace, with flames roaring with a sound like the passage of air; the heart will be represented by hollow boxes or baskets, the bladder by round, bag-shaped objects or, more generally, by hollow ones. A dream caused by stimuli arising from the male sexual organs may cause the dreamer to find the top part of a clarinet in the street or the mouth-piece of a tobacco-pipe, or again, a piece of fur. Here the clarinet and the tobacco-pipe represent the approximate shape of the male organ, while the fur stands for the pubic hair. In the case of a sexual dream in a woman, the narrow space where the thighs come together may be represented by a narrow courtyard surrounded by houses, while the vagina may be symbolized by a soft, slippery and very narrow foot-path leading across the yard, along which the dreamer has to pass, in order, perhaps, to take a gentleman a letter.' (Ibid., 34.) It is of special importance that, at the end of dreams with a somatic stimulus, such as these, the dream-imagination often throws aside its veil, as it were, by openly revealing the organ concerned or its function. Thus a dream 'with a dental stimulus' usually ends by the dreamer picturing himself pulling a tooth out of his mouth. [Ibid., 35.]

Dream-imagination may, however, not merely direct its attention to the *form* of the stimulating organ; it may equally well symbolize the substance contained in that organ. In this way, a dream with an intestinal stimulus may lead the dreamer along muddy streets, or one with a urinary stimulus may lead him to a foaming stream. Or the stimulus as such, the nature of the excitement it produces, or the object it desires, may be symbolically represented. Or the dream-ego may enter into concrete relations with the symbols of its own state; for instance, in the case of painful stimuli the dreamer may engage in a desperate struggle with fierce dogs or savage bulls, or a woman in a sexual dream may find herself pursued by a naked man. [Ibid., 35 f.] Quite apart from the wealth of the means that it employs, the symbolizing activity of the imagination remains the central force in every dream. [Ibid., 36.] The task of penetrating more deeply into the nature of this imagination and of finding a place for it in a system of philosophical thought is attempted by Volkelt in the pages of his book. But, though it is well and feelingly written, it remains excessively hard to understand for anyone whose early education has not prepared him for a sympathetic grasp of the conceptual constructions of philosophy.

There is no utilitarian function attached to Scherner's symbolizing imagination. The mind plays in its sleep with the stimuli that impinge upon it. One might almost suspect that it plays with them mischievously. But I might also be asked whether my detailed examination of Scherner's theory of dreams can serve any utilitarian purpose, since its arbitrary character and its disobedience to all the rules of research seem only too obvious. By way of rejoinder, I might register a protest against the arrogance which would dismiss Scherner's theory unexamined. His theory is built upon the impression made by his dreams upon a man who considered them with the greatest attention and seems to have had a great personal gift for investigating the obscure things of the mind. Moreover it deals with a subject that for thousands of years has been regarded by mankind as enigmatic, no doubt, but also as important in itself and its implications—a subject to the elucidation of which exact science, on its own admission, has contributed little apart from an attempt (in direct opposition to popular feeling) to deny it any meaning or significance. And finally it may honestly be said that in attempting to explain dreams it is not easy to avoid being fantastic. Ganglion cells can be fantastic too. The passage which I quoted on p. 104 from a sober and exact investigator like Binz, and which describes the way in which the dawn of awakening steals over the mass of sleeping cells in the cerebral cortex, is no less fantastic—and no less improbable—than Scherner's attempts at interpretation. I hope to be able to show that behind the latter there is an element of reality, though it has only been vaguely perceived and lacks the attribute of universality which should characterize a theory of dreams. Meanwhile the contrast between Scherner's theory and the medical one will show us the extremes between which explanations of dream-life doubtfully oscillate to this very day.[1]

(H)

THE RELATIONS BETWEEN DREAMS AND MENTAL DISEASES

When we speak of the relation of dreams to mental disorders we may have three things in mind: (1) aetiological and clinical connections, as when a dream represents a psychotic state, or introduces it, or is left over from it; (2) modifications to which dream-life is subject in cases of mental disease; and (3) intrinsic connections between dreams and psychoses, analogies pointing to their being essentially akin. These numerous relations between the two groups of phenomena were a favourite topic among medical writers in earlier times and have become so once again today, as is

---

[1] [Scherner's theories are further discussed on pp. 245 ff. and 360.]

shown by the bibliographies of the subject collected by Spitta [1882, 196 f. and 319 f.], Radestock [1879, 217], Maury [1878, 124 f.] and Tissié [1898, 77 f.]. Quite recently Sante de Sanctis has turned his attention to this subject.[1] It will be enough for the purpose of my thesis if I do no more than touch upon this important question.

As regards the clinical and aetiological connections between dreams and psychoses, the following observations may be given as samples. Hohnbaum [1830, 124], quoted by Krauss [1858, 619], reports that a first outbreak of delusional insanity often originates in an anxious or terrifying dream, and that the dominant idea is connected with the dream. Sante de Sanctis brings forward similar observations in cases of paranoia and declares that in some of these the dream was the 'vraie cause déterminante de la folie.'[2] The psychosis, says de Sanctis, may come to life at a single blow with the appearance of the operative dream which brings the delusional material to light; or it may develop slowly in a series of further dreams, which have still to overcome a certain amount of doubt. In one of his cases the significant dream was followed by mild hysterical attacks and later by a condition of anxious melancholia. Féré [1886] (quoted by Tissié, 1898 [78]) reports a dream which resulted in a hysterical paralysis. In these instances the dreams are represented as the aetiology of the mental disorder; but we should be doing equal justice to the facts if we said that the mental disorder made its first appearance in dream-life, that it first broke through in a dream. In some further examples the pathological symptoms are contained in dream-life, or the psychosis is limited to dream-life. Thus Thomayer (1897) draws attention to certain anxiety-dreams which he thinks should be regarded as equivalents of epileptic fits. Allison [1868] (quoted by Radestock, 1879 [225]) has described a 'nocturnal insanity,' in which the patient appears completely healthy during the day but is regularly subject at night to hallucinations, fits of frenzy, etc. Similar observations are reported by de Sanctis [1899, 226] (a dream in an alcoholic patient which was equivalent to a paranoia, and which represented voices accusing his wife of unfaithfulness) and Tissié. The latter (1898, [147 ff.]) gives copious recent examples in which acts of a pathological nature, such

---

[1] [*Footnote added* 1914:] Among later writers who deal with these relations are Féré [1887], Ideler [1862], Lasègue [1881], Pichon [1896], Régis [1894], Vespa [1897], Giessler [1888, etc.], Kazowsky [1901], Pachantoni [1909], etc.

[2] ['The true determining cause of insanity.']

as conduct based on delusional premises and obsessive impulses, were derived from dreams. Guislain [1833] describes a case in which sleep was replaced by an intermittent insanity.

There can be no doubt that alongside of the psychology of dreams physicians will some day have to turn their attention to a *psychopathology* of dreams.

In cases of recovery from mental diseases it can often be quite clearly observed that, while functioning is normal during the day, dream-life is still under the influence of the psychosis. According to Krauss (1859, 270), Gregory first drew attention to this fact. Macario [1847], quoted by Tissié [1898, 89], describes how a manic patient, a week after his complete recovery, was still subject in his dreams to the flight of ideas and the violent passions which were characteristic of his illness.

Very little research has hitherto been carried out into the modifications occurring in dream-life during chronic psychoses.[1] On the other hand, attention was long ago directed to the underlying kinship between dreams and mental disorders, exhibited in the wide measure of agreement between their manifestations. Maury (1854, 124) tells us that Cabanis (1802) was the first to remark on them, and after him Lélut [1852], J. Moreau (1855) and, in particular, Maine de Biran [1834, 111 ff.] the philosopher. No doubt the comparison goes back still earlier. Radestock (1879, 217) introduces the chapter in which he deals with it by a number of quotations drawing an analogy between dreams and madness. Kant writes somewhere [1764]: 'The madman is a waking dreamer.' Krauss (1859, 270) declares that 'insanity is a dream dreamt while the senses are awake.' Schopenhauer [1862, 1, 246] calls dreams a brief madness and madness a long dream. Hagen [1846, 812] describes delirium as dream-life induced not by sleep but by illness. Wundt [1878, 662] writes: 'We ourselves, in fact, can experience in dreams almost all the phenomena to be met with in insane asylums.'

Spitta (1882, 199), in much the same way as Maury (1854), enumerates as follows the different points of agreement which constitute the basis for this comparison: '(1) Self-consciousness is suspended or at least retarded, which results in a lack of insight into the nature of the condition, with consequent inability to feel surprise and loss of moral consciousness. (2) Perception by the sense organs is modified: being diminished in

---

[1] [This question was later examined by Freud himself (1922b, end of Section B).]

dreams but as a rule greatly increased in insanity. (3) Inter-connection of ideas occurs exclusively according to the laws of association and reproduction; ideas thus fall into sequences automatically and there is a consequent lack of proportion in the relation between ideas (exaggerations and illusions). All this leads to (4) an alteration or in some cases a reversal of personality and occasionally of character traits (perverse conduct).'

Radestock (1879, 219) adds a few more features—analogies between the *material* in the two cases: 'The majority of hallucinations and illusions occur in the region of the senses of sight and hearing and of coenaesthesia. As in the case of dreams, the senses of smell and taste provide the fewest elements.—Both in patients suffering from fever and in dreamers memories arise from the remote past; both sleeping and sick men recollect things which waking and healthy men seem to have forgotten.' The analogy between dreams and psychoses is only fully appreciated when it is seen to extend to the details of expressive movement and to particular characteristics of facial expression.

'A man tormented by physical and mental suffering obtains from dreams what reality denies him: health and happiness. So too in mental disease there are bright pictures of happiness, grandeur, eminence and wealth. The supposed possession of property and the imaginary fulfilment of wishes—the withholding or destruction of which actually affords a psychological basis for insanity—often constitute the chief content of a delirium. A woman who has lost a loved child experiences the joys of motherhood in her delirium; a man who has lost his money believes himself immensely rich; a girl who has been deceived feels that she is tenderly loved.'

(This passage from Radestock is actually a summary of an acute observation made by Griesinger (1861, 106), who shows quite clearly that ideas in dreams and in psychoses have in common the characteristic of being *fulfilments of wishes*. My own researches have taught me that in this fact lies the key to a psychological theory of both dreams and psychoses.)

'The chief feature of dreams and of insanity lies in their eccentric trains of thought and their weakness of judgement.' In both states [Radestock continues] we find an over-valuation of the subject's own mental achievements which seems senseless to a sober view; the rapid sequence of ideas in dreams is paralleled by the flight of ideas in psychoses. In both there is a complete lack of sense of time. In dreams the personality may be split— when, for instance, the dreamer's own knowledge is divided between two persons and when, in the dream, the extraneous ego corrects the actual one. This is precisely on a par with the splitting of the personality that is familiar to us in hallucinatory paranoia; the dreamer too hears his own thoughts pronounced by extraneous voices. Even chronic delusional ideas have their analogy in stereotyped recurrent pathological dreams (*le rêve obsédant*).—It not infrequently happens that after recovering from a delirium patients will say that the whole period of their illness seems to them like a not unpleasant dream: indeed they will sometimes tell us that even during the illness they have occasionally had a feeling that they are only caught up in a dream—as is often the case in dreams occurring in sleep.

After all this, it is not surprising that Radestock sums up his views, and those of many others, by declaring that 'insanity, an abnormal pathological phenomenon, is to be regarded as an intensification of the periodically recurrent normal condition of dreaming.' (Ibid., 228.)

Krauss (1859, 270 f.) has sought to establish what is perhaps a still more intimate connection between dreams and insanity than can be demonstrated by an analogy between these external manifestations. This connection he sees in their aetiology or rather in the sources of their excitation. The fundamental element common to the two states lies according to him, as we have seen [pp. 70 f.], in organically determined sensations, in sensations derived from somatic stimuli, in the coenaesthesia which is based upon contributions arising from all the organs. (Cf. Peisse, 1857, 2, 21, quoted by Maury, 1878, 52.)

The indisputable analogy between dreams and insanity, extending as it does down to their characteristic details, is one of the most powerful props of the medical theory of dream-life, which regards dreaming as a useless and disturbing process and as the expression of a reduced activity of the mind. Nevertheless it is not to be expected that we shall find the ultimate explanation of dreams in the direction of mental disorders; for the unsatisfactory state of our knowledge of the origin of these latter conditions is generally recognized. It is quite likely, on the contrary, that a modification of our attitude towards dreams will at the same time affect our views upon the internal mechanism of mental disorders and that we shall be working towards an explanation of the psychoses while we are endeavouring to throw some light on the mystery of dreams.[1]

---

[1] [A discussion of the relation between dreams and psychoses will be found in Lecture 29 of the *New Introductory Lectures* (Freud, 1933a).]

POSTSCRIPT, 1909

The fact that I have not extended my account of the literature dealing with the problems of dreams to cover the period between the first and second editions of this book stands in need of a justification. It may strike the reader as an unsatisfactory one, but for me it was none the less decisive. The motives which led me to give any account at all of the way in which earlier writers have dealt with dreams were exhausted with the completion of this introductory chapter; to continue the task would have cost me an extraordinary effort—and the result would have been of very little use or instruction. For the intervening nine years have produced nothing new or valuable either in factual material or in opinions that might throw light on the subject. In the majority of publications that have appeared during the interval my work has remained unmentioned and unconsidered. It has, of course, received least attention from those who are engaged in what is described as 'research' into dreams, and who have thus provided a shining example of the repugnance to learning anything new which is characteristic of men of science. In the ironical words of Anatole France, '*les savants ne sont pas curieux.*' If there were such a thing in science as a right to retaliate, I should certainly be justified in my turn in disregarding the literature that has been issued since the publication of this book. The few notices of it that have appeared in scientific periodicals show so much *lack* of understanding and so much *mis*understanding that my only reply to the critics would be to suggest their reading the book again—or perhaps, indeed, merely to suggest their reading it.

A large number of dreams have been published and analysed in accordance with my directions in papers by physicians who have decided to adopt the psycho-analytic therapeutic procedure, as well as by other authors.[1] In so far as these writings have gone beyond a mere confirmation of my views I have included their findings in the course of my exposition. I have added a second bibliography at the end of the volume containing

---

[1] [In the 1909 and 1911 editions only, there was a parenthesis at this point containing the names of Jung, Abraham, Riklin, Muthmann and Stekel. In 1909 only, the next sentence read: 'But these publications have merely confirmed my views and not added anything to them.']

a list of the most important works that have appeared since this book was first published.[1] The extensive monograph on dreams by Sante de Sanctis (1899), of which a German translation appeared soon after its issue, was published almost simultaneously with my *Interpretation of Dreams*, so that neither I nor the Italian author was able to comment upon each other's work. I have unfortunately been unable to escape the conclusion that his painstaking volume is totally deficient in ideas—so much so, in fact, that it would not even lead one to suspect the existence of the problems with which I have dealt.

Only two publications require to be mentioned which come near to my own treatment of the problems of dreams. Hermann Swoboda (1904), a youthful philosopher, has undertaken the task of extending to psychical events the discovery of a biological periodicity (in 23-day and 28-day periods) made by Wilhelm Fliess [1906].[2] In the course of his highly imaginative work he has endeavoured to use this key for the solution, among other problems, of the riddle of dreams. His findings would seem to underestimate the significance of dreams; the subject-matter of a dream, on his view, is to be explained as an assemblage of all the memories which, on the night on which it is dreamt, complete one of the biological periods, whether for the first or for the nth time. A personal communication from the author led me at first to suppose that he himself no longer took this theory seriously, but it seems that this was a mistaken conclusion on my part.[3] At a later stage [see below, pp. 190 ff.] I shall report upon some observations which I made in connection with Swoboda's suggestion but which led me to no convincing conclusion. I was the more pleased when, in an unexpected quarter, I made the chance discovery of a view of dreams which coincides entirely with the core of my own theory. It is impossible, for chronological reasons, that the statement in question can have been influenced by my book. I must therefore hail it as the single discoverable instance in the literature of the subject of an

---

[1] [See the Editor's Introduction, pp. xii f. and xx.]

[2] [An account of Fliess's theories and of his relations with Swoboda is given in Section IV of Kris's introduction to Freud's correspondence with Fliess (Freud, 1950a).]

[3] [In its present form this sentence dates from 1911. In 1909 it read: 'A personal communication from the author to the effect that he himself no longer supports these views exempts me from giving them serious consideration.' The following sentence was added in 1911.]

independent thinker who is in agreement with the essence of my theory of dreams. The book which contains the passage upon dreaming which I have in mind appeared in its second edition in 1900 under the title of *Phantasien eines Realisten* by 'Lynkeus.' [First edition, 1899.][1]

POSTSCRIPT, 1914

The preceding plea of justification was written in 1909. I am bound to admit that since then the situation has changed; my contribution to the interpretation of dreams is no longer neglected by writers on the subject. The new state of affairs, however, has now made it quite out of the question for me to extend my previous account of the literature. *The Interpretation of Dreams* has raised a whole series of fresh considerations and problems which have been discussed in a great variety of ways. I cannot give an account of these works, however, before I have expounded those views of my own on which they are based. I have therefore dealt with whatever seems to me of value in the latest literature at its appropriate place in the course of the discussion which now follows.

---

[1] [*Footnote added* 1930:] Cf: my paper on Josef Popper-Lynkeus and the theory of dreams (1923 *f.*). [Freud wrote a further paper on the subject (1932*c*). The passage referred to in the text above will be found quoted in full below in a footnote on p. 325 f.]

CHAPTER II

THE METHOD OF INTERPRETING DREAMS:
AN ANALYSIS OF A SPECIMEN DREAM

THE title that I have chosen for my work makes plain which of the traditional approaches to the problem of dreams I am inclined to follow. The aim which I have set before myself is to show that dreams are capable of being interpreted; and any contributions I may be able to make towards the solution of the problems dealt with in the last chapter will only arise as by-products in the course of carrying out my proper task. My presumption that dreams can be interpreted at once puts me in opposition to the ruling theory of dreams and in fact to every theory of dreams with the single exception of Scherner's [pp. 109 ff.]; for 'interpreting' a dream implies assigning a 'meaning' to it—that is, replacing it by something which fits into the chain of our mental acts as a link having a validity and importance equal to the rest. As we have seen, the scientific theories of dreams leave no room for any problem of interpreting them, since in their view a dream is not a mental act at all, but a somatic process signalizing its occurrence by indications registered in the mental apparatus. Lay opinion has taken a different attitude throughout the ages. It has exercised its indefeasible right to behave inconsistently; and, though admitting that dreams are unintelligible and absurd, it cannot bring itself to declare that they have no significance at all. Led by some obscure feeling, it seems to assume that, in spite of everything, every dream has a meaning, though a hidden one, that dreams are designed to take the place of some other process of thought, and that we have only to undo the substitution correctly in order to arrive at this hidden meaning.

Thus the lay world has from the earliest times concerned itself with 'interpreting' dreams and in its attempts to do so it has made use of two essentially different methods.

The first of these procedures considers the content of the dream as a whole and seeks to replace it by another content which is intelligible and in certain respects analogous to the original one. This is 'symbolic' dream-interpreting; and it inevitably breaks down when faced by dreams which are not merely unintelligible but also confused. An example of this procedure is to be seen in the explanation of Pharaoh's dream propounded by Joseph in the Bible. The seven fat kine followed by seven lean kine that ate up the fat kine—all this was a symbolic substitute for a prophecy of seven years of famine in the land of Egypt which should consume all that was brought forth in the seven years of plenty. Most of the artificial dreams constructed by imaginative writers are designed for a symbolic interpretation of this sort: they reproduce the writer's thoughts under a disguise which is regarded as harmonizing with the recognized characteristics of dreams.[1] The idea of dreams being chiefly concerned with the future and being able to foretell it—a remnant of the old prophetic significance of dreams—provides a reason for transposing the meaning of the dream, when it has been arrived at by symbolic interpretation, into the future tense. It is of course impossible to give instructions upon the *method* of arriving at a symbolic interpretation. Success must be a question of hitting on a clever idea, of direct intuition, and for that reason it was possible for dream-interpretation by means of symbolism to be exalted into an artistic activity dependent on the possession of peculiar gifts.[2]

---

[1] [*Footnote added* 1909:] I found by chance in *Gradiva*, a story written by Wilhelm Jensen, a number of artificial dreams which were perfectly correctly constructed and could be interpreted just as though they had not been invented but had been dreamt by real people. In reply to an enquiry, the author confirmed the fact that he had no knowledge of my theory of dreams. I have argued that the agreement between my researches and this writer's creations is evidence in favour of the correctness of my analysis of dreams. (See Freud, 1907*a*.)

[2] [*Footnote added* 1914:] Aristotle [*De divinatione per somnum*, II (*Trans.*, 1935, 383)] remarked in this connection that the best interpreter of dreams was the man who could best grasp similarities; for dream-pictures, like pictures on water, are pulled out of shape by movement, and the most successful interpreter is the man who can detect the truth from the misshapen picture. (Büchsenschütz, 1868, 65.)

The second of the two popular methods of interpreting dreams is far from making any such claims. It might be described as the '*decoding*' method, since it treats dreams as a kind of cryptography in which each sign can be translated into another sign having a known meaning, in accordance with a fixed key. Suppose, for instance, that I have dreamt of a letter and also of a funeral. If I consult a 'dream-book,' I find that 'letter' must be translated by 'trouble' and 'funeral' by 'betrothal.' It then remains for me to link together the keywords which I have deciphered in this way and, once more, to transpose the result into the future tense. An interesting modification of the process of decoding, which to some extent corrects the purely mechanical character of its method of transposing, is to be found in the book written upon the interpretation of dreams [*Oneirocritica*] by Artemidorus of Daldis.[1] This method takes into account not only the content of the dream but also the character and circumstances of the dreamer; so that the same dream-element will have a

---

[1] [*Footnote added* 1914:] Artemidorus of Daldis, who was probably born at the beginning of the second century A.D., has left us the most complete and painstaking study of dream-interpretation as practised in the Graeco-Roman world. As Theodor Gomperz (1866, 7 f.) points out, he insisted on the importance of basing the interpretation of dreams on observation and experience, and made a rigid distinction between his own art and others that were illusory. The principle of his interpretative art, according to Gomperz, is identical with magic, the principle of association. A thing in a dream means what it recalls to the mind—to the dream-interpreter's mind, it need hardly be said. An insuperable source of arbitrariness and uncertainty arises from the fact that the dream-element may recall *various* things to the interpreter's mind and may recall something different to different interpreters. The technique which I describe in the pages that follow differs in one essential respect from the ancient method: it imposes the task of interpretation upon the dreamer himself. It is not concerned with what occurs to the *interpreter* in connection with a particular element of the dream, but with what occurs to the *dreamer.*—Recent reports, however, from a missionary, Father Tfinkdji (1913, [516–17 and 523]), show that modern dream-interpreters in the East also make free use of the dreamer's collaboration. He writes as follows of dream-interpreters among the Arabs of Mesopotamia: 'Pour interpréter exactement un songe, les oniromanciens les plus habiles s'informent de ceux qui les consultent de toutes les circonstances qu'ils regardent nécessaires pour la bonne explication. . . . En un mot, nos oniromanciens ne laissent aucune circonstance leur échapper et ne donnent l'interprétation désirée avant d'avoir parfaitement saisi et reçu toutes les interrogations désirables.' ['In order to give a precise interpretation of a dream, the most skilful dream-diviners find out from those who

different meaning for a rich man, a married man or, let us say, an orator, from what it has for a poor man, a bachelor or a merchant. The essence of the decoding procedure, however, lies in the fact that the work of interpretation is not brought to bear on the dream as a whole but on each portion of the dream's content independently, as though the dream were a geological conglomerate in which each fragment of rock required a separate assessment. There can be no question that the invention of the decoding method of interpretation was suggested by disconnected and confused dreams.[2]

It cannot be doubted for a moment that neither of the two popular procedures for interpreting dreams can be employed for a scientific treatment of the subject. The symbolic method is restricted in its application and incapable of being laid down on general lines. In the case of the decoding method everything depends on the trustworthiness of the 'key'—the dream-book, and of this we have no guarantee. Thus one might feel

---

consult them all the circumstances which they consider essential in order to arrive at a right explanation. . . . In short, these dream-diviners do not allow a single point to escape them and only give their interpretation after they have completely mastered the replies to all the necessary enquiries.'] Among these enquiries are habitually included questions as to the dreamer's closest family relations—his parents, wife and children—as well as such a typical formula as: 'Habuistine in hac nocte copulam conjugalem ante vel post somnium?' ['Did you copulate with your wife that night before or after you had the dream?']—'L'idée dominante dans l'interprétation des songes consiste à expliquer le rêve par son opposée.' ['The principal idea in interpreting dreams lies in explaining a dream by its opposite.']

[2] [Footnote added 1909:] Dr. Alfred Robitsek has pointed out to me that the oriental 'dream-books' (of which ours are wretched imitations) base the greater number of their interpretations of dream-elements upon similarity of sounds and resemblance between words. The fact that these connections inevitably disappear in translation accounts for the unintelligibility of the renderings in our own popular dream-books. The extraordinarily important part played by punning and verbal quibbles in the ancient civilizations of the East may be studied in the writings of Hugo Winckler [the famous archaeologist].—[Added 1911:] The nicest instance of a dream-interpretation which has reached us from ancient times is based on a play upon words. It is told by Artemidorus [Book IV, Chap. 24, Krauss's translation, 1881, 255]: 'I think too that Aristander gave a most happy interpretation to Alexander of Macedon when he had surrounded Tyre [Τύρος] and was besieging it but was feeling uneasy and disturbed because of the length of time the siege was taking. Alexander dreamt he saw a satyr

tempted to agree with the philosophers and the psychiatrists and, like them, rule out the problem of dream-interpretation as a purely fanciful task.[2] But I have been taught better. I have been driven to realize that here once more we have one of those not infrequent cases in which an ancient and jealously held popular belief seems to be nearer the truth than the judgement of the prevalent science of today. I must affirm that dreams really have a meaning and that a scientific procedure for interpreting them is possible.

My knowledge of the procedure was reached in the following manner. I have been engaged for many years (with a therapeutic aim in view) in unravelling certain psycho-pathological structures—hysterical phobias, obsessional ideas, and so on. I have been doing so, in fact, ever since I learnt from an important communication by Josef Breuer that as regards these structures (which are looked on as pathological symptoms) unravelling them coincides with removing them.[3] (Cf. Breuer and Freud, 1895.) If a pathological idea of this sort can be traced back to the elements in the patient's mental life from which it originated, it simultaneously crumbles away and the patient is freed from it. Considering the impotence of our other therapeutic efforts and the puzzling nature of these disorders, I felt tempted to follow the path marked out by Breuer, in spite of every difficulty, till a complete explanation was reached. I shall have on another occasion to report at length upon the form finally taken

---

[σάτυρος] dancing on his shield. Aristander happened to be in the neighborhood of Tyre, in attendance on the king during his Syrian campaign. By dividing the word for satyr into σά and τύρος he encouraged the king to press home the siege so that he became master of the city.' (σά Τύρος = Tyre is thine.)— Indeed, dreams are so closely related to linguistic expression that Ferenczi [1910] has truly remarked that every tongue has its own dream-language. It is impossible as a rule to translate a dream into a foreign language and this is equally true, I fancy, of a book such as the present one. [*Added* 1930:] Nevertheless Dr. A. A. Brill of New York, and others after him, have succeeded in translating *The Interpretation of Dreams.*

[2] After I had completed my manuscript I came across a work by Stumpf (1899) which agrees with my views in seeking to prove that dreams have a meaning and can be interpreted. He effects his interpretations, however, by means of a symbolism of an allegorical character without any guarantee of the general validity of his procedure.

[3] ['*Auflösung*' and '*Lösung*' in the original.]

by this procedure and the results of my labours. It was in the course of these psycho-analytic studies that I came upon dream-interpretation. My patients were pledged to communicate to me every idea or thought that occurred to them in connection with some particular subject; amongst other things they told me their dreams and so taught me that a dream can be inserted into the psychical chain that has to be traced backwards in the memory from a pathological idea. It was then only a short step to treating the dream itself as a symptom and to applying to dreams the method of interpretation that had been worked out for symptoms.

This involves some psychological preparation of the patient. We must aim at bringing about two changes in him: an increase in the attention he pays to his own psychical perceptions and the elimination of the criticism by which he normally sifts the thoughts that occur to him. In order that he may be able to concentrate his attention on his self-observation it is an advantage for him to lie in a restful attitude and shut his eyes.[1] It is necessary to insist explicitly on his renouncing all criticism of the thoughts that he perceives. We therefore tell him that the success of the psychoanalysis depends on his noticing and reporting whatever comes into his head and not being misled, for instance, into suppressing an idea because it strikes him as unimportant or irrelevant or because it seems to him meaningless. He must adopt a completely impartial attitude to what occurs to him, since it is precisely his critical attitude which is responsible for his being unable, in the ordinary course of things, to achieve the desired unravelling of his dream or obsessional idea or whatever it may be.

I have noticed in my psycho-analytical work that the whole frame of mind of a man who is reflecting is totally different from that of a man who is observing his own psychical processes. In reflection there is one more psychical activity at work than in the most attentive self-observation, and this is shown amongst other things by the tense looks and wrinkled forehead of a person pursuing his reflections as compared with the restful expression of a self-observer. In both cases attention[2] must be concentrated, but the man who is reflecting is also exercising his *critical* faculty; this leads him to reject some of the ideas that occur to him after perceiving them, to cut short oth-

---

[1] [The stress upon the advisability of shutting the eyes (a remnant of the old hypnotic procedure) was very soon dropped. See, for instance, the account of psycho-analytic technique in Freud (1904a), where it is specifically mentioned that the analyst does *not* ask the patient to shut his eyes.]

[2] [The function of attention is discussed below (p. 590).]

ers without following the trains of thought which they would open up to him, and to behave in such a way towards still others that they never become conscious at all and are accordingly suppressed before being perceived. The self-observer on the other hand need only take the trouble to suppress his critical faculty. If he succeeds in doing that, innumerable ideas come into his consciousness of which he could otherwise never have got hold. The material which is in this way freshly obtained for his self-perception makes it possible to interpret both his pathological ideas and his dream-structures. What is in question, evidently, is the establishment of a psychical state which, in its distribution of psychical energy (that is, of mobile attention), bears some analogy to the state before falling asleep—and no doubt also to hypnosis. As we fall asleep, 'involuntary ideas' emerge, owing to the relaxation of a certain deliberate (and no doubt also critical) activity which we allow to influence the course of our ideas while we are awake. (We usually attribute this relaxation to 'fatigue.') As the involuntary ideas emerge they change into visual and acoustic images. (Cf. the remarks by Schleiermacher and others quoted above on pp. 78 f. [and 99 f.].)[1] In the state used for the analysis of dreams and pathological ideas, the patient purposely and deliberately abandons this activity and employs the psychical energy thus saved (or a portion of it) in attentively following the involuntary thoughts which now emerge, and which—and here the situation differs from that of falling asleep—retain the character of ideas. *In this way the 'involuntary' ideas are transformed into 'voluntary' ones.*

The adoption[2] of the required attitude of mind towards ideas that seem to emerge 'of their own free will' and the abandonment of the critical function that is normally in operation against them seem to be hard of achievement for some people. The 'involuntary thoughts' are liable to release a most violent resistance, which seeks to prevent their emergence. If we may trust that great poet and philosopher Friedrich Schiller, however, poetic creation must demand an exactly similar attitude. In a passage in his correspondence with Körner—we have to thank Otto Rank for unearthing it—Schiller (writing on December 1, 1788) replies to his friend's complaint of insufficient productivity: 'The ground for your complaint

---

[1] [*Footnote added* 1919:] Silberer (1909, 1910 and 1912) has made important contributions to dream-interpretation by directly observing this transformation of ideas into visual images. [See below, pp. 358 f. and 507 f.]

[2] [This paragraph was added in 1909, and the first sentence of the next paragraph modified accordingly.]

seems to me to lie in the constraint imposed by your reason upon your imagination. I will make my idea more concrete by a simile. It seems a bad thing and detrimental to the creative work of the mind if Reason makes too close an examination of the ideas as they come pouring in—at the very gateway, as it were. Looked at in isolation, a thought may seem very trivial or very fantastic; but it may be made important by another thought that comes after it, and, in conjunction with other thoughts that may seem equally absurd, it may turn out to form a most effective link. Reason cannot form any opinion upon all this unless it retains the thought long enough to look at it in connection with the others. On the other hand, where there is a creative mind, Reason—so it seems to me—relaxes its watch upon the gates, and the ideas rush in pell-mell, and only then does it look them through and examine them in a mass.—You critics, or whatever else you may call yourselves, are ashamed or frightened of the momentary and transient extravagances which are to be found in all truly creative minds and whose longer or shorter duration distinguishes the thinking artist from the dreamer. You complain of your unfruitfulness because you reject too soon and discriminate too severely.'

Nevertheless what Schiller describes as a relaxation of the watch upon the gates of Reason, the adoption of an attitude of uncritical self-observation, is by no means difficult. Most of my patients achieve it after their first instructions. I myself can do so very completely, by the help of writing down my ideas as they occur to me. The amount of psychical energy by which it is possible to reduce critical activity and increase the intensity of self-observation varies considerably according to the subject on which one is trying to fix one's attention.

Our first step in the employment of this procedure teaches us that what we must take as the object of our attention is not the dream as a whole but the separate portions of its content. If I say to a patient who is still a novice: 'What occurs to you in connection with this dream?' as a rule his mental horizon becomes a blank. If, however, I put the dream before him cut up into pieces, he will give me a series of associations to each piece, which might be described as the 'background thoughts' of that particular part of the dream. Thus the method of dream-interpretation which I practise already differs in this first important respect from the popular, historic and legendary method of interpretation by means of symbolism and approximates to the second or 'decoding' method. Like the latter, it employs interpretation *en détail* and not *en masse*; like the latter, it regards dreams from the very first as being of a composite character, as being conglomerates of psychical formations. [Cf. pp. 427 f. and 457.][1]

In the course of my psycho-analyses of neurotics I must already have analysed over a thousand dreams; but I do not propose to make use of this material in my present introduction to the technique and theory of dream-interpretation. Apart from the fact that such a course would be open to the objection that these are the dreams of neuropaths, from which no valid inferences could be made as to the dreams of normal people, there is quite another reason which forces this decision upon me. The subject to which these dreams of my patients lead up is always, of course, the case history which underlies their neurosis. Each dream would therefore necessitate a lengthy introduction and an investigation of the nature and aetiological determinants of the psychoneuroses. But these questions are in themselves novelties and highly bewildering and would distract attention from the problem of dreams. On the contrary, it is my intention to make use of my present elucidation of dreams as a preliminary step towards solving the more difficult problems of the psychology of the neuroses.[2] If, however, I forego my principal material, the dreams of my neurotic patients, I must not be too particular about what is left to me. All that remains are such dreams as have been reported to me from time to time by normal persons of my acquaintance, and such others as have been quoted as instances in the literature dealing with dream-life. Unluckily, however, none of these dreams are accompanied by the analysis without which I cannot discover a dream's meaning. My procedure is not so convenient as the popular decoding method which translates any given piece of a dream's content by a fixed key. I, on the contrary, am prepared to find that the same piece of

---

[1] [The technique of dream-interpretation is further discussed below (p. 526 ff.). See also the first two sections of Freud (1923c). The quite other question of the part played by dream-interpretation in the technique of therapeutic psycho-analysis is considered in Freud (1911e).]

[2] [At the beginning of Section E of Chapter VII, Freud reflects upon the difficulties imposed upon his exposition of the subject by this programme, which is already laid down in his preface to the first edition (p. xxiii). As he points out on p. 170 f. and again on p. 175 n., he is often led into disregarding it. In spite of his declared intention, he makes use of many of his patients' dreams, and more than once (e.g. on p. 173 f.) enters into a discussion of the mechanism of neurotic symptoms.]

content may conceal a different meaning when it occurs in various people or in various contexts. Thus it comes about that I am led to my own dreams, which offer a copious and convenient material, derived from an approximately normal person and relating to multifarious occasions of daily life. No doubt I shall be met by doubts of the trustworthiness of 'self-analyses' of this kind; and I shall be told that they leave the door open to arbitrary conclusions. In my judgement the situation is in fact more favourable in the case of *self*-observation than in that of other people; at all events we may make the experiment and see how far self-analysis takes us with the interpretation of dreams. But I have other difficulties to over-come, which lie within myself. There is some natural hesitation about re-vealing so many intimate facts about one's mental life; nor can there be any guarantee against misinterpretation by strangers. But it must be possi-ble to overcome such hesitations. 'Tout psychologiste,' writes Delboeuf [1885], 'est obligé de faire l'aveu même de ses faiblesses s'il croit par là jeter du jour sur quelque problème obscur.'[1] And it is safe to assume that my readers too will very soon find their initial interest in the indiscretions which I am bound to make replaced by an absorbing immersion in the psychological problems upon which they throw light.[2]

Accordingly I shall proceed to choose out one of my own dreams and demonstrate upon it my method of interpretation. In the case of every such dream some remarks by way of preamble will be necessary.—And now I must ask the reader to make my interests his own for quite a while, and to plunge, along with me, into the minutest details of my life; for a transference of this kind is peremptorily demanded by our interest in the hidden meaning of dreams.

Preamble

During the summer of 1895 I had been giving psychoanalytic treatment to a young lady who was on very friendly terms with me and my family. It will be readily understood that a mixed relationship such as this may

---

[1] ['Every psychologist is under an obligation to confess even his own weaknesses, if he thinks that it may throw light upon some obscure problem.']

[2] I am obliged to add, however, by way of qualification of what I have said above, that in scarcely any instance have I brought forward the *complete* interpretation of one of my own dreams, as it is known to me. I have probably been wise in not putting too much faith in my readers' discretion.

be a source of many disturbed feelings in a physician and particularly in a psychotherapist. While the physician's personal interest is greater, his authority is less; any failure would bring a threat to the old-established friendship with the patient's family. This treatment had ended in a partial success; the patient was relieved of her hysterical anxiety but did not lose all her somatic symptoms. At that time I was not yet quite clear in my mind as to the criteria indicating that a hysterical case history was finally closed, and I proposed a solution to the patient which she seemed unwilling to accept. While we were thus at variance, we had broken off the treatment for the summer vacation.—One day I had a visit from a junior colleague, one of my oldest friends, who had been staying with my patient, Irma, and her family at their country resort. I asked him how he had found her and he answered: 'She's better, but not quite well.' I was conscious that my friend Otto's words, or the tone in which he spoke them, annoyed me. I fancied I detected a reproof in them, such as to the effect that I had promised the patient too much; and, whether rightly or wrongly, I attributed the supposed fact of Otto's siding against me to the influence of my patient's relatives, who, as it seemed to me, had never looked with favour on the treatment. However, my disagreeable impression was not clear to me and I gave no outward sign of it. The same evening I wrote out Irma's case history, with the idea of giving it to Dr. M. (a common friend who was at that time the leading figure in our circle) in order to justify myself. That night (or more probably the next morning) I had the following dream, which I noted down immediately after waking.[1]

Dream of July 23rd–24th, 1895

A large hall—numerous guests, whom we were receiving.—Among them was Irma. I at once took her on one side, as though to answer her letter and to reproach her for not having accepted my 'solution' yet. I said to her: 'If you still get pains, it's really only your fault.' She replied: 'If you only knew what pains

---

[1] [*Footnote added* 1914:] This is the first dream which I submitted to a detailed interpretation. [Freud describes some first groping attempts at the analysis of his own dreams in *Studies on Hysteria* (Breuer and Freud, 1895). They will be found mentioned in the course of the long footnote attached to the entry of May 15 in the Case History of Frau Emmy von N. This passage is quoted in full in the Editor's Introduction (pp. xiii f.).]

I've got now in my throat and stomach and abdomen—it's choking me'—I was alarmed and looked at her. She looked pale and puffy. I thought to myself that after all I must be missing some organic trouble. I took her to the window and looked down her throat, and she showed signs of recalcitrance, like women with artificial dentures. I thought to myself that there was really no need for her to do that.—She then opened her mouth properly and on the right I found a big white[1] patch; at another place I saw extensive whitish grey scabs upon some remarkable curly structures which were evidently modelled on the turbinal bones of the nose.—I at once called in Dr. M., and he repeated the examination and confirmed it. . . . Dr. M. looked quite different from usual; he was very pale, he walked with a limp and his chin was clean-shaven. . . . My friend Otto was now standing beside her as well, and my friend Leopold was percussing her through her bodice and saying: 'She has a dull area low down on the left.' He also indicated that a portion of the skin on the left shoulder was infiltrated. (I noticed this, just as he did, in spite of her dress.) . . . M. said: 'There's no doubt it's an infection, but no matter; dysentery will supervene and the toxin will be eliminated.' . . . We were directly aware, too, of the origin of her infection. Not long before, when she was feeling unwell, my friend Otto had given her an injection of a preparation of propyl, propyls . . . propionic acid . . . trimethylamin (and I saw before me the formula for this printed in heavy type). . . . Injections of that sort ought not to be made so thoughtlessly. . . . And probably the syringe had not been clean.

This dream has one advantage over many others. It was immediately clear what events of the previous day provided its starting-point. My preamble makes that plain. The news which Otto had given me of Irma's condition and the case history which I had been engaged in writing till far into the night continued to occupy my mental activity even after I was asleep. Nevertheless, no one who had only read the preamble and the content of the dream itself could have the slightest notion of what the dream meant. I myself had no notion. I was astonished at the symptoms of which Irma complained to me in the dream, since they were not the same as those for which I had treated her. I smiled at the senseless idea of an injection of propionic acid and at Dr. M.'s consoling reflections. Towards its end the dream seemed to me to be more obscure and compressed than it was at the beginning. In order to discover the meaning of all this it was necessary to undertake a detailed analysis.

---

[1] [The word 'white' is omitted, no doubt accidentally, in the 1942 edition only.]

Analysis

The hall—numerous guests, whom we were receiving. We were spending that summer at Bellevue, a house standing by itself on one of the hills adjoining the Kahlenberg.[1] The house had formerly been designed as a place of entertainment and its reception-rooms were in consequence unusually lofty and hall-like. It was at Bellevue that I had the dream, a few days before my wife's birthday. On the previous day my wife had told me that she expected that a number of friends, including Irma, would be coming out to visit us on her birthday. My dream was thus anticipating this occasion: it was my wife's birthday and a number of guests, including Irma, were being received by us in the large hall at Bellevue.

I reproached Irma for not having accepted my solution; I said: 'If you still get pains, it's your own fault.' I might have said this to her in waking life, and I may actually have done so. It was my view at that time (though I have since recognized it as a wrong one) that my task was fulfilled when I had informed a patient of the hidden meaning of his symptoms: I considered that I was not responsible for whether he accepted the solution or not—though this was what success depended on. I owe it to this mistake, which I have now fortunately corrected, that my life was made easier at a time when, in spite of all my inevitable ignorance, I was expected to produce therapeutic successes.—I noticed, however, that the words which I spoke to Irma in the dream showed that I was specially anxious not to be responsible for the pains which she still had. If they were her fault they could not be mine. Could it be that the purpose of the dream lay in this direction?

Irma's complaint: pains in her throat and abdomen and stomach; it was choking her. Pains in the stomach were among my patient's symptoms but were not very prominent; she complained more of feelings of nausea and disgust. Pains in the throat and abdomen and constriction of the throat played scarcely any part in her illness. I wondered why I decided upon this choice of symptoms in the dream but could not think of any explanation at the moment.

She looked pale and puffy. My patient always had a rosy complexion. I began to suspect that someone else was being substituted for her.

I was alarmed at the idea that I had missed an organic illness. This, as may well be believed, is a perpetual source of anxiety to a specialist whose

---

[1] [A hill which is a favourite resort in the immediate neighbourhood of Vienna.]

practice is almost limited to neurotic patients and who is in the habit of attributing to hysteria a great number of symptoms which other physicians treat as organic. On the other hand, a faint doubt crept into my mind—from where, I could not tell—that my alarm was not entirely genuine. If Irma's pains had an organic basis, once again I could not be held responsible for curing them; my treatment only set out to get rid of *hysterical* pains. It occurred to me, in fact, that I was actually *wishing* that there had been a wrong diagnosis; for, if so, the blame for my lack of success would also have been got rid of.

I took her to the window to look down her throat. She showed some recalcitrance, like women with false teeth. I thought to myself that really there was no need for her to do that. I had never had any occasion to examine Irma's oral cavity. What happened in the dream reminded me of an examination I had carried out some time before of a governess: at a first glance she had seemed a picture of youthful beauty, but when it came to opening her mouth she had taken measures to conceal her plates. This led to recollections of other medical examinations and of little secrets revealed in the course of them—to the satisfaction of neither party. *'There was really no need for her to do that'* was no doubt intended in the first place as a compliment to Irma; but I suspected that it had another meaning besides. (If one carries out an analysis attentively, one gets a feeling of whether or not one has exhausted all the background thoughts that are to be expected.) The way in which Irma stood by the window suddenly reminded me of another experience. Irma had an intimate woman friend of whom I had a very high opinion. When I visited this lady one evening I had found her by a window in the situation reproduced in the dream, and her physician, the same Dr. M., had pronounced that she had a diphtheritic membrane. The figure of Dr. M. and the membrane reappear later in the dream. It now occurred to me that for the last few months I had had every reason to suppose that this other lady was also a hysteric. Indeed, Irma herself had betrayed the fact to me. What did I know of her condition? One thing precisely: that, like my Irma of the dream, she suffered from hysterical choking. So in the dream I had replaced my patient by her friend. I now recollected that I had often played with the idea that she too might ask me to relieve her of her symptoms. I myself, however, had thought this unlikely, since she was of a very reserved nature. She was *recalcitrant*, as was shown in the dream. Another reason was that *there was no need for her to do it:* she had so far shown herself strong enough to master her condition without outside help. There still remained a few features that I could not attach either to Irma or to her friend: *pale; puffy; false teeth.* The false teeth took me to the governess whom I have already mentioned; I now felt inclined to be satisfied with *bad* teeth. I then thought of someone else to whom these features might be alluding. She again was not one of my patients, nor should I have liked to have her as a patient, since I had noticed that she was bashful in my presence and I could not think she would make an amenable patient. She was usually pale, and once, while she had been in specially good health, she had looked puffy.[1] Thus I had been comparing my patient Irma with two other people who would also have been recalcitrant to treatment. What could the reason have been for my having exchanged her in the dream for her friend? Perhaps it was that I should have *liked* to exchange her: either I felt more sympathetic towards her friend or had a higher opinion of her intelligence. For Irma seemed to me foolish because she had not accepted my solution. Her friend would have been wiser, that is to say she would have yielded sooner. She would then have *opened her mouth properly*, and have told me more than Irma.[2]

What I saw in her throat: a white patch and turbinal bones with scabs on them. The white patch reminded me of diphtheritis and so of Irma's friend, but also of a serious illness of my eldest daughter's almost two years earlier and of the fright I had had in those anxious days. The scabs on the turbinal bones recalled a worry about my own state of health. I was making frequent use of cocaine at that time to reduce some troublesome nasal swellings, and I had heard a few days earlier that one of my women patients who had followed my example had developed an extensive necrosis

---

[1] The still unexplained complaint about *pains in the abdomen* could also be traced back to this third figure. The person in question was, of course, my own wife; the pains in the abdomen reminded me of one of the occasions on which I had noticed her bashfulness. I was forced to admit to myself that I was not treating either Irma or my wife very kindly in this dream; but it should be observed by way of excuse that I was measuring them both by the standard of the good and amenable patient.

[2] I had a feeling that the interpretation of this part of the dream was not carried far enough to make it possible to follow the whole of its concealed meaning. If I had pursued my comparison between the three women, it would have taken me far afield.—There is at least one spot in every dream at which it is unplumbable—a navel, as it were, that is its point of contact with the unknown. [Cf. p. 528.]

of the nasal mucous membrane. I had been the first to recommend the use of cocaine, in 1885,[1] and this recommendation had brought serious reproaches down on me. The misuse of that drug had hastened the death of a dear friend of mine. This had been before 1895 [the date of the dream].

I at once called in Dr. M., and he repeated the examination. This simply corresponded to the position occupied by M. in our circle. But the *'at once'* was sufficiently striking to require a special explanation.[2] It reminded me of a tragic event in my practice. I had on one occasion produced a severe toxic state in a woman patient by repeatedly prescribing what was at that time regarded as a harmless remedy (sulphonal), and had hurriedly turned for assistance and support to my experienced senior colleague. There was a subsidiary detail which confirmed the idea that I had this incident in mind. My patient—who succumbed to the poison—had the same name as my eldest daughter. It had never occurred to me before, but it struck me now almost like an act of retribution on the part of destiny. It was as though the replacement of one person by another was to be continued in another sense: this Mathilde for that Mathilde, an eye for an eye and a tooth for a tooth. It seemed as if I had been collecting all the occasions which I could bring up against myself as evidence of lack of medical conscientiousness.

Dr. M. was pale, had a clean-shaven chin and walked with a limp. This was true to the extent that his unhealthy appearance often caused his friends anxiety. The two other features could only apply to someone else. I thought of my elder brother, who lives abroad, who is clean-shaven and whom, if I remembered right, the M. of the dream closely resembled. We had had news a few days earlier that he was walking with a limp owing to an arthritic affection of his hip. There must, I reflected, have been some reason for my fusing into one the two figures in the dream. I then remembered that I had a similar reason for being in an ill-humour with each of them: they had both rejected a certain suggestion I had recently laid before them.

---

[1] [This is a misprint (which occurs in every German edition) for '1884,' the date of Freud's first paper on cocaine. A full account of Freud's work in connection with cocaine will be found in Chapter VI of the first volume of Ernest Jones's life of Freud. From this it appears that the 'dear friend' was Fleischl von Marxow (see p. 487 *n.*). Further indirect allusions to this episode will be found on pp. 194 f., 228, 237 f. and 490.]

[2] [See below, p. 517.]

My friend Otto was now standing beside the patient and my friend Leopold was examining her and indicated that there was a dull area low down on the left. My friend Leopold was also a physician and a relative of Otto's. Since they both specialized in the same branch of medicine, it was their fate to be in competition with each other, and comparisons were constantly being drawn between them. Both of them acted as my assistants for years while I was still in charge of the neurological out-patients' department of a children's hospital.[1] Scenes such as the one represented in the dream used often to occur there. While I was discussing the diagnosis of a case with Otto, Leopold would be examining the child once more and would make an unexpected contribution to our decision. The difference between their characters was like that between the bailiff Bräsig and his friend Karl:[2] one was distinguished for his quickness, while the other was slow but sure. If in the dream I was contrasting Otto with the prudent Leopold, I was evidently doing so to the advantage of the latter. The comparison was similar to the one between my disobedient patient Irma and the friend whom I regarded as wiser than she was. I now perceived another of the lines along which the chain of thought in the dream branched off: from the sick child to the children's hospital.—*The dull area low down on the left* seemed to me to agree in every detail with one particular case in which Leopold had struck me by his thoroughness. I also had a vague notion of something in the nature of a metastatic affection; but this may also have been a reference to the patient whom I should have liked to have in the place of Irma. So far as I had been able to judge, she had produced an imitation of a tuberculosis.

A portion of the skin on the left shoulder was infiltrated. I saw at once that this was the rheumatism in my own shoulder, which I invariably notice if I sit up late into the night. Moreover the wording in the dream was most ambiguous: '*I noticed this, just as he did. . . .*' I noticed it in my own body, that is. I was struck, too, by the unusual phrasing: 'a portion of the skin was infiltrated.' We are in the habit of speaking of 'a left upper posterior infiltration,' and this would refer to the lung and so once more to tuberculosis.

---

[1] [For details of this hospital see Section II of Kris's introduction to the Fliess correspondence (Freud, 1950*a*).]

[2] [The two chief figures in the once popular novel, *Ut mine Stromtid*, written in Mecklenburg dialect, by Fritz Reuter (1862–4). There is an English translation, *An Old Story of My Farming Days* (London, 1878).]

In spite of her dress. This was in any case only an interpolation. We naturally used to examine the children in the hospital undressed: and this would be a contrast to the manner in which adult female patients have to be examined. I remembered that it was said of a celebrated clinician that he never made a physical examination of his patients except through their clothes. Further than this I could not see. Frankly, I had no desire to penetrate more deeply at this point.

Dr. M. said: 'It's an infection, but no matter. Dysentery will supervene and the toxin will be eliminated.' At first this struck me as ridiculous. But nevertheless, like all the rest, it had to be carefully analysed. When I came to look at it more closely it seemed to have some sort of meaning all the same. What I discovered in the patient was a local diphtheritis. I remembered from the time of my daughter's illness a discussion on diphtheritis and diphtheria, the latter being the general infection that arises from the local diphtheritis. Leopold indicated the presence of a general infection of this kind from the existence of a dull area, which might thus be regarded as a metastatic focus. I seemed to think, it is true, that metastases like this do not in fact occur with diphtheria: it made me think rather of pyaemia.

No matter. This was intended as a consolation. It seemed to fit into the context as follows. The content of the preceding part of the dream had been that my patient's pains were due to a severe organic affection. I had a feeling that I was only trying in that way to shift the blame from myself. Psychological treatment could not be held responsible for the persistence of diphtheritic pains. Nevertheless I had a sense of awkwardness at having invented such a severe illness for Irma simply in order to clear myself. It looked so cruel. Thus I was in need of an assurance that all would be well in the end, and it seemed to me that to have put the consolation into the mouth precisely of Dr. M. had not been a bad choice. But here I was taking up a superior attitude towards the dream, and this itself required explanation.

And why was the consolation so nonsensical?

Dysentery. There seemed to be some remote theoretical notion that morbid matter can be eliminated through the bowels. Could it be that I was trying to make fun of Dr. M.'s fertility in producing far-fetched explanations and making unexpected pathological connections? Something else now occurred to me in relation to dysentery. A few months earlier I had taken on the case of a young man with remarkable difficulties associated with defaecating, who had been treated by other physicians as a case of 'anaemia accompanied by malnutrition.' I had recognized it as a hysteria, but had been unwilling to try him with my psychotherapeutic treatment and had sent him on a sea voyage. Some days before, I had had a despairing letter from him from Egypt, saying that he had had a fresh attack there which a doctor had declared was dysentery. I suspected that the diagnosis was an error on the part of an ignorant practitioner who had allowed himself to be taken in by the hysteria. But I could not help reproaching myself for having put my patient in a situation in which he might have contracted some organic trouble on top of his hysterical intestinal disorder. Moreover 'dysentery' sounds not unlike 'diphtheria'—a word of ill omen which did not occur in the dream.[1]

Yes, I thought to myself, I must have been making fun of Dr. M. with the consoling prognosis 'Dysentery will supervene,' etc.: for it came back to me that, years before, he himself had told an amusing story of a similar kind about another doctor. Dr. M. had been called in by him for consultation over a patient who was seriously ill, and had felt obliged to point out, in view of the very optimistic view taken by his colleague, that he had found albumen in the patient's urine. The other, however, was not in the least put out: '*No matter,*' he had said, 'the albumen will soon be eliminated!'—I could no longer feel any doubt, therefore, that this part of the dream was expressing derision at physicians who are ignorant of hysteria. And, as though to confirm this, a further idea crossed my mind: 'Does Dr. M. realize that the symptoms in his patient (Irma's friend) which give grounds for fearing tuberculosis also have a hysterical basis? Has he spotted this hysteria? or has he been taken in by it?'

But what could be my motive for treating this friend of mine so badly? That was a very simple matter. Dr. M. was just as little in agreement with my 'solution' as Irma herself. So I had already revenged myself in this dream on two people: on Irma with the words 'If you still get pains, it's your own fault,' and on Dr. M. by the wording of the nonsensical consolation that I put into his mouth.

We were directly aware of the origin of the infection. This direct knowledge in the dream was remarkable. Only just before we had had no knowledge of it, for the infection was only revealed by Leopold.

When she was feeling unwell, my friend Otto had given her an injection. Otto had in fact told me that during his short stay with Irma's family he had been called in to a neighbouring hotel to give an injection to someone who had suddenly felt unwell. These injections reminded me once more of my

---

[1] [The German words '*Dysenterie*' and '*Diphtherie*' are more alike than the English ones.]

unfortunate friend who had poisoned himself with cocaine [see p. 136 *n*.]. I had advised him to use the drug internally [i.e. orally] only, while morphia was being withdrawn; but he had at once given himself cocaine *injections.*

A preparation of propyl . . . propyls . . . propionic acid. How could I have come to think of this? During the previous evening, before I wrote out the case history and had the dream, my wife had opened a bottle of liqueur, on which the word 'Ananas'[1] appeared and which was a gift from our friend Otto: for he has a habit of making presents on every possible occasion. It was to be hoped, I thought to myself, that some day he would find a wife to cure him of the habit.[2] This liqueur gave off such a strong smell of fusel oil that I refused to touch it. My wife suggested our giving the bottle to the servants, but I—with even greater prudence—vetoed the suggestion, adding in a philanthropic spirit that there was no need for *them* to be poisoned either. The smell of fusel oil (amyl . . .) evidently stirred up in my mind a recollection of the whole series—propyl, methyl, and so on—and this accounted for the propyl preparation in the dream. It is true that I carried out a substitution in the process: I dreamt of propyl after having smelt amyl. But substitutions of this kind are perhaps legitimate in organic chemistry.

Trimethylamin. I saw the chemical formula of this substance in my dream, which bears witness to a great effort on the part of my memory. Moreover the formula was printed in heavy type, as though there had been a desire to lay emphasis on some part of the context as being of quite special importance. What was it, then, to which my attention was to be directed in this way by trimethylamin? It was to a conversation with another friend who had for many years been familiar with all my writings during the period of their gestation, just as I had been with his.[3] He had at that time confided some ideas to me on the subject of the chemistry of

---

[1] I must add that the sound of the word 'Ananas' bears a remarkable resemblance to that of my patient Irma's family name.

[2] [*Footnote added* 1909, but omitted again from 1925 onwards:] In this respect the dream did not turn out to be prophetic. But in another respect it *was*. For my patient's 'unsolved' gastric pains, for which I was so anxious not to be blamed, turned out to be the forerunners of a serious disorder caused by gall-stones.

[3] [This was Wilhelm Fliess, the Berlin biologist and nose and throat specialist, who exercised a great influence on Freud during the years immediately preceding the publication of this book, and who figures frequently, though as a rule anonymously, in its pages. See Freud (1950*a*).]

the sexual processes, and had mentioned among other things that he believed that one of the products of sexual metabolism was trimethylamin. Thus this substance led me to sexuality, the factor to which I attributed the greatest importance in the origin of the nervous disorders which it was my aim to cure. My patient Irma was a young widow; if I wanted to find an excuse for the failure of my treatment in her case, what I could best appeal to would no doubt be this fact of her widowhood, which her friends would be so glad to see changed. And how strangely, I thought to myself, a dream like this is put together! The other woman, whom I had as a patient in the dream instead of Irma, was also a young widow.

I began to guess why the formula for trimethylamin had been so prominent in the dream. So many important subjects converged upon that one word. Trimethylamin was an allusion not only to the immensely powerful factor of sexuality, but also to a person whose agreement I recalled with satisfaction whenever I felt isolated in my opinions. Surely this friend who played so large a part in my life must appear again elsewhere in these trains of thought. Yes. For he had a special knowledge of the consequences of affections of the nose and its accessory cavities; and he had drawn scientific attention to some very remarkable connections between the turbinal bones and the female organs of sex. (Cf. the three curly structures in Irma's throat.) I had had Irma examined by him to see whether her gastric pains might be of nasal origin. But he suffered himself from suppurative rhinitis, which caused me anxiety; and no doubt there was an allusion to this in the pyaemia which vaguely came into my mind in connection with the metastases in the dream.[1]

Injections of that sort ought not to be made so thoughtlessly. Here an accusation of thoughtlessness was being made directly against my friend Otto. I seemed to remember thinking something of the same kind that afternoon when his words and looks had appeared to show that he was siding against me. It had been some such notion as: 'How easily his thoughts are influenced! How thoughtlessly he jumps to conclusions!'— Apart from this, this sentence in the dream reminded me once more of my dead friend who had so hastily resorted to cocaine injections. As I have said, I had never contemplated the drug being given by injection.

---

[1] [The analysis of this part of the dream is further elaborated below (pp. 310 ff.). It had already been used by Freud as an example of the mechanism of displacement in Section 21 of Part I of his very early 'Project for a Scientific Psychology,' written in the autumn of 1895 and printed as an Appendix to Freud (1950a).]

I noticed too that in accusing Otto of thoughtlessness in handling chemical substances I was once more touching upon the story of the unfortunate Mathilde, which gave grounds for the same accusation against myself. Here I was evidently collecting instances of my conscientiousness, but also of the reverse.

And probably the syringe had not been clean. This was yet another accusation against Otto, but derived from a different source. I had happened the day before to meet the son of an old lady of eighty-two, to whom I had to give an injection of morphia twice a day.[1] At the moment she was in the country and he told me that she was suffering from phlebitis. I had at once thought it must be an infiltration caused by a dirty syringe. I was proud of the fact that in two years I had not caused a single infiltration; I took constant pains to be sure that the syringe was clean. In short, I was conscientious. The phlebitis brought me back once more to my wife, who had suffered from thrombosis during one of her pregnancies; and now three similar situations came to my recollection involving my wife, Irma and the dead Mathilde. The identity of these situations had evidently enabled me to substitute the three figures for one another in the dream.

I have now completed the interpretation of the dream.[2] While I was carrying it out I had some difficulty in keeping at bay all the ideas which were bound to be provoked by a comparison between the content of the dream and the concealed thoughts lying behind it. And in the meantime the 'meaning' of the dream was borne in upon me. I became aware of an intention which was carried into effect by the dream and which must have been my motive for dreaming it. The dream fulfilled certain wishes which were started in me by the events of the previous evening (the news given me by Otto and my writing out of the case history). The conclusion of the dream, that is to say, was that I was not responsible for the persistence of Irma's pains, but that Otto was. Otto had in fact annoyed me by his remarks about Irma's incomplete cure, and the dream gave me my revenge by throwing the reproach back on to him. The dream acquitted

---

[1] [This old lady makes frequent appearances in Freud's writings at this period. See below, pp. 258 f., and *The Psychopathology of Everyday Life* (1901*b*), Chapter VIII *(b* and *g)* and Chapter VII (*Cb*). Her death is reported in a letter to Fliess of July 8, 1901 (Freud, 1950*a*, Letter 145).]

[2] [*Footnote added* 1909:] Though it will be understood that I have not reported everything that occurred to me during the process of interpretation.

me of the responsibility for Irma's condition by showing that it was due to other factors—it produced a whole series of reasons. The dream represented a particular state of affairs as I should have wished it to be. *Thus its content was the fulfilment of a wish and its motive was a wish.* Thus much leapt to the eyes. But many of the details of the dream also became intelligible to me from the point of view of wish-fulfilment. Not only did I revenge myself on Otto for being too hasty in taking sides against me by representing him as being too hasty in his medical treatment (in giving the injection); but I also revenged myself on him for giving me the bad liqueur which had an aroma of fusel oil. And in the dream I found an expression which united the two reproaches: the injection was of a preparation of propyl. This did not satisfy me and I pursued my revenge further by contrasting him with his more trustworthy competitor. I seemed to be saying: 'I like *him* better than *you*.' But Otto was not the only person to suffer from the vials of my wrath. I took revenge as well on my disobedient patient by exchanging her for one who was wiser and less recalcitrant. Nor did I allow Dr. M. to escape the consequences of his contradiction but showed him by means of a clear allusion that he was an ignoramus on the subject. (*'Dysentery will supervene,'* etc.) Indeed I seemed to be appealing from him to someone else with greater knowledge (to my friend who had told me of trimethylamin) just as I had turned from Irma to her friend and from Otto to Leopold. 'Take these people away! Give me three others of my choice instead! Then I shall be free of these undeserved reproaches!' The groundlessness of the reproaches was proved for me in the dream in the most elaborate fashion. *I* was not to blame for Irma's pains, since she herself was to blame for them by refusing to accept my solution. *I* was not concerned with Irma's pains, since they were of an organic nature and quite incurable by psychological treatment. Irma's pains could be satisfactorily explained by her widowhood (cf. the trimethylamin) which *I* had no means of altering. Irma's pains had been caused by Otto giving her an incautious injection of an unsuitable drug—a thing *I* should never have done. Irma's pains were the result of an injection with a dirty needle, like my old lady's phlebitis—whereas *I* never did any harm with my injections. I noticed, it is true, that these explanations of Irma's pains (which agreed in exculpating me) were not entirely consistent with one another, and indeed that they were mutually exclusive. The whole plea—for the dream was nothing else—reminded one vividly of the defence put forward by the man who was charged by one of his neighbours with having given him back a borrowed kettle in a damaged condition. The defendant asserted first, that he had given it back undamaged; secondly, that the kettle had a hole in it when he borrowed it; and thirdly, that he had never borrowed a kettle from his neighbour at all. So much the better: if only a single one of these three lines of defence were to be accepted as valid, the man would have to be acquitted.[1]

Certain other themes played a part in the dream, which were not so obviously connected with my exculpation from Irma's illness: my daughter's illness and that of my patient who bore the same name, the injurious effect of cocaine, the disorder of my patient who was travelling in Egypt, my concern about my wife's health and about that of my brother and of Dr. M., my own physical ailments, my anxiety about my absent friend who suffered from suppurative rhinitis. But when I came to consider all of these, they could all be collected into a single group of ideas and labelled, as it were, 'concern about my own and other people's health—professional conscientiousness.' I called to mind the obscure disagreeable impression I had when Otto brought me the news of Irma's condition. This group of thoughts that played a part in the dream enabled me retrospectively to put this transient impression into words. It was as though he had said to me: 'You don't take your medical duties seriously enough. You're not conscientious; you don't carry out what you've undertaken.' Thereupon, this group of thoughts seemed to have put itself at my disposal, so that I could produce evidence of how highly conscientious I was, of how deeply I was concerned about the health of my relations, my friends and my patients. It was a noteworthy fact that this material also included some disagreeable memories, which supported my friend Otto's accusation rather than my own vindication. The material was, as one might say, impartial; but nevertheless there was an unmistakable connection between this more extensive group of thoughts which underlay the dream and the narrower subject of the dream which gave rise to the wish to be innocent of Irma's illness.

I will not pretend that I have completely uncovered the meaning of this dream or that its interpretation is without a gap. I could spend much more time over it, derive further information from it and discuss fresh problems raised by it. I myself know the points from which further trains of thought could be followed. But considerations which arise in the case

---

[1] [This anecdote is discussed by Freud in relation to this passage in Chapter II, Section 8, and Chapter VII, Section 2, of his book on jokes. (Freud, 1905c.)]

of every dream of my own restrain me from pursuing my interpretative work. If anyone should feel tempted to express a hasty condemnation of my reticence, I would advise him to make the experiment of being franker than I am. For the moment I am satisfied with the achievement of this one piece of fresh knowledge. If we adopt the method of interpreting dreams which I have indicated here, we shall find that dreams really have a meaning and are far from being the expression of a fragmentary activity of the brain, as the authorities have claimed. *When the work of interpretation has been completed, we perceive that a dream is the fulfilment of a wish.*[1]

---

[1] [In a letter to Fliess on June 12, 1900 (Freud, 1950*a*, Letter 137), Freud describes a later visit to Bellevue, the house where he had this dream. 'Do you suppose,' he writes, 'that some day a marble tablet will be placed on the house, inscribed with these words?—

> In This House, on July 24th, 1895
> the Secret of Dreams was Revealed
> to Dr. Sigm. Freud

At the moment there seems little prospect of it.']

CHAPTER III

A DREAM IS THE FULFILMENT OF A WISH

WHEN, after passing through a narrow defile, we suddenly emerge upon
a piece of high ground, where the path divides and the finest prospects
open up on every side, we may pause for a moment and consider in
which direction we shall first turn our steps.[1] Such is the case with us,
now that we have surmounted the first interpretation of a dream. We find
ourselves in the full daylight of a sudden discovery. Dreams are not to be
likened to the unregulated sounds that rise from a musical instrument
struck by the blow of some external force instead of by a player's hand
[cf. p. 104 f.]; they are not meaningless, they are not absurd; they do not
imply that one portion of our store of ideas is asleep while another portion is beginning to wake. On the contrary, they are psychical phenomena
of complete validity—fulfilments of wishes; they can be inserted into the
chain of intelligible waking mental acts; they are constructed by a highly
complicated activity of the mind.

But no sooner have we begun to rejoice at this discovery than we are
assailed by a flood of questions. If, as we are told by dream-interpretation,

---

[1] [In a letter to Fliess of August 6, 1899 (Freud, 1950a, Letter 114), Freud describes the opening chapters of this book as follows: 'The whole thing is planned
on the model of an imaginary walk. First comes the dark wood of the authorities
(who cannot see the trees), where there is no clear view and it is easy to go astray.
Then there is a cavernous defile through which I lead my readers—my specimen
dream with its peculiarities, its details, its indiscretions and its bad jokes—and
then, all at once, the high ground and the open prospect and the question:
"Which way do you want to go?"']

147

a dream represents a fulfilled wish, what is the origin of the remarkable and puzzling form in which the wish-fulfilment is expressed? What alteration have the dream-thoughts undergone before being changed into the manifest dream which we remember when we wake up? How does that alteration take place? What is the source of the material that has been modified into the dream? What is the source of the many peculiarities that are to be observed in the dream-thoughts—such, for instance, as the fact that they may be mutually contradictory? (Cf. the analogy of the borrowed kettle on pp. 143 f.) Can a dream tell us anything new about our internal psychical processes? Can its content correct opinions we have held during the day?

I propose that for the moment we should leave all these questions on one side and pursue our way further along one particular path. We have learnt that a dream can represent a wish as fulfilled. Our first concern must be to enquire whether this is a universal characteristic of dreams or whether it merely happened to be the content of the particular dream (the dream of Irma's injection) which was the first that we analysed. For even if we are prepared to find that every dream has a meaning and a psychical value, the possibility must remain open of this meaning not being the same in every dream. Our first dream was the fulfilment of a wish; a second one might turn out to be a fulfilled fear; the content of a third might be a reflection; while a fourth might merely reproduce a memory. Shall we find other wishful dreams besides this one? or are there perhaps no dreams but wishful ones?

It is easy to prove that dreams often reveal themselves without any disguise as fulfilments of wishes; so that it may seem surprising that the language of dreams was not understood long ago. For instance, there is a dream that I can produce in myself as often as I like—experimentally, as it were. If I eat anchovies or olives or any other highly salted food in the evening, I develop thirst during the night which wakes me up. But my waking is preceded by a dream; and this always has the same content, namely, that I am drinking. I dream I am swallowing down water in great gulps, and it has the delicious taste that nothing can equal but a cool drink when one is parched with thirst. Then I wake up and have to have a real drink. This simple dream is occasioned by the thirst which I become aware of when I wake. The thirst gives rise to a wish to drink, and the dream shows me that wish fulfilled. In doing so it is performing a function—which it was easy to divine. I am a good sleeper and not accustomed to be woken by any physical need. If I can succeed in appeasing my thirst by *dreaming* that I am drinking, then I need not wake up in order to quench it. This, then, is a dream of convenience. Dreaming has taken the place of action, as it often does elsewhere in life. Unluckily my need for water to quench my thirst cannot be satisfied by a dream in the same way as my thirst for revenge against my friend Otto and Dr. M.; but the good intention is there in both cases. Not long ago this same dream of mine showed some modification. I had felt thirsty even before I fell asleep, and I had emptied a glass of water that stood on the table beside my bed. A few hours later during the night I had a fresh attack of thirst, and this had inconvenient results. In order to provide myself with some water I should have had to get up and fetch the glass standing on the table by my wife's bed. I therefore had an appropriate dream that my wife was giving me a drink out of a vase; this vase was an Etruscan cinerary urn which I had brought back from a journey to Italy and had since given away. But the water in it tasted so salty (evidently because of the ashes in the urn) that I woke up. It will be noticed how conveniently everything was arranged in this dream. Since its only purpose was to fulfil a wish, it could be completely egoistical. A love of comfort and convenience is not really compatible with consideration for other people. The introduction of the cinerary urn was probably yet another wish-fulfilment. I was sorry that the vase was no longer in my possession—just as the glass of water on my wife's table was out of my reach. The urn with its ashes fitted in, too, with the salty taste in my mouth which had now grown stronger and which I knew was bound to wake me.[1]

---

[1] Weygandt (1893, 41) was aware of the occurrence of thirst dreams, for he writes: 'The sensation of thirst is perceived with greater precision than any other; it always gives rise to an idea of its being quenched. The manner in which the thirst is represented as being quenched in the dream varies, and derives its special form from some near-by memory. Another general feature in these cases is that immediately after the idea of the thirst being quenched there follows a disappointment over the small effect produced by the imaginary refreshment.' Weygandt, however, overlooks the fact that this reaction of a dream to a stimulus is one which holds good universally. Other people who are attacked by thirst in the night may wake up without having had a dream; but that is no objection to my experiment. It merely shows that they are worse sleepers than I am.—[*Added* 1914:] Compare in this connection Isaiah xxix, 8: 'It shall even be as when an hungry man dreameth, and, behold, he eateth; but he awaketh, and his soul is empty: or as when a thirsty man dreameth, and, behold, he drinketh; but he awaketh, and, behold, he is faint, and his soul hath appetite.'

Dreams of convenience like these were very frequent in my youth. Having made it a practice as far back as I can remember to work late into the night, I always found it difficult to wake early. I used then to have a dream of being out of bed and standing by the washing-stand; after a while I was no longer able to disguise from myself the fact that I was really still in bed, but in the meantime I had had a little more sleep. A slothful dream of this kind, which was expressed in a particularly amusing and elegant form, has been reported to me by a young medical colleague who seems to share my liking for sleep. The landlady of his lodgings in the neighbourhood of the hospital had strict instructions to wake him in time every morning but found it no easy job to carry them out. One morning sleep seemed peculiarly sweet. The landlady called through the door: 'Wake up, Herr Pepi! It's time to go to the hospital!' In response to this he had a dream that he was lying in bed in a room in the hospital, and that there was a card over the bed on which was written: 'Pepi H., medical student, age 22.' While he was dreaming, he said to himself, 'As I'm already *in* the hospital, there's no need for me to go there'—and turned over and went on sleeping. In this way he openly confessed the motive for his dream.[1]

Here is another dream in which once again the stimulus produced its effect during actual sleep. One of my women patients, who had been obliged to undergo an operation on her jaw which had taken an unfavourable course, was ordered by her doctors to wear a cooling apparatus on the side of her face day and night. But as soon as she fell asleep she used to throw it off. One day, after she had once more thrown the apparatus on the floor, I was asked to speak to her seriously about it. 'This time I really couldn't help it,' she answered. 'It was because of a dream I had in the night. I dreamt I was in a box at the opera and very much enjoying the performance. But Herr Karl Meyer was in the nursing-home and complaining bitterly of pains in his jaw. So I told myself that as I hadn't any pain I didn't need the apparatus; and I threw it away.' The dream of this poor sufferer seems almost like a concrete representation of a phrase that sometimes forces its way on to people's lips in unpleasant situations: 'I must say I could think of something more agreeable than this.' The dream gives a picture of this more agreeable thing. The Herr

---

[3] [This dream was reported by Freud in a letter to Fliess, dated March 4, 1895 (Freud, 1950*a*, Letter 22)—the earliest recorded hint at the wish-fulfilment theory.]

Karl Meyer on to whom the dreamer transplanted her pains was the most indifferent young man of her acquaintance that she could call to mind.

The wish-fulfilment can be detected equally easily in some other dreams which I have collected from normal people. A friend of mine, who knows my theory of dreams and has told his wife of it, said to me one day: 'My wife has asked me to tell you that she had a dream yesterday that she was having her period. You can guess what that means.' I could indeed guess it. The fact that this young married woman dreamt that she was having her period meant that she had missed her period. I could well believe that she would have been glad to go on enjoying her freedom a little longer before shouldering the burden of motherhood. It was a neat way of announcing her first pregnancy. Another friend of mine wrote and told me that, not long before, his wife had dreamt that she had noticed some milk stains on the front of her vest. This too was an announcement of pregnancy, but not of a first one. The young mother was wishing that she might have more nourishment to give her second child than she had had for her first.

A young woman had been cut off from society for weeks on end while she nursed her child through an infectious illness. After the child's recovery, she had a dream of being at a party at which, among others, she met Alphonse Daudet, Paul Bourget, and Marcel Prévost; they were all most affable to her and highly amusing. All of the authors resembled their portraits, except Marcel Prévost, of whom she had never seen a picture; and he looked like . . . the disinfection officer who had fumigated the sickroom the day before and who had been her first visitor for so long. Thus it seems possible to give a complete translation of the dream: 'It's about time for something more amusing than this perpetual sick-nursing.'

These examples will perhaps be enough to show that dreams which can only be understood as fulfilments of wishes and which bear their meaning upon their faces without disguise are to be found under the most frequent and various conditions. They are mostly short and simple dreams, which afford a pleasant contrast to the confused and exuberant compositions that have in the main attracted the attention of the authorities. Nevertheless, it will repay us to pause for a moment over these simple dreams. We may expect to find the very simplest forms of dreams in *children*, since there can be no doubt that their psychical productions are less complicated than those of adults. Child psychology, in my opinion, is destined to perform the same useful services for adult psychology that the investigation of the structure or development of the lower animals has performed for research into the structure of the higher classes of animals. Few deliberate efforts have hitherto been made to make use of child psychology for this purpose.

The dreams of young children are frequently[1] pure wish-fulfilments and are in that case[2] quite uninteresting compared with the dreams of adults. They raise no problems for solution; but on the other hand they are of inestimable importance in proving that, in their essential nature, dreams represent fulfilments of wishes. I have been able to collect a few instances of such dreams from material provided by my own children.

I have to thank an excursion which we made to the lovely village of Hallstatt[3] in the summer of 1896 for two dreams: one of these was dreamt by my daughter, who was then eight and a half, and the other by her brother of five and a quarter. I must explain by way of preamble that we had been spending the summer on a hillside near Aussee, from which, in fine weather, we enjoyed a splendid view of the Dachstein. The Simony Hütte could be clearly distinguished through a telescope. The children made repeated attempts at seeing it through the telescope—I cannot say with what success. Before our excursion I had told the children that Hallstatt lay at the foot of the Dachstein. They very much looked forward to the day. From Hallstatt we walked up the Echerntal, which delighted the children with its succession of changing landscapes. One of them, however, the five-year-old boy, gradually became fretful. Each time a new mountain came into view he asked if that was the Dachstein and I had to say, 'No, only one of the foothills.' After he had asked the question several times, he fell completely silent; and he refused point-blank to come with us up the steep path to the waterfall. I thought he was tired. But next morning he came to me with a radiant face and said: 'Last night I dreamt we were at the Simony Hütte.' I understood him then. When I had spoken about the Dachstein, he had expected to climb the mountain in the course of our ex-

---

[1] [This word was added in 1911. The following comment upon this qualifying adverb appears in *Gesammelte Schriften*, **3** (1925), 21: 'Experience has shown that distorted dreams, which stand in need of interpretation, are already found in children of four or five; and this is in full agreement with our theoretical views on the determining conditions of distortion in dreams.']

[2] [Before 1911: 'for that reason.']

[3] [In the Salzkammergut district of Upper Austria.—'Echerntal' (below) is misprinted 'Escherntal' in all the German editions.]

cursion to Hallstatt and to find himself at close quarters with the hut which there had been so much talk about in connection with the telescope. But when he found that he was being fobbed off with foothills and a waterfall, he felt disappointed and out of spirits. The dream was a compensation. I tried to discover its details, but they were scanty: 'You have to climb up steps for six hours'—which was what he had been told.

The same excursion stirred up wishes in the eight-and-a-half-year-old girl as well—wishes which had to be satisfied in a dream. We had taken our neighbour's twelve-year-old son with us to Hallstatt. He was already a full-blown gallant, and there were signs that he had engaged the young lady's affections. Next morning she told me the following dream: 'Just fancy! I had a dream that Emil was one of the family and called you "Father" and "Mother" and slept with us in the big room like the boys. Then Mother came in and threw a handful of big bars of chocolate, wrapped up in blue and green paper, under our beds.' Her brothers, who have evidently not inherited a faculty for understanding dreams, followed the lead of the authorities and declared that the dream was nonsense. The girl herself defended one part of the dream at least; and it throws light on the theory of the neuroses to learn *which* part. 'Of course it's nonsense Emil being one of the family; but the part about the bars of chocolate isn't.' It had been precisely on that point that I had been in the dark, but the girl's mother now gave me the explanation. On their way home from the station the children had stopped in front of a slot-machine from which they were accustomed to obtain bars of chocolate of that very kind, wrapped in shiny metallic paper. They had wanted to get some; but their mother rightly decided that the day had already fulfilled enough wishes and left this one over to be fulfilled by the dream. I myself had not observed the incident. But the part of the dream which had been proscribed by my daughter was immediately clear to me. I myself had heard our well-behaved guest telling the children on the walk to wait till Father and Mother caught up with them. The little girl's dream turned this temporary kinship into permanent adoption. Her affection was not yet able to picture any other forms of companionship than those which were represented in the dream and which were based on her relation to her brothers. It was of course impossible to discover without questioning her why the bars of chocolate were thrown under the beds.

A friend of mine has reported a dream to me which was very much like my son's. The dreamer was an eight-year-old girl. Her father had started off with several children on a walk to Dornbach,[1] with the idea of visiting the Rohrer Hütte. As it was getting late, however, he had turned back, promising the children to make up for the disappointment another time. On their way home they had passed the signpost that marks the path up to the Hameau. The children had then asked to be taken up to the Hameau; but once again for the same reason they had to be consoled with the promise of another day. Next morning the eight-year-old girl came to her father and said in satisfied tones: 'Daddy, I dreamt last night that you went with us to the Rohrer Hütte and the Hameau.' In her impatience she had anticipated the fulfilment of her father's promises.

Here is an equally straightforward dream, provoked by the beauty of the scenery at Aussee in another of my daughters, who was at that time three and a quarter. She had crossed the lake for the first time, and the crossing had been too short for her: when we reached the landing-stage she had not wanted to leave the boat and had wept bitterly. Next morning she said: 'Last night I went on the lake.' Let us hope that her dream-crossing had been of a more satisfying length.

My eldest boy, then eight years old, already had dreams of his phantasies coming true: he dreamt that he was driving in a chariot with Achilles and that Diomede was the charioteer. As may be guessed, he had been excited the day before by a book on the legends of Greece which had been given to his elder sister.

If I may include words spoken by children in their sleep under the heading of dreams, I can at this point quote one of the most youthful dreams in my whole collection. My youngest daughter, then nineteen months old, had had an attack of vomiting one morning and had consequently been kept without food all day. During the night after this day of starvation she was heard calling out excitedly in her sleep: 'Anna Fweud, stwawbewwies, wild stwaw-bewwies, omblet, pudden!' At that time she was in the habit of using her own name to express the idea of taking posession of something. The menu included pretty well everything that must have seemed to her to make up a desirable meal. The fact that strawberries appeared in it in two varieties was a demonstration against the domestic health regulations. It was based upon the circumstance, which she had no doubt observed, that her nurse had attributed her in-

---

[1] [In the hills just outside Vienna.]

disposition to a surfeit of strawberries. She was thus retaliating in her dream against this unwelcome verdict.[1]

Though we think highly of the happiness of childhood because it is still innocent of sexual desires, we should not forget what a fruitful source of disappointment and renunciation, and consequently what a stimulus to dreaming, may be provided by the other of the two great vital instincts.[2] Here is another instance of this. My nephew, aged 22 months, had been entrusted with the duty of congratulating me on my birthday and of presenting me with a basket of cherries, which are still scarcely in season at that time of year. He seems to have found the task a hard one, for he kept on repeating 'Chewwies in it' but could not be induced to hand the present over. However, he found a means of compensation. He had been in the habit every morning of telling his mother that he had a dream of the 'white soldier'—a Guards officer in his white cloak whom he had once gazed at admiringly in the street. On the day after his birthday sacrifice he awoke with a cheerful piece of news, which could only have originated from a dream: 'Hermann eaten all the chewwies!'[3]

I do not myself know what animals dream of. But a proverb, to which my attention was drawn by one of my students, does claim to know.

---

[1] The same feat was accomplished shortly afterwards by a dream produced by this little girl's grandmother—their combined ages came to some seventy years. She had been obliged to go without food for a whole day on account of a disturbance due to a floating kidney. During the following night, no doubt imagining herself back in the heyday of her girlhood, she dreamt that she had been 'asked out' to both of the principal meals and been served at both with the most appetizing delicacies.—[The little girl's dream had been reported to Fliess not long after its occurrence (Freud, 1950a, Letter 73 of October 31, 1897).]

[2] [*Footnote added* 1911:] A closer study of the mental life of children has taught us, to be sure, that sexual instinctual forces, in infantile form, play a large enough part, and one that has been too long overlooked, in the psychical activity of children. Closer study, too, has given us grounds for feeling some doubt in regard to the happiness of childhood as it has been constructed by adults in retrospect. Cf. my *Three Essays on the Theory of Sexuality* (1905d).—[The remarkable inconsistency between this sentence in the text and several other passages (e.g. on pp. 273 ff. below) is commented on in the editor's preface to the last-mentioned work in the seventh volume of the Standard Edition.]

[3] [*Footnote added* 1911:] The fact should be mentioned that children soon begin to have more complicated and less transparent dreams, and that, on the other hand, adults in certain circumstances often have dreams of a similarly simple, infantile

character. The wealth of unexpected material that may occur in the dreams of children of four or five is shown by examples in my 'Analysis of a Phobia in a Five-Year-Old Boy' (1909*b*) and in Jung (1910*a*).—[*Added* 1914:] For analytical interpretations of children's dreams see also von Hug-Hellmuth (1911 and 1913), Putnam (1912), van Raalte (1912), Spielrein (1913) and Tausk (1913). Children's dreams are also reported by Bianchieri (1912), Busemann (1909 and 1910), Doglia and Bianchieri (1910–11) and, in particular, Wiggam (1909), who lays stress on their trend towards wish-fulfilment.—[*Added* 1911:] On the other hand, dreams of an infantile type seem to occur in adults with special frequency when they find themselves in unusual external circumstances. Thus Otto Nordenskjöld (1904, **1**, 336 f.) writes as follows of the members of his expedition while they were wintering in the Antarctic: 'The direction taken by our innermost thoughts was very clearly shown by our dreams, which were never more vivid or numerous than at this time. Even those of us who otherwise dreamt but rarely had long stories to tell in the morning when we exchanged our latest experiences in this world of the imagination. They were all concerned with the outside world which was now so remote from us, though they were often adapted to our actual circumstances. One of my companions had a particularly characteristic dream of being back in his school class-room, where it was his task to skin miniature seals which had been specially prepared for instructional purposes. Eating and drinking, however, were the pivot round which our dreams most often revolved. One of us, who had a special gift for attending large luncheon parties during the night, was proud if he was able to report in the morning that he had "got through a three-course dinner." Another of us dreamt of tobacco, of whole mountains of tobacco; while a third dreamt of a ship in full sail coming in across open water. Yet another dream is worth repeating. The postman brought round the mail and gave a long explanation of why we had had to wait so long for it: he had delivered it at the wrong address and had only succeeded in recovering it with great difficulty. We dreamt, of course, of still more impossible things. But there was a most striking lack of imaginativeness shown by almost all the dreams that I dreamt myself or heard described. It would certainly be of great psychological interest if all these dreams could be recorded. And it will easily be understood how much we longed for sleep, since it could offer each one of us everything that he most eagerly desired.' [This passage is much abbreviated in the English translation of Nordenskjöld's book (1905, 290).]—[*Added* 1914:] According to Du Prel (1885, 231), 'Mungo Park, when he was almost dying of thirst on one of his African journeys, dreamt unceasingly of the well-watered valleys and meadows of his home. Similarly, Baron Trenck, suffering torments of hunger while he was a prisoner in the fortress at Magdeburg, dreamt of being surrounded by sumptuous meals; and George Back, who took part in Franklin's first expedition, when he was almost dying of starvation as a result of his fearful privations, dreamt constantly and regularly of copious meals.'

'What,' asks the proverb, 'do geese dream of?' And it replies: 'Of maize.'[1] The whole theory that dreams are wish-fulfilments is contained in these two phrases.[2]

It will be seen that we might have arrived at our theory of the hidden meaning of dreams most rapidly merely by following linguistic usage. It is true that common language sometimes speaks of dreams with contempt. (The phrase '*Träume sind Schäume* [Dreams are froth]' seems intended to support the scientific estimate of dreams.) But, on the whole, ordinary usage treats dreams above all as the blessed fulfillers of wishes. If ever we find our expectation surpassed by the event, we exclaim in our delight: 'I should never have imagined such a thing even in my wildest dreams.'[3]

---

[1] [*Footnote added* 1911:] A Hungarian proverb quoted by Ferenczi [1910] goes further and declares that 'pigs dream of acorns and geese dream of maize.'— [*Added* 1914:] A Jewish proverb runs: 'What do hens dream of?—Of millet.' (Bernstein and Segel, 1908, 116.)

[2] [*Footnote added* 1914:] I am far from seeking to maintain that I am the first writer to have had the idea of deriving dreams from wishes. (Cf. the opening sentences of my next chapter.) Those who attach any importance to anticipations of this kind may go back to classical antiquity and quote Herophilus, a physician who lived under the first Ptolemy. According to Büchsenschütz (1868, 33), he distinguished three sorts of dreams: those which are sent by the gods, those which are natural and arise when the mind forms a picture of something that is agreeable to it and will come about, and those which are of a mixed nature and which arise of their own accord from the emergence of pictures in which we see what we wish for. J. Stärcke (1913, [248]) has drawn attention to a dream in Scherner's collection which that writer himself describes as the fulfilment of a wish. Scherner (1861, 239) writes: 'The dreamer's imagination fulfilled her waking wish so promptly, simply because that wish was emotionally active in her.' Scherner classes this dream among 'dreams of mood'; alongside it he places 'dreams of erotic yearning' in men and women, and 'dreams of ill-temper.' There is clearly no question of Scherner attributing any more importance to wishes in the instigation of dreams than to any other waking mental state: still less is there any question of his having related wishes to the essential nature of dreaming.

[3] [Children's dreams (including many of those recorded in this chapter) and dreams of an infantile type are discussed in Lecture VIII of Freud's *Introductory Lectures* (1916–17) and more briefly in Section III of his short study *On Dreams* (1901*a*) (Standard Ed., **5**, 643 f.).]

CHAPTER IV

DISTORTION IN DREAMS

IF I proceed to put forward the assertion that the meaning of *every* dream is the fulfilment of a wish, that is to say that there cannot be any dreams but wishful dreams, I feel certain in advance that I shall meet with the most categorical contradiction.

'There is nothing new,' I shall be told, 'in the idea that *some* dreams are to be regarded as wish-fulfilments; the authorities noticed that fact long ago. Cf. Radestock (1879, 137 f.), Volkelt (1875, 110 f.), Purkinje (1846, 456), Tissié (1890, 70), Simon (1888, 42, on the hunger dreams of Baron Trenck while he was a prisoner), and a passage in Griesinger (1845, 89).[1] But to assert that there are no dreams other than wish-fulfilment dreams is only one more unjustifiable generalization, though fortunately one which it is easy to disprove. After all, plenty of dreams occur which contain the most distressing subject-matter but never a sign of any wish-fulfilment. Eduard von Hartmann, the philosopher of pessimism, is probably furthest removed from the wish-fulfilment theory. In his *Philosophie des Unbewussten* (1890, **2**, 344) he writes: "When it comes to dreams, we find all the annoyances of waking life carried over into the state of sleep; the only thing we do *not* find is what can to some extent reconcile an educated man to life—scientific and artistic enjoyment. . . ." But even less disgruntled observers

---

[1] [*Footnote added* 1914:] A writer as early as Plotinus, the Neo-platonist, is quoted by Du Prel (1885, 276) as saying: 'When our desires are aroused, imagination comes along and, as it were, presents us with the objects of those desires.' [*Ennead*, iv, 4, 17.]

have insisted that pain and un-pleasure are more common in dreams than pleasure: for instance, Scholz (1893, 57), Volkelt (1875, 80), and others. Indeed two ladies, Florence Hallam and Sarah Weed (1896, 499), have actually given statistical expression, based on a study of their own dreams, to the preponderance of unpleasure in dreaming. They find that 57.2 per cent of dreams are "disagreeable" and only 28.6 per cent positively "pleasant." And apart from these dreams, which carry over into sleep the various distressing emotions of life, there are anxiety-dreams, in which that most dreadful of all unpleasurable feelings holds us in its grasp till we awaken. And the commonest victims of these anxiety-dreams are precisely children,[1] whose dreams you have described as undisguised wish-fulfilments.'

It does in fact look as though anxiety-dreams make it impossible to assert as a general proposition (based on the examples quoted in my last chapter) that dreams are wish-fulfilments; indeed they seem to stamp any such proposition as an absurdity.

Nevertheless, there is no great difficulty in meeting these apparently conclusive objections. It is only necessary to take notice of the fact that my theory is not based on a consideration of the manifest content of dreams but refers to the thoughts which are shown by the work of interpretation to lie behind dreams. We must make a contrast between the *manifest* and the *latent* content of dreams. There is no question that there are dreams whose manifest content is of the most distressing kind. But has anyone tried to interpret such dreams? to reveal the latent thoughts behind them? If not, then the two objections raised against my theory will not hold water: it still remains possible that distressing dreams and anxiety-dreams, when they have been interpreted, may turn out to be fulfilments of wishes.[2]

When in the course of a piece of scientific work we come upon a problem which is difficult to solve, it is often a good plan to take up a second problem along with the original one—just as it is easier to crack two nuts

---

[1] Cf. Debacker (1881) on pavor nocturnus.

[2] [*Footnote added* 1909:] It is hard to credit the obstinacy with which readers and critics of this book shut their eyes to this consideration and overlook the fundamental distinction between the manifest and latent content of dreams.—[*Added* 1914:] On the other hand, nothing in the literature of the subject comes so near to my hypothesis as a passage in James Sully's essay 'The Dream as a Revelation' (1893, 364). The fact that I am only now quoting it for the first time is no sign of disparagement: 'It would seem then, after all, that dreams are not the utter nonsense they have been said to be by such authorities as Chaucer, Shakespeare

together than each separately. Thus we are not only faced by the question 'How can distressing dreams and anxiety-dreams be wish-fulfilments?'; our reflections enable us to add a second question: 'Why is it that dreams with an indifferent content, which turn out to be wish-fulfilments, do not express their meaning undisguised?' Take, for instance, the dream which I treated at such length of Irma's injection. It was not by any means of a distressing nature and interpretation showed it as a striking example of the fulfilment of a wish. But why should it have needed any interpretation at all? Why did it not say what it meant straight out? At first sight the dream of Irma's injection gave no impression that it represented a wish of the dreamer's as fulfilled. My readers will have had no such impression; but neither did I myself before I carried out the analysis. Let us describe this behaviour of dreams, which stands in so much need of explanation, as 'the phenomenon of distortion in dreams.' Thus our second problem is: what is the origin of dream-distortion?

A number of possible solutions of the problem may at once occur to us: as, for instance, that some incapacity exists during sleep for giving direct expression to our dream-thoughts. But the analysis of certain dreams forces us to adopt another explanation of distortion in dreams. I will exemplify this by another dream of my own. Once again this will involve me in a variety of indiscretions; but a thorough elucidation of the problem will compensate for my personal sacrifice.

PREAMBLE.—In the spring of 1897 I learnt that two professors at our university had recommended me for appointment as *professor extraordinarius*.[1] The news surprised and greatly delighted me, since it implied

---

and Milton. The chaotic aggregations of our night-fancy have a significance and communicate new knowledge. Like some letter in cypher, the dream-inscription when scrutinized closely loses its first look of balderdash and takes on the aspect of a serious, intelligible message. Or, to vary the figure slightly, we may say that, like some palimpsest, the dream discloses beneath its worthless surface-characters traces of an old and precious communication.' [Freud prints the two last sentences in spaced type.]

[1] [Roughly equivalent to an Assistant Professor. All such appointments in Austria were made by the Minister of Education. The fact of this recommendation is reported by Freud in a letter to Fliess of February 8, 1897 (Freud, 1950a, Letter 58) and the dream itself is mentioned on March 15, 1897 (ibid., Letter 85).— The 'denominational considerations' mentioned below relate, of course, to anti-Semitic feeling, which was already rife in Vienna during the last years of the nineteenth century.]

recognition by two eminent men, which could not be put down to any considerations of a personal kind. But I at once warned myself not to attach any expectations to the event. During the last few years the Ministry had disregarded recommendations of that sort; and several of my colleagues who were my seniors in age and at least my equals in merit had been waiting vainly for appointment. I had no reason to believe that I should be more fortunate. I therefore determined to meet the future with resignation. So far as I knew, I was not an ambitious man; I was following my profession with gratifying success even without the advantages afforded by a title. Moreover there was no question of my pronouncing the grapes sweet or sour: they hung far too high over my head.

One evening I had a visit from a friend—one of the men whose example I had taken as a warning to me. For a considerable time he had been a candidate for promotion to a professorship, a rank which in our society turns its holder into a demi-god to his patients. Less resigned than I was, however, he was in the habit of paying his respects from time to time in the offices of the Ministry with a view to advancing his prospects. He had been paying one of these visits just before calling on me. He told me that on this occasion he had driven the exalted official into a corner and had asked straight out whether the delay over his appointment was not in fact due to denominational considerations. The reply had been that, in view of the present state of feeling, it was no doubt true that, for the moment, His Excellency was not in a position, etc., etc. 'At least I know where I am now,' my friend had concluded. It was not news to me, though it was bound to strengthen my feeling of resignation; for the same denominational considerations applied to my own case.

On the morning after this visit I had the following dream, which was remarkable among other things for its form. It consisted of two thoughts and two pictures—each thought being succeeded by a picture. I shall, however, report only the first half of the dream here, since the other half has no connection with the purpose for which I am describing the dream.

> I. . . . *My friend R. was my uncle.—I had a great feeling of affection for him.*
> II. *I saw before me his face, somewhat changed. It was as though it had been drawn out lengthways. A yellow beard that surrounded it stood out especially clearly.*

Then followed the two other pieces which I shall pass over—once more a thought followed by a picture.

The interpretation of the dream took place as follows.

When, during the course of the morning, the dream came into my head, I laughed aloud and said: 'The dream's nonsense!' But it refused to go away and followed me about all day, till at last in the evening I began to reproach myself: 'If one of your patients who was interpreting a dream could find nothing better to say than that it was nonsense, you would take him up about it and suspect that the dream had some disagreeable story at the back of it which he wanted to avoid becoming aware of. Treat yourself in the same way. Your opinion that the dream is nonsense only means that you have an internal resistance against interpreting it. Don't let yourself be put off like this.' So I set about the interpretation.

'*R. was my uncle.*' What could that mean? I never had more than one uncle—Uncle Josef.[1] There was an unhappy story attached to him. Once—more than thirty years ago—in his eagerness to make money, he allowed himself to be involved in a transaction of a kind that is severely punished by the law, and he was in fact punished for it. My father, whose hair turned grey from grief in a few days, used always to say that Uncle Josef was not a bad man but only a simpleton; those were his words. So that if my friend R. was my Uncle Josef, what I was meaning to say was that R. was a simpleton. Hardly credible and most disagreeable!—But there was the face which I saw in the dream with its elongated features and yellow beard. My uncle did in fact have a face like that, elongated and framed in a handsome fair beard. My friend R. had originally been extremely dark; but when black-haired people begin to turn grey they pay for the splendour of their youth. Hair by hair, their black beards go through an unpleasing change of colour: first they turn to a reddish brown, then to a yellowish brown, and only then to a definite grey. My friend R.'s beard was at that time passing through this stage—and so, incidentally, was my own, as I had noticed with dissatisfaction. The face

---

[1] It is astonishing to observe the way in which my memory—my waking memory—was narrowed at this point, for the purposes of the analysis. Actually I have known five of my uncles, and loved and honoured one of them. But at the moment at which I overcame my resistance to interpreting the dream I said to myself that I never had more than one uncle—the one that was intended in the dream.

that I saw in the dream was at once my friend R.'s and my uncle's. It was like one of Galton's composite photographs. (In order to bring out family likenesses, Galton used to photograph several faces on the same plate [1907, 6 ff. and 221 ff.].) So there could be no doubt that I really did mean that my friend R. was a simpleton—like my Uncle Josef.

I still had no idea at all what could be the purpose of this comparison, against which I continued to struggle. It did not go very deep, after all, since my uncle was a criminal, whereas my friend R. bore an unblemished character . . . except for having been fined for knocking a boy down with his bicycle. Could I have had that crime in mind? That would have been making fun of the comparison. At this point I remembered another conversation which I had had a few days earlier with another colleague, N., and, now I came to think of it, upon the same subject. I had met N. in the street. He too had been recommended for a professorship. He had heard of the honour that had been paid me and had offered me his congratulations on it; but I had unhesitatingly refused to accept them. 'You are the last person,' I had said, 'to make that kind of joke; you know what such a recommendation is worth from your own experience.' 'Who can say?' he had answered—jokingly, it seemed; 'there was something definite against *me*. Don't you know that a woman once started legal proceedings against me? I needn't assure you that the case was dismissed. It was a disgraceful attempt at blackmail; and I had the greatest difficulty in saving the prosecutrix from being punished. But perhaps they may be using this at the Ministry as an excuse for not appointing me. But *you* have an unblemished character.' This told me who the criminal was, and at the same time showed me how the dream was to be interpreted and what its purpose was. My Uncle Josef represented my two colleagues who had not been appointed to professorships—the one as a simpleton and the other as a criminal. I now saw too why they were represented in this light. If the appointment of my friends R. and N. had been postponed for 'denominational' reasons, my own appointment was also open to doubt; if, however, I could attribute the rejection of my two friends to other reasons, which did not apply to me, my hopes would remain untouched. This was the procedure adopted by my dream: it made one of them, R., into a simpleton and the other, N., into a criminal, whereas *I* was neither the one nor the other; thus we no longer had anything in common; I could rejoice at my appointment to a professorship, and I could avoid drawing the distressing conclusion that R.'s report of what the high official had said to him must apply equally to me.

But I felt obliged to proceed still further with my interpretation of the dream; I felt I had not yet finished dealing with it satisfactorily. I was still uneasy over the light-heartedness with which I had degraded two of my respected colleagues in order to keep open my own path to a professorship. My dissatisfaction with my conduct, however, had diminished since I had come to realize the worth that was to be attached to expressions in dreams. I was prepared to deny through thick and thin that I really considered that R. was a simpleton and that I really disbelieved N.'s account of the blackmailing affair. Nor did I believe that Irma was really made dangerously ill through being injected with Otto's preparation of propyl. In both these cases what my dreams had expressed was only *my wish that it might be so.* The assertion in which my wish was realized sounded less absurd in the later dream than in the earlier one; it made cleverer use of the actual facts in its construction, like a well-designed slander of the kind that makes people feel that 'there's something in it.' For one of the professors in his own faculty had voted against my friend R., and my friend N. had himself innocently provided me with the material for my aspersions. Nevertheless, I must repeat, the dream seemed to me to stand in need of further elucidation.

I then recalled that there was still a piece of the dream which the interpretation had not touched. After the idea had occurred to me that R. was my uncle, I had had a warm feeling of affection for him in the dream. Where did that feeling belong? I had naturally never had any feeling of affection for my Uncle Josef. I had been fond of my friend R. and had esteemed him for many years; but if I had gone up to him and expressed my sentiments in terms approaching the degree of affection I had felt in the dream, there could be no doubt that he would have been astonished. My affection for him struck me as ungenuine and exaggerated—like the judgement of his intellectual qualities which I had expressed by fusing his personality with my uncle's, though *there* the exaggeration had been in the opposite direction. But a new light began to dawn on me. The affection in the dream did not belong to the latent content, to the thoughts that lay behind the dream; it stood in contradiction to them and was calculated to conceal the true interpretation of the dream. And probably that was precisely its *raison d'être.* I recalled my resistance against embarking on the interpretation, how long I had put it off and how I had declared that the dream was sheer nonsense. My psycho-analytic treatments taught me how a repudiation of that kind was to be interpreted: it had no value as a judgement but was simply an expression of emotion. If my little daughter did not want an apple that was offered to her, she asserted that the apple tasted sour without having tasted it. And if my patients behaved like the child, I knew that they were concerned with an idea which they wanted to repress. The same was true of my dream. I did not want to interpret it, because the interpretation contained something that I was struggling against. When I had completed the interpretation I learnt what it was that I had been struggling against—namely, the assertion that R. was a simpleton. The affection that I felt for R. could not be derived from the latent dream-thoughts; but no doubt it originated from this struggle of mine. If my dream was distorted in this respect from its latent content—and distorted into its opposite—then the affection that was manifest in the dream served the purpose of this distortion. In other words, distortion was shown in this case to be deliberate and to be a means of *dissimulation*. My dream-thoughts had contained a slander against R.; and, in order that I might not notice this, what appeared in the dream was the opposite, a feeling of affection for him.

It seemed as though this might be a discovery of general validity. It is true that, as was shown by the instances quoted in Chapter III, there are some dreams which are undisguised fulfilments of wishes. But in cases where the wish-fulfilment is unrecognizable, where it has been disguised, there must have existed some inclination to put up a defence against the wish; and owing to this defence the wish was unable to express itself except in a distorted shape. I will try to seek a social parallel to this internal event in the mind. Where can we find a similar distortion of a psychical act in social life? Only where two persons are concerned, one of whom possesses a certain degree of power which the second is obliged to take into account. In such a case the second person will distort his psychical acts or, as we might put it, will dissimulate. The politeness which I practise every day is to a large extent dissimulation of this kind; and when I interpret my dreams for my readers I am obliged to adopt similar distortions. The poet complains of the need for these distortions in the words:

> Das Beste, was du wissen kannst,
> Darfst du den Buben doch nicht sagen.[1]

---

[1] [Mephistopheles, in Goethe's *Faust*, Part I [Scene 4]: 'After all, the best of what you know may not be told to boys.'—These were favourite lines of Freud's. He uses them again on p. 461 below. He had already quoted them in letters to Fliess of December 3, 1897, and February 9, 1898 (Freud, 1950*a*, Letters 77 and 83); and, towards the end of his life, on the occasion of his reception of the Goethe prize in 1930, he applied them to Goethe himself. (Freud, 1930*e*.)]

A similar difficulty confronts the political writer who has disagreeable truths to tell to those in authority. If he presents them undisguised, the authorities will suppress his words—after they have been spoken, if his pronouncement was an oral one, but beforehand, if he had intended to make it in print. A writer must beware of the censorship,[1] and on its account he must soften and distort the expression of his opinion. According to the strength and sensitiveness of the censorship he finds himself compelled either merely to refrain from certain forms of attack, or to speak in allusions in place of direct references, or he must conceal his objectionable pronouncement beneath some apparently innocent disguise: for instance, he may describe a dispute between two Mandarins in the Middle Kingdom, when the people he really has in mind are officials in his own country. The stricter the censorship, the more far-reaching will be the disguise and the more ingenious too may be the means employed for putting the reader on the scent of the true meaning.[2]

---

[1] [This analogy, which makes its first appearance in this passage in connection with dreams, had already been used in connection with paranoia at the end of Freud's second paper on the neuropsychoses of defence (1896*b*) and more generally in Section 2 of his chapter on psychotherapy in *Studies on Hysteria* (Breuer and Freud, 1895).]

[2] [*Footnote added* 1919:] Frau Dr. H. von Hug-Hellmuh (1915) has recorded a dream which is perhaps better fitted than any to justify my choice of nomenclature. In this example the dream-distortion adopted the same methods as the postal censorship for expunging passages which were objectionable to it. The postal censorship makes such passages unreadable by blacking them out; the dream censorship replaced them by an incomprehensible mumble.

In order to make the dream intelligible, I must explain that the dreamer, a cultivated and highly esteemed lady, was fifty years of age. She was the widow of an officer of high rank who had died some twelve years previously and was the mother of grown sons, one of whom was in the field at the time of the dream.

Here then is the dream—which deals with 'love services' in wartime. ['*Liebesdienste*' means in the first instance 'services performed for love,' i.e. 'unremunerated services'; but the term obviously courts another interpretation.] 'The patient went to Garrison Hospital No. 1 and informed the sentry at the gate that she must speak to the Chief Medical Officer (mentioning a name that was unknown to her) as she wanted to volunteer for service at the hospital. She pronounced the word "service" in such a way that the N.C.O. at once understood that she meant "love service." Since she was an elderly lady, after some hesitation he allowed her to pass. Instead of finding the Chief Medical Officer, however, she reached a large and gloomy apartment in which a number of officers and army doctors were

The fact that the phenomena of censorship and of dream-distortion correspond down to their smallest details justifies us in presuming that they are similarly determined. We may therefore suppose that dreams are given their shape in individual human beings by the operation of two psychical forces (or we may describe them as currents or systems); and that one of these forces constructs the wish which is expressed by the dream, while the other exercises a censorship upon this dream-wish and, by the use of that censorship, forcibly brings about a distortion in the expression of the wish. It remains to enquire as to the nature of the power enjoyed by this second agency which enables it to exercise its censorship. When we bear in mind that the latent dream-thoughts are not conscious before an analysis has

---

standing and sitting round a long table. She approached a staff surgeon with her request, and he understood her meaning after she had said only a few words. The actual wording of her speech in the dream was: "I and many other women and girls in Vienna are ready to . . ." at this point in the dream her words turned into a mumble ". . . for the troops—officers and other ranks without distinction." She could tell from the expressions on the officers' faces, partly embarrassed and partly sly, that everyone had understood her meaning correctly. The lady went on: "I'm aware that our decision must sound surprising, but we mean it in bitter earnest. No one asks a soldier in the field whether he wishes to die or not." There followed an awkward silence of some minutes. The staff surgeon then put his arm round her waist and said: "Suppose, madam, it actually came to . . . (mumble)." She drew away from him, thinking to herself: "He's like all the rest of them," and replied: "Good gracious, I'm an old woman and I might never come to that. Besides, there's one condition that must be observed: age must be respected. It must never happen that an elderly woman . . . (mumble) . . . a mere boy. That would be terrible." "I understand perfectly," replied the staff surgeon. Some of the officers, and among them one who had been a suitor of hers in her youth, laughed out loud. The lady then asked to be taken to the Chief Medical Officer, with whom she was acquainted, so that the whole matter could be thrashed out; but she found, to her consternation, that she could not recall his name. Nevertheless, the staff surgeon, most politely and respectfully, showed her the way up to the second floor by a very narrow, iron, spiral staircase, which led directly from the room to the upper storeys of the building. As she went up she heard an officer say: "That's a tremendous decision to make—no matter whether a woman's young or old! Splendid of her!" Feeling simply that she was doing her duty, she walked up an interminable staircase.—The dream was repeated twice in the course of a few weeks, with, as the lady remarked, some quite unimportant and meaningless modifications.'

[Some further comments on this dream will be found in Freud's *Introductory Lectures* (1916–17), Lecture IX.]

been carried out, whereas the manifest content of the dream is consciously remembered, it seems plausible to suppose that the privilege enjoyed by the second agency is that of permitting thoughts to enter consciousness. Nothing, it would seem, can reach consciousness from the first system without passing the second agency; and the second agency allows nothing to pass without exercising its rights and making such modifications as it thinks fit in the thought which is seeking admission to consciousness. Incidentally, this enables us to form a quite definite view of the 'essential nature' of consciousness: we see the process of a thing becoming conscious as a specific psychical act, distinct from and independent of the process of the formation of a presentation or idea; and we regard consciousness as a sense organ which perceives data that arise elsewhere. It can be demonstrated that these basic assumptions are absolutely indispensable to psychopathology. We must, however, postpone our further consideration of them to a later stage. [See Chapter VII, particularly Section F, pp. 605 ff.]

If this picture of the two psychical agencies and their relation to consciousness is accepted, there is a complete analogy in political life to the extraordinary affection which I felt in my dream for my friend R., who was treated with such contumely during the dream's interpretation. Let us imagine a society in which a struggle is in process between a ruler who is jealous of his power and an alert public opinion. The people are in revolt against an unpopular official and demand his dismissal. But the autocrat, to show that he need take no heed of the popular wish, chooses that moment for bestowing a high distinction upon the official, though there is no other reason for doing so. In just the same way my second agency, which commands the approaches to consciousness, distinguished my friend R. by a display of excessive affection simply because the wishful impulses belonging to the first system, for particular reasons of their own on which they were intent at the moment, chose to condemn him as a simpleton.[1]

These considerations may lead us to feel that the interpretation of dreams may enable us to draw conclusions as to the structure of our mental

---

[1] [The analysis of this dream is continued on pp. 213 ff.—*Footnote added* 1911:] Hypocritical dreams of this description are not uncommon events in my own case or in that of other people. [They are further discussed below, pp. 477 ff.] While I was engaged in working out a certain scientific problem, I was troubled for several nights in close succession by a somewhat confusing dream which had as its subject a reconciliation with a friend whom I had dropped many years before. On the fourth or fifth occasion I at last succeeded in understanding the

apparatus which we have hoped for in vain from philosophy. I do not propose, however, to follow this line of thought [which is taken up in Chapter VII]; but, having cleared up the matter of distortion in dreams, I shall go back to the problem from which we started. The question raised was how dreams with a distressing content can be resolved into wish-fulfilments. We now see that this is possible if dream-distortion has occurred and if the distressing content serves only to disguise something that is wished for. Bearing in mind our assumption of the existence of two psychical agencies, we can further say that distressing dreams do in fact contain something which is distressing to the *second* agency, but something which at the same time fulfils a wish on the part of the *first* agency. They are wishful dreams in so far as every dream arises from the first agency; the relation of the second agency towards dreams is of a *defensive* and not of a *creative* kind.[1] If we were to restrict ourselves to considering what the second agency contributes to dreams, we could never arrive at an understanding of them: all the conundrums which the authorities have observed in dreams would remain unsolved.

The fact that dreams really have a secret meaning which represents the fulfilment of a wish must be proved afresh in each particular case by analysis. I shall therefore select a few dreams with a distressing content and attempt to analyse them. Some of them are the dreams of hysterical patients which require lengthy preambles and an occasional excursus into the psychical processes characteristic of hysteria. But I cannot escape this aggravation of the difficulties of presenting my argument. [See p. 128.]

As I have already explained [pp. 125 f.], when I undertake the analytic treatment of a psychoneurotic patient his dreams are invariably discussed between us. In the course of these discussions I am obliged to give him

---

meaning of the dream. It was an incitement to abandon my last remnants of consideration for the person in question and to free myself from him completely, and it had been hypocritically disguised as its opposite. [Cf. p. 482.] I have reported elsewhere [1910*l*, reprinted below, p. 408 *n*.] a 'hypocritical Oedipus dream,' dreamt by a man, in which the hostile impulses and death-wishes contained in the dream-thoughts were replaced by manifest affection. Another kind of hypocritical dream will be mentioned below in Chapter VI [pp. 479 ff.]. [The friend referred to in this footnote was evidently Fliess. Cf. Section IV of Kris's introduction to Freud's correspondence with Fliess (Freud, 1950*a*).]

[1] [*Footnote added* 1930:] Later [pp. 482 *n*. and 558 ff.] we shall also come across instances in which, on the contrary, a dream expresses a wish on the part of the *second* agency.

all the psychological explanations which have enabled me myself to reach an understanding of his symptoms. I am thereupon subjected to a remorseless criticism, certainly no less severe than I have to expect from the members of my own profession. And my patients invariably contradict my assertion that all dreams are fulfilments of wishes. Here, then, are some instances from the material of dreams that have been brought up against me as evidence to the contrary.

'You're always saying to me,' began a clever woman patient of mine, 'that a dream is a fulfilled wish. Well, I'll tell you a dream whose subject was the exact opposite—a dream in which one of my wishes was *not* fulfilled. How do you fit that in with your theory? This was the dream:

I wanted to give a supper-party, but I had nothing in the house but a little smoked salmon. I thought I would go out and buy something, but remembered then that it was Sunday afternoon and all the shops would be shut. Next I tried to ring up some caterers, but the telephone was out of order. So I had to abandon my wish to give a supper-party.'

I answered, of course, that analysis was the only way of deciding on the meaning of the dream; though I admitted that at first sight it seemed sensible and coherent and looked like the reverse of a wish-fulfilment. 'But what material did the dream arise from? As you know, the instigation to a dream is always to be found in the events of the previous day.'

ANALYSIS.—My patient's husband, an honest and capable wholesale butcher, had remarked to her the day before that he was getting too stout and therefore intended to start on a course of weight-reduction. He proposed to rise early, do physical exercises, keep to a strict diet, and above all accept no more invitations to supper.—She laughingly added that her husband, at the place where he regularly lunched, had made the acquaintance of a painter, who had pressed him to be allowed to paint his portrait, as he had never seen such expressive features. Her husband however had replied in his blunt manner that he was much obliged, but he was sure the painter would prefer a piece of a pretty young girl's behind to the whole of his face.[1]

---

[1] Cf. the phrase 'sitting for one's portrait' and Goethe's lines:

> Und wenn er keinen Hintern hat,
> Wie mag der Edle sitzen?

> [And if he hasn't a behind,
> How can his Lordship sit?
> (From 'Totalität,' 1814–15.)]

She was very much in love with her husband now and teased him a lot. She had begged him, too, not to give her any caviare.

I asked her what that meant; and she explained that she had wished for a long time that she could have a caviare sandwich every morning but had grudged the expense. Of course her husband would have let her have it at once if she had asked him. But, on the contrary, she had asked him *not* to give her any caviare, so that she could go on teasing him about it.

This explanation struck me as unconvincing. Inadequate reasons like this usually conceal unconfessed motives. They remind one of Bernheim's hypnotized patients. When one of these carries out a post-hypnotic suggestion and is asked why he is acting in this way, instead of saying that he has no idea, he feels compelled to invent some obviously unsatisfactory reason. The same was no doubt true of my patient and the caviare. I saw that she was obliged to create an unfulfilled wish for herself in her actual life; and the dream represented this renunciation as having been put into effect. But why was it that she stood in need of an unfulfilled wish?

The associations which she had so far produced had not been sufficient to interpret the dream. I pressed her for some more. After a short pause, such as would correspond to the overcoming of a resistance, she went on to tell me that the day before she had visited a woman friend of whom she confessed she felt jealous because her (my patient's) husband was constantly singing her praises. Fortunately this friend of hers is very skinny and thin and her husband admires a plumper figure. I asked her what she had talked about to her thin friend. Naturally, she replied, of that lady's wish to grow a little stouter. Her friend had enquired, too: 'When are you going to ask us to another meal? You always feed one so well.'

The meaning of the dream was now clear, and I was able to say to my patient: 'It is just as though when she made this suggestion you said to yourself: "A likely thing! I'm to ask you to come and eat in my house so that you may get stout and attract my husband still more! I'd rather never give another supper-party." What the dream was saying to you was that you were unable to give any supper-parties, and it was thus fulfilling your wish not to help your friend to grow plumper. The fact that what people eat at parties makes them stout had been brought home to you by your husband's decision not to accept any more invitations to supper in the interests of his plan to reduce his weight.' All that was now lacking was some coincidence to confirm the solution. The smoked salmon in the dream had not yet been accounted for. 'How,' I asked, 'did you arrive at the salmon that came into your dream?' 'Oh,' she replied, 'smoked salmon is my friend's favourite dish.' I happen to be acquainted with the lady in question myself, and I can confirm the fact that she grudges herself salmon no less than my patient grudges herself caviare.

The same dream admits of another and subtler interpretation, which in fact becomes unavoidable if we take a subsidiary detail into account. (The two interpretations are not mutually contradictory, but both cover the same ground; they are a good instance of the fact that dreams, like all other psychopathological structures, regularly have more than one meaning.) My patient, it will be remembered, at the same time as she was occupied with her dream of the renunciation of a wish, was also trying to bring about a renounced wish (for the caviare sandwich) in real life. Her friend had also given expression to a wish—to become stouter—and it would not have been surprising if my patient had dreamt that her friend's wish was unfulfilled; for my patient's own wish was that her friend's wish (to put on weight) should not be fulfilled. But instead of this she dreamt that one of her *own* wishes was not fulfilled. Thus the dream will acquire a new interpretation if we suppose that the person indicated in the dream was not herself but her friend, that she had put herself in her friend's place, or, as we might say, that she had 'identified' herself with her friend. I believe she had in fact done this; and the circumstance of her having brought about a renounced wish in real life was evidence of this identification.

What is the meaning of hysterical identification? It requires a somewhat lengthy explanation. Identification is a highly important factor in the mechanism of hysterical symptoms. It enables patients to express in their symptoms not only their own experiences but those of a large number of other people; it enables them, as it were, to suffer on behalf of a whole crowd of people and to act all the parts in a play single-handed. I shall be told that this is not more than the familiar hysterical imitation, the capacity of hysterics to imitate any symptoms in other people that may have struck their attention—sympathy, as it were, intensified to the point of reproduction. This, however, does no more than show us the path along which the psychical process in hysterical imitation proceeds. The path is something different from the mental act which proceeds along it. The latter is a little more complicated than the common picture

of hysterical imitation; it consists in the unconscious drawing of an inference, as an example will make clear. Supposing a physician is treating a
woman patient, who is subject to a particular kind of spasm, in a hospital
ward among a number of other patients. He will show no surprise if he
finds one morning that this particular kind of hysterical attack has found
imitators. He will merely say: 'The other patients have seen it and copied
it; it's a case of psychical infection.' That is true; but the psychical infection has occurred along some such lines as these. As a rule, patients know
more about one another than the doctor does about any of them; and after the doctor's visit is over they turn their attention to one another. Let
us imagine that this patient had her attack on a particular day; then the
others will quickly discover that it was caused by a letter from home, the
revival of some unhappy love-affair, or some such thing. Their sympathy
is aroused and they draw the following inference, though it fails to penetrate into consciousness: 'If a cause like this can produce an attack like
this, I may have the same kind of attack since I have the same grounds for
having it.' If this inference were capable of entering consciousness, it
might possibly give rise to a *fear* of having the same kind of attack. But
in fact the inference is made in a different psychical region, and consequently results in the actual realization of the dreaded symptom. Thus
identification is not simple imitation but *assimilation* on the basis of a
similar aetiological pretension; it expresses a resemblance and is derived
from a common element which remains in the unconscious.

Identification is most frequently used in hysteria to express a common
sexual element. A hysterical woman identifies herself in her symptoms
most readily—though not exclusively—with people with whom she has
had sexual relations or with people who have had sexual relations with the
same people as herself. Linguistic usage takes this into account, for two
lovers are spoken of as being 'one.' In hysterical phantasies, just as in
dreams, it is enough for purposes of identification that the subject should
have *thoughts* of sexual relations without their having necessarily taken
place in reality. Thus the patient whose dream I have been discussing was
merely following the rules of hysterical processes of thought in expressing
her jealousy of her friend (which incidentally she herself knew was unjustified) by taking her place in the dream and identifying herself with her
by creating a symptom—the renounced wish. The process might be expressed verbally thus: my patient put herself in her friend's place in the
dream because her friend was taking my patient's place with her husband

and because she (my patient) wanted to take her friend's place in her husband's high opinion.[1]

A contradiction to my theory of dreams produced by another of my women patients (the cleverest of all my dreamers) was resolved more simply, but upon the same pattern: namely that the non-fulfilment of one wish meant the fulfilment of another. One day I had been explaining to her that dreams are fulfilments of wishes. Next day she brought me a dream in which she was travelling down with her mother-in-law to the place in the country where they were to spend their holidays together. Now I knew that she had violently rebelled against the idea of spending the summer near her mother-in-law and that a few days earlier she had successfully avoided the propinquity she dreaded by engaging rooms in a far distant resort. And now her dream had undone the solution she had wished for: was not this the sharpest possible contradiction of my theory that in dreams wishes are fulfilled? No doubt; and it was only necessary to follow the dream's logical consequence in order to arrive at its interpretation. The dream showed that I was wrong. *Thus it was her wish that I might be wrong, and her dream showed that wish fulfilled.* But her wish that I might be wrong, which was fulfilled in connection with her summer holidays, related in fact to another and more serious matter. For at about the same time I had inferred from the material produced in her analysis that at a particular period of her life something must have occurred that was of importance in determining her illness. She had disputed this, since she had no recollection of it; but soon afterwards it had turned out that I was right.

---

[1] I myself regret the insertion into my argument of excerpts from the psychopathology of hysteria. [See p. 128 f.] Their fragmentary presentation and detachment from their context cannot fail to detract from their enlightening effect. If, however, they serve to indicate the intimate connection between the topic of dreams and that of the psychoneuroses, they will have fulfilled the purpose for which they are inserted.—[This is Freud's first published discussion of identification, though he had referred to it earlier, in his correspondence with Fliess (e.g. in Letter 58 of February 8, 1897, and Manuscript L of May 2, 1897). Though he touched upon the subject here and there in later publications, his first lengthy consideration of it after the present one was more than twenty years later—in Chapter VII of *Group Psychology* (Freud, 1921c). The different topic of identification as part of the dream-work is discussed below on pp. 336 f.]

Thus her wish that I might be wrong, which was transformed into her dream of spending her holidays with her mother-in-law, corresponded to a well-justified wish that the events of which she was then becoming aware for the first time might never have occurred.

I have ventured to interpret—without any analysis, but only by a guess—a small episode which occurred to a friend of mine who was in the same class as I was all through our career at a secondary school. One day he listened to a lecture which I gave before a small audience on the novel idea that dreams were wish-fulfilments. He went home and dreamt that *he had lost all his cases* (he was a barrister) and afterwards arraigned me on the subject. I evaded the issue by telling him that after all one can't win *all* one's cases. But to myself I thought: 'Considering that for eight whole years I sat on the front bench as top of the class while he drifted about somewhere in the middle, he can hardly fail to nourish a wish, left over from his schooldays, that some day or other *I* may come a complete cropper.'

A dream of a gloomier kind was also brought up against me by a patient as an objection to the theory of wishful dreams.

The patient, who was a young girl, began thus: 'As you will remember, my sister has only one boy left now—Karl; she lost his elder brother, Otto, while I was still living with her. Otto was my favourite; I more or less brought him up. I'm fond of the little one too, but of course not nearly so fond as I was of the one who died. Last night, then, I dreamt that *I saw Karl lying before me dead. He was lying in his little coffin with his hands folded and with candles all round—in fact just like little Otto, whose death was such a blow to me.* Now tell me, what can that mean? You know me. Am I such a wicked person that I can wish my sister to lose the one child she still has? Or does the dream mean that I would rather Karl were dead than Otto whom I was so much fonder of?'

I assured her that this last interpretation was out of the question. And after reflecting a little I was able to give her the correct interpretation of the dream, which she afterwards confirmed. I was able to do so because I was familiar with the whole of the dreamer's previous history.

The girl had early been left an orphan and had been brought up in the house of a much older sister. Among the friends who visited at the house was a man who made a lasting impression on her heart. For a time it had seemed as though her scarcely acknowledged relations with him would lead to marriage; but this happy outcome was brought to nothing by her sister, whose motives were never fully explained. After the breach the man ceased to visit the house; and shortly after the death of little Otto, on to whom she had meanwhile turned her affection, my patient herself set up on her own. She did not succeed, however, in freeing herself from her attachment to her sister's friend. Her pride bade her avoid him; but she was unable to transfer her love to any of the other admirers who presented themselves later. Whenever it was announced that the object of her affections, who was by profession a literary man, was to give a lecture anywhere, she was invariably in the audience; and she took every possible opportunity of seeing him from a distance on neutral ground. I remembered that she had told me the day before that the Professor was going to a particular concert and that she intended to go to it as well so as to enjoy a glimpse of him once more. That had been on the day before the dream, and the concert was to take place on the day on which she told me the dream. It was therefore easy for me to construct the correct interpretation, and I asked her whether she could think of anything that happened after little Otto's death. She answered at once: 'Of course; the Professor came to see us again after a long absence, and I saw him once more beside little Otto's coffin.' This was exactly what I had expected, and I interpreted the dream in this way: 'If now the other boy were to die, the same thing would happen. You would spend the day with your sister and the Professor would be certain to come to offer his condolences, so that you would see him again under the same conditions as the other time. The dream means no more than your wish to see him once more, a wish which you are inwardly struggling against. I know you have a ticket for today's concert in your pocket. Your dream was a dream of impatience: it anticipated the glimpse you are to have of him today by a few hours.'

In order to conceal her wish, she had evidently chosen a situation in which such wishes are usually suppressed, a situation in which one is so much filled with grief that one has no thought of love. Yet it is quite possible that even in the real situation of which the dream was an exact replica, beside the coffin of the elder boy whom she had loved still more, she may have been unable to suppress her tender feelings for the visitor who had been absent so long.[1]

A similar dream of another woman patient had a different explanation. When she was young she had been remarkable for her ready wit and

---

[1] [This dream is referred to again on pp. 266 f. and 469; it is also briefly recorded in Section IX of Freud, 1901*a* (Standard Ed., **5**, 675).]

cheerful disposition; and these characteristics were still to be seen, at all events in the ideas that occurred to her during the treatment. In the course of a longish dream, this lady imagined that she saw her only, fifteen-year-old daughter lying dead 'in a case.' She had half a mind to use the scene as an objection to the wish-fulfilment theory, though she herself suspected that the detail of the 'case' must point the way to another view of the dream.[1] In the course of the analysis she recalled that at a party the evening before there had been some talk about the English word 'box' and the various ways in which it could be translated into German—such as 'Schachtel' ['case'], 'Loge' ['box at the theatre'], 'Kasten' ['chest'], 'Ohrfeige' ['box on the ear'], and so on. Other portions of the same dream enabled us to discover further that she had guessed that the English 'box' was related to the German 'Büchse' ['receptacle'], and that she had then been plagued by a recollection that 'Büchse' is used as a vulgar term for the female genitals. If some allowance was made for the limits of her knowledge of topographical anatomy, it might be presumed, therefore, that the child lying in the case meant an embryo in the womb. After being enlightened up to this point, she no longer denied that the dream-picture corresponded to a wish of hers. Like so many young married women, she had been far from pleased when she became pregnant; and more than once she had allowed herself to wish that the child in her womb might die. Indeed, in a fit of rage after a violent scene with her husband, she had beaten with her fists on her body so as to hit the child inside it. Thus the dead child was in fact the fulfilment of a wish, but of a wish that had been put aside fifteen years earlier. It is scarcely to be wondered at if a wish that was fulfilled after such a long delay was not recognized. Too much had changed in the interval.[2]

I shall have to return to the group of dreams to which the last two examples belong (dreams dealing with the death of relatives of whom the dreamer is fond) when I come to consider 'typical' dreams [pp. 266 ff.]. I shall then be able to show from further instances that, in spite of their unwished-for contents, all such dreams must be interpreted as wish-fulfilments.

---

[1] Like the smoked salmon in the dream of the abandoned supper-party. [See above, p. 172 f.]

[2] [This dream is further discussed on p. 267 and is also reported briefly in Lecture XIII of Freud's *Introductory Lectures* (1916–17).]

I owe the following dream, not to a patient, but to an intelligent jurist of my acquaintance. He told it to me, once again, in order to restrain me from rash generalizing on the theory of wishful dreams. 'I dreamt,' said my informant, 'that *I came up to my house with a lady on my arm. A closed carriage was standing in front of it and a man came up to me, showed me his credentials as a police officer and requested me to follow him. I asked him to allow me a little time to put my affairs in order.* Can you suppose that I have a wish to be arrested?'—Of course not, I could only agree. Do you happen to know the charge on which you were arrested?—'Yes, for infanticide, I believe.'—Infanticide? But surely you're aware that that's a crime that can only be committed by a mother on a newborn child?—'Quite true.'[1]—And what were the circumstances in which you had the dream? What happened on the previous evening?—'I would prefer not to tell you. It's a delicate matter.'—Nevertheless I shall have to hear it; otherwise we shall have to give up the idea of interpreting the dream.—'Very well then, listen. I didn't spend last night at home but with a lady who means a great deal to me. When we woke up in the morning there was a further passage between us, after which I went to sleep again and had the dream I described to you.'—Is she a married woman?—'Yes.'—And you don't want to have a child by her?—'Oh, no; that might give us away.'—So you don't practice normal intercourse?—'I take the precaution of withdrawing before ejaculation.'—I think I may assume that you had used this device several times during the night, and that after repeating it in the morning you felt a little uncertain whether you had carried it out successfully.—'That's possible, no doubt.'—In that case your dream was the fulfilment of a wish. It gave you a reassurance that you had not procreated a child, or, what amounts to the same thing, that you had killed a child. The intermediate links are easily indicated. You remember that a few days ago we were talking about marriage difficulties and how inconsistent it is that there should be no objection to carrying out intercourse in such a way that no fertilization takes place, whereas any interference when once the ovum and semen have come together and a foetus has been formed is punished as a crime. We went on to recall the mediaeval controversy over the exact point of

---

[1] It often happens that the account first given of a dream is incomplete and that the memory of the omitted portions only emerges in the course of analysis. These subsequently added portions regularly turn out to provide the key to the dream's interpretation. Cf. the discussion below on the forgetting of dreams [pp. 522 ff.].

time at which the soul enters the foetus, since it is not until after that that the concept of murder becomes applicable. No doubt, too, you know Lenau's gruesome poem ['Das tote Glück'] in which child murder and child prevention are equated.—'Oddly enough I happened to think of Lenau this morning, quite by chance, as it seemed.'—An after-echo of your dream. And now I can show you another incidental wish-fulfilment contained in your dream. You came up to your house with the lady on your arm. Thus you were bringing her home,[1] instead of spending the night in her house as you did in reality. There may be more than one reason why the wish-fulfilment which constitutes the core of the dream was disguised in such a disagreeable form. Perhaps you have learned from my paper on the aetiology of anxiety neurosis [Freud, 1895b] that I regard *coitus interruptus* as one of the aetiological factors in the development of neurotic anxiety? It would tally with this if, after carrying out sexual intercourse in this way several times, you were left in an uneasy mood which afterwards became an element in the construction of your dream. Moreover, you made use of this moodiness to help disguise the wish-fulfilment. [Cf. p. 492.] Incidentally, your reference to infanticide has not been explained. How did you come to light on this specifically feminine crime?— 'I must admit that some years ago I became involved in an occurrence of that kind. I was responsible for a girl's trying to avoid the consequence of a love-affair with me by means of an abortion. I had nothing to do with her carrying out her intention, but for a long time I naturally felt very nervous in case the business came out.'—I quite understand that. This recollection provides a second reason why you must have been worried by your suspicion that your device might have gone wrong.[2]

A young physician who heard me describe this dream during a course of lectures must have been greatly struck by it, for he promptly re-dreamt it, applying the same pattern of thought to another theme. The day before, he had sent in his income tax return, which he had filled in perfectly honestly, since he had very little to declare. He then had a dream that *an acquaintance of his came to him from a meeting of the tax commissioners and informed him that, while no objection had been raised to any of the other tax returns, general suspicion had been aroused by his and a heavy fine had been imposed on him.* The dream was a poorly disguised fulfilment of his wish

---

[1] [The German '*heimführen*' means both 'to bring home' and 'to marry.']

[2] [This dream was recorded in Draft I, attached to Freud's letter to Fliess of May 2, 1897 (Freud, 1950a, Letter 61).]

to be known as a doctor with a large income. It recalls the well-known story of the girl who was advised not to accept a suitor because he had a violent temper and would be sure to beat her if they were married. 'If only he'd begun beating me already!' the girl replied. Her wish to be married was so intense that she was ready to take the threatened unpleasantness into the bargain, and even went so far as to turn it into a wish.

The very frequent dreams,[1] which appear to stand in contradiction to my theory because their subject-matter is the frustration of a wish or the occurrence of something clearly unwished-for, may be brought together under the heading of 'counter-wish dreams.' If these dreams are considered as a whole, it seems to me possible to trace them back to two principles; I have not yet mentioned one of these, although it plays a large part not only in people's dreams but in their lives as well. One of the two motive forces leading to such dreams is the wish that I may be wrong. These dreams appear regularly in the course of my treatments when a patient is in a state of resistance to me; and I can count almost certainly on provoking one of them after I have explained to a patient for the first time my theory that dreams are fulfilment of wishes.[2] Indeed, it is to be expected that the same thing will happen to some of the readers of the present book: they will be quite ready to have one of their wishes frustrated in a dream if only their wish that I may be wrong can be fulfilled.

The same point is illustrated by one last dream of the kind which I will quote from a patient under treatment. This was the dream of a girl who had succeeded in her struggle to continue her treatment with me against the will of her relatives and of the authorities whose opinions had been consulted. *She dreamt that her people forbade her to go on coming to me. She then reminded me of a promise I had given her that if necessary I would continue the treatment without a fee. To this I replied: 'I cannot make any allowances in money matters.'* It must be admitted that it was not easy to point to the wish-fulfilment in this instance. But in all such cases one discovers a second riddle, the solution of which helps one to solve the original one. What was the origin of the words she put into my mouth? Of course I had said nothing of the kind to her; but one of her brothers,

---

[1] [This paragraph and the next were added in 1909.]

[2] [*Footnote added* 1911:] During the last few years similar 'counter-wish dreams' have repeatedly been reported to me by people who have heard me lecturing, as a reaction to first making the acquaintance of my 'wishful' theory of dreams.

and the one by whom she was most influenced, had been good enough to attribute this sentiment to me. The dream was thus intended to prove her brother right. And it was not only in her dreams that she insisted on his being right; the same idea dominated her whole life and it was the motive of her illness.

A dream[1] which seems at first sight to put special difficulties in the way of the wish-fulfilment theory was dreamt and interpreted by a physician, and reported by August Stärcke (1911): '*I saw upon my left index-finger the first indication [Primäraffekt] of syphilis on the terminal phalange.*' The reflection that, apart from the dream's unwished-for content, it appears to be clear and coherent, might dissuade us from analysing it. If, however, we are prepared to face the trouble involved, we shall find that '*Primäraffekt*' was equivalent to a '*prima affectio*' (a first love), and that the repellent ulcer turned out, to quote Stärcke's words, to 'stand for wish-fulfilments that were highly charged with emotion.'

The second motive for counter-wish dreams[2] is so obvious that it is easy to overlook it, as I did myself for some considerable time. There is a masochistic component in the sexual constitution of many people, which arises from the reversal of an aggressive, sadistic component into its opposite.[3] Those who find their pleasure, not in having *physical* pain inflicted on them, but in humiliation and mental torture, may be described as 'mental masochists.' It will at once be seen that people of this kind can have counter-wish dreams and unpleasurable dreams, which are none the less wish-fulfilments since they satisfy their masochistic inclinations. I will quote one such dream, produced by a young man who in his earlier years had greatly tormented his elder brother, to whom he had a homosexual attachment. His character having undergone a fundamental change, he had the following dream, which was in three pieces: *I. His elder brother was chaffing him. II. Two grown men were caressing each other with a homosexual purpose. III. His brother had sold the business of which he himself had looked forward to becoming the director.* He awoke from the last dream with the most distressing feelings. Nevertheless it was a masochistic wishful dream, and might be translated thus: 'It would serve me right if my brother were to confront me with this sale as a punishment for all the torments he had to put up with from me.'

---

[1] [This paragraph was added in 1914.]
[2] [This paragraph was added in 1909.]
[3] [The author's amended views on this subject will be found in Freud, 1924c.]

I hope that the foregoing examples will be enough (till the next objection is raised) to make it seem plausible that even dreams with a distressing content are to be construed as wish-fulfilments.[1] Nor will anyone regard it as a chance coincidence that the interpretation of these dreams has brought us up each time against topics about which people are loth to speak or to think. The distressing feeling aroused by these dreams is no doubt identical with the repugnance which tends (usually with success) to restrain us from discussing or mentioning such topics, and which each of us has to overcome if we nevertheless find ourselves compelled to embark on them. But the unpleasurable feeling which thus recurs in dreams does not disprove the existence of a wish. Everyone has wishes that he would prefer not to disclose to other people, and wishes that he will not admit even to himself. On the other hand, we are justified in linking the unpleasurable character of all these dreams with the fact of dream-distortion. And we are justified in concluding that these dreams are distorted and the wish-fulfilment contained in them disguised to the point of being unrecognizable precisely owing to the repugnance felt for the topic of the dream or for the wish derived from it and to an intention to repress them. The distortion in the dream is thus shown in fact to be an act of the censorship. We shall be taking into account everything that has been brought to light by our analysis of unpleasurable dreams if we make the following modification in the formula in which we have sought to express the nature of dreams: *a dream is a (disguised) fulfilment of a (suppressed or repressed) wish.*[2]

There remain to be discussed anxiety-dreams as a special sub-species of dreams with a distressing content. The notion of regarding these as wishful dreams will meet with very little sympathy from the unenlightened.

---

[1] [The following sentence was included in the text, in a slightly different form, in 1919 and printed as a footnote in 1925:] 'I must point out that the subject is not yet finally disposed of; I shall return to it later on.' [See pp. 557.]

[2] [*Footnote added* 1914:] A great living writer, who, as I have been told, refuses to hear anything of psycho-analysis or the interpretation of dreams, has independently arrived at an almost identical formula for the nature of dreams. He speaks of a dream as 'the unauthorized emergence of suppressed desires and wishes, under false features and name.' (Spitteler, 1914, 1.)

[*Added* 1911:] I shall anticipate questions which will be discussed later by quoting at this point Otto Rank's enlargement and modification of the above basic formula: 'On the basis and with the help of repressed, infantile sexual material, dreams regularly represent present-day, and also as a rule erotic, wishes as fulfilled, in a veiled and symbolically disguised shape.' (Rank, 1910, [519].)

Nevertheless I can deal with anxiety-dreams very briefly at this point. They do not present us with a new aspect of the dream-problem; what they face us with is the whole question of neurotic anxiety. The anxiety that we feel in a dream is only *apparently* explained by the dream's content. If we submit the content of the dream to analysis, we find that the anxiety in the dream is no better justified by the dream's content than, let us say, the anxiety in a phobia is justified by the idea to which the phobia relates. No doubt it is true, for instance, that it is possible to fall out of a window and that there is therefore reason for exercising a certain degree of caution in the neighbourhood of a window; but we cannot see why the anxiety felt in a phobia on this subject is so great and pursues the patient far beyond its occasion.[1] We find then that the same thing may be validly asserted both of phobias and of anxiety-dreams: in both cases the anxiety is only superficially attached to the idea that accompanies it; it originates from another source.

[*Added* 1925:] I have nowhere stated that I adopted Rank's formula as my own. The shorter version, as stated in the text above, seems to me adequate. But the mere fact of my having mentioned Rank's modification has been enough to unleash countless accusations against psychoanalysis of having asserted that 'all dreams have a sexual content.'

If this sentence is taken in the sense in which it was intended, it merely shows the unconscientious manner in which critics are accustomed to perform their functions, and the readiness with which opponents overlook the clearest statements if they do not give scope to their aggressive inclinations. For only a few pages earlier [pp. 152 ff.] I had mentioned the variety of the wishes whose fulfilments are to be found in children's dreams (wishes to take part in an excursion or a sail on a lake, or to make up for a missed meal, and so on); and in other passages I had discussed dreams of hunger [p. 155 *n*.], dreams stimulated by thirst [pp. 148 f.] or by excretory needs, and dreams of mere convenience [p. 150]. Even Rank himself made no absolute assertion. The words he used were 'also *as a rule* erotic wishes,' and what he said can be amply confirmed in the dreams of most adults.

The situation would be different if 'sexual' was being used by my critics in the sense in which it is now commonly employed in psychoanalysis—in the sense of 'Eros.' But my opponents are scarcely likely to have had in mind the interesting problem of whether all dreams are created by 'libidinal' instinctual forces as contrasted with 'destructive' ones. [Cf. Freud, *The Ego and the Id*, Chapter IV (Freud, 1923*b*).]

[1] [This particular form of phobia, the fear of falling out of windows, was referred to by Freud in a letter to Fliess of December 12, 1896 (Freud, 1950*a*, Letter 53), and again much later in his paper on 'Dreams and Telepathy' (Freud, 1922*a*).]

Since this intimate connection exists between anxiety in dreams and in neuroses, in discussing the former I must refer to the latter. In a short paper on anxiety-neurosis (Freud, 1895*b*), I argued some time ago that neurotic anxiety is derived from sexual life and corresponds to libido which has been diverted from its purpose and has found no employment.[1] Since then this formula has met the test of time; and it enables us now to infer from it that anxiety-dreams are dreams with a sexual content, the libido belonging to which has been transformed into anxiety. There will be an opportunity later to support this assertion by the analysis of some neurotic patients' dreams.[2] In the course, too, of a further attempt to arrive at a theory of dreams, I shall have occasion to discuss once more the determinants of anxiety-dreams and their compatibility with the theory of wish-fulfilment.

---

[1] [The author's later views on the relation between libido and anxiety will be found in his *Inhibitions, Symptoms and Anxiety* (1926*d*).]

[2] [Freud evidently changed his mind on this point: see pp. 578 ff., where, however, two anxiety-dreams are analysed and the whole subject of anxiety-dreams is again discussed.]

CHAPTER V

THE MATERIAL AND SOURCES OF DREAMS

WHEN the analysis of the dream of Irma's injection showed us that a dream could be the fulfilment of a wish, our interest was at first wholly absorbed by the question of whether we had come upon a universal characteristic of dreams, and for the time being we stifled our curiosity about any other scientific problems that may have arisen during the work of the interpretation. Having followed one path to its end, we may now retrace our steps and choose another starting-point for our rambles through the problems of dream-life: for the time being, we may leave the topic of wish-fulfilment on one side, though we are still far from having exhausted it.

Now that the application of our procedure for interpreting dreams enables us to disclose a *latent* content in them which is of far greater significance than their *manifest* one, the pressing task at once arises of re-examining one by one the various problems raised by dreams, to see whether we may not now be in a position to find satisfactory solutions for the conundrums and contradictions which seemed intractable so long as we were only acquainted with the manifest content.

In the first chapter I have given a detailed account of the views of the authorities on the relation of dreams with waking life [Section A] and on the origin of the material of dreams [Section C]. No doubt, too, my readers will recall the three characteristics of memory in dreams [Section B], which have been so often remarked on but which have never been explained:

(1) Dreams show a clear preference for the impressions of the immediately preceding days [pp. 50 f.]. Cf. Robert [1886, 46], Strümpell [1877, 39], Hildebrandt [1875, 11] and Hallam and Weed [1896, 410 f.].

(2) They make their selection upon different principles from our waking memory, since they do not recall what is essential and important but what is subsidiary and unnoticed. [Pp. 51 ff.]

(3) They have at their disposal the earliest impressions of our childhood and even bring up details from that period of our life which, once again, strike us as trivial and which in our waking state we believe to have been long since forgotten. [Pp. 48 ff.][1]

All these peculiarities shown by dreams in their choice of material have, of course, only been studied by earlier writers in connection with their *manifest* content.

(A)

RECENT AND INDIFFERENT MATERIAL IN DREAMS

If I examine my own experience on the subject of the origin of the elements included in the content of dreams, I must begin with an assertion that in every dream it is possible to find a point of contact with the experiences of the previous day. This view is confirmed by every dream that I look into, whether my own or anyone else's. Bearing this fact in mind, I am able, on occasion, to begin a dream's interpretation by looking for the event of the previous day which set it in motion; in many instances, indeed, this is the easiest method.[2] In the two dreams which I have analysed in detail in my last chapters (the dream of Irma's injection and the dream of my uncle with a yellow beard) the connection with the previous day is so obvious as to require no further comment. But in order to show the regularity with which such a connection can be traced, I will go through the records of my own dreams and give some instances. I shall only quote enough of the dream to indicate the source we are looking for:

---

[1] The view adopted by Robert [1886, 9 f.] that the purpose of dreams is to unburden our memory of the useless impressions of daytime [cf. pp. 105 f.] is plainly no longer tenable if indifferent memory images from our childhood appear at all frequently in dreams. Otherwise we could only conclude that dreams perform their function most inadequately.

[2] [The different ways of beginning the interpretation of a dream are discussed in Section I of Freud, 1923*c*.]

(1) *I was visiting a house into which I had difficulty in gaining admittance . . . ; in the meantime I kept a lady* WAITING.

Source: I had had a conversation with a female relative the evening before in which I had told her that she would have to *wait* for a purchase she wanted to make till . . . etc.

(2) *I had written a* MONOGRAPH *on a certain* (indistinct) *species of plant.*

Source: That morning I had seen a *monograph* on the genus Cyclamen in the window of a bookshop. [See below, pp. 193 ff.]

(3) *I saw two women in the street,* A MOTHER AND DAUGHTER, *the latter of whom was a patient of mine.*

Source: One of my patients had explained to me the previous evening the difficulties her *mother* was putting in the way of her continuing her treatment.

(4) *I took out a subscription in S. and R.'s bookshop for a periodical costing* TWENTY FLORINS *a year.*

Source: My wife had reminded me the day before that I still owed her *twenty florins* for the weekly household expenses.

(5) *I received a* COMMUNICATION *from the Social Democratic Committee, treating me as though I were a* MEMBER.

Source: I had received *communications* simultaneously from the Liberal Election *Committee* and from the Council of the Humanitarian League, of which latter body I was in fact *a member.*

(6) *A man standing on* A CLIFF IN THE MIDDLE OF THE SEA, IN THE STYLE OF BÖCKLIN.

Source: Dreyfus on the *Ile du Diable;* I had had news at the same time from my relatives in *England,* etc.

The question may be raised whether the point of contact with the dream is invariably the events of the *immediately* preceding day or whether it may go back to impressions derived from a rather more extensive period of the most recent past. It is unlikely that this question involves any matter of theoretical importance; nevertheless I am inclined to decide in favour of the exclusiveness of the claims of the day immediately preceding the dream—which I shall speak of as the 'dream-day.' Whenever it has seemed at first that the source of a dream was an impression two or three days earlier, closer enquiry has convinced me that the impression had been recalled on the previous day and thus that it was possible to show that a reproduction of the impression, occurring on the previous day, could be inserted between the day of the original event and the time of the dream; moreover it has been possible to indicate the contingency on the previous day which may have led to the recalling of the older impression.

On the other hand[1] I do not feel convinced that there is any regular interval of biological significance between the instigating daytime impression and its recurrence in the dream. (Swoboda, 1904, has mentioned an initial period of eighteen hours in this connection.)[2]

---

[1] [This paragraph was added in 1909.]

[2] [*Footnote added* 1911:] As I have mentioned in a postscript to my first chapter (p. 120), Hermann Swoboda [1904] has made a far-reaching application to the mental field of the biological periodic intervals of 23 and 28 days discovered by Wilhelm Fliess [1906]. He has asserted in particular that these periods determine the emergence of the elements which appear in dreams. No essential modification in dream-interpretation would be involved if this fact were to be established; it would merely provide a fresh source of origin of dream-material. I have, however, recently made some investigations upon my own dreams, to test how far the 'theory of periodicity' is applicable to them. For this purpose I chose some specially outstanding dream-elements the time of whose appearance in real life could be determined with certainty.

I. DREAM OF OCTOBER 1ST–2ND, 1910

(Fragment) . . . *Somewhere in Italy. Three daughters were showing me some small curios, as though we were in an antique shop, and were sitting on my lap. I commented on one of the objects: 'Why, you got that from me,' and saw plainly before me a small profile relief with the clear-cut features of Savonarola.*

When had I last seen a portrait of Savonarola? My travel-diary proved that I had been in Florence on September 4th and 5th. While I was there I thought I would show my travelling companion the medallion bearing the fanatical monk's features, let into the pavement of the Piazza della Signoria, which marks the place where he was burned. I pointed it out to him, I believe, on the morning of the 3rd. [Misprinted '5th' in recent editions.] Between this impression and its reappearance in the dream 27 + 1 days elapsed—Fliess's 'female period.' Unluckily for the conclusiveness of this example, however, I must add that on the actual 'dream-day' I had a visit (for the first time since my return) from a capable but gloomy-looking medical colleague of mine whom I had many years before nicknamed 'Rabbi Savonarola.' He introduced a patient to me who was suffering from the effects of an accident to the Pontebba express, in which I myself had travelled a week earlier, and my thoughts were thus led back to my recent visit to Italy. The appearance in the content of the dream of the outstanding element 'Savonarola' is thus accounted for by my colleague's visit on the dream-day; and the interval of 28 days is deprived of its significance.

II. Dream of October 10th–11th, 1910

I was once more working at chemistry in the University laboratory. Hofrat L. invited me to come somewhere and walked in front of me along the corridor, holding a lamp or some other instrument before him in his uplifted hand and with his head stretched forward in a peculiar attitude, with a clear-sighted (? far-sighted) look about him. Then we crossed an open space. . . . (The remainder was forgotten.)

The most outstanding point in the content of this dream was the way in which Hofrat L. held the lamp (or magnifying glass) before him, with his eyes peering into the distance. It was many years since I had last seen him; but I knew at once that he was only a substitute figure in the place of someone else, someone greater than he—Archimedes, whose statue stands near the Fountain of Arethusa at Syracuse in that very attitude, holding up his burning-glass and peering out towards the besieging army of the Romans. When did I see that statue for the first (and last) time? According to my diary it was on the evening of September 17th; and between then and the time of the dream 13 + 10 = 23 days had elapsed—Fliess's 'male period.'

Unfortunately, when we go into the interpretation of this dream in greater detail, we once again find that the coincidence loses some of its conclusiveness. The exciting cause of the dream was the news I received on the dream-day that the clinic, in whose lecture room I was able by courtesy to deliver my lectures, was shortly to be removed to another locality. I took it for granted that its new situation would be very out of the way and told myself that in that case I might just as well not have a lecture room at my disposal at all. From that point my thoughts must have gone back to the beginning of my career as University Lecturer when I in fact had no lecture room and when my efforts to get hold of one met with little response from the powerfully placed Hofrats and Professors. In those circumstances I had gone to L., who at that time held the office of Dean of the Faculty and who I believed was friendlily disposed to me, to complain of my troubles. He promised to help me, but I heard nothing more from him. In the dream he was Archimedes, giving me a ποῦ στῶ [footing] and himself leading me to the new locality. Anyone who is an adept at interpretation will guess that the dream-thoughts were not exactly free from ideas of vengeance and self-importance. It seems clear, in any case, that without this exciting cause Archimedes would scarcely have found his way into my dream that night; nor am I convinced that the powerful and still recent impression made on me by the statue in Syracuse might not have produced its effect after some different interval of time.

III. Dream of October 2nd–3rd, 1910

(Fragment) . . . *Something about Professor Oser, who had drawn up the menu for me himself, which had a very soothing effect. . . .* (Some more that was forgotten.)

Havelock Ellis [1911, 224],[1] who has also given some attention to this point, declares that he was unable to find any such periodicity in his dreams in spite of looking for it. He records a dream of being in Spain and of wanting to go to a place called Daraus, Varaus or Zaraus. On waking he could not recall any such place-name, and put the dream on one side. A few months later he discovered that Zaraus was in fact the name of a station on the line between San Sebastian and Bilbao, through which his train had passed 250 days before he had the dream.

I believe, then, that the instigating agent of every dream is to be found among the experiences which one has not yet 'slept on.' Thus the relations of a dream's content to impressions of the most recent past (with the single exception of the day immediately preceding the night of the dream) differ in no respect from its relations to impressions dating from any remoter period. Dreams can select their material from any part of the dreamer's life, provided only that there is a train of thought linking the experience of the dream-day (the 'recent' impressions) with the earlier ones.

But why this preference for recent impressions? We shall form some notion on this point, if we submit one of the dreams in the series I have just quoted [p. 189] to a fuller analysis. For this purpose I shall choose the

---

This dream was a reaction to a digestive disturbance that day, which made me consider whether I should go to one of my colleagues to have a dietary prescribed for me. My reason for choosing Oser for that purpose, who had died in the course of the summer, went back to the death of another University teacher whom I greatly admired, which had occurred shortly before (on October 1st). When had Oser died? and when had I heard of his death? According to a paragraph in the papers he had died on August 22nd. I had been in Holland at that time and had my Vienna newspaper sent on to me regularly; so that I must have read of his death on August 24th or 25th. But here the interval no longer corresponds to either period. It amounts to 7 + 30 + 2 = 39 days or possibly 40 days. I could not recall having spoken or thought of Oser in the meantime.

Intervals such as this one, which cannot be fitted into the theory of periodicity without further manipulation, occur far more frequently in my dreams than intervals which *can* be so fitted. The only relation which I find occurs with regularity is the relation which I have insisted upon in the text and which connects the dream with some impression of the dream-day.

[1] [This paragraph was added in 1914.]

Dream of the Botanical Monograph

I had written a monograph on a certain plant. The book lay before me and I was at the moment turning over a folded coloured plate. Bound up in each copy there was a dried specimen of the plant, as though it had been taken from a herbarium.

Analysis

That morning I had seen a new book in the window of a bookshop, bearing the title *The Genus Cyclamen*—evidently a *monograph* on that plant.

Cyclamens, I reflected, were my wife's *favourite flowers* and I reproached myself for so rarely remembering to *bring* her *flowers*, which was what she liked.—The subject of '*bring flowers*' recalled an anecdote which I had recently repeated to a circle of friends and which I had used as evidence in favour of my theory that forgetting is very often determined by an unconscious purpose and that it always enables one to deduce the secret intentions of the person who forgets.[1] A young woman was accustomed to receiving a bouquet of flowers from her husband on her birthday. One year this token of his affection failed to appear, and she burst into tears. Her husband came in and had no idea why she was crying till she told him that today was her birthday. He clasped his hand to his head and exclaimed: 'I'm so sorry, but I'd quite forgotten. I'll go out at once and fetch your *flowers*.' But she was not to be consoled; for she recognized that her husband's forgetfulness was a proof that she no longer had the same place in his thoughts as she had formerly.—This lady, Frau L., had met my wife two days before I had the dream, had told her that she was feeling quite well and enquired after me. Some years ago she had come to me for treatment.

I now made a fresh start. Once, I recalled, I really *had* written something in the nature of a *monograph on a plant*, namely a dissertation on the *coca-plant* [Freud, 1884e], which had drawn Karl Koller's attention to

---

[1] [The theory was published a few months after the date of the dream, in Freud (1898b), and then incorporated in *The Psychopathology of Everyday Life* (Freud, 1901b).]

the anaesthetic properties of cocaine. I had myself indicated this application of the alkaloid in my published paper, but I had not been thorough enough to pursue the matter further.[1] This reminded me that on the morning of the day after the dream—I had not found time to interpret it till the evening—I had thought about cocaine in a kind of daydream. If ever I got glaucoma, I had thought, I should travel to Berlin and get myself operated on, incognito, in my friend's [Fliess's] house, by a surgeon recommended by him. The operating surgeon, who would have no idea of my identity, would boast once again of how easily such operations could be performed since the introduction of cocaine; and I should not give the slightest hint that I myself had had a share in the discovery. This phantasy had led on to reflections of how awkward it is, when all is said and done, for a physician to ask for medical treatment for himself from his professional colleagues. The Berlin eye-surgeon would not know me, and I should be able to pay his fees like anyone else. It was not until I had recalled this daydream that I realized that the recollection of a specific event lay behind it. Shortly after Koller's discovery, my father had in fact been attacked by glaucoma; my friend Dr. Königstein, the ophthalmic surgeon, had operated on him; while Dr. Koller had been in charge of the cocaine anaesthesia and had commented on the fact that this case had brought together all of the three men who had had a share in the introduction of cocaine.

My thoughts then went on to the occasion when I had last been reminded of this business of the cocaine. It had been a few days earlier, when I had been looking at a copy of a *Festschrift* in which grateful pupils had celebrated the jubilee of their teacher and laboratory director. Among the laboratory's claims to distinction which were enumerated in this book I had seen a mention of the fact that Koller had made his discovery there of the anaesthetic properties of cocaine. I then suddenly perceived that my dream was connected with an event of the previous evening. I had walked home precisely with Dr. Königstein and had got into conversation with him about a matter which never fails to excite my feelings whenever it is raised. While I was talking to him in the entrance-hall, Professor *Gärtner* [Gardener] and his wife had joined us; and I could not help congratulating them both on their *blooming* looks. But Professor Gärtner was one of the authors of the *Festschrift* I have just mentioned, and may well have reminded me of it. Moreover, the Frau L., whose disappointment on

---

[1] [See footnote 1, p. 136.]

her birthday I described earlier, was mentioned—though only, it is true, in another connection—in my conversation with Dr. Königstein.

I will make an attempt at interpreting the other determinants of the content of the dream as well. There was *a dried specimen of the plant* included in the monograph, as though it had been a *herbarium*. This led me to a memory from my secondary school. Our headmaster once called together the boys from the higher forms and handed over the school's herbarium to them to be looked through and cleaned. Some small worms—bookworms—had found their way into it. He does not seem to have had much confidence in my helpfulness, for he handed me only a few sheets. These, as I could still recall, included some Crucifers. I never had a specially intimate contact with botany. In my preliminary examination in botany I was also given a Crucifer to identify—and failed to do so. My prospects would not have been too bright, if I had not been helped out by my theoretical knowledge. I went on from the Cruciferae to the Compositae. It occurred to me that artichokes were Compositae, and indeed I might fairly have called them my *favourite flowers*. Being more generous than I am, my wife often brought me back these favourite flowers of mine from the market.

I saw the monograph which I had written *lying before me*. This again led me back to something. I had had a letter from my friend [Fliess] in Berlin the day before in which he had shown his power of visualization: 'I am very much occupied with your dream-book. *I see it lying finished before me and I see myself turning over its pages.*'[1] How much I envied him his gift as a seer! If only *I* could have seen it lying finished before me!

The folded coloured plate. While I was a medical student I was the constant victim of an impulse only to learn things out of *monographs*. In spite of my limited means, I succeeded in getting hold of a number of volumes of the proceedings of medical societies and was enthralled by their *coloured plates*. I was proud of my hankering for thoroughness. When I myself had begun to publish papers, I had been obliged to make my own drawings to illustrate them and I remembered that one of them had been so wretched that a friendly colleague had jeered at me over it. There followed, I could not quite make out how, a recollection from very early youth. It had once amused my father to hand over a book with *coloured plates* (an account of

---

[1] [Freud's reply to this letter from Fliess is dated March 10, 1898 (Freud, 1950a, Letter 84); so that the dream must have occurred not more than a day or two earlier.]

a journey through Persia) for me and my eldest sister to destroy. Not easy to justify from the educational point of view! I had been five years old at the time and my sister not yet three; and the picture of the two of us blissfully pulling the book to pieces (leaf by leaf, like an *artichoke*, I found myself saying) was almost the only plastic memory that I retained from that period of my life. Then, when I became a student, I had developed a passion for collecting and owning books, which was analogous to my liking for learning out of monographs: a *favourite hobby*. (The idea of '*favourite*' had already appeared in connection with cyclamens and artichokes.) I had become a *bookworm*. I had always, from the time I first began to think about myself, referred this first passion of mine back to the childhood memory I have mentioned. Or rather, I had recognized that the childhood scene was a 'screen memory' for my later bibliophile propensities.[1] And I had early discovered, of course, that passions often lead to sorrow. When I was seventeen I had run up a largish account at the bookseller's and had nothing to meet it with; and my father had scarcely taken it as an excuse that my inclinations might have chosen a worse outlet. The recollection of this experience from the later years of my youth at once brought back to my mind the conversation with my friend Dr. Königstein. For in the course of it we had discussed the same question of my being blamed for being too much absorbed in my *favourite hobbies*.

For reasons with which we are not concerned, I shall not pursue the interpretation of this dream any further, but will merely indicate the direction in which it lay. In the course of the work of analysis I was reminded of my conversation with Dr. Königstein, and I was brought to it from more than one direction. When I take into account the topics touched upon in that conversation, the meaning of the dream becomes intelligible to me. All the trains of thought starting from the dream—the thoughts about my wife's and my own favourite flowers, about cocaine, about the awkwardness of medical treatment among colleagues, about my preference for studying monographs and about my neglect of certain branches of science such as botany—all of these trains of thought, when they were further pursued, led ultimately to one or other of the many ramifications of my conversation with Dr. Königstein. Once again the dream, like the one we first analysed—the dream of Irma's injection—turns out to have been in the nature of a self-justification, a plea on behalf of my own rights. In-

---

[1] Cf. my paper on screen memories [Freud, 1899*a*].

deed, it carried the subject that was raised in the earlier dream a stage further and discussed it with reference to fresh material that had arisen in the interval between the two dreams. Even the apparently indifferent form in which the dream was couched turns out to have had significance. What it meant was: 'After all, I'm the man who wrote the valuable and memorable paper (on cocaine),' just as in the earlier dream I had said on my behalf: 'I'm a conscientious and hard-working student.' In both cases what I was insisting was: 'I may allow myself to do this.' There is, however, no need for me to carry the interpretation of the dream any further, since my only purpose in reporting it was to illustrate by an example the relation between the content of a dream and the experience of the previous day which provoked it. So long as I was aware only of the dream's *manifest* content, it appeared to be related only to a *single* event of the dream-day. But when the analysis was carried out, a *second* source of the dream emerged in another experience of the same day. The first of these two impressions with which the dream was connected was an indifferent one, a subsidiary circumstance: I had seen a book in a shop-window whose title attracted my attention for a moment but whose subject-matter could scarcely be of interest to me. The second experience had a high degree of psychical importance: I had had a good hour's lively conversation with my friend the eye-surgeon; in the course of it I had given him some information which was bound to affect both of us closely, and I had had memories stirred up in me which had drawn my attention to a great variety of internal stresses in my own mind. Moreover, the conversation had been interrupted before its conclusion because we had been joined by acquaintances.

We must now ask what was the relation of the two impressions of the dream-day to each other and to the dream of the subsequent night. In the manifest content of the dream only the *indifferent* impression was alluded to, which seems to confirm the notion that dreams have a preference for taking up unimportant details of waking life. All the strands of the interpretation, on the other hand, led to the *important* impression, to the one which had justifiably stirred my feelings. If the sense of the dream is judged, as it can only rightly be, by its latent content as revealed by the analysis, a new and significant fact is unexpectedly brought to light. The conundrum of why dreams are concerned only with worthless fragments of waking life seems to have lost all its meaning; nor can it any longer be maintained that waking life is not pursued further in dreams and that dreams are thus psychical activity wasted upon foolish material. The contrary is true: our dream-thoughts are dominated by the same material that has occupied us during the day and we only bother to dream of things which have given us cause for reflection in the daytime.

Why is it, then, that, though the occasion of my dreaming was a daytime impression by which I had been justifiably stirred, I nevertheless actually dreamt of something indifferent? The most obvious explanation, no doubt, is that we are once more faced by one of the phenomena of dream-distortion, which in my last chapter I traced to a psychical force acting as a censorship. My recollection of the monograph on the genus Cyclamen would thus serve the purpose of being an *allusion* to the conversation with my friend, just as the 'smoked salmon' in the dream of the abandoned supper-party [pp. 172 f.] served as an *allusion* to the dreamer's thought of her woman friend. The only question is as to the intermediate links which enabled the impression of the monograph to serve as an allusion to the conversation with the eye-surgeon, since at first sight there is no obvious connection between them. In the example of the abandoned supper-party the connection was given at once: 'smoked salmon,' being the friend's favourite dish, was an immediate constituent of the group of ideas which were likely to be aroused in the dreamer's mind by the personality of her friend. In this later example there were two detached impressions which at a first glance only had in common the fact of their having occurred on the same day: I had caught sight of the monograph in the morning and had had the conversation the same evening. The analysis enabled us to solve the problem as follows: connections of this kind, when they are not present in the first instance, are woven retrospectively between the ideational content of one impression and that of the other. I have already drawn attention to the intermediate links in the present case by the words I have italicized in my record of the analysis. If there had been no influences from another quarter, the idea of the monograph on the Cyclamen would only, I imagine, have led to the idea of its being my wife's favourite flower, and possibly also to Frau L.'s absent bouquet. I scarcely think that these background thoughts would have sufficed to evoke a dream. As we are told in *Hamlet*:

> There needs no ghost, my lord, come from the grave
> To tell us this.

But, lo and behold, I was reminded in the analysis that the man who interrupted our conversation was called *Gärtner* [Gardener] and that I had thought his wife looked *blooming*. And even as I write these words I recall that one of my patients, who bore the charming name of *Flora*, was for a time the pivot of our discussion. These must have been the intermediate links, arising from the botanical group of ideas, which formed the bridge between the two experiences of that day, the indifferent and the stirring one. A further set of connections was then established—those surrounding the idea of cocaine, which had every right to serve as a link between the figure of Dr. Königstein and a botanical monograph which I had written; and these connections strengthened the fusion between the two groups of ideas so that it became possible for a portion of the one experience to serve as an allusion to the other one.

I am prepared to find this explanation attacked on the ground of its being arbitrary or artificial. What, it may be asked, would have happened if Professor Gärtner and his wife with her blooming looks had not come up to us or if the patient we were talking about had been called Anna instead of Flora? The answer is simple. If these chains of thought had been absent others would no doubt have been selected. It is easy enough to construct such chains, as is shown by the puns and riddles that people make every day for their entertainment. The realm of jokes knows no boundaries. Or, to go a stage further, if there had been no possibility of forging enough intermediate links between the two impressions, the dream would simply have been different. Another indifferent impression of the same day—for crowds of such impressions enter our minds and are then forgotten—would have taken the place of the 'monograph' in the dream, would have linked up with the subject of the conversation and would have represented it in the content of the dream. Since it was in fact the monograph and not any other idea that was chosen to serve this function, we must suppose that it was the best adapted for the connection. There is no need for us to emulate Lessing's Hänschen Schlau and feel astonished that 'only the rich people own the most money.'[1]

A psychological process by which, according to our account, indifferent experiences take the place of psychically significant ones, cannot fail to arouse suspicion and bewilderment. It will be our task in a later chapter [Chapter VI, Section B (pp. 322 ff.)] to make the peculiarities of this apparently irrational operation more intelligible. At this point we are only

---

[1] [From one of Lessing's *Sinngedichte* (epigrams in verse). A further lengthy discussion of this dream will be found below (pp. 300 ff.).]

concerned with the *effects* of a process whose reality I have been driven to assume by innumerable and regularly recurrent observations made in analysing dreams. What takes place would seem to be something in the nature of a 'displacement'—of psychical emphasis, shall we say?—by means of intermediate links; in this way, ideas which originally had only a *weak* charge of intensity take over the charge from ideas which were originally *intensely* cathected[1] and at last attain enough strength to enable them to force an entry into consciousness. Displacements of this kind are no surprise to us where it is a question of dealing with quantities of *affect* or with motor activities in general. When a lonely old maid transfers her affection to animals, or a bachelor becomes an enthusiastic collector, when a soldier defends a scrap of coloured cloth—a flag—with his life's blood, when a few seconds' extra pressure in a handshake means bliss to a lover, or when, in *Othello*, a lost handkerchief precipitates an outburst of rage— all of these are instances of psychical displacements to which we raise no objection. But when we hear that a decision as to what shall reach our consciousness and what shall be kept out of it—what we shall *think*, in short—has been arrived at in the same manner and on the same principles, we have an impression of a pathological event and, if such things happen in waking life, we describe them as errors in thought. I will anticipate the conclusions to which we shall later be led, and suggest that the psychical process which we have found at work in dream-displacement, though it cannot be described as a pathological disturbance, nevertheless differs from the normal and is to be regarded as a process of a more *primary* nature. [See below, Chapter VII, Section E, pp. 585 ff.]

Thus the fact that the content of dreams includes remnants of trivial experiences is to be explained as a manifestation of dream-distortion (by displacement); and it will be recalled that we came to the conclusion that dream-distortion was the product of a censorship operating in the passage-way between two psychical agencies. It is to be expected that the analysis of a dream will regularly reveal its true, psychically significant source in waking life, though the emphasis has been displaced from the recollection of that source on to that of an indifferent one. This explanation brings us into complete conflict with Robert's theory [pp. 105 ff.], which ceases to be of any service to us. For the fact which Robert sets out to explain is a nonexistent one. His acceptance of it rests on a misunderstanding, on his

---

[1] [Charged with psychical energy. See Editor's Introduction, p. xvi f.]

failure to replace the *apparent* content of dreams by their *real* meaning. And there is another objection that can be raised to Robert's theory. If it were really the business of dreams to relieve our memory of the 'dregs' of daytime recollections by a special psychical activity, our sleep would be more tormented and harder worked than our mental life while we are awake. For the number of indifferent impressions from which our memory would need to be protected is clearly immensely large: the night would not be long enough to cope with such a mass. It is far more likely that the process of forgetting indifferent impressions goes forward without the active intervention of our psychical forces.

Nevertheless we must not be in a hurry to take leave of Robert's ideas without further consideration. [See pp. 577 f.] We have still not explained the fact that one of the indifferent impressions of waking life, one, moreover, dating from the day preceding the dream, invariably contributes towards the dream's content. The connections between this impression and the true source of the dream in the unconscious are not always there ready-made; as we have seen, they may only be established retrospectively, in the course of the dream-work,[1] with a view, as it were, to making the intended displacement feasible. There must therefore be some compelling force in the direction of establishing connections precisely with a recent, though indifferent, impression; and the latter must possess some attribute which makes it especially suitable for this purpose. For if that were not so, it would be just as easy for the dream-thoughts to displace their emphasis on to an unimportant component in their *own* circle of ideas.

The following observations may help us towards clearing up this point. If in the course of a single day we have two or more experiences suitable for provoking a dream, the dream will make a combined reference to them as a single whole; *it is under a necessity to combine them into a unity.* Here is an instance. One afternoon during the summer I entered a railway compartment in which I found two acquaintances who were strangers to each other. One of them was an eminent medical colleague and the other was a member of a distinguished family with which I had professional relations. I introduced the two gentlemen to each other, but all through the long journey they conducted their conversation with me as a go-between, so that I presently found myself discussing various topics alternately, first with the

---

[1] [This is the first mention of the fundamentally important concept to which the whole of the sixth and longest chapter of the book is devoted.]

one and then with the other. I asked my doctor friend to use his influence on behalf of a common acquaintance of ours who was just starting a medical practice. The doctor replied that he was convinced of the young man's capacity, but that his homely appearance would make it hard for him to make his way in families of the better class; to which I replied that that was the very reason why he needed influential assistance. Turning to my other fellow-traveller, I enquired after the health of his aunt—the mother of one of my patients—who was lying seriously ill at the time. During the night following the journey I had a dream that the young friend on whose behalf I had pleaded was sitting in a fashionable drawing room in a select company composed of all the distinguished and wealthy people of my acquaintance and, with the easy bearing of a man of the world, was delivering a funeral oration on the old lady (who was already dead so far as my dream was concerned), the aunt of my second fellow-traveller. (I must confess that I had not been on good terms with that lady.) Thus my dream had, once again, worked out connections between the two sets of impressions of the previous day and had combined them into a single situation.

Many experiences such as this lead me to assert that the dream-work is under some kind of necessity to combine all the sources which have acted as stimuli for the dream into a single unity in the dream itself.[1]

I will now proceed to the question of whether the instigating source of a dream, revealed by analysis, must invariably be a recent (and significant) event or whether an internal experience, that is, the *recollection* of a psychically important event—a train of thought—can assume the rôle of a dream-instigator. The answer, based upon a large number of analyses, is most definitely in favour of the latter alternative. A dream can be instigated by an internal process which has, as it were, become a recent event, owing to thought-activity during the previous day.

---

[1] The tendency of the dream-work to fuse into a single action all events of interest which occur simultaneously has already been remarked on by several writers; e.g. Delage (1891, 41) and Delboeuf (1885, 237), who speaks of '*rapprochement forcé*' ['enforced convergence']. [Freud himself had stated this principle in the passage in *Studies on Hysteria* (Breuer and Freud, 1895) quoted in the Editor's Introduction (p. xiv).—At this point the following sentence was added in 1909 and included in every edition up to that of 1922, after which it was omitted: 'In a later chapter (on the dream-work) we shall come across this compelling impulse towards combining as an instance of "condensation"—another kind of primary psychical process.' (Cf. pp. 248 and 296 ff.)]

This seems to be the appropriate moment for tabulating the different conditions to which we find that the sources of dreams are subject. The source of a dream may be either—

(*a*) a recent and psychically significant experience which is represented in the dream directly,[1] or

(*b*) several recent and significant experiences which are combined into a single unity by the dream,[2] or

(*c*) one or more recent and significant experiences which are represented in the content of the dream by a mention of a contemporary but indifferent experience,[3] or

(*d*) an internal significant experience (e.g. a memory or a train of thought), which is in that case *invariably* represented in the dream by a mention of a recent but indifferent impression.[4]

It will be seen that in interpreting dreams we find one condition always fulfilled: one component of the content of the dream is a repetition of a recent impression of the previous day. This impression that is to be represented in the dream may either itself belong to the circle of ideas surrounding the actual instigator of the dream—whether as an essential or as a trivial portion of it—or it may be derived from the field of an indifferent impression which has been brought into connection with the ideas surrounding the dream-instigator by more or less numerous links. The apparent multiplicity of governing conditions is in fact merely dependent upon the two alternatives of whether a displacement has or has not taken place; and it is worth pointing out that we are enabled by these alternatives to explain the range of contrast between different dreams just as easily as the medical theory is enabled to do by its hypothesis of brain cells ranging from partial to total wakefulness. (See above, pp. 107 ff.)

It will further be observed, if we consider these four possible cases, that a psychical element which is significant but not recent (e.g. a train of thought or a memory) can be replaced, for the purpose of forming a dream, by an element which is recent but indifferent, provided only that two conditions are fulfilled: (1) the content of the dream must be connected with a recent experience, and (2) the instigator of the dream must

---

[1] As in the dream of Irma's injection [pp. 131 ff.] and in the dream of my uncle with the yellow beard [pp. 163 ff.].

[2] As in the young doctor's funeral oration [pp. 201 f.].

[3] As in the dream of the botanical monograph [pp. 193 ff.].

[4] Most of my patients' dreams during analysis are of this kind.

remain a psychically significant process. Only in one case—case (*a*)—are both of these conditions fulfilled by one and the same impression. It is to be noticed, moreover, that indifferent impressions which are capable of being used for constructing a dream so long as they are recent lose that capacity as soon as they are a day (or at the most a few days) older. From this we must conclude that the freshness of an impression gives it some kind of psychical value for purposes of dream-construction equivalent in some way to the value of emotionally coloured memories or trains of thought. The basis of the value which thus attaches to recent impressions in connection with the construction of dreams will only become evident in the course of our subsequent psychological discussions.[1]

In this connection it will be noticed, incidentally, that modifications in our mnemic and ideational material may take place during the night unobserved by our consciousness. We are often advised that before coming to a final decision on some subject we should 'sleep on it,' and this advice is evidently justified. But here we have passed from the psychology of dreams to that of sleep, and this is not the last occasion on which we shall be tempted to do so.[2]

---

[1] See the passage on 'transference' in Chapter VII [pp. 562 ff.].

[2] [*Footnote added* 1919:] An important contribution to the part played by recent material in the construction of dreams has been made by Pötzl (1917) in a paper which carries a wealth of implications. In a series of experiments Pötzl required the subjects to make a drawing of what they had consciously noted of a picture exposed to their view in a tachistoscope [an instrument for exposing an object to view for an extremely short time]. He then turned his attention to the dreams dreamt by the subjects during the following night and required them once more to make drawings of appropriate portions of these dreams. It was shown unmistakably that those details of the exposed picture which had not been noted by the subject provided material for the construction of the dream, whereas those details which had been consciously perceived and recorded in the drawing made after the exposure did not recur in the manifest content of the dream. The material that was taken over by the dream-work was modified by it for the purposes of dream-construction in its familiar 'arbitrary' (or, more properly, 'autocratic') manner. The questions raised by Pötzl's experiment go far beyond the sphere of dream-interpretation as dealt with in the present volume. In passing, it is worth remarking on the contrast between this new method of studying the formation of dreams experimentally and the earlier, crude technique for introducing into the dream stimuli which interrupted the subject's sleep. [Cf. p. 243 *n.* 2.]

An objection, however, may be raised which threatens to upset these last conclusions. If indifferent impressions can only find their way into a dream provided they are recent, how does it happen that the content of dreams also includes elements from an earlier period of life which at the time when they were recent possessed, to use Strümpell's words [1877, 40 f.], no psychical value, and should therefore have been long since forgotten—elements, that is to say, which are neither fresh nor psychically significant?

This objection can be completely dealt with by a reference to the findings of the psycho-analysis of neurotics. The explanation is that the displacement which replaces psychically important by indifferent material (alike in dreaming and in thinking) has in these cases already taken place at the early period of life in question and since then become fixed in the memory. These particular elements which were originally indifferent are indifferent no longer, since taking over (by means of displacement) the value of psychically significant material. Nothing that has *really* remained indifferent can be reproduced in a dream.

The reader will rightly conclude from the foregoing arguments that I am asserting that there are no indifferent dream-instigators—and consequently no 'innocent' dreams. Those are, in the strictest and most absolute sense, my opinions—if I leave on one side the dreams of children and perhaps brief reactions in dreams to sensations felt during the night. Apart from this, what we dream is either manifestly recognizable as psychically significant, or it is distorted and cannot be judged till the dream has been interpreted, after which it will once more be found to be significant. Dreams are never concerned with trivialities; we do not allow our sleep to be disturbed by trifles.[1] The apparently innocent dreams turn out to be quite the reverse when we take the trouble to analyse them. They are, if I may say so, wolves in sheep's clothing. Since this is another point upon which I may expect to be contradicted, and since I am glad of an opportunity of showing dream-distortion at work, I will select a number of 'innocent' dreams from my records and submit them to analysis.

---

[1] [*Footnote added* 1914:] Havelock Ellis, a friendly critic of this book, writes (1911, 166): 'This is the point at which many of us are no longer able to follow Freud.' Havelock Ellis has not, however, carried out any analyses of dreams and refuses to believe how impossible it is to base one's judgement on their manifest content.

I

An intelligent and cultivated young woman, reserved and undemonstrative in her behaviour, reported as follows: *I dreamt that I arrived too late at the market and could get nothing either from the butcher or from the woman who sells vegetables.* An innocent dream, no doubt; but dreams are not as simple as that, so I asked to be told it in greater detail. She thereupon gave me the following account. *She dreamt she was going to the market with her cook, who was carrying the basket. After she had asked for something, the butcher said to her: 'That's not obtainable any longer,' and offered her something else, adding, 'This is good too.' She rejected it and went on to the woman who sells vegetables, who tried to get her to buy a peculiar vegetable that was tied up in bundles but was of a black colour. She said: 'I don't recognize that; I won't take it.'*

The dream's connection with the previous day was quite straightforward. She had actually gone to the market too late and had got nothing. The situation seemed to shape itself into the phrase *'Die Fleischbank war schon geschlossen* ['the meat-shop was closed']. I pulled myself up: was not that, or rather its opposite, a vulgar description of a certain sort of slovenliness in a man's dress?[1] However, the dreamer herself did not use the phrase; she may perhaps have avoided using it. Let us endeavour, then, to arrive at an interpretation of the details of the dream.

When anything in a dream has the character of direct speech, that is to say, when it is said or heard and not merely thought (and it is easy as a rule to make the distinction with certainty), then it is derived from something actually spoken in waking life—though, to be sure, this something is merely treated as raw material and may be cut up and slightly altered and, more especially, divorced from its context.[2] In carrying out an interpretation, one method is to start from spoken phrases of this kind. What, then, was the origin of the butcher's remark *'That's not obtainable any longer'*? The answer was that it came from me myself. A few days earlier I had ex-

---

[1] ['*Du hast deine Fleischbank offen*' ('your meat-shop's open'): Viennese slang for 'your fly is undone.']

[2] See my discussion of speeches in dreams in my chapter on the dream-work [pp. 427 ff.]. Only one writer on the subject seems to have recognized the source of spoken phrases occurring in dreams, namely Delboeuf (1885, 226), who compares them to *clichés.* [This dream is briefly recorded in Section VII of Freud's short essay *On Dreams* (1901*a*); Standard Ed., **5**, 668.]

plained to the patient that the earliest experiences of childhood were '*not obtainable any longer* as such,' but were replaced in analysis by 'transferences' and dreams.[1] So *I* was the butcher and she was rejecting these transferences into the present of old habits of thinking and feeling.—What, again, was the origin of her own remark in the dream '*I don't recognize that; I won't take it*'? For the purposes of the analysis this had to be divided up. '*I don't recognize that*' was something she had said the day before to her cook, with whom she had had a dispute; but at the time she had gone on: '*Behave yourself properly!*' At this point there had clearly been a displacement. Of the two phrases that she had used in the dispute with her cook, she had chosen the insignificant one for inclusion in the dream. But it was only the suppressed one, '*Behave yourself properly!*' that fitted in with the rest of the content of the dream: those would have been the appropriate words to use if someone had ventured to make improper suggestions and had forgotten 'to close his meat-shop.' The allusions underlying the incident with the vegetable-seller were a further confirmation that our interpretation was on the right track. A vegetable that is sold tied up in bundles (lengthways, as the patient added afterwards) and is also black, could only be a dream-combination of asparagus and black (Spanish) radishes. No knowledgeable person of either sex will ask for an interpretation of asparagus. But the other vegetable—'*Schwarzer Rettig*' ['black radish']—can be taken as an exclamation—'*Schwarzer, rett' dich!*' ['Blacky! Be off!']—[2], and accordingly it too seems to hint at the same sexual topic which we suspected at the very beginning, when we felt inclined to introduce the phrase about the meat-shop being closed into the original account of the dream. We need not enquire now into the full meaning of the dream. So much is quite clear: it *had* a meaning and that meaning was far from innocent.[3]

---

[1] [This passage is referred to in a footnote to a discussion of childhood memories in Section V of Freud's case history of the 'Wolf Man' (1918*b*).]

[2] [It seems probable that this is a reminiscence of a picture puzzle or rebus of the kind so common in the pages of *Fliegende Blätter* and similar comic papers.]

[3] If anyone is curious to know, I may add that the dream concealed a phantasy of my behaving in an improper and sexually provocative manner, and of the patient putting up a defence against my conduct. If this interpretation seems incredible, I need only point to the numerous instances in which doctors have charges of the same kind brought against them by hysterical women. But in such cases the phantasy emerges into consciousness undisguised and in the form of a delusion, instead of being distorted and appearing only as a dream.—[*Added* 1909:] This dream occurred at the beginning of the patient's psycho-analytic treatment. It was

II

Here is another innocent dream, dreamt by the same patient, and in a sense a counterpart to the last one. *Her husband asked her: 'Don't you think we ought to have the piano tuned?' And she replied: 'It's not worth while; the hammers need reconditioning in any case.'*

Once again this was a repetition of a real event of the previous day. Her husband had asked this question and she had made some such reply. But what was the explanation of her dreaming it? She told me that the piano was a *disgusting* old *box*, that it made an *ugly noise*, that it had been in her husband's possession before their marriage,[1] and so on. But the key to the solution was only given by her words: '*It's not worth while.*' These were derived from a visit she had paid the day before to a woman friend. She had been invited to take off her jacket, but had refused with the words: 'Thank you, but *it's not worth while*; I can only stop a minute.' As she was telling me this, I recollected that during the previous day's analysis she had suddenly caught hold of her jacket, one of the buttons having come undone. Thus it was as though she were saying: 'Please don't look; *it's not worth while.*' In the same way 'box' ['*Kasten*'] was a substitute for a 'chest' ['*Brustkasten*']; and the interpretation of the dream led us back at once to the time of her physical development at puberty, when she had begun to be dissatisfied by her figure. We can hardly doubt that it led back to still earlier times, if we take the word '*disgusting*' into account and the '*ugly noise*,' and if we remember how often—both in *doubles entendres* and in dreams—the lesser hemispheres of a woman's body are used, whether as contrasts or as substitutes, for the larger ones.

III

I will interrupt this series for a moment and insert a short innocent dream produced by a young man. He dreamt that *he was putting on his winter overcoat once more, which was a dreadful thing.* The ostensible reason for

---

not until later that I learnt that she had been repeating in it the initial trauma from which her neurosis had arisen. I have since then come across the same behaviour in other patients; having been exposed to a sexual assault in their childhood, they seek, as it were, to bring about a repetition of it in their dreams.

[1] This last was a substitute for the opposite idea, as the course of the analysis will make clear.

this dream was a sudden return of cold weather. If we look more closely, however, we shall notice that the two short pieces that make up the dream are not in complete harmony. For what could there be 'dreadful' about putting on a heavy or thick overcoat in cold weather? Moreover, the innocence of the dream was decidedly upset by the first association that occurred to the dreamer in the analysis. He recalled that a lady confided to him the day before that her youngest child owed its existence to a torn condom. On that basis he was able to reconstruct his thoughts. A thin condom was dangerous, but a thick one was bad. The condom was suitably represented as an overcoat, since one slips into both of them. But an occurrence such as the lady described to him would certainly be 'dreadful' for an unmarried man. And now let us return, to our innocent lady dreamer.

IV

She was putting a candle into a candlestick; but the candle broke so that it wouldn't stand up properly. The girls at her school said she was clumsy; but the mistress said it was not her fault.

Yet again the occasion for the dream was a real event. The day before she had actually put a candle into a candlestick, though it did not break. Some transparent symbolism was being used in this dream. A candle is an object which can excite the female genitals; and, if it is broken, so that it cannot stand up properly, it means that the man is impotent. (*'It was not her fault.'*) But could a carefully brought-up young woman, who had been screened from the impact of anything ugly, have known that a candle might be put to such a use? As it happened, she was able to indicate how it was that she obtained this piece of knowledge. Once when they were in a rowing boat on the Rhine, another boat had passed them with some students in it. They were in high spirits and were singing, or rather shouting, a song:

> Wenn die Königin von Schweden,
> Bei geschlossenen Fensterläden
> Mit Apollokerzen . . .[1]

---

[1] ['When the Queen of Sweden, behind closed shutters, . . . with Apollo candles.' 'Apollo candles' was the trade name of a familiar brand of candles. This is an extract from a well-known students' song, which has innumerable similar stanzas. The missing word is *'onaniert'* ('masturbates').]

She either failed to hear or did not understand the last word and had to get her husband to give her the necessary explanation. The verse was replaced in the content of the dream by an innocent recollection of some job she had done clumsily when she was at school, and the replacement was made possible owing to the common element of *closed shutters*. The connection between the topics of masturbation and impotence is obvious enough. The 'Apollo' in the latent content of this dream linked it with an earlier one in which the virgin Pallas figured. Altogether far from innocent.

V

In order that we may not be tempted to draw conclusions too easily from dreams as to the dreamer's actual life, I will add one more dream of the same patient's, which once more has an innocent appearance. '*I dreamt,*' she said, '*of what I really did yesterday: I filled a small trunk so full of books that I had difficulty in shutting it and I dreamt just what really happened.*' In this instance the narrator herself laid the chief emphasis on the agreement between the dream and reality. [Cf. pp. 54 *n.* 2 and 384.] All such judgements on a dream and comments upon it, though they have made themselves a place in waking thought, invariably form in fact part of the latent content of the dream, as we shall find confirmed by other examples later on [pp. 453 ff.]. What we were being told, then, was that what the dream described had really happened the day before. It would take up too much space to explain how it was that the idea occurred to me of making use of the English language in the interpretation. It is enough to say that once again what was in question was a little 'box' (cf. the dream of the dead child in the 'case,' pp. 177 f.) which was so full that nothing more could get into it. Anyhow nothing bad this time.

In all of these 'innocent' dreams the motive for the censorship is obviously the sexual factor. This, however, is a subject of prime importance which I must leave on one side.

(B)

INFANTILE MATERIAL AS A SOURCE OF DREAMS

Like every other writer on the subject, with the exception of Robert, I have pointed out as a third peculiarity of the content of dreams that it may include impressions which date back to earliest childhood, and which seem not to be accessible to waking memory. It is naturally hard to determine how rarely or how frequently this occurs, since the origin of the dream-elements in question is not recognized after waking. Proof that what we are dealing with are impressions from childhood must therefore be established by external evidence and there is seldom an opportunity for doing this. A particularly convincing example is that given by Maury [1878, 143 f., quoted on p. 49 above] of the man who determined one day to revisit his old home after an absence of more than twenty years. During the night before his departure he dreamt that he was in a totally unknown place and there met an unknown man in the street and had a conversation with him. When he reached his home, he found that the unknown place was a real one in the immediate neighbourhood of his native town, and the unknown man in the dream turned out to be a friend of his dead father's who was still living there. This was conclusive evidence that he had seen both the man and the place in his childhood. This dream is also to be interpreted as a dream of impatience like that of the girl with the concert-ticket in her pocket (pp. 176 ff.), that of the child whose father had promised to take her on an excursion to the Hameau (cf. pp. 153 f.), and similar ones. The motives which led the dreamers to reproduce one particular impression from their childhood rather than any other cannot, of course, be discovered without an analysis.

Someone who attended a course of lectures of mine and boasted that his dreams very seldom underwent distortion reported to me that not long before he had dreamt of seeing *his former tutor in bed with the nurse* who had been with his family till his eleventh year. In the dream he had identified the locality where the scene occurred. His interest had been aroused and he had reported the dream to his elder brother, who had laughingly confirmed the truth of what he had dreamt. His brother remembered it very well, as he had been six years old at the time. The lovers had been in the habit of making the elder boy drunk with beer, whenever circumstances were favourable for intercourse during the night. The younger boy—the dreamer—who was then three years old and slept in the room with the nurse, was not regarded as an impediment. [See also p. 231.]

There is another way in which it can be established with certainty without the assistance of interpretation that a dream contains elements from childhood. This is where the dream is of what has been called the 'recurrent' type: that is to say, where a dream was first dreamt in childhood and then constantly reappears from time to time during adult sleep.[1] I am able to add to the familiar examples of such dreams a few from my own records, though I have never myself experienced one. A physician in his thirties told me that from the earliest days of his childhood to the present time a yellow lion frequently appeared in his dreams; he was able to give a minute description of it. This lion out of his dreams made its appearance one day in bodily form, as a china ornament that had long disappeared. The young man then learnt from his mother that this object had been his favourite toy during his early childhood, though he himself had forgotten the fact.[2]

If we turn now from the manifest content of dreams to the dream-thoughts which only analysis uncovers, we find to our astonishment that experiences from childhood also play a part in dreams whose content would never have led one to suppose it. I owe a particularly agreeable and instructive example of a dream of this kind to my respected colleague of

---

[1] [See above, p. 73 *n.* Some remarks on 'recurrent' dreams will be found in Freud's 'Fragment of an Analysis of a Case of Hysteria' (1905*e*), at the end of the synthesis of Dora's first dream (Section II). Cf. below, p. 577 *n.*]

[2] [The following further dream appeared at this point in the first edition (1900) only. A note in *Ges. Schriften*, **3** (1925), 38, remarks that it was rightly omitted in all subsequent editions: 'Dreams of this sort are of a *typical* character and correspond not to memories but to phantasies, whose meaning it is not hard to guess.' Here are the cancelled sentences: 'One of my women patients dreamt the same dream—a scene filled with anxiety—four or five times during her thirty-eighth year. She was being pursued, fled into a room, shut the door, and then opened it again to take out the key, which was on the outside of the door. She had a feeling that if she failed something frightful would happen. She got hold of the key, locked the door from the inside and gave a sigh of relief. I cannot say to what age we should assign this little scene, in which, of course, she had only played the part of an audience.']

the yellow lion. After reading Nansen's narrative of his polar expedition, he had a dream of being in a field of ice and of giving the gallant explorer galvanic treatment for an attack of sciatica from which he was suffering. In the course of analysing the dream, he thought of a story dating from his childhood, which alone, incidentally, made the dream intelligible. One day, when he was a child of three or four, he had heard the grownups talking of voyages of discovery and had asked his father whether that was a serious illness. He had evidently confused '*Reisen*' ['voyages'] with '*Reissen*' ['gripes'], and his brothers and sisters saw to it that he never forgot this embarrassing mistake.

There was a similar instance of this when, in the course of my analysis of the dream of the monograph on the genus Cyclamen [see above p. 195 f.], I stumbled upon the childhood memory of my father, when I was a boy of five, giving me a book illustrated with coloured plates to destroy. It may perhaps be doubted whether this memory really had any share in determining the form taken by the content of the dream or whether it was not rather that the process of analysis built up the connection subsequently. But the copious and intertwined associative links warrant our accepting the former alternative: cyclamen—favourite flower—favourite food— artichokes; pulling to pieces like an artichoke, leaf by leaf (a phrase constantly ringing in our ears in relation to the piecemeal dismemberment of the Chinese Empire)—herbarium—bookworms, whose favourite food is books. Moreover I can assure my readers that the ultimate meaning of the dream, which I have not disclosed, is intimately related to the subject of the childhood scene.

In the case of another group of dreams, analysis shows us that the actual wish which instigated the dream, and the fulfilment of which is represented by the dream, is derived from childhood; so that, to our surprise, *we find the child and the child's impulses still living on in the dream.*

At this point I shall once more take up the interpretation of a dream which we have already found instructive—the dream of my friend R. being my uncle. [See pp. 162 ff.] We have followed its interpretation to the point of recognizing clearly as one of its motives my wish to be appointed to a professorship; and we explained the affection I felt in the dream for my friend R. as a product of opposition and revolt against the slanders upon my two colleagues which were contained in the dream-thoughts. The dream was one of my own; I may therefore continue its analysis by saying that my feelings were not yet satisfied by the solution that had so far been reached. I knew that my waking judgement upon the colleagues who were so ill-used in the dream-thoughts would have been a very different one; and the force of my wish not to share their fate in the matter of the appointment struck me as insufficient to explain the contradiction between my waking and dreaming estimates of them. If it was indeed true that my craving to be addressed with a different tide was as strong as all that, it showed a pathological ambition which I did not recognize in myself and which I believed was alien to me. I could not tell how other people who believed they knew me would judge me in this respect. It might be that I was really ambitious; but, if so, my ambition had long ago been transferred to objects quite other than the title and rank of *professor extraordinarius*.

What, then, could have been the origin of the ambitiousness which produced the dream in me? At that point I recalled an anecdote I had often heard repeated in my childhood. At the time of my birth an old peasant-woman had prophesied to my proud mother that with her first-born child she had brought a great man into the world. Prophecies of this kind must be very common: there are so many mothers filled with happy expectations and so many old peasant-women and others of the kind who make up for the loss of their power to control things in the present world by concentrating it on the future. Nor can the prophetess have lost anything by her words. Could this have been the source of my thirst for grandeur? But that reminded me of another experience, dating from my later childhood, which provided a still better explanation. My parents had been in the habit, when I was a boy of eleven or twelve, of taking me with them to the Prater.[1] One evening, while we were sitting in a restaurant there, our attention had been attracted by a man who was moving from one table to another and, for a small consideration, improvising a verse upon any topic presented to him. I was despatched to bring the poet to our table and he showed his gratitude to the messenger. Before enquiring what the chosen topic was to be, he had dedicated a few lines to myself; and he had been inspired to declare that I should probably grow up to be a Cabinet Minister. I still remembered quite well what an impression this second prophecy had made on me. Those were the days of the '*Bürger*' Ministry.[2] Shortly before, my father had brought home portraits of these middle-class profes-

---

[1] [The famous park on the outskirts of Vienna.]

[2] [The 'Middle-class Ministry'—a government of liberal complexion, elected after the new Austrian constitution was established in 1867.]

sional men—Herbst, Giskra, Unger, Berger and the rest—and we had il-
luminated the house in their honour. There had even been some Jews
among them. So henceforth every industrious Jewish schoolboy carried a
Cabinet Minister's portfolio in his satchel. The events of that period no
doubt had some bearing on the fact that up to a time shortly before I entered the University it had been my intention to study Law; it was only at
the last moment that I changed my mind. A ministerial career is definitely
barred to a medical man. But now to return to my dream. It began to
dawn on me that my dream had carried me back from the dreary present
to the cheerful hopes of the days of the '*Bürger*' Ministry, and that the wish
that it had done its best to fulfil was one dating back to those times. In
mishandling my two learned and eminent colleagues because they were
Jews, and in treating the one as a simpleton and the other as a criminal, I
was behaving as though I were the Minister, I had put myself in the Minister's place. Turning the tables on His Excellency with a vengeance! He
had refused to appoint me *professor extraordinarius* and I had retaliated in
the dream by stepping into his shoes.[1]

In another instance it became apparent that, though the wish which
instigated the dream was a present-day one, it had received a powerful reinforcement from memories that stretched far back into childhood. What
I have in mind is a series of dreams which are based upon a longing to
visit Rome. For a long time to come, no doubt, I shall have to continue
to satisfy that longing in my dreams: for at the season of the year when it
is possible for me to travel, residence in Rome must be avoided for reasons of health.[2] For instance, I dreamt once that I was looking out of a
railway-carriage window at the Tiber and the Ponte Sant' Angelo. The
train began to move off, and it occurred to me that I had not so much as
set foot in the city. The view that I had seen in my dream was taken from

---

[1] [In an amusing letter to Fliess of March 11, 1902 (Freud, 1950*a*, Letter 152),
Freud tells the story of how he came actually to be appointed to a professorship,
two years after the publication of this book.]

[2] [*Footnote added* 1909:] I discovered long since that it only needs a little courage
to fulfil wishes which till then have been regarded as unattainable; [*added* 1925:]
and thereafter became a constant pilgrim to Rome. [The correspondence with
Fliess (Freud, 1950*a*) gives repeated evidence of the emotional importance to
Freud of the idea of visiting Rome. He first fulfilled this wish in the summer of
1901 (Letter 146).]

a well-known engraving which I had caught sight of for a moment the day before in the sitting-room of one of my patients. Another time someone led me to the top of a hill and showed me Rome half-shrouded in mist; it was so far away that I was surprised at my view of it being so clear. There was more in the content of this dream than I feel prepared to detail; but the theme of 'the promised land seen from afar' was obvious in it. The town which I saw in this way for the first time, shrouded in mist, was—Lübeck, and the prototype of the hill was—at Gleichenberg.[1] In a third dream I had at last got to Rome, as the dream itself informed me; but I was disappointed to find that the scenery was far from being of an urban character. *There was a narrow stream of dark water; on one side of it were black cliffs and on the other meadows with big white flowers. I noticed a Herr Zucker* (whom I knew slightly) *and determined to ask him the way to the city.* I was clearly making a vain attempt to see in my dream a city which I had never seen in my waking life. Breaking up the landscape in the dream into its elements, I found that the white flowers took me to Ravenna, which I have visited and which, for a time at least, superseded Rome as capital of Italy. In the marshes round Ravenna we found the loveliest water-lilies growing in black water. Because we had had such difficulty in picking them out of the water, the dream made them grow in meadows like the narcissi at our own Aussee. The dark cliff, so close to the water, reminded me vividly of the valley of the Tepl near Karlsbad. '*Karlsbad*' enabled me to explain the curious detail of my having asked Herr Zucker the way. The material out of which the dream was woven included at this point two of those facetious Jewish anecdotes which contain so much profound and often bitter worldly wisdom and which we so greatly enjoy quoting in our talk and letters.[2] Here is the first one: the '*constitution*' story. An impecunious Jew had stowed himself away without a ticket in the fast train to *Karlsbad*. He was caught, and each time tickets were inspected he was taken out of the train and treated more and more severely. At one of the stations on his *via dolorosa* he met an acquaintance, who asked him where he was travelling to. 'To Karlsbad,' was his reply, 'if

---

[1] [An Austrian spa in Styria, not far from Graz.]

[2] [In a letter to Fliess of June 12, 1897 (Freud, 1950*a*, Letter 65), Freud mentions that he is making a collection of these anecdotes, of which he was to make great use in his book on jokes (Freud, 1905*c*). The first of the present anecdotes is alluded to more than once in his letters, and Rome and Karlsbad come to be identified as symbols of unattainable aims (e.g. in Letters 112 and 130).]

my constitution can stand it.' My memory then passed on to another story: of a Jew who could not speak French and had been recommended when he was in Paris to ask the way to the rue Richelieu. Paris itself had for many long years been another goal of my longings; and the blissful feelings with which I first set foot on its pavement seemed to me a guarantee that others of my wishes would be fulfilled as well. 'Asking the way,' moreover, was a direct allusion to *Rome*, since it is well known that all roads lead there. Again, the name *Zucker* [sugar] was once more an allusion to *Karlsbad*; for we are in the habit of prescribing treatment there for anyone suffering from the *constitutional* complaint of diabetes.[1] The instigation to this dream had been a proposal made by my friend in Berlin that we should meet in Prague at Easter. What we were going to discuss there would have included something with a further connection with 'sugar' and 'diabetes.'

A fourth dream, which occurred soon after the last one, took me to Rome once more. I saw a street-corner before me and was surprised to find so many posters in German stuck up there.[2] I had written to my friend with prophetic foresight the day before to say that I thought Prague might not be an agreeable place for a German to walk about in. Thus the dream expressed at the same time a wish to meet him in Rome instead of in a Bohemian town, and a desire, probably dating back to my student days, that the German language might be better tolerated in Prague. Incidentally, I must have understood Czech in my earliest childhood, for I was born in a small town in Moravia which has a Slav population. A Czech nursery rhyme, which I heard in my seventeenth year, printed itself on my memory so easily that I can repeat it to this day, though I have no notion what it means. Thus there was no lack of connections with my early childhood in these dreams either.

It was on my last journey to Italy, which, among other places, took me past Lake Trasimene, that finally—after having seen the Tiber and sadly turned back when I was only fifty miles from Rome—I discovered the way in which my longing for the eternal city had been reinforced by impressions from my youth. I was in the act of making a plan to by-pass Rome next year and travel to Naples, when a sentence occurred to me

---

[1] [The German word for 'diabetes' is '*Zuckerkrankheit*' ('sugar-disease').]

[2] [This dream is discussed in a letter to Fliess of December 3, 1897 (Freud, 1950*a*, Letter 77). The meeting in Prague was probably in the early part of the same year (see Letter 58, of February 8, 1897).]

which I must have read in one of our classical authors:[1] 'Which of the two, it may be debated, walked up and down his study with the greater impatience after he had formed his plan of going to Rome—Winckelmann, the Vice-Principal, or Hannibal, the Commander-in-Chief?' I had actually been following in Hannibal's footsteps. Like him, I had been fated not to see Rome; and he too had moved into the Campagna when everyone had expected him in Rome. But Hannibal, whom I had come to resemble in these respects, had been the favourite hero of my later school days. Like so many boys of that age, I had sympathized in the Punic Wars not with the Romans but with the Carthaginians. And when, in the higher classes I began to understand for the first time what it meant to belong to an alien race, and anti-semitic feelings among the other boys warned me that I must take up a definite position, the figure of the Semitic general rose still higher in my esteem. To my youthful mind Hannibal and Rome symbolized the conflict between the tenacity of Jewry and the organization of the Catholic church. And the increasing importance of the effects of the anti-semitic movement upon our emotional life helped to fix the thoughts and feelings of those early days. Thus the wish to go to Rome had become in my dream-life a cloak and symbol for a number of other passionate wishes. Their realization was to be pursued with all the perseverance and single-mindedness of the Carthaginian, though their fulfilment seemed at the moment just as little favoured by destiny as was Hannibal's lifelong wish to enter Rome.

At that point I was brought up against the event in my youth whose power was still being shown in all these emotions and dreams. I may have been ten or twelve years old, when my father began to take me with him on his walks and reveal to me in his talk his views upon things in the world we live in. Thus it was, on one such occasion, that he told me a story to show me how much better things were now than they had been in his days. 'When I was a young man,' he said, 'I went for a walk one Saturday in the streets of your birthplace; I was well dressed, and had a new fur cap on my head. A Christian came up to me and with a single blow knocked off my cap into the mud and shouted: "Jew! get off the pavement!"' 'And what did you do?' I asked. 'I went into the roadway and picked up my cap,' was his quiet reply. This struck me as unheroic conduct on the part

---

[1] [*Footnote added* 1925:] The author in question must no doubt have been Jean Paul.—[His decision to visit Rome was the turning-point in the career of Winckelmann, the eighteenth-century founder of classical archaeology.]

of the big, strong man who was holding the little boy by the hand. I contrasted this situation with another which fitted my feelings better: the scene in which Hannibal's father, Hamilcar Barca,[1] made his boy swear before the household altar to take vengeance on the Romans. Ever since that time Hannibal had had a place in my phantasies.

I believe I can trace my enthusiasm for the Carthaginian general a step further back into my childhood; so that once more it would only have been a question of a transference of an already formed emotional relation on to a new object. One of the first books that I got hold of when I had learnt to read was Thiers' history of the Consulate and Empire. I can still remember sticking labels on the flat backs of my wooden soldiers with the names of Napoleon's marshals written on them. And at that time my declared favourite was already Masséna (or to give the name its Jewish form, Manasseh).[2] (No doubt this preference was also partly to be explained by the fact that my birthday fell on the same day as his, exactly a hundred years later.)[3] Napoleon himself lines up with Hannibal owing to their both having crossed the Alps. It may even be that the development of this martial ideal is traceable still further back into my childhood: to the times when, at the age of three, I was in a close relation, sometimes friendly but sometimes warlike, with a boy a year older than myself, and to the wishes which the relation must have stirred up in the weaker of us.[4]

The deeper one carries the analysis of a dream, the more often one comes upon the track of experiences in childhood which have played a part among the sources of that dream's latent content.

We have already seen (on p. 53) that a dream very seldom reproduces recollections in such a way that they constitute, without abbreviation or modification, the *whole* of its manifest content. Nevertheless there are some undoubted instances of this happening: and I can add a few more, relating, once more, to childhood scenes. One of my patients was presented in a dream with an almost undistorted reproduction of a sexual

---

[1] [*Footnote added* 1909:] In the first edition the name of Hasdrubal appeared instead: a puzzling mistake, which I have explained in my *Psychopathology of Everyday Life* (1901*b*), Chapter X (2).

[2] [*Footnote added* 1930:] Incidentally, doubts have been thrown on the Marshal's Jewish origin.

[3] [This sentence was added in 1914.]

[4] [A fuller account of this will be found on pp. 433 f. and 488 f.]

episode, which was at once recognizable as a true recollection. His memory of the event had, in fact, never been completely lost in waking life, though it had become greatly obscured, and its revival was a consequence of work previously done in analysis. At the age of twelve, the dreamer had gone to visit a school friend who was laid up in bed, when the latter, by what was probably an accidental movement, uncovered his body. At the sight of his friend's genitals, my patient had been overcome by some sort of compulsion and had uncovered himself too and caught hold of the other's penis. His friend looked at him with indignation and astonishment; whereupon, overcome by embarrassment, he let go. This scene was repeated in a dream twenty-three years later, including all the details of his feelings at the time. It was modified, however, to this extent, that the dreamer assumed the passive instead of the active role, while the figure of his school-friend was replaced by someone belonging to his contemporary life. (See also p. 211 f.)

It is true that as a rule the childhood scene is only represented in the dream's manifest content by an allusion, and has to be arrived at by an interpretation of the dream. Such instances, when they are recorded, cannot carry much conviction, since as a rule there is no other evidence of these childhood experiences having occurred: if they date back to a very early age they are no longer recognized as memories. The general justification for inferring the occurrence of these childhood experiences from dreams is provided by a whole number of factors in psycho-analytic work, which are mutually consistent and thus seem sufficiently trustworthy. If I record some of these inferred childhood experiences torn from their context for the purposes of dream-interpretation, they may perhaps create little impression, especially as I shall not even be able to quote all the material on which the interpretations were based. Nevertheless I shall not allow this to deter me from relating them.

I

All the dreams of one of my women patients were characterized by her being 'rushed': she would be in a violent rush to get somewhere in time not to miss a train, and so on. In one dream *she was going to call on a woman friend; her mother told her to take a cab and not to walk; but she ran instead and kept on falling down.*—The material which came up in analysis led to memories of *rushing* about and romping as a child. One particular dream recalled the favourite children's game of saying a sentence '*Die Kuh rannte, bis sie fiel*' ['The cow ran till it fell'] so quickly that it sounds as though it were a single [nonsensical] word—another *rush* in fact. All these innocent rushings-about with little girl friends were remembered because they took the place of other, less innocent ones.

II

Here is another woman patient's dream: *She was in a big room in which all sorts of machines were standing, like what she imagined an orthopaedic institute to be. She was told I had no time and that she must have her treatment at the same time as five others. She refused, however, and would not lie down in the bed—or whatever it was—that was meant for her. She stood in the corner and waited for me to say it wasn't true. Meanwhile the others were laughing at her and saying it was just her way of 'carrying on.'— Simultaneously, it was as though she was making a lot of small squares.*

The first part of the content of this dream related to the treatment and was a transference on to me. The second part contained an allusion to a scene in childhood. The two parts were linked together by the mention of the bed.

The *orthopaedic institute* referred back to a remark I had made in which I had compared the treatment, alike in its length and in its nature, to an *orthopaedic* one. When I started her treatment I had been obliged to tell her that for the time being *I had not much time for her*, though later I should be able to give her a whole hour daily. This had stirred up her old sensitiveness, which is a principal trait in the character of children inclined to hysteria: they are insatiable for love. My patient had been the youngest of a family of six children (hence: *at the same time as five others*) and had therefore been her father's favourite; but even so she seems to have felt that her adored father devoted too little of his time and attention to her.—Her *waiting for me to say it wasn't true* had the following origin. A young tailor's apprentice had brought her a dress and she had given him the money for it. Afterwards she had asked her husband whether if the boy lost the money she would have to pay it over again. Her husband, to *tease* her, had said that was so. (The *teasing* in the dream.) She kept on asking over and over again and *waited for him to say after all it wasn't true*. It was then possible to infer that in the latent content of the dream she had had a thought of whether she would have to pay me twice as much if I gave her twice as much time—a thought which she felt was avaricious or *filthy*. (Uncleanliness in childhood is often replaced in dreams by avariciousness for money; the link between the two is the word 'filthy.'[1]) If the whole passage about *waiting for me to say*, etc., was intended in the dream as a circumlocution for the word 'filthy,' then her '*standing in the corner*' and '*not lying down in the bed*' would fit in with it as constituents of a scene from her childhood: a scene in which she had dirtied her bed and been punished by being made to stand in the corner, with a threat that her father would not love her any more and her brothers and sisters would laugh at her, and so on.—The *small squares* related to her little niece, who had shown her the arithmetical trick of arranging the digits in nine squares (I believe this is correct) so that they add up in all directions to fifteen.

III

A man dreamt as follows: *He saw two boys struggling—barrel-maker's boys, to judge by the implements lying around. One of the boys threw the other down; the boy on the ground had earrings with blue stones. He hurried towards the offender with his stick raised, to chastise him. The latter fled for protection to a woman, who was standing by a wooden fence, as though she was his mother. She was a woman of the working classes and her back was turned to the dreamer. At last she turned round and gave him a terrible look so that he ran off in terror. The red flesh of the lower lids of her eyes could be seen standing out.*

The dream had made copious use of trivial events of the previous day. He had in fact seen two boys in the street, one of whom threw the other down. When he hurried up to stop the fight they had both taken to their heels.—*Barrel-maker's boys.* This was only explained by a subsequent dream in which he used the phrase '*knocking the bottom out of a barrel.*'—From his experience he believed that *earrings with blue stones* were mostly worn by prostitutes. A line from a well-known piece of doggerel about *two boys* then occurred to him: 'The other boy was called Marie' (i.e. was a girl).—*The woman standing.* After the scene with the two boys he had gone for a walk along the bank of the Danube and had profited by the loneliness of the spot to micturate against *a wooden fence*. Further on, a

---

[1] [This point was later enlarged upon by Freud (1908*b*). But it already occurs in a letter to Fliess of December 22, 1897 (Freud, 1950*a*, Letter 79).]

respectably dressed elderly lady had smiled at him in a very friendly manner and had wanted to give him her visiting-card. Since the woman in the dream was standing in the same position as he had been in when he was micturating, it must have been a question of a micturating woman. This tallies with her terrible *look* and the *red flesh standing out*, which could only relate to the gaping of the genitals caused by stooping. This, seen in his childhood, reappeared, in later memory as '*proud flesh*'—as a wound.

The dream combined two opportunities he had had as a little boy of seeing little girls' genitals: when they were *thrown down* and when they were *micturating*. And from the other part of the context it emerged that he had a recollection of being *chastised* or threatened by his father for the sexual curiosity he had evinced on these occasions.

IV

Behind the following dream (dreamt by an elderly lady) there lay a whole quantity of childhood memories, combined, as best they might be, into a single phantasy.

She went out in a violent rush to do some commissions. In the Graben[1] *she sank down on her knees, as though she was quite broken-down. A large number of people collected round her, especially cab-drivers; but no one helped her up. She made several vain attempts, and she must at last have succeeded, for she was put into a cab which was to take her home. Someone threw a big, heavily-laden basket (like a shopping-basket) in through the window after her.*

This was the same lady who always felt 'rushed' in her dreams, just as she had rushed and romped about when she was a child. [See above, p. 220 f.] The first scene in the dream was evidently derived from the sight of a horse fallen down; in the same way the word '*broken-down*' referred to horse-racing. In her youth she had ridden horses, and no doubt when she was still younger she had actually *been* a horse. The *falling down* was related to a memory from very early childhood of the seventeen-year-old son of the house-porter who had fallen down in the street in an epileptic fit and been brought home in a carriage. She had of course only *heard* about this, but the idea of epileptic fits (of the '*falling* sickness') had obtained a hold on her imagination and had later influenced the form taken by her own hysterical attacks.—If a woman dreams of falling, it almost

---

[1] [One of the principal shopping centres in Vienna.]

invariably has a sexual sense: she is imagining herself as a '*fallen woman.*' The present dream in particular scarcely left any room for doubt, since the place where my patient fell was the Graben, a part of Vienna notorious as a promenade for prostitutes. The *shopping-basket* [*Korb*] led to more than one interpretation. It reminded her of the numerous *rebuffs* [*Körbe*][1] which she had dealt out to her suitors, as well as of those which she complained of having later received herself. This also connected with the fact that *no one helped her up*, which she herself explained as a rebuff. The *shopping-basket* further reminded her of phantasies which had already come up in her analysis, in which she was married far beneath her and had to go marketing herself. And lastly it might serve as the mark of a servant. At this point further childhood recollections emerged. First, of a cook who had been dismissed for stealing, and who had *fallen on her knees* and begged to be forgiven. She herself had been twelve at the time. Then, of a housemaid who had been dismissed on account of a love-affair with the family *coachman* (who incidentally married her subsequently). Thus this memory was also one of the sources of the coachmen (*drivers*)[2] in the dream (who, in contradistinction to the actual coachman, failed to raise the fallen woman). There remained to be explained the fact of the basket being *thrown in after her* and *through the window*. This reminded her of *handing in* luggage to be *sent off* by rail, of the country custom of lovers climbing in through their sweethearts' *window*, and of other little episodes from her life in the country: how a gentleman had thrown some *blue plums* to a lady *through the window* of her room, and how her own younger sister had been scared by the village idiot looking in *through her window*. An obscure memory from her tenth year then began to emerge, of a nurse in the country who had had love-scenes (which the girl might have seen something of) with one of the servants in the house and who, along with her lover, had been *sent off, thrown out* (the opposite of the dream-image '*thrown in*')—a story that we had already approached from several other directions. A servant's luggage or trunk is referred to contemptuously in Vienna as 'seven *plums*': 'pack up your seven plums and out you go!'

My records naturally include a large collection of patients' dreams the analysis of which led to obscure or entirely forgotten impressions of child-

---

[1] [The word '*Korb*' ('basket') is commonly used for the rejection of an offer of marriage.]

[2] [The German word is the same (*Kutscher*) in both cases.]

hood, often going back to the first three years of life. But it would be unsafe to apply any conclusions drawn from them to dreams in general. The persons concerned were in every instance neurotics and in particular hysterics; and it is possible that the part played by childhood scenes in their dreams might be determined by the nature of their neurosis and not by the nature of dreams. Nevertheless, in analysing my own dreams—and, after all, I am not doing so on account of any gross pathological symptoms—it happens no less frequently that in the latent content of a dream I come unexpectedly upon a scene from childhood, and that all at once a whole series of my dreams link up with the associations branching out from some experience of my childhood. I have already given some instances of this [pp. 215–19], and I shall have others to give in a variety of connections. I cannot, perhaps, bring this section to a better close than by reporting one or two dreams of mine in which recent occasions and long-forgotten experiences of childhood came together as sources of the dream.

I

Tired and hungry after a journey, I went to bed, and the major vital needs began to announce their presence in my sleep; I dreamt as follows:

I went into a kitchen in search of some pudding. Three women were standing in it; one of them was the hostess of the inn and was twisting something about in her hands, as though she was making Knödel [dumplings]. She answered that I must wait till she was ready. (These were not definite spoken words.) *I felt impatient and went off with a sense of injury. I put on an overcoat. But the first I tried on was too long for me. I took it off, rather surprised to find it was trimmed with fur. A second one that I put on had a long strip with a Turkish design let into it. A stranger with a long face and a short pointed beard came up and tried to prevent my putting it on, saying it was his. I showed him then that it was embroidered all over with a Turkish pattern. He asked: 'What have the Turkish (designs, stripes . . .) to do with you?' But we then became quite friendly with each other.*

When I began analysing this dream, I thought quite unexpectedly of the first novel I ever read (when I was thirteen, perhaps); as a matter of fact I began at the end of the first volume. I have never known the name of the novel or of its author; but I have a vivid memory of its ending. The hero went mad and kept calling out the names of the three women who had brought the greatest happiness and sorrow into his life. One of these

names was *Pélagie*. I still had no notion what this recollection was going
to lead to in the analysis. In connection with the three women I thought
of the three Fates who spin the destiny of man, and I knew that one of the
three women—the inn-hostess in the dream—was the mother who gives
life, and furthermore (as in my own case) gives the living creature its first
nourishment. Love and hunger, I reflected, meet at a woman's breast. A
young man who was a great admirer of feminine beauty was talking
once—so the story went—of the good-looking wet-nurse who had suckled
him when he was a baby: 'I'm sorry,' he remarked, 'that I didn't make a
better use of my opportunity.' I was in the habit of quoting this anecdote
to explain the factor of 'deferred action' in the mechanism of the psychoneuroses.[1]—One of the Fates, then, was rubbing the palms of her
hands together as though she was making dumplings: a queer occupation
for a Fate, and one that cried out for an explanation. This was provided by
another and earlier memory of my childhood. When I was six years old
and was given my first lessons by my mother, I was expected to believe that
we were all made of earth and must therefore return to earth. This did not
suit me and I expressed doubts of the doctrine. My mother thereupon
rubbed the palms of her hands together—just as she did in making
dumplings, except that there was no dough between them—and showed
me the blackish scales of *epidermis* produced by the friction as a proof that
we were made of earth. My astonishment at this ocular demonstration
knew no bounds and I acquiesced in the belief which I was later to hear
expressed in the words: '*Du bist der Natur einen Tod schuldig.*'[2] So they
really were Fates that I found in the kitchen when I went into it—as I had
so often done in my childhood when I was hungry, while my mother,
standing by the fire, had admonished me that I must wait till dinner was

---

[1] [A reference to a superseded theory of the mechanism of hysteria, described in
  the later sections of Part II of Freud's early 'Project for a Scientific Psychology'
  (Freud, 1950*a*).]

[2] ['Thou owest Nature a death.' Evidently a reminiscence of Prince Hal's remark
  to Falstaff in *1 Henry IV*, v. 1: 'Thou owest God a death.' Freud uses the same
  words and ascribes them to Shakespeare in a letter to Fliess of February 6, 1899
  (Freud, 1950*a*, Letter 104).]—Both of the emotions that were attached to these
  childhood scenes—astonishment and submission to the inevitable—had occurred in a dream which I had had shortly before this one and which had first
  reminded me of this event in my childhood.

ready.—And now for the dumplings—the *Knödel!* One at least of my teachers at the University—and precisely the one to whom I owe my histological knowledge (for instance of the *epidermis*) would infallibly be reminded by the name *Knödl* of a person against whom he had been obliged to take legal action for *plagiarizing* his writings. The idea of plagiarizing—of appropriating whatever one can, even though it belongs to someone else—clearly led on to the second part of the dream, in which I was treated as though I were the thief who had for some time carried on his business of stealing overcoats in the lecture-rooms. I had written down the word 'plagiarizing,' without thinking about it, because it occurred to me; but now I noticed that it could form a bridge [*Brücke*] between different pieces of the dream's manifest content. A chain of associations (*Pélagie—plagiarizing—plagiostomes*[1] or sharks [*Haifische*]—*a fish's swimming-bladder* [*Fischblase*]) connected the old novel with the case of Knödl and with the overcoats, which clearly referred to implements used in sexual technique [see p. 208 f.]. (Cf. Maury's alliterative dreams [on pp. 87 f.].) No doubt it was a very far-fetched and senseless chain of thought; but I could never have constructed it in waking life unless it had already been constructed by the dream-work. And, as though the need to set up forced connections regarded *nothing* as sacred, the honoured name of Brücke[2] (cf. the verbal *bridge* above) reminded me of the Institute in which I spent the happiest hours of my student life, free from all other desires—

> So wird's Euch an der Weisheit *Brüsten*
> Mit jedem Tage mehr gelüsten[3]

—in complete contrast to the desires which were now *plaguing* me in my dreams. Finally there came to mind another much respected teacher—his name, Fleischl ['*Fleisch*' = 'meat'], like Knödl, sounded like something to

---

[1] I have deliberately avoided enlarging upon the plagiostomes; they reminded me of an unpleasant occasion on which I had disgraced myself in connection with this same University teacher.

[2] [For Brücke and Fleischl (below) see footnote, p. 487.]

[3] ['Thus, at the *breasts* of Wisdom clinging,
Thou'lt find each day a greater rapture bringing.'
Goethe, *Faust*, Part I, [Scene 4]
(Bayard Taylor's translation).]

eat—and a distressing scene in which *scales of epidermis* played a part (my mother and the inn-hostess) as well as *madness* (the novel) and a drug from the dispensary[1] which removes *hunger:* cocaine.

I might pursue the intricate trains of thought further along these lines and explain fully the part of the dream which I have not analysed; but I must desist at this point because the personal sacrifice demanded would be too great. I will only pick out one thread, which is qualified to lead us straight to one of the dream-thoughts underlying the confusion. The stranger with the long face and pointed beard who tried to prevent my putting on the overcoat bore the features of a shop-keeper at Spalato from whom my wife had bought a quantity of *Turkish* stuffs. He was called Popović, an equivocal name,[2] on which a humorous writer, Stettenheim, has already made a suggestive comment: 'He told me his name and blushingly pressed my hand.' Once again I found myself misusing a name, as I already had done with Pélagie, Knödl, Brücke and Fleischl. It could scarcely be denied that playing about with names like this was a kind of childish naughtiness. But if I indulged in it, it was as an act of retribution; for my own name had been the victim of feeble witticisms like these on countless occasions.[3] Goethe, I recalled, had remarked somewhere upon people's sensitiveness about their names: how we seem to have grown into them like our *skin*. He had said this *à propos* of a line written on his name by Herder:

'Der du von Göttern abstammst, von Gothen oder vom Kote.'—'So seid ihr Götterbilder auch zu Staub.'[4]

I noticed that my digression on the subject of the misuse of names was only leading up to this complaint. But I must break off here.—My wife's

---

[1] [In German '*lateinische Küche*' (literally, 'Latin kitchen').—Cf. footnote 1, p. 136.]
[2] ['*Popo*' is a childish word for 'bottom.']
[3] '*Freud*' is the German word for 'joy.']
[4] [The first of these lines comes from a facetious note written by Herder to Goethe with a request for the loan of some books: 'Thou who art the offspring of gods or of Goths or of dung—(Goethe, send them to me!)' The second line, a further free association of Freud's, is taken from the well-known recognition scene in Goethe's *Iphigenie auf Tauris*. Iphigenia, hearing from Pylades of the death of so many heroes during the siege of Troy, exclaims: 'So you too, divine figures, have turned to dust!']

purchase made at Spalato reminded me of another purchase, made at Cattaro,[1] which I had been too cautious over, so that I had lost an opportunity of making some nice acquisitions. (Cf. the neglected opportunity with the wet-nurse.) For one of the thoughts which my hunger introduced into the dream was this: 'One should never neglect an opportunity, but always take what one can even when it involves doing a small wrong. One should never neglect an opportunity, since life is short and death inevitable.' Because this lesson of 'carpe diem' had among other meanings a sexual one, and because the desire it expressed did not stop short of doing wrong, it had reason to dread the censorship and was obliged to conceal itself behind a dream. All kinds of thoughts having a *contrary* sense then found voice: memories of a time when the dreamer was content with *spiritual* food, restraining thoughts of every kind and even threats of the most revolting sexual punishments.

II

The next dream calls for a rather long preamble:

I had driven to the Western Station [in Vienna] to take the train for my summer holiday at Aussee, but had arrived on the platform while an earlier train, going to Ischl, was still standing in the station. There I had seen Count Thun[2] who was once again travelling to Ischl for an audience with the Emperor. Though it was raining, he had arrived in an open carriage. He had walked straight in through the entrance for the Local Trains. The ticket inspector at the gate had not recognized him and had tried to take his ticket, but he had waved the man aside with a curt motion of his hand and without giving any explanation. After the train for Ischl had gone out, I ought by rights to have left the platform again and returned to the waiting room; and it had cost me some trouble to arrange matters so that I was allowed to stop on the platform. I had passed the time in keeping a look-out to see if anyone came along and tried to get a reserved compartment by exercising some sort of 'pull.' I had intended in that case to make a loud

---

[1] [Spalato and Cattaro: both towns on the Dalmatian coast.]

[2] [Austrian politician (1847–1916) of reactionary views; an upholder of Bohemian self-government as against the German nationalists; Austrian premier 1898–9.—Ischl, in Upper Austria, where the Court regularly spent the summer months.]

protest: that is to say to claim equal rights. Meantime I had been humming
a tune to myself which I recognized as Figaro's aria from *Le Nozze di Figaro:*

> Se vuol ballare, signor contino,
> Se vuol ballare, signor contino,
> Il chitarino le suonerò[1]

(It is a little doubtful whether anyone else would have recognized the tune.)

The whole evening I had been in high spirits and in a combative
mood. I had chaffed my waiter and my cab-driver—without, I hope,
hurting their feelings. And now all kinds of insolent and revolutionary
ideas were going through my head, in keeping with Figaro's words and
with my recollections of Beaumarchais' comedy which I had seen acted
by the *Comédie française*. I thought of the phrase about the great gentlemen who had taken the trouble to be born, and of the *droit du Seigneur*
which Count Almaviva tried to exercise over Susanna. I thought, too, of
how our malicious opposition journalists made jokes over Count Thun's
name, calling him instead 'Count Nichtsthun.'[2] Not that I envied him.
He was on his way to a difficult audience with the Emperor, while *I* was
the real Count Do-nothing—just off on my holidays. There followed all
sorts of enjoyable plans for the holidays. At this point a gentleman came
on to the platform whom I recognized as a Government invigilator at
medical examinations, and who by his activities in that capacity had won
the flattering nickname of 'Government bedfellow.'[3] He asked to be given
a first-class half-compartment to himself in virtue of his official position,
and I heard one railwayman saying to another: 'Where are we to put the
gentleman with the half first-class ticket?'[4] This, I thought to myself, was
a fine example of privilege; after all *I* had paid the full first-class fare. And
I did in fact get a compartment to myself, but not in a corridor coach, so
that there would be no lavatory available during the night. I complained
to an official without any success; but I got my own back on him by sug-

---

[1] ['If my Lord Count is inclined to go dancing,
    If my Lord Count is inclined to go dancing,
    I'll be quite ready to play him a tune . . .']
[2] ['Count Do-nothing.' '*Thun*' is the German word for 'to do.']
[3] ['*Beischläfer*,' literally 'one who sleeps with someone' because he used to go to
    sleep instead of invigilating.]
[4] [Being a government official, he had been able to buy his ticket at half-rates.]

gesting that he should at all events have a hole made in the floor of the compartment to meet the possible needs of passengers. And in fact I did wake up at a quarter to three in the morning with a pressing need to micturate, having had the following dream:

A crowd of people, a meeting of students.—A count (Thun or Taaffe[1]) was speaking. He was challenged to say something about the Germans, and declared with a contemptuous gesture that their favourite flower was colt's foot, and put some sort of dilapidated leaf—or rather the crumpled skeleton of a leaf—into his buttonhole. I fired up—so I fired up,[2] though I was surprised at my taking such an attitude.

(Then, less distinctly:) *It was as though I was in the Aula,[3] trances were cordoned off and we had to escape. I made my way through a series of beautifully furnished rooms, evidently ministerial or public apartments, with furniture upholstered in a colour between brown and violet; at last I came to a corridor, in which a housekeeper was sitting, an elderly stout woman. I avoided speaking to her, but she evidently thought I had a right to pass, for she asked whether she should accompany me with the lamp. I indicated to her, by word or gesture, that she was to stop on the staircase; and I felt I was being very cunning in thus avoiding inspection at the exit. I got downstairs and found a narrow and steep ascending path, along which I went.*

(Becoming indistinct again) . . . *It was as though the second problem was to get out of the town, just as the first one had been to get out of the house. I was driving in a cab and ordered the driver to drive me to a station. 'I can't drive with you along the railway-line itself,' I said, after he had raised some objection, as though I had overtired him. It was as if I had already driven with him for some of the distance one normally travels by train. The stations were cordoned off. I wondered whether to go to Krems or Znaim,[4] but reflected that*

---

[1] Austrian politician (1833–95); premier 1870–1 and 1879–93. Like Count Thun, he favoured some degree of independence for the non-German parts of the Empire.]

[2] This repetition crept into my record of the dream, apparently through inadvertence. I have let it stand, since the analysis showed that it was significant. [The German is '*ich fahre auf*'; '*fahren*' also means 'to drive' or 'to travel' and is used repeatedly in these senses later in the dream. See on this point p. 441 *n*.]

[3] [The great ceremonial hall of the University.]

[4] [Krems in Lower Austria and Znaim in Moravia were neither of them Imperial residences.—Graz is the capital of the province of Styria.]

the Court would be in residence there, so I decided in favour of Graz, or some such place. I was now sitting in the compartment, which was like a carriage on the Stadtbahn [the suburban railway]; *and in my buttonhole I had a peculiar plaited, long-shaped object, and beside it some violet-brown violets made of a stiff material. This greatly struck people.* (At this point the scene broke off.)

Once more I was in front of the station, but this time in the company of an elderly gentleman. I thought of a plan for remaining unrecognized; and then saw that this plan had already been put into effect. It was as though thinking and experiencing were one and the same thing. He appeared to be blind, at all events with one eye, and I handed him a male glass urinal (which we had to buy or had bought in town). So I was a sick-nurse and had to give him the urinal because he was blind. If the ticket-collector were to see us like that, he would be certain to let us get away without noticing us. Here the man's attitude and his micturating penis appeared in plastic form. (This was the point at which I awoke, feeling a need to micturate.)

The dream as a whole gives one the impression of being in the nature of a phantasy in which the dreamer was carried back to the Revolutionary year 1848. Memories of that year had been recalled to me by the [Emperor Francis Joseph's] Jubilee in 1898, as well as by a short trip which I had made to *the Wachau*, in the course of which I had visited Emmersdorf,[1] the place of retirement of the student-leader Fischhof, to whom certain elements in the manifest content of the dream may allude. My associations then led me to England and to my brother's house there. He used often to tease his wife with the words 'Fifty Years Ago' (from the title of one of Lord Tennyson's poems),[2] which his children used then to correct to '*fifteen years* ago.' This revolutionary phantasy, however, which was

---

[1] [The Wachau is a stretch of the Danube valley some fifty miles above Vienna.— *Footnote added* 1925:] This is a mistake, but not a slip this time. I only learnt later that the Emmersdorf in the Wachau is not to be identified with the place of the same name which was the refuge of the revolutionary leader Fischhof. [A reference to this mistake will be found in *The Psychopathology of Everyday Life* (Freud, 1901*b*), Chapter X (3).]

[2] [No poem by Tennyson seems to bear this title. The reference is perhaps to his ode 'On the Jubilee of Queen Victoria,' in which the words 'fifty years' (though not 'fifty years ago') occur repeatedly. Or, alternatively, the allusion may be to the second 'Locksley Hall': 'Sixty Years After.']

derived from ideas aroused in me by seeing Count Thun, was like the façade of an Italian church in having no organic relation with the structure lying behind it. But it differed from those façades in being disordered and full of gaps, and in the fact that portions of the interior construction had forced their way through into it at many points.

The first situation in the dream was an amalgam of several scenes, which I can separate out. The insolent attitude adopted by the Count in the dream was copied from a scene at my secondary school when I was *fifteen years* old. We had hatched a conspiracy against an unpopular and ignorant master, the moving spirit of which had been one of my schoolfellows who since those days seemed to have taken *Henry VIII* of *England* as his model. The leadership in the chief assault was allotted to me, and the signal for open revolt was a discussion on the significance of the Danube to Austria (cf. *the Wachau*). One of our fellow-conspirators had been the only aristocratic boy in the class, who, on account of his remarkable length of limb, was called 'the Giraffe.' He was standing up, like the Count in my dream, having been taken to task by the school tyrant, the *German language* master. The *favourite flower* and the *putting into his buttonhole* of something in the nature of a flower (which last made me think of some orchids which I had brought the same day for a woman friend and also of a rose of Jericho[1]) were a striking reminder of the scene in one of Shakespeare's historical plays [*3 Henry VI*, I. 1] which represented the beginning of the Wars of the *Red* and *White* Roses. (The mention of *Henry VIII* opened the way to this recollection.)—From there it was only a short step to red and white carnations. (Two little couplets, one in *German* and the other in *Spanish*, slipped into the analysis at this point:

> Rosen, Tulpen, Nelken,
> alle Blumen welken.

> *Isabelita*, no llores,
> que se marchitan las flores.[2]

The appearance of a *Spanish* couplet led back to *Figaro*.) Here in Vienna white carnations had become an emblem of anti-semitism, and red ones

---

[1] [The 'Resurrection plant,' whose dried fronds unfold under moisture.]

[2] ['Roses, tulips, carnations: every flower fades.' (Lines often found in nineteenth century 'common-place books.')—'*Isabelita*, do not weep because the flowers fade.']

of the Social Democrats. Behind this lay a recollection of a piece of antisemitic provocation during a railway journey in the lovely Saxon countryside (cf. *Anglo-Saxon*).—The third scene which contributed to the formation of the first situation in the dream dated from my early student days. There was a discussion in a *German* students' club on the relation of philosophy to the natural sciences. I was a green youngster, full of materialistic theories, and thrust myself forward to give expression to an extremely one-sided point of view. Thereupon someone who was my senior and my superior, someone who has since then shown his ability as a leader of men and an organizer of large groups (and who also, incidentally, bears a name derived from the Animal Kingdom[1]), stood up and gave us a good talking-to: he too, he told us, had fed swine in his youth and returned repentant to his father's house. *I fired up* (as I did in the dream) and replied boorishly ['*saugrob*,' literally 'swinishly gross'] that since I now knew that he had fed *swine* in his youth I was no longer *surprised* at the tone of his speeches. (In the dream I was *surprised* at my German-nationalist attitude. [Cf. p. 358.]) There was a general uproar and I was called upon from many sides to withdraw my remarks, but I refused to do so. The man I had insulted was too sensible to look upon the incident as a *challenge*, and let the affair drop.

The remaining elements of this first situation in the dream were derived from deeper layers. What was the meaning of the Count's pronouncement about colt's foot? To find the answer, I followed a train of associations: colt's foot ['*Huflattich*,' literally 'hoof lettuce']—lettuce—salad—dog-in-the-manger ['*Salathund*,' literally 'salad dog']. Here was a whole collection of terms of abuse: 'Gir-affe' ['*Affe*' is the German for 'ape'], 'swine,' 'dog'—and I could have arrived at 'donkey' if I had made a détour through another name and insulted yet another academic teacher. Moreover, I translated 'colt's foot'—whether rightly or wrongly I could not tell—by the French '*pisse-en-lit*'.[2] This information was derived from Zola's *Germinal*, in which a child was told to pick some of that plant for salad. The French word for 'dog'—'*chien*'—reminded me of the major function ('*chier*' in French, compared with '*pisser*' for the minor one). Soon, I thought, I should have collected examples of impropri-

---

[1] [Presumably Viktor Adler ('eagle'), the Austrian Social Democrat leader (1852–1918). Cf.'*Adler*' on p. 235 below.]

[1] ['*Pissenlit*' actually means 'dandelion.']

ety in all three states of matter—solid, liquid and gaseous;—for this same book, *Germinal*, which had plenty to do with the approaching revolution, contained an account of a very peculiar sort of competition—for the production of a gaseous excretion known by the name of '*flatus*.'[1] I now saw that the path leading to *flatus* had been prepared far ahead: from *flowers*, through the *Spanish* couplet, *Isabelita*, *Isabella* and Ferdinand, *Henry VIII*, *English* history, and the Armada which sailed against *England*, after whose defeat a medal was struck, bearing the inscription '*Flavit* et dissipati sunt,'[2] since the stormblast had scattered the Spanish fleet. I had thought, half seriously, of using those words as the heading to the chapter on 'Therapy,' if ever I got so far as producing a detailed account of my theory and treatment of hysteria.

Turning now to the second episode of the dream, I am unable to deal with it in such detail—out of consideration for the censorship. For I was putting myself in the place of an exalted personage of those revolutionary times, who also had an adventure with an eagle [*Adler*] and is said to have suffered from incontinence of the bowels, and so on. I thought to myself that *I should not be justified in passing* the censorship at this point, even though the greater part of the story was told me by a Hofrat (a *consiliarius aulicus* [court councillor]—cf. *Aula*). The series of public rooms in the dream were derived from His Excellency's saloon carriage, of which I had succeeded in getting a glimpse. But the 'rooms' [*Zimmer*] also meant 'women' [*Frauenzimmer*] as is often the case in dreams[3]—in this instance 'public women.' In the figure of the housekeeper I was showing my lack of gratitude towards a witty elderly lady and ill repaying her hospitality and the many good stories that I heard while I was stopping in her

---

[1] Not in fact in *Germinal* but in *La terre*: a mistake which I only observed after I had completed the analysis.—Notice the occurrence of the same letters in '*Huflattich*' ['colt's foot'] and '*flatus*.'

[2] ['He blew and they were scattered.'—*Footnote added* 1925:] An unsolicited biographer, Dr. Fritz Wittels [1924, 21; Engl. trans. (1924), 28] has charged me with having omitted the name of Jehovah from the above motto. [*Added* 1930:] The English medallion bears the deity's name in Hebrew lettering on a cloud in the background. It is so placed that it can be taken as being part either of the design or of the inscription.—[The idea of using the words as a motto at the head of a chapter on therapy is mentioned in a letter to Fliess of January 3, 1897 (Freud, 1950a, Letter 54).]

[3] ['*Frauenzimmer*,' literally 'women's apartment,' is commonly used in German as a slightly derogatory word for 'woman.' Cf. p. 367.]

house.—The allusion to the lamp went back to Grillparzer,[1] who introduced a charming episode of a similar kind, which he had actually experienced, into his tragedy about Hero and Leander, *Des Meeres und der Liebe Wellen* ['The *Waves of the Sea* and of Love']—the Armada and the *storm*.[2]

I must also refrain from any detailed analysis of the two remaining episodes of the dream.[3] I will merely pick out the elements leading to the two childhood scenes on whose account alone I embarked upon a discussion of this dream. It will rightly be suspected that what compels me to make this suppression is sexual material; but there is no need to rest content with this explanation. After all, there are many things which one has to keep secret from other people but of which one makes no secret to oneself; and the question here is not as to why I am obliged to conceal the solution but as to the motives for the *internal* censorship which hid the true content of the dream from myself. I must therefore explain that the analysis of these three [last] episodes of the dream showed that they were impertinent boastings, the issue of an absurd megalomania which had long been suppressed in my waking life and a few of whose ramifications had even made their way into the dream's manifest content (e.g. '*I felt I was being very cunning*'), and which incidentally accounted for my exuberant spirits during the evening before I had the dream. The boasting extended to all spheres; for instance, the mention of *Graz* went back to the slang phrase 'What's the price of Graz?' which expresses the self-satisfaction of a person who feels extremely well-off. The first episode of the dream may also be included among the boastings by anyone who will bear in mind the great Rabelais' incomparable account of the life and deeds of Gargantua and his son Pantagruel.

Here is the material relating to the two childhood scenes which I have promised my readers. I had bought a *new* trunk for the journey, of a *brownish violet* colour. This colour appears more than once in the dream:

---

[1] [The well-known Austrian dramatist (1791–1872).]

[2] [*Footnote added* 1911:] In an interesting paper, Silberer (1910) has tried to show from this part of my dream that the dream-work can succeed in reproducing not only the latent dream-thoughts but also the psychical processes that take place during the formation of dreams. (This is what he terms 'the functional phenomenon.') [See below, pp. 507 ff.—*Added* 1914:] But he is, I think, overlooking the fact that 'the psychical processes that take place during the formation of dreams' were, like the rest, part of the *material* of my thoughts. In this boastful dream I was evidently proud of having discovered those processes.

[3] [The first of these is in fact further analysed on pp. 440 ff.]

the *violet-brown violets made of a stiff material* and beside them a thing known as a '*Mädchenfänger*' ['girl-catcher']¹—and the furniture in the ministerial apartments. It is commonly believed by children that *people are struck* by anything *new*. The following scene from my childhood has been described to me, and my memory of the description has taken the place of my memory of the scene itself. It appears that when I was two years old I still occasionally *wetted the bed*, and when I was reproached for this I *consoled* my father by promising to buy him a nice *new red* bed in N., the nearest town of any size. This was the origin of the parenthetical phrase in the dream to the effect that *we had bought or had to buy the* urinal in town: one must keep one's promises. (Notice, too, the juxtaposition in symbolism of the male urinal and the female trunk or box. [Cf. pp. 177 f.]) This promise of mine exhibited all the megalomania of childhood. We have already come across the significant part played in dreams by children's difficulties in connection with micturition (cf. the dream reported on p. 222). We have also learned from the psychoanalysis of neurotic subjects the intimate connection between bed-wetting and the character trait of ambition.²

When I was seven or eight years old there was another domestic scene, which I can remember very clearly. One evening before going to sleep I disregarded the rules which modesty lays down and obeyed the calls of nature in my parents' bedroom while they were present. In the course of his reprimand, my father let fall the words: 'The boy will come to nothing.' This must have been a frightful blow to my ambition, for references to this scene are still constantly recurring in my dreams and are always linked with an enumeration of my achievements and successes, as though I wanted to say: 'You see, I *have* come to something.' This scene, then, provided the material for the final episode of the dream, in which—in revenge, of course—the roles were interchanged. The older man (clearly my father, since his blindness in one eye referred to his unilateral glaucoma)³ was now micturating in

---

¹ [This word, ordinarily used in the sense of 'rake' (see footnote 3 on p. 238), seems here to be the slang name of some sort of buttonhole. Cf. corresponding terms such as 'fascinator' and 'beaucatcher' used in America for women's head-dresses.]

² [This sentence was added in 1914. The first mention of the connection seems to have been made in the last paragraph of Freud's paper on 'Character and Anal Erotism' (1908*b*).]

³ There is another interpretation. He was one-eyed like Odin, the father-god.— *Odhins Trost* [*Odin's Consolation*, a mythological novel by Felix Dahn (1880)]— The *consolation* I offered him in the first childhood scene of buying him a new bed.

front of me, just as I had in front of him in my childhood. In the reference to his glaucoma I was reminding him of the cocaine, which had helped him in the operation [cf. pp. 194 f.], as though I had in that way kept my promise. Moreover, I was making fun of him; I had to hand him the urinal because he was blind, and I revelled in allusions to my discoveries in connection with the theory of hysteria, of which I felt so proud.[1]

The two scenes of micturition from my childhood were in any case closely linked to the topic of megalomania; but their emergence while I was travelling to Aussee was further assisted by the chance circumstance that there was no lavatory attached to my compartment and that I had reason to anticipate the predicament which in fact arose in the morning. I awoke with the sensations of a physical need. One might, I think, be inclined to suppose that these sensations were the actual provoking agent of the dream; but I would prefer to take another view, namely that the desire to micturate was only called up by the dream-thoughts. It is quite unusual for me to be disturbed in my sleep by physical needs of any kind, especially at the hour at which I awoke on this occasion—a quarter to three in the morning. And I may meet a further objection by remarking that upon other journeys under more comfortable conditions I have

---

[1] Here is some further interpretative material. Handing him the glass [urinal] reminded me of the story of the peasant at the optician's, trying glass after glass and still not being able to read.—(Peasant-*catcher* [*Bauernfänger*, 'sharper']: girl-*catcher* [*Mädchenfänger*] in the preceding episode of the dream.)—The way in which the father in Zola's *La terre* was treated among the peasants after he had grown feeble-minded.—The tragic requital that lay in my father's soiling his bed like a child during the last days of his life [cf. p. 437], hence my appearance in the dream as a *sick-nurse.*—'*Here it was as though thinking and experiencing were one and the same thing.*' This recalled a strongly revolutionary literary play by Oskar Panizza ['*Das Liebeskonzil*' (1895)], in which God the Father is ignominiously treated as a paralytic old man. In his case will and deed were represented as one and the same thing, and he had to be restrained from cursing and swearing by one of his archangels, a kind of Ganymede, because his imprecations would be promptly fulfilled.—My making *plans* was a reproach against my father dating from a later period. And indeed the whole rebellious content of the dream, with its *lèse majesté* and its derision of the higher authorities, went back to rebellion against my father. A Prince is known as the father of his country; the father is the oldest, first, and for children the only authority, and from his autocratic power the other social authorities have developed in the course of the history of human civilization—except in so far as the 'matriarchy' calls for a

scarcely ever felt a need to micturate when I have woken up early. But in any case it will do no harm to leave the point unresolved.[1]

My experiences in analysing dreams have drawn my attention to the fact that trains of thought reaching back to earliest childhood lead off even from dreams which seem at first sight to have been completely interpreted, since their sources and instigating wish have been discovered without difficulty. I have therefore been compelled to ask myself whether this characteristic may not be a further essential precondition of dreaming. Stated in general terms, this would imply that every dream was linked in its manifest content with recent experiences and in its latent content with the most ancient experiences. And I have in fact been able to show in my analysis of hysteria that these ancient experiences have remained recent in the proper sense of the word up to the immediate present. It is still extremely hard to demonstrate the truth of this suspicion; and I shall have to return in another connection (Chapter VII, [pp. 553 ff.]) to a consideration of the probable part played by the earliest experiences of childhood in the formation of dreams.

Of the three characteristics of memory in dreams enumerated at the beginning of this chapter, one—the preference for non-essential materials

---

qualification of this assertion.—The phrase '*thinking and experiencing were one and the same thing*' had a reference to the explanation of hysterical symptoms, and the '*male urinal*' belonged in the same connection. I need not explain to a Viennese the principle of the '*Gschnas.*' It consists in constructing what appear to be rare and precious objects out of trivial and preferably comic and worthless materials (for instance, in making armour out of saucepans, wisps of straw and dinner rolls)—a favourite pastime at bohemian parties here in Vienna. I had observed that this is precisely what hysterical subjects do: alongside what has really happened to them, they unconsciously build up frightful or perverse imaginary events which they construct out of the most innocent and everyday material of their experience. It is to these phantasies that their symptoms are in the first instance attached and not to their recollections of real events, whether serious or equally innocent. This revelation had helped me over a number of difficulties and had given me particular pleasure. What made it possible for me to refer to this by means of the dream-element of the 'male urinal' was as follows. I had been told that at the latest '*Gschnas*'-night a poisoned chalice belonging to Lucrezia Borgia had been exhibited; its central and principal constituent had been a *male urinal* of the type used in hospitals.

[1] [This dream is further discussed on pp. 440 ff.]

in the content of dreams—has been satisfactorily cleared up by being traced back to dream-distortion. We have been able to confirm the existence of the other two—the emphasis upon recent and upon infantile material—but we have not been able to account for them on the basis of the motives that lead to dreaming. These two characteristics, whose explanation and appreciation remain to be discovered, must be kept in mind. Their proper place must be looked for elsewhere—either in the psychology of the state of sleep or in the discussion of the structure of the mental apparatus upon which we shall later embark, after we have learnt that the interpretation of dreams is like a window through which we can get a glimpse of the interior of that apparatus. [See Chapter VII.]

There is, however, another inference following from these last dream-analyses to which I will draw attention at once. Dreams frequently seem to have more than one meaning. Not only, as our examples have shown, may they include several wish-fulfilments one alongside the other; but a succession of meanings or wish-fulfilments may be superimposed on one another, the bottom one being the fulfilment of a wish dating from earliest childhood. And here again the question arises whether it might not be more correct to assert that this occurs 'invariably' rather than 'frequently.'[1]

(C)

THE SOMATIC SOURCES OF DREAMS

If one tries to interest an educated layman in the problems of dreams and, with that end in view, asks him what in his opinion are the sources from which they arise, one finds as a rule that he feels confident of possessing the answer to this part of the question. He thinks at once of the

---

[1] [*Footnote added* 1914:] The fact that the meanings of dreams are arranged in superimposed layers is one of the most delicate, though also one of the most interesting, problems of dream-interpretation. Anyone who forgets this possibility will easily go astray and be led into making untenable assertions upon the nature of dreams. Yet it is still a fact that far too few investigations have been made into this matter. Hitherto the only thorough piece of research has been Otto Rank's [1912*a*] into the fairly regular stratification of symbols in dreams provoked by pressure of the bladder. [See below, pp. 412 ff.]

effects produced on the construction of dreams by digestive disturbances or difficulties—'dreams come from indigestion' [cf. p. 54]—by postures accidentally assumed by the body and by other small incidents during sleep. It never seems to occur to him that when all these factors have been taken into account anything is left over that needs explaining.

I have already discussed at length in the opening chapter (Section C) the part assigned by scientific writers to somatic sources of stimulation in the formation of dreams; so that here I need only recall the results of that enquiry. We found that three different kinds of somatic sources of stimulation were distinguished: objective sensory stimuli arising from external objects, internal states of excitation of the sense organs having only a subjective basis, and somatic stimuli derived from the interior of the body. We noticed moreover that the authorities were inclined to push into the background, or to exclude entirely, any possible *psychical* sources of dreams, as compared with these somatic stimuli (cf. p. 71). In our examination of the claims made on behalf of somatic sources of stimulation we arrived at the following conclusions. The significance of *objective* excitations of the sense organs (consisting partly of chance stimuli during sleep and partly of excitations such as cannot fail to impinge even upon a sleeping mind) is established from numerous observations and has been experimentally confirmed (cf. pp. 55 f.). The part played by *subjective* sensory excitations seems to be demonstrated by the recurrence in dreams of hypnagogic sensory images (cf. pp. 62 f.). And lastly it appears that, though it is impossible to prove that the images and ideas occurring in our dreams can be traced back to *internal* somatic stimuli to the extent to which this has been asserted to be the case, nevertheless this origin finds support in the universally recognized influence exercised upon our dreams by states of excitation in our digestive, urinary and sexual organs [cf. pp. 68 f.].

It would appear, then, that 'nervous stimulation' and 'somatic stimulation' are the somatic sources of dreams—that is to say, according to many writers, their sole source.

On the other hand, we have already found a number of doubts expressed, which seemed to imply a criticism, not indeed of the *correctness*, but of the *adequacy* of the theory of somatic stimulation.

However secure the supporters of this theory might feel in its factual basis—especially as far as accidental and external nervous stimuli are concerned, since these can be traced in the content of dreams without any trouble at all—not one of them could fail to perceive that it is impossible to attribute the wealth of ideational material in dreams to external nervous stimuli alone. Miss Mary Whiton Calkins (1893, 312) examined her own and another person's dreams for six weeks with this question in mind. She found that in only 13.2 per cent and 6.7 per cent of them respectively was it possible to trace the element of external sense-perception; while only two cases in the collection were derivable from organic sensations. Here we have statistical confirmation of what I had been led to suspect from a hasty survey of my own experiences.

It has often been proposed to separate off 'dreams due to nervous stimulation' from other forms of dreams as a subspecies that has been thoroughly investigated. Thus Spitta [1882, 233] divides dreams into 'dreams due to nervous stimulation' and 'dreams due to association.' This solution was, however, bound to remain unsatisfactory so long as it was impossible to demonstrate the link between the somatic sources of a dream and its ideational content. Thus, in addition to the first objection—the insufficient frequency of external sources of stimulation—there was a second one—the insufficient explanation of dreams afforded by such sources. We have a right to expect the supporters of this theory to give us explanations of two points: first, why it is that the external stimulus of a dream is not perceived in its true character but is invariably misunderstood (cf. the alarm-clock dreams on pp. 59 f.); and secondly, why it is that the reaction of the perceiving mind to these misunderstood stimuli should lead to results of such unpredictable variety.

By way of answer to these questions, Strümpell (1877, 108 f.) tells us that, because the mind is withdrawn from the external world during sleep, it is unable to give a correct interpretation of objective sensory stimuli and is obliged to construct illusions on the basis of what is in many respects an indeterminate impression. To quote his own words: 'As soon as a sensation or complex of sensations or a feeling or a psychical process of any kind arises in the mind during sleep as a result of an external or internal nervous stimulus and is perceived by the mind, that process calls up sensory images from the circle of experiences left over in the mind from the waking state—that is to say, earlier perceptions—which are either bare or accompanied by their appropriate psychical values. The process surrounds itself, as it were, with a larger or smaller number of images of this kind and through them the impression derived from the nervous stimulus acquires its psychical value. We speak here (just as we usually do in the case of waking behaviour) of the sleeping mind "interpreting" the impressions made by the nervous stimulus. The outcome of this interpretation is what we describe as a "dream due to nervous stimulation," that is, a dream whose components are determined by a nervous stimulus producing its psychical effects in the mind according to the laws of reproduction.' [Cf. pp. 60 f., 83 f. and 87.]

Wundt [1874, 656 f.] is saying something essentially identical with this theory when he asserts that the ideas occurring in dreams are derived, for the most part at least, from sensory stimuli, including especially co-enaesthetic sensations, and are for that reason mainly imaginative illusions and probably only to a small extent pure mnemic ideas intensified into hallucinations. [Cf. pp. 71 f.] Strümpell (1877, 84) has hit upon an apt simile for the relation which subsists on this theory between the contents of a dream and its stimuli, when he writes that 'it is as though the ten fingers of a man who knows nothing of music were wandering over the keys of a piano.' [Cf. pp. 104 f. and 147.] Thus a dream is not, on this view, a mental phenomenon based on psychical motives, but the outcome of a physiological stimulus which is expressed in psychical symptoms because the apparatus upon which the stimulus impinges is capable of no other form of expression. A similar presupposition also underlies, for instance, the famous analogy by means of which Meynert attempted to explain obsessive ideas: the analogy of a clock-face on which certain figures stand out by being more prominently embossed than the rest.[1]

However popular the theory of the somatic stimulation of dreams may have become and however attractive it may seem, its weak point is easily displayed. Every somatic dream-stimulus which requires the sleeping mental apparatus to interpret it by the construction of an illusion may give rise to an unlimited number of such attempts at interpretation—that is to say, it may be represented in the content of the dream by an immense variety of ideas.[2] But the theory put forward by Strümpell and Wundt is incapable

---

[1] [This has not been traced in Meynert's published writings.]

[2] [*Footnote added* 1914:] Mourly Vold [1910–12] has produced a two-volume work containing detailed and precise reports of a series of experimentally produced dreams. [Cf. pp. 70.] I should recommend a study of this work to anyone who wishes to convince himself of how little light is thrown on the content of individual dreams by the conditions of the experiments described in it and of how little help in general is afforded by such experiments towards an understanding of the problems of dreams. [See, however, p. 204 *n.*]

of producing any motive governing the relation between an external stimulus and the dream-idea chosen for its interpretation—is incapable, that is, of explaining what Lipps (1883, 170) describes as the 'remarkable choice often made' by these stimuli 'in the course of their productive activity.' Objections have further been raised against the presupposition upon which the whole theory of illusion is based—the presupposition that the sleeping mind is incapable of recognizing the true nature of objective sensory stimuli. Burdach, the physiologist, showed us long ago that even in sleep the mind is very well able to interpret correctly the sense impressions that reach it and to react in accordance with that correct interpretation; for he recalled the fact that particular sense impressions which seem important to the sleeper can be excepted from the general neglect to which such impressions are subjected during sleep (as in the case of a nursing mother or wet-nurse and her charge), and that a sleeper is much more certain to be woken by the sound of his own name than by any indifferent auditory impression— all of which implies that the mind distinguishes between sensations during sleep (cf. pp. 82). Burdach went on to infer from these observations that what we must presume during the state of sleep is not an *incapacity to interpret* sensory stimuli but a *lack of interest* in them. The same arguments which were used by Burdach in 1830 were brought forward once more without any modifications by Lipps in 1883 in his criticism of the theory of somatic stimulation. Thus the mind seems to behave like the sleeper in the anecdote. When someone asked him if he was asleep, he replied 'No.' But when his questioner went on to say: 'Then lend me ten florins,' he took refuge in a subterfuge and replied: 'I'm asleep.'

The inadequacy of the theory of the somatic stimulation of dreams can be demonstrated in other ways. Observation shows that external stimuli do not necessarily compel me to dream, even though such stimuli appear in the content of my dream when and if I do dream. Supposing, let us say, that I am subjected to a tactile stimulus while I am asleep. A variety of different reactions are then open to me. I may disregard it, and when I wake up I may find, for instance, that my leg is uncovered or that there is some pressure on my arm; pathology provides very numerous instances in which various powerfully exciting sensory and motor stimuli can remain without effect during sleep. Or again, I may be aware of the sensation in my sleep—I may be aware of it, as one might say, 'through' my sleep—(which is what happens as a rule in the case of painful stimuli) but without my weaving the pain into a dream. And thirdly, I may react to the stimulus by waking up so as to get rid of it.[1] It is only as a fourth possibility that the nervous stimulus may cause me to dream. Yet the other possibilities are realized at least as frequently as this last one of constructing a dream. And this could not happen unless the motive for dreaming lay *elsewhere than in somatic sources of stimulation.*

Certain other writers—Scherner [1861] and Volkelt [1875], the philosopher, who adopted Scherner's views—formed a just estimate of the gaps which I have here indicated in the explanation of dreams as being due to somatic stimulation. These writers attempted to define more precisely the mental activities which lead to the production of such variegated dream-images from the somatic stimuli; in other words, they sought to regard dreaming once again as something essentially *mental*— as a psychical activity. [Cf. pp. 109 ff.] Scherner did not merely depict the psychical characteristics unfolded in the production of dreams in terms charged with poetic feeling and glowing with life; he believed, too, that he had discovered the principle according to which the mind deals with the stimuli presented to it. On his view, the dream-work, when the imagination is set free from the shackles of daytime, seeks to give a *symbolic* representation of the nature of the organ from which the stimulus arises and of the nature of the stimulus itself. Thus he provides a kind of 'dream-book' to serve as a guide to the interpretation of dreams, which makes it possible to deduce from the dream-images inferences as to the somatic feelings, the state of the organs and the character of the stimuli concerned. 'Thus the image of a cat expresses a state of angry ill-temper, and the image of a smooth and lightly-coloured loaf of bread stands for physical nudity.' [Volkelt, 1875, 32.] The human body as a whole is pictured by the dream-imagination as a house and the separate organs of the body by portions of a house. In 'dreams with a dental stimulus,' an entrance-hall with a high, vaulted roof corresponds to the oral cavity and a staircase to the descent from the throat to the oesophagus. 'In dreams due to headaches, the top of the head is represented by the ceiling of a room covered with disgusting, toad-like spiders.' [Ibid., 33 f.] A variety of such symbols are employed by dreams to represent the same organ. 'Thus the

---

[1] [*Footnote added* 1919:] Cf. Landauer (1918) on behaviour during sleep. Anyone can observe persons asleep carrying out actions which obviously have a meaning. A man asleep is not reduced to complete idiocy; on the contrary, he is capable of logical and deliberate acts.

breathing lung will be symbolically represented by a blazing furnace, with flames roaring with a sound like the passage of air; the heart will be represented by hollow boxes, or baskets, the bladder by round, bag-shaped objects or, more generally, by hollow ones.' [Ibid., 34.] 'It is of special importance that at the end of a dream the organ concerned or its function is often openly revealed, and as a rule in relation to the dreamer's own body. Thus a dream with a dental stimulus usually ends by the dreamer picturing himself pulling a tooth out of his mouth.' [Ibid., 35.]

This theory of dream-interpretation cannot be said to have been very favourably received by other writers on the subject. Its main feature seems to be its extravagance; and there has even been hesitation in recognizing such justification as, in my opinion, it can lay claim to. As will have been seen, it involves a revival of dream-interpretation by means of *symbolism*— the same method that was employed in antiquity, except that the field from which interpretations are collected is restricted within the limits of the human body. Its lack of any technique of interpreting that can be grasped scientifically must greatly narrow the application of Scherner's theory. It seems to leave the door open to arbitrary interpretations, especially as in its case, too, the same stimulus can be represented in the dream-content in a variety of different ways. Thus even Scherner's disciple, Volkelt, found himself unable to confirm the view that the body was represented by a house. Objections are also bound to arise from the fact that once again the mind is saddled with the dream-work as a useless and aimless function; for, according to the theory we are discussing, the mind is content with making phantasies about the stimulus with which it is occupied, without the remotest hint at anything in the nature of *disposing* of the stimulus.

There is one particular criticism, however, which is gravely damaging to Scherner's theory of the symbolization of somatic stimuli. These stimuli are present at all times and it is generally held that the mind is more accessible to them during sleep than when it is awake. It is difficult to understand, then, why the mind does not dream continuously all through the night, and, indeed, dream every night of all the organs. An attempt may be made to avoid this criticism by adding the further condition that in order to arouse dream-activity it is necessary for *special* excitations to proceed from the eyes, ears, teeth, intestines, etc. But the difficulty then arises of proving the objective nature of such increases of stimulus—which is only possible in a small number of cases. If dreams of flying are a symbolization of the rising and sinking of the lobes of the lungs [cf. p. 69], then, as Strümpell [1877, 119] has already pointed out, either such dreams would have to be much more frequent than they are or it would be necessary to prove an increase in the activity of breathing in the course of them. There is a third possibility, which is the most probable of all, namely that special motives may be temporarily operative which direct the attention to visceral sensations that are uniformly present at all times. This possibility, however, carries us beyond the scope of Scherner's theory.

The value of the views put forward by Scherner and Volkelt lies in the fact that they draw attention to a number of characteristics of the content of dreams which call for explanation and seem to promise fresh discoveries. It is perfectly true that dreams contain symbolizations of bodily organs and functions, that water in a dream often points to a urinary stimulus, and that the male genitals can be represented by an upright stick or a pillar, and so on. In the case of dreams in which the field of vision is full of movement and bright colours, in contrast to the drabness of other dreams, it is scarcely possible not to interpret them as 'dreams with a visual stimulus'; nor can one dispute the part played by illusions in the case of dreams characterized by noise and a confusion of voices. Scherner [1861, 167] reports a dream of two rows of pretty, fair-haired boys standing opposite each other on a bridge, and of their attacking each other and then going back to their original position, till at last the dreamer saw himself sitting down on a bridge and pulling a long tooth out of his jaw. Similarly Volkelt [1875, 52] reports a dream in which two rows of drawers in a cupboard played a part and which once more ended with the dreamer pulling out a tooth. Dream-formations such as these, which are recorded in great numbers by the two authors, forbid our dismissing Scherner's theory as an idle invention without looking for its kernel of truth. [See p. 360.] The task, then, that faces us is to find an explanation of another kind for the supposed symbolization of what is alleged to be a dental stimulus.[1]

Throughout the whole of this discussion of the theory of the somatic sources of dreams I have refrained from making use of the argument based upon my dream-analyses. If it can be proved, by a procedure which other writers have not employed upon their dream-material, that dreams possess a value of their own as psychical acts, that wishes are the motive for their construction and that experiences of the preceding day provide the immediate material for their content, then any other theory of dreams, which

---

[1] [These dreams are further considered on pp. 395 ff.]

neglects so important a procedure of research and accordingly represents dreams as a useless and puzzling psychical reaction to somatic stimuli, stands condemned without there being any necessity for specific criticisms. Otherwise—and this seems highly improbable—there would have to be two quite different kinds of dreaming, one of which has come only under *my* observation and the other only under that of the earlier authorities. All that remains, therefore, is to find a place in my theory of dreams for the facts upon which the current theory of the somatic stimulation of dreams is based.

We have already taken the first step in this direction by advancing the thesis (see pp. 201 f.) that the dream-work is under the necessity of combining into a unity all instigations to dreaming which are active simultaneously. We found that, when two or more experiences capable of creating an impression are left over from the previous day, the wishes derived from them are combined in a single dream, and similarly that the psychically significant impression and the indifferent experiences from the previous day are brought together in the dream-material, provided always that it is possible to set up communicating ideas between them. Thus a dream appears to be a reaction to everything that is simultaneously present in the sleeping mind as currently active material. So far as we have hitherto analysed the material of dreams, we have seen it as a collection of psychical residues and memory-traces, to which (on account of the preference shown for recent and infantile material) we have been led to attribute a hitherto indefinable quality of being 'currently active.' We can foresee, then, without any great difficulty, what will happen if fresh material in the form of sensations is added during sleep to these currently active memories. It is once again owing to the fact of their being currently active that these sensory excitations are of importance for the dream; they are united with the other currently active psychical material to furnish what is used for the construction of the dream. To put it another way, stimuli arising during sleep are worked up into a wish-fulfilment the other constituents of which are the familiar psychical 'day's residues.' This combination *need* not occur; as I have already pointed out, there is more than one way of reacting to a somatic stimulus during sleep. When it *does* occur, it means that it has been possible to find ideational material to serve as the content of the dream of such a sort as to be able to represent both kinds of source of the dream—the somatic and the psychical.

The essential nature of the dream is not altered by the fact of somatic material being added to its psychical sources: a dream remains the fulfilment of a wish, no matter in what way the expression of that wish-fulfilment is determined by the currently active material.

I am prepared to leave room at this point for the operation of a number of special factors which can lend a varying importance to external stimuli in relation to dreams. As I picture it, a combination of individual factors, physiological and accidental, produced by the circumstances of the moment, is what determines how a person shall behave in particular cases of comparatively intense objective stimulation during sleep. The habitual or accidental depth of his sleep, taken in conjunction with the intensity of the stimulus, will make it possible in one case for him to suppress the stimulus so that his sleep is not interrupted and in another case will compel him to wake up or will encourage an attempt to overcome the stimulus by weaving it into a dream. In accordance with these various possible combinations, external objective stimuli will find expression in dreams with greater or less frequency in one person than in another. In my own case, since I am an excellent sleeper and obstinately refuse to allow anything to disturb my sleep, it very rarely happens that external causes of excitation find their way into my dreams; whereas psychical motives obviously cause me to dream very easily. In fact I have only noted a single dream in which an objective and painful source of stimulus is recognizable; and it will be most instructive to examine the effect which the external stimulus produced in this particular dream.

I was riding on a grey horse, timidly and awkwardly to begin with, as though I were only reclining upon it. I met one of my colleagues, P., who was sitting high on a horse, dressed in a tweed suit, and who drew my attention to something (probably to my bad seat). I now began to find myself sitting more and more firmly and comfortably on my highly intelligent horse, and noticed that I was feeling quite at home up there. My saddle was a kind of bolster, which completely filled the space between its neck and crupper. In this way I rode straight in between two vans. After riding some distance up the street, I turned round and tried to dismount, first in front of a small open chapel that stood in the street frontage. Then I actually did dismount in front of another chapel that stood near it. My hotel was in the same street; I might have let the horse go to it on its own, but I preferred to lead it there. It was as though I should have felt ashamed to arrive at it on horseback. A hotel 'boots' was standing in front of the hotel; he showed me a note of mine that had been found, and laughed at me over it. In the note was written, doubly underlined: 'No food' and then another remark (indistinct) *such as 'No work,' together with a vague idea that I was in a strange town in which I was doing no work.*

It would not be supposed at first sight that this dream originated un der the influence, or rather under the compulsion, of a painful stimulus. But for some days before I had been suffering from boils which made every movement a torture; and finally a boil the size of an apple had risen at the base of my scrotum, which caused me the most unbearable pain with every step I took. Feverish lassitude, loss of appetite and the hard work with which I nevertheless carried on—all these had combined with the pain to depress me. I was not properly capable of discharging my medical duties. There was, however, one activity for which, in view of the nature and situation of my complaint, I should certainly have been less fitted than for any other, and that was—riding. And this was precisely the activity in which the dream landed me: it was the most energetic denial of my illness that could possibly be imagined. I cannot in fact ride, nor have I, apart from this, had dreams of riding. I have only sat on a horse once in my life and that was without a saddle, and I did not enjoy it. But in this dream I was riding as though I had no boil on my perineum—or rather *because I wanted not to have one.* My saddle, to judge from its description, was the poultice which had made it possible for me to fall asleep. Under its assuaging influence I had probably been unaware of my pain during the first hours of sleep. The painful feelings had then announced themselves and sought to wake me; whereupon the dream came and said soothingly: 'No! Go on sleeping! There's no need to wake up. You haven't got a boil; for you're riding on a horse, and it's quite certain that you couldn't ride if you had a boil in that particular place.' And the dream was successful. The pain was silenced, and I went on sleeping.

But the dream was not content with 'suggesting away' my boil by obstinately insisting upon an idea that was inconsistent with it and so behaving like the hallucinatory delusion of the mother who had lost her child or the merchant whose losses had robbed him of his fortune.[1] The details of the sensation which was being repudiated and of the picture which was employed in order to repress that sensation also served the

---

[1] Cf. the passage in Griesinger [1861, 106, referred to on pp. 116] and my remarks in my second paper on the neuro-psychoses of defence (Freud, 1896*b*). [Actually the reference seems to be to a paragraph near the end of Freud's *first* paper on that subject (Freud, 1894*a*).]

dream as a means of connecting *other* material that was currently active in my mind with the situation in the dream and of giving that material representation. I was riding on a *grey* horse, whose colour corresponded precisely to the *pepper-and-salt* colour of the suit my colleague P. was wearing when I had last met him in the country. The cause of my boils had been ascribed to my eating *highly-spiced* food—an aetiology that was at least preferable to the *sugar* [diabetes] which might also occur to one in connection with boils. My friend P. liked to ride *the high horse* over me ever since he had taken over one of my women patients on whom I had pulled off some remarkable *feats*. (In the dream I began by riding tangentially—like the *feat* of a trick-rider.) But in fact, like the horse in the anecdote of the Sunday horseman,[1] this patient had taken me wherever she felt inclined. Thus the horse acquired the symbolic meaning of a woman patient. (It was *highly intelligent* in the dream.) '*I felt quite at home up there*' referred to the position I had occupied in this patient's house before I was replaced by P. Not long before, one of my few patrons among the leading physicians in this city had remarked to me in connection with this same house: 'You struck me as being firmly in the saddle there.' It was a remarkable *feat*, too, to be able to carry on my psychotherapeutic work for eight or ten hours a day while I was having so much pain. But I knew that I could not go on long with my peculiarly difficult work unless I was in completely sound physical health; and my dream was full of gloomy allusions to the situation in which I should then find myself. (The *note* which neurasthenics bring with them to show the doctor; *no work, no food*.) In the course of further interpretation I saw that the dream-work had succeeded in finding a path from the wishful situation of riding to some scenes of quarrelling from my very early childhood which must have occurred between me and a nephew of mine, a year my senior, who was at present living in England. [Cf. pp. 433 f.] Furthermore, the dream had derived some of its elements from my travels in Italy: the street in the dream was composed of impressions of Verona and Siena. A still deeper interpretation led to sexual dream-thoughts, and I recalled the meaning which references to Italy seem to have had in the dreams of a woman patient who had never visited that lovely country: '*gen Italien* [to Italy]'— '*Genitalien* [genitals]'; and this was connected, too, with the house in

---

[1] [In a letter to Fliess of July 7, 1898 (Freud, 1950a, Letter 92), Freud describes 'the famous principle of Itzig, the Sunday horseman: "Itzig, where are you riding to?"—"Don't ask *me*! Ask the horse!"']

which I had preceded my friend P. as physician, as well as with the situation of my boil.

In another dream[1] I similarly succeeded in warding off a threatened interruption of my sleep which came this time from a sensory stimulus. In this case it was only by chance, however, that I was able to discover the link between the dream and its accidental stimulus and thus to understand the dream. One morning at the height of summer, while I was staying at a mountain resort in the Tyrol, I woke up knowing I had had a dream that *the Pope was dead.* I failed to interpret this dream—a non-visual one—and only remembered as part of its basis that I had read in a newspaper a short time before that his Holiness was suffering from a slight indisposition. In the course of the morning, however, my wife asked me if I had heard the frightful noise made by the pealing of bells that morning. I had been quite unaware of them, but I now understood my dream. It had been a reaction on the part of my need for sleep to the noise with which the pious Tyrolese had been trying to wake me. I had taken my revenge on them by drawing the inference which formed the content of the dream, and I had then continued my sleep without paying any more attention to the noise.

The dreams quoted in earlier chapters included several which might serve as instances of the working-over of such so-called nervous stimuli. My dream of drinking water in great gulps [p. 148] is an example. The somatic stimulus was apparently its only source, and the wish derived from the sensation (the thirst, that is) was apparently its only motive. The case is similar with other simple dreams in which a somatic stimulus seems able by itself to construct a wish. The dream of the woman patient who threw off the cooling apparatus from her cheek during the night [pp. 150 f.] presents an unusual method of reacting to a painful stimulus with a wish-fulfilment: it appears as though the patient succeeded temporarily in making herself analgesic, while ascribing her pains to someone else.

My dream of the three Fates [pp. 225 ff.] was clearly a hunger dream. But it succeeded in shifting the craving for nourishment back to a child's longing for his mother's breast, and it made use of an innocent desire as

---

[1] [This paragraph was added in 1914. The dream had already been very briefly recorded in Freud, 1913*h* (No. 1); it will also be found in Lecture V of Freud, 1916–17.]

a screen for a more serious one which could not be so openly displayed. My dream about Count Thun [pp. 231 ff.] showed how an accidental physical need can be linked up with the most intense (but at the same time the most intensely suppressed) mental impulses. And a case such as that related by Garnier (1872, **1,** 476) of how the First Consul wove the noise of an exploding bomb into a battle dream before he woke up from it [p. 58 f.] reveals with quite special clarity the nature of the sole motive that leads mental activity to concern itself with sensations during sleep. A young barrister,[1] fresh from his first important bankruptcy proceedings, who dropped asleep one afternoon, behaved in just the same way as the great Napoleon. He had a dream of a certain G. Reich of *Husyatin* [a town in Galicia] whom he had come across during a bankruptcy case; the name 'Husyatin' kept on forcing itself on his notice, till he woke up and found that his wife (who was suffering from a bronchial catarrh) was having a violent fit of coughing [in German '*husten*'].

Let us compare this dream of the first Napoleon (who, incidentally, was an extremely sound sleeper) with that of the sleepy student who was roused by his landlady and told that it was time to go to the hospital, and who proceeded to dream that he was in bed at the hospital and then slept on, under the pretext that as he was already in the hospital there was no need for him to get up and go there [p. 150]. This latter dream was clearly a dream of convenience. The dreamer admitted his motive for dreaming without any disguise; but at the same time he gave away one of the secrets of dreaming in general. All dreams are in a sense dreams of convenience: they serve the purpose of prolonging sleep instead of waking up. *Dreams are the* GUARDIANS *of sleep and not its disturbers.* We shall have occasion elsewhere to justify this view of them in relation to awakening factors of a *psychical* kind [see below pp. 577]; but we are already in a position to show that it is applicable to the part played by objective external stimuli. Either the mind pays no attention at all to occasions for sensation during sleep—if it is able to do this despite the intensity of the stimuli and the significance which it knows attaches to them; or it makes use of a dream in order to deny the stimuli; or, thirdly, if it is obliged to recognize them, it seeks for an interpretation of them which will make the currently active sensation into a component part of a situation which is wished for and which is consistent with sleeping. The currently active

---

[1] [This sentence and the next were added in 1909.]

sensation is woven into a dream *in order to rob it of reality.* Napoleon could sleep on—with a conviction that what was trying to disturb him was only a dream-memory of the thunder of the guns at Arcole.[1]

Thus the wish to sleep (which the conscious ego is concentrated upon, and which, together with the dream-censorship and the 'secondary revision' which I shall mention later [pp. 493 ff.]*, constitute the conscious ego's share in dreaming) must in every case be reckoned as one of the motives for the formation of dreams, and every successful dream is a fulfilment of that wish.*[2] We shall discuss elsewhere [pp. 570 ff.] the relations subsisting between this universal, invariably present and unchanging wish to sleep and the other wishes, of which now one and now another is fulfilled by the content of the dream. But we have found in the wish to sleep the factor that is able to fill the gap in the theory of Strümpell and Wundt [pp. 243 f.] and to explain the perverse and capricious manner in which external stimuli are interpreted. The correct interpretation, which the sleeping mind is perfectly capable of making, would involve an active interest and would require that sleep should be brought to an end; for that reason, of all the possible interpretations, only those are admitted which are consistent with the absolute censorship exercised by the wish to sleep. 'It is the nightingale and not the lark.' For if it were the lark it would mean the end of the lovers' night. Among the interpretations of the stimulus which are accordingly admissible, that one is then selected which can provide the best link with the wishful impulses lurking in the mind. Thus everything is unambiguously determined and nothing is left to arbitrary decision. The misinterpretation is not an illusion but, as one might say, an evasion. Here once again, however, just as when, in obedience to the dream-censorship, a substitution is effected by displacement, we have to admit that we are faced by an act which deviates from normal psychical processes.

When external nervous stimuli and internal somatic stimuli are intense enough to force psychical attention to themselves, then—provided

---

[1] The two sources from which I know this dream do not agree in their account of it.

[2] [The portion of this sentence in parentheses was not included in the first or second edition (1900 and 1909). The phrase 'which the conscious ego is concentrated upon, and which, together with the dream-censorship, constitute the conscious ego's contribution to dreaming' was added in 1911. The phrase 'and the "secondary revision" which we shall mention later' was added as a footnote in 1914 and incorporated in the text in 1930.]

that their outcome *is* dreaming and not waking up—they serve as a fixed point for the formation of a dream, a nucleus in its material; a wish-fulfilment is then looked for that shall correspond to this nucleus, just as (see above, pp. 248) intermediate ideas are looked for between two psychical dream-stimuli. To that extent it is true that in a number of dreams the content of the dream is dictated by the somatic element. In this extreme instance it may even happen that a wish which is not actually a currently active one is called up for the sake of constructing a dream. A dream, however, has no alternative but to represent a wish in the situation of having been fulfilled; it is, as it were, faced with the problem of looking for a wish which can be represented as fulfilled by the currently active sensation. If this immediate material is of a painful or distressing kind, that does not necessarily mean that it cannot be used for the construction of a dream. The mind has wishes at its disposal whose fulfilment produces unpleasure. This seems self-contradictory; but it becomes intelligible when we take into account the presence of two psychical agencies and a censorship between them.

As we have seen, there are 'repressed' wishes in the mind, which belong to the first system and whose fulfilment is opposed by the second system. In saying that there are such wishes I am not making a historical statement to the effect that they once existed and were later abolished. The theory of repression, which is essential to the study of the psychoneuroses, asserts that these repressed wishes *still* exist—though there is a simultaneous inhibition which holds them down. Linguistic usage hits the mark in speaking of the 'suppression' [i.e. the 'pressing down'] of these impulses. The psychical arrangements that make it possible for such impulses to force their way to realization remain in being and in working order. Should it happen, however, that a suppressed wish of this kind is carried into effect, and that its inhibition by the second system (the system that is admissible to consciousness) is defeated, this defeat finds expression as unpleasure. In conclusion: if sensations of an unpleasurable nature arising from somatic sources occur during sleep, the dream-work makes use of that event in order to represent—subject to the continuance of the censorship to a greater or less degree—the fulfilment of some wish which is normally suppressed.[1]

---

[1] [This whole subject is further discussed in Section C of Chapter VII; see especially pp. 557 ff. Cf. also pp. 284 and 492.]

This state of affairs is what makes possible one group of anxiety-dreams—dream-structures unpropitious from the point of view of the wish-theory. A second group of them reveal a different mechanism; for anxiety in dreams may be psychoneurotic anxiety: it may originate from psychosexual excitations—in which case the anxiety corresponds to repressed libido. Where this is so, the anxiety, like the whole anxiety-dream, has the significance of a neurotic symptom, and we come near the limit at which the wish-fulfilling purpose of dreams breaks down. [See pp. 183 ff. and 579 ff.] But there are some anxiety-dreams [—those of the first group—] in which the feeling of anxiety is determined somatically—where, for instance, there happens to be difficulty in breathing owing to disease of the lungs or heart—and in such cases the anxiety is exploited in order to assist the fulfilment in the form of dreams of energetically suppressed wishes which, if they had been dreamt about for *psychical* reasons, would have led to a similar release of anxiety. But there is no difficulty in reconciling these two apparently different groups. In both groups of dreams two psychical factors are involved: an inclination towards an affect and an ideational content; and these are intimately related to each other. If one of them is currently active, it calls up the other even in a dream; in the one case the somatically determined anxiety calls up the suppressed ideational content, and in the other the ideational content with its accompanying sexual excitation, having been set free from repression, calls up a release of anxiety. We can put it that in the first case a somatically determined affect is given a psychical interpretation; while in the other case, though the whole is psychically determined, the content which had been suppressed is easily replaced by a somatic interpretation appropriate to anxiety. The difficulties which all this offers to our understanding have little to do with dreams: they arise from the fact that we are here touching on the problem of the generation of anxiety and on the problem of repression.

There can be no doubt that physical coenaesthesia [or diffuse general sensibility, see p. 66 f.] is among the internal somatic stimuli which can dictate the content of dreams. It can do so, not in the sense that it can provide the dream's content, but in the sense that it can force upon the dream-thoughts a choice of the material to be represented in the content by putting forward one part of the material as being appropriate to its own character and by holding back another part. Apart from this, the coenaesthetic feelings left over from the preceding day link themselves up, no doubt, with the psychical residues which have such an important influence on dreams. This general mood may persist unchanged in the dream or it may be mastered, and thus, if it is unpleasurable, may be changed into its opposite.[1]

Thus, in my opinion, somatic sources of stimulation during sleep (that is to say, sensations during sleep), unless they are of unusual intensity, play a similar part in the formation of dreams to that played by recent but indifferent impressions left over from the previous day. I believe, that is, that they are brought in to help in the formation of a dream if they fit in appropriately with the ideational content derived from the dream's psychical sources, but otherwise not. They are treated like some cheap material always ready to hand, which is employed whenever it is needed, in contrast to a precious material which itself prescribes the way in which it shall be employed. If, to take a simile, a patron of the arts brings an artist some rare stone, such as a piece of onyx, and asks him to create a work of art from it, then the size of the stone, its colour and markings, help to decide what head or what scene shall be represented in it. Whereas in the case of a uniform and plentiful material such as marble or sandstone, the artist merely follows some idea that is present in his own mind. It is only in this way, so it seems to me, that we can explain the fact that dream-content provided by somatic stimuli of no unusual intensity fails to appear in every dream or every night. [Cf. pp. 246.][2]

I can perhaps best illustrate my meaning by an example, which, moreover, will bring us back to dream-interpretation.

One day I had been trying to discover what might be the meaning of the feelings of being inhibited, of being glued to the spot, of not being able to get something done, and so on, which occur so often in dreams and are so closely akin to feelings of anxiety. That night I had the following dream:

I was very incompletely dressed and was going upstairs from a flat on the ground floor to a higher storey. I was going up three steps at a time and was delighted at my agility. Suddenly I saw a maid-servant coming down the stairs—coming towards me, that is. I felt ashamed and tried to hurry, and at

---

[1] [Cf. pp. 492 ff.—This last sentence was added in 1914.]

[2] [*Footnote added* 1914:] Rank has shown in a number of papers [1910, 1912*a* and 1912*b*] that certain arousal dreams produced by organic stimuli (dreams with a urinary stimulus and dreams of emission or orgasm) are especially suited to demonstrate the struggle between the need to sleep and the claims of organic needs, as well as the influence of the latter upon the content of dreams. [See pp. 412 ff.]

this point the feeling of being inhibited set in: I was glued to the steps and unable to budge from the spot.

Analysis.—The situation in the dream is taken from everyday reality. I occupy two flats in a house in Vienna, which are connected only by the public staircase. My consulting-room and study are on the upper ground floor and my living rooms are one storey higher. When, late in the evening, I have finished my work down below, I go up the stairs to my bedroom. On the evening before I had the dream, I had in fact made this short journey in rather disordered dress—that is to say, I had taken off my collar and tie and cuffs. In the dream this had been turned into a higher degree of undress, but, as usual, an indeterminate one. [Cf. p. 263.] I usually go upstairs two or three steps at a time; and this was recognized in the dream itself as a wish-fulfilment: the ease with which I achieved it reassured me as to the functioning of my heart. Further, this method of going upstairs was an effective contrast to the inhibition in the second half of the dream. It showed me—what needed no proving—that dreams find no difficulty in representing motor acts carried out to perfection. (One need only recall dreams of flying.)

The staircase up which I was going, however, was not the one in my house. At first I failed to recognize it and it was only the identity of the person who met me that made it clear to me what locality was intended. This person was the maid-servant of the old lady whom I was visiting twice a day in order to give her injections [cf. p. 142]; and the staircase, too, was just like the one in her house which I had to go up twice a day.

Now how did this staircase and this female figure come to be in my dream? The feeling of shame at not being completely dressed is no doubt of a sexual nature; but the maid-servant whom I dreamt about was older than I am, surly and far from attractive. The only answer to the problem that occurred to me was this. When I paid my morning visits to this house I used as a rule to be seized with a desire to clear my throat as I went up the stairs and the product of my expectoration would fall on the staircase. For on neither of these floors was there a spittoon; and the view I took was that the cleanliness of the stairs should not be maintained at my expense but should be made possible by the provision of a spittoon. The concierge, an equally elderly and surly woman (but of cleanly instincts, as I was prepared to admit), looked at the matter in a different light. She would lie in wait for me to see whether I should again make free of the stairs, and, if she found that I did, I used to hear her grumbling audibly; and for several days afterwards she would omit the usual greeting when we met. The day before I had the dream the concierge's party had received a reinforcement in the shape of the maid-servant. I had, as usual, concluded my hurried visit to the patient, when the servant stopped me in the hall and remarked: 'You might have wiped your boots, doctor, before you came into the room today. You've made the red carpet all dirty again with your feet.' This was the only claim the staircase and the maid-servant had to appearing in my dream.

There was an internal connection between my running up the stairs and my spitting on the stairs. Pharyngitis as well as heart trouble are both regarded as punishments for the vice of smoking. And on account of that habit my reputation for tidiness was not of the highest with the authorities in my own house any more than in the other; so that the two were fused into one in the dream.

I must postpone my further interpretation of this dream till I can explain the origin of the typical dream of being incompletely dressed. I will only point out as a provisional conclusion to be drawn from the present dream that a sensation of inhibited movement in dreams is produced whenever the particular context requires it. The cause of this part of the dream's content cannot have been that some special modification in my powers of movement had occurred during my sleep, since only a moment earlier I had seen myself (almost as though to confirm this fact) running nimbly up the stairs.[1]

(D)

TYPICAL DREAMS

We are not in general in a position to interpret another person's dream unless he is prepared to communicate to us the unconscious thoughts that lie behind its content. The practical applicability of our method of interpreting dreams is in consequence severely restricted.[2] We have seen that, as a general rule, each person is at liberty to construct his dream-world according to his individual peculiarities and so to make it unintelligible to

---

[1] [The feeling of inhibition in dreams is discussed at length on pp. 350 ff. The present dream is further analysed on pp. 265 f. It was reported in a letter to Fliess of May 31, 1897. (Freud, 1950a, Letter 64.)]

[2] [*Footnote added* 1925:] This assertion that our method of interpreting dreams cannot be applied unless we have access to the dreamer's associative material requires supplementing: our interpretative activity is in one instance independent

other people. It now appears, however, that, in complete contrast to this, there are a certain number of dreams which almost everyone has dreamt alike and which we are accustomed to assume must have the same meaning for everyone. A special interest attaches, moreover, to these typical dreams because they presumably arise from the same sources in every case and thus seem particularly well qualified to throw light on the sources of dreams.

It is therefore with quite particular anticipations that we shall attempt to apply our technique of dream-interpretation to these typical dreams; and it is with great reluctance that we shall have to confess that our art disappoints our expectations precisely in relation to this material. If we attempt to interpret a typical dream, the dreamer fails as a rule to produce the associations which would in other cases have led us to understand it, or else his associations become obscure and insufficient so that we cannot solve our problem with their help. We shall learn in a later portion of this work [Section E of Chapter VI, pp. 363 ff.] why this is so and how we can make up for this defect in our technique. My readers will also discover why it is that at the present point I am able to deal only with a few members of the group of typical dreams and must postpone my consideration of the rest until this later point in my discussion. [See pp. 394 ff.][1]

(α) Embarrassing Dreams of Being Naked

Dreams of being naked or insufficiently dressed in the presence of strangers sometimes occur with the additional feature of there being a complete absence of any such feeling as shame on the dreamer's part. We

---

of these associations—if, namely, the dreamer has employed *symbolic* elements in the content of the dream. In such cases we make use of what is, strictly speaking, a second and auxiliary method of dream-interpretation. (See below [pp. 371 f.].) [In the edition of 1911 only, the following footnote appeared at this point: 'Apart from cases in which the dreamer makes use of symbols which are familiar to us for the purpose of representing his latent dream-thoughts (see below).']

[1] [This paragraph in its present form dates from 1914. It was in the edition of that year (the fourth) that the section on symbolism was added to Chapter VI. This led to considerable alterations in the present section, much of the material in which was transferred to the new section. (See Editor's Introduction, p. xiii.)]

are only concerned here, however, with those dreams of being naked in which one *does* feel shame and embarrassment and tries to escape or hide, and is then overcome by a strange inhibition which prevents one from moving and makes one feel incapable of altering one's distressing situation. It is only with this accompaniment that the dream is typical; without it, the gist of its subject-matter may be included in every variety of context or may be ornamented with individual trimmings. Its essence [in its typical form] lies in a distressing feeling in the nature of shame and in the fact that one wishes to hide one's nakedness, as a rule by locomotion, but finds one is unable to do so. I believe the great majority of my readers will have found themselves in this situation in dreams.

The nature of the undress involved is customarily far from clear. The dreamer may say 'I was in my chemise,' but this is rarely a distinct picture. The kind of undress is usually so vague that the description is expressed as an alternative: 'I was in my chemise or petticoat.' As a rule the defect in the dreamer's toilet is not so grave as to appear to justify the shame to which it gives rise. In the case of a man who has worn the Emperor's uniform, nakedness is often replaced by some breach of the dress regulations: 'I was walking in the street without my sabre and saw some officers coming up,' or 'I was without my necktie,' or 'I was wearing civilian check trousers,' and so on.

The people in whose presence one feels ashamed are almost always strangers, with their features left indeterminate. In the typical dream it never happens that the clothing which causes one so much embarrassment is objected to or so much as noticed by the onlookers. On the contrary, they adopt indifferent or (as I observed in one particularly clear dream) solemn and stiff expressions of face. This is a suggestive point.

The embarrassment of the dreamer and the indifference of the onlookers offer us, when taken together, a contradiction of the kind that is so common in dreams. It would after all be more in keeping with the dreamer's feelings if strangers looked at him in astonishment and derision or with indignation. But this objectionable feature of the situation has, I believe, been got rid of by wish-fulfilment, whereas some force has led to the retention of the other features; and the two portions of the dream are consequently out of harmony with each other. We possess an interesting piece of evidence that the dream in the form in which it appears—partly distorted by wish-fulfilment—has not been rightly understood. For it has become the basis of a fairy tale which is familiar to us all in Hans Andersen's version, *The*

Emperor's New Clothes, and which has quite recently been put into verse by Ludwig Fulda[1] in his ['dramatic fairy tale'] *Der Talisman*. Hans Andersen's fairy tale tells us how two impostors weave the Emperor a costly garment which, they say, will be visible only to persons of virtue and loyalty. The Emperor walks out in this invisible garment, and all the spectators, intimidated by the fabric's power to act as a touchstone, pretend not to notice the Emperor's nakedness.

This is just the situation in our dream. It is hardly rash to assume that the unintelligibility of the dream's content as it exists in the memory has led to its being recast in a form designed to make sense of the situation. That situation, however, is in the process deprived of its original meaning and put to extraneous uses. But, as we shall see later, it is a common thing for the conscious thought-activity of a second psychical system to misunderstand the content of a dream in this way, and this misunderstanding must be regarded as one of the factors in determining the final form assumed by dreams.[2] Moreover we shall learn that similar misunderstandings (taking place, once again, within one and the same psychical personality) play a major part in the construction of obsessions and phobias.

In the case of our dream we are in a position to indicate the material upon which the misinterpretation is based. The impostor is the dream and the Emperor is the dreamer himself; the moralizing purpose of the dream reveals an obscure knowledge of the fact that the latent dream-content is concerned with forbidden wishes that have fallen victim to repression. For the context in which dreams of this sort appear during my analyses of neurotics leaves no doubt that they are based upon memories from earliest childhood. It is only in our childhood that we are seen in inadequate clothing both by members of our family and by strangers—nurses, maid-servants, and visitors; and it is only then that we feel no shame at our nakedness.[3] We can observe how undressing has an almost intoxicating effect on many children even in their later years, instead of making them feel ashamed. They laugh and jump about and slap themselves, while their mother, or whoever else may be there, reproves them

---

[1] [German playwright, 1862–1939.]

[2] [This process of 'secondary revision' forms the subject of Section I of Chapter VI (pp. 493 ff.). Its application to this same fairy tale is discussed in a letter to Fliess of July 7, 1897 (Freud, 1950a, Letter 66).]

[3] A child plays a part in the fairy tale as well; for it was a small child who suddenly exclaimed: 'But he has nothing on!'

and says: 'Ugh! Shocking! You mustn't ever do that!' Children frequently manifest a desire to exhibit. One can scarcely pass through a country village in our part of the world without meeting some child of two or three who lifts up his little shirt in front of one—in one's honour, perhaps. One of my patients has a conscious memory of a scene in his eighth year, when at bed-time he wanted to dance into the next room where his little sister slept, dressed in his nightshirt, but was prevented by his nurse. In the early history of neurotics an important part is played by exposure to children of the opposite sex; in paranoia delusions of being observed while dressing and undressing are to be traced back to experiences of this kind; while among persons who have remained at the stage of perversion there is one class in which this infantile impulse has reached the pitch of a symptom—the class of 'exhibitionists.'[1]

When we look back at this unashamed period of childhood it seems to us a Paradise; and Paradise itself is no more than a group phantasy of the childhood of the individual. That is why mankind were naked in Paradise and were without shame in one another's presence; till a moment arrived when shame and anxiety awoke, expulsion followed, and sexual life and the tasks of cultural activity began. But we can regain this Paradise every night in our dreams. I have already [p. 239] expressed a suspicion that impressions of earliest childhood (that is, from the prehistoric epoch until about the end of the third year of life) strive to achieve reproduction, from their very nature and irrespectively perhaps of their actual content, and that their repetition constitutes the fulfilment of a wish. Thus dreams of being naked are dreams of exhibiting.[2]

The core of a dream of exhibiting lies in the figure of the dreamer himself (not as he was as a child but as he appears at the present time) and his inadequate clothing (which emerges indistinctly, whether owing to superimposed layers of innumerable later memories of being in undress or

---

[1] [This allusion to the perversions as remnants of infantile sexual activity foreshadows Freud's analysis of the sexual instinct in his *Three Essays* (1950d).]

[2] [*Footnote added* 1911:] Ferenczi [1910] has recorded a number of interesting dreams of being naked dreamt by *women*. There was no difficulty in tracing these back to the infantile desire to exhibit; but they differed in some respects from the 'typical' dreams of being naked which I have discussed in the text.— [The penultimate sentence in the paragraph above seems to adumbrate some of the ideas put forward twenty years later in *Beyond the Pleasure Principle* (Freud, 1920g).]

as a result of the censorship). Added to these are the figures of the people in whose presence the dreamer feels ashamed. I know of no instance in which the actual spectators of the infantile scene of exhibiting have appeared in the dream; a dream is scarcely ever a simple memory. Curiously enough, the people upon whom our sexual interest was directed in childhood are omitted in all the reproductions which occur in dreams, in hysteria and in obsessional neurosis. It is only in paranoia that these spectators reappear and, though they remain invisible, their presence is inferred with fanatical conviction. What takes their place in dreams—'a lot of strangers' who take no notice of the spectacle that is offered—is nothing more nor less than the wishful contrary of the single familiar individual before whom the dreamer exposed himself. Incidentally, 'a lot of strangers' frequently appear in dreams in many other connections, and they always stand as the wishful contrary of 'secrecy.'[1] It is to be noticed that even in paranoia, where the original state of things is restored, this reversal into a contrary is observed. The subject feels that he is no longer alone, he has no doubt that he is being observed, but the observers are 'a lot of strangers' whose identity is left curiously vague.

In addition to this, repression plays a part in dreams of exhibiting; for the distress felt in such dreams is a reaction on the part of the second system against the content of the scene of exhibiting having found expression in spite of the ban upon it. If the distress was to be avoided, the scene should never have been revived.

We shall return later [pp. 350 ff.] to the feeling of being inhibited. It serves admirably in dreams to represent a conflict in the will or a negative. The unconscious purpose requires the exhibiting to proceed; the censorship demands that it shall be stopped.

There can be no doubt that the connections between our typical dreams and fairy tales and the material of other kinds of creative writing are neither few nor accidental. It sometimes happens that the sharp eye of a creative writer has an analytic realization of the process of transformation of which he is habitually no more than the tool. If so, he may follow the process in a reverse direction and so trace back the imaginative writing to a dream. One of my friends has drawn my attention to the following pas-

---

[1] [This point is also mentioned towards the end of Freud's paper on 'Screen Memories' (1899a).—*Footnote added* 1909:] For obvious reasons the presence of 'the whole family' in a dream has the same significance.

sage in Gottfried Keller's *Der grüne Heinrich* [Part III, Chapter 2]: 'I hope, my dear Lee, that you may never learn from your own personal experience the peculiar and *piquant* truth of the plight of Odysseus when he appeared, naked and covered with mud, before the eyes of Nausicaä and her maidens! Shall I tell you how that can happen? Let us look into our example. If you are wandering about in a foreign land, far from your home and from all that you hold dear, if you have seen and heard many things, have known sorrow and care, and are wretched and forlorn, then without fail you will dream one night that you are coming near to your home; you will see it gleaming and shining in the fairest colours, and the sweetest, dearest and most beloved forms will move towards you. Then suddenly you will become aware that you are in rags, naked and dusty. You will be seized with a nameless shame and dread, you will seek to find covering and to hide yourself, and you will awake bathed in sweat. This, so long as men breathe, is the dream of the unhappy wanderer; and Homer has evoked the picture of his plight from the deepest and eternal nature of man.'

The deepest and eternal nature of man, upon whose evocation in his hearers the poet is accustomed to rely, lies in those impulses of the mind which have their roots in a childhood that has since become prehistoric. Suppressed and forbidden wishes from childhood break through in the dream behind the exile's unobjectionable wishes which are capable of entering consciousness; and that is why the dream which finds concrete expression in the legend of Nausicaä ends as a rule as an anxiety-dream.

My own dream (recorded on p. 257 f.) of running upstairs and of soon afterwards finding myself glued to the steps was equally a dream of exhibiting, since it bears the essential marks of being one. It should be possible, therefore, to trace it back to experiences during my childhood, and if these could be discovered they should enable us to judge how far the maidservant's behaviour to me—her accusing me of dirtying the carpet—helped to give her her place in my dream. I can, as it happens, provide the necessary particulars. In a psycho-analysis one learns to interpret propinquity in time as representing connection in subject-matter. [See below, p. 330.] Two thoughts which occur in immediate sequence without any apparent connection are in fact part of a single unity which has to be discovered; in just the same way, if I write an '*a*' and a '*b*' in succession, they have to be pronounced as a single syllable '*ab*.' The same is true of dreams. The staircase dream to which I have referred was one of a series of dreams; and I understood the interpretation of the other members of the series. Since this particular dream was surrounded by the others it must have dealt with the same subject. Now these other dreams were based on a recollection of a nurse in whose charge I had been from some date during my earliest infancy till I was two and a half. I even retain an obscure conscious memory of her. According to what I was told not long ago by my mother, she was old and ugly, but very sharp and efficient. From what I can infer from my own dreams her treatment of me was not always excessive in its amiability and her words could be harsh if I failed to reach the required standard of cleanliness. And thus the maid-servant, since she had undertaken the job of carrying on this educational work, acquired the right to be treated in my dream as a reincarnation of the prehistoric old nurse. It is reasonable to suppose that the child loved the old woman who taught him these lessons, in spite of her rough treatment of him.[1]

(β) Dreams of the Death of Persons of Whom the Dreamer is Fond

Another group of dreams which may be described as typical are those containing the death of some loved relative—for instance, of a parent, of a brother or sister, or of a child. Two classes of such dreams must at once be distinguished: those in which the dreamer is unaffected by grief, so that on awakening he is astonished at his lack of feeling, and those in which the dreamer feels deeply pained by the death and may even weep bitterly in his sleep.

We need not consider the dreams of the first of these classes, for they have no claim to be regarded as 'typical.' If we analyse them, we find that they have some meaning other than their apparent one, and that they are intended to conceal some other wish. Such was the dream of the aunt who saw her sister's only son lying in his coffin. (See pp. 176 f.) It did not mean that she wished her little nephew dead; as we have seen, it merely

---

[1] Here is an 'over-interpretation' of the same dream. Since '*spuken* [haunting]' is an activity of *spirits*, '*spucken* [spitting] on the stairs' might be loosely rendered as '*esprit d'escalier.*' This last phrase is equivalent to lack of ready repartee ['*Schlagfertigkeit,*' literally 'readiness to strike']—a failing to which I must in fact plead guilty. Was my nurse, I wonder, equally wanting in that quality? [This nurse is referred to at the end of Chapter IV of *The Psychopathology of Everyday Life* (Freud, 1901*b*) and in greater detail in his letters to Fliess of October 3 and 4 and October 15, 1897 (Freud, 1950*a*, Letters 70 and 71).]

concealed a wish to see a particular person of whom she was fond and whom she had not met for a long time—a person whom she had once before met after a similarly long interval beside the coffin of another nephew. This wish, which was the true content of the dream, gave no occasion for grief, and no grief, therefore, was felt in the dream. It will be noticed that the affect felt in the dream belongs to its latent and not to its manifest content, and that the dream's *affective* content has remained untouched by the distortion which has overtaken its *ideational* content.[1]

Very different are the dreams of the other class—those in which the dreamer imagines the death of a loved relative and is at the same time painfully affected. The meaning of such dreams, as their content indicates, is a wish that the person in question may die. And since I must expect that the feelings of all of my readers and any others who have experienced similar dreams will rebel against my assertion, I must try to base my evidence for it on the broadest possible foundation.

I have already discussed a dream which taught us that the wishes which are represented in dreams as fulfilled are not always present-day wishes. They may also be wishes of the past which have been abandoned, overlaid and repressed, and to which we have to attribute some sort of continued existence only because of their re-emergence in a dream. They are not dead in our sense of the word but only like the shades in the Odyssey, which awoke to some sort of life as soon as they had tasted blood. In the dream of the dead child in the 'case' (pp. 177 f.) what was involved was a wish which had been an immediate one fifteen years earlier and was frankly admitted as having existed at that time. I may add—and this may not be without its bearing upon the theory of dreams—that even behind this wish there lay a memory from the dreamer's earliest childhood. When she was a small child—the exact date could not be fixed with certainty—she had heard that her mother had fallen into a deep depression during the pregnancy of which she had been the fruit and had passionately wished that the child she was bearing might die. When the dreamer herself was grown-up and pregnant, she merely followed her mother's example.

If anyone dreams, with every sign of pain, that his father or mother or brother or sister has died, I should never use the dream as evidence that

---

[1] [See the discussion on affects in dreams in Chapter VII, Section H (especially p. 469).]

he wishes for that person's death *at the present time.* The theory of dreams does not require as much as that; it is satisfied with the inference that this death has been wished for at some time or other during the dreamer's childhood. I fear, however, that this reservation will not appease the objectors; they will deny the possibility of their *ever* having had such a thought with just as much energy as they insist that they harbour no such wishes now. I must therefore reconstruct a portion of the vanished mental life of children on the basis of the evidence of the present.[1]

Let us first consider the relation of children to their brothers and sisters. I do not know why we presuppose that that relation must be a loving one; for instances of hostility between adult brothers and sisters force themselves upon everyone's experience and we can often establish the fact that the disunity originated in childhood or has always existed. But it is further true that a great many adults, who are on affectionate terms with their brothers and sisters and are ready to stand by them today, passed their childhood on almost unbroken terms of enmity with them. The elder child ill-treats the younger, maligns him and robs him of his toys; while the younger is consumed with impotent rage against the elder, envies and fears him, or meets his oppressor with the first stirrings of a love of liberty and a sense of justice. Their parents complain that the children do not get on with one another, but cannot discover why. It is easy to see that the character of even a good child is not what we should wish to find it in an adult. Children are completely egoistic; they feel their needs intensely and strive ruthlessly to satisfy them—especially as against the rivals, other children, and first and foremost as against their brothers and sisters. But we do not on that account call a child 'bad,' we call him 'naughty'; he is no more answerable for his evil deeds in our judgement than in the eyes of the law. And it is right that this should be so; for we may expect that, before the end of the period which we count as childhood, altruistic impulses and morality will awaken in the little egoist and (to use Meynert's terms [e.g. 1892, 169 ff.]) a secondary ego will overlay and inhibit the primary one. It is true, no doubt, that morality does not set in simultaneously all along the line and that the length of non-moral childhood varies in different individuals. If this morality fails to develop,

---

[1] [*Footnote added* 1909:] Cf. my 'Analysis of a Phobia in a Five-Year-Old Boy' (1909*b*) and my paper 'On the Sexual Theories of Children' (1908*c*).

we like to talk of 'degeneracy,' though what in fact faces us is an inhibition in development. After the primary character has already been overlaid by later development, it can still be laid bare again, at all events in part, in cases of hysterical illness. There is a really striking resemblance between what is known as the hysterical character and that of a naughty child. Obsessional neurosis, on the contrary, corresponds to a supermorality imposed as a reinforcing weight upon fresh stirrings of the primary character.

Many people, therefore, who love their brothers and sisters and would feel bereaved if they were to die, harbour evil wishes against them in their unconscious, dating from earlier times; and these are capable of being realized in dreams.

It is of quite particular interest, however, to observe the behaviour of small children up to the age of two or three or a little older towards their younger brothers and sisters. Here, for instance, was a child who had so far been the only one; and now he was told that the stork had brought a new baby. He looked the new arrival up and down and then declared decisively: 'The stork can take him away again!'[1] I am quite seriously of the opinion that a child can form a just estimate of the set-back he has to expect at the hands of the little stranger. A lady of my acquaintance, who is on very good terms today with a sister four years her junior, tells me that she greeted the news of her first arrival with this qualification: 'But all the same I shan't give her my red cap!' Even if a child only comes to realize the situation later on, his hostility will date from that moment. I know of a case in which a little girl of less than three tried to strangle an infant in its cradle because she felt that its continued presence boded her no good. Children at that time of life are capable of jealousy of any degree of intensity and obviousness. Again, if it should happen that the baby sister does in fact disappear after a short while, the elder child will find the whole affection of the household once more concentrated upon himself.

---

[1] [*Footnote added* 1909:] The three-and-a-half-year-old Hans (whose phobia was the subject of the analysis mentioned in the preceding footnote) exclaimed shortly after the birth of a sister, while he was suffering from a feverish sore throat: 'I don't *want* a baby sister!' [Freud, 1909*b*, Section I.] During his neurosis eighteen months later he frankly confessed to a wish that his mother might drop the baby into the bath so that she would die. [Ibid., Section H (April 11).] At the same time, Hans was a good-natured and affectionate child, who soon grew fond of this same sister and particularly enjoyed taking her under his wing.

If after that the stork should bring yet another baby, it seems only logical that the little favourite should nourish a wish that his new competitor may meet with the same fate as the earlier one, so that he himself may be as happy as he was originally and during the interval.[1] Normally, of course, this attitude of a child towards a younger brother or sister is a simple function of the difference between their ages. Where the gap in time is sufficiently long, an elder girl will already begin to feel the stirring of her maternal instincts towards the helpless new-born baby.

Hostile feelings towards brothers and sisters must be far more frequent in childhood than the unseeing eye of the adult observer can perceive.[2]

In the case of my own children, who followed each other in rapid succession, I neglected the opportunity of carrying out observations of this kind; but I am now making up for this neglect by observing a small nephew, whose autocratic rule was upset, after lasting for fifteen months, by the appearance of a female rival. I am told, it is true, that the young man behaves in the most chivalrous manner to his little sister, that he kisses her hand and strokes her; but I have been able to convince myself that even before the end of his second year he made use of his powers of speech for the purpose of criticizing someone whom he could not fail to regard as superfluous. Whenever the conversation touched upon her he used to intervene in it and exclaim petulantly: 'Too 'ickle! too 'ickle!' During the last few months the baby's growth has made enough progress to place her beyond this particular ground for contempt, and the little boy has found a different basis for his assertion that she does not deserve

---

[1] [*Footnote added* 1914:] Deaths that are experienced in this way in childhood may quickly be forgotten in the family; but psychoanalytic research shows that they have a very important influence on subsequent neuroses.

[2] [*Footnote added* 1914:] Since this was written, a large number of observations have been made and recorded in the literature of psycho-analysis upon the originally hostile attitude of children towards their brothers and sisters and one of their parents. The [Swiss] author and poet Spitteler has given us a particularly genuine and naïve account of this childish attitude, derived from his own childhood [1914, 40]: 'Moreover there was a second Adolf there: a little creature who they alleged was my brother, though I could not see what use he was and still less why they made as much fuss of him as of me myself. I was sufficient so far as I was concerned; why should I want a brother? And he was not merely useless, he was positively in the way. When I pestered my grandmother, he wanted to pester her too. When I was taken out in the perambulator, he sat opposite to me and took up half the space, so that we were bound to kick each other with our feet.'

so much attention: at every suitable opportunity he draws attention to the fact that she has no teeth.[1] We all of us recollect how the eldest girl of another of my sisters, who was then a child of six, spent half-an-hour in insisting upon each of her aunts in succession agreeing with her: 'Lucie can't understand that yet, can she?' she kept asking. Lucie was her rival—two and a half years her junior.

In none of my women patients, to take an example, have I failed to come upon this dream of the death of a brother or sister, which tallies with an increase in hostility. I have only found a single exception; and it was easy to interpret this as a confirmation of the rule. On one occasion during an analytic session I was explaining this subject to a lady, since in view of her symptom its discussion seemed to me relevant. To my astonishment she replied that she had never had such a dream. Another dream, however, occurred to her, which ostensibly had no connection with the topic—a dream which she had first dreamt when she was four years old and at that time the youngest of the family, and which she had dreamt repeatedly since: *A whole crowd of children—all her brothers, sisters and cousins of both sexes—were romping in a field. Suddenly they all grew wings, flew away and disappeared.* She had no idea what this dream meant; but it is not hard to recognize that in its original form it had been a dream of the death of all her brothers and sisters, and had been only slightly influenced by the censorship. I may venture to suggest the following analysis. On the occasion of the death of one of this crowd of children (in this instance the children of two brothers had been brought up together as a single family) the dreamer, not yet four years old at the time, must have asked some wise grown-up person what became of children when they were dead. The reply must have been: 'They grow wings and turn into little angels.' In the dream which followed upon this piece of information all the dreamer's brothers and sisters had wings like angels and—which is the main point—flew away. Our little baby-killer was left alone, strange to say: the only survivor of the whole crowd! We can hardly be wrong in supposing that the fact of the children romping in a *field* before flying away points to butterflies. It is as though the child was led by the same chain of thought as the peoples of antiquity to picture the soul as having a butterfly's wings.

---

[1] [*Footnote added* 1909:] Little Hans, when he was three and a half, gave vent to a crushing criticism of his sister in the same words. It was because of her lack of teeth, he supposed, that she was unable to talk. [Freud, 1909*b*, Section I.]

At this point someone will perhaps interrupt: 'Granted that children have hostile impulses towards their brothers and sisters, how can a child's mind reach such a pitch of depravity as to wish for the *death* of his rivals or of playmates stronger than himself, as though the death penalty were the only punishment for every crime?' Anyone who talks like this has failed to bear in mind that a child's idea of being 'dead' has nothing much in common with ours apart from the word. Children know nothing of the horrors of corruption, of freezing in the ice-cold grave, of the terrors of eternal nothingness—ideas which grown-up people find it so hard to tolerate, as is proved by all the myths of a future life. The fear of death has no meaning to a child; hence it is that he will play with the dreadful word and use it as a threat against a playmate: 'If you do that again, you'll die, like Franz!' Meanwhile the poor mother gives a shudder and remembers, perhaps, that the greater half of the human race fail to survive their childhood years. It was actually possible for a child, who was over eight years old at the time, coming home from a visit to the Natural History Museum, to say to his mother: 'I'm so fond of you, Mummy: when you die I'll have you stuffed and I'll keep you in this room, so that I can see you *all* the time.' So little resemblance is there between a child's idea of being dead and our own![1]

To children, who, moreover, are spared the sight of the scenes of suffering which precede death, being 'dead' means approximately the same as being 'gone'—not troubling the survivors any longer. A child makes no distinction as to how this absence is brought about: whether it is due to a journey, to a dismissal, to an estrangement, or to death.[2] If, during a child's prehistoric epoch, his nurse has been dismissed, and if soon after-

---

[1] [*Footnote added* 1909:] I was astonished to hear a highly intelligent boy of ten remark after the sudden death of his father: 'I know father's dead, but what I can't understand is why he doesn't come home to supper.'—[*Added* 1919:] Further material on this subject will be found in the first [seven] volumes of the periodical *Imago* [1912–21], under the standing rubric of '*Vom wahren Wesen der Kinderseele*' ['The True Nature of the Child Mind'], edited by Frau Dr. H. von Hug-Hellmuth.

[2] [*Footnote added* 1919:] An observation made by a parent who had a knowledge of psycho-analysis caught the actual moment at which his highly intelligent four-year-old daughter perceived the distinction between being 'gone' and being 'dead.' The little girl had been troublesome at meal-time and noticed that one of the maids at the pension where they were staying was looking at her askance.

wards his mother has died, the two events are superimposed on each other in a single series in his memory as revealed in analysis. When people are absent, children do not miss them with any great intensity; many mothers have learnt this to their sorrow when, after being away from home for some weeks on a summer holiday, they are met on their return by the news that the children have not once asked after their mummy. If their mother does actually make the journey to that 'undiscover'd country, from whose bourn no traveller returns,' children seem at first to have forgotten her, and it is only later on that they begin to call their dead mother to mind.

Thus if a child has reasons for wishing the absence of another, there is nothing to restrain him from giving his wish the form of the other child being dead. And the psychical reaction to dreams containing death-wishes proves that, in spite of the different content of these wishes in the case of children, they are nevertheless in some way or other the same as wishes expressed in the same terms by adults.[1]

If, then, a child's death-wishes against his brothers and sisters are explained by the childish egoism which makes him regard them as his rivals, how are we to explain his death-wishes against his parents, who surround him with love and fulfil his needs and whose preservation that same egoism should lead him to desire?

A solution of this difficulty is afforded by the observation that dreams of the death of parents apply with preponderant frequency to the parent who is of the same sex as the dreamer: that men, that is, dream mostly of their father's death and women of their mother's. I cannot pretend that this is universally so, but the preponderance in the direction I have indicated is so evident that it requires to be explained by a factor of general

---

'I wish Josefine was dead,' was the child's comment to her father. 'Why dead?' enquired her father soothingly; 'wouldn't it do if she went away?' 'No,' replied the child; 'then she'd come back again.' The unbounded self-love (the narcissism) of children regards any interference as an act of *lèse majesté*; and their feelings demand (like the Draconian code) that any such crime shall receive the one form of punishment which admits of no degrees.

[1] [The adult attitude to death is discussed by Freud more particularly in the second essay of his *Totem and Taboo* (1912–13), Section 3(*c*), in his paper on 'The Three Caskets' (1913*f*) and in the second part of his 'Thoughts on War and Death' (1915*b*).]

importance.[1] It is as though—to put it bluntly—a sexual preference were making itself felt at an early age: as though boys regarded their fathers and girls their mothers as their rivals in love, whose elimination could not fail to be to their advantage.

Before this idea is rejected as a monstrous one, it is as well in this case, too, to consider the real relations obtaining—this time between parents and children. We must distinguish between what the cultural standards of filial piety demand of this relation and what everyday observation shows it in fact to be. More than one occasion for hostility lies concealed in the relation between parents and children—a relation which affords the most ample opportunities for wishes to arise which cannot pass the censorship.

Let us consider first the relation between father and son. The sanctity which we attribute to the rules laid down in the Decalogue has, I think, blunted our powers of perceiving the real facts. We seem scarcely to venture to observe that the majority of mankind disobey the Fifth Commandment. Alike in the lowest and in the highest strata of human society filial piety is wont to give way to other interests. The obscure information which is brought to us by mythology and legend from the primaeval ages of human society gives an unpleasing picture of the father's despotic power and of the ruthlessness with which he made use of it. Kronos devoured his children, just as the wild boar devours the sow's litter; while Zeus emasculated his father[2] and made himself ruler in his place. The more unrestricted was the rule of the father in the ancient family, the more must the son, as his destined successor, have found himself in the position of an enemy, and the more impatient must he have been to become ruler himself through his father's death. Even in our middle-class families fathers are as a rule inclined to refuse their sons independence and the means necessary

---

[1] [*Footnote added* 1925:] The situation is often obscured by the emergence of a self-punitive impulse, which threatens the dreamer, by way of a moral reaction, with the loss of the parent whom he loves.

[2] [*Footnote added* 1909:] Or so he is reported to have done according to some myths. According to others, emasculation was only carried out by Kronos on his father Uranus. [This passage is discussed in Chapter X (3) of *The Psychopathology of Everyday Life* (Freud, 1901*b*).] For the mythological significance of this theme, cf. Rank, 1909, [*added* 1914:] and Rank, 1912*c*, Chapter IX, Section 2.— [These sentences in the text are, of course, an early hint at the line of thought developed later by Freud in his *Totem and Taboo* (1912–13).]

to secure it and thus to foster the growth of the germ of hostility which is inherent in their relation. A physician will often be in a position to notice how a son's grief at the loss of his father cannot suppress his satisfaction at having at length won his freedom. In our society today fathers are apt to cling desperately to what is left of a now sadly antiquated *potestas patris familias*; and an author who, like Ibsen, brings the immemorial struggle between fathers and sons into prominence in his writings may be certain of producing his effect.

Occasions for conflict between a daughter and her mother arise when the daughter begins to grow up and long for sexual liberty, but finds herself under her mother's tutelage; while the mother, on the other hand, is warned by her daughter's growth that the time has come when she herself must abandon her claims to sexual satisfaction.

All of this is patent to the eyes of everyone. But it does not help us in our endeavour to explain dreams of a parent's death in people whose piety towards their parents has long been unimpeachably established. Previous discussions, moreover, will have prepared us to learn that the death-wish against parents dates back to earliest childhood.

This supposition is confirmed with a certainty beyond all doubt in the case of psychoneurotics when they are subjected to analysis. We learn from them that a child's sexual wishes—if in their embryonic stage they deserve to be so described—awaken very early, and that a girl's first affection is for her father[1] and a boy's first childish desires are for his mother. Accordingly, the father becomes a disturbing rival to the boy and the mother to the girl; and I have already shown in the case of brothers and sisters how easily such feelings can lead to a death-wish. The parents too give evidence as a rule of sexual partiality: a natural predilection usually sees to it that a man tends to spoil his little daughters, while his wife takes her sons' part; though both of them, where their judgement is not disturbed by the magic of sex, keep a strict eye upon their children's education. The child is very well aware of this partiality and turns against that one of his parents who is opposed to showing it. Being loved by an adult does not merely bring a child the satisfaction of a special need; it also means that he will get what he wants in every other respect as well. Thus he will be following his own sexual instinct and at the same time giving fresh strength to the inclination shown by his parents if his choice between them falls in with theirs.

---

[1] [Freud's views on this point were later modified. Cf. Freud, 1925*j* and 1931*b*.]

The signs of these infantile preferences are for the most part over-looked; yet some of them are to be observed even after the first years of childhood. An eight-year-old girl of my acquaintance, if her mother is called away from the table, makes use of the occasion to proclaim herself her successor: '*I*'m going to be Mummy now. Do you want some more greens, Karl? Well, help yourself, then!' and so on. A particularly gifted and lively girl of four, in whom this piece of child psychology is especially transparent, declared quite openly: 'Mummy can go away now. Then Daddy must marry me and I'll be his wife.' Such a wish occurring in a child is not in the least inconsistent with her being tenderly attached to her mother. If a little boy is allowed to sleep beside his mother when his father is away from home, but has to go back to the nursery and to some-one of whom he is far less fond as soon as his father returns, he may easily begin to form a wish that his father should *always* be away, so that he himself could keep his place beside his dear, lovely Mummy. One obvious way of attaining this wish would be if his father were dead; for the child has learnt one thing by experience—namely that 'dead' people, such as Granddaddy, are always away and never come back.

Though observations of this kind on small children fit in perfectly with the interpretation I have proposed, they do not carry such complete conviction as is forced upon the physician by psycho-analyses of adult neurotics. In the latter case dreams of the sort we are considering are in-troduced into the analysis in such a context that it is impossible to avoid interpreting them as *wishful* dreams.

One day one of my women patients was in a distressed and tearful mood. 'I don't want ever to see my relations again,' she said, 'they must think me horrible.' She then went on, with almost no transition, to say that she remembered a dream, though of course she had no idea what it meant. When she was four years old she had a dream that *a lynx or fox*[1] *was walking on the roof; then something had fallen down or she had fallen down; and then her mother was carried out of the house dead*—and she wept bitterly. I told her that this dream must mean that when she was a child she had wished she could see her mother dead, and that it must be on ac-count of the dream that she felt her relations must think her horrible. I had scarcely said this when she produced some material which threw light

---

[1] [The German names for these animals are very much alike: '*Luchs*' and '*Fuchs*.']

on the dream. 'Lynx-eye' was a term of abuse that had been thrown at her by a street-urchin when she was a very small child. When she was three years old, a tile off the roof had fallen on her mother's head and made it bleed violently.

I once had an opportunity of making a detailed study of a young woman who passed through a variety of psychical conditions. Her illness began with a state of confusional excitement during which she displayed a quite special aversion to her mother, hitting and abusing her whenever she came near her bed, while at the same period she was docile and affectionate towards a sister who was many years her senior. This was followed by a state in which she was lucid but somewhat apathetic and suffered from badly disturbed sleep. It was during this phase that I began treating her and analysing her dreams. An immense number of these dreams were concerned, with a greater or less degree of disguise, with the death of her mother: at one time she would be attending an old woman's funeral, at another she and her sister would be sitting at table dressed in mourning. There could be no question as to the meaning of these dreams. As her condition improved still further, hysterical phobias developed. The most tormenting of these was a fear that something might have happened to her mother. She was obliged to hurry home, wherever she might be, to convince herself that her mother was still alive. This case, taken in conjunction with what I had learnt from other sources, was highly instructive: it exhibited, translated as it were into different languages, the various ways in which the psychical apparatus reacted to one and the same exciting idea. In the confusional state, in which, as I believe, the second psychical agency was overwhelmed by the normally suppressed first one, her unconscious hostility to her mother found a powerful *motor* expression. When the calmer condition set in, when the rebellion was suppressed and the domination of the censorship re-established, the only region left open in which her hostility could realize the wish for her mother's death was that of dreaming. When a normal state was still more firmly established, it led to the production of her exaggerated worry about her mother as a hysterical counter-reaction and defensive phenomenon. In view of this it is no longer hard to understand why hysterical girls are so often attached to their mothers with such exaggerated affection.

On another occasion I had an opportunity of obtaining a deep insight into the unconscious mind of a young man whose life was made almost impossible by an obsessional neurosis. He was unable to go out into the street because he was tortured by the fear that he would kill everyone he met. He spent his days in preparing his alibi in case he might be charged with one of the murders committed in the town. It is unnecessary to add that he was a man of equally high morals and education. The analysis (which, incidentally, led to his recovery) showed that the basis of this distressing obsession was an impulse to murder his somewhat over-severe father. This impulse, to his astonishment, had been consciously expressed when he was seven years old, but it had, of course, originated much earlier in his childhood. After his father's painful illness and death, the patient's obsessional self-reproaches appeared—he was in his thirty-first year at the time—taking the shape of a phobia transferred on to strangers. A person, he felt, who was capable of wanting to push his own father over a precipice from the top of a mountain was not to be trusted to respect the lives of those less closely related to him; he was quite right to shut himself up in his room.[1]

In my experience, which is already extensive, the chief part in the mental lives of all children who later become psychoneurotics is played by their parents. Being in love with the one parent and hating the other are among the essential constituents of the stock of psychical impulses which is formed at that time and which is of such importance in determining the symptoms of the later neurosis. It is not my belief, however, that psychoneurotics differ sharply in this respect from other human beings who remain normal—that they are able, that is, to create something absolutely new and peculiar to themselves. It is far more probable—and this is confirmed by occasional observations on normal children—that they are only distinguished by exhibiting on a magnified scale feelings of love and hatred to their parents which occur less obviously and less intensely in the minds of most children.

This discovery is confirmed by a legend that has come down to us from classical antiquity: a legend whose profound and universal power to move can only be understood if the hypothesis I have put forward in regard to the psychology of children has an equally universal validity. What I have in mind is the legend of King Oedipus and Sophocles' drama which bears his name.

Oedipus, son of Laïus, King of Thebes, and of Jocasta, was exposed as an infant because an oracle had warned Laïus that the still unborn child

---

[1] [This patient is referred to again on p. 465.]

would be his father's murderer. The child was rescued, and grew up as a prince in an alien court, until, in doubts as to his origin, he too questioned the oracle and was warned to avoid his home since he was destined to murder his father and take his mother in marriage. On the road leading away from what he believed was his home, he met King Laïus and slew him in a sudden quarrel. He came next to Thebes and solved the riddle set him by the Sphinx who barred his way. Out of gratitude the Thebans made him their king and gave him Jocasta's hand in marriage. He reigned long in peace and honour, and she who, unknown to him, was his mother bore him two sons and two daughters. Then at last a plague broke out and the Thebans made enquiry once more of the oracle. It is at this point that Sophocles' tragedy opens. The messengers bring back the reply that the plague will cease when the murderer of Laïus has been driven from the land.

> But he, where is he? Where shall now be read
> The fading record of this ancient guilt?[1]

The action of the play consists in nothing other than the process of revealing, with cunning delays and ever-mounting excitement—a process that can be likened to the work of a psycho-analysis—that Oedipus himself is the murderer of Laïus, but further that he is the son of the murdered man and of Jocasta. Appalled at the abomination which he has unwittingly perpetrated, Oedipus blinds himself and forsakes his home. The oracle has been fulfilled.

Oedipus Rex is what is known as a tragedy of destiny. Its tragic effect is said to lie in the contrast between the supreme will of the gods and the vain attempts of mankind to escape the evil that threatens them. The lesson which, it is said, the deeply moved spectator should learn from the tragedy is submission to the divine will and realization of his own impotence. Modern dramatists have accordingly tried to achieve a similar tragic effect by weaving the same contrast into a plot invented by themselves. But the spectators have looked on unmoved while a curse or an oracle was fulfilled in spite of all the efforts of some innocent man: later tragedies of destiny have failed in their effect.

If *Oedipus Rex* moves a modern audience no less than it did the contemporary Greek one, the explanation can only be that its effect does not lie in

---

[1] [Lewis Campbell's translation (1883), lines 108 f.]

the contrast between destiny and human will, but is to be looked for in the particular nature of the material on which that contrast is exemplified. There must be something which makes a voice within us ready to recognize the compelling force of destiny in the *Oedipus*, while we can dismiss as merely arbitrary such dispositions as are laid down in [Grillparzer's] *Die Ahnfrau* or other modern tragedies of destiny. And a factor of this kind is in fact involved in the story of King Oedipus. His destiny moves us only because it might have been ours—because the oracle laid the same curse upon us before our birth as upon him. It is the fate of all of us, perhaps, to direct our first sexual impulse towards our mother and our first hatred and our first murderous wish against our father. Our dreams convince us that that is so. King Oedipus, who slew his father Laïus and married his mother Jocasta, merely shows us the fulfilment of our own childhood wishes. But, more fortunate than he, we have meanwhile succeeded, in so far as we have not become psychoneurotics, in detaching our sexual impulses from our mothers and in forgetting our jealousy of our fathers. Here is one in whom these primaeval wishes of our childhood have been fulfilled, and we shrink back from him with the whole force of the repression by which those wishes have since that time been held down within us. While the poet, as he unravels the past, brings to light the guilt of Oedipus, he is at the same time compelling us to recognize our own inner minds, in which those same impulses, though suppressed, are still to be found. The contrast with which the closing Chorus leaves us confronted—

. . . Fix on Oedipus your eyes,
Who resolved the dark enigma, noblest champion and most wise.
Like a star his envied fortune mounted beaming far and wide:
Now he sinks in seas of anguish, whelmed beneath a raging tide . . .[1]

—strikes as a warning at ourselves and our pride, at us who since our childhood have grown so wise and so mighty in our own eyes. Like Oedipus, we live in ignorance of these wishes, repugnant to morality, which have been forced upon us by Nature, and after their revelation we may all of us well seek to close our eyes to the scenes of our childhood.[2]

---

[1] [Lewis Campbell's translation, lines 1524 ff.]

[2] [*Footnote added* 1914:] None of the findings of psycho-analytic research has provoked such embittered denials, such fierce opposition—or such amusing contortions—on

There is an unmistakable indication in the text of Sophocles' tragedy itself that the legend of Oedipus sprang from some primaeval dream-material which had as its content the distressing disturbance of a child's relation to his parents owing to the first stirrings of sexuality. At a point when Oedipus, though he is not yet enlightened, has begun to feel troubled by his recollection of the oracle, Jocasta consoles him by referring to a dream which many people dream, though, as she thinks, it has no meaning:

> Many a man ere now in dreams hath lain
> With her who bare him. He hath least annoy
> Who with such omens troubleth not his mind.[1]

Today, just as then, many men dream of having sexual relations with their mothers, and speak of the fact with indignation and astonishment. It is clearly the key to the tragedy and the complement to the dream of the dreamer's father being dead. The story of Oedipus is the reaction of the imagination to these two typical dreams. And just as these dreams, when dreamt by adults, are accompanied by feelings of repulsion, so too the legend must include horror and self-punishment. Its further modification originates once again in a misconceived secondary revision of the material, which has sought to exploit it for theological purposes. (Cf. the dream-material in dreams of exhibiting, pp. 261 ff.) The attempt to harmonize

---

the part of critics as this indication of the childhood impulses towards incest which persist in the unconscious. An attempt has even been made recently to make out, in the face of all experience, that the incest should only be taken as 'symbolic.'— Ferenczi (1912) has proposed an ingenious 'over-interpretation' of the Oedipus myth, based on a passage in one of Schopenhauer's letters.—[*Added* 1919:] Later studies have shown that the 'Oedipus complex,' which was touched upon for the first time in the above paragraphs in the *Interpretation of Dreams*, throws a light of undreamt-of importance on the history of the human race and the evolution of religion and morality. (See my *Totem and Taboo*, 1912–13 [Essay IV].)—[Actually the gist of this discussion of the Oedipus complex and of the *Oedipus Rex*, as well as of what follows on the subject of *Hamlet*, had already been put forward by Freud in a letter to Fliess as early as October 15th, 1897. (See Freud, 1950a, Letter 71.) A still earlier hint at the discovery of the Oedipus complex was included in a letter of May 31st, 1897. (Ibid., Draft N.)—The actual term 'Oedipus complex' seems to have been first used by Freud in his published writings in the first of his 'Contributions to the Psychology of Love' (1910h).]

[1] [Lewis Campbell's translation, lines 982 ff.]

divine omnipotence with human responsibility must naturally fail in connection with this subject-matter just as with any other.

Another of the great creations of tragic poetry, Shakespeare's *Hamlet*, has its roots in the same soil as *Oedipus Rex*.[1] But the changed treatment of the same material reveals the whole difference in the mental life of these two widely separated epochs of civilization: the secular advance of repression in the emotional life of mankind. In the *Oedipus* the child's wishful phantasy that underlies it is brought into the open and realized as it would be in a dream. In *Hamlet* it remains repressed; and—just as in the case of a neurosis—we only learn of its existence from its inhibiting consequences. Strangely enough, the overwhelming effect produced by the more modern tragedy has turned out to be compatible with the fact that people have remained completely in the dark as to the hero's character. The play is built up on Hamlet's hesitations over fulfilling the task of revenge that is assigned to him; but its text offers no reasons or motives for these hesitations and an immense variety of attempts at interpreting them have failed to produce a result. According to the view which was originated by Goethe and is still the prevailing one today, Hamlet represents the type of man whose power of direct action is paralysed by an excessive development of his intellect. (He is 'sicklied o'er with the pale cast of thought.') According to another view, the dramatist has tried to portray a pathologically irresolute character which might be classed as neurasthenic. The plot of the drama shows us, however, that Hamlet is far from being represented as a person incapable of taking any action. We see him doing so on two occasions: first in a sudden outburst of temper, when he runs his sword through the eavesdropper behind the arras, and secondly in a premeditated and even crafty fashion, when, with all the callousness of a Renaissance prince, he sends the two courtiers to the death that had been planned for himself. What is it, then, that inhibits him in fulfilling the task set him by his father's ghost? The answer, once again, is that it is the peculiar nature of the task. Hamlet is able to do anything— except take vengeance on the man who did away with his father and took that father's place with his mother, the man who shows him the repressed wishes of his own childhood realized. Thus the loathing which should drive him on to revenge is replaced in him by self-reproaches, by scruples of con-

---

[1] [This paragraph was printed as a footnote in the first edition (1900) and included in the text from 1914 onward.]

science, which remind him that he himself is literally no better than the sinner whom he is to punish. Here I have translated into conscious terms what was bound to remain unconscious in Hamlet's mind; and if anyone is inclined to call him a hysteric, I can only accept the fact as one that is implied by my interpretation. The distaste for sexuality expressed by Hamlet in his conversation with Ophelia fits in very well with this: the same distaste which was destined to take possession of the poet's mind more and more during the years that followed, and which reached its extreme expression in *Timon of Athens*. For it can of course only be the poet's own mind which confronts us in Hamlet. I observe in a book on Shakespeare by Georg Brandes (1896) a statement that *Hamlet* was written immediately after the death of Shakespeare's father (in 1601), that is, under the immediate impact of his bereavement and, as we may well assume, while his childhood feelings about his father had been freshly revived. It is known, too, that Shakespeare's own son who died at an early age bore the name of 'Hamnet,' which is identical with 'Hamlet.' Just as *Hamlet* deals with the relation of a son to his parents, so *Macbeth* (written at approximately the same period) is concerned with the subject of childlessness. But just as all neurotic symptoms, and, for that matter, dreams, are capable of being 'over-interpreted' and indeed need to be, if they are to be fully understood, so all genuinely creative writings are the product of more than a single motive and more than a single impulse in the poet's mind, and are open to more than a single interpretation. In what I have written I have only attempted to interpret the deepest layer of impulses in the mind of the creative writer.[1]

---

[1] [*Footnote added* 1919:] The above indications of a psycho-analytic explanation of *Hamlet* have since been amplified by Ernest Jones and defended against the alternative views put forward in the literature of the subject. (See Jones, 1910a [and, in a completer form, 1949].)—[*Added* 1930:] Incidentally, I have in the meantime ceased to believe that the author of Shakespeare's works was the man from Stratford. [See Freud, 1930e]—[*Added* 1919:] Further attempts at an analysis of *Macbeth* will be found in a paper of mine [Freud, 1916d] and in one by Jekels (1917).—[The first part of this footnote was included in a different form in the edition of 1911 but omitted from 1914 onwards: 'The views on the problem of *Hamlet* contained in the above passage have since been confirmed and supported with fresh arguments in an extensive study by Dr. Ernest Jones of Toronto (1910a). He has also pointed out the relation between the material in *Hamlet* and the myths of the birth of heroes discussed by Rank (1909).'—Freud further discussed *Hamlet* in a posthumously published sketch dealing with 'Psychopathic Characters on the Stage' (1942b), probably written in 1905 or 1906.]

I cannot leave the subject of typical dreams of the death of loved relatives, without adding a few more words to throw light on their significance for the theory of dreams in general. In these dreams we find the highly unusual condition realized of a dream-thought formed by a repressed wish entirely eluding censorship and passing into the dream without modification. There must be special factors at work to make this event possible, and I believe that the occurrence of these dreams is facilitated by two such factors. Firstly, there is no wish that seems more remote from us than this one: 'we couldn't even *dream*'—so we believe—of wishing such a thing. For this reason the dream-censorship is not armed to meet such a monstrosity, just as Solon's penal code contained no punishment for parricide. Secondly, in this case the repressed and unsuspected wish is particularly often met half-way by a residue from the previous day in the form of a *worry* about the safety of the person concerned. This worry can only make its way into the dream by availing itself of the corresponding wish; while the wish can disguise itself behind the worry that has become active during the day. [Cf. pp. 594 f.] We may feel inclined to think that things are simpler than this and that one merely carries on during the night and in dreams with what one has been turning over in one's mind during the day; but if so we shall be leaving dreams of the death of people of whom the dreamer is fond completely in the air and without any connection with our explanation of dreams in general, and we shall thus be clinging quite unnecessarily to a riddle which is perfectly capable of solution.

It is also instructive to consider the relation of these dreams to anxiety-dreams. In the dreams we have been discussing, a repressed wish has found a means of evading censorship—and the distortion which censorship involves. The invariable concomitant is that painful feelings are experienced in the dream. In just the same way anxiety-dreams only occur if the censorship has been wholly or partly overpowered; and, on the other hand, the overpowering of the censorship is facilitated if anxiety has already been produced as an immediate sensation arising from somatic sources. [Cf. above, pp. 255 ff.] We can thus plainly see the purpose for which the censorship exercises its office and brings about the distortion of dreams: it does so *in order to prevent the generation of anxiety or other forms of distressing affect.*

I have spoken above [p. 268] of the egoism of children's minds, and I may now add, with a hint at a possible connection between the two facts, that dreams have the same characteristic. All of them are completely ego-istic:[1] the beloved ego appears in all of them, even though it may be disguised. The wishes that are fulfilled in them are invariably the ego's wishes, and if a dream seems to have been provoked by an altruistic interest, we are only being deceived by appearances. Here are a few analyses of instances which seem to contradict this assertion.

I

A child of under four years old reported having dreamt that *he had seen a big dish with a big joint of roast meat and vegetables on it. All at once the joint had been eaten up—whole and without being cut up. He had not seen the person who ate it.*[2]

Who can the unknown person have been whose sumptuous banquet of meat was the subject of the little boy's dream? His experiences during the dream-day must enlighten us on the subject. By doctor's orders he had been put on a milk diet for the past few days. On the evening of the dream-day he had been naughty, and as a punishment he had been sent to bed without his supper. He had been through this hunger-cure once before and had been very brave about it. He knew he would get nothing, but would not allow himself to show by so much as a single word that he was hungry. Education had already begun to have an effect on him: it found expression in this dream, which exhibits the beginning of dream-distortion. There can be no doubt that the person whose wishes were

---

[1] [Cf. end of footnote below, pp. 288. See also pp. 338 f.]

[2] [This dream, which was dreamt by Fliess's son Robert, is mentioned in Freud's letters to Fliess of August 8 and 20, 1899. (Freud, 1950a, Letters 114 and 116.)]— The appearance in dreams of things of great size and in great quantities and amounts, and of exaggeration generally, may be another childish characteristic. Children have no more ardent wish than to be big and grown-up and to get as much of things as grown-up people do. They are hard to satisfy, know no such word as 'enough' and insist insatiably on a repetition of things which they have enjoyed or whose taste they liked. It is only the civilizing influence of education that teaches them moderation and how to be content or resigned. Everyone knows that neurotics are equally inclined to be extravagant and immoderate. [Children's love of repetition was alluded to by Freud towards the end of the sixth section of Chapter VII of his book on jokes (Freud, 1905c) and again discussed near the beginning of Chapter V of *Beyond the Pleasure Principle* (1920g).]

aimed at this lavish meal—a meat meal, too—was himself. But since he knew he was not allowed it, he did not venture to sit down to the meal himself, as hungry children do in dreams. (Cf. my little daughter Anna's dream of strawberries on p. 163.) The person who ate the meal remained anonymous.

II

I dreamt one night that I saw in the window of a bookshop a new volume in one of the series of monographs for connoisseurs which I am in the habit of buying—monographs on great artists, on world history, on famous cities, etc. *The new series was called 'Famous Speakers' or 'Speeches' and its first volume bore the name of Dr. Lecher.*

When I came to analyse this, it seemed to me improbable that I should be concerned in my dreams with the fame of Dr. Lecher, the non-stop speaker of the German Nationalist obstructionists in Parliament. The position was that a few days earlier I had taken on some new patients for psychological treatment, and was now obliged to talk for ten or eleven hours every day. So it was I myself who was a non-stop speaker.

III

Another time I had a dream that a man I knew on the staff of the University said to me: '*My son, the Myops.*' Then followed a dialogue made up of short remarks and rejoinders. After this, however, there was yet a third piece of dream in which I myself and my sons figured. So far as the dream's latent content was concerned, Professor M. and his son were men of straw—a mere screen for me and my eldest son. I shall have to return to this dream later, on account of another of its features. [See pp. 449 ff.]

IV

The dream which follows is an instance of really low egoistic feelings concealed behind affectionate worry.

My friend Otto was looking ill. His face was brown and he had protruding eyes.

Otto is my family doctor, and I owe him more than I can ever hope to repay: he has watched over my children's health for many years, he has treated them successfully when they have been ill, and, in addition, whenever circumstances have given him an excuse, he has given them presents. [See p. 140.] He had visited us on the dream-day, and my wife had remarked that he looked tired and strained. That night I had my dream, which showed him with some of the signs of Basedow's [Graves'] disease. Anyone who interprets this dream without regard for my rules will conclude that I was worried about my friend's health and that this worry was realized in the dream. This would not only contradict my assertion that dreams are wish-fulfilments, but my other assertion, too, that they are accessible only to egoistic impulses. But I should be glad if anyone interpreting the dream in this way would be good enough to explain to me why my fears on Otto's behalf should have lighted on *Basedow's* disease—a diagnosis for which his actual appearance gives not the slightest ground. My analysis, on the other hand, brought up the following material from an occurrence six years earlier. A small group of us, which included Professor R., were driving in pitch darkness through the forest of N., which lay some hours' drive from the place at which we were spending our summer holidays. The coachman, who was not perfectly sober, spilt us, carriage and all, over an embankment, and it was only by a piece of luck that we all escaped injury. We were obliged, however, to spend the night in a neighbouring inn, at which the news of our accident brought us a lot of sympathy. A gentleman, with unmistakable signs of Basedow's disease—incidentally, just as in the dream, only the brown discoloration of the skin of the face and the protruding eyes, but no goitre—placed himself entirely at our disposal and asked what he could do for us. Professor R. replied in his decisive manner: 'Nothing except to lend me a nightshirt.' To which the fine gentleman rejoined: 'I'm sorry, but I can't do that,' and left the room.

As I continued my analysis, it occurred to me that Basedow was the name not only of a physician but also of a famous educationalist. (In my waking state I no longer felt quite so certain about this.[1]) But my friend Otto was the person whom I had asked to watch over my children's physical education, especially at the age of puberty (hence the nightshirt), in case anything happened to me. By giving my friend Otto in the dream the symptoms of our noble helper, I was evidently saying that if anything happened to me he would do just as little for the children as Baron L. had

---

[1] [Though in fact it was correct. He was an eighteenth-century follower of Rousseau.]

done on that occasion in spite of his kind offers of assistance. This seems to be sufficient evidence of the egoistic lining of the dream.[1]

But where was its wish-fulfilment to be found? Not in my avenging myself on my friend Otto, whose fate it seems to be to be ill-treated in my dreams[2]; but in the following consideration. At the same time as I represented Otto in the dream as Baron L., I had identified myself with someone else, namely Professor R.; for just as in the anecdote R. had made a request to Baron L., so I had made a request to Otto. And that is the point. Professor R., with whom I should really not venture to compare myself in the ordinary way, resembled me in having followed an independent path outside the academic world and had only achieved his well-merited title late in life. So once again I was wanting to be a Professor! Indeed the words 'late in life' were themselves a wish-fulfilment; for they implied that I should live long enough to see my boys through the age of puberty myself.[3]

(γ) Other Typical Dreams

I have no experience of my own of other kinds of typical dreams, in which the dreamer finds himself flying through the air to the accompaniment of agreeable feelings or falling with feelings of anxiety; and whatever

---

[1] [*Footnote added* 1911:] When Ernest Jones was giving a scientific lecture on the egoism of dreams before an American audience, a learned lady objected to this unscientific generalization, saying that the author of the present work could only judge of the dreams of Austrians and had no business to speak of the dreams of Americans. So far as she was concerned, she was certain that all her dreams were strictly altruistic.—[*Added* 1925:] By way of excuse for this patriotic lady, I may remark that the statement that dreams are entirely egoistic [p. 284 f.] must not be misunderstood. Since anything whatever that occurs in preconscious thought can pass into a dream (whether into its actual content or into the latent dream-thoughts) that possibility is equally open to altruistic impulses. In the same way, an affectionate or erotic impulse towards someone else, if it is present in the unconscious, can appear in a dream. The truth in the assertion made in the text above is thus restricted to the fact that among the unconscious instigators of a dream we very frequently find egoistic impulses which seem to have been overcome in waking life.

[2] [Cf. the dream of Irma's injection in Chapter II (pp. 131 ff.).]

[3] [This dream is further discussed on pp. 556 and 560.]

I have to say on the subject is derived from psycho-analyses.[1] The information provided by the latter forces me to conclude that these dreams, too, reproduce impressions of childhood; they relate, that is, to games involving movement, which are extraordinarily attractive to children. There cannot be a single uncle who has not shown a child how to fly by rushing across the room with him in his outstretched arms, or who has not played at letting him fall by riding him on his knee and then suddenly stretching out his leg, or by holding him up high and then suddenly pretending to drop him. Children are delighted by such experiences and never tire of asking to have them repeated, especially if there is something about them that causes a little fright or giddiness. In after years they repeat these experiences in dreams; but in the dreams they leave out the hands which held them up, so that they float, or fall unsupported. The delight taken by young children in games of this kind (as well as in swings and see-saws) is well known; and when they come to see acrobatic feats in a circus their memory of such games is revived.[2] Hysterical attacks in boys sometimes consist merely in reproductions of feats of this kind, carried out with great skill. It not uncommonly happens that these games of movement, though innocent in themselves, give rise to sexual feelings.[3] Childish 'romping'

---

[1] [The first sentence of this paragraph appeared in the original edition (1900) but was thereafter dropped until 1925. The remainder of the paragraph, together with the next one, were added in 1909, and in 1914 transferred to Chapter VI, Section E (where they will also be found, on p. 404 below). In the 1930 edition they were included in *both* places.]

[2] [*Footnote added* 1925:] Analytic research has shown us that in addition to pleasure derived from the organs concerned, there is another factor which contributes to the delight taken by children in acrobatic performances and to their repetition in hysterical attacks. This other factor is a memory-image, often unconscious, of an observation of sexual intercourse, whether between human beings or animals.

[3] A young medical colleague, who is quite free from any kind of nervous trouble, has given me the following information on this point: 'I know from my own experience that in my childhood I had a peculiar sensation in my genitals when I was on a swing and especially when the downward motion reached its greatest momentum. And though I cannot say I really enjoyed this sensation I must describe it as a pleasurable one.'—Patients have often told me that the first pleasurable erections that they can remember occurred in their boyhood while they were climbing about.—Psycho-analysis makes it perfectly certain that the first sexual impulses frequently have their roots in games involving romping and wrestling played during childhood. [This topic was elaborated by Freud in the last section of the second of his *Three Essays on the Theory of Sexuality* (1905*d*).]

['*Hetzen*'], if I may use a word which commonly describes all such activities, is what is being repeated in dreams of flying, falling, giddiness and so on; while the pleasurable feelings attached to these experiences are transformed into anxiety. But often enough, as every mother knows, romping among children actually ends in squabbling and tears.

Thus I have good grounds for rejecting the theory that what provokes dreams of flying and falling is the state of our tactile feelings during sleep or sensations of the movement of our lungs, and so on. [Cf. pp. 69 f.] In my view these sensations are themselves reproduced as part of the memory to which the dream goes back: that is to say, they are part of the *content* of the dream and not its source.

I cannot, however, disguise from myself that I am unable to produce any complete explanation of this class of typical dreams.[1] My material has left me in the lurch precisely at this point. I must, however, insist upon the general assertion that all the tactile and motor sensations which occur in these typical dreams are called up immediately there is any psychical reason for making use of them and that they can be disregarded when no such need for them arises. [Cf. p. 257.] I am also of the opinion that the relation of these dreams to infantile experiences has been established with certainty from the indications I have found in the analyses of psychoneurotics. I am not able to say, however, what other meanings may become attached to the recollection of such sensations in the course of later life—different meanings, perhaps, in every individual case, in spite of the typical appearance of the dreams; and I should be glad to be able to fill up the gap by a careful analysis of clear instances. If anyone feels surprised that, in spite of the frequency precisely of dreams of flying, falling and pulling out teeth, etc., I should be complaining of lack of material on this particular topic, I must explain that I myself have not experienced any dreams of the kind since I turned my attention to the subject of dream-interpretation. The dreams of neurotics, moreover, of which I might otherwise avail myself, cannot always be interpreted—not, at least, in many cases, so as to reveal the whole of their concealed meaning; a particular psychical force, which was concerned with the original constructing of the neurosis and is brought into operation once again when attempts are made at resolving it, prevents us from interpreting such dreams down to their last secret.

---

[1] [In the original edition (1900) the following paragraph (the first on examination dreams) *preceded* this one, and the present paragraph concluded the chapter. Thereafter this paragraph was altogether omitted until 1925.]

(δ) EXAMINATION DREAMS

Everyone who has passed the Matriculation examination at the end of his school studies complains of the obstinacy with which he is pursued by anxiety-dreams of having failed, or of being obliged to take the examination again, etc. In the case of those who have obtained a University degree this typical dream is replaced by another one which represents them as having failed in their University Finals; and it is in vain that they object, even while they are still asleep, that for years they have been practising medicine or working as University lecturers or heads of offices. The ineradicable memories of the punishments that we suffered for our evil deeds in childhood become active within us once more and attach themselves to the two crucial points in our studies—the '*dies irae, dies illa*' of our stiffest examinations. The 'examination anxiety' of neurotics owes its intensification to these same childhood fears. After we have ceased to be school-children, our punishments are no longer inflicted on us by our parents or by those who brought us up or later by our schoolmasters. The relentless causal chains of real life take charge of our further education, and now we dream of Matriculation or Finals (and who has not trembled on those occasions, even if he was well-prepared for the examination?) whenever, having done something wrong or failed to do something properly, we expect to be punished by the event—whenever, in short, we feel the burden of responsibility.

For a further explanation of examination dreams[1] I have to thank an experienced colleague [Stekel], who once declared at a scientific meeting that so far as he knew dreams of Matriculation only occur in people who have successfully passed it and never in people who have failed in it. It would seem, then, that anxious examination dreams (which, as has been confirmed over and over again, appear when the dreamer has some responsible activity ahead of him next day and is afraid there may be a fiasco) search for some occasion in the past in which great anxiety has turned out to be unjustified and has been contradicted by the event. This, then, would be a very striking instance of the content of a dream being misunderstood by the waking agency. [See pp. 262.] What is regarded as

---

[1] [This paragraph and the next one were added in 1909. In the editions of 1909 and 1911 only, the words 'the true explanation' took the place of 'a further explanation.']

an indignant protest against the dream: 'But I'm a doctor, etc., already!' would in reality be the consolation put forward by the dream, and would accordingly run: 'Don't be afraid of tomorrow! Just think how anxious you were before your Matriculation, and yet nothing happened to you. You're a doctor, etc., already.' And the anxiety which is attributed to the dream would really have arisen from the day's residues.

Such tests as I have been able to make of this explanation on myself and on other people, though they have not been sufficiently numerous, have confirmed its validity. For instance, I myself failed in Forensic Medicine in my Finals; but I have never had to cope with this subject in dreams, whereas I have quite often been examined in Botany, Zoology or Chemistry. I went in for the examination in these subjects with well-founded anxiety; but, whether by the grace of destiny or of the examiners, I escaped punishment. In my dreams of school examinations, I am invariably examined in History, in which I did brilliantly—though only, it is true, because [in the oral examination] my kindly master (the one-eyed benefactor of another dream, see p. 50) did not fail to notice that on the paper of questions which I handed him back I had run my fingernail through the middle one of the three questions included, to warn him not to insist upon that particular one. One of my patients, who decided not to sit for his Matriculation the first time but passed it later, and who subsequently failed in his army examination and never got a commission, has told me that he often dreams of the former of these examinations but never of the latter.[1]

The interpretation of examination dreams is faced by the difficulty which I have already referred to as characteristic of the majority of typical dreams [p. 259].[2] It is but rarely that the material with which the dreamer

---

[1] [At this point in the 1909 edition the following paragraph appeared: 'The colleague whom I have mentioned above (Dr. Stekel) has drawn attention to the fact that the word we use for Matriculation, "*Matura*," also means "maturity"; he claims to have observed that "*Matura*" dreams very often appear when a sexual test lies ahead for the next day, when, that is, the fiasco that is dreaded may lie in an insufficient release of potency.' In the 1911 edition the following sentence was added: 'A German colleague has, as I think rightly, objected to this that the name of this examination in Germany—"*Abiturium*"—does not bear this double meaning.' This whole paragraph was omitted from 1914 onwards. In 1925 it was replaced by the new final paragraph of the chapter. The subject was discussed by Stekel himself in 1909, 464 and 471.]

[2] [This paragraph was added in 1914.]

provides us in associations is sufficient to interpret the dream. It is only by collecting a considerable number of examples of such dreams that we can arrive at a better understanding of them. Not long ago I came to the conclusion that the objection 'You're a doctor, etc., already' does not merely conceal a consolation but also signifies a reproach. This would have run: 'You're quite old now, quite far advanced in life, and yet you go on doing these stupid, childish things.' This mixture of self-criticism and consolation would thus correspond to the latent content of examination dreams. If so, it would not be surprising if the self-reproaches for being 'stupid' and 'childish' in these last examples referred to the repetition of reprehensible sexual acts.

Wilhelm Stekel,[1] who put forward the first interpretation of dreams of Matriculation ['*Matura*'], was of the opinion that they regularly related to sexual tests and sexual maturity. My experience has often confirmed his view.[2]

---

[1] [This paragraph was added in 1925.]

[2] [In the 1909 and 1911 editions this chapter was continued with a discussion of other kinds of 'typical' dreams. But from 1914 onwards this further discussion was transferred to Chapter VI, Section E, after the newly introduced material dealing with dream-symbolism. See p. 394 f. below. (Cf. Editor's Introduction, p. xiii.)]

CHAPTER VI

THE DREAM-WORK[1]

EVERY attempt that has hitherto been made to solve the problem of dreams has dealt directly with their manifest content as it is presented in our memory. All such attempts have endeavoured to arrive at an interpretation of dreams from their *manifest* content or (if no interpretation was attempted) to form a judgement as to their nature on the basis of that same manifest content. We are alone in taking something else into account. We have introduced a new class of psychical material between the manifest content of dreams and the conclusions of our enquiry: namely, their *latent* content, or (as we say) the 'dream-thoughts,' arrived at by means of our procedure. It is from these dream-thoughts and not from a dream's manifest content that we disentangle its meaning. We are thus presented with a new task which had no previous existence: the task, that is, of investigating the relations between the manifest content of dreams and the latent dream-thoughts, and of tracing out the processes by which the latter have been changed into the former.

The dream-thoughts and the dream-content are presented to us like two versions of the same subject-matter in two different languages. Or, more properly, the dream-content seems like a transcript of the dream-thoughts into another mode of expression, whose characters and syntactic laws it is our business to discover by comparing the original and the translation. The

---

[1] [Lecture XI of Freud's *Introductory Lectures* (1916–17) deals with the dream-work on a much less extensive scale.]

dream-thoughts are immediately comprehensible, as soon as we have learnt them. The dream-content, on the other hand, is expressed as it were in a pictographic script, the characters of which have to be transposed individually into the language of the dream-thoughts. If we attempted to read these characters according to their pictorial value instead of according to their symbolic relation, we should clearly be led into error. Suppose I have a picture-puzzle, a rebus, in front of me. It depicts a house with a boat on its roof, a single letter of the alphabet, the figure of a running man whose head has been conjured away, and so on. Now I might be misled into raising objections and declaring that the picture as a whole and its component parts are nonsensical. A boat has no business to be on the roof of a house, and a headless man cannot run. Moreover, the man is bigger than the house; and if the whole picture is intended to represent a landscape, letters of the alphabet are out of place in it since such objects do not occur in nature. But obviously we can only form a proper judgement of the rebus if we put aside criticisms such as these of the whole composition and its parts and if, instead, we try to replace each separate element by a syllable or word that can be represented by that element in some way or other. The words which are put together in this way are no longer nonsensical but may form a poetical phrase of the greatest beauty and significance. A dream is a picture-puzzle of this sort and our predecessors in the field of dream-interpretation have made the mistake of treating the rebus as a pictorial composition: and as such it has seemed to them nonsensical and worthless.

(A)

THE WORK OF CONDENSATION

The first thing that becomes clear to anyone who compares the dream-content with the dream-thoughts is that a work of *condensation* on a large scale has been carried out. Dreams are brief, meagre and laconic in comparison with the range and wealth of the dream-thoughts. If a dream is written out it may perhaps fill half a page. The analysis setting out the dream-thoughts underlying it may occupy six, eight or a dozen times as much space. This relation varies with different dreams; but so far as my experience goes its direction never varies. As a rule one underestimates the amount of compression that has taken place, since one is inclined to regard the dream-thoughts that have been brought to light as the complete material, whereas if the work of interpretation is carried further it may reveal still more thoughts concealed behind the dream I have already had occasion to point out [cf. pp. 252 f.] that it is in fact never possible to be sure that a dream has been completely interpreted.[1] Even if the solution seems satisfactory and without gaps, the possibility always remains that the dream may have yet another meaning. Strictly speaking, then, it is impossible to determine the amount of condensation.

There is an answer, which at first sight seems most plausible, to the argument that the great lack of proportion between the dream-content and the dream-thoughts implies that the psychical material has undergone an extensive process of condensation in the course of the formation of the dream. We very often have an impression that we have dreamt a great deal all through the night and have since forgotten most of what we dreamt. On this view, the dream which we remember when we wake up would only be a fragmentary remnant of the total dream-work; and this, if we could recollect it in its entirety, might well be as extensive as the dream-thoughts. There is undoubtedly some truth in this: there can be no question that dreams can be reproduced most accurately if we try to recall them as soon as we wake up and that our memory of them becomes more and more incomplete towards evening. But on the other hand it can be shown that the impression that we have dreamt a great deal more than we can reproduce is very often based on an illusion, the origin of which I shall discuss later. [Cf. pp. 494 and 520.] Moreover the hypothesis that condensation occurs during the dream-work is not affected by the possibility of dreams being forgotten, since this hypothesis is proved to be correct by the quantities of ideas which are related to each individual piece of the dream which has been retained. Even supposing that a large piece of the dream has escaped recollection, this may merely have prevented our having access to another group of dream-thoughts. There is no justification for supposing that the lost pieces of the dream would have related to the same thoughts which we have already reached from the pieces of the dream that have survived.[2]

---

[1] [This subject is discussed at length in Freud, 1925*i*, Section A.]

[2] [*Footnote added* 1914:] The occurrence of condensation in dreams has been hinted at by many writers. Du Prel (1885, 85) has a passage in which he says it is absolutely certain that there has been a process of condensation of the groups of ideas in dreams.

In view of the very great number of associations produced in analysis to each individual element of the content of a dream, some readers may be led to doubt whether, as a matter of principle, we are justified in regarding as part of the dream-thoughts all the associations that occur to us during the subsequent analysis—whether we are justified, that is, in supposing that all these thoughts were already active during the state of sleep and played a part in the formation of the dream. Is it not more probable that new trains of thought have arisen in the course of the analysis which had no share in forming the dream? I can only give limited assent to this argument. It is no doubt true that some trains of thought arise for the first time during the analysis. But one can convince oneself in all such cases that these new connections are only set up between thoughts which were already linked in some other way in the dream-thoughts.[1] The new connections are, as it were, loop-lines or short-circuits, made possible by the existence of other and deeper-lying connecting paths. It must be allowed that the great bulk of the thoughts which are revealed in analysis were already active during the process of forming the dream; for, after working through a string of thoughts which seem to have no connection with the formation of a dream, one suddenly comes upon one which is represented in its content and is indispensable for its interpretation, but which could not have been reached except by this particular line of approach. I may here recall the dream of the botanical monograph [pp. 193 ff.], which strikes one as the product of an astonishing amount of condensation, even though I have not reported its analysis in full.

How, then, are we to picture psychical conditions during the period of sleep which precedes dreams? Are all the dream-thoughts present alongside one another? or do they occur in sequence? or do a number of trains of thoughts start out simultaneously from different centres and afterwards unite? There is no need for the present, in my opinion, to form any plastic idea of psychical conditions during the formation of dreams. It must not be forgotten, however, that we are dealing with an *unconscious* process of thought, which may easily be different from what we perceive during purposive reflection accompanied by consciousness.

---

[1] [This question is mentioned again on pp. 326 f. and discussed at very much greater length in the last part of Section A of Chapter VII (pp. 529 f.). See especially pp. 534 f.]

The unquestionable fact remains, however, that the formation of dreams is based on a process of condensation. How is that condensation brought about?

When we reflect that only a small minority of all the dream-thoughts revealed are represented in the dream by one of their ideational elements, we might conclude that condensation is brought about by *omission*: that is, that the dream is not a faithful translation or a point-for-point projection of the dream-thoughts, but a highly incomplete and fragmentary version of them. This view, as we shall soon discover, is a most inadequate one. But we may take it as a provisional starting-point and go on to a further question. If only a few elements from the dream-thoughts find their way into the dream-content, what are the conditions which determine their selection?

In order to get some light on this question we must turn our attention to those elements of the dream-content which must have fulfilled these conditions. And the most favourable material for such an investigation will be a dream to the construction of which a particularly intense process of condensation has contributed. I shall accordingly begin by choosing for the purpose the dream which I have already recorded on pp. 193 ff.

I

The Dream of the Botanical Monograph

Content of the Dream.—*I had written a monograph on an (unspecified) genus of plants. The book lay before me and I was at the moment turning over a folded coloured plate. Bound up in the copy there was a dried specimen of the plant.*

The element in this dream which stood out most was the *botanical monograph*. This arose from the impressions of the dream-day: I had in fact seen a monograph on the genus Cyclamen in the window of a bookshop. There was no mention of this genus in the content of the dream; all that was left in it was the monograph and its relation to botany. The 'botanical monograph' immediately revealed its connection with the *work upon cocaine* which I had once written. From 'cocaine' the chains of thought led on the one hand to the *Festschrift* and to certain events in a University laboratory, and on the other hand to my friend Dr. Königstein, the eye surgeon, who had had a share in the introduction of cocaine. The figure of Dr. Königstein further reminded me of the interrupted conversation which I had had with him the evening before and of my various reflections upon the payment for medical services among colleagues. This conversation was the actual currently active instigator of the dream; the monograph on the Cyclamen was also a currently active impression, but one of an indifferent nature. As I perceived, the 'botanical monograph' in the dream turned out to be an 'intermediate common entity' between the two experiences of the previous day: it was taken over unaltered from the indifferent impression and was linked with the psychically significant event by copious associative connections.

Not only the compound idea, 'botanical monograph,' however, but each of its components, 'botanical' and 'monograph' separately, led by numerous connecting paths deeper and deeper into the tangle of dream-thoughts. 'Botanical' was related to the figure of Professor *Gärtner* [Gardener], the *blooming* looks of his wife, to my patient *Flora* and to the lady [Frau L.] of whom I had told the story of the forgotten *flowers*. Gärtner led in turn to the laboratory and to my conversation with Königstein. My two patients [Flora and Frau L.] had been mentioned in the course of this conversation. A train of thought joined the lady with the flowers to my wife's *favourite flowers* and thence to the title of the monograph which I had seen for a moment during the day. In addition to these, 'botanical' recalled an episode at my secondary school and an examination while I was at the University. A fresh topic touched upon in my conversation with Dr. Königstein—my *favourite* hobbies—was joined, through the intermediate link of what I jokingly called my *favourite flower*, the artichoke, with the train of thought proceeding from the forgotten flowers. Behind 'artichokes' lay, on the one hand, my thoughts about Italy[1] and, on the other hand, a scene from my childhood which was the opening of what have since become my intimate relations with books. Thus 'botanical' was a regular nodal point in the dream. Numerous trains of thought converged upon it, which, as I can guarantee, had appropriately entered into the context of the conversation with Dr. Königstein. Here we find ourselves in a factory of thoughts where, as in the 'weaver's masterpiece'—

---

[1] [This seems to be a reference to an element in the dream-thoughts not previously mentioned.]

Ein Tritt tausend Fäden regt,
Die Schifflein herüber hinüber schiessen,
Die Fäden ungesehen fliessen,
Ein Schlag tausend Verbindungen schlägt.[1]

So, too, 'monograph' in the dream touches upon two subjects: the one-sidedness of my studies and the costliness of my favourite hobbies. This first investigation leads us to conclude that the elements 'botanical' and 'monograph' found their way into the content of the dream because they possessed copious contacts with the majority of the dream-thoughts, because, that is to say, they constituted 'nodal points' upon which a great number of the dream-thoughts converged, and because they had several meanings in connection with the interpretation of the dream. The explanation of this fundamental fact can also be put in another way: each of the elements of the dream's content turns out to have been 'overdetermined'— to have been represented in the dream-thoughts many times over.

We discover still more when we come to examine the remaining constituents of the dream in relation to their appearance in the dream-thoughts. The *coloured plate* which I was unfolding led (see the analysis, pp. 195 f.) to a new topic, my colleagues' criticisms of my activities, and to one which was already represented in the dream, my favourite hobbies; and it led, in addition, to the childhood memory in which I was pulling to pieces a book with coloured plates. The *dried specimen of the plant* touched upon the episode of the herbarium at my secondary school and specially stressed that memory.

The nature of the relation between dream-content and dream-thoughts thus becomes visible. Not only are the elements of a dream determined by the dream-thoughts many times over, but the individual dream-thoughts are represented in the dream by several elements. Associative paths lead from one element of the dream to several dream-thoughts, and from one dream-thought to several elements of the dream. Thus a dream is not constructed

---

[1] [. . . a thousand threads one treadle throws,
Where fly the shuttles hither and thither,
Unseen the threads are knit together,
And an infinite combination grows.
                    Goethe, *Faust*, Part I [Scene 4]
                    (Bayard Taylor's translation).]

by each individual dream-thought, or group of dream-thoughts, finding (in abbreviated form) separate representation in the content of the dream—in the kind of way in which an electorate chooses parliamentary representatives; a dream is constructed, rather, by the whole mass of dream-thoughts being submitted to a sort of manipulative process in which those elements which have the most numerous and strongest supports acquire the right of entry into the dream-content—in a manner analogous to election by *scrutin de liste*. In the case of every dream which I have submitted to an analysis of this kind I have invariably found these same fundamental principles confirmed: the elements of the dream are constructed out of the whole mass of dream-thoughts and each one of those elements is shown to have been determined many times over in relation to the dream-thoughts.

It will certainly not be out of place to illustrate the connection between dream-content and dream-thoughts by a further example, which is distinguished by the specially ingenious interweaving of their reciprocal relations. It is a dream produced by one of my patients—a man whom I was treating for claustrophobia. It will soon become clear why I have chosen to give this exceptionally clever dream-production the title of

II

'A LOVELY DREAM'

He was driving with a large party to X Street, in which there was an unpretentious inn. (This is not the case.) There was a play being acted inside it. At one moment he was audience, at another actor. When it was over, they had to change their clothes so as to get back to town. Some of the company were shown into rooms on the ground floor and others into rooms on the first floor. Then a dispute broke out. The ones up above were angry because the ones down below were not ready, and they could not come downstairs. His brother was up above and he was down below and he was angry with his brother because they were so much pressed. (This part was obscure.) Moreover, it had been decided and arranged even when they first arrived who was to be up above and who was to be down below. Then he was walking by himself up the rise made by X Street in the direction of town. He walked with such difficulty and so laboriously that he seemed glued to the spot. An elderly gentleman

*came up to him and began abusing the King of Italy. At the top of the rise he
was able to walk much more easily.*

His difficulty in walking up the rise was so distinct that after waking
up he was for some time in doubt whether it was a dream or reality.

We should not think very highly of this dream, judging by its manifest
content. In defiance of the rules, I shall begin its interpretation with the
portion which the dreamer described as being the most distinct.

The difficulty which he dreamt of and probably actually experienced
during the dream—the laborious climbing up the rise accompanied by
dyspnoea—was one of the symptoms which the patient had in fact exhibited years before and which had at that time been attributed, along with
certain other symptoms, to tuberculosis. (The probability is that this was
hysterically simulated.) The peculiar sensation of inhibited movement
that occurs in this dream is already familiar to us from dreams of exhibiting [see pp. 261 ff.] and we see once more that it is material available at
any time for any other representational purpose. [Cf. p. 350 f.] The piece
of the dream-content which described how the climb began by being difficult and became easy at the end of the rise reminded me, when I heard
it, of the masterly introduction to Alphonse Daudet's *Sappho*. That well-
known passage describes how a young man carries his mistress upstairs in
his arms; at first she is as light as a feather, but the higher he climbs the
heavier grows her weight. The whole scene foreshadows the course of
their love-affair, which was intended by Daudet as a warning to young
men not to allow their affections to be seriously engaged by girls of humble origin and a dubious past.[1] Though I knew that my patient had been
involved in a love-affair which he had recently broken off with a lady on
the stage, I did not expect to find my guess at an interpretation justified.
Moreover the situation in *Sappho* was the *reverse* of what it had been in
the dream. In the dream the climbing had been difficult to begin with
and had afterwards become easy; whereas the symbolism in the novel only
made sense if something that had been begun lightly ended by becoming
a heavy burden. But to my astonishment my patient replied that my interpretation fitted in very well with a piece he had seen at the theatre the
evening before. It was called *Rund um Wien* [*Round Vienna*] and gave a

---

[1] [*Footnote added* 1911:] What I have written below in the section on symbolism
about the significance of dreams of climbing [p. 368 n. 2] throws light upon the
imagery chosen by the novelist.

picture of the career of a girl who began by being respectable, who then became a *demi-mondaine* and had *liaisons* with men in high positions and so '*went up in the world*,' but who ended by '*coming down in the world*.' The piece had moreover reminded him of another, which he had seen some years earlier, called *Von Stufe zu Stufe* [*Step by Step*], and which had been advertised by a poster showing a staircase with a flight of *steps*.

To continue with the interpretation. The actress with whom he had had this latest, eventful *liaison* had lived in X Street. There is nothing in the nature of an inn in that street. But when he was spending part of the summer in Vienna on the lady's account he had put up [German '*abgestiegen*,' literally '*stepped down*'] at a small hotel in the neighbourhood. When he left the hotel he had said to his cab-driver: 'Anyhow I'm lucky not to have picked up any vermin.' (This, incidentally, was another of his phobias.) To this the driver had replied: 'How could anyone put up at such a place! It's not a hotel, it's only an *inn*.'

The idea of an inn at once recalled a quotation to his mind:

> Bei einem *Wirte* wundermild,
> Da war ich jüngst zu Gaste.[1]

The host in Uhland's poem was an *apple-tree*; and a second quotation now carried on his train of thought:

> FAUST (*mit der Jungen tanzend*):
> > Einst hatt' ich *einen schönen* Traum;
> > Da sah ich einen *Apfelbaum*,
> > Zwei schöne Äpfel glänzten dran,
> > Sie reizten mich, *ich stieg hinan*.
> DIE SHÖNE:
> > Der Äpfelchen begehrt ihr sehr,
> > Und schon vom Paradiese her.
> > Von Freuden fühl' ich mich bewegt,
> > Dass auch mein Garten solche trägt.[2]

---

[1] [Literally: 'I was lately a guest at an inn with a most gentle host'.
(Uhland, *Wanderlieder*, 8, 'Einkehr.')]
[2] [FAUST (*dancing with the Young Witch*):
A lovely dream once came to me,
And I beheld an *apple-tree*,

There cannot be the faintest doubt what the apple-tree and the apples stood for. Moreover, lovely breasts had been among the charms which had attracted the dreamer to his actress.

The context of the analysis gave us every ground for supposing that the dream went back to an impression in childhood. If so, it must have referred to the wet-nurse of the dreamer, who was by then a man almost thirty years old. For an infant the breasts of his wet-nurse are nothing more nor less than an inn. The wet-nurse, as well as Daudet's *Sappho*, seem to have been allusions to the mistress whom the patient had recently dropped.

The patient's (elder) brother also appeared in the content of the dream, the brother being *up above* and the patient himself *down below*. This was once again the reverse of the actual situation; for, as I knew, the brother had lost his social position while the patient had maintained his. In repeating the content of the dream to me, the dreamer had avoided saying that his brother was up above and he himself 'on the ground floor.' That would have put the position too clearly, since here in Vienna if we say someone is '*on the ground floor*' we mean that he has lost his money and his position—in other words, that he has '*come down in the world.*' Now there must have been a reason for some of this part of the dream being represented by its *reverse*. Further, the reversal must hold good of some other relation between dream-thoughts and dream-content as well [cf. below, pp. 341 f.]; and we have a hint of where to look for this reversal. It must evidently be at the end of the dream, where once again there was a reversal of the difficulty in going upstairs as described in *Sappho*. We can then easily see what reversal is intended. In *Sappho* the man carried a woman who was in a sexual relation to him; in the dream-thoughts the position was *reversed*, and a woman was carrying a man. And since this can only happen in childhood, the reference was once more to the wet-nurse bearing the weight of the

---

On which two lovely apples shone;
They charmed me so, *I climbed thereon.*
THE LOVELY WITCH:
Apples have been desired by you,
Since first in Paradise they grew;
And I am moved with joy to know
That such within my garden grow.
    Goethe, *Faust*, Part I [Scene 21, Walpurgisnacht]
        (Bayard Taylor's translation, slightly modified).]

infant in her arms. Thus the end of the dream made a simultaneous reference to Sappho and to the wet-nurse.

Just as the author of the novel, in choosing the name 'Sappho,' had in mind an allusion to Lesbian practices, so too the pieces of the dream that spoke of people '*up above*' and '*down below*' alluded to phantasies of a sexual nature which occupied the patient's mind and, as suppressed desires, were not without a bearing on his neurosis. (The interpretation of the dream did not itself show us that what were thus represented in the dream were phantasies and not recollections of real events; an analysis only gives us the *content* of a thought and leaves it to us to determine its reality. Real and imaginary events appear in dreams at first sight as of equal validity; and that is so not only in dreams but in the production of more important psychical structures.)[1]

A 'large party' meant, as we already know [see pp. 263 f.], a secret. His brother was simply the representative (introduced into the childhood scene by a 'retrospective phantasy')[2] of all his later rivals for a woman's affection. The episode of the gentleman who abused the King of Italy related once again, *via* the medium of a recent and in itself indifferent experience, to people of lower rank pushing their way into higher society. It was just as though the child at the breast was being given a warning parallel to the one which Daudet had given to young men.[3]

To provide a third opportunity for studying condensation in the formation of dreams, I will give part of the analysis of another dream, which I owe to an elderly lady undergoing psycho-analytic treatment. As was to be expected from the severe anxiety-states from which the patient suffered, her dreams contained a very large number of sexual thoughts, the first realization of which both surprised and alarmed her. Since I shall not

---

[1] [Freud is probably referring here to the discovery which he had recently made that the infantile sexual traumas apparently revealed in his analyses of neurotic patients were in fact very often phantasies. See Freud, 1906*a*.]

[2] [Phantasies of this kind had been discussed by Freud previously, in the latter part of his paper on 'Screen Memories' (1899*a*).]

[3] The imaginary nature of the situation relating to the dreamer's wet-nurse was proved by the objectively established fact that in his case the wet-nurse had been his mother. I may recall in this connection the anecdote, which I repeated on p. 226, of the young man who regretted that he had not made better use of his opportunities with his wet-nurse. A regret of the same kind was no doubt the source of the present dream.

be able to pursue the interpretation of the dream to the end, its material will appear to fall into several groups without any visible connection.

III

'The May-Beetle[1] Dream'

CONTENT OF THE DREAM.—*She called to mind that she had two may-beetles in a box and that she must set them free or they would suffocate. She opened the box and the may-beetles were in an exhausted state. One of them flew out of the open window; but the other was crushed by the casement while she was shutting it at someone's request. (Signs of disgust.)*

ANALYSIS.—Her husband was temporarily away from home, and her fourteen-year-old daughter was sleeping in the bed beside her. The evening before, the girl had drawn her attention to a moth which had fallen into her tumbler of water; but she had not taken it out and felt sorry for the poor creature next morning. The book she had been reading during the evening had told how some boys had thrown a cat into boiling water, and had described the animal's convulsions. These were the two precipitating causes of the dream—in themselves indifferent. She then pursued the subject of *cruelty to animals* further. Some years before, while they were spending the summer at a particular place, her daughter had been very cruel to animals. She was collecting butterflies and asked the patient for some *arsenic* to kill them with. On one occasion a moth with a pin through its body had gone on flying about the room for a long time; another time some caterpillars which the child was keeping to turn into chrysalises starved to death. At a still more tender age the same child used to tear the wings off *beetles* and butterflies. But today she would be horrified at all these cruel actions—she had grown so kind-hearted.

The patient reflected over this contradiction. It reminded her of another contradiction, between appearance and character, as George Eliot displays it in *Adam Bede*: one girl who was pretty, but vain and stupid, and another who was ugly, but of high character; a nobleman who seduced the silly girl, and a working man who felt and acted with true nobility. How

---

[1] [The commoner English equivalent for the German '*Maikäfer*' is 'cockchafer.' For the purposes of this dream, however, a literal translation is to be preferred.]

impossible it was, she remarked, to recognize that sort of thing in people! Who would have guessed, to look at *her*, that she was tormented by sensual desires?

In the same year in which the little girl had begun collecting butterflies, the district they were in had suffered from a serious plague of *may-beetles*. The children were furious with the beetles and crushed them unmercifully. At that time my patient had seen a man who tore the wings off may-beetles and then ate their bodies. She herself had been born in *May* and had been married in *May*. Three days after her marriage she had written to her parents at home saying how happy she was. But it had been far from true.

The evening before the dream she had been rummaging among some old letters and had read some of them—some serious and some comic—aloud to her children. There had been a most amusing letter from a piano-teacher who had courted her when she was a girl, and another from an admirer of *noble birth*.[1]

She blamed herself because one of her daughters had got hold of a 'bad' book by Maupassant.[2] The *arsenic* that the girl had asked for reminded her of the *arsenic pills* which restored the Due de Mora's youthful strength in [Daudet's] *Le Nabab*.

'Set them free' made her think of a passage in the *Magic Flute*:

> Zur Liebe kann ich dich nicht zwingen,
> Doch geb ich dir *die Freiheit* nicht.[3]

'May-beetles' also made her think of Kätchen's words:

> Verliebt ja wie ein *Käfer* bist du mir.[4]

---

[1] This had been the true instigator of the dream.

[2] An interpolation is required at this point: 'books of that kind are *poison* to a girl.' The patient herself had dipped into forbidden books a great deal when she was young.

[3] [Fear not, to love I'll ne'er compel thee;
Yet 'tis too soon to *set thee free*.
(Sarastro to Pamina in the *Finale* to Act I.—
E. J. Dent's translation.)]

[4] ['You are madly in love with me.' Literally: 'You are in love with me like a *beetle*.' From Kleist's *Kätchen von Heilbronn*, IV, 2.]—A further train of thought led to the same poet's *Penthesilea*, and to the idea of *cruelty* to a lover.

And in the middle of all this came a quotation from *Tannhäuser*:

> Weil du von *böser* Lust beseelt . . .[1]

She was living in a perpetual worry about her absent husband. Her fear that something might happen to him on his journey was expressed in numerous waking phantasies. A short time before, in the course of her analysis, she had lighted among her unconscious thoughts upon a complaint about her husband 'growing senile.' The wishful thought concealed by her present dream will perhaps best be conjectured if I mention that, some days before she dreamt it, she was horrified, in the middle of her daily affairs, by a phrase in the imperative mood which came into her head and was aimed at her husband: 'Go and hang yourself!' It turned out that a few hours earlier she had read somewhere or other that when a man is hanged he gets a powerful erection. The wish for an erection was what had emerged from repression in this horrifying disguise. 'Go and hang yourself!' was equivalent to: 'Get yourself an erection at any price!' Dr. Jenkins's arsenic pills in *Le Nabab* fitted in here. But my patient was also aware that the most powerful aphrodisiac, cantharides (commonly known as 'Spanish flies'), was prepared from *crushed beetles*. This was the drift of the principal part of the dream's content.

The opening and shutting of *windows* was one of the main subjects of dispute between her and her husband. She herself was aerophilic in her sleeping habits; her husband was aerophobic. *Exhaustion* was the chief symptom which she complained of at the time of the dream.

In all three of the dreams which I have just recorded, I have indicated by italics the points at which one of the elements of the dream-content re-appears in the dream-thoughts, so as to show clearly the multiplicity of connections arising from the former. Since, however, the analysis of none of these dreams has been traced to its end, it will perhaps be worth while to consider a dream whose analysis has been recorded exhaustively, so as to show how its content is over-determined. For this purpose I will take the dream of Irma's injection [pp. 131 ff.]. It will be easy to see from

---

[1] [Literally: 'Because thou wast inspired by such *evil pleasure*.' This is presumably a recollection of the opening phrase of the Pope's condemnation reported by Tannhäuser in the last scene of the opera. The actual words are: 'Hast du so böse Lust getheilt'—'Since thou hast shared such evil pleasure.']

that example that the work of condensation makes use of more than one method in the construction of dreams.

The principal figure in the dream-content was my patient Irma. She appeared with the features which were hers in real life, and thus, in the first instance, represented herself. But the position in which I examined her by the window was derived from someone else, the lady for whom, as the dream-thoughts showed, I wanted to exchange my patient. In so far as Irma appeared to have a diphtheritic membrane, which recalled my anxiety about my eldest daughter, she stood for that child and, behind her, through her possession of the same name as my daughter, was hidden the figure of my patient who succumbed to poisoning. In the further course of the dream the figure of Irma acquired still other meanings, without any alteration occurring in the visual picture of her in the dream. She turned into one of the children whom we had examined in the neurological department of the children's hospital, where my two friends revealed their contrasting characters. The figure of my own child was evidently the stepping-stone towards this transition. The same 'Irma's' recalcitrance over opening her mouth brought an allusion to another lady whom I had once examined, and, through the same connection, to my wife. Moreover, the pathological changes which I discovered in her throat involved allusions to a whole series of other figures.

None of these figures whom I lighted upon by following up 'Irma' appeared in the dream in bodily shape. They were concealed behind the dream figure of 'Irma,' which was thus turned into a collective image with, it must be admitted, a number of contradictory characteristics. Irma became the representative of all these other figures which had been sacrificed to the work of condensation, since I passed over to *her*, point by point, everything that reminded me of *them*.

There is another way in which a 'collective figure' can be produced for purposes of dream-condensation, namely by uniting the actual features of two or more people into a single dream-image. It was in this way that the Dr. M. of my dream was constructed. He bore the name of Dr. M., he spoke and acted like him; but his physical characteristics and his malady belonged to someone else, namely to my eldest brother. One single feature, his pale appearance, was doubly determined, since it was common to both of them in real life.

Dr. R. in my dream about my uncle with the yellow beard [pp. 162 ff.] was a similar composite figure. But in his case the dream-image was constructed in yet another way. I did not combine the features of one person with those of another and in the process omit from the memory-picture certain features of each of them. What I did was to adopt the procedure by means of which Galton produced family portraits: namely by projecting two images on to a single plate, so that certain features common to both are emphasized, while those which fail to fit in with one another cancel one another out and are indistinct in the picture. In my dream about my uncle the fair beard emerged prominently from a face which belonged to two people and which was consequently blurred; incidentally, the beard further involved an allusion to my father and myself through the intermediate idea of growing grey.

The construction of collective and composite figures is one of the chief methods by which condensation operates in dreams. I shall presently have occasion to deal with them in another context. [See pp. 336 f.]

The occurrence of the idea of 'dysentery' in the dream of Irma's injection also had a multiple determination: first owing to its phonetic similarity to 'diphtheria' [see p. 138 f.], and secondly owing to its connection with the patient whom I had sent to the East and whose hysteria was not recognized.

Another interesting example of condensation in this dream was the mention in it of 'propyls' [pp. 140]. What was contained in the dream-thoughts was not 'propyls' but 'amyls.' It might be supposed that a single displacement had taken place at this point in the construction of the dream. This was indeed the case. But the displacement served the purposes of condensation, as it proved by the following addition to the analysis of the dream. When I allowed my attention to dwell for a moment longer on the word 'propyls,' it occurred to me that it sounded like 'Propylaea.' But there are Propylaea not only in Athens but in Munich.[1] A year before the dream I had gone to Munich to visit a friend who was seriously ill at the time—the same friend who was unmistakably alluded to in the dream by the word 'trimethylamin' which occurred immediately after 'propyls.'

I shall pass over the striking way in which here, as elsewhere in dream-analyses, associations of the most various inherent importance are used for laying down thought-connections as though they were of equal weight, and shall yield to the temptation to give, as it were, a plastic picture of the process by which the amyls in the dream-thoughts were replaced by propyls in the dream-content.

---

[1] [A ceremonial portico on the model of the Athenian one.]

On the one hand we see the group of ideas attached to my friend Otto, who did not understand me, who sided against me, and who made me a present of liqueur with an aroma of amyl. On the other hand we see—linked to the former group by its very contrast—the group of ideas attached to my friend in Berlin [Wilhelm Fliess], who *did* understand me, who would take my side, and to whom I owed so much valuable information, dealing, amongst other things, with the chemistry of the sexual processes.

The recent exciting causes—the actual instigators of the dream—determined what was to attract my attention in the 'Otto' group; the amyl was among these selected elements, which were predestined to form part of the dream-content. The copious 'Wilhelm' group was stirred up precisely through being in contrast to 'Otto,' and those elements in it were emphasized which echoed those which were already stirred up in 'Otto.' All through the dream, indeed, I kept on turning from someone who annoyed me to someone else who could be agreeably contrasted with him; point by point, I called up a friend against an opponent. Thus the amyl in the 'Otto' group produced memories from the field of chemistry in the other group; in this manner the trimethylamin, which was supported from several directions, found its way into the dream-content. 'Amyls' itself might have entered the dream-content unmodified; but it came under the influence of the 'Wilhelm' group. For the whole range of memories covered by that name was searched through in order to find some element which could provide a two-sided determination for 'amyls.' 'Propyls' was closely associated with 'amyls,' and Munich from the 'Wilhelm' group with its 'propylaea' came halfway to meet it. The two groups of ideas converged in 'propyls-propylaea'; and, as though by an act of compromise, this intermediate element was what found its way into the dream-content. Here an intermediate common entity had been constructed which admitted of multiple determination. It is obvious, therefore, that multiple determination must make it easier for an element to force its way into the dream-content. In order to construct an intermediate link of this kind, attention is without hesitation displaced from what is actually intended on to some neighbouring association.

Our study of the dream of Irma's injection has already enabled us to gain some insight into the processes of condensation during the formation of dreams. We have been able to observe certain of their details, such as how preference is given to elements that occur several times over in the dream-thoughts, how new unities are formed (in the shape of collective figures and composite structures), and how intermediate common entities are constructed. The further questions of the *purpose* of condensation and of the factors which tend to produce it will not be raised till we come to consider the whole question of the psychical processes at work in the formation of dreams. [See pp. 345 f. and Chapter VII, Section E, especially pp. 592 ff.] We will be content for the present with recognizing the fact that dream-condensation is a notable characteristic of the relation between dream-thoughts and dream-content.

The work of condensation in dreams is seen at its clearest when it handles words and names. It is true in general that words are treated in dreams as though they were concrete things, and for that reason they are apt to be combined in just the same way as presentations of concrete things.[1] Dreams of this sort offer the most amusing and curious neologisms.[2]

I

On one occasion a medical colleague had sent me a paper he had written, in which the importance of a recent physiological discovery was, in my opinion, overestimated, and in which, above all, the subject was treated in too emotional a manner. The next night I dreamt a sentence which clearly referred to this paper: '*Its written in a positively norekdal style.*' The analysis of the word caused me some difficulty at first. There could be no doubt that it was a parody of the [German] superlatives '*kolossal*' and '*pyramidal*'; but its origin was not so easy to guess. At last I saw that the monstrosity was composed of the two names 'Nora' and 'Ekdal'— characters in two well-known plays of Ibsen's. [*A Doll's House* and *The Wild Duck*.] Some time before, I had read a newspaper article on Ibsen by the same author whose latest work I was criticizing in the dream.

---

[1] [The relation between presentations of words and of things was discussed by Freud very much later, in the last pages of his paper on the Unconscious (1915e).]

[2] [A dream involving a number of verbal conceits is reported by Freud in Chapter V (10) of his *Psychopathology of Everyday Life* (1901b).—The examples which follow are, as will be seen, for the most part untranslatable. See Editor's Introduction (p. xxi).]

One of my women patients told me a short dream which ended in a meaningless verbal compound. She dreamt she was with her husband at a peasant festivity and said: '*This will end in a general "Maistollmütz."*' In the dream she had a vague feeling that it was some kind of pudding made with maize—a sort of polenta. Analysis divided the word into '*Mais*' ['maize'], '*toll*' ['mad'], '*mannstoll*' ['nymphomaniac'—literally 'mad for men'] and *Olmütz* [a town in Moravia]. All these fragments were found to be remnants of a conversation she had had at table with her relatives. The following words lay behind '*Mais*' (in addition to a reference to the recently opened Jubilee Exhibition[1]): '*Meissen*' (a Meissen [Dresden] porcelain figure representing a bird); '*Miss*' (her relatives' English governess had just gone to *Olmütz*); and '*mies*' (a Jewish slang term, used jokingly to mean 'disgusting'). A long chain of thoughts and associations led off from each syllable of this verbal hotchpotch.

A young man, whose door-bell had been rung late one night by an acquaintance who wanted to leave a visiting-card on him, had a dream that night: *A man had been working till late in the evening to put his house-telephone in order. After he had gone, it kept on ringing—not continuously, but with detached rings. His servant fetched the man back, and the latter remarked: 'It's a funny thing that even people who are "tutelrein" as a rule are quite unable to deal with a thing like this.'*

It will be seen that the indifferent exciting cause of the dream only covers one element of it. That episode only obtained any importance from the fact that the dreamer put it in the same series as an earlier experience which, though equally indifferent in itself, was given a substitutive meaning by his imagination. When he was a boy, living with his father, he had upset a glass of water over the floor while he was half-asleep. The flex of the house-telephone had been soaked through and its *continuous*

---

[1] [To commemorate the jubilee of the Emperor Francis Joseph, which was celebrated in 1898.]

ringing had disturbed his father's sleep. Since the continuous ringing corresponded to getting wet, the *'detached rings'* were used to represent drops falling. The word *'tutelrein'* could be analysed in three directions, and led in that way to three of the subjects represented in the dream-thoughts. *'Tutel'* is a legal term for 'guardianship' ['tutelage']. *'Tutel'* (or possibly *'Tuttel'*) is also a vulgar term for a woman's breast. The remaining portion of the word, *'rein'* ['clean'], combined with the first part of *'Zimmertelegraph'* ['house-telephone'], forms *'zimmerrein'* ['house-trained']—which is closely connected with making the floor wet, and, in addition, sounded very much like the name of a member of the dreamer's family.[1]

IV

In a confused dream of my own of some length, whose central point seemed to be a sea voyage, it appeared that the next stopping place was called *'Hearsing'* and the next after that *'Fliess'.* This last word was the

---

[1] In waking life this same kind of analysis and synthesis of syllables—a syllabic chemistry, in fact—plays a part in a great number of jokes: 'What is the cheapest way of obtaining silver? You go down an avenue of silver poplars [*Pappeln*, which means both "poplars" and "babbling"] and call for silence. The babbling then ceases and the silver is released.' The first reader and critic of this book—and his successors are likely to follow his example—protested that 'the dreamer seems to be too ingenious and amusing.' This is quite true so long as it refers only to the dreamer; it would only be an objection if it were to be extended to the dream-interpreter. In waking reality I have little claim to be regarded as a wit. If my dreams seem amusing, that is not on my account, but on account of the peculiar psychological conditions under which dreams are constructed; and the fact is intimately connected with the theory of jokes and the comic. Dreams become ingenious and amusing because the direct and easiest pathway to the expression of their thoughts is barred: they are forced into being so. The reader can convince himself that my patients' dreams seem at least as full of jokes and puns as my own, or even fuller.—[*Added* 1909:] Nevertheless this objection led me to compare the technique of jokes with the dream-work; and the results are to be found in the book which I published on *Jokes and their Relation to the Unconscious* (1905c). [In particular in Chapter VI.—Towards the end of this chapter Freud remarks that dream-jokes are bad jokes, and explains why this should be so. The same point is made in Lecture XV of the *Introductory Lectures* (1916–17.)—The 'first reader' referred to above was Fliess, and the question is dealt with in a letter to him of September 11, 1899 (Freud, 1950a, Letter 118)].

name of my friend in B[erlin], who has often been the goal of my travels. 'Hearsing' was a compound. One part of it was derived from the names of places on the suburban railway near Vienna, which so often end in 'ing': Hietzing, Liesing, Mödling (Medelitz, *'meae deliciae,'* was its old name—that is *'meine Freud?'* ['my delight']). The other part was derived from the English word 'hearsay.' This suggested slander and established the dream's connection with its indifferent instigator of the previous day: a poem in the periodical *Fliegende Blätter* about a slanderous dwarf called 'Sagter Hatergesagt' ['He-says Says-he']. If the syllable 'ing' were to be added to the name 'Fliess' we should get 'Vlissingen,' which was in fact the stopping-place on the sea voyage made by my brother whenever he visited us from England. But the English name for Vlissingen is 'Flushing,' which in English means 'blushing' and reminded me of the patients I have treated for ereutophobia, and also of a recent paper on that neurosis by Bechterew which had caused me some annoyance.

V

On another occasion I had a dream which consisted of two separate pieces. The first piece was the word 'Autodidasker,' which I recalled vividly. The second piece was an exact reproduction of a short and harmless phantasy which I had produced some days before. This phantasy was to the effect that when I next saw Professor N. I must say to him: 'The patient about whose condition I consulted you recently is in fact only suffering from a neurosis, just as you suspected.' Thus the neologism 'Autodidasker' must satisfy two conditions: firstly, it must bear or represent a composite meaning; and secondly, that meaning must be solidly related to the intention I had reproduced from waking life of making amends to Professor N.

The word 'Autodidasker' could easily be analysed into 'Autor' [Author], 'Autodidakt' [self-taught] and 'Lasker,' with which I also associated the name of Lassalle.[1] The first of these words led to the precipitating

---

[1] [Ferdinand Lassalle, founder of the German Social Democratic movement, was born at Breslau in 1825 and died in 1864. Eduard Lasker (1829–1884), born at Jarotschin, not far from Breslau, was one of the founders of the National Liberal Party in Germany. Both were of Jewish origin.]

cause of the dream—this time a significant one. I had given my wife several volumes by a well-known [Austrian] writer who was a friend of my brother's, and who, as I have learnt, was a native of my own birth-place: J. J. David. One evening she had told me of the deep impression that had been made on her by the tragic story in one of David's books of how a man of talent went to the bad; and our conversation had turned to a discussion of the gifts of which we saw signs in our own children. Under the impact of what she had been reading, my wife expressed concern about the children, and I consoled her with the remark that those were the very dangers which could be kept at bay by a good up-bringing. My train of thought was carried further during the night; I took up my wife's concern and wove all kinds of other things into it. A remark made by the author to my brother on the subject of marriage showed my thoughts a by-path along which they might come to be represented in the dream. This path led to Breslau, where a lady with whom we were very friendly had gone to be married and settle down. The concern I felt over the danger of coming to grief over a woman—for that was the kernel of my dream-thoughts— found an example in Breslau in the cases of Lasker and Lassalle which made it possible to give a simultaneous picture of the two ways in which this fatal influence can be exercised.[1] '*Cherchez la femme*,' the phrase in which these thoughts could be summarized, led me, taken in another sense, to my still unmarried brother, whose name is Alexander. I now perceived that 'Alex,' the shortened form of the name by which we call him, has almost the same sound as an anagram of 'Lasker,' and that this factor must have had a share in leading my thoughts along the by-path by way of Breslau.

The play which I was making here upon names and syllables had a still further sense, however. It expressed a wish that my brother might have a happy domestic life, and it did so in this way. In Zola's novel of an artist's life, *L'oeuvre*, the subject of which must have been close to my dream-thoughts, its author, as is well known, introduced himself and his own domestic happiness as an episode. He appears under the name of 'Sandoz.' The transformation was probably arrived at as follows. If 'Zola' is written backwards (the sort of thing children are so fond of doing), we arrive at

---

[1] Lasker died of tabes, that is, as a result of an infection (syphilis) contracted from a woman; Lassalle, as everyone knows, fell in a duel on account of a woman. [George Meredith's *Tragic Comedians* is based on his story.]

'Aloz.' No doubt this seemed too undisguised. He therefore replaced 'Al,' which is the first syllable of 'Alexander' by 'Sand,' which is the third syllable of the same name; and in this way 'Sandoz' came into being. My own 'Autodidasker' arose in much the same fashion.

I must now explain how my phantasy of telling Professor N. that the patient we had both examined was only suffering from a neurosis made its way into the dream. Shortly before the end of my working year, I began the treatment of a new patient who quite baffled my powers of diagnosis. The presence of a grave organic disease—perhaps some degeneration of the spinal cord—strongly suggested itself but could not be established. It would have been tempting to diagnose a neurosis (which would have solved every difficulty), if only the patient had not repudiated with so much energy the sexual history without which I refuse to recognize the presence of a neurosis. In my embarrassment I sought help from the physician whom I, like many other people, respect more than any as a man and before whose authority I am readiest to bow. He listened to my doubts, told me they were justified, and then gave his opinion: 'Keep the man under observation; it must be a neurosis.' Since I knew he did not share my views on the aetiology of the neuroses, I did not produce my counter-argument, but I made no concealment of my scepticism. A few days later I informed the patient that I could do nothing for him and recommended him to seek other advice. Whereupon, to my intense astonishment, he started apologizing for having lied to me. He had been too much ashamed of himself, he said, and went on to reveal precisely the piece of sexual aetiology which I had been expecting and without which I had been unable to accept his illness as a neurosis. I was relieved but at the same time humiliated. I had to admit that my consultant, not being led astray by considering the anamnesis, had seen more clearly than I had. And I proposed to tell him as much when I next met him—to tell him that *he* had been right and I wrong.

This was precisely what I did in the dream. But what sort of a wish-fulfilment can there have been in confessing that I was wrong? To be wrong was, however, just what I *did* wish. I wanted to be wrong in my fears, or, more precisely, I wanted my wife, whose fears I had adopted in the dream-thoughts, to be wrong. The subject round which the question of right or wrong revolved in the dream was not far removed from what the dream-thoughts were really concerned with. There was the same alternative between organic and functional damage caused by a woman, or, more properly, by sexuality: tabetic paralysis or neurosis? (The manner of Lassalle's death could be loosely classed in the latter category.)

In this closely knit and, when it was carefully interpreted, very transparent dream, Professor N. played a part not only on account of this analogy and of my wish to be wrong, and on account of his incidental connections with Breslau and with the family of our friend who had settled there after her marriage—but also on account of the following episode which occurred at the end of our consultation. When he had given his opinion and so concluded our medical discussion, he turned to more personal subjects: 'How many children have you got now?'— 'Six.'—He made a gesture of admiration and concern.—'Girls or boys?'—'Three and three: they are my pride and my treasure.'—'Well, now, be on your guard! Girls are safe enough, but bringing up boys leads to difficulties later on.'—I protested that mine had been very well behaved so far. Evidently this second diagnosis, on the future of my boys, pleased me no more than the earlier one, according to which my patient was suffering from a neurosis. Thus these two impressions were bound up together by their contiguity, by the fact of their having been experienced both at once; and in taking the story of the neurosis into my dream, I was substituting it for the conversation about up-bringing, which had more connection with the dream-thoughts, since it touched so closely upon the worries later expressed by my wife. So even my fear that N. might be right in what he said about the difficulty of bringing up boys had found a place in the dream, for it lay concealed behind the representation of my wish that I myself might be wrong in harbouring such fears. The same phantasy served unaltered to represent both of the opposing alternatives.

VI

'Early this morning,[1] between dreaming and waking, I experienced a very nice example of verbal condensation. In the course of a mass of dream-fragments that I could scarcely remember, I was brought up short, as it were, by a word which I saw before me as though it were half written and half printed. The word was "*erzefilisch*," and it formed part of a sentence

---

[1] Quoted from Marcinowski [1911.] [This paragraph was added in 1914.]

which slipped into my conscious memory apart from any context and in complete isolation: "That has an *erzefilisch* influence on the sexual emotions." I knew at once that the word ought really to have been "*erzieherisch*" ["educational"]. And I was in doubt for some time whether the second "*e*" in "*erzefilisch*" should not have been an "*i*."[1] In that connection the word "syphilis" occurred to me and, starting to analyse the dream while I was still half asleep, I racked my brains in an effort to make out how that word could have got into my dream, since I had nothing to do with the disease either personally or professionally. I then thought of "erzehlerisch" [another nonsense word], and this explained the "e" of the second syllable of "*erzefilisch*" by reminding me that the evening before I had been asked by our governess [*Erzieherin*] to say something to her on the problem of prostitution, and had given her Hesse's book on prostitution in order to influence her emotional life—for this had not developed quite normally; after which I had talked [erzählt] a lot to her on the problem. I then saw all at once that the word "syphilis" was not to be taken literally, but stood for "poison"— of course in relation to sexual life. When translated, therefore, the sentence in the dream ran quite logically: "My talk [*Erzählung*] was intended to have an educational [*erzieherisch*] influence on the emotional life of our governess [*Erzieherin*]; but I fear it may at the same time have had a poisonous effect." "*Erzefilisch*" was compounded from "*erzäh-*" and "*erzieh-*."'

The verbal malformations in dreams greatly resemble those which are familiar in paranoia but which are also present in hysteria and obsessions. The linguistic tricks performed by children,[2] who sometimes actually treat words as though they were objects and moreover invent new languages and artificial syntactic forms, are the common source of these things in dreams and psychoneuroses alike.

The analysis of the nonsensical verbal forms that occur in dreams[3] is particularly well calculated to exhibit the dream-work's achievements in

---

[1] [This ingenious example of condensation turns upon the pronunciation of the second syllable—the stressed syllable—of the nonsense word. If it is '*ze*,' it is pronounced roughly like the English 'tsay,' thus resembling the second syllable of '*erzählen*' and of the invented '*erzehlerisch*.' If it is '*zi*,' it is pronounced roughly like the English 'tsee,' thus resembling the second syllable of '*erzieherisch*,' as well as (less closely) the first syllable of 'syphilis.']

[2] See Chapter IV of Freud's book on jokes (1905*c*).]

[3] [This paragraph was added in 1916.]

the way of condensation. The reader should not conclude from the paucity of the instances which I have given that material of this kind is rare or observed at all exceptionally. On the contrary, it is very common. But as a result of the fact that dream-interpretation is dependent upon psycho-analytic treatment, only a very small number of instances are observed and recorded and the analyses of such instances are as a rule only intelligible to experts in the pathology of the neuroses. Thus a dream of this kind was reported by Dr. von Karpinska (1914) containing the nonsensical verbal form: '*Svingnum elvi.*' It is also worth mentioning those cases in which a word appears in a dream which is not in itself meaningless but which has lost its proper meaning and combines a number of other meanings to which it is related in just the same way as a 'meaningless' word would be. This is what occurred, for instance, in the ten-year-old boy's dream of a 'category' which was recorded by Tausk (1913). 'Category' in that case meant 'female genitals' and to 'categorate' meant the same as 'to micturate.'

Where spoken sentences occur in dreams and are expressly distinguished as such from thoughts, it is an invariable rule that the words spoken in the dream are derived from spoken words remembered in the dream-material. The text of the speech is either retained unaltered or expressed with some slight displacement. A speech in a dream is often put together from various recollected speeches, the text remaining the same but being given, if possible, several meanings, or one different from the original one. A spoken remark in a dream is not infrequently no more than an allusion to an occasion on which the remark in question was made.[1]

---

[1] [*Footnote added* 1909:] Not long ago I found a single exception to this rule in the case of a young man who suffered from obsessions while retaining intact his highly developed intellectual powers. The spoken words which occurred in his dreams were not derived from remarks which he had heard or made himself. They contained the undistorted text of his obsessional thoughts, which in his waking life only reached his consciousness in a modified form. [This young man was the subject of Freud's case history of an obsessional neurotic (the 'Rat Man'); a reference to this point will be found there (Freud, 1909*d*) near the beginning of Section 11(A).—The question of spoken words in dreams is dealt with much more fully below on pp. 427 ff.]

(B)

THE WORK OF DISPLACEMENT

In making our collection of instances of condensation in dreams, the existence of another relation, probably of no less importance, had already become evident. It could be seen that the elements which stand out as the principal components of the manifest content of the dream are far from playing the same part in the dream-thoughts. And, as a corollary, the converse of this assertion can be affirmed: what is clearly the essence of the dream-thoughts need not be represented in the dream at all. The dream is, as it were, differently centred from the dream-thoughts—its content has different elements as its central point. Thus in the dream of the botanical monograph [pp. 193 ff.], for instance, the central point of the dream-content was obviously the element 'botanical'; whereas the dream-thoughts were concerned with the complications and conflicts arising between colleagues from their professional obligations, and further with the charge that I was in the habit of sacrificing too much for the sake of my hobbies. The element 'botanical' had no place whatever in this core of the dream-thoughts, unless it was loosely connected with it by an antithesis—the fact that botany never had a place among my favourite studies. In my patient's *Sappho* dream [pp. 302 ff.] the central position was occupied by climbing up and down and being up above and down below; the dream-thoughts, however, dealt with the dangers of sexual relations with people of an inferior social class. So that only a single element of the dream-thoughts seems to have found its way into the dream-content, though that element was expanded to a disproportionate extent. Similarly, in the dream of the may-beetles [pp. 307 ff.], the topic of which was the relations of sexuality to cruelty, it is true that the factor of cruelty emerged in the dream-content; but it did so in another connection and without any mention of sexuality, that is to say, divorced from its context and consequently transformed into something extraneous. Once again, in my dream about my uncle [pp. 162 ff.], the fair beard which formed its centre-point seems to have had no connection in its meaning with my ambitious wishes which, as we saw, were the core of the dream-thoughts. Dreams such as these give a justifiable impression of 'displacement.' In complete contrast to these examples, we can see that in the dream of Irma's injection [pp. 131 ff.] the different elements were able to retain, during the process of constructing the dream, the approximate place which they occupied in the dream-thoughts. This further relation between the dream-thoughts and the dream-content, wholly variable as it is in its sense or direction, is calculated at first to create astonishment. If we are considering a psychical process in normal life and find that one out of its several component ideas has been picked out and has acquired a special degree of vividness in consciousness, we usually regard this effect as evidence that a specially high amount of psychical value—some particular degree of interest—attaches to this predominant idea. But we now discover that, in the case of the different elements of the dream-thoughts, a value of this kind does not persist or is disregarded in the process of dream-formation. There is never any doubt as to which of the elements of the dream-thoughts have the highest psychical value; we learn that by direct judgement. In the course of the formation of a dream these essential elements, charged, as they are, with intense interest, may be treated as though they were of small value, and their place may be taken in the dream by other elements, of whose small value in the dream-thoughts there can be no question. At first sight it looks as though no attention whatever is paid to the psychical intensity[1] of the various ideas in making the choice among them for the dream, and as though the only thing considered is the greater or less degree of multiplicity of their determination. What appears in dreams, we might suppose, is not what is *important* in the dream-thoughts but what occurs in them several times over. But this hypothesis does not greatly assist our understanding of dream-formation, since from the nature of things it seems clear that the two factors of multiple determination and inherent psychical value must necessarily operate in the same sense. The ideas which are most important among the dream-thoughts will almost certainly be those which occur most often in them, since the different dream-thoughts will, as it were, radiate out from them. Nevertheless a dream can reject elements which are thus both highly stressed in themselves and reinforced from many directions, and can select for its content other elements which possess only the second of these attributes.

In order to solve this difficulty we shall make use of another impression derived from our enquiry [in the previous section] into the over-determination of the dream-content. Perhaps some of those who have read

---

[1] *Psychical* intensity or value or the degree of interest of an idea is of course to be distinguished from *sensory* intensity or the intensity of the image presented.

that enquiry may already have formed an independent conclusion that the overdetermination of the elements of dreams is no very important discovery, since it is a self-evident one. For in analysis we start out from the dream-elements and note down all the associations which lead off from them; so that there is nothing surprising in the fact that in the thought-material arrived at in this way we come across these same elements with peculiar frequency. I cannot accept this objection; but I will myself put into words something that sounds not unlike it. Among the thoughts that analysis brings to light are many which are relatively remote from the kernel of the dream and which look like artificial interpolations made for some particular purpose. That purpose is easy to divine. It is precisely *they* that constitute a connection, often a forced and far-fetched one, between the dream-content and the dream-thoughts; and if these elements were weeded out of the analysis the result would often be that the component parts of the dream-content would be left not only without overdetermination but without any satisfactory determination at all. We shall be led to conclude that the multiple determination which decides what shall be included in a dream is not always a primary factor in dream-construction but is often the secondary product of a psychical force which is still unknown to us. Nevertheless multiple determination must be of importance in choosing what particular elements shall enter a dream, since we can see that a considerable expenditure of effort is used to bring it about in cases where it does not arise from the dream-material unassisted.

It thus seems plausible to suppose that in the dream-work a psychical force is operating which on the one hand strips the elements which have a high psychical value of their intensity, and on the other hand, *by means of over-determination*, creates from elements of low psychical value new values, which afterwards find their way into the dream-content. If that is so, a *transference and displacement of psychical intensities* occurs in the process of dream-formation, and it is as a result of these that the difference between the text of the dream-content and that of the dream-thoughts comes about. The process which we are here presuming is nothing less than the essential portion of the dream-work; and it deserves to be described as 'dream-displacement.' Dream-displacement and dream-condensation are the two governing factors to whose activity we may in essence ascribe the form assumed by dreams.

Nor do I think we shall have any difficulty in recognizing the psychical force which manifests itself in the facts of dream-displacement. The consequence of the displacement is that the dream-content no longer resembles the core of the dream-thoughts and that the dream gives no more than a distortion of the dream-wish which exists in the unconscious. But we are already familiar with dream-distortion. We traced it back to the censorship which is exercised by one psychical agency in the mind over another. [See pp. 167 ff.] Dream-displacement is one of the chief methods by which that distortion is achieved. *Is fecit cui profuit.*[1] We may assume, then, that dream-displacement comes about through the influence of the same censorship—that is, the censorship of endopsychic defence.[2]

---

[1] [The old legal tag: 'He did the deed who gained by it.']

[2] [*Footnote added* 1909:] Since I may say that the kernel of my theory of dreams lies in my derivation of dream-distortion from the censorship, I will here insert the last part of a story from *Phantasien eines Realisten* [*Phantasies of a Realist*] by 'Lynkeus' (Vienna, 2nd edition, 1900 [1st edition, 1899]), in which I have found this principal feature of my theory once more expounded. [See above, Postscript, 1909, to Chapter I, pp. 120 f.; also Freud, 1923*f* and 1932*c*.] The title of the story is 'Träumen wie Wachen,' ['Dreaming Like Waking']:

'About a man who has the remarkable attribute of never dreaming nonsense. . . .

'"This splendid gift of yours, for dreaming as though you were waking, is a consequence of your virtues, of your kindness, your sense of justice, and your love of truth; it is the moral serenity of your nature which makes me understand all about you."

'"But when I think the matter over properly," replied the other, "I almost believe that everyone is made like me, and that no one at all ever dreams nonsense. Any dream which one can remember clearly enough to describe it afterwards— any dream, that is to say, which is not a fever-dream—must *always* make sense, and it cannot possibly be otherwise. For things that were mutually contradictory could not group themselves into a single whole. The fact that time and space are often thrown into confusion does not affect the true content of the dream, since no doubt neither of them are of significance for its real essence. We often do the same thing in waking life. Only think of fairy tales and of the many daring products of the imagination, which are full of meaning and of which only a man without intelligence could say: 'This is nonsense, for it's impossible.'"

'"If only one always knew how to interpret dreams in the right way, as you have just done with mine!" said his friend.

'"That is certainly no easy task; but with a little attention on the part of the dreamer himself it should no doubt always succeed.—You ask why it is that for the most part it does *not* succeed? In you other people there seems always to be something that lies concealed in your dreams, something unchaste in a special and higher sense, a certain secret quality in your being which it is hard to follow. And that is why your dreams so often seem to be without meaning or even to be nonsense. But in the deepest sense this is not in the least so; indeed, it cannot be so at all—for it is always the same man, whether he is awake or dreaming."'

The question of the interplay of these factors—of displacement, condensation and overdetermination—in the construction of dreams, and the question which is a dominant factor and which a subordinate one—all of this we shall leave aside for later investigation. [See e.g. pp. 415 ff.] But we can state provisionally a second condition which must be satisfied by those elements of the dream-thoughts which make their way into the dream: *they must escape the censorship imposed by resistance.*[1] And henceforward in interpreting dreams we shall take dream-displacement into account as an undeniable fact.

(C)

THE MEANS OF REPRESENTATION IN DREAMS

In the process of transforming the latent thoughts into the manifest content of a dream we have found two factors at work: dream-condensation and dream-displacement. As we continue our investigation we shall, in addition to these, come across two further determinants which exercise an undoubted influence on the choice of the material which is to find access to the dream.

But first, even at the risk of appearing to bring our progress to a halt, I should like to take a preliminary glance at the processes involved in carrying out the interpretation of a dream. I cannot disguise from myself that the easiest way of making those processes clear and of defending their trustworthiness against criticism would be to take some particular dream as a sample, go through its interpretation (just as I have done with the dream of Irma's injection in my second chapter), and then collect the dream-thoughts which I have discovered and go on to reconstruct from them the process by which the dream was formed—in other words, to complete a dream-analysis by a dream-synthesis. I have in fact carried out that task for my own instruction on several specimens; but I cannot reproduce them here, since I am forbidden to do so for reasons connected with the nature of the psychical material involved—reasons which are of many kinds and which will be accepted as valid by any reasonable person. Such

---

[1] [The first condition being that they must be overdetermined. (See pp. 324 f.)]

considerations interfered less in the *analysis* of dreams, since an analysis could be incomplete and nevertheless retain its value, even though it penetrated only a small way into the texture of the dream. But in the case of the synthesis of a dream I do not see how it can be convincing unless it is complete. I could only give a complete *synthesis* of dreams dreamt by people unknown to the reading public. Since, however, this condition is fulfilled only by my patients, who are neurotics, I must postpone this part of my exposition of the subject till I am able—in another volume—to carry the psychological elucidation of neuroses to a point at which it can make contact with our present topic.[1]

My attempts at building up dreams by synthesis from the dream-thoughts have taught me that the material which emerges in the course of interpretation is not all of the same value. One part of it is made up of the essential dream-thoughts—those, that is, which completely replace the dream, and which, if there were no censorship of dreams, would be sufficient in themselves to replace it. The other part of the material is usually to be regarded as of less importance. Nor is it possible to support the view that all the thoughts of this second kind had a share in the formation of the dream. (See pp. 298 and 535.) On the contrary, there may be associations among them which relate to events that occurred *after* the dream, between the times of dreaming and interpreting. This part of the material includes all the connecting paths that led from the manifest dream-content to the latent dream-thoughts, as well as the intermediate and linking associations by means of which, in the course of the process of interpretation, we came to discover these connecting paths.[2]

---

[1] [*Footnote added* 1909:] Since writing the above words, I have published a complete analysis and synthesis of two dreams in my 'Fragment of the Analysis of a Case of Hysteria' [Freud, 1905*e* (Sections II and III). See also the synthesis of the 'Wolf Man's' dream in Section IV of Freud (1918*b*).—*Added* 1914:] Otto Rank's analysis, 'Ein Traum, der sich selbst deutet' ['A Dream which Interprets Itself,' 1910], deserves mention as the most complete interpretation that has been published of a dream of considerable length.

[2] [The last four sentences (beginning with 'the other part of the material') date in their present form from 1919. In editions earlier than that, this passage ran as follows: 'The other part of the material may be brought together under the term "collaterals." As a whole, they constitute the paths over which the true wish, which arises from the dream-thoughts, passes before becoming the dream-wish. The first set of these "collaterals" consist in derivatives from the dream-thoughts proper; they are, schematically regarded, displacements from what is essential to

We are here interested only in the essential dream-thoughts. These usually emerge as a complex of thoughts and memories of the most intricate possible structure, with all the attributes of the trains of thought familiar to us in waking life. They are not infrequently trains of thought starting out from more than one centre, though having points of contact. Each train of thought is almost invariably accompanied by its contradictory counterpart, linked with it by antithetical association.

The different portions of this complicated structure stand, of course, in the most manifold logical relations to one another. They can represent foreground and background, digressions and illustrations, conditions, chains of evidence and counter-arguments. When the whole mass of these dream-thoughts is brought under the pressure of the dream-work, and its elements are turned about, broken into fragments and jammed together— almost like pack-ice—the question arises of what happens to the logical connections which have hitherto formed its framework. What representation do dreams provide for 'if,' 'because,' 'just as,' 'although,' 'either—or,' and all the other conjunctions without which we cannot understand sentences or speeches?

In the first resort our answer must be that dreams have no means at their disposal for representing these logical relations between the dream-thoughts. For the most part dreams disregard all these conjunctions, and it is only the substantive content of the dream-thoughts that they take over and manipulate.[1] The restoration of the connections which the dream-work has destroyed is a task which has to be performed by the interpretative process.

The incapacity of dreams to express these things must lie in the nature of the psychical material out of which dreams are made. The plastic arts of painting and sculpture labour, indeed, under a similar limitation as

---

what is inessential. A second set of them comprise the thoughts that connect these inessential elements (which have become important owing to displacement) with one another, and extend from them to the dream-content. Finally, a third set consist in the associations and trains of thought by means of which the work of interpretation leads us from the dream-content to the second group of collaterals. It need not be supposed that the whole of this third set were necessarily also concerned in the formation of the dream.' With reference to this passage Freud remarks in *Ges. Schr.*, ‡ (1925), 55 that he has dropped the term 'collaterals.' In fact, however, the term has survived below on p. 535.]

[1] [A qualification of this statement will be found below, p. 458 n.]

compared with poetry, which can make use of speech; and here once again the reason for their incapacity lies in the nature of the material which these two forms of art manipulate in their effort to express something. Before painting became acquainted with the laws of expression by which it is governed, it made attempts to get over this handicap. In ancient paintings small labels were hung from the mouths of the persons represented, containing in written characters the speeches which the artist despaired of representing pictorially.

At this point an objection may perhaps be raised in dispute of the idea that dreams are unable to represent logical relations. For there are dreams in which the most complicated intellectual operations take place, statements are contradicted or confirmed, ridiculed or compared, just as they are in waking thought. But here again appearances are deceitful. If we go into the interpretation of dreams such as these, we find that the whole of this *is part of the material of the dream-thoughts and is not a representation of intellectual work performed during the dream itself.* What is reproduced by the ostensible thinking in the dream is the *subject-matter* of the dream-thoughts and not the *mutual relations between them*, the assertion of which constitutes thinking. I shall bring forward some instances of this. [See pp. 449 ff.] But the easiest point to establish in this connection is that all spoken sentences which occur in dreams and are specifically described as such are unmodified or slightly modified reproductions of speeches which are also to be found among the recollections in the material of the dream-thoughts. A speech of this kind is often no more than an allusion to some event included among the dream-thoughts, and the meaning of the dream may be a totally different one. [See pp. 427 ff.]

Nevertheless, I will not deny that critical thought-activity which is not a mere repetition of material in the dream-thoughts *does* have a share in the formation of dreams. I shall have to elucidate the part played by this factor at the end of the present discussion. It will then become apparent that this thought-activity is not produced by the dream-thoughts but by the dream itself after it has already, in a certain sense, been completed. [See the last Section of this Chapter (p. 493).]

Provisionally, then, it may be said that the logical relations between the dream-thoughts are not given any separate representation in dreams. For instance, if a contradiction occurs in a dream, it is either a contradiction of the dream itself or a contradiction derived from the subject-matter of one of the dream-thoughts. A contradiction in a dream can only correspond in an exceedingly indirect manner to a contradiction *between* the dream-thoughts. But just as the art of painting eventually found a way of expressing, by means other than the floating labels, at least the *intention* of the words of the personages represented—affection, threats, warnings, and so on—so too there is a possible means by which dreams can take account of some of the logical relations between their dream-thoughts, by making an appropriate modification in the method of representation characteristic of dreams. Experience shows that different dreams vary greatly in this respect. While some dreams completely disregard the logical sequence of their material, others attempt to give as full an indication of it as possible. In doing so dreams depart sometimes more and sometimes less widely from the text that is at their disposal for manipulation. Incidentally dreams vary similarly in their treatment of the *chronological* sequence of the dream-thoughts, if such a sequence has been established in the unconscious (as, for instance, in the dream of Irma's injection. [Pp. 131 ff.]).

What means does the dream-work possess for indicating these relations in the dream-thoughts which it is so hard to represent? I will attempt to enumerate them one by one.

In the first place, dreams take into account in a general way the connection which undeniably exists between all the portions of the dream-thoughts by combining the whole material into a single situation or event. They reproduce *logical connection* by *simultaneity in time*. Here they are acting like the painter who, in a picture of the School of Athens or of Parnassus, represents in one group all the philosophers or all the poets. It is true that they were never in fact assembled in a single hall or on a single mountain-top; but they certainly form a group in the conceptual sense.

Dreams carry this method of reproduction down to details. Whenever they show us two elements close together, this guarantees that there is some specially intimate connection between what correspond to them among the dream-thoughts. In the same way, in our system of writing, '*ab*' means that the two letters are to be pronounced in a single syllable. If a gap is left between the '*a*' and the '*b*,' it means that the '*a*' is the last letter of one word and the '*b*' is the first of the next one.[1] So, too, collocations in dreams do not consist of any chance, disconnected portions of the

---

[1] [This simile is a favourite one of Freud's. He uses it above on p. 265 and again in the middle of Section I of the case history of Dora (1905*c*). It is possibly derived from a lyric of Goethe's ('Schwer in Waides Busch') in which the same image occurs.]

dream-material, but of portions which are fairly closely connected in the dream-thoughts as well.

For representing *causal relations* dreams have two procedures which are in essence the same. Suppose the dream-thoughts run like this: 'Since this was so and so, such and such was bound to happen.' Then the commoner method of representation would be to introduce the dependent clause as an introductory dream and to add the principal clause as the main dream. If I have interpreted aright, the temporal sequence may be reversed. But the more extensive part of the dream always corresponds to the principal clause.

One of my women patients once produced an excellent instance of this way of representing causality in a dream which I shall later record fully. [See pp. 361 ff.; also discussed on pp. 335 and 340.] It consisted of a short prelude and a very diffuse piece of dream which was centred to a marked degree on a single theme and might be entitled 'The Language of Flowers.' The introductory dream was as follows: *She went into the kitchen, where her two maids were, and found fault with them for not having got her 'bite of food' ready. At the same time she saw a very large quantity of common kitchen crockery standing upside down in the kitchen to drain; it was piled up in heaps. The two maids went to fetch some water and had to step into a kind of river which came right up to the house or into the yard.* The main dream then followed, beginning thus: *She was descending from a height over some strangely constructed palisades, and felt glad that her dress was not caught in them . . .* etc.

The introductory dream related to the dreamer's parents' home. No doubt she had often heard her mother using the words that occurred in the dream. The heaps of common crockery were derived from a modest hardware shop which was located in the same building. The other part of the dream contained a reference to her father, who used always to run after the maids and who eventually contracted a fatal illness during a flood. (The house stood near a river-bank.) Thus the thought concealed behind the introductory dream ran as follows: 'Because I was born in this house, in such mean and depressing circumstances . . .' The main dream took up the same thought and presented it in a form modified by wish-fulfilment: 'I am of high descent.' Thus the actual underlying thought was: 'Because I am of such low descent, the course of my life has been so and so.'

The division of a dream into two unequal parts does not invariably, so far as I can see, signify that there is a causal relation between the thoughts behind the two parts. It often seems as though the same material were being represented in the two dreams from different points of view. (This is certainly the case where a series of dreams during one night end in an emission or orgasm—a series in which the somatic need finds its way to progressively clearer expression.)[1] Or the two dreams may have sprung from separate centres in the dream-material, and their content may overlap, so that what is the centre in one dream is present as a mere hint in the other, and *vice versa*. But in a certain number of dreams a division into a shorter preliminary dream and a longer sequel does in fact signify that there is a causal relation between the two pieces.

The other method of representing a causal relation is adapted to less extensive material and consists in one image in the dream, whether of a person or thing, being transformed into another. The existence of a causal relation is only to be taken seriously if the transformation actually occurs before our eyes and not if we merely notice that one thing has appeared in the place of another.

I have said that the two methods of representing a causal relation were in essence the same. In both cases causation is represented by temporal sequence: in one instance by a sequence of dreams and in the other by the direct transformation of one image into another. In the great majority of cases, it must be confessed, the causal relation is not represented at all but is lost in the confusion of elements which inevitably occurs in the process of dreaming.

The alternative 'either—or' cannot be expressed in dreams in any way whatever. Both of the alternatives are usually inserted in the text of the dream as though they were equally valid. The dream of Irma's injection contains a classic instance of this. Its latent thoughts clearly ran [see p. 143]: 'I am not responsible for the persistence of Irma's pains; the responsibility lies *either* in her recalcitrance to accepting my solution, *or* in the unfavourable sexual conditions under which she lives and which I cannot alter, or in the fact that her pains are not hysterical at all but of an organic nature.' The dream, on the other hand, fulfilled *all* of these possibilities (which were almost mutually exclusive), and did not hesitate to add a fourth solution, based on the dream-wish. After interpreting the dream, I proceeded to insert the 'either—or' into the context of the dream-thoughts.

---

[1] [This sentence was added in 1914. The point is further mentioned on p. 350 and discussed at greater length on pp. 412–14. The whole subject of dreams occurring on the same night is dealt with on pp. 348 ff.]

If, however, in reproducing a dream, its narrator feels inclined to make use of an 'either—or'—e.g. 'it was either a garden or a sitting-room'—what was present in the dream-thoughts was not an alternative but an 'and,' a simple addition. An 'either—or' is mostly used to describe a dream-element that has a quality of vagueness—which, however, is capable of being resolved. In such cases the rule for interpretation is: treat the two apparent alternatives as of equal validity and link them together with an 'and.'

For instance, on one occasion a friend of mine was stopping in Italy and I had been without his address for a considerable time. I then had a dream of receiving a telegram containing this address. I saw it printed in blue on the telegraph form. The first word was vague:

'*Via*,' perhaps
or '*Villa*' }; the second was clear: '*Secerno*.'
or possibly even ('*Casa*')

The second word sounded like some Italian name and reminded me of discussions I had had with my friend on the subject of etymology. It also expressed my anger with him for having kept his address *secret* from me for so long. On the other hand, each of the three alternatives for the first word turned out on analysis to be an independent and equally valid starting-point for a chain of thoughts.[1]

During the night before my father's funeral I had a dream of a printed notice, placard or poster—rather like the notices forbidding one to smoke in railway waiting-rooms—on which appeared either

'You are requested to close the eyes'
or,   'You are requested to close an eye.'

I usually write this in the form:

the
'You are requested to close   eye(s).'
an

---

[1] [This dream will be found described in greater detail in Freud's letter to Fliess (the friend in question) of April 28, 1897. See Freud, 1950*a*, Letter 60.]

Each of these two versions had a meaning of its own and led in a different direction when the dream was interpreted. I had chosen the simplest possible ritual for the funeral, for I knew my father's own views on such ceremonies. But some other members of the family were not sympathetic to such puritanical simplicity and thought we should be disgraced in the eyes of those who attended the funeral. Hence one of the versions: 'You are requested to close an eye,' i.e. to 'wink at' or 'overlook.' Here it is particularly easy to see the meaning of the vagueness expressed by the 'either—or.' The dream-work failed to establish a unified wording for the dream-thoughts which could at the same time be ambiguous, and the two main lines of thought consequently began to diverge even in the manifest content of the dream.[1]

In a few instances the difficulty of representing an alternative is got over by dividing the dream into two pieces of equal length.

The way in which dreams treat the category of contraries and contradictories is highly remarkable. It is simply disregarded. 'No' seems not to exist so far as dreams are concerned.[2] They show a particular preference for combining contraries into a unity or for representing them as one and the same thing. Dreams feel themselves at liberty, moreover, to represent any element by its wishful contrary; so there is no way of deciding at a first glance whether any element that admits of a contrary is present in the dream-thoughts as a positive or as a negative.[3]

---

[1] [This dream is reported by Freud in a letter to Fliess of November 2, 1896. (See Freud, 1950*a*, Letter 50.) It is there stated to have occurred during the night *after* the funeral.]

[2] [Qualifications of this assertion occur on pp. 341, 351 f. and 442 f.—In its first wording the dream referred to closing the dead man's eyes as a filial duty.]

[3] [*Footnote added* 1911:] I was astonished to learn from a pamphlet by K. Abel, *The Antithetical Meaning of Primal Words* (1884) (cf. my review of it, 1910*e*)— and the fact has been confirmed by other philologists—that the most ancient languages behave exactly like dreams in this respect. In the first instance they have only a single word to describe the two contraries at the extreme ends of a series of qualities or activities (e.g. 'strong-weak,' 'old-young,' 'far-near,' 'bind-sever'); they only form distinct terms for the two contraries by a secondary process of making small modifications in the common word. Abel demonstrates this particularly from Ancient Egyptian; but he shows that there are distinct traces of the same course of development in the Semitic and Indo-Germanic languages as well. [See also p. 477.]

In one of the dreams recorded just above, the first clause of which has already been interpreted ('because my descent was such and such' [see p. 331]), the dreamer saw herself climbing down over some palisades holding a blossoming branch in her hand. In connection with this image she thought of the angel holding a spray of lilies in pictures of the Annunciation—her own name was Maria—and of girls in white robes walking in Corpus Christi processions, when the streets are decorated with green branches. Thus the blossoming branch in the dream without any doubt alluded to sexual innocence. However, the branch was covered with *red* flowers, each of which was like a camellia. By the end of her walk—so the dream went on—the blossoms were already a good deal faded. There then followed some unmistakable allusions to menstruation. Accordingly, the same branch which was carried like a lily and as though by an innocent girl was at the same time an allusion to the *Dame aux camélias* who, as we know, usually wore a white camellia, except during her periods, when she wore a red one. The same blossoming branch (cf. 'des Mädchens Blüten' ['the maiden's blossoms'] in Goethe's poem 'Der Müllerin Verrat') represented both sexual innocence and its contrary. And the same dream which expressed her joy at having succeeded in passing through life immaculately gave one glimpses at certain points (e.g. in the fading of the blossoms) of the contrary train of ideas—of her having been guilty of various sins against sexual purity (in her childhood, that is). In analysing the dream it was possible clearly to distinguish the two trains of thought, of which the consoling one seemed the more superficial and the self-reproachful one the deeper-lying—trains of thought which were diametrically opposed to each other but whose similar though contrary elements were represented by the same elements in the manifest dream.[1]

One and one only of these logical relations is very highly favoured by the mechanism of dream-formation; namely, the relation of similarity, consonance or approximation—the relation of 'just as.' This relation, unlike any other, is capable of being represented in dreams in a variety of ways.[2] Parallels or instances of 'just as' inherent in the material of the dream-thoughts constitute the first foundations for the construction of a

---

[1] [The dream is fully reported on p. 361 below.]
[2] [*Footnote added* 1914:] Cf. Aristotle's remark on the qualifications of a dream-interpreter quoted above on p. 122 n.

dream; and no inconsiderable part of the dream-work consists in creating fresh parallels where those which are already present cannot find their way into the dream owing to the censorship imposed by resistance. The representation of the relation of similarity is assisted by the tendency of the dream-work towards condensation.

Similarity, consonance, the possession of common attributes—all these are represented in dreams by unification, which may either be present already in the material of the dream thoughts or may be freshly constructed. The first of these possibilities may be described as 'identification' and the second as 'composition.' Identification is employed where *persons* are concerned; composition where *things* are the material of the unification. Nevertheless composition may also be applied to persons. Localities are often treated like persons.

In identification, only one of the persons who are linked by a common element succeeds in being represented in the manifest content of the dream, while the second or remaining persons seem to be suppressed in it. But this single covering figure appears in the dream in all the relations and situations which apply either to him or to the figures which he covers. In composition, where this is extended to persons, the dream-image contains features which are peculiar to one or other of the persons concerned but not common to them; so that the combination of these features leads to the appearance of a new unity, a composite figure. The actual process of composition can be carried out in various ways. On the one hand, the dream-figure may bear the name of one of the persons related to it—in which case we simply know directly, in a manner analogous to our waking knowledge, that this or that person is intended—while its visual features may belong to the other person. Or, on the other hand, the dream-image itself may be composed of visual features belonging in reality partly to the one person and partly to the other. Or again the second person's share in the dream-image may lie, not in its visual features, but in the gestures that we attribute to it, the words that we make it speak, or the situation in which we place it. In this last case the distinction between identification and the construction of a composite figure begins to lose its sharpness.[1]

---

[1] [On the subject of composite figures cf. also pp. 310 ff. The next three sentences were added in 1911. The final sentence of the paragraph was added in 1914.— 'Identification' in this passage is evidently being used in a sense different from that discussed on pp. 173 ff.]

But it may also happen that the formation of a composite figure of this kind is unsuccessful. If so, the scene in the dream is attributed to *one* of the persons concerned, while the other (and usually the more important one) appears as an attendant figure without any other function. The dreamer may describe the position in such a phrase as: 'My mother was there as well.' (Stekel.) An element of this kind in the dream-content may be compared to the 'determinatives' used in hieroglyphic script, which are not meant to be pronounced but serve merely to elucidate other signs.

The common element which justifies, or rather causes, the combination of the two persons may be represented in the dream or may be omitted from it. As a rule the identification or construction of a composite person takes place for the very purpose of avoiding the representation of the common element. Instead of saying: 'A has hostile feelings towards me and so has *B*,' I make a composite figure out of *A* and *B* in the dream, or I imagine *A* performing an act of some other kind which is characteristic of *B*. The dream-figure thus constructed appears in the dream in some quite new connection, and the circumstance that it represents both *A* and *B* justifies me in inserting at the appropriate point in the dream the element which is common to both of them, namely a hostile attitude towards me. It is often possible in this way to achieve quite a remarkable amount of condensation in the content of a dream; I can save myself the need for giving a direct representation of very complicated circumstances relating to one person, if I can find another person to whom some of these circumstances apply equally. It is easy to see, too, how well this method of representation by means of identification can serve to evade the censorship due to resistance, which imposes such severe conditions upon the dream-work. What the censorship objects to may lie precisely in certain ideas which, in the material of the dream-thoughts, are attached to a particular person; so I proceed to find a second person, who is also connected with the objectionable material, but only with part of it. The contact between the two persons upon this censorable point now justifies me in constructing a composite figure characterized by indifferent features derived from both. This figure, arrived at by identification or composition, is then admissible to the dream-content without censorship, and thus, by making use of dream-condensation, I have satisfied the claims of the dream-censorship.

When a common element between two persons is represented in a dream, it is usually a hint for us to look for another, concealed common element whose representation has been made impossible by the censorship.

A displacement in regard to the common element has been made in order, as it were, to facilitate its representation. The fact that the composite figure appears in the dream with an indifferent common element leads us to conclude that there is another far from indifferent common element present in the dream-thoughts.

Accordingly, identification or the construction of composite figures serves various purposes in dreams: firstly to represent an element common to two persons, secondly to represent a *displaced* common element, and thirdly, too, to express a merely *wishful* common element. Since wishing that two persons had a common element frequently coincides with exchanging one for the other, this latter relation is also expressed in dreams by means of identification. In the dream of Irma's injection, I wished to exchange her for another patient: I wished, that is, that the other woman might be my patient just as Irma was. The dream took this wish into account by showing me a person who was called Irma, but who was examined in a position in which I had only had occasion to see the other woman [pp. 133 f.]. In the dream about my uncle an exchange of this kind became the central point of the dream: I identified myself with the Minister by treating and judging my colleagues no better than he did. [P. 215.]

It is my experience, and one to which I have found no exception, that every dream deals with the dreamer himself. Dreams are completely egoistical.[1] Whenever my own ego does not appear in the content of the dream, but only some extraneous person, I may safely assume that my own ego lies concealed, by identification, behind this other person; I can insert my ego into the context. On other occasions, when my own ego *does* appear in the dream, the situation in which it occurs may teach me that some other person lies concealed, by identification, behind my ego. In that case the dream should warn me to transfer on to myself, when I am interpreting the dream, the concealed common element attached to this other person. There are also dreams in which my ego appears along with other people who, when the identification is resolved, are revealed once again as my ego. These identifications should then make it possible for me to bring into contact with my ego certain ideas whose acceptance has been forbidden by the censorship. Thus my ego may be represented in a dream several times over, now directly and now through identifica-

---

[1] [*Footnote added* 1925:] Cf. the footnote on pp. 288.

tion with extraneous persons. By means of a number of such identifications it becomes possible to condense an extraordinary amount of thought-material.[1] The fact that the dreamer's own ego appears several times, or in several forms, in a dream is at bottom no more remarkable than that the ego should be contained in a conscious thought several times or in different places or connections—e.g. in the sentence 'when *I* think what a healthy child *I* was.'[2]

Identifications in the case of proper names of *localities* are resolved even more easily than in the case of persons, since here there is no interference by the ego, which occupies such a dominating place in dreams. In one of my dreams about Rome (see pp. 217 f.), the place in which I found myself was called Rome, but I was astonished at the quantity of German posters at a street-corner. This latter point was a wish-fulfilment, which at once made me think of Prague; and the wish itself may perhaps have dated from a German-nationalist phase which I passed through during my youth, but have since got over.[3] At the time at which I had the dream there was a prospect of my meeting my friend [Fliess] in Prague; so that the identification of Rome and Prague can be explained as a wishful common element: I would rather have met my friend in Rome than in Prague and would have liked to exchange Prague for Rome for the purpose of this meeting.

The possibility of creating composite structures stands foremost among the characteristics which so often lend dreams a fantastic appearance, for it introduces into the content of dreams elements which could never have been objects of actual perception.[4] The psychical process of constructing composite images in dreams is evidently the same as when we imagine or portray a centaur or a dragon in waking life. The only difference is that what determines the production of the imaginary figure in waking life is the impression which the new structure itself is intended to make; whereas

---

[1] When I am in doubt behind which of the figures appearing in the dream my ego is to be looked for, I observe the following rule: the person who in the dream feels an emotion which I myself experience in my sleep is the one who conceals my ego.

[2] [This sentence was added in 1925. The point is dealt with further in Freud, 1923c, Section X.]

[3] [Cf. the 'Revolutionary' dream, pp. 231 f. and 233 f.]

[4] [Some amusing instances are given at the end of Section IV of Freud's short essay on dreams (1901a); Standard Ed., 5, 651.]

the formation of the composite structure in a dream is determined by a factor extraneous to its actual shape—namely the common element in the dream-thoughts. Composite structures in dreams can be formed in a great variety of ways. The most naïve of these procedures merely represents the attributes of one thing to the accompaniment of a knowledge that they also belong to something else. A more painstaking technique combines the features of both objects into a new image and in so doing makes clever use of any similarities that the two objects may happen to possess in reality. The new structure may seem entirely absurd or may strike us as an imaginative success, according to the material and to the ingenuity with which it is put together. If the objects which are to be condensed into a single unity are much too incongruous, the dream-work is often content with creating a composite structure with a comparatively distinct nucleus, accompanied by a number of less distinct features. In that case the process of unification into a single image may be said to have failed. The two representations are superimposed and produce something in the nature of a contest between the two visual images. One might arrive at similar representations in a drawing, if one tried to illustrate the way in which a general concept is formed from a number of individual perceptual images.

Dreams are, of course, a mass of these composite structures. I have given some examples of them in dreams that I have already analysed; and I will now add a few more. In the dream reported below on pp. 361 ff. [also above, p. 335], which describes the course of the patient's life 'in the language of flowers,' the dream-ego held a blossoming branch in her hand which, as we have seen, stood both for innocence and for sexual sinfulness. The branch, owing to the way in which the blossoms were placed on it, also reminded the dreamer of *cherry*-blossom; the blossoms themselves, regarded individually, were *camellias*, and moreover the general impression was of an *exotic* growth. The common factor among the elements of this composite structure was shown by the dream-thoughts. The blossoming branch was composed of allusions to gifts made to her in order to win, or attempt to win, her favour. Thus she had been given *cherries* in her childhood and, later in life, a *camellia*-plant; while '*exotic*' was an allusion to a much-travelled naturalist who had tried to win her favour with a flower-drawing.—Another of my women patients produced in one of her dreams a thing that was intermediate between a bathing-hut at the seaside, an outside closet in the country and an attic in a town house. The first two elements have in common a connection with people naked and undressed; and their combination with the third element leads to the conclusion that (in her childhood) an attic had also been a scene of undressing.—Another dreamer,[1] a man, produced a composite locality out of two places where 'treatments' are carried out: one of them being my consulting-room and the other the place of entertainment where he had first made his wife's acquaintance.—A girl dreamt, after her elder brother had promised to give her a feast of caviare, that this same brother's legs were *covered all over with black grains of caviare.* The element of '*contagion*' (in the moral sense) and a recollection of a rash in her childhood, which had covered her legs all over with red spots, instead of black ones, had been combined with the *grains of caviare* into a new concept—namely the concept of '*what she had got from her brother.*' In this dream, as in others, parts of the human body were treated like objects.—In a dream recorded by Ferenczi [1910],[2] a composite image occurred which was made up from the figure of a *doctor* and of a *horse* and was also dressed in a *nightshirt.* The element common to these three components was arrived at in the analysis after the woman-patient had recognized that the nightshirt was an allusion to her father in a scene from her childhood. In all three cases it was a question of an object of her sexual curiosity. When she was a child she had often been taken by her nurse to a military stud-farm where she had ample opportunities of gratifying what was at that time her still uninhibited curiosity.

I have asserted above [p. 334] that dreams have no means of expressing the relation of a contradiction, a contrary or a 'no.' I shall now proceed to give a first denial of this assertion.[3] One class of cases which can be comprised under the heading of 'contraries' are, as we have seen [p. 338], simply represented by identification—cases, that is, in which the idea of an exchange or substitution can be brought into connection with the contrast. I have given a number of instances of this. Another class of contraries in the dream-thoughts, falling into a category which may be described as 'contrariwise' or 'just the reverse,' find their way into dreams in the following remarkable fashion, which almost deserves to be described as a joke. The 'just the reverse' is not itself represented in the dream-content, but reveals its presence in the material through the fact that some piece of the dream-content, which has already been constructed and happens (for some other reason) to be adjacent to it, is—as it were by an afterthought—turned

---

[1] [This sentence was added in 1909.]
[2] [The remainder of this paragraph was added in 1911.]
[3] [Others will be found below on pp. 351 f. and 442 f.]

round the other way. The process is more easily illustrated than described. In the interesting 'Up and Down' dream (pp. 319 ff.) the representation of the climbing in the dream was the reverse of what it was in its prototype in the dream-thoughts—that is, in the introductory scene from Daudet's *Sappho*: in the dream the climbing was difficult at first but easier later, while in the Daudet scene it was easy at first but more and more difficult later. Further, the 'up above' and 'down below' in the dreamer's relation to his brother were represented the other way round in the dream. This pointed to the presence of a reversed or contrary relation between two pieces of the material in the dream-thoughts; and we found it in the dreamer's childhood phantasy of being carried by his wet-nurse, which was the reverse of the situation in the novel, where the hero was carrying his mistress. So too in my dream of Goethe's attack on Herr M. (see below, pp. 447 ff.) there is a similar 'just the reverse' which has to be put straight before the dream can be successfully interpreted. In the dream Goethe made an attack on a young man, Herr M.; in the real situation contained in the dream-thoughts a man of importance, my friend [Fliess], had been attacked by an unknown young writer. In the dream I based a calculation on the date of Goethe's death; in reality the calculation had been made from the year of the paralytic patient's birth. The thought which turned out to be the decisive one in the dream-thoughts was a contradiction of the idea that Goethe should be treated as though he were a lunatic. 'Just the reverse,' said [the underlying meaning of] the dream, 'if you don't understand the book, it's *you* [the critic] that are feeble-minded, and not the author.' I think, moreover, that all these dreams of turning things round the other way include a reference to the contemptuous implications of the idea of 'turning one's back on something.'[1] (E.g. the dreamer's turning round in relation to his brother in the *Sappho* dream [pp. 305 f.].) It is remarkable to observe, moreover,[2] how frequently reversal is employed precisely in dreams arising from repressed homosexual impulses.

Incidentally,[3] reversal, or turning a thing into its opposite, is one of the means of representation most favoured by the dream-work and one which is capable of employment in the most diverse direction. It serves in the first

---

[1] [The German '*Kehrseite*' can mean both 'reverse' and 'backside.' Cf. the vulgar English phrase 'arse upwards' for 'upside down,' 'the wrong way round.']

[2] [This sentence was added in 1911.]

[3] [This and the next paragraph were added in 1909.]

place to give expression to the fulfilment of a wish in reference to some particular element of the dream-thoughts. 'If only it had been the other way round!' This is often the best way of expressing the ego's reaction to a disagreeable fragment of memory. Again, reversal is of quite special use as a help to the censorship, for it produces a mass of distortion in the material which is to be represented, and this has a positively paralysing effect, to begin with, on any attempt at understanding the dream. For that reason, if a dream obstinately declines to reveal its meaning, it is always worth while to see the effect of reversing some particular elements in its manifest content, after which the whole situation often becomes immediately clear.

And, apart from the reversal of subject-matter, *chronological* reversal must not be overlooked. Quite a common technique of dream-distortion consists in representing the outcome of an event or the conclusion of a train of thought at the beginning of a dream and of placing at its end the premises on which the conclusion was based or the causes which led to the event. Anyone who fails to bear in mind this technical method adopted by dream-distortion will be quite at a loss when confronted with the task of interpreting a dream.[1]

In some instances, indeed,[2] it is only possible to arrive at the meaning of a dream after one has carried out quite a number of reversals of its content in various respects. For instance, in the case of a young obsessional

---

[1] [*Footnote added* 1909:] Hysterical attacks sometimes make use of the same kind of chronological reversal in order to disguise their meaning from observers. For instance, a hysterical girl needed to represent something in the nature of a brief romance in one of her attacks—a romance of which she had had a phantasy in her unconscious after an encounter with someone on the suburban railway. She imagined how the man had been attracted by the beauty of her foot and had spoken to her while she was reading; whereupon she had gone off with him and had had a passionate love-scene. Her attack *began* with a representation of this love-scene by convulsive twitching of her body, accompanied by movements of her lips to represent kissing and tightening of her arms to represent embracing. She then hurried into the next room, sat down on a chair, raised her skirt so as to show her foot, pretended to be reading a book and spoke to me (that is, answered me).—[*Added* 1914:] Cf. in this connection what Artemidorus says: 'In interpreting the images seen in dreams one must sometimes follow them from the beginning to the end and sometimes from the end to the beginning. . .' [Book I, Chapter XI, Krauss's translation (1881), 20.]

[2] [This paragraph was added in 1911.]

neurotic, there lay concealed behind one of his dreams the memory of a death-wish dating from his childhood and directed against his father, of whom he had been afraid. Here is the text of the dream: *His father was scolding him for coming home so late.* The context in which the dream occurred in the psycho-analytic treatment and the dreamer's associations showed, however, that the original wording must have been that *he* was angry with his *father*, and that in his view his father always came home too *early* (i.c. too soon). He would have preferred it if his father had not come home *at all*, and this was the same thing as a death-wish against his father. (See pp. 272 f.) For as a small boy, during his father's temporary absence, he had been guilty of an act of sexual aggression against someone, and as a punishment had been threatened in these words: 'Just you wait till your father comes back!'

If we wish to pursue our study of the relations between dream-content and dream-thoughts further, the best plan will be to take dreams themselves as our point of departure and consider what certain *formal* characteristics of the method of representation in dreams signify in relation to the thoughts underlying them. Most prominent among these formal characteristics, which cannot fail to impress us in dreams, are the differences in sensory intensity between particular dream-images and in the distinctness of particular parts of dreams or of whole dreams as compared with one another.

The differences in intensity between particular dream-images cover the whole range extending between a sharpness of definition which we feel inclined, no doubt unjustifiably, to regard as greater than that of reality and an irritating vagueness which we declare characteristic of dreams because it is not completely comparable to any degree of indistinctness which we ever perceive in real objects. Furthermore we usually describe an impression which we have of an indistinct object in a dream as 'fleeting,' while we feel that those dream-images which are more distinct have been perceived for a considerable length of time. The question now arises what it is in the material of the dream-thoughts that determines these differences in the vividness of particular pieces of the content of a dream.

We must begin by countering certain expectations which almost inevitably present themselves. Since the material of a dream may include real sensations experienced during sleep, it will probably be presumed that these, or the elements in the dream derived from them, are given prominence in the dream-content by appearing with special intensity; or, conversely, that whatever is very specially vivid in a dream can be traced back to real sensations during sleep. In my experience, however, this has never been confirmed. It is not the case that the elements of a dream which are derivatives of real impressions during sleep (i.e. of nervous stimuli) are distinguished by their vividness from other elements which arise from memories. The factor of reality counts for nothing in determining the intensity of dream-images.

Again, it might be expected that the *sensory* intensity (that is, the vividness) of particular dream-images would be related to the *psychical* intensity of the elements in the dream-thoughts corresponding to them. In the latter, psychical intensity coincides with psychical *value*: the most intense elements are also the most important ones—those which form the centre-point of the dream-thoughts. We know, it is true, that these are precisely elements which, on account of the censorship, cannot as a rule make their way into the content of the dream; nevertheless, it might well be that their immediate derivatives which represent them in the dream might bear a higher degree of intensity, without necessarily on that account forming the centre of the dream. But this expectation too is disappointed by a comparative study of dreams and the material from which they are derived. The intensity of the elements in the one has no relation to the intensity of the elements in the other: the fact is that a complete 'transvaluation of all psychical values' [in Nietzsche's phrase] takes place between the material of the dream-thoughts and the dream. A direct derivative of what occupies a dominating position in the dream-thoughts can often only be discovered precisely in some transitory element of the dream which is quite overshadowed by more powerful images.

The intensity of the elements of a dream turns out to be determined otherwise—and by two independent factors. In the first place, it is easy to see that the elements by which the wish-fulfilment is expressed are represented with special intensity. [See pp. 561 f.] And in the second place, analysis shows that the most vivid elements of a dream are the starting-point of the most numerous trains of thought—that the most vivid elements are also those with the most numerous determinants. We shall not be altering the sense of this empirically based assertion if we put it in these terms: the greatest intensity is shown by those elements of a dream on whose formation the greatest amount of condensation has been expended. [Cf. pp. 592.] We may expect that it will eventually turn out to be possible to express this determinant and the other (namely relation to the wish-fulfilment) in a single formula.

The problem with which I have just dealt—the causes of the greater or less intensity or clarity of particular elements of a dream—is not to be confounded with another problem, which relates to the varying clarity of whole dreams or sections of dreams. In the former case clarity is contrasted with vagueness, but in the latter case it is contrasted with confusion. Nevertheless it cannot be doubted that the increase and decrease of the qualities in the two scales run parallel. A section of a dream which strikes us as perspicuous usually contains intense elements; a dream which is obscure, on the other hand, is composed of elements of small intensity. Yet the problem presented by the scale which runs from what is apparently clear to what is obscure and confused is far more complicated than that of the varying degrees of vividness of dream-elements. Indeed, for reasons which will appear later, the former problem cannot yet be discussed. [See pp. 504 f.]

In a few cases we find to our surprise that the impression of clarity or indistinctness given by a dream has no connection at all with the make-up of the dream itself but arises from the material of the dream-thoughts and is a constituent of it. Thus I remember a dream of mine which struck me when I woke up as being so particularly well-constructed, flawless and clear that, while I was still half-dazed with sleep, I thought of introducing a new category of dreams which were not subject to the mechanisms of condensation and displacement but were to be described as 'phantasies during sleep.' Closer examination proved that this rarity among dreams showed the same gaps and flaws in its structure as any other; and for that reason I dropped the category of 'dream-phantasies.'[1] The content of the dream, when it was arrived at, represented me as laying before my friend [Fliess] a difficult and long-sought theory of bisexuality; and the wish-fulfilling power of the dream was responsible for our regarding this theory (which, incidentally, was not given in the dream) as clear and flawless. Thus what I had taken to be a judgement on the completed dream was actually a part, and indeed the essential part, of the dream-content. The dream-work had in this case encroached, as it were, upon my first waking

---

[1] [*Footnote added* 1930:] Whether rightly I am now uncertain. [Freud argues in favour of there being such a category in some remarks at the end of the discussion of his first example in his paper on 'Dreams and Telepathy' (1922*a*).]

thoughts and had conveyed to me as a *judgement* upon the dream the part of the material of the dream-thoughts which it had not succeeded in representing accurately in the dream.[1] I once came across a precise counterpart to this in a woman-patient's dream during analysis. To begin with she refused altogether to tell it me, 'because it was so indistinct and muddled.' At length, protesting repeatedly that she felt no certainty that her account was correct, she informed me that several people had come into the dream—she herself, her husband and her father—and that it was as though she had not known whether her husband was her father, or who her father was, or something of that sort. This dream, taken in conjunction with her associations during the analytic session, showed beyond a doubt that it was a question of the somewhat commonplace story of a servant-girl who was obliged to confess that she was expecting a baby but was in doubts as to 'who the (baby's) father really was.'[2] Thus here again the lack of clarity shown by the dream was a part of the material which instigated the dream: part of this material, that is, was represented in the form of the dream. *The form of a dream or the form in which it is dreamt is used with quite surprising frequency for representing its concealed subject-matter.*[3]

Glosses on a dream, or apparently innocent comments on it, often serve to disguise a portion of what has been dreamt in the subtlest fashion, though in fact betraying it. For instance, a dreamer remarked that at one point 'the dream had been wiped away'; and the analysis led to an infantile recollection of his listening to someone wiping himself after defaecating. Or here is another example which deserves to be recorded in detail. A young man had a very clear dream which reminded him of some phantasies of his boyhood that had remained conscious. He dreamt that it was evening and that he was in a hotel at a summer resort. He mistook the number of his room and went into one in which an elderly lady and her two daughters were undressing and going to bed. He proceeded: 'Here there are some gaps in the dream; there's something missing. Finally there was a man in the room who tried to throw me out, and I had

---

[1] [This subject is discussed much more fully below, on pp. 452 ff.]

[2] Her accompanying hysterical symptoms were amenorrhoea and great depression (which was this patient's chief symptom). [This dream is discussed on pp. 453 f.]

[3] [The last sentence was added in 1909, and from 1914 onwards was printed in spaced type. The next paragraph was added in 1911.]

to have a struggle with him.' He made vain endeavours to recall the gist and drift of the boyish phantasy to which the dream was evidently alluding; until at last the truth emerged that what he was in search of was already in his possession in his remark about the obscure part of the dream. The 'gaps' were the genital apertures of the women who were going to bed; and 'there's something missing' described the principal feature of the female genitalia. When he was young he had had a consuming curiosity to see a woman's genitals and had been inclined to hold to the infantile sexual theory according to which women have male organs.

An analogous recollection of another dreamer assumed a very similar shape.[1] He dreamt as follows: *'I was going into the Volksgarten Restaurant with Fräulein K. . . . then came an obscure patch, an interruption . . . then I found myself in the salon of a brothel, where I saw two or three women, one of them in her chemise and drawers.'*

ANALYSIS.—Fräulein K. was the daughter of his former chief, and, as he himself admitted, a substitute sister of his own. He had seldom had an opportunity of talking to her, but they once had a conversation in which 'it was just as though we had become aware of our sex, it was as though I were to say: "I'm a man and you're a woman."' He had only once been inside the restaurant in question, with his brother-in-law's sister, a girl who meant nothing at all to him. Another time he had gone with a group of three ladies as far as the entrance of the same restaurant. These ladies were his sister, his sister-in-law and the brother-in-law's sister who has just been mentioned. All of them were highly indifferent to him, but all three fell into the class of 'sister.' He had only seldom visited a brothel— only two or three times in his life.

The interpretation was based on the 'obscure patch' and the 'interruption' in the dream, and put forward the view that in his boyish curiosity he had occasionally, though only seldom, inspected the genitals of a sister who was a few years his junior. Some days later he had a conscious recollection of the misdeed alluded to by the dream.

The content of all dreams that occur during the same night forms part of the same whole; the fact of their being divided into several sections, as well as the grouping and number of those sections—all of this has a meaning and may be regarded as a piece of information arising from the

---

[1] [This and the two following paragraphs were added in 1914.]

latent dream-thoughts.[1] In interpreting dreams consisting of several main sections or, in general, dreams occurring during the same night, the possibility should not be overlooked that separate and successive dreams of this kind may have the same meaning, and may be giving expression to the same impulses in different material. If so, the first of these homologous dreams to occur is often the more distorted and timid, while the succeeding one will be more confident and distinct.

Pharaoh's dreams in the Bible of the kine and the ears of corn, which were interpreted by Joseph, were of this kind. They are reported more fully by Josephus (*Ancient History of the Jews*, Book 2, Chapter 5) than in the Bible. After the King had related his first dream, he said: 'After I had seen this vision, I awaked out of my sleep; and, being in disorder, and considering with myself what this appearance should be, I fell asleep again, and saw another dream, more wonderful than the foregoing, which did more affright and disturb me . . .' After hearing the King's account of the dream, Joseph replied: 'This dream, O King, although seen under two forms, signifies one and the same event . . .' [Whiston's translation, 1874, **1,** 127–8.]

In his 'Contribution to the Psychology of Rumour,' Jung (1910b), describes how the disguised erotic dream of a school-girl was understood by her school-friends without any interpreting and how it was further elaborated and modified. He remarks in connection with one of these dream stories: 'The final thought in a long series of dream-images contains precisely what the first image in the series had attempted to portray. The censorship keeps the complex at a distance as long as possible by a succession of fresh symbolic screens, displacements, innocent disguises, etc.' (Ibid., 87.) Scherner (1861, 166) was well acquainted with this peculiarity of the method of representation in dreams and describes it, in connection with his theory of organic stimuli [see pp. 111 f.], as a special law: 'Lastly, however, in all symbolic dream-structures which arise from particular nervous stimuli, the imagination observes a general law: at the beginning of a dream it depicts the object from which the stimulus arises only by the remotest and most inexact allusions, but at the end, when the

---

[1] [This sentence was added in 1909. The remainder of this paragraph, and the three following ones, were added in 1911. Freud deals with the subject again towards the end of Lecture XXIX of his *New Introductory Lectures* (1933a). It has already been touched upon on pp. 331 ff., and is mentioned again on p. 413, p. 452 *n.* and p. 528.]

pictorial effusion has exhausted itself, it nakedly presents the stimulus it-self, or, as the case may be, the organ concerned or the function of that organ, and therewith the dream, having designated its actual organic cause, achieves its end. . . .'

Otto Rank (1910) has produced a neat confirmation of this law of Scherner's. A girl's dream reported by him was composed of two separate dreams dreamt, with an interval between them, during the same night, the second of which ended with an orgasm. It was possible to carry out a detailed interpretation of this second dream even without many contri-butions from the dreamer; and the number of connections between the contents of the two dreams made it possible to see that the first dream represented in a more timid fashion the same thing as the second. So that the second, the dream with the orgasm, helped towards the complete ex-planation of the first. Rank rightly bases upon this example a discussion of the general significance of dreams of orgasm or emission for the theory of dreaming. [See pp. 412 ff.]

Nevertheless in my experience it is only rarely that one is in a position to interpret the clarity or confusion of a dream by the presence of cer-tainty or doubt in its material. Later on I shall have to disclose a factor in dream-formation which I have not yet mentioned and which exercises the determining influence upon the scale of these qualities in any particular dream. [See pp. 504 f.]

Sometimes, in a dream in which the same situation and setting have persisted for some time, an interruption will occur which is described in these words: 'But then it was as though at the same time it was another place, and there such and such a thing happened.' After a while the main thread of the dream may be resumed, and what interrupted it turns out to be a subordinate clause in the dream-material—an interpolated thought. A conditional in the dream-thoughts has been represented in the dream by simultaneity: 'if' has become 'when.'

What is the meaning of the sensation of inhibited movement which appears so commonly in dreams and verges so closely upon anxiety? One tries to move forward but finds oneself glued to the spot, or one tries to reach something but is held up by a series of obstacles. A train is on the point of departure but one is unable to catch it. One raises one's hand to avenge an insult but finds it powerless. And so forth. We have already met with this sensation in dreams of exhibiting [pp. 256 ff.; cf. also p. 302], but have not as yet made any serious attempt to interpret it. An easy but insufficient answer would be to say that motor paralysis prevails in sleep and that we become aware of it in the sensation we are discussing. But it may be asked why in that case we are not perpetually dreaming of these inhibited movements; and it is reasonable to suppose that this sensation, though one which can be summoned up at any moment during sleep, serves to facilitate some particular kind of representation, and is only aroused when the material of the dream-thoughts needs to be represented in that way.

This 'not being able to do anything' does not always appear in dreams as a sensation but is sometimes simply a part of the content of the dream. A case of this sort seems to me particularly well qualified to throw light on the meaning of this feature of dreaming. Here is an abridged version of a dream in which I was apparently charged with dishonesty. *The place was a mixture of a private sanatorium and several other institutions. A man-servant appeared to summon me to an examination. I knew in the dream that something had been missed and that the examination was due to a suspicion that I had appropriated the missing article.* (The analysis showed that the examination was to be taken in two senses and included a medical examination.) *Conscious of my innocence and of the fact that I held the position of a consultant in the establishment, I accompanied the servant quietly. At the door we were met by another servant, who said, pointing to me: 'Why have you brought him? He's a respectable person.' I then went, unattended, into a large hall, with machines standing in it, which reminded me of an Inferno with its hellish instruments of punishment. Stretched out on one apparatus I saw one of my colleagues, who had every reason to take some notice of me; but he paid no attention. I was then told I could go. But I could not find my hat and could not go after all.*

The wish-fulfilment of the dream evidently lay in my being recognized as an honest man and told I could go. There must therefore have been all kinds of material in the dream-thoughts containing a contradiction of this. That I could go was a sign of my absolution. If therefore something happened at the end of the dream which prevented my going, it seems plausible to suppose that the suppressed material containing the contradiction was making itself felt at that point. My not being able to find my hat meant accordingly: 'After all you're not an honest man.' Thus the 'not being able to do something' in this dream was a way of expressing a contradiction—a 'no'—so that my earlier statement [p. 334] that dreams cannot express a 'no' requires correction.[1]

In other dreams, in which the 'not carrying out' of a movement occurs as a sensation and not simply as a situation, the sensation of the inhibition of a movement gives a more forcible expression to the same contradiction— it expresses a volition which is opposed by a counter-volition. Thus the sensation of the inhibition of a movement represents a conflict of will. [Cf. p. 264.] We shall learn later [pp. 567] that the motor paralysis accompanying sleep is precisely one of the fundamental determinants of the psychical process during dreaming. Now an impulse transmitted along the motor paths is nothing other than a volition, and the fact of our being so certain that we shall feel that impulse inhibited during sleep is what makes the whole process so admirably suited for representing an act of volition and a 'no' which opposes it. It is also easy to see, on my explanation of anxiety, why the sensation of an inhibition of will approximates so closely to anxiety and is so often linked with it in dreams. Anxiety is a libidinal impulse which has its origin in the unconscious and is inhibited by the preconscious.[2] When, therefore, the sensation of inhibition is linked with anxiety in a dream, it must be a question of an act of volition which was at one time capable of generating libido—that is, it must be a question of a sexual impulse.

---

[1] In the complete analysis there was a reference to an event in my childhood, reached by the following chain of association. 'Der Mohr hat seine Schuldigkeit getan, der Mohr *kann gehen*.' ['The Moor has done his duty, the Moor *can go*.' (Schiller, *Fiesco*, III, 4.) '*Schuldigkeit*' ('duty') is actually a misquotation for '*Arbeit*' ('work').] Then came a facetious conundrum: 'How old was the Moor when he had done his duty?'—'One year old, because then he could go ['*gehen*'—both 'to go' and 'to walk'].' (It appears that I came into the world with such a tangle of black hair that my young mother declared I was a little Moor.)—My not being able to find my hat was an occurrence from waking life which was used in more than one sense. Our housemaid, who was a genius at putting things away, had hidden it.—The end of this dream also concealed a rejection of some melancholy thoughts about death: 'I am far from having done my duty, so I must not go yet.'—Birth and death were dealt with in it, just as they had been in the dream of Goethe and the paralytic patient, which I had dreamt a short time before. (See pp. 342, 447 ff. [and 456 ff.].)

[2] [*Footnote added* 1930:] In the light of later knowledge this statement can no longer stand. [Cf. p. 185, *n*. 2. See also p. 503 *n*.]

I shall deal elsewhere (see below [pp. 493 f.]) with the meaning and psychical significance of the judgement which often turns up in dreams expressed in the phrase 'after all this is only a dream.'[1] Here I will merely say in anticipation that it is intended to detract from the importance of what is being dreamt. The interesting and allied problem, as to what is meant when some of the content of a dream is described in the dream itself as 'dreamt'—the enigma of the 'dream within a dream'—has been solved in a similar sense by Stekel [1909, 459 ff.], who has analysed some convincing examples. The intention is, once again, to detract from the importance of what is 'dreamt' in the dream, to rob it of its reality. What is dreamt in a dream after waking from the 'dream within a dream' is what the dream-wish seeks to put in the place of an obliterated reality. It is safe to suppose, therefore, that what has been 'dreamt' in the dream is a representation of the reality, the true recollection, while the continuation of the dream, on the contrary, merely represents what the dreamer wishes. To include something in a 'dream within a dream' is thus equivalent to wishing that the thing described as a dream had never happened. In other words,[2] if a particular event is inserted into a dream as a dream by the dream-work itself, this implies the most decided confirmation of the reality of the event—the strongest *affirmation* of it. The dream-work makes use of dreaming as a form of repudiation, and so confirms the discovery that dreams are wish-fulfilments.[3]

(D)

CONSIDERATIONS OF REPRESENTABILITY

We have been occupied so far with investigating the means by which dreams represent the relations between the dream-thoughts. In the course of this investigation, however, we have more than once touched upon the further topic of the general nature of the modifications which the material

---

[1] [This paragraph (except for its penultimate sentence and part of its last sentence) was added in 1911.]

[2] [This sentence was added in 1919.]

[3] [The last clause was added in 1919.]

of the dream-thoughts undergoes for the purpose of the formation of a dream. We have learnt that that material, stripped to a large extent of its relations, is submitted to a process of compression, while at the same time displacements of intensity between its elements necessarily bring about a psychical transvaluation of the material. The displacements we have hitherto considered turned out to consist in the replacing of some one particular idea by another in some way closely associated with it, and they were used to facilitate condensation in so far as, by their means, instead of *two* elements, a single common element intermediate between them found its way into the dream. We have not yet referred to any other sort of displacement. Analyses show us, however, that another sort exists and that it reveals itself in a change in the *verbal expression* of the thoughts concerned. In both cases there is a displacement along a chain of associations; but a process of such a kind can occur in various psychical spheres, and the outcome of the displacement may in one case be that one element is replaced by another, while the outcome in another case may be that a single element has its *verbal form* replaced by another.

This second species of displacement which occurs in dream-formation is not only of great theoretical interest but is also specially well calculated to explain the appearance of fantastic absurdity in which dreams are disguised. The direction taken by the displacement usually results in a colourless and abstract expression in the dream-thought being exchanged for a pictorial and concrete one. The advantage, and accordingly the purpose, of such a change jumps to the eyes. A thing that is pictorial is, from the point of view of a dream, a thing that is *capable of being represented*: it can be introduced into a situation in which abstract expressions offer the same kind of difficulties to representation in dreams as a political leading article in a newspaper would offer to an illustrator. But not only representability, but the interests of condensation and the censorship as well, can be the gainers from this exchange. A dream-thought is unusable so long as it is expressed in an abstract form; but when once it has been transformed into pictorial language, contrasts and identifications of the kind which the dream-work requires, and which it creates if they are not already present, can be established more easily than before between the new form of expression and the remainder of the material underlying the dream. This is so because in every language concrete terms, in consequence of the history of their development, are richer in associations than conceptual ones. We may suppose that a good part of the intermediate work done during the formation of a dream, which seeks to reduce the dispersed dream-thoughts to the most succinct and unified expression possible, proceeds along the line of finding appropriate verbal transformations for the individual thoughts. Any one thought, whose form of expression may happen to be fixed for other reasons, will operate in a determinant and selective manner on the possible forms of expression allotted to the other thoughts, and it may do so, perhaps, from the very start—as is the case in writing a poem. If a poem is to be written in rhymes, the second line of a couplet is limited by two conditions: it must express an appropriate meaning, and the expression of that meaning must rhyme with the first line. No doubt the best poem will be one in which we fail to notice the intention of finding a rhyme, and in which the two thoughts have, by mutual influence, chosen from the very start a verbal expression which will allow a rhyme to emerge with only slight subsequent adjustment.

In a few instances a change of expression of this kind assists dream-condensation even more directly, by finding a form of words which owing to its ambiguity is able to give expression to more than one of the dream-thoughts. In this way the whole domain of verbal wit is put at the disposal of the dream-work. There is no need to be astonished at the part played by words in dream-formation. Words, since they are the nodal points of numerous ideas, may be regarded as predestined to ambiguity; and the neuroses (e.g. in framing obsessions and phobias), no less than dreams, make unashamed use of the advantages thus offered by words for purposes of condensation and disguise.[1] It is easy to show that dream-distortion too profits from displacement of expression. If one ambiguous word is used instead of two unambiguous ones the result is misleading; and if our everyday, sober method of expression is replaced by a pictorial one, our understanding is brought to a halt, particularly since a dream never tells us whether its elements are to be interpreted literally or in a figurative sense or whether they are to be connected with the material of the dream-thoughts directly or through the intermediary of some interpolated phraseology.[2] In interpreting any dream-element it is in general doubtful

---

[1] [*Footnote added* 1909:] See my volume on jokes (1905*c*) [especially the later part of Chapter VI] and the use of 'verbal bridges' in the solution of neurotic symptoms. [See, e.g., the synthesis of Dora's first dream at the end of Section II of Freud, 1905*e* (where the term 'switch-words' is also used), and the solution of the 'Rat Man's' rat-obsession in Section I(G) of Freud, 1909*d*.]

[2] [The remainder of this paragraph was added as a footnote in 1909 and included in the text in 1914.]

(*a*) whether it is to be taken in a positive or negative sense (as an antithetic relation),

(*b*) whether it is to be interpreted historically (as a recollection),

(*c*) whether it is to be interpreted symbolically, or

(*d*) whether its interpretation is to depend on its wording. Yet, in spite of all this ambiguity, it is fair to say that the productions of the dream-work, which, it must be remembered, *are not made with the intention of being understood*, present no greater difficulties to their translators than do the ancient hieroglyphic scripts to those who seek to read them.

I have already given several examples of representations in dreams which are only held together by the ambiguity of their wording. (For instance, 'She opened her mouth properly' in the dream of Irma's injection [p. 135] and 'I could not go after all' in the dream which I last quoted [pp. 351].) I will now record a dream in which a considerable part was played by the turning of abstract thought into pictures. The distinction between dream-interpretation of this kind and interpretation by means of symbolism can still be drawn quite sharply. In the case of symbolic dream-interpretation the key to the symbolization is arbitrarily chosen by the interpreter; whereas in our cases of verbal disguise the keys are generally known and laid down by firmly established linguistic usage. If one has the right idea at one's disposal at the right moment, one can solve dreams of this kind wholly or in part even independently of information from the dreamer.

A lady of my acquaintance had the following dream: *She was at the Opera. A Wagner opera was being performed, and had lasted till a quarter to eight in the morning. There were tables set out in the stalls, at which people were eating and drinking. Her cousin, who had just got back from his honeymoon, was sitting at one of the tables with his young wife, and an aristocrat was sitting beside them. Her cousin's wife, so it appeared, had brought him back with her from the honeymoon, quite openly, just as one might bring back a hat. In the middle of the stalls there was a high tower, which had a platform on top of it surrounded by an iron railing. High up at the top was the conductor, who had the features of Hans Richter. He kept running round the railing, and was perspiring violently; and from that position he was conducting the orchestra, which was grouped about the base of the tower. She herself was sitting in a box with a woman friend* (whom I knew). *Her younger sister wanted to hand her up a large lump of coal from the stalls, on the ground that she had not known it would be so long, and must be simply freezing by now. (As though the boxes required to be heated during the long performance.)*

Even though the dream was well focused on a single situation, yet in other respects it was sufficiently senseless: the tower in the middle of the stalls, for instance, with the conductor directing the orchestra from the top of it! And above all the coal that her sister handed up to her! I deliberately refrained from asking for an analysis of the dream. But since I had some knowledge of the dreamer's personal relations, I was able to interpret certain pieces of it independently of her. I know she had had a great deal of sympathy for a musician whose career had been prematurely cut short by insanity. So I decided to take the tower in the stalls metaphorically. It then emerged that the man whom she had wanted to see in Hans Richter's place *towered high above* the other members of the orchestra. The tower might be described as a composite picture formed by apposition. The lower part of its structure represented the man's greatness; the railing at the top, behind which he was running round like a prisoner or an animal in a cage—this was an allusion to the unhappy man's name[1]— represented his ultimate fate. The two ideas might have been brought together in the word '*Narrenturm*.'[2]

Having thus discovered the mode of representation adopted by the dream, we might attempt to use the same key for solving its second apparent absurdity—the coal handed up to the dreamer by her sister. 'Coal' must mean 'secret love':

> Kein Feuer, keine *Kohle*
> kann brennen so heiss
> als wie *heimliche Liebe*,
> von der niemand nichts weiss.[3]

She herself and her woman friend had been left unmarried [German '*sitzen geblieben*,' literally 'left sitting']. Her younger sister, who still had prospects of marriage, handed her up the coal 'because she had not known *it would be so long*.' The dream did not specify *what* would be so

---

[1] [*Footnote added* 1925:] Hugo Wolf.
[2] [Literally 'Fools' Tower'—an old term for an insane asylum.]
[3] [No *fire*, no *coal*
So hotly glows
As *secret love*
Of which no one knows.
German *Volkslied*.]

long. If it were a story, we should say 'the performance'; but since it is a dream, we may take the phrase as an independent entity, decide that it was used ambiguously and add the words 'before she got married.' Our interpretation of 'secret love' is further supported by the mention of the dreamer's cousin sitting with his wife in the stalls, and by the *open* love-affair attributed to the latter. The dream was dominated by the antithesis between secret and open love and between the dreamer's own fire and the coldness of the young wife. In both cases, moreover, there was someone 'highly-placed'—a term applying equally to the aristocrat and to the musician on whom such high hopes had been pinned.[1]

The foregoing discussion has led us at last to the discovery of a third factor[2] whose share in the transformation of the dream-thoughts into the dream-content is not to be underrated: namely, *considerations of representability in the peculiar psychical material of which dreams make use*—for the most part, that is, representability in visual images. Of the various subsidiary thoughts attached to the essential dream-thoughts, those will be preferred which admit of visual representation; and the dream-work does not shrink from the effort of recasting unadaptable thoughts into a new verbal form—even into a less usual one—provided that that process facilitates representation and so relieves the psychological pressure caused by constricted thinking. This pouring of the content of a thought into another mould may at the same time serve the purposes of the activity of condensation and may create connections, which might not otherwise have been present, with some other thought; while this second thought itself may already have had its original form of expression changed, with a view to meeting the first one half-way.

Herbert Silberer (1909)[3] has pointed out a good way of directly observing the transformation of thoughts into pictures in the process of forming dreams and so of studying this one factor of the dream-work in isolation. If, when he was in a fatigued and sleepy condition, he set himself some intellectual task, he found that it often happened that the thought escaped him and that in its place a picture appeared, which he was then able to recognize as a substitute for the thought. Silberer describes these substitutes

---

[1] [The element of absurdity in this dream is commented upon on p. 444.]
[2] [The two previous ones being condensation and displacement.]
[3] [This paragraph and the subsequent quotation from Silberer were added in 1914.]

by the not very appropriate term of 'auto-symbolic.' I will here quote a few examples from Silberer's paper [ibid., 519–22], and I shall have occasion, on account of certain characteristics of the phenomena concerned, to return to them later. [See pp. 507 ff.]

'*Example* 1.—I thought of having to revise an uneven passage in an essay.

'*Symbol.*—I saw myself planing a piece of wood.'

'*Example* 5.—I endeavoured to bring home to myself the aim of certain metaphysical studies which I was proposing to make. Their aim, I reflected, was to work one's way through to ever higher forms of consciousness and layers of existence, in one's search for the bases of existence.

'*Symbol.*—I was pushing a long knife under a cake, as though to lift out a slice.

'*Interpretation.*—My motion with the knife meant the "working my way through" which was in question. . . . Here is the explanation of the symbolism. It is from time to time my business at meals to cut up a cake and distribute the helpings. I perform the task with a long, flexible knife—which demands some care. In particular, to lift out the slices cleanly after they have been cut offers certain difficulties; the knife must be pushed carefully *under* the slice (corresponding to the slow "working my way through" to reach the "bases"). But there is yet more symbolism in the picture. For the cake in the symbol was a "Dobos" cake—a cake with a number of "layers" through which, in cutting it, the knife has to penetrate (the "layers" of consciousness and thought).'

'*Example* 9.—I had lost the thread in a train of thought. I tried to find it again, but had to admit that the starting-point had completely escaped me.

'*Symbol.*—Part of a compositor's forme, with the last lines of type fallen away.'

In view of the part played by jokes, quotations, songs and proverbs in the mental life of educated people, it would fully agree with our expectations if disguises of such kinds were used with extreme frequency for representing dream-thoughts. What, for instance, is the meaning in a dream of a number of carts, each filled with a different sort of vegetable? They stand for a wishful contrast to '*Kraut und Rüben*' [literally, 'cabbages and turnips'], that is to say to 'higgledy-piggledy,' and accordingly signify 'disorder.' I am surprised that this dream has only been reported to me once.[1]

---

[1] [*Footnote added* 1925:] I have in fact never met with this image again; so I have lost confidence in the correctness of the interpretation.

A dream-symbolism of universal validity has only emerged in the case of a few subjects, on the basis of generally familiar allusions and verbal substitutes. Moreover a good part of this symbolism is shared by dreams with psychoneuroses, legends and popular customs.[1]

Indeed, when we look into the matter more closely, we must recognize the fact that the dream-work is doing nothing original in making substitutions of this kind. In order to gain its ends—in this case the possibility of a representation unhampered by censorship—it merely follows the paths which it finds already laid down in the unconscious; and it gives preference to those transformations of the repressed material which can also become conscious in the form of jokes or allusions and of which the phantasies of neurotic patients are so full. At this point we suddenly reach an understanding of Scherner's dream-interpretations, whose essential correctness I have defended elsewhere [pp. 109 ff. and 247]. The imagination's pre-occupation with the subject's own body is by no means peculiar to dreams or characteristic only of them. My analyses have shown me that it is habitually present in the unconscious thoughts of neurotics, and that it is derived from sexual curiosity, which, in growing youths or girls, is directed to the genitals of the other sex, and to those of their own as well. Nor, as Scherner [1861] and Volkelt [1875] have rightly insisted, is a house the only circle of ideas employed for symbolizing the body; and this is equally true of dreams and of the unconscious phantasies of neurosis. It is true that I know patients who have retained an architectural symbolism for the body and the genitals. (Sexual interest ranges far beyond the sphere of the external genitalia.) For these patients pillars and columns represent the legs (as they do in the *Song of Solomon*), every gateway stands for one of the bodily orifices (a 'hole'), every water-pipe is a reminder of the urinary apparatus, and so on. But the circle of ideas centring round plant-life or the kitchen may just as readily be chosen to conceal sexual images.[2] In the former case the way has been well prepared by linguistic usage, itself the precipitate of imaginative similes reaching back to remote antiquity: e.g. the Lord's vineyard, the seed, and the maiden's garden in the *Song of Solomon*. The ugliest as well as the most intimate details of sexual life may be thought and dreamt of in seemingly innocent allusions to activities in the kitchen; and the symptoms of hysteria could never be interpreted if we

---

[1] [The subject of dream-symbolism is treated at length in the next section.]

[2] [*Footnote added* 1914:] Abundant evidence of this is to be found in the three supplementary volumes to Fuchs (1909–12).

forgot that sexual symbolism can find its best hiding-place behind what is commonplace and inconspicuous. There is a valid sexual meaning behind the neurotic child's intolerance of blood or raw meat, or his nausea at the sight of eggs or macaroni, and behind the enormous exaggeration in neurotics of the natural human dread of snakes. Wherever neuroses make use of such disguises they are following paths along which all humanity passed in the earliest periods of civilization—paths of whose continued existence today, under the thinnest of veils, evidence is to be found in linguistic usages, superstitions and customs.

I will now append the 'flowery' dream dreamt by one of my women patients which I have already [p. 331] promised to record. I have indicated in small capitals those elements in it that are to be given a sexual interpretation. The dreamer quite lost her liking for this pretty dream after it had been interpreted.

(*a*) INTRODUCTORY DREAM: *She went into the kitchen, where her two maidservants were, and found fault with them for not having got her 'bite of food' ready. At the same time she saw quite a quantity of crockery standing upside down to drain, common crockery piled up in heaps.* Later addition: *The two maidservants went to fetch some water and had to step into a kind of river which came right up to the house into the yard.*[1]

(*b*) MAIN DREAM[2]: *She was descending from a height*[3] *over some strangely constructed palisades or fences, which were put together into large panels, and consisted of small squares of wattling.*[4] *It was not intended for climbing over; she had trouble in finding a place to put her feet in and felt glad that her dress had not been caught anywhere, so that she had stayed respectable as she went along.*[5] *She was holding a* BIG BRANCH *in her hand*[6]*; actually it was like a tree, covered over with* RED BLOSSOMS*, branching and spreading out.*[7] *There*

---

[1] For the interpretation of this introductory dream, which is to be interpreted as a causal dependent clause, see p. 331. [Cf. also pp. 335 and 340.]

[2] Describing the course of her life.

[3] Her high descent: a wishful antithesis to the introductory dream.

[4] A composite picture, uniting two localities: what were known as the 'attics' of her family home, where she used to play with her brother, the object of her later phantasies, and a farm belonging to a bad uncle who used to tease her.

[5] A wishful antithesis to a real recollection of her uncle's farm, where she used to throw off her clothes in her sleep.

[6] Just as the angel carries a sprig of lilies in pictures of the Annunciation.

[7] For the explanation of this composite image see p. 354: innocence, menstruation, *La dame aux camélias*.

*was an idea of their being cherry-*BLOSSOM; *but they also looked like double* CAMELLIAS, *though of course those do not grow on trees. As she went down, first she had one, then suddenly* TWO, *and later again* ONE.[1] *When she got down, the lower* BLOSSOMS *were already a good deal* FADED. *Then she saw, after she had got down, a manservant who—she felt inclined to say—was combing a similar tree, that is to say he was using a* PIECE OF WOOD *to drag out some* THICK TUFTS OF HAIR *that were hanging down from it like moss. Some other workmen had cut down similar branches from a* GARDEN *and thrown them into the* ROAD, *where they* LAY ABOUT, *so that* A LOT OF PEOPLE TOOK SOME. *But she asked whether that was all right—whether she might* TAKE ONE TOO.[2] *A young* MAN (someone she knew, a stranger) *was standing in the garden; she went up to him to ask how* BRANCHES *of that kind could be* TRANSPLANTED INTO HER OWN GARDEN.[3] *He embraced her; whereupon she struggled and asked him what he was thinking of and whether he thought people could embrace her like that. He said there was no harm in that: it was allowed.[4] He then said he was willing to go into the* OTHER GARDEN *with her, to show her how the planting was done, and added something she could not quite understand: 'Anyhow, I need three* YARDS (later she gave it as: *three square yards*) *or three fathoms of ground.' It was as though he were asking her for something in return for his willingness, as though he intended* TO COMPENSATE HIMSELF *in her garden, or as though he wanted to* CHEAT *some law or other, to get some advantage from it without causing her harm. Whether he really showed her something, she had no idea.*

This dream, which I have brought forward on account of its symbolic elements, may be described as a 'biographical' one. Dreams of this kind occur frequently during psycho-analysis, but perhaps only rarely outside it.[5]

---

[1] Referring to the multiplicity of the people involved in her phantasy.

[2] That is whether she might pull one down, i.e. masturbate. ['*Sich einen herunterreissen*' or '*ausreissen*' (literally, 'to pull one down' or 'out') are vulgar German terms equivalent to the English 'to toss oneself off.' Freud had already drawn attention to this symbolism at the end of his paper on 'Screen Memories' (1899*a*); see also below, pp. 400 f.]

[3] The branch had long since come to stand for the male genital organ; incidentally it also made a plain allusion to her family name.

[4] This, as well as what next follows, related to marriage precautions.

[5] [This paragraph was added in 1925.—*Footnote added* (to the preceding paragraph) 1911:] A similar 'biographical' dream will be found below as the third of my examples of dream-symbolism [p. 377.] Another one has been recorded at length by Rank [1910], and another, which must be read 'in reverse,' by Stekel

I naturally have at my disposal[1] a superfluity of material of this kind, but to report it would involve us too deeply in a consideration of neurotic conditions. It all leads to the same conclusion, namely that there is no necessity to assume that any peculiar symbolizing activity of the mind is operating in the dream-work, but that dreams make use of any symbolizations which are already present in unconscious thinking, because they fit in better with the requirements of dream-construction on account of their representability and also because as a rule they escape censorship.

(E)

REPRESENTATION BY SYMBOLS IN DREAMS—SOME FURTHER TYPICAL DREAMS[2]

The analysis of this last, biographical, dream is clear evidence that I recognized the presence of symbolism in dreams from the very beginning. But it was only by degrees and as my experience increased that I arrived

---

(1909, 486).—[A reference to 'biographical' dreams will be found near the end of Freud's 'History of the Psycho-Analytic Movement' (1914*d*).]

[1] [In the first three editions, 1900, 1909 and 1911, this paragraph was preceded by another, which was omitted from 1914 onwards. The deleted paragraph ran as follows: 'I must mention another circle of ideas which often serves as a disguise for sexual material both in dreams and in neuroses: namely ideas connected with changing house. "Changing house" may easily be replaced by the word "*Ausziehen*" [meaning both "moving house" and "undressing,"] and is thus connected with the subject of "clothing." If there is also a lift or elevator in the dream, we shall be reminded of the English word "to lift," that is, "to lift one's clothes."']

[2] [With the exception of two paragraphs (on p. 404) none of Section E of this chapter appeared in the first edition of the book. As explained in the Editor's Introduction (p. xiii), much of the material was added in the 1909 and 1911 editions, but in them it was included in Chapter V under the heading of 'Typical Dreams' (Section D of that chapter). In the edition of 1914 the present section was first constituted, partly from the material previously added to Chapter V and partly from further new material. Still more material was added in subsequent editions. In view of these complications, in this section a date has been added in square brackets at the end of each paragraph. It will be understood from what has been said that material dated 1909 and 1911 originally appeared in Chapter V and was transferred to its present position in 1914.]

at a full appreciation of its extent and significance, and I did so under the influence of the contributions of Wilhelm Stekel (1911), about whom a few words will not be out of place here. [1925.]

That writer, who has perhaps damaged psycho-analysis as much as he has benefited it, brought forward a large number of unsuspected translations of symbols; to begin with they were met with scepticism, but later they were for the most part confirmed and had to be accepted. I shall not be belittling the value of Stekel's services if I add that the sceptical reserve with which his proposals were received was not without justification. For the examples by which he supported his interpretations were often unconvincing, and he made use of a method which must be rejected as scientifically untrustworthy. Stekel arrived at his interpretations of symbols by way of intuition, thanks to a peculiar gift for the direct understanding of them. But the existence of such a gift cannot be counted upon generally, its effectiveness is exempt from all criticism and consequently its findings have no claim to credibility. It is as though one sought to base the diagnosis of infectious diseases upon olfactory impressions received at the patient's bedside—though there have undoubtedly been clinicians who could accomplish more than other people by means of the sense of smell (which is usually atrophied) and were really able to diagnose a case of enteric fever by smell. [1925.]

Advances in psycho-analytic experience have brought to our notice patients who have shown a direct understanding of dream-symbolism of this kind to a surprising extent. They were often sufferers from dementia praecox, so that for a time there was an inclination to suspect every dreamer who had this grasp of symbols of being a victim of that disease.[1] But such is not the case. It is a question of a personal gift or peculiarity which has no visible pathological significance. [1925.]

When we have become familiar with the abundant use made of symbolism for representing sexual material in dreams, the question is bound to arise of whether many of these symbols do not occur with a permanently fixed meaning, like the 'grammalogues' in shorthand; and we shall feel tempted to draw up a new 'dream-book' on the decoding principle [see pp. 123 f.]. On that point there is this to be said: this symbolism is not peculiar to dreams, but is characteristic of unconscious ideation, in

---

[1] [Freud remarks elsewhere (1913a) that, just as the presence of dementia praecox facilitates the interpretation of symbols, so an obsessional neurosis makes it more difficult.]

particular among the people, and it is to be found in folklore, and in popular myths, legends, linguistic idioms, proverbial wisdom and current jokes, to a more complete extent than in dreams. [1909.]

It would therefore carry us far beyond the sphere of dream-interpretation if we were to do justice to the significance of symbols and discuss the numerous, and to a large extent still unsolved, problems attaching to the concept of a symbol.[1] We must restrict ourselves here to remarking that representation by a symbol is among the indirect methods of representation, but that all kinds of indications warn us against lumping it in with other forms of indirect representation without being able to form any clear conceptual picture of their distinguishing features. In a number of cases the element in common between a symbol and what it represents is obvious; in others it is concealed and the choice of the symbol seems puzzling. It is precisely these latter cases which must be able to throw light upon the ultimate meaning of the symbolic relation, and they indicate that it is of a genetic character. Things that are symbolically connected today were probably united in the prehistoric times by conceptual and linguistic identity.[2] The symbolic relation seems to be a relic and a mark of former identity. In this connection we may observe how in a number of cases the use of a common symbol extends further than the use of a common language, as was already pointed out by Schubert (1814).[3] A number of symbols are as old as language itself, while others (e.g. 'airship,' 'Zeppelin') are being coined continuously down to the present time. [1914.]

---

[1] [*Footnote* 1911:] Cf. the works of Bleuler [1910] and of his Zürich pupils, Maeder [1908], Abraham [1909], etc., on symbolism, and the non-medical writers to whom they refer (Kleinpaul, etc.). [*Added* 1914:] What is most to the point on this subject will be found in Rank and Sachs (1913, Chapter I). [*Added* 1925:] See further Jones (1916).

[2] [*Footnote added* 1925:] This view would be powerfully supported by a theory put forward by Dr. Hans Sperber (1912). He is of the opinion that all primal words referred to sexual things but afterwards lost their sexual meaning through being applied to other things and activities which were compared with the sexual ones.

[3] [This last clause was added in 1919.—*Footnote* 1914:] For instance, according to Ferenczi [see Rank, 1912*a*, 100], a ship moving on the water occurs in dreams of micturition in Hungarian dreamers, though the term '*schiffen*' ['to ship'; cf. vulgar English 'to pump-ship'] is unknown in that language. (See also pp. 380 below.) In dreams of speakers of French and other Romance languages a room is used to symbolize a woman, though these languages have nothing akin to the German expression '*Frauenzimmer.*' [See p. 235 *n*.]

Dreams make use of this symbolism for the disguised representation of their latent thoughts. Incidentally, many of the symbols are habitually or almost habitually employed to express the same thing. Nevertheless, the peculiar plasticity of the psychical material [in dreams] must never be forgotten. Often enough a symbol has to be interpreted in its proper meaning and not symbolically; while on other occasions a dreamer may derive from his private memories the power to employ as sexual symbols all kinds of things which are not ordinarily employed as such.[1] If a dreamer has a choice open to him between a number of symbols, he will decide in favour of the one which is connected in its subject-matter with the rest of the material of his thoughts—which, that is to say, has individual grounds for its acceptance in addition to the typical ones. [1909; last sentence 1914.]

Though the later investigations since the time of Scherner have made it impossible to dispute the existence of dream-symbolism—even Havelock Ellis [1911, 109] admits that there can be no doubt that our dreams are full of symbolism—yet it must be confessed that the presence of symbols in dreams not only facilitates their interpretation but also makes it more difficult. As a rule the technique of interpreting according to the dreamer's free associations leaves us in the lurch when we come to the symbolic elements in the dream-content. Regard for scientific criticism forbids our returning to the arbitrary judgement of the dream-interpreter, as it was employed in ancient times and seems to have been revived in the reckless interpretations of Stekel. We are thus obliged, in dealing with those elements of the dream-content which must be recognized as symbolic, to adopt a combined technique, which on the one hand rests on the dreamer's associations and on the other hand fills the gaps from the interpreter's knowledge of symbols. We must combine a critical caution in resolving symbols with a careful study of them in dreams which afford particularly clear instances of their use, in order to disarm any charge of arbitrariness in dream-interpretation. The uncertainties which still attach to our activities as interpreters of dreams spring in part from our incomplete knowledge, which can be progressively improved as we advanced further, but in part from certain characteristics of dream-symbols themselves. They frequently have more than one or even several meanings, and, as

---

[1] [In the editions of 1909 and 1911 only, the following sentence appeared at this point: 'Moreover the ordinarily used sexual symbols are not invariably unambiguous.']

with Chinese script, the correct interpretation can only be arrived at on each occasion from the context. This ambiguity of the symbols links up with the characteristic of dreams for admitting of 'over-interpretation' [see p. 313]—for representing in a single piece of content thoughts and wishes which are often widely divergent in their nature. [1914.]

Subject to these qualifications and reservations I will now proceed. The Emperor and Empress (or the King and Queen) as a rule really represent the dreamer's parents; and a Prince or Princess represents the dreamer himself or herself. [1909.] But the same high authority is attributed to great men as to the Emperor; and for that reason Goethe, for instance, appears as a father-symbol in some dreams (Hitschmann, 1913.) [1919.]—All elongated objects, such as sticks, tree-trunks and umbrellas (the opening of these last being comparable to an erection) may stand for the male organ [1909]—as well as all long, sharp weapons, such as knives, daggers and pikes [1911]. Another frequent though not entirely intelligible symbol of the same thing is a nail-file—possibly on account of the rubbing up and down. [1909.]—Boxes, cases, chests, cupboards and ovens represent the uterus [1909], and also hollow objects, ships, and vessels of all kinds [1919].—Rooms in dreams are usually women ('*Frauenzimmer*' [see p. 235 *n*.]); if the various ways in and out of them are represented, this interpretation is scarcely open to doubt. [1909.][1] In this connection interest in whether the room is open or locked is easily intelligible. (Cf. Dora's first dream in my 'Fragment of an Analysis of a Case of Hysteria,' 1905*e* [Footnote near the beginning of Section II].) There is no need to name explicitly the key that unlocks the room; in his ballad of Count Eberstein, Uhland has used the symbolism of locks and keys to construct a charming piece of bawdry. [1911.]—A dream of going through a suite of rooms is a

---

[1] [*Footnote added* 1919:] 'One of my patients, who was living in a boarding-house, dreamt that *he met one of the maidservants and asked her what her number was. To his surprise she answered*: "14". He had in fact started a liaison with this girl and had paid several visits to her in her bedroom. She had not unnaturally been afraid that the landlady might become suspicious, and, on the day before the dream, she had proposed that they should meet in an unoccupied room. This room was actually "No. 14," while in the dream it was the woman herself who bore this number. It would hardly be possible to imagine clearer proof of an identification between a woman and a room.' (Jones, 1914*a*.) Cf. Artemidorus, *Oneirocritica*, Book II, Chapter X: 'Thus, for instance, a bedchamber stands for a wife, if such there be in the house.' (*Trans.* F. S. Krauss, 1881, 110.)

brothel or harem dream. [1909.] But, as Sachs [1914] has shown by some neat examples, it can also be used (by antithesis) to represent marriage. [1914.]—We find an interesting link with the sexual researches of child-hood when a dreamer dreams of two rooms which were originally one, or when he sees a familiar room divided into two in the dream, or vice versa. In childhood the female genitals and the anus are regarded as a single area—the 'bottom' (in accordance with the infantile 'cloaca theory')[1]; and it is not until later that the discovery is made that this region of the body comprises two separate cavities and orifices. [1919.]—Steps, ladders or staircases, or, as the case may be, walking up or down them, are represen-tations of the sexual act.[2]—Smooth walls over which the dreamer climbs, the façades of houses, down which he lowers himself—often in great anxiety—correspond to erect human bodies, and are probably repeating in the dream recollections of a baby's climbing up his parents or nurse. The 'smooth' walls are men; in his fear the dreamer often clutches hold of 'pro-jections' in the façades of houses. [1911.]—Tables, tables laid for a meal, and boards also stand for women—no doubt by antithesis, since the con-tours of their bodies are eliminated in the symbols. [1909.] 'Wood' seems, from its linguistic connections, to stand in general for female 'material.' The name of the Island of 'Madeira' means 'wood' in Portuguese [1911.]

---

[1] [See the section on 'Theories of Birth' in the second of Freud's *Three Essays on the Theory of Sexuality* (1905*d*).]

[2] [*Footnote* 1911:] I will repeat here what I have written on this subject elsewhere (Freud, 1910*d*): 'A little time ago I heard that a psychologist whose views are somewhat different from ours had remarked to one of us that, when all was said and done, we did undoubtedly exaggerate the hidden sexual significance of dreams: his own commonest dream was of going upstairs, and surely there could not be anything sexual in *that*. We were put on the alert by this objection, and began to turn our attention to the appearance of steps, staircases and ladders in dreams, and were soon in a position to show that staircases (and analogous things) were unquestionably symbols of copulation. It is not hard to discover the basis of the comparison: we come to the top in a series of rhythmical movements and with increasing breathlessness and then, with a few rapid leaps, we can get to the bottom again. Thus the rhythmical pattern of copulation is reproduced in going upstairs. Nor must we omit to bring in the evidence of linguistic usage. It shows us that "mounting" [German "*steigen*"] is used as a direct equivalent for the sexual act. We speak of a man as a "*Steiger*" [a "mounter"] and of "*nach-steigen*" ["to run after," literally "to climb after"]. In French the steps on a stair-case are called "*marches*" and "*un vieux marcheur*" has the same meaning as our "*ein alter Steiger*" ["an old rake"].' [Cf. also pp. 302 ff.]

Since 'bed and board' constitute marriage, the latter often takes the place of the former in dreams and the sexual complex of ideas is, so far as may be, transposed on to the eating complex. [1909.]—As regards articles of clothing, a woman's hat can very often be interpreted with certainty as a genital organ, and, moreover, as a *man's*. The same is true of an overcoat [German 'Mantel'], though in this case it is not clear to what extent the use of the symbol is due to a verbal assonance. In men's dreams a necktie often appears as a symbol for the penis. No doubt this is not only because neckties are long, dependent objects and peculiar to men, but also because they can be chosen according to taste—a liberty which, in the case of the object symbolized, is forbidden by Nature.[1] Men who make use of this symbol in dreams are often very extravagant in ties in real life and own whole collections of them. [1911.]—It is highly probable that all complicated machinery and apparatus occurring in dreams stand for the genitals (and as a rule male ones [1919])—in describing which dream-symbolism is as indefatigable as the 'joke-work.'[2] [1909.] Nor is there any doubt that all weapons and tools are used as symbols for the male organ: e.g. ploughs, hammers, rifles, revolvers, daggers, sabres, etc. [1919.]—In the same way many landscapes in dreams, especially any containing bridges or wooded hills, may clearly be recognized as descriptions of the genitals. [1911.] Marcinowski [1912*a*] has published a collection of dreams illustrated by their dreamers with drawings that ostensibly represent landscapes and other localities occurring in the dreams. These drawings bring out very clearly the distinction between a dream's manifest and latent meaning. Whereas to the innocent eye they appear as plans, maps, and so on, closer inspection shows that they represent the human body, the genitals, etc., and only then do the dreams become intelligible. (See in this connection Pfister's papers [1911–12 and 1913] on cryptograms and puzzle-pictures.)

---

[1] [*Footnote added* 1914:] Compare the drawing made by a nineteen-year-old manic patient reproduced in *Zbl. Psychoanal.*, **2**, 675. [Rohrschach, 1912.] It represents a man with a necktie consisting of a snake which is turning in the direction of a girl. See also the story of 'The Bashful Man' in *Anthropophyteia*, **6**, 334: A lady went into a bathroom, and there she came upon a gentleman who scarcely had time to put on his shirt. He was very much embarrassed, but hurriedly covering his throat with the front part of his shirt, he exclaimed: 'Excuse me, but I've not got my necktie on.'

[2] [See Freud's volume on jokes (1905*c*), in which he introduced the term 'joke-work' (on the analogy of 'dream-work') to designate the psychological processes involved in the production of jokes.]

[1914.] In the case of unintelligible neologisms, too, it is worth considering whether they may not be put together from components with a sexual meaning. [1911.]—Children in dreams often stand for the genitals; and, indeed, both men and women are in the habit of referring to their genitals affectionately as their 'little ones.' [1909.] Stekel [1909, 473] is right in recognizing a 'little brother' as the penis. [1925.] Playing with a little child, beating it, etc., often represent masturbation in dreams. [1911.]—To represent castration symbolically, the dream-work makes use of baldness, haircutting, falling out of teeth and decapitation. If one of the ordinary symbols for a penis occurs in a dream doubled or multiplied, it is to be regarded as a warding-off of castration.[1] The appearance in dreams of lizards—animals whose tails grow again if they are pulled off—has the same significance. (Cf. the lizard-dream on pp. 45 f.)—Many of the beasts which are used as genital symbols in mythology and folklore play the same part in dreams: e.g. fishes, snails, cats, mice (on account of the pubic hair), and above all those most important symbols of the male organ—snakes. Small animals and vermin represent small children—for instance, undesired brothers and sisters. Being plagued with vermin is often a sign of pregnancy. [1919.]—A quite recent symbol of the male organ in dreams deserves mention: the air-ship, whose use in this sense is justified by its connection with flying as well as sometimes by its shape. [1911.]

A number of other symbols have been put forward, with supporting instances, by Stekel, but have not yet been sufficiently verified. [1911.] Stekel's writings, and in particular his *Die Sprache des Traumes* [1911], contain the fullest collection of interpretations of symbols. Many of these show penetration, and further examination has proved them correct: for instance, his section on the symbolism of death. But this author's lack of a critical faculty and his tendency to generalization at all costs throw doubts upon other of his interpretations or render them unusable; so that it is highly advisable to exercise caution in accepting his conclusions. I therefore content myself with drawing attention to only a few of his findings. [1914.]

According to Stekel, 'right' and 'left' in dreams have an ethical sense. 'The right-hand path always means the path of righteousness and the left-hand one that of crime. Thus "left" may represent homosexuality, incest or perversion, and "right" may represent marriage, intercourse with a prosti-

---

[1] [This point is elaborated in Section II of Freud's paper on 'The Uncanny' (1919*h*). See also Freud's posthumously published paper (written in 1922) on Medusa's head (1940*c*), and below, p. 421.]

tute and so on, always looked at from the subject's individual moral stand-point.' (Stekel, 1909, 466 ff.)—Relatives in dreams usually play the part of genitals (ibid., 473). I can only confirm this in the case of sons, daughters and younger sisters[1]—that is only so far as they fall into the category of 'little ones.' On the other hand I have come across undoubted cases in which 'sisters' symbolized the breasts and 'brothers' the larger hemispheres.—Stekel explains failing to catch up with a carriage as regret at a difference in age which cannot be caught up with (ibid., 479).—Luggage that one travels with is a load of sin, he says, that weighs one down (loc. cit.). [1911.] But precisely luggage often turns out to be an unmistakable symbol of the dreamer's own genitals. [1914.] Stekel also assigns fixed symbolic meanings to numbers, such as often appear in dreams [ibid. 497 ff.]. But these explanations seem neither sufficiently verified nor generally valid, though his interpretations usually appear plausible in the individual cases. [1911.][2] In any case the number three has been confirmed from many sides as a symbol of the male genitals. [1914.][3]

One of the generalizations put forward by Stekel concerns the double significance of genital symbols. [1914.] 'Where,' he asks, 'is there a symbol which—provided that the imagination by any means admits of it—cannot be employed both in a male and in a female sense?' [1911, 73.] In any case the clause in parenthesis removes much of the certainty from this assertion, since in fact the imagination does not always admit of it. But I think it is worth while remarking that in my experience Stekel's generalization cannot be maintained in the face of the greater complexity of the facts. In addition to symbols which can stand with equal frequency for the male and for the female genitals, there are some which designate one of the sexes predominantly or almost exclusively, and yet others which are known *only* with a male or a female meaning. For it is a fact that the imagination does not admit of long, stiff objects and weapons being used as symbols of the female genitals, or of hollow objects, such as chests, cases, boxes, etc., being used as symbols for the male ones. It is true that the tendency of

---

[1] [And, apparently, younger brothers, see above, p. 370.]

[2] [At this point, in the 1911 edition only, the following sentence appeared: 'In Wilhelm Stekel's recently published volume, *Die Sprache des Traumes*, which appeared too late for me to notice it, there is to be found (1911, 72 f.) a list of the commonest sexual symbols which is intended to show that all sexual symbols can be employed bisexually.']

[3] [A discussion of the number nine will be found in Section 3 of Freud (1923*d*).]

dreams and of unconscious phantasies to employ sexual symbols bisexually betrays an archaic characteristic; for in childhood the distinction between the genitals of the two sexes is unknown and the same kind of genitals are attributed to both of them. [1911.] But it is possible, too, to be misled into wrongly supposing that a sexual symbol is bisexual, if one forgets that in some dreams there is a general inversion of sex, so that what is male is represented as female and *vice versa*. Dreams of this kind may, for instance, express a woman's wish to be a man. [1925.]

The genitals can also be represented in dreams by other parts of the body: the male organ by a hand or a foot and the female genital orifice by the mouth or an ear or even an eye. The secretions of the human body— mucus, tears, urine, semen, etc.—can replace one another in dreams. This last assertion of Stekel's [1911, 49], which is on the whole correct, has been justifiably criticized by Reitler (1913b) as requiring some qualification: what in fact happens is that significant secretions, such as semen, are replaced by indifferent ones. [1919.]

It is to be hoped that these very incomplete hints may serve to encourage others to undertake a more painstaking general study of the subject [1909.][1] I myself have attempted to give a more elaborate account of dream-symbolism in my *Introductory Lectures on Psycho-Analysis* (1916– 17 [Lecture X]). [1919.]

I shall now append a few examples of the use of these symbols in dreams, with the idea of showing how impossible it becomes to arrive at the interpretation of a dream if one excludes dream-symbolism, and how irresistibly one is driven to accept it in many cases. [1911.] At the same time, however, I should like to utter an express warning against over- estimating the importance of symbols in dream-interpretation, against re- stricting the work of translating dreams merely to translating symbols and against abandoning the technique of making use of the dreamer's associ- ations. The two techniques of dream-interpretation must be complemen- tary to each other; but both in practice and in theory the first place continues to be held by the procedure which I began by describing and

---

[1] [*Footnote added* 1911:] However much Scherner's view of dream-symbolism may differ from the one developed in these pages, I must insist that he is to be regarded as the true discoverer of symbolism in dreams, and that the investiga- tions of psycho-analysis have at last brought recognition to his book, published as it was so many years ago (in 1861), and for so long regarded as fantastic.

which attributes a decisive significance to the comments made by the dreamer, while the translation of symbols, as I have explained it, is also at our disposal as an auxiliary method. [1909.]

I

A Hat as a Symbol of a Man (or of Male Genitals) (1911)[1]

(Extract from the dream of a young woman suffering from agoraphobia as a result of fears of seduction.)

'*I was walking in the street in the summer, wearing a straw hat of peculiar shape; its middle-piece was bent upwards and its side-pieces hung downwards*' (the description became hesitant at this point) '*in such a way that one side was lower than the other. I was cheerful and in a self-confident frame of*

---

[1] [This dream and the two next ones were first published in a paper entitled 'Additional Examples of Dream-Interpretation' (1911*a*). The paper was introduced by the following paragraphs, which have never been reprinted in German:

'*Some Instances of Dream-Symbols.*—Of the many objections that have been raised against the procedure of psycho-analysis, the strangest, and, perhaps, one might add, the most ignorant, seems to me to be doubt as to the existence of symbolism in dreams and the unconscious. For no one who carries out psychoanalyses can avoid assuming the presence of such symbolism, and the resolution of dreams by symbols has been practised from the earliest times. On the other hand, I am ready to admit that the occurrence of these symbols should be subject to particularly strict proof in view of their great multiplicity.

'In what follows I have put together some examples from my most recent experience: cases in which a solution by means of a particular symbol strikes me as especially revealing. By this means a dream acquires a meaning which it could otherwise never have found; it falls into place in the chain of the dreamer's thoughts and its interpretation is recognized by the subject himself.

'On a point of technique I may remark that a dreamer's associations are apt to fail precisely in connection with the symbolic elements of dreams. In my record of these few selected examples I have tried to draw a sharp line between the work of the patient (or dreamer) himself and my own interventions.'

The paper ended with some shorter examples, which will be found reprinted in Section F of this chapter (Nos. 2, 3 and 4 on pp. 417 f.). In the original paper these were introduced as follows:

mind; and, as I passed a group of young officers, I thought: "None of you can do me any harm!"'

Since nothing occurred to her in connection with the hat in the dream, I said: 'No doubt the hat was a male genital organ, with its middle-piece sticking up and its two side-pieces hanging down. It may seem strange, perhaps, that a hat should be a man, but you will remember the phrase *"Unter die Haube kommen"* ["to find a husband" (literally "to come under the cap")].' I intentionally gave her no interpretation of the detail about the two side-pieces hanging down unevenly; though it is precisely details of this kind that must point the way in determining an interpretation. I went on to say that as she had a husband with such fine genitals there was no need for her to be afraid of the officers—no need, that is, for her to wish for anything from them, since as a rule she was prevented from going for a walk unprotected and unaccompanied owing to her phantasies of being seduced. I had already been able to give her this last explanation of her anxiety on several occasions upon the basis of other material.

The way in which the dreamer reacted to this material was most remarkable. She withdrew her description of the hat and maintained that she had never said that the two side-pieces hung down. I was too certain of what I had heard to be led astray, and stuck to my guns. She was silent for a while and then found enough courage to ask what was meant by one of her husband's testes hanging down lower than the other and whether it was the same in all men. In this way the remarkable detail of the hat was explained and the interpretation accepted by her.

At the time my patient told me this dream I had long been familiar with the hat-symbol. Other, less transparent cases had led me to suppose that a hat can also stand for female genitals.[1]

'*Some Rarer Forms of Representation.*—I have mentioned "considerations of representability" as one of the factors that influence the formation of dreams. In the process of transforming a thought into a visual image a peculiar faculty is revealed by dreamers, and an analyst is rarely equal to following it with his guesses. It will therefore give him real satisfaction if the intuitive perception of the dreamer—the creator of these representations—is able to explain their meaning.']

[1] [*Footnote* 1911:] Cf. an example of this in Kirchgraber (1912). Stekel (1909, 475) records a dream in which a hat with a feather standing up crooked in the middle of it symbolized an (impotent) man. [Freud suggested an explanation of hat symbolism in a later paper (1916c).]

11

**A 'LITTLE ONE' AS THE GENITAL ORGAN—
'BEING RUN OVER' AS A SYMBOL OF
SEXUAL INTERCOURSE [1911]**

(Another dream of the same agoraphobic patient.)

Her mother sent her little daughter away, so that she had to go by herself. Then she went in a train with her mother and saw her little one walk straight on to the rails so that she was bound to be run over. She heard the cracking of her bones. (This produced an uncomfortable feeling in her but no real horror.) Then she looked round out of the window of the railway-carriage to see whether the parts could not be seen behind. Then she reproached her mother for having made the little one go by herself.

ANALYSIS.—It is no easy matter to give a complete interpretation of the dream. It formed part of a cycle of dreams and can only be fully understood if it is taken in connection with the others. There is difficulty in obtaining in sufficient isolation the material necessary for establishing the symbolism.—In the first place, the patient declared that the train journey was to be interpreted historically, as an allusion to a journey she had taken when she was leaving a sanatorium for nervous diseases, with whose director, needless to say, she had been in love. Her mother had fetched her away, and the doctor had appeared at the station and handed her a bouquet of flowers as a parting present. It had been very awkward that her mother should have witnessed this tribute. At this point, then, her mother figured as interfering with her attempts at a love affair; and this had in fact been the part played by that severe lady during the patient's girlhood.—Her next association related to the sentence: 'she looked round to see whether the parts could not be seen from behind.' The façade of the dream would of course lead one to think of the parts of her little daughter who had been run over and mangled. But her association led in quite another direction. She recollected having once seen her father naked in the bathroom from behind; she went on to talk of the distinctions between the sexes, and laid stress on the fact that a man's genitals can be seen even from behind but a woman's cannot. In this connection she herself interpreted 'the little one' as meaning the genitals and 'her little one'—she had a four-year-old daughter—as her own genitals. She reproached her mother with having expected her to live as though she had no genitals, and pointed out that the same reproach was expressed in the opening sentence of the dream: 'her mother sent her little one away, so that she had to go by herself.' In her imagination 'going by herself in the streets' meant not having a man, not having any sexual relations ('*coire*' in Latin [from which 'coitus' is derived] means literally 'to go with')—and she disliked that. Her accounts all went to show that when she was a girl she had in fact suffered from her mother's jealousy owing to the preference shown her by her father.[1]

The deeper interpretation of this dream was shown by another dream of the same night, in which the dreamer identified herself with her brother. She had actually been a boyish girl, and had often been told that she should have been a boy. This identification with her brother made it particularly clear that 'the little one' meant a genital organ. Her mother was threatening him (or her) with castration, which could only have been a punishment for playing with her penis; thus the identification also proved that she herself had masturbated as a child—a memory which till then she had only had as applied to her brother. The information supplied by the second dream showed that she must have come to know about the male organ at an early age and have afterwards forgotten it. Further, the second dream alluded to the infantile sexual theory according to which girls are boys who have been castrated. [Cf. Freud, 1908*c*.] When I suggested to her that she had had this childish belief, she at once confirmed the fact by telling me that she had heard the anecdote of the little boy's saying to the little girl: 'Cut off?' and of the little girl's replying: 'No, always been like that.'

Thus the sending away of the little one (of the genital organ) in the first dream was also related to the threat of castration. Her ultimate complaint against her mother was for not having given birth to her as a boy.

The fact that 'being run over' symbolizes sexual intercourse would not be obvious from this dream, though it has been confirmed from many other sources.

---

[1] [In the 1911 edition only, the following sentence was added at this point: 'Stekel [1909, 473], basing himself on a very common idiomatic usage, has suggested that the "little one" is a symbol of the male or female genitals.']

III

The Genitals Represented by Buildings, Stairs and Shafts [1911][1]

(The dream of a young man inhibited by his father-complex.)

He was going for a walk with his father in a place which must certainly have been the Prater,[2] since he saw the rotunda, with a small annex in front of it *to which a* captive balloon *was attached, though it looked rather* limp. *His father asked him what all this was for; he was surprised at his asking, but explained it to him. Then they came into a courtyard which had a large sheet of tin laid out in it. His father wanted to* pull off *a large piece of it, but first looked around to see if anyone was watching. He told him that he need only tell the foreman and he could take some without any bother. A* staircase *led down from this yard into a* shaft, *whose walls were cushioned in some soft material, rather like a leather armchair. At the end of the shaft was a longish platform and then another* shaft *started....*

Analysis.—This dreamer belonged to a type whose therapeutic prospects are not favourable: up to a certain point they offer no resistance at all to analysis, but from then onwards turn out to be almost inaccessible. He interpreted this dream almost unaided. 'The Rotunda,' he said, 'was my genitals and the captive balloon in front of it was my penis, whose limpness I have reason to complain of.' Going into greater detail, then, we may translate the Rotunda as the bottom (habitually regarded by children as part of the genitals) and the small annex in front of it as the scrotum. His father asked him in the dream what all this was, that is, what was the purpose and function of the genitals. It seemed plausible to reverse this situation and turn the dreamer into the questioner. Since he had in fact never questioned his father in this way, we had to look upon the dream-thought as a wish, or take it as a conditional clause, such as: 'If I had asked my father for sexual enlightenment...' We shall presently find the continuation of this thought in another part of the dream.

---

[1] [This dream and its interpretation are reproduced in Freud's *Introductory Lectures* (1916–17), Lecture XII, No. 7.]

[2] [See footnote, p. 214.]

The courtyard in which the sheet of tin was spread out is not to be taken symbolically in the first instance. It was derived from the business premises of the dreamer's father. For reasons of discretion I have substituted 'tin' for another material in which his father actually dealt: but I have made no other change in the wording of the dream. The dreamer had entered his father's business and had taken violent objection to the somewhat dubious practices on which the firm's earnings in part depended. Consequently the dream-thought I have just interpreted may have continued in this way: '(If I had asked him), he would have deceived me just as he deceives his customers.' As regards the 'pulling off' which served to represent his father's dishonesty in business, the dreamer himself produced a second explanation—namely that it stood for masturbating. Not only was I already familiar with this interpretation (see p. 362 *n.* 2 above), but there was something to confirm it by the fact that the secret nature of masturbation was represented by its reverse: it might be done openly. Just as we should expect, the masturbatory activity was once again displaced on to the dreamer's father, like the questioning in the first scene of the dream. He promptly interpreted the shaft as a vagina, having regard to the soft cushioning of its walls. I added from my own knowledge derived elsewhere that climbing down, like climbing up in other cases, described sexual intercourse in the vagina. (See my remarks [in Freud 1910*d*], quoted above, p. 368 *n.* 2.)

The dreamer himself gave a biographical explanation of the fact that the first shaft was followed by a longish platform and then by another shaft. He had practised intercourse for a time but had then given it up on account of inhibitions, and he now hoped to be able to resume it by the help of the treatment. The dream became more indistinct, however, towards the end, and it must seem probable to anyone who is familiar with these things that the influence of another topic was already making itself felt in the second scene of the dream, and was hinted at by the father's business, by his deceitful conduct and by the interpretation of the first shaft as a vagina: all this pointed to a connection with the dreamer's mother.[1]

---

[1] [The following additional paragraph was appended to this dream on its first publication (in Freud, 1911*a*): 'This dream as a whole belongs to the not uncommon class of "biographical" dreams, in which the dreamer gives a survey of his sexual life in the form of a continuous narrative. (See the example [on pp. 361 ff.])—The frequency with which buildings, localities and landscapes are employed as symbolic representations of the body, and in particular (with constant reiteration) of the genitals, would certainly deserve a comprehensive study, illustrated by numerous examples.']

IV

The Male Organ Represented by Persons and the Female Organ by a Landscape [1911]

(The dream of an uneducated woman whose husband was a policeman, reported by B. Dattner.)

'. . . Then someone broke into the house and she was frightened and called out for a policeman. But he had quietly gone into a church,[1] to which a number of steps[2] led up, accompanied by two tramps. Behind the church there was a hill[3] and above it a thick wood.[4] The policeman was dressed in a helmet, brass collar and cloak.[5] He had a brown beard. The two tramps, who went along peaceably with the policeman, had sack-like aprons tied round their middles.[6] In front of the church a path led up to the hill; on both sides of it there grew grass and brushwood, which became thicker and thicker and, at the top of the hill, turned into a regular wood.'

V

Dreams of Castration in Children [1919]

(a) A boy aged three years and five months, who obviously disliked the idea of his father's returning from the front, woke up one morning in a disturbed and excited state. He kept on repeating: 'Why was Daddy carrying his head on a plate? Last night Daddy was carrying his head on a plate.'

(b) A student who is now suffering from a severe obsessional neurosis remembers having repeatedly had the following dream during his sixth year: He went to the hairdresser's to have his hair cut. A big, severe-looking woman came up to him and cut his head off. He recognized the woman as his mother.

---

[1] 'Or chapel (= vagina).'
[2] 'Symbol of copulation.'
[3] '*Mons veneris*.'
[4] 'Pubic hair.'
[5] 'According to an expert, demons in cloaks and hoods are of a phallic character.'
[6] 'The two halves of the scrotum.'

VI

Urinary Symbolism [1914]

The series of drawings reproduced [on p. 624] were found by Ferenczi in a Hungarian comic paper called *Fidibusz*, and he at once saw how well they could be used to illustrate the theory of dreams. Otto Rank has already reproduced them in a paper (1912*a*, [99]).

The drawings bear the title 'A French Nurse's Dream'; but it is only the last picture, showing the nurse being woken up by the child's screams, that tells us that the seven previous pictures represent the phases of a dream. The first picture depicts the stimulus which should have caused the sleeper to wake: the little boy has become aware of a need and is asking for help in dealing with it. But in the dream the dreamer, instead of being in the bedroom, is taking the child for a walk. In the second picture she has already led him to a street corner where he is micturating—and she can go on sleeping. But the arousal stimulus continues; indeed, it increases. The little boy, finding he is not being attended to, screams louder and louder. The more imperiously he insists upon his nurse waking up and helping him, the more insistent becomes the dream's assurance that everything is all right and that there is no need for her to wake up. At the same time, the dream translates the increasing stimulus into the increasing dimensions of its symbols. The stream of water produced by the micturating boy becomes mightier and mightier. In the fourth picture it is already large enough to float a rowing boat; but there follow a gondola, a sailing-ship and finally a liner. The ingenious artist has in this way cleverly depicted the struggle between an obstinate craving for sleep and an inexhaustible stimulus towards waking.

VII

A Staircase Dream [1911]

(Reported and Interpreted by Otto Rank.)[1]

'I have to thank the same colleague to whom I owe the dream with a dental stimulus [recorded on pp. 399 ff. below] for an equally transparent emission dream:

---

[1] [Apparently not published elsewhere.]

"'I was running down the staircase [of a block of flats] in pursuit of a little girl who had done something to me, in order to punish her. At the foot of the stairs someone (a grown-up woman?) stopped the child for me. I caught hold of her; but I don't know whether I hit her, for I suddenly found myself on the middle of the staircase copulating with the child (as it were in the air). It was not a real copulation; I was only rubbing my genitals against her external genitals, and while I did so I saw them extremely distinctly, as well as her head, which was turned upwards and sideways. During the sexual act I saw hanging above me to my left (also as it were in the air) two small paintings— landscapes representing a house surrounded by trees. At the bottom of the smaller of these, instead of the painter's signature, I saw my own first name, as though it were intended as a birthday present for me. Then I saw a label in front of the two pictures, which said that cheaper pictures were also to be had. (I then saw myself very indistinctly as though I were lying in bed on the landing) and I was woken up by the feeling of wetness caused by the emission I had had.'*

'Interpretation.—On the evening of the dream-day the dreamer had been in a bookshop, and as he was waiting to be attended to he had looked at some pictures which were on view there and which represented subjects similar to those in the dream. He went up close to one small picture which had particularly pleased him, to look at the artist's name—but it had been quite unknown to him.

'Later the same evening, when he was with some friends, he had heard a story of a Bohemian servant-girl who boasted that her illegitimate child had been "made on the stairs." The dreamer had enquired the details of this rather unusual event and had learnt that the servant-girl had gone home with her admirer to her parents' house, where there had been no opportunity for sexual intercourse, and in his excitement the man had copulated with her on the stairs. The dreamer had made a joking allusion to a malicious expression used to describe adulterated wines, and had said that in fact the child came of a "cellar-stair vintage."

'So much for the connections with the previous day, which appeared with some insistence in the dream-content and were reproduced by the dreamer without any difficulty. But he brought up no less easily an old fragment of infantile recollection which had also found its use in the dream. The staircase belonged to the house where he had spent the greater part of his childhood and, in particular, where he had first made conscious acquaintance with the problems of sex. He had frequently played on this staircase and, among other things, used to slide down the banisters, riding astride on them—which had given him sexual feelings. In the dream, too, he rushed down the stairs extraordinarily fast—so fast, indeed, that, according to his own specific account, he did not put his feet down on the separate steps but "flew" down them, as people say. If the infantile experience is taken into account, the beginning part of the dream seems to represent the factor of sexual excitement.—But the dreamer had also often romped in a sexual way with the neighbours' children on this same staircase and in the adjacent building, and had satisfied his desires in just the same way as he did in the dream.

'If we bear in mind that Freud's researches into sexual symbolism (1910*d* [see above, p. 368 *n*.]) have shown that stairs and going upstairs in dreams almost invariably stand for copulation, the dream becomes quite transparent. Its motive force, as indeed was shown by its outcome— an emission—was of a purely libidinal nature. The dreamer's sexual excitement was awakened during his sleep—this being represented in the dream by his rushing down the stairs. The sadistic element in the sexual excitement, based on the romping in childhood, was indicated by the pursuit and overpowering of the child. The libidinal excitement increased and pressed towards sexual action—represented in the dream by his catching hold of the child and conveying it to the middle of the staircase. Up to that point the dream was only *symbolically* sexual and would have been quite unintelligible to any inexperienced dream-interpreter. But symbolic satisfaction of that kind was not enough to guarantee a restful sleep, in view of the strength of the libidinal excitation. The excitation led to an orgasm and thus revealed the fact that the whole staircase-symbolism represented copulation.—The present dream offers a specially clear confirmation of Freud's view that one of the reasons for the use of going upstairs as a sexual symbol is the rhythmical character of both activities: for the dreamer expressly stated that the most clearly defined element in the whole dream was the rhythm of the sexual act and its up and down motion.

'I must add a word with regard to the two pictures which, apart from their real meaning, also figured in a symbolic sense as "*Weibsbilder.*"[1] This was shown at once by there being a large picture and a small picture, just as a large (or grown-up) girl and a small one appeared in the dream. The fact that "cheaper pictures were also to be had" led to the prostitute-

---

[1] [Literally 'pictures of women'—a common German idiom for 'women.']

complex; while on the other hand the appearance of the dreamer's first name on the small picture and the idea of its being intended as a birthday present for him were hints at the parental complex. ("Born on the stairs" = "begotten by copulation.")

'The indistinct final scene, in which the dreamer saw himself lying in bed on the landing and had a feeling of wetness, seems to have pointed the way beyond infantile masturbation still further back into childhood and to have had its prototype in similarly pleasurable scenes of bed-wetting.'

VIII

A Modified Staircase Dream [1911]

One of my patients, a man whose sexual abstinence was imposed on him by a severe neurosis, and whose [unconscious] phantasies were fixed upon his mother, had repeated dreams of going upstairs in her company. I once remarked to him that a moderate amount of masturbation would probably do him less harm than his compulsive self-restraint, and this provoked the following dream:

His piano-teacher reproached him for neglecting his piano-playing, and for not practising Mocheles' 'Etudes' and Clementi's 'Gradus ad Parnassum.'

By way of comment, he pointed out that '*Gradus*' are also 'steps'; and that the key-board itself is a staircase, since it contains scales [ladders].

It is fair to say that there is no group of ideas that is incapable of representing sexual facts and wishes.

IX

The Feeling of Reality and the Representation of Repetition [1919]

A man who is now thirty-five years old reported a dream which he remembered clearly and claimed to have had at the age of four. *The lawyer who had charge of his father's will*—he had lost his father when he was three—*brought two large pears. He was given one of them to eat; the other lay on the window-sill in the sitting-room.* He awoke with a conviction of the reality of what he had dreamt and kept obstinately asking his mother for the second pear, and insisted that it was on the window-sill. His mother had laughed at this.

ANALYSIS.—The lawyer was a jovial old gentleman who, the dreamer seemed to remember, had really once brought some pears along. The window-sill was as he had seen it in the dream. Nothing else occurred to him in connection with it—only that his mother had told him a dream shortly before. She had had two birds sitting on her head and had asked herself when they would fly away; they did not fly away; but one of them flew to her mouth and sucked at it.

The failure of the dreamer's associations gave us a right to attempt an interpretation by symbolic substitution. The two pears—'*pommes ou poires*'—were his mother's breasts which had given him nourishment; the window-sill was the projection formed by her bosom—like balconies in dreams of houses (see p. 368). His feeling of reality after waking was justified, for his mother had really suckled him, and had done so, in fact, for far longer than the usual time and his mother's breast was still available to him.[1] The dream must be translated: 'Give (or show) me your breast again, Mother, that I used to drink from in the past.' 'In the past' was represented by his eating one of the pears; 'again' was represented by his longing for the other. The *temporal repetition* of an act is regularly shown in dreams by the *numerical multiplication* of an object.

It is most remarkable, of course, that symbolism should already be playing a part in the dream of a four-year-old child. But this is the rule and not the exception. It may safely be asserted that dreamers have symbolism at their disposal from the very first.

The following uninfluenced recollection by a lady who is now twenty-seven shows at what an early age symbolism is employed outside dream-life as well as inside it. *She was between three and four years old. Her nurse-maid took her to the lavatory along with a brother eleven months her junior and a girl cousin of an age between the other two, to do their small business before going out for a walk. Being the eldest, she sat on the seat, while the other two sat on chambers. She asked her cousin: 'Have you got a purse too? Walter's got a little sausage; I've got a purse.' Her cousin replied: 'Yes, I've*

---

[1] [Cf. p. 210. This point—the fact that a specially strong feeling after waking of the reality of the dream or of some part of it actually relates to the latent dream-thoughts—is insisted upon by Freud in a passage towards the end of Chapter II of his study on Jensen's *Gradiva* (1907a) and in the course of his first comments on the 'Wolf Man's' dream (Section IV of Freud, 1918b).]

got a purse too.' The nursemaid heard what they said with much amusement and reported the conversation to the children's mother, who reacted with a sharp reprimand.

I will here interpolate a dream (recorded in a paper by Alfred Robitsek, 1912), in which the beautifully chosen symbolism made an interpretation possible with only slight assistance from the dreamer.

x

'The Question of Symbolism in the Dreams of Normal Persons' [1914]

'One objection which is frequently brought forward by opponents of psycho-analysis, and which has lately been voiced by Havelock Ellis (1911, 168), argues that though dream-symbolism may perhaps occur as a product of the neurotic mind, it is not to be found in normal persons. Now psycho-analytic research finds no fundamental, but only quantitative, distinctions between normal and neurotic life; and indeed the analysis of dreams, in which repressed complexes are operative alike in the healthy and the sick, shows a complete identity both in their mechanisms and in their symbolism. The naïve dreams of healthy people actually often contain a much simpler, more perspicuous and more characteristic symbolism than those of neurotics; for in the latter, as a result of the more powerful workings of the censorship and of the consequently more far-reaching dream-distortion, the symbolism may be obscure and hard to interpret. The dream recorded below will serve to illustrate this fact. It was dreamt by a girl who is not neurotic but is of a somewhat prudish and reserved character. In the course of conversation with her I learnt that she was engaged, but that there were some difficulties in the way of her marriage which were likely to lead to its postponement. Of her own accord she told me the following dream.

"I arrange the centre of a table with flowers for a birthday." [1] In reply to a question she told me that in the dream she seemed to be in her own home (where she was not at present living) and had "a feeling of happiness."

---

[1] [In the present analysis all the material printed in italics occurs in English in the original, exactly as here reproduced.]

'"Popular" symbolism made it possible for me to translate the dream unaided. It was an expression of her bridal wishes: the table with its floral centre-piece symbolized herself and her genitals; she represented her wishes for the future as fulfilled, for her thoughts were already occupied with the birth of a baby; so her marriage lay a long way behind her.

'I pointed out to her that "*the 'centre' of a table*" was an unusual expression (which she admitted), but I could not of course question her further directly on that point. I carefully avoided suggesting the meaning of the symbols to her, and merely asked her what came into her head in connection with the separate parts of the dream. In the course of the analysis her reserve gave place to an evident interest in the interpretation and to an openness made possible by the seriousness of the conversation.

'When I asked what flowers they had been, her first reply was: "*expensive flowers; one has to pay for them*," and then that they had been "*lilies of the valley, violets and pinks or carnations.*" I assumed that the word "lily" appeared in the dream in its popular sense as a symbol of chastity; she confirmed this assumption, for her association to "lily" was "*purity.*" "*Valley*" is a frequent female symbol in dreams; so that the chance combination of the two symbols in the English name of the flower was used in the dream-symbolism to stress the preciousness of her virginity—"*expensive flowers, one has to pay for them*"—and to express her expectation that her husband would know how to appreciate its value. The phrase "expensive flowers," etc., as will be seen, had a different meaning in the case of each of the three flower-symbols.

'"*Violets*" was ostensibly quite asexual; but, very boldly, as it seemed to me, I thought I could trace a secret meaning for the word in an unconscious link with the French word "*viol*" ["rape"]. To my surprise the dreamer gave as an association the English word "*violate.*" The dream had made use of the great chance similarity between the words "*violet*" and "*violate*"—the difference in their pronunciation lies merely in the different stress upon their final syllables—in order to express "in the language of flowers" the dreamer's thoughts on the violence of defloration (another term that employs flower symbolism) and possibly also a masochistic trait in her character. A pretty instance of the "verbal bridges" [see p. 355 n.] crossed by the paths leading to the unconscious. The words "*one has to pay for them*" signified having to pay with her life for being a wife and a mother.

'In connection with "*pinks*," which she went on to call "*carnations*," I thought of the connection between that word and "carnal." But the dreamer's association to it was "*colour.*" She added that "*carnations*" were the flowers which her *fiancé*" gave her frequently and in great numbers. At the end of her remarks she suddenly confessed of her own accord that she had not told the truth: what had occurred to her had not been "*colour*" but "*incarnation*"—the word I had expected. Incidentally "*colour*" itself was not a very remote association, but was determined by the meaning of "*carnation*" (flesh-colour)—was determined, that is, by the same complex. This lack of straightforwardness showed that it was at this point that resistance was greatest, and corresponded to the fact that this was where the symbolism was most clear and that the struggle between libido and its repression was at its most intense in relation to this phallic theme. The dreamer's comment to the effect that her *fiancé* frequently gave her flowers of that kind was an indication not only of the double sense of the word "*carnations*" but also of their phallic meaning in the dream. The gift of flowers, an exciting factor of the dream derived from her current life, was used to express an exchange of sexual gifts: she was making a gift of her virginity and expected a full emotional and sexual life in return for it. At this point, too, the words "*expensive flowers, one has to pay for them*" must have had what was no doubt literally a financial meaning.—Thus the flower symbolism in this dream included virginal feminity, masculinity and an allusion to defloration by violence. It is worth pointing out in this connection that sexual flower symbolism, which, indeed, occurs very commonly in other connections, symbolizes the human organs of sex by blossoms, which are the sexual organs of plants. It may perhaps be true in general that gifts of flowers between lovers have this unconscious meaning.

'The birthday for which she was preparing in the dream meant, no doubt, the birth of a baby. She was identifying herself with her *fiancé*, and was representing him as "arranging" her for a birth—that is, as copulating with her. The latent thought may have run: "If I were he, I wouldn't wait—I would deflower my *fiancée* without asking her leave—I would use violence." This was indicated by the word "*violate*," and in this way the sadistic component of the libido found expression.

'In a deeper layer of the dream, the phrase "*I arrange . . .*" must no doubt have an auto-erotic, that is to say, an infantile, significance.

'The dreamer also revealed an awareness, which was only possible to her in a dream, of her physical deficiency: she saw herself like a table, without projections, and on that account laid all the more emphasis on the preciousness of the "*centre*"—on another occasion she used the words, "*a centre-piece of flowers*"—that is to say, on her virginity. The horizontal attribute of a table must also have contributed something to the symbol.

'The concentration of the dream should be observed: there was nothing superfluous in it, every word was a symbol.

'Later on the dreamer produced an addendum to the dream: "*I decorate the flowers with green crinkled paper.*" She added that it was "*fancy paper*" of the sort used for covering common flowerpots. She went on: "*to hide untidy things, whatever was to be seen, which was not pretty to the eye; there is a gap, a little space in the flowers. The paper looks like velvet or moss.*"—To "*decorate*" she gave the association "*decorum,*" as I had expected. She said the green colour predominated, and her association to it was "*hope*"—another link with pregnancy.—In this part of the dream the chief factor was not identification with a man; ideas of shame and self-revelation came to the fore. She was making herself beautiful for him and was admitting physical defects which she felt ashamed of and was trying to correct. Her associations "*velvet*" and "*moss*" were a clear indication of a reference to pubic hair.

'This dream, then, gave expression to thoughts of which the girl was scarcely aware in her waking life—thoughts concerned with sensual love and its organs. She was being "arranged for a birthday"—that is, she was being copulated with. The fear of being deflowered was finding expression, and perhaps, too, ideas of pleasurable suffering. She admitted her physical deficiencies to herself and overcompensated for them by an overvaluation of her virginity. Her shame put forward as an excuse for the signs of sensuality the fact that its purpose was the production of a baby. Material considerations, too, alien to a lover's mind, found their way to expression. The affect attaching to this simple dream—a feeling of happiness—indicated that powerful emotional complexes had found satisfaction in it.'

Ferenczi (1917)[1] has justly pointed out that the meaning of symbols and the significance of dreams can be arrived at with particular ease from the dreams of precisely those people who are uninitiated into psycho-analysis.

At this point I shall interpose a dream dreamt by a contemporary historical figure. I am doing so because in it an object that would in any case appropriately represent a male organ has a further attribute which established it in the clearest fashion as a phallic symbol. The fact of a riding whip growing to an endless length could scarcely be taken to mean any-

---

[1] [This paragraph was added in 1919.]

thing but an erection. Apart from this, too, the dream is an excellent instance of the way in which thoughts of a serious kind, far removed from
anything sexual, can come to be represented by infantile sexual material.

XI

A DREAM OF BISMARCK'S [1919][1]

In his *Gedanken und Erinnerungen* [1898, **2**, 194; English translation
by A. J. Butler, *Bismarck, the Man and the Statesman*, 1898, **2**, 209 f.] Bismarck quotes a letter written by him to the Emperor William I on December 18th, 1881, in the course of which the following passage occurs:
"Your Majesty's communication encourages me to relate a dream which
I had in the Spring of 1863, in the hardest days of the Conflict, from
which no human eye could see any possible way out. I dreamt (as I related the first thing next morning to my wife and other witnesses) that I
was riding on a narrow Alpine path, precipice on the right, rocks on the
left. The path grew narrower, so that the horse refused to proceed, and it
was impossible to turn round or dismount, owing to lack of space. Then,
with my whip in my left hand, I struck the smooth rock and called on
God. The whip grew to an endless length, the rocky wall dropped like a
piece of stage scenery and opened out a broad path, with a view over hills
and forests, like a landscape in Bohemia; there were Prussian troops with
banners, and even in my dream the thought came to me at once that I
must report it to your Majesty. This dream was fulfilled, and I woke up
rejoiced and strengthened. . . .'"

'The action of this dream falls into two sections. In the first part the
dreamer found himself in an *impasse* from which he was miraculously rescued in the second part. The difficult situation in which the horse and its
rider were placed is an easily recognizable dream-picture of the statesman's
critical position, which he may have felt with particular bitterness as he
thought over the problems of his policy on the evening before the dream.
In the passage quoted above Bismarck himself uses the same simile [of
there being no possible "way out"] in describing the hopelessness of his
position at the time. The meaning of the dream-picture must therefore

---

[1] From a paper by Hanns Sachs [1913.]

have been quite obvious to him. We are at the same time presented with a fine example of Silberer's "functional phenomenon" [cf. pp. 507 ff.]. The process taking place in the dreamer's mind—each of the solutions attempted by his thoughts being met in turn by insuperable obstacles, while nevertheless he could not and might not tear himself free from the consideration of those problems—were most appropriately depicted by the rider who could neither advance nor retreat. His pride, which forbade his thinking of surrendering or resigning, was expressed in the dream by the words "it was impossible to turn round or dismount." In his quality of a man of action who exerted himself unceasingly and toiled for the good of others, Bismarck must have found it easy to liken himself to a horse; and in fact he did so on many occasions, for instance, in his well-known saying: "A good horse dies in harness." In this sense the words "the horse refused to proceed" meant nothing more nor less than that the over-tired statesman felt a need to turn away from the cares of the immediate present, or, to put it another way, that he was in the act of freeing himself from the bonds of the reality principle by sleeping and dreaming. The wish-fulfilment which became so prominent in the second part of the dream, was already hinted at in the words "Alpine path." No doubt Bismarck already knew at that time that he was going to spend his next vacation in the Alps—at Gastein; thus the dream, by conveying him thither, set him free at one blow from all the burdens of State business.

'In the second part of the dream, the dreamer's wishes were represented as fulfilled in two ways: undisguisedly and obviously, and, in addition, symbolically. Their fulfilment was represented symbolically by the disappearance of the obstructive rock and the appearance in its place of a broad path—the "way out," which he was in search of, in its most convenient form; and, it was represented undisguisedly in the picture of the advancing Prussian troops. In order to explain this prophetic vision there is no need whatever for constructing mystical hypotheses; Freud's theory of wish-fulfilment fully suffices. Already at the time of this dream Bismarck desired a victorious war against Austria as the best escape from Prussia's internal conflicts. Thus the dream was representing this wish as fulfilled, just as is postulated by Freud, when the dreamer saw the Prussian troops with their banners in Bohemia, that is, in enemy country. The only peculiarity of the case was that the dreamer with whom we are here concerned was not content with the fulfilment of his wish in a dream but knew how to achieve it in *reality*. One feature which cannot fail to strike anyone familiar with the psycho-analytic technique of interpretation is the riding whip—which grew to an "endless length." Whips, sticks, lances and similar objects are familiar to us as phallic symbols; but when a whip further possesses the most striking characteristic of a phallus, its extensibility, scarcely a doubt can remain. The exaggeration of the phenomenon, its growing to an "endless length," seems to hint at a hypercathexis[1] from infantile sources. The fact that the dreamer took the whip in his hand was a clear allusion to masturbation, though the reference was not, of course, to the dreamer's contemporary circumstances but to childish desires in the remote past. The interpretation discovered by Dr. Stekel [1909, 466 ff.] that in dreams "left" stands for what is wrong, forbidden and sinful is much to the point here, for it might very well be applied to masturbation carried out in childhood in the face of prohibition. Between this deepest infantile stratum and the most superficial one, which was concerned with the statesman's immediate plans, it is possible to detect an intermediate layer which was related to both the others. The whole episode of a miraculous liberation from need by striking a rock and at the same time calling on God as a helper bears a remarkable resemblance to the Biblical scene in which Moses struck water from a rock for the thirsting Children of Israel. We may unhesitatingly assume that this passage was familiar in all its details to Bismarck, who came of a Bible-loving Protestant family. It would not be unlikely that in this time of conflict Bismarck should compare himself with Moses, the leader, whom the people he sought to free rewarded with rebellion, hatred and ingratitude. Here, then, we should have the connection with the dreamer's contemporary wishes. But on the other hand the Bible passage contains some details which apply well to a masturbation phantasy. Moses seized the rod in the face of God's command and the Lord punished him for this transgression by telling him that he must die without entering the Promised Land. The prohibited seizing of the rod (in the dream an unmistakably phallic one), the production of fluid from its blow, the threat of death—in these we find all the principal factors of infantile masturbation united. We may observe with interest the process of revision which has welded together these two heterogeneous pictures (originating, the one from the mind of a statesman of genius, and the other

---

[1] [Sachs seems to be using the word simply to mean an 'additional cathexis' and not in the special sense in which Freud uses it below on pp. 590 f., 599, and 611.]

from the impulses of the primitive mind of a child) and which has by that means succeeded in eliminating all the distressing factors. The fact that seizing the rod was a forbidden and rebellious act was no longer indicated except symbolically by the "left" hand which performed it. On the other hand, God was called on in the manifest content of the dream as though to deny as ostentatiously as possible any thought of a prohibition or secret. Of the two prophecies made by God to Moses—that he should see the Promised Land but that he should not enter it—the first is clearly represented as fulfilled ("the view over hills and forests"), while the second, highly distressing one was not mentioned at all. The water was probably sacrificed to the requirements of secondary revision [cf. pp. 493 ff.], which successfully endeavoured to make this scene and the former one into a single unity; instead of water, the rock itself fell.

'We should expect that at the end of an infantile masturbation phantasy, which included the theme of prohibition, the child would wish that the people in authority in his environment should learn nothing of what had happened. In the dream this wish was represented by its opposite, a wish to report to the King immediately what had happened. But this reversal fitted in excellently and quite unobtrusively into the phantasy of victory contained in the superficial layer of dream-thoughts and in a portion of the manifest content of the dream. A dream such as this of victory and conquest is often a cover for a wish to succeed in an *erotic* conquest; certain features of the dream, such as, for instance, that an obstacle was set in the way of the dreamer's advance but that after he had made use of the extensible whip a broad path opened out, might point in that direction, but they afford an insufficient basis for inferring that a definite trend of thoughts and wishes of that kind ran through the dream. We have here a perfect example of completely successful dream-distortion. Whatever was obnoxious in it was worked over so that it never emerged through the surface layer that was spread over it as a protective covering. In consequence of this it was possible to avoid any release of anxiety. The dream was an ideal case of a wish successfully fulfilled without infringing the censorship; so that we may well believe that the dreamer awoke from it "rejoiced and strengthened."'

As a last example, here is

XII

A Chemist's Dream [1909]

This was dreamt by a young man who was endeavouring to give up his habit of masturbating in favour of sexual relations with women. Preamble.—On the day before he had the dream he had been instructing a student on the subject of Grignard's reaction, in which magnesium is dissolved in absolutely pure ether through the catalytic action of iodine. Two days earlier, when the same reaction was being carried out, an explosion had occurred which had burnt the hand of one of the workers.

Dream.—(I) *He was supposed to be making phenyl-magnesium-bromide. He saw the apparatus with particular distinctness, but had substituted himself for the magnesium. He now found himself in a singularly unstable state. He kept on saying to himself: 'This is all right, things are working, my feet are beginning to dissolve already, my knees are getting soft.' Then he put out his hands and felt his feet. Meanwhile (how, he could not tell) he pulled his legs out of the vessel and said to himself once more: 'This can't be right. Yes it is, though.' At this point he partly woke up and went through the dream to himself, so as to be able to report it to me. He was positively frightened of the solution[1] of the dream. He felt very much excited during this period of semi-sleep and kept repeating: 'Phenyl, phenyl.'*

(II) He was at ——ing with his whole family and was due to be at the Schottentor[2] at half-past eleven to meet a particular lady. But he only woke at half-past eleven, and said to himself: 'It's too late. You can't get there before half-past twelve.' The next moment he saw the whole family sitting round the table; he saw his mother particularly clearly and the maidservant carrying the soup-tureen. So he thought: 'Well, as we've started dinner, it's too late for me to go out.'

Analysis.—He had no doubt that even the first part of the dream had some connection with the lady whom he was to meet. (He had had the dream during the night before the expected *rendez-vous*.) He thought the student to whom he had given the instructions a particularly unpleasant

---

[1] [German '*Auflösung*'; also the word used above for 'dissolving.']
[2] ['——ing,' was presumably a suburb of Vienna (see p. 315 f.); the Schottentor is near the middle of the town.]

person. He had said to him: 'That's not right,' because the magnesium showed no signs of being affected. And the student had replied, as though he were quite unconcerned: 'No, nor it is.' The student must have stood for himself (the patient), who was just as indifferent about the analysis as the student was about the synthesis. The 'he' in the dream who carried out the operation stood for me. How unpleasant I must think him for being so indifferent about the result!

On the other hand, he (the patient) was the material which was being used for the analysis (or synthesis). What was in question was the success of the treatment. The reference to his legs in the dream reminded him of an experience of the previous evening. He had been having a dancing-lesson and had met a lady of whom he had been eager to make a conquest. He clasped her to himself so tightly that on one occasion she gave a scream. As he relaxed his pressure against her legs, he felt her strong responsive pressure against the lower part of his thighs as far down as his knees—the point mentioned in his dream. So that in this connection it was the woman who was the magnesium in the retort—things were working at last. He was feminine in relation to me, just as he was masculine in relation to the woman. If it was working with the lady it was working with him in the treatment. His feeling himself and the sensations in his knees pointed to masturbation and fitted in with his fatigue on the previous day.—His appointment with the lady had in fact been for half-past eleven. His wish to miss it by oversleeping and to stay with his sexual objects at home (that is, to keep to masturbation) corresponded to his resistance.

In connection with his repeating the word 'phenyl,' he told me that he had always been very fond of all these radicals ending in '-yl,' because they were so easy to use: benzyl, acetyl, etc. This explained nothing. But when I suggested 'Schlemihl' to him as another radical in the series,[1] he laughed heartily and told me that in the course of the summer he had read a book by Marcel Prévost in which there was a chapter on 'Les exclus de l'amour' which in fact included some remarks upon 'les Schlémiliés.' When he read them he had said to himself: 'This is just what I'm like.'—If he had missed the appointment it would have been another example of his 'Schlemihlness.'

It would seem that the occurrence of sexual symbolism in dreams has already been experimentally confirmed by some work carried out by

---

[1] ['Schlemihl,' which rhymes with the words ending in '-yl,' is a word of Hebrew origin commonly used in German to mean an unlucky, incompetent person.]

K. Schrötter, on lines proposed by H. Swoboda. Subjects under deep hypnosis were given suggestions by Schrötter, and these led to the production of dreams a large part of whose content was determined by the suggestions. If he gave a suggestion that the subject should dream of normal or abnormal sexual intercourse, the dream, in obeying the suggestion, would make use of symbols familiar to us from psycho-analysis in place of the sexual material. For instance, when a suggestion was made to a female subject that she should dream of having homosexual intercourse with a friend, the friend appeared in the dream carrying a shabby hand-bag with a label stuck on it bearing the words 'Ladies only.' The woman who dreamt this was said never to have had any knowledge of symbolism in dreams or of their interpretation. Difficulties are, however, thrown in the way of our forming an opinion of the value of these interesting experiments by the unfortunate circumstance that Dr. Schrötter committed suicide soon after making them. The only record of them is to be found in a preliminary communication published in the *Zentralblatt für Psychoanalyse* (Schrötter, 1912). [1914.]

Similar findings were published by Roffenstein in 1923. Some experiments made by Betlheim and Hartmann (1924) were of particular interest, since they made no use of hypnosis. These experimenters related anecdotes of a coarsely sexual character to patients suffering from Korsakoff's syndrome and observed the distortions which occurred when the anecdotes were reproduced by the patients in these confusional states. They found that the symbols familiar to us from the interpretation of dreams made their appearance (e.g. going upstairs, stabbing and shooting as symbols of copulation, and knives and cigarettes as symbols of the penis). The authors attached special importance to the appearance of the symbol of a staircase, for, as they justly observed, 'no conscious desire to distort could have arrived at a symbol of such a kind.' [1925.]

It is only now, after we have properly assessed the importance of symbolism in dreams that it becomes possible for us to take up the theme of typical dreams, which was broken off on p. 293 above. [1914.] I think we are justified in dividing such dreams roughly into two classes: those which really always have the same meaning, and those which, in spite of having the same or a similar content, must nevertheless be interpreted in the greatest variety of ways. Among typical dreams of the first class I have already [pp. 291 ff.] dealt in some detail with examination dreams. [1909.]

Dreams of missing a train deserve to be put alongside examination dreams on account of the similarity of their affect, and their explanation shows that we shall be right in doing so. They are dreams of consolation for another kind of anxiety felt in sleep—the fear of dying. 'Departing' on a journey is one of the commonest and best authenticated symbols of death. These dreams say in a consoling way: 'Don't worry, you won't die (depart),' just as examination dreams say soothingly: 'Don't be afraid, no harm will come to you this time either.' The difficulty of understanding both these kinds of dreams is due to the fact that the feeling of anxiety is attached precisely to the expression of consolation. [1911.][1]

The meaning of dreams 'with a dental stimulus' [cf. p. 247],[2] which I often had to analyse in patients, escaped me for a long time because, to my surprise, there were invariably too strong resistances against their interpretation. Overwhelming evidence left me at last in no doubt that in males the motive force of these dreams was derived from nothing other than the masturbatory desires of the pubertal period. I will analyse two dreams of this kind, one of which is also a 'flying dream'. They were both dreamt by the same person, a young man with strong homosexual leanings, which were, however, inhibited in real life.

He was attending a performance of 'Fidelio' and was sitting in the stalls at the Opera beside L., a man who was congenial to him and with whom he would have liked to make friends. Suddenly he flew through the air right across the stalls, put his hand in his mouth and pulled out two of his teeth.

He himself said of the flight that it was as though he was being 'thrown' into the air. Since it was a performance of *Fidelio*, the words:

Wer ein holdes Weib errungen . . .

might have seemed appropriate. But the gaining of even the loveliest woman was not among the dreamer's wishes. Two other lines were more to the point:

---

[1] [In the 1911 edition only, the following sentence appeared at this point: 'Death symbols are dealt with at length in the recently published volume by Stekel (1911).']

[2] [This and the following six paragraphs date from 1909.]

> Wem der grosse Wurf gelungen,
> Eines Freundes Freund zu sein . . .[1]

The dream in fact contained this 'great throw,' which, however, was not only a wish-fulfilment. It also concealed the painful reflection that the dreamer had often been unlucky in his attempts at friendship, and had been 'thrown out.' It concealed, too, his fear that this misfortune might be repeated in relation to the young man by whose side he was enjoying the performance of *Fidelio*. And now followed what the fastidious dreamer regarded as a shameful confession: that once, after being rejected by one of his friends, he had masturbated twice in succession in the state of sensual excitement provoked by his desire.

Here is the second dream: *He was being treated by two University professors of his acquaintance instead of by me. One of them was doing something to his penis. He was afraid of an operation. The other was pushing against his mouth with an iron rod; so that he lost one or two of his teeth. He was tied up with four silk cloths.*

It can scarcely be doubted that his dream had a sexual meaning. The silk cloths identified him with a homosexual whom he knew. The dreamer had never carried out coitus and had never aimed at having sexual intercourse with men in real life; and he pictured sexual intercourse on the model of the pubertal masturbation with which he had once been familiar.

The many modifications of the typical dream with a dental stimulus (dreams, for instance, of a tooth being pulled out by someone else, etc.) are, I think, to be explained in the same way.[2] It may, however, puzzle us

---

[1]   [Wem der grosse Wurf gelungen,
       Eines Freundes Freund zu sein,
       Wer ein holdes Weib errungen. . .

'He who has won the *great throw* of becoming the friend of a friend, he who has gained a lovely woman . . . !' These are the opening lines of the second stanza of Schiller's *Hymn to Joy*, which was set to music by Beethoven in his Choral Symphony. But the third of these lines (the one first quoted above by Freud) is in fact also the opening line of the last section of the final Chorus in Beethoven's opera *Fidelio*—his librettist having apparently plagiarized Schiller.]

[2] [*Footnote added* 1914:] A tooth being pulled out by someone else in a dream is as a rule to be interpreted as castration (like having one's hair cut by a barber, according

to discover how 'dental stimuli' have come to have this meaning. But I should like to draw attention to the frequency with which sexual repression makes use of transpositions from a lower to an upper part of the body.[1] Thanks to them it becomes possible in hysteria for all kinds of sensations and intentions to be put into effect, if not where they properly belong—in relation to the genitals, at least in relation to other, unobjectionable parts of the body. One instance of a transposition of this kind is the replacement of the genitals by the face in the symbolism of unconscious thinking. Linguistic usage follows the same line in recognizing the buttocks ['*Hinterbacken*,' literally 'back-cheeks'] as homologous to the cheeks, and by drawing a parallel between the '*labia*' and the lips which frame the aperture of the mouth. Comparisons between nose and penis are common, and the similarity is made more complete by the presence of hair in both places. The one structure which affords no possibility of an analogy is the teeth; and it is precisely this combination of similarity and dissimilarity which makes the teeth so appropriate for representational purposes when pressure is being exercised by sexual repression.

I cannot pretend that the interpretation of dreams with a dental stimulus as dreams of masturbation—an interpretation whose correctness seems to me beyond doubt—has been entirely cleared up.[2] I have given what explanation I can and must leave what remains unsolved. But I may draw attention to another parallel to be found in linguistic usage. In our part of the world the act of masturbation is vulgarly described as '*sich einen ausreissen*' or '*sich einen herunterreissen*' [literally, 'pulling one out' or 'pulling one down'].[3] I know nothing of the source of this terminology or of the imagery on which it is based; but 'a tooth' would fit very well into the first of the two phrases.

---

to Stekel). A distinction must in general be made between dreams with a dental stimulus and dentist dreams, such as those recorded by Coriat (1913).

[1] [Instances of this will be found in the case history of 'Dora' (Freud, 1905*e*). The comparison which follows had been drawn by Freud in a letter to Fliess of January 16, 1899 (Freud, 1950*a*, Letter 102).]

[2] [*Footnote added* 1909:] A communication by C. G. Jung informs us that dreams with a dental stimulus occurring in women have the meaning of birth dreams.— [*Added* 1919:] Ernest Jones [1914*b*] has brought forward clear confirmation of this. The element in common between this interpretation and the one put forward above lies in the fact that in both cases (castration and birth) what is in question is the separation of a part of the body from the whole.

[3] [*Footnote added* 1911:] Cf. the 'biographical' dream on p. 362, *n*. 2.

According to popular belief dreams of teeth being pulled out are to be interpreted as meaning the death of a relative, but psycho-analysis can at most confirm this interpretation only in the joking sense I have alluded to above. In this connection, however, I will quote a dream with a dental stimulus that has been put at my disposal by Otto Rank.[1]

'A colleague of mine, who has for some time been taking a lively interest in the problems of dream-interpretation, has sent me the following contribution to the subject of dreams with a dental stimulus.

'"A short time ago I had a dream that *I was at the dentist's and he was drilling a back tooth in my lower jaw. He worked on it so long that the tooth became useless. He then seized it with a forceps and pulled it out with an effortless ease that excited my astonishment. He told me not to bother about it, for it was not the tooth that he was really treating, and put it on the table, where the tooth (as it now seemed to me, an upper incisor) fell apart into several layers. I got up from the dentist's chair, went closer to it with a feeling of curiosity, and raised a medical question which interested me. The dentist explained to me, while he separated out the various portions of the strikingly white tooth and crushed them up (pulverized them) with an instrument, that it was connected with puberty and that it was only before puberty that teeth came out so easily, and that in the case of women the decisive factor was the birth of a child.*

'"I then became aware (while I was half asleep, I believe) that the dream had been accompanied by an emission, which I could not attach with certainty, however, to any particular part of the dream; I was most inclined to think that it had already occurred while the tooth was being pulled out.

'"I then went on to dream of an occurrence which I can no longer recall, but which ended *with my leaving my hat and coat somewhere (possibly in the dentist's cloakroom) in the hope that someone would bring them after me, and with my hurrying off, dressed only in my overcoat, to catch a train which was starting. I succeeded at the last moment in jumping on to the hindmost carriage where someone was already standing. I was not able, though, to make my way into the inside of the carriage, but was obliged to travel in an uncomfortable situation from which I tried, successfully in the end, to escape.*

---

[1] [This paragraph and the quotation from Rank which follows were first included in 1911. The quotation is from Rank 1911c. Cf. the same dreamer's staircase dream on pp. 380 f.]

We entered a big tunnel and two trains, going in the opposite direction to us, passed through our train as if it were the tunnel. I was looking into a carriage window as though I were outside.

"'The following experiences and thoughts from the previous day provide material for an interpretation of the dream:

"'(I.) I had in fact been having dental treatment recently, and at the time of the dream I was having continual pain in the tooth in the lower jaw which was being drilled in the dream and at which the dentist had, again in reality, worked longer than I liked. On the morning of the dream-day I had once more been to the dentist on account of the pain; and he had suggested to me that I should have another tooth pulled out in the same jaw as the one he had been treating, saying that the pain probably came from this other one. This was a 'wisdom tooth' which I was cutting just then. I had raised a question touching his medical conscience in that connection.

"'(II.) On the afternoon of the same day, I had been obliged to apologize to a lady for the bad temper I was in owing to my toothache; whereupon she had told me she was afraid of having a root pulled out, the crown of which had crumbled away almost entirely. She thought that pulling out 'eye-teeth' was especially painful and dangerous, although on the other hand one of her acquaintances had told her that it was easier to pull out teeth in the upper jaw, which was where hers was. This acquaintance had also told her that he had once had the wrong tooth pulled out under an anaesthetic, and this had increased her dread of the necessary operation. She had then asked me whether 'eye-teeth' were molars or canines, and what was known about them. I pointed out to her on the one hand the superstitious element in all these opinions, though at the same time I emphasized the nucleus of truth in certain popular views. She was then able to repeat to me what she believed was a very old and widespread popular belief—that if a pregnant woman had toothache she would have a boy.

"'(III.) This saying interested me in connection with what Freud says in his *Interpretation of Dreams* on the typical meaning of dreams with a dental stimulus as substitutes for masturbation, since in the popular saying (quoted by the lady) a tooth and male genitals (or a boy) were also brought into relation with each other. On the evening of the same day, therefore, I read through the relevant passage in the *Interpretation of Dreams* and found there amongst other things the following statements whose influence upon my dream may be observed just as clearly as that of the other two experiences I have mentioned. Freud writes of dreams with a dental stimulus that 'in males the motive force of these dreams was derived from nothing other than the masturbatory desires of the pubertal period' [p. 396]. And further: 'The many modifications of the typical dream with a dental stimulus (dreams, for instance, of a tooth being pulled out by someone else, etc.) are, I think, to be explained in the same way. It may, however, puzzle us to discover how "dental stimuli" should have come to have this meaning. But I should like to draw attention to the frequency with which sexual repression makes use of transpositions from a lower to an upper part of the body.' (In the present dream from the lower jaw to the upper jaw.) 'Thanks to them it becomes possible in hysteria for all kinds of sensations and intentions to be put into effect, if not where they properly belong—in relation to the genitals, at least in re lation to other, unobjectionable parts of the body' [p. 398]. And again: 'But I may draw attention to another parallel to be found in linguistic us age. In our part of the world the act of masturbation is vulgarly described as "sich einen ausreissen" or "sich einen herunterreissen"' [p. 398]. I was al ready familiar with this expression in my early youth as a description of masturbation, and no experienced dream-interpreter will have any diffi culty in finding his way from here to the infantile material underlying the dream. I will only add that the ease with which the tooth in the dream, which after its extraction turned into an upper incisor, came out, re minded me of an occasion in my childhood on which I myself pulled out a loose upper front tooth easily and without pain. This event, which I can still remember clearly today in all its details, occurred at the same early period to which my first conscious attempts at masturbation go back. (This was a screen memory.)

'"Freud's reference to a statement by C. G. Jung to the effect that 'dreams with a dental stimulus occurring in women have the meaning of birth dreams' [p. 398 footnote], as well as the popular belief in the signifi cance of toothache in pregnant women, accounted for the contrast drawn in the dream between the decisive factor in the case of females and of males (puberty). In this connection I recall an earlier dream of mine which I had soon after a visit to the dentist and in which I dreamt that the gold crowns which had just been fixed fell out; this annoyed me very much in the dream on account of the considerable expense in which I had been in volved and which I had not yet quite got over at the time. This other dream now became intelligible to me (in view of a certain experience of mine) as a recognition of the material advantages of masturbation over object-love: the latter, from an economic point of view, was in every respect less desirable (cf. the gold crowns)[1]; and I believe that the lady's remark about the significance of toothache in pregnant women had reawakened these trains of thought in me."

'So much for the interpretation put forward by my colleague, which is most enlightening and to which, I think, no objections can be raised. I have nothing to add to it, except, perhaps, a hint at the probable meaning of the second part of the dream. This seems to have represented the dreamer's transition from masturbation to sexual intercourse, which was apparently accomplished with great difficulty—(cf. the tunnel through which the trains went in and out in various directions) as well as the danger of the latter (cf. pregnancy and the overcoat [see p. 208 f.]). The dreamer made use for this purpose of the verbal bridges "*Zahn-ziehen (Zug)*" and "*Zahn-reissen (Reisen)*."[2]

'On the other hand, theoretically, the case seems to me interesting in two respects. In the first place, it brings evidence in favour of Freud's discovery that ejaculation in a dream accompanies the act of pulling out a tooth. In whatever form the emission may appear, we are obliged to regard it as a masturbatory satisfaction brought about without the assistance of any mechanical stimulation. Moreover, in this case, the satisfaction accompanying the emission was not, as it usually is, directed to an object, even if only to an imaginary one, but had no object, if one may say so; it was completely auto-erotic, or at the most showed a slight trace of homosexuality (in reference to the dentist).

'The second point which seems to me to deserve emphasis is the following. It may plausibly be objected that there is no need at all to regard the present case as confirming Freud's view, since the events of the previous day would be sufficient in themselves to make the content of the dream intelligible. The dreamer's visit to the dentist, his conversation with the lady and his reading of the *Interpretation of Dreams* would quite sufficiently explain how he came to produce this dream, especially as his sleep was disturbed by toothache; they would even explain, if need be, how the dream served to dispose of the pain which was disturbing his sleep—by means of the idea of getting rid of the painful tooth and by simultaneously

---

[1] [The crown (*Krone*) was at this time the Austrian monetary unit.]

[2] ['*Zahn-ziehen*' = 'to pull out a tooth'; '*Zug*' (from the same root as '*ziehen*') = 'train' or 'pull.' '*Zahn-reissen*' = 'to pull out a tooth'; '*Reisen*' (pronounced not much unlike '*reissen*') = 'to travel.']

drowning with libido the painful sensation which the dreamer feared. But even if we make the greatest possible allowance for all this, it cannot be seriously maintained that the mere reading of Freud's explanations could have established in the dreamer the connection between pulling out a tooth and the act of masturbation, or could even have put that connection into operation, unless it had been laid down long since, as the dreamer himself admits it was (in the phrase "*sich einen ausreissen*"). This connection may have been revived not only by his conversation with the lady but by a circumstance which he reported subsequently. For in reading the *Interpretation of Dreams* he had been unwilling, for comprehensible reasons, to believe in this typical meaning of dreams with a dental stimulus, and had felt a desire to know whether that meaning applied to all dreams of that sort. The present dream confirmed the fact that this was so, at least as far as he was concerned, and thus showed him why it was that he had been obliged to feel doubts on the subject. In this respect too, therefore, the dream was the fulfilment of a wish—namely, the wish to convince himself of the range of application and the validity of this view of Freud's.'

The second group of typical dreams included those in which the dreamer flies or floats in the air, falls, swims, etc. What is the meaning of such dreams? It is impossible to give a general reply. As we shall hear, they mean something different in every instance; it is only the raw material of sensations contained in them which is always derived from the same source. [1909.]

The information provided by psycho-analyses forces me to conclude that these dreams, too, reproduce impressions of childhood; they relate, that is, to games involving movement, which are extraordinarily attractive to children. There cannot be a single uncle who has not shown a child how to fly by rushing across the room with him in his outstretched arms, or who has not played at letting him fall by riding him on his knee and then suddenly stretching out his leg, or by holding him up high and then suddenly pretending to drop him. Children are delighted by such experiences and never tire of asking to have them repeated, especially if there is something about them that causes a little fright or giddiness. In after years they repeat these experiences in dreams; but in the dreams they leave out the hands which held them up, so that they float or fall unsupported. The delight taken by young children in games of this kind (as well as in swings and see-saws) is well known; when they come to see acrobatic feats in a circus their memory of such games is revived. Hysterical attacks in boys sometimes consist merely in reproductions of feats of this kind, carried out with great skill. It not uncommonly happens that these games of movement, though innocent in themselves, give rise to sexual feelings. Childish romping ['*Hetzen*'], if I may use a word which commonly describes all such activities, is what is being repeated in dreams of flying, falling, giddiness and so on; while the pleasurable feelings attached to these experiences are transformed into anxiety. But, often enough, as every mother knows, romping among children actually ends in squabbling and tears. [1900.]

Thus I have good grounds for rejecting the theory that what provokes dreams of flying and falling is the state of our tactile feelings during sleep or sensations of the movement of our lungs, and so on. In my view these sensations are themselves reproduced as part of the memory to which the dream goes back: that is to say, they are part of the *content* of the dream and not its source. [1900.][1]

This material, then, consisting of sensations of movement of similar kinds and derived from the same source, is used to represent dreamthoughts of every possible sort. Dreams of flying or floating in the air (as a rule, pleasurably toned) require the most various interpretations; with some people these interpretations have to be of an individual character, whereas with others they may even be of a typical kind. One of my women patients used very often to dream that she was floating at a certain height over the street without touching the ground. She was very short, and she dreaded the contamination involved in contact with other people. Her floating dream fulfilled her two wishes, by raising her feet from the ground and lifting her head into a higher stratum of air. In other women I have found that flying dreams expressed a desire 'to be like a bird'; while other dreamers became angels during the night because they had not been called angels during the day. The close connection of flying with the idea of birds explains how it is that in men flying dreams usually have a grossly sensual meaning;[2] and we shall not be surprised when we hear that some dreamer or other is very proud of his powers of flight. [1909.]

---

[1] [*Footnote added* 1930:] These remarks on dreams of movement are repeated here, since the present context requires them. See above, pp. 289 f. [where some additional footnotes will be found.]

[2] [See p. 581, *n.* 4.]

Dr. Paul Federn (of Vienna [and later of New York]) has put forward[1] the attractive theory that a good number of these flying dreams are dreams of erection; for the remarkable phenomenon of erection, around which the human imagination has constantly played, cannot fail to be impressive, involving as it does an apparent suspension of the laws of gravity. (Cf. in this connection the winged phalli of the ancients.) [1911.]

It is a remarkable fact that Mourly Vold, a sober-minded investigator of dreams and one who is disinclined to interpretation of any kind, also supports the erotic interpretation of flying or floating dreams (Vold, 1910–12, **2**, 791). He speaks of the erotic factor as 'the most powerful motive for floating dreams,' draws attention to the intense feeling of vibration in the body that accompanies such dreams and points to the frequency with which they are connected with erections or emissions. [1914.]

Dreams of falling, on the other hand, are more often characterized by anxiety. Their interpretation offers no difficulty in the case of women, who almost always accept the symbolic use of falling as a way of describing a surrender to an erotic temptation. Nor have we yet exhausted the infantile sources of dreams of falling. Almost every child has fallen down at one time or other and afterwards been picked up and petted; or if he has fallen out of his cot at night, has been taken into bed with his mother or nurse. [1909.]

People who have frequent dreams of swimming and who feel great joy in cleaving their way through the waves, and so on, have as a rule been bed-wetters and are repeating in their dreams a pleasure which they have long learnt to forgo. We shall learn presently [pp. 410 ff.] from more than one example what it is that dreams of swimming are most easily used to represent. [1909.]

The interpretation of dreams of fire justifies the nursery law which forbids a child to 'play with fire'—so that he shall not wet his bed at night. For in their case, too, there is an underlying recollection of the enuresis of childhood. In my 'Fragment of an Analysis of a Case of Hysteria' [1905e, Part II, Dora's first dream], I have given a complete analysis and synthesis of a fire-dream of this kind in connection with the dreamer's

---

[1] [At a meeting of the Vienna Psycho-Analytical Society. See his subsequent paper on the subject (Federn, 1914, 126).]

case history, and I have shown what impulses of adult years this infantile material can be used to represent. [1911.]

It would be possible to mention a whole number of other 'typical' dreams if we take the term to mean that the same manifest dream-content is frequently to be found in the dreams of different dreamers. For instance we might mention dreams of passing through narrow streets or of walking through whole suites of rooms [cf. p. 235], and dreams of burglars—against whom, incidentally, nervous people take precautions *before* they go to sleep [cf. p. 413 f.]. Dreams of being pursued by wild animals (or by bulls or horses) [cf. p. 419] or of being threatened with knives, daggers or lances—these last two classes being characteristic of the manifest content of the dreams of people who suffer from anxiety—and many more. An investigation specially devoted to this material would thoroughly repay the labour involved. But instead of this I have two[1] observations to make, though these do not apply exclusively to typical dreams. [1909.]

The more one is concerned with the solution of dreams, the more one is driven to recognize that the majority of the dreams of adults deal with sexual material and give expression to erotic wishes. A judgement on this point can be formed only by those who really analyse dreams, that is to say, who make their way through their manifest content to the latent dream-thoughts, and never by those who are satisfied with making a note of the manifest content alone (like Näcke, for instance, in his writings on sexual dreams). Let me say at once that this fact is not in the least surprising but is in complete harmony with the principles of my explanation of dreams. No other instinct has been subjected since childhood to so much suppres-

---

[1] [This 'two' is a vestige of the 1909 and 1911 editions, in which the whole discussion on 'typical' dreams was contained in Chapter V. The first observation, introduced by a 'I,' began with the paragraph which now follows and continued to the end of the present Section E—to p. 414. The second observation, introduced by a 'II,' immediately followed; it was the passage beginning on p. 364 with the words 'When we have become familiar' and continuing to the words 'another example of his "Schlemihlness"' on p. 394, with which, in those two editions, Chapter V ended. In later editions, of course, both these passages have become very greatly enlarged by the accretion of fresh material. In the 1909 edition the two observations together only occupied about five pages, as compared with forty-two in 1930.]

sion as the sexual instinct with its numerous components (cf. my *Three Essays on the Theory of Sexuality*, 1905*d*); from no other instinct are so many and such powerful unconscious wishes left over, ready to produce dreams in a state of sleep. In interpreting dreams we should never forget the significance of sexual complexes, though we should also, of course, avoid the exaggeration of attributing exclusive importance to them. [1909.]

We can assert of many dreams, if they are carefully interpreted, that they are bisexual, since they unquestionably admit of an 'over-interpretation' in which the dreamer's homosexual impulses are realized—impulses, that is, which are contrary to his normal sexual activities. To maintain, however, as do Stekel (1911, [71]) and Adler (1910, etc.), that *all* dreams are to be interpreted bisexually appears to me to be a generalization which is equally undemonstrable and unplausible and which I am not prepared to support. In particular, I cannot dismiss the obvious fact that there are numerous dreams which satisfy needs other than those which are erotic in the widest sense of the word: dreams of hunger and thirst, dreams of convenience, etc. So, too, such statements as that 'the spectre of death is to be found behind every dream' (Stekel [1911, 34]), or that 'every dream shows an advance from the feminine to the masculine line' (Adler [1910]), appear to me to go far beyond anything that can be legitimately maintained in dream-interpretation. [1911.]

The assertion that all dreams require a sexual interpretation, against which critics rage so incessantly, occurs nowhere in my *Interpretation of Dreams*. It is not to be found in any of the numerous editions of this book and is in obvious contradiction to other views expressed in it. [1919.][1]

I have already shown elsewhere [pp. 206 ff.] that strikingly innocent dreams may embody crudely erotic wishes, and I could confirm this by many new instances. But it is also true that many dreams which appear to be *indifferent* and which one would not regard as in any respect peculiar lead back on analysis to wishful impulses which are unmistakably sexual and often of an unexpected sort. Who, for instance, would have suspected the presence of a sexual wish in the following dream before it had been interpreted? The dreamer gave this account of it: *Standing back a little behind two stately palaces was a little house with closed doors. My wife led me along the piece of street up to the little house and pushed the door open; I then slipped quickly and easily into the inside of a court which rose in an*

---

[1] [This point is more fully dealt with on p. 194, footnote.]

incline. Anyone, however, who has had a little experience in translating dreams will at once reflect that penetrating into narrow spaces and opening closed doors are among the commonest sexual symbols, and will easily perceive in this dream a representation of an attempt at *coitus a tergo* (between the two stately buttocks of the female body). The narrow passage rising in an incline stood, of course, for the vagina. The assistance attributed by the dreamer to his wife forces us to conclude that in reality it was only consideration for her that restrained the dreamer from making attempts of this kind. It turned out that on the dream-day a girl had come to live in the dreamer's household who had attracted him and had given him the impression that she would raise no great objections to an approach of that kind. The little house between the two palaces was a reminiscence of the Hradshin [Citadel] in Prague and was a further reference to the same girl, who came from that place. [1909.]

When I insist to one of my patients on the frequency of Oedipus dreams, in which the dreamer has sexual intercourse with his own mother, he often replies: 'I have no recollection of having had any such dream.' Immediately afterwards, however, a memory will emerge of some other inconspicuous and indifferent dream, which the patient has dreamt repeatedly. Analysis then shows that this is in fact a dream with the same content—once more an Oedipus dream. I can say with certainty that *disguised* dreams of sexual intercourse with the dreamer's mother are many times more frequent than straightforward ones. [1909.][1]

---

[1] [*Footnote added* 1911:] I have published elsewhere a typical example of a disguised Oedipus dream of this kind. [Freud 1910*l*; now reprinted at the end of this footnote.] Another example, with a detailed analysis, has been published by Otto Rank (1911*a*).—[*Added* 1914:] For some other disguised Oedipus dreams, in which eye-symbolism is prominent, see Rank (1913). Other papers on eye-dreams and eye-symbolism, by Eder [1913], Ferenczi [1913] and Reitler [1913*a*] will be found in the same place. The blinding in the legend of Oedipus, as well as elsewhere, stands for castration.—[*Added* 1911:] Incidentally, the symbolic interpretation of undisguised Oedipus dreams was not unknown to the ancients. Rank (1910, 534) writes: 'Thus Julius Caesar is reported to have had a dream of sexual intercourse with his mother which was explained by the dream-interpreters as a favourable augury for his taking possession of the earth (Mother Earth). The oracle given to the Tarquins is equally well known, which prophesied that the conquest of Rome would fall to that one of them who should first kiss his mother ("*osculum matri tulerit*"). This was interpreted by Brutus as referring to Mother Earth. ("*Terram osculo contigit, scilicet quod ea communis mater*

In some dreams of landscapes or other localities emphasis is laid in the dream itself on a convinced feeling of having been there once before. (Occurrences of '*déjà vu*' in dreams have a special meaning.[1]) These places are

---

omnium mortalium esset." ["He kissed the earth, saying it was the common mother of all mortals."] Livy, **I**, 56.)'—[*Added* 1914:] Compare in this connection the dream of Hippias reported by Herodotus (VI, 107 [*Trans.* 1922, 259]): 'As for the Persians, they were guided to Marathon by Hippias son of Pisistratus. Hippias in the past night had seen a vision in his sleep wherein he thought that he lay with his own mother; he interpreted this dream to signify that he should return to Athens and recover his power, and so die an old man in his own mother-country.'—[*Added* 1911:] These myths and interpretations reveal a true psychological insight. I have found that people who know that they are preferred or favoured by their mother give evidence in their lives of a peculiar self-reliance and an unshakable optimism which often seem like heroic attributes and bring actual success to their possessors.

[This reprint of the short paper by Freud (1910*l*) which is mentioned at the beginning of the present footnote was added here in 1925:]

'TYPICAL EXAMPLE OF A DISGUISED OEDIPUS DREAM: A man dreamt that *he had a secret liaison with a lady whom someone else wanted to marry. He was worried in case this other man might discover the liaison and the proposed marriage come to nothing. He therefore behaved in a very affectionate way to the man. He embraced him and kissed him.*—There was only one point of contact between the content of this dream and the facts of the dreamer's life. He had a secret *liaison* with a married woman; and an ambiguous remark made by her husband, who was a friend of his, led him to suspect that the husband might have noticed something. But in reality there was something else involved, all mention of which was avoided in the dream but which alone provided a key to its understanding. The husband's life was threatened by an organic illness. His wife was prepared for the possibility of his dying suddenly, and the dreamer was consciously occupied with an intention to marry the young widow after her husband's death. This external situation placed the dreamer in the constellation of the Oedipus dream. His wish was capable of killing the man in order to get the woman as his wife. The dream expressed this wish in a hypocritically distorted form. Instead of her being married already, he made out that someone else wanted to marry her, which corresponded to his own secret intentions; and his hostile wishes towards her husband were concealed behind demonstrations of affection which were derived from his memory of his relations with his own father in childhood.' [Hypocritical dreams are discussed on pp. 169 *n*. and 477 ff.]

[1] [This last sentence was interpolated in 1914. The phenomenon of '*déjà vu*' in general is discussed by Freud in Chapter XII (D) of his *Psychopathology of Everyday Life* (1901*b*) and in another short paper (Freud, 1914*a*). See also below p. 454.]

invariably the genitals of the dreamer's mother; there is indeed no other place about which one can assert with such conviction that one has been there once before. [1909.]

On one occasion only I was perplexed by an obsessional neurotic who told me a dream in which he was visiting a house that he had been in *twice* before. But this particular patient had told me a considerable time before of an episode during his sixth year. On one occasion he had been sharing his mother's bed and misused the opportunity by inserting his finger into her genitals while she was asleep. [1914.]

A large number of dreams,[1] often accompanied by anxiety and having as their content such subjects as passing through narrow spaces or being in water, are based upon phantasies of intra-uterine life, of existence in the womb and of the act of birth. What follows was the dream of a young man who, in his imagination, had taken advantage of an intra-uterine opportunity of watching his parents copulating.

He was in a deep pit with a window in it like the one in the Semmering Tunnel.[2] At first he saw an empty landscape through the window, but then invented a picture to fit the space, which immediately appeared and filled in the gap. The picture represented a field which was being ploughed up deeply by some implement; and the fresh air together with the idea of hard work which accompanied the scene, and the blue-black clods of earth, produced a lovely impression. He then went on further and saw a book upon education open in front of him . . . and was surprised that so much attention was devoted in it to the sexual feelings (of children); and this led him to think of me.

And here is a pretty water dream, dreamt by a woman patient, which served a special purpose in the treatment. *At her summer holiday resort, by the Lake of——, she dived into the dark water just where the pale moon was mirrored in it.*

Dreams like this one are birth dreams. Their interpretation is reached by reversing the event reported in the manifest dream; thus, instead of 'diving into the water' we have 'coming out of the water,' i.e. being born.[3] We can discover the locality from which a child is born by calling to mind

---

[1] [This paragraph and the three following ones date from 1909.]

[2] [A tunnel some 70 miles from Vienna on the main line to the southwest.]

[3] [*Footnote added* 1914:] For the mythological significance of birth from the water see Rank (1909).

the slang use of the word '*lune*' in French [viz. 'bottom']. The pale moon was thus the white bottom which children are quick to guess that they came out of. What was the meaning of the patient's wishing to be born at her summer holiday resort? I asked her and she replied without hesitation: 'Isn't it just as though I had been reborn through the treatment?' Thus the dream was an invitation to me to continue treating her at the holiday resort—that is, to visit her there. Perhaps there was a very timid hint in it, too, of the patient's wish to become a mother herself.[1]

I will quote another birth-dream, together with its interpretation, from a paper by Ernest Jones [1910*b*].[2] '*She stood on the sea-shore watching a small boy, who seemed to be hers, wading into the water. This he did till the water covered him and she could only see his head bobbing up and down near the surface. The scene then changed into the crowded hall of an hotel. Her husband left her, and she "entered into conversation with" a stranger.* The second half of the dream revealed itself in the analysis as representing a flight from her husband and the entering into intimate relations with a third person. . . . The first part of the dream was a fairly evident birth-phantasy. In dreams as in mythology, the delivery of the child *from* the uterine waters is commonly presented by distortion as the entry of the child *into* water; among many others, the births of Adonis, Osiris, Moses and Bacchus are well-known illustrations of this. The bobbing up and down of the head into the water at once recalled to the patient the sensation of quickening she had experienced in her only pregnancy. Thinking of the boy going into the water induced a reverie in which she saw herself taking him out of the water, carrying him to a nursery, washing him and dressing him, and installing him in her household.

'The second half of the dream therefore represented thoughts concerning the elopement, that belonged to the first half of the underlying latent

---

[1] [*Footnote* 1909:] It was not for a long time that I learned to appreciate the importance of phantasies and unconscious thoughts about life in the womb. They contain an explanation of the remarkable dread that many people have of being buried alive; and they also afford the deepest unconscious basis for the belief in survival after death, which merely represents a projection into the future of this uncanny life before birth. *Moreover, the act of birth is the first experience of anxiety, and thus the source and prototype of the affect of anxiety.* [Cf. a much later discussion of this in a passage near the beginning of Chapter VIII of Freud's *Inhibitions, Symptoms and Anxiety* (1926*d*).]

[2] [This paragraph and the following one were added in 1914.]

content; the first half of the dream corresponded with the second half of
the latent content, the birth-phantasy. Besides this inversion in order, further inversions took place in each half of the dream. In the first half the
child *entered* the water, and then his head bobbed; in the underlying
dream-thoughts first the quickening occurred and then the child *left* the
water (a double inversion). In the second half her husband left her; in the
dream-thoughts she left her husband.'

Abraham (1909, 22 ff.) has reported another birth-dream, dreamt by
a young woman who was facing her first confinement. A subterranean
channel led directly into the water from a place in the floor of her room
(genital canal—amniotic fluid). She raised a trap-door in the floor and a
creature dressed in brown fur, very much resembling a seal, promptly appeared. This creature turned out to be the dreamer's younger brother, to
whom she had always been like a mother. [1911.]

Rank [1912a] has shown from a series of dreams that birth-dreams
make use of the same symbolism as dreams with a urinary stimulus. The
erotic stimulus is represented in the latter as a urinary stimulus; and the
stratification of meaning in these dreams corresponds to a change that has
come over the meaning of the symbol since infancy. [1914.]

This is an appropriate point at which to return to a topic that was broken off in an earlier chapter (p. 257):[1] the problem of the part played in the
formation of dreams by organic stimuli which disturb sleep. Dreams which
come about under their influence openly exhibit not only the usual tendency to wish-fulfilment and to serving the end of convenience, but very
often a perfectly transparent symbolism as well; for it not infrequently happens that a stimulus awakens a dreamer *after a vain attempt has been made
to deal with it in a dream under a symbolic disguise.* This applies to dreams
of emission or orgasm as well as to those provoked by a need to micturate
or defaecate. 'The peculiar nature of emission dreams not only puts us in a
position to reveal directly certain sexual symbols which are already known
as being typical, but which have nevertheless been violently disputed; it also
enables us to convince ourselves that some apparently innocent situations
in dreams are no more than a symbolic prelude to crudely sexual scenes.
The latter are as a rule represented undisguisedly in the relatively rare emission dreams, whereas they culminate often enough in anxiety dreams,
which have the same result of awakening the sleeper.' [Rank, ibid., 55.]

---

[1] [This paragraph and the three following ones date from 1919.]

The symbolism of dreams with a urinary stimulus is especially transparent and has been recognized from the earliest times. The view was already expressed by Hippocrates that dreams of fountains and springs indicate a disorder of the bladder (Havelock Ellis [1911, 164]). Scherner [1861, 189] studied the multiplicity of the symbolism of urinary stimuli and asserted that 'any urinary stimulus of considerable strength invariably passes over into stimulation of the sexual regions and symbolic representations of them. . . . Dreams with a urinary stimulus are often at the same time representatives of sexual dreams.' [Ibid., 192.]

Otto Rank, whose discussion in his paper on the stratification of symbols in arousal dreams [Rank, 1912a] I am here following, has made it seem highly probable that a great number of dreams with a urinary stimulus have in fact been caused by a *sexual* stimulus which has made a first attempt to find satisfaction regressively in the infantile form of urethral erotism. [Ibid., 78.] Those cases are particularly instructive in which the urinary stimulus thus set up leads to awakening and emptying the bladder, but in which the dream is nevertheless continued and the need then expressed in undisguisedly erotic imagery.[1]

Dreams with an intestinal stimulus throw light in an analogous fashion on the symbolism involved in them, and at the same time confirm the connection between gold and faeces which is also supported by copious evidence from social anthropology. (See Freud, 1908b; Rank, 1912a; Dattner, 1913; and Reik, 1915.) 'Thus, for instance, a woman who was receiving medical treatment for an intestinal disorder dreamt of someone who was burying a treasure in the neighbourhood of a little wooden hut which looked like a rustic out-door closet. There was a second part to the dream in which she was wiping the behind of her little girl who had dirtied herself.' [Rank, 1912a, 55.]

Rescue dreams are connected with birth dreams. In women's dreams, to rescue, and especially to rescue from the water, has the same significance

---

[1] [*Footnote* 1919:] 'The same symbols which occur in their infantile aspect in bladder dreams, appear with an eminently sexual meaning in their "recent" aspects: Water = urine = semen = amniotic fluid; ship = "pump ship" (micturate) = uterus (box); to get wet = enuresis = copulation = pregnancy; to swim = full bladder = abode of the unborn; rain = micturate = symbol of fertility; travel (starting, getting out) = getting out of bed = sexual intercourse (honeymoon); micturate = emission.' (Rank, 1912a, 95.)

as giving birth; but the meaning is modified if the dreamer is a man.[1] [1911.]

Robbers, burglars and ghosts, of whom some people feel frightened before going to bed, and who sometimes pursue their victims after they are asleep, all originate from one and the same class of infantile reminiscence. They are the nocturnal visitors who rouse children and take them up to prevent their wetting their beds, or who lift the bedclothes to make sure where they have put their hands in their sleep. Analyses of some of these anxiety-dreams have made it possible for me to identify these nocturnal visitors more precisely. In every case the robbers stood for the sleeper's father, whereas the ghosts corresponded to female figures in white nightgowns. [1909.]

(F)

SOME EXAMPLES—CALCULATIONS AND SPEECHES IN DREAMS[2]

Before assigning the fourth of the factors which govern the formation of dreams to its proper place [cf. pp. 493 ff.], I propose to quote a number of examples from my collection. These will serve partly to illustrate the interplay between the three factors already known to us and partly to provide confirmatory evidence for what have hitherto been unsupported assertions or to indicate some conclusions which inevitably follow from them. In giving an account of the dream-work, I have found very great difficulty in backing my findings by examples. Instances in support of particular

---

[1] [*Footnote* 1911:] A dream of this kind has been reported by Pfister (1909). For the symbolic meaning of rescuing see Freud, 1910*d*, and Freud, 1910*h*. [*Added* 1914:] See also Rank (1911*b*) and Reik (1911). [*Added* 1919:] See further, Rank (1914). [A dream of rescue from the water will be found in the second case discussed by Freud in his paper on 'Dreams and Telepathy' (1922*a*).]

[2] [As in the case of Section E, a large part of the first half of the present section was added to the work in its later editions. The date of the first inclusion of each paragraph will accordingly be found attached to it in square brackets. The second half of the section (from p. 423 onwards) dates from the first edition.— Another collection of examples of dream-analyses will be found in the twelfth of Freud's *Introductory Lectures* (1916–17).]

propositions carry conviction only if they are treated in the context of the interpretation of a dream as a whole. If they are torn from their context they lose their virtue; while, on the other hand, a dream-interpretation which is carried even a little way below the surface quickly becomes so voluminous as to make us lose the thread of the train of thought which it was designed to illustrate. This technical difficulty must serve as my excuse if in what follows I string together all sorts of things, whose only common bond is their connection with the contents of the preceding sections of this chapter. [1900.]

I will begin by giving a few instances of peculiar or unusual modes of representation in dreams.

A lady had the following dream: *A servant girl was standing on a ladder as if she were cleaning a window, and had a chimpanzee with her and a gorilla-cat* (the dreamer afterwards corrected this to *an angora cat*). *She hurled the animals at the dreamer; the chimpanzee cuddled up to her, which was very disgusting.*—This dream achieved its purpose by an extremely simple device: it took a figure of speech literally and gave an exact representation of its wording. 'Monkey,' and animals' names in general, are used as invectives; and the situation in the dream meant neither more nor less than 'hurling invectives.' In the course of the present series of dreams we shall come upon a number of other instances of the use of this simple device during the dream-work. [1900.]

Another dream adopted a very similar procedure. *A woman had a child with a remarkably deformed skull. The dreamer had heard that the child had grown like that owing to its position in the uterus. The doctor said that the skull might be given a better shape by compression, but that that would damage the child's brain. She reflected that as he was a boy it would do him less harm.*—This dream contained a plastic representation of the abstract concept of 'impressions on children' which the dreamer had met with in the course of the explanations given her during her treatment. [1900.]

The dream-work adopted a slightly different method in the following instance. The dream referred to an excursion to the Hilmteich[1] near Graz. *The weather outside was fearful. There was a wretched hotel, water was dripping from the walls of the room, the bedclothes were damp.* (The latter part of the dream was reported less directly than I have given it.) The meaning of the dream was 'superfluous.' This abstract idea, which was present in

---

[1] [A stretch of water in the outskirts of the town.]

the dream-thoughts, was in the first instance given a somewhat forced twist and put into some such form as 'overflowing,' 'flowing over' or 'fluid'—after which it was represented in a number of similar pictures: water outside, water on the walls inside, water in the dampness of the bed-clothes—everything flowing or 'overflowing.' [1900.]

We shall not be surprised to find that, for the purpose of representation in dreams, the spelling of words is far less important than their sound, especially when we bear in mind that the same rule holds good in rhyming verse. Rank (1910, 482) has recorded in detail, and analysed very fully, a girl's dream in which the dreamer described how she was walking through the fields and cutting off rich ears ['*Ähren*'] of barley and wheat. A friend of her youth came towards her, but she tried to avoid meeting him. The analysis showed that the dream was concerned with a kiss—an 'honourable kiss' ['*Kuss in Ehren*' pronounced the same as '*Ähren*,' literally, 'kiss in honour']¹. In the dream itself the '*Ähren*,' which had to be cut off, not pulled off, figured as ears of corn, while, condensed with 'Ehren,' they stood for a whole number of other [latent] thoughts. [1911.]

On the other hand, in other cases, the course of linguistic evolution has made things very easy for dreams. For language has a whole number of words at its command which originally had a pictorial and concrete significance, but are used today in a colourless and abstract sense. All that the dream need do is to give these words their former, full meaning or to go back a little way to an earlier phase in their development. A man had a dream, for instance, of his brother being in a *Kasten* ['box']. In the course of interpretation the *Kasten* was replaced by a *Schrank* ['cupboard'—also used abstractly for 'barrier,' 'restriction']. The dream-thought had been to the effect that his brother ought to restrict himself ['*sich einschränken*']—instead of the dreamer doing so.² [1909.]

Another man dreamt that he climbed to the top of a mountain which commanded a quite unusually *extensive view*. Here he was identifying himself with a brother of his who was the editor of a *survey* which dealt with far Eastern affairs. [1911.]

---

¹ [The reference is to a German proverb: '*Einen Kuss in Ehren kann niemand verwehren*' ('No one can refuse an honourable kiss'). The dreamer had in reality been given her first kiss as she was walking through a cornfield—a kiss among the ears of corn.]

² [This instance and the next are also quoted (with somewhat different comments) in respectively the seventh and eighth of Freud's *Introductory Lectures* (1916–17).]

In *Der Grüne Heinrich*[1] a dream is related in which a mettlesome horse was rolling about in a beautiful field of oats, each grain of which was 'a sweet almond, a raisin and a new penny piece . . . wrapped up together in red silk and tied up with a bit of pig's bristle.' The author (or dreamer) gives us an immediate interpretation of this dream-picture: the horse felt agreeably tickled and called out 'Der Hafer sticht mich!'[2] [1914.]

According to Henzen [1890] dreams involving puns and turns of speech occur particularly often in the old Norse sagas, in which scarcely a dream is to be found which does not contain an ambiguity or a play upon words. [1914.]

It would be a work in itself to collect these modes of representation and to classify them according to their underlying principles. [1909.] Some of these representations might almost be described as jokes, and they give one a feeling that one would never have understood them without the dreamer's help. [1911.]

(1) A man dreamt that he was asked someone's name, but could not think of it. He himself explained that what this meant was that 'he would never dream of such a thing.' [1911.]

(2)[3] A woman patient told me a dream in which *all the people were especially big*. 'That means,' she went on, 'that the dream must be to do with events in my early childhood, for at that time, of course, all grown-up people seemed to me enormously big.' [Cf. p. 62 *n*.] She herself did not appear in the content of this dream.—The fact of a dream referring to childhood may also be expressed in another way, namely by a translation of time into space. The characters and scenes are seen as though they were at a great distance, at the end of a long road, or as though they were being looked at through the wrong end of a pair of opera-glasses. [1911.]

(3) A man who in his working life tended to use abstract and indefinite phraseology, though he was quite sharp-witted in general, dreamt on one occasion that *he arrived at a railway station just as a train was coming*

---

[1] [Part IV, Chapter 6, of Gottfried Keller's novel.]
[2] [Literally: 'The oats are pricking me,' but with the idiomatic meaning of 'Prosperity has spoiled me.']
[3] [This and the two following examples were first published in a short paper, '*Nachträge zur Traumdeutung*' (Freud, 1911a). See above, p. 373 *n*.]

in. What then happened was that the platform moved towards the train, while the train stopped still—an absurd reversal of what actually happens. This detail was no more than an indication that we should expect to find another reversal in the dream's content. [Cf. p. 341.] The analysis of the dream led to the patient's recollecting some picture-books in which there were illustrations of men standing on their heads and walking on their hands. [1911.]

(4) Another time the same dreamer told me a short dream which was almost reminiscent of the technique of a rebus. He dreamt that *his uncle gave him a kiss in an automobile.* He went on at once to give me the interpretation, which I myself would never have guessed: namely that it meant auto-erotism. The content of this dream might have been produced as a joke in waking life.[1] [1911.]

(5) A man dreamt that *he was pulling a woman out from behind a bed.* The meaning of this was that he was giving her preference.[2] (1914.)

(6) A man dreamt that *he was an officer sitting at a table opposite the Emperor.* This meant that he was putting himself in opposition to his father. [1914.]

(7) A man dreamt that *he was treating someone for a broken limb.* The analysis showed that the broken bone ['*Knochenbruch*'] stood for a broken marriage ['*Ehebruch*,' properly 'adultery'].[3] [1914.]

(8) The time of day in dreams very often stands for the age of the dreamer at some particular period in his childhood. Thus, in one dream,

---

[1] ['*Auto*' is the ordinary German word for 'motor-car.'—This dream is reported in slightly different terms in Freud's *Introductory Lectures* (1916–17), Lecture XV.]

[2] [The point here is a purely verbal one, depending on the similarity of the German words for 'pulling out' ('*hervorziehen*') and 'giving preference to' ('*vorziehen*'). This dream is also quoted in Freud, *Introductory Lectures* (1916–17), Lecture VII. Nos. 5, 6, 8 and 9 of the present set of examples were published first in Freud, 1913*h*.]

[3] [This example is also quoted in Freud's *Introductory Lectures* (1916–17), Lecture XI, where, in a footnote, a 'symptomatic act' is reported, which confirms this particular interpretation.]

'a quarter past five in the morning' meant the age of five years and three months, which was significant, since that was the dreamer's age at the time of the birth of his younger brother. [1914.]

(9) Here is another method of representing ages in a dream. A woman dreamt that *she was walking with two little girls whose ages differed by fifteen months*. She was unable to recall any family of her acquaintance to whom this applied. She herself put forward the interpretation that the two children both represented herself and that the dream was reminding her that the two traumatic events of her childhood were separated from each other by precisely that interval. One had occurred when she was three and a half, the other when she was four and three-quarters. [1914.]

(10) It is not surprising that a person undergoing psycho-analytic treatment should often dream of it and be led to give expression in his dreams to the many thoughts and expectations to which the treatment gives rise. The imagery most frequently chosen to represent it is that of a journey, usually by motor-car, as being a modern and complicated vehicle. The speed of the car will then be used by the patient as an opportunity for giving vent to ironical comments.—If 'the unconscious,' as an element in the subject's waking thoughts, has to be represented in a dream, it may be replaced very appropriately by subterranean regions.—These, where they occur *without* any reference to analytic treatment, stand for the female body or the womb.—'Down below' in dreams often relates to the genitals, 'up above,' on the contrary, to the face, mouth or breast.—Wild beasts are as a rule employed by the dream-work to represent passionate impulses of which the dreamer is afraid, whether they are his own or those of other people. (It then needs only a slight displacement for the wild beasts to come to represent the people who are possessed by these passions. We have not far to go from here to cases in which a dreaded father is represented by a beast of prey or a dog or wild horse—a form of representation recalling totemism.)[1] It might be said that the wild beasts are used to represent the libido, a force dreaded by the ego and combated by means of repression. It often happens, too, that the dreamer separates off his neurosis, his 'sick personality,' from himself and depicts it as an independent person. [1919.]

---

[1] [See Freud, *Totem and Taboo* (1912–13), Chapter IV, Section 3.]

(11) Here is an example recorded by Hanns Sachs (1911): 'We know from Freud's *Interpretation of Dreams* that the dream-work makes use of different methods for giving a sensory form to words or phrases. If, for instance, the expression that is to be represented is an ambiguous one, the dream-work may exploit the fact by using the ambiguity as a switch-point: where one of the meanings of the word is present in the dream-thoughts the other one can be introduced into the manifest dream. This was the case in the following short dream in which ingenious use was made for representational purposes of appropriate impressions of the previous day. I was suffering from a cold on the "dream-day," and I had therefore decided in the evening that, if I possibly could, I would avoid getting out of bed during the night. I seemed in the dream merely to be continuing what I had been doing during the day. I had been engaged in sticking press-cuttings into an album and had done my best to put each one in the place where it belonged. I dreamt that *I was trying to paste a cutting into the album. But it wouldn't go on to the page* ("*er geht nicht auf die Seite*"), *which caused me much pain.* I woke up and became aware that the pain in the dream persisted in the form of a pain in my inside, and I was compelled to abandon the decision I had made before going to bed. My dream, in its capacity of guardian of my sleep, had given me the illusion of a fulfilment of my wish to stop in bed, by means of a plastic representation of the ambiguous phrase "*er geht nicht auf die Seite*" ["he isn't going to the lavatory"].' [1914.]

We can go so far as to say that the dream-work makes use, for the purpose of giving a visual representation of the dream-thoughts, of any methods within its reach, whether waking criticism regards them as legitimate or illegitimate. This lays the dream-work open to doubt and derision on the part of everyone who has only *heard* of dream-interpretation but never practised it. Stekel's book, *Die Sprache des Traumes* (1911), is particularly rich in examples of this kind. I have, however, avoided quoting instances from it, on account of the author's lack of critical judgement and of the arbitrariness of his technique, which give rise to doubts even in unprejudiced minds. [Cf. p. 363 f.] [1919.]

(12) [1914.] The following examples are taken from a paper by V. Tausk (1914) on the use of clothes and colours in dreaming.

(*a*) A. dreamt of *seeing a former governess of his in a dress of black luster* ['*Lüster*'] *which fitted very tight across her buttocks.*—This was explained as meaning that the governess was lustful ['*lüstern*'].

(*b*) C. dreamt of *seeing a girl on the——Road, who was bathed in white light and was wearing a white blouse.*— The dreamer had had intimate relations with a Miss White for the first time on this road.

(*c*) Frau D. dreamt of *seeing the eighty-year-old Viennese actor Blasel lying on a sofa in full armour* [*'in voller Rüstung'*]. *He began jumping over tables and chairs, drew a dagger, looked at himself in the looking-glass and brandished the dagger in the air as though he was fighting an imaginary enemy.*—Interpretation: The dreamer suffered from a long-standing affection of the bladder [*'Blase'*]. She lay on a sofa for her analysis; when she looked at herself in a looking-glass, she thought privately that in spite of her age and illness she still looked hale and hearty [*'rüstig'*].

(13) [1919.] A 'Great Achievement' in a Dream.—A man dreamt that *he was a pregnant woman lying in bed. He found the situation very disagreeable. He called out: 'I'd rather be . . .'* (during the analysis, after calling to mind a nurse, he completed the sentence with the words 'breaking stones'). *Behind the bed there was hanging a map, the bottom edge of which was kept stretched by a strip of wood. He tore the strip of wood down by catching hold of its two ends. It did not break across but split into two halves lengthways. This action relieved him and at the same time helped on delivery.*

Without any assistance he interpreted tearing down the strip [*'Leiste'*] as a great achievement [*'Leistung'*]. He was escaping from his uncomfortable situation (in the treatment) by tearing himself out of his feminine attitude. . . . The absurd detail of the strip of wood not simply breaking but splitting lengthways was explained thus: the dreamer recalled that this combination of doubling and destroying was an allusion to castration. Dreams very often represent castration by the presence of two penis symbols as the defiant expression of an antithetical wish [cf. p. 370]. Incidentally, the '*Leiste*' ['groin'] is a part of the body in the neighbourhood of the genitals. The dreamer summed up the interpretation of the dream as meaning that he had got the better of the threat of castration which had led to his adopting a feminine attitude.[1]

---

[1] [This example was first published as a separate paper (1914*e*). In reprinting it here, Freud omitted a passage, which occurred originally after the words 'by tearing himself out of his feminine attitude.' The omitted passage (which has never been reprinted) deals with Silberer's 'functional phenomenon,' discussed below, on pp. 507 ff. It ran as follows: 'No objection can be made to this interpretation of the patient's; but I would not describe it as "functional" simply because his

(14) [1919.] In an analysis which I was conducting in French a dream came up for interpretation in which I appeared as an elephant. I naturally asked the dreamer why I was represented in that form. '*Vous me trompez*' ['you are deceiving me'] was his reply ('*trompe*' = 'trunk').

The dream-work can often succeed in representing very refractory material, such as proper names, by a far-fetched use of out-of-the-way associations. In one of my dreams *old Brücke*[1] *had set me the task of making a dissection; . . . I fished something out that looked like a piece of crumpled silver-paper.* (I shall return to this dream later [see pp. 459 ff.].) The association to this (at which I arrived with some difficulty) was 'stanniol.'[2] I then perceived that I was thinking of the name of Stannius, the author of a dissertation on the nervous system of fish, which I had greatly admired in my youth. The first scientific task which my teacher [Brücke] set me was in fact concerned with the nervous system of a fish, Ammocoetes [Freud, 1877a]. It was clearly impossible to make use of the name of this fish in a picture puzzle. [1900].

At this point I cannot resist recording a very peculiar dream, which also deserves to be noticed as having been dreamt by a child, and which can easily be explained analytically. 'I remember having often dreamt when I was a child,' said a lady, '*that God wore a paper cocked-hat on his head.* I used very often to have a hat of that sort put on my head at meals, to prevent my being able to look at the other children's plates, to see how big their helpings were. As I had heard that God was omniscient, the

---

dream-thoughts related to his attitude in the treatment. Thoughts of that kind serve as "material" for the construction of dreams like anything else. It is hard to see why the thoughts of a person under analysis should not be concerned with his behaviour during treatment. [Cf. also p. 236, n. 3.] The distinction between "material" and "functional" phenomena in Silberer's sense is of significance only where—as was the case in Silberer's well-known self-observations as he was falling asleep [see pp. 358 ff.]—there is an *alternative* between the subject's attention being directed either to some piece of thought-content present in his mind *or* to his own actual psychical state, and not where that state itself constitutes the content of his thoughts.' Freud also remarked in parenthesis that in any case the 'absurd detail of the strip of wood not simply breaking but splitting lengthways' could not be 'functional.']

[1] [See footnote, p. 487.]

[2] [Silver paper = tin-foil; stanniol is a derivative of tin (stannium).]

meaning of the dream was that I knew everything—even in spite of the hat that had been put on my head.'[1] [1909.]

The nature of the dream-work[2] and the way in which it plays about with its material, the dream-thoughts, are instructively shown when we come to consider numbers and calculations that occur in dreams. Moreover, numbers in dreams are regarded superstitiously as being especially significant in regard to the future.[3] I shall therefore select a few instances of this kind from my collection.

I

Extract from a dream dreamt by a lady shortly before her treatment came to an end: *She was going to pay for something. Her daughter took 3 florins and 65 kreuzers from her (the mother's) purse. The dreamer said to her: 'What are you doing? It only costs 21 kreuzers.'*[4] Owing to my knowledge of the dreamer's circumstances, this bit of dream was intelligible to me without any further explanation on her part. The lady came from abroad and her daughter was at school in Vienna. She was in a position to carry on her treatment with me as long as her daughter remained in Vienna. The girl's school year was due to end in three weeks and this also meant the end of the lady's treatment. The day before the dream, the head-mistress had asked her whether she would not consider leaving her daughter at school for another year. From this suggestion she had evidently gone on to reflect that in that case she might also continue her treatment. This was what the dream referred to. One year is equal to 365

---

[1] [This dream is also discussed in Freud, *Introductory Lectures* (1916–17), Lecture VII.]

[2] [The remainder of the present section (F), with the exception of Example IV on p. 426, appeared in the original edition (1900).]

[3] [This point is discussed by Freud in Chapter XII (7) of his *Psycho-pathology of Everyday Life* (1901b) and in Section II of his paper on 'The Uncanny' (1919h).]

[4] [The old Austrian currency in florins and kreuzers was not replaced until after the first publication of this book. 1 florin (= 100 kreuzers) was at that time approximately equivalent to an English 1s. 10d. or an American 40 cents. Accordingly, of the sums mentioned in this dream and the next, 3 fl. 65 would have been about 6s. or $1.25; 21 kr. about 4d. or 7½ cents; 1 fl. 50 about 2s. 6d. or 62½ cents; and 150 fl. about £12 10s. or $62.50.]

days. The three weeks which remained both of the school-year and of the treatment were equivalent to 21 days (though the hours of treatment would be less than this). The numbers, which in the dream-thoughts referred to periods of time, were attached in the dream itself to sums of money—not but what there was a deeper meaning involved, for 'time is money.' 365 kreuzers only amount to 3 florins and 65 kreuzers; and the smallness of the sums that occurred in the dream was obviously the result of wish-fulfilment. The dreamer's wish reduced the cost both of the treatment and of the year's school-fees.

II

The numbers which occurred in another dream involved more complicated circumstances. A lady who, though she was still young, had been married for a number of years, received news that an acquaintance of hers, Elise L., who was almost exactly her contemporary, had just become engaged. Thereupon she had the following dream. *She was at the theatre with her husband. One side of the stalls was completely empty. Her husband told her that Elise L. and her fiancé had wanted to go too; but had only been able to get bad seats—three for 1 florin 50 kreuzers[1]—and of course they could not take those. She thought it would not really have done any harm if they had.*

What was the origin of the 1 florin 50 kreuzers? It came from what was in fact an indifferent event of the previous day. Her sister-in-law had been given a present of 150 florins by her husband and had been in a hurry to get rid of them by buying a piece of jewellery. It is to be noticed that 150 florins is a *hundred* times as much as 1 florin 50 kreuzers. Where did the *three* come from which was the number of the theatre tickets? The only connection here was that her newly-engaged friend was the same number of months—*three*—her junior. The solution of the dream was arrived at with the discovery of the meaning of the empty stalls. They were an unmodified allusion to a small incident which had given her husband a good excuse for teasing her. She had planned to go to one of the plays that had been announced for the coming week and had taken the trouble to buy tickets several days ahead, and had therefore had to pay a booking fee.

---

[1] [See previous footnote.]

When they got to the theatre they found that one side of the house was almost empty. There had been *no need for her to be in such a hurry.*

Let me now put the dream-thoughts in place of the dream. 'It was *absurd* to marry so early. There was *no need for me to be in such a hurry.* I see from Elise L.'s example that I should have got a husband in the end. Indeed, I should have got one *a hundred times* better' (a *treasure*) 'if I had only *waited*' (in antithesis to her sister-in-law's *hurry*). 'My money' (or dowry) 'could have bought *three* men just as good.'

It will be observed that the meaning and context of the numbers have been altered to a far greater extent in this dream than in the former one. The processes of modification and distortion have gone further here; and this is to be explained by the dream-thoughts in this case having to overcome a specially high degree of endopsychic resistance before they could obtain representation. Nor should we overlook the fact that there was an element of absurdity in the dream, namely the *three* seats being taken by *two* people. I will anticipate my discussion of absurdity in dreams [pp. 434 ff.] by pointing out that this absurd detail in the content of the dream was intended to represent the most strongly emphasized of the dream-thoughts, viz., 'it was *absurd* to marry so early.' The absurdity which had to find a place in the dream was ingeniously supplied by the number 3, which was itself derived from a quite immaterial point of distinction between the two people under comparison—the 3 months' difference between their ages. The reduction of the actual 150 florins to 1 florin 50 corresponded to the *low value* assigned by the dreamer to her husband (or treasure), in her suppressed thoughts.[1]

III

The next example exhibits the methods of calculation employed by dreams, which have brought them into so much disrepute. A man had a dream that *he was settled in a chair at the B.'s*—a family with which he had been formerly acquainted—*and said to them: 'It was a great mistake your*

---

[1] [This dream is more elaborately analysed at various points in Freud's *Introductory Lectures* (1916–17), particularly at the end of Lecture VII and in two places in Lecture XIV. It and the preceding dream are also recorded in Section VII of Freud's work *On Dreams* (1901a), *Standard Ed.*, 5, 669.]

not letting me have Mali.'—*'How old are you?' he then went on to ask the*
girl.—*'I was born in 1882,' she replied.*—*'Oh, so you're 28, then.'*

Since the dream dates from 1898 this was evidently a miscalculation,
and the dreamer's inability to do sums would deserve to be compared
with that of a general paralytic unless it could be explained in some other
way. My patient was one of those people who, whenever they happen to
catch sight of a woman, cannot let her alone in their thoughts. The patient who for some months used regularly to come next after him in my
consulting room, and whom he thus ran into, was a young lady; he used
constantly to make enquiries about her and was most anxious to create a
good impression with her. It was she whose age he estimated at 28 years.
So much by way of explanation of the result of the ostensible calculation.
1882, incidentally, was the year in which the dreamer had married.—I
may add that he was unable to resist entering into conversation with the
two other members of the female sex whom he came across in my
house—the two maids (neither of them by any means youthful), one or
other of whom used to open the door to him; he explained their lack of
response as being due to their regarding him as an elderly gentleman of
settled habits.

IV[1]

Here is another dream dealing with figures, which is characterized by
the clarity of the manner in which it was determined, or rather, overdetermined. I owe both the dream and its interpretation to Dr. B. Dattner. 'The landlord of my block of flats, who is a police-constable, dreamt
that *he was on street duty.* (This was a wish-fulfilment.) *An inspector came
up to him, who had the number 22 followed by 62 or 26, on his collar. At
any rate there were several twos on it.*

'The mere fact that in reporting the dream the dreamer broke up the
number 2262 showed that its components had separate meanings. He recalled that the day before there had been some talk at the police station
about the men's length of service. The occasion for it was an inspector
who had retired on his pension at the age of 62. The dreamer had only
served for 22 years, and it would be 2 years and 2 months before he

---

[1] [This example was added in 1911.]

would be eligible for a 90 per cent pension. The dream represented in the first place the fulfilment of a long-cherished wish of the dreamer's to reach the rank of inspector. The superior officer with "2262" on his collar was the dreamer himself. He was on street duty—another favourite wish of his—he had served his remaining 2 years and 2 months and now, like the 62-year-old inspector, he could retire on a full pension.'[1]

When we take together these and some other examples which I shall give later [pp. 456 ff.], we may safely say that the dream-work does not in fact carry out any calculations at all, whether correctly or incorrectly; it merely throws into the *form* of a calculation numbers which are present in the dream-thoughts and can serve as allusions to matter that cannot be represented in any other way. In this respect the dream-work is treating numbers as a medium for the expression of its purpose in precisely the same way as it treats any other idea, including proper names and speeches that occur recognizably as verbal presentations. [See next paragraph but one.]

For the dream-work cannot actually *create* speeches. [See above, pp. 206 f. and 321.] However much speeches and conversations, whether reasonable or unreasonable in themselves, may figure in dreams, analysis invariably proves that all that the dream has done is to extract from the dream-thoughts fragments of speeches which have really been made or heard. It deals with these fragments in the most arbitrary fashion. Not only does it drag them out of their context and cut them in pieces, incorporating some portions and rejecting others, but it often puts them together in a new order, so that a speech which appears in the dream to be a connected whole turns out in analysis to be composed of three or four detached fragments. In producing this new version, a dream will often abandon the meaning that the words originally had in the dream-thoughts and give them a fresh one.[2] If we look closely into a speech that occurs in a dream, we shall find that it consists on the one hand of relatively clear and compact portions and on the

---

[1] [*Footnote added* 1914:] For analyses of other dreams containing numbers, see Jung [1911], Marcinowski [1912*b*] and others. These often imply very complicated operations with numbers, which have been carried out by the dreamer with astonishing accuracy. See also Jones (1912*a*).

[2] [*Footnote added* 1909:] in this respect neuroses behave exactly like dreams. I know a patient one of whose symptoms is that, involuntarily and against her will, she hears—i.e. hallucinates—songs or fragments of songs, without being able to understand what part they play in her mental life. (Incidentally, she is

other hand of portions which serve as connecting matter and have probably been filled in at a later stage, just as, in reading, we fill in any letters or syllables that may have been accidentally omitted. Thus speeches in dreams have a structure similar to that of breccia, in which largish blocks of various kinds of stone are cemented together by a binding medium. [Cf. p. 457.]

Strictly speaking, this description applies only to such speeches in dreams as possess something of the sensory quality of speech, and which are described by the dreamer himself as being speeches. Other sorts of speeches, which are not, as it were, felt by him as having been heard or

---

certainly not paranoiac.) Analysis has shown that, by allowing herself a certain amount of licence, she puts the text of these songs to false uses. For instance in the lines from [Agathe's aria in Weber's *Freischütz*] *'Leise, leise, Fromme Weise!'* [literally, 'Softly, softly, devout melody'] the last word was taken by her unconscious as though it was spelt *'Waise'* [= 'orphan,' thus making the lines read 'Softly, softly, pious orphan,'] the orphan being herself. Again *'O du selige, o du fröhliche'* ['Oh thou blessèd and happy . . .'] is the opening of a Christmas carol; by not continuing the quotation to the word 'Christmastide' she turned it into a bridal song.—The same mechanism of distortion can also operate in the occurrence of an idea *unaccompanied* by hallucination. Why was it that one of my patients was pestered by the recollection of a poem that he had had to learn in his youth: *'Nächtlich am Busento lispeln . . .'* ['By night on the Busento whispering . . .']? Because his imagination went no further than the first part of this quotation: *'Nächtlich am Busen,'* ['By night on the bosom.']

We are familiar with the fact that this same technical trick is used by parodists. Included in a series of 'Illustrations to the German Classics' published in *Fliegende Blätter* [the well-known comic paper] was one which illustrated Schiller's *'Siegesfest,'* with the following quotation attached to it:

> Und des frisch erkämpften Weibes
> Freut sich der Atrid und strickt . . .

> [The conqu'ring son of Atreus sits
> At his fair captive's side and knits. . . .]

Here the quotation broke off. In the original the lines continue:

> . . . Um den Reiz des schönen Leibes
> Seine Anne hochbeglückt.

> [. . . His joyful and triumphant arms
> About her body's lovely charms.]

spoken (that is, which have no acoustic or motor accompaniments in the dream), are merely thoughts such as occur in our waking thought-activity and are often carried over unmodified into our dreams. Another copious source of undifferentiated speeches of this kind, though one which it is difficult to follow up, seems to be provided by material that has been *read*. But whatever stands out markedly in dreams as a speech can be traced back to real speeches which have been spoken or heard by the dreamer.

Instances showing that speeches in dreams have this origin have already been given by me in the course of analysing dreams which I have quoted for quite other purposes. Thus, in the 'innocent' market dream reported on p. 206, the spoken words 'that's not obtainable any longer' served to identify me with the butcher, while one portion of the other speech, 'I don't recognize that; I won't take it,' was actually responsible for making the dream an 'innocent' one. The dreamer, it will be remembered, having had some suggestion made to her on the previous day by her cook, had replied with the words: 'I don't recognize that; behave yourself properly!' The innocent-sounding *first* part of this speech was taken into the dream by way of allusion to its *second* part, which fitted excellently into the phantasy underlying the dream, but would at the same time have betrayed it.

Here is another example, which will serve instead of many, all of them leading to the same conclusion.

The dreamer was in a big courtyard in which some dead bodies were being burnt. 'I'm off,' he said, 'I can't bear the sight of it.' (This was not definitely a speech.) He then met two butcher's boys. 'Well,' he asked, 'did it taste nice?' 'No,' one of them answered, 'not a bit nice'—as though it had been human flesh.

The innocent occasion of the dream was as follows. The dreamer and his wife had paid a visit after supper to their neighbours, who were excellent people but not precisely *appetizing*. The hospitable old lady was just having her supper and had tried to *force* him (there is a phrase with a sexual sense used jokingly among men to render this idea[1]) to taste some of it. He had declined, saying he had no appetite left: 'Get along!' she had replied, 'you can manage it,' or words to that effect. He had therefore been obliged to taste it and had complimented her on it, saying: 'That was very nice.' When he was once more alone with his wife he had grumbled at his neighbour's insistence and also at the quality of the food. The thought, 'I

---

[1] ['*Notzüchtigen*, '"to force sexually,' 'to rape,' is so used in place of '*nötigen*, '"to force' (in the ordinary sense).]

can't bear the sight of it,' which in the dream too failed to emerge as a speech in the strict sense, was an allusion to the physical charms of the lady from which the invitation had come, and it must be taken as meaning that he had no desire to look at them.

More instruction can be derived from another dream, which I shall report in this connection on account of the very distinct speech which formed its centre-point, although I shall have to put off explaining it fully till I come to discuss affect in dreams [pp. 466 ff.]. I had a very clear dream. *I had gone to Brücke's laboratory at night, and, in response to a gentle knock on the door, I opened it to* (the late) *Professor Fleischl,*[1] *who came in with a number of strangers and, after exchanging a few words, sat down at his table.* This was followed by a second dream. *My friend Fl.* [Fliess] *had come to Vienna unobtrusively in July. I met him in the street in conversation with my* (deceased) *friend P., and went with them to some place where they sat opposite each other as though they were at a small table. I sat in front at its narrow end. Fl. spoke about his sister and said that in three quarters of an hour she was dead, and added some such words as 'that was the threshold.' As P. failed to understand him,*[2] *Fl. turned to me and asked me how much I had told P. about his affairs. Whereupon, overcome by strange emotions, I tried to explain to Fl. that P.* (could not understand anything at all, of course, because he) *was not alive. But what I actually said—and I myself noticed the mistake—was,* 'Non vixit.' *I then gave P. a piercing look. Under my gaze he turned pale; his form grew indistinct and his eyes a sickly blue—and finally he melted away. I was highly delighted at this and I now realized that Ernst Fleischl, too, had been no more than an apparition, a 'revenant'* ['ghost'—literally, 'one who returns']; *and it seemed to me quite possible that people of that kind only existed as long as one liked and could be got rid of if someone else wished it.*

This fine specimen includes many of the characteristics of dreams—the fact that I exercised my critical faculties during the dream and myself noticed my mistake when I said *'Non vixit'* instead of *'Non vivit'* [that is, 'he did not live' instead of 'he is not alive'], my unconcerned dealings with people who were dead and were recognized as being dead in the dream itself, the absurdity of my final inference and the great satisfaction it gave me. This dream exhibits so many of these puzzling features, indeed, that I would give a great deal to be able to present the complete solution of its

---

[1] [See footnote on p. 487 for an explanation of the persons concerned.]
[2] [This detail is analysed below on p. 517.]

conundrums. But in point of fact I am incapable of doing so—of doing, that is to say, what I did in the dream, of sacrificing to my ambition people whom I greatly value. Any concealment, however, would destroy what I know very well to be the dream's meaning; and I shall therefore content myself, both here and in a later context [pp. 485 ff.], with selecting only a few of its elements for interpretation.

The central feature of the dream was a scene in which I annihilated P. with a look. His eyes changed to a strange and uncanny blue and he melted away. This scene was unmistakably copied from one which I had actually experienced. At the time I have in mind I had been a demonstrator at the Physiological Institute and was due to start work early in the morning. It came to Brücke's ears that I sometimes reached the students' laboratory late. One morning he turned up punctually at the hour of opening and awaited my arrival. His words were brief and to the point. But it was not they that mattered. What overwhelmed me were the terrible blue eyes with which he looked at me and by which I was reduced to nothing—just as P. was in the dream, where, to my relief, the roles were reversed. No one who can remember the great man's eyes, which retained their striking beauty even in his old age, and who has ever seen him in anger, will find it difficult to picture the young sinner's emotions.

It was a long time, however, before I succeeded in tracing the origin of the 'Non vixit' with which I passed judgement in the dream. But at last it occurred to me that these two words possessed their high degree of clarity in the dream, not as words heard or spoken, but as words *seen*. I then knew at once where they came from. On the pedestal of the Kaiser Josef Memorial in the Hofburg [Imperial Palace] in Vienna the following impressive words are inscribed:

> Saluti patriae vixit
> non diu sed totus.[1]

---

[1] ['For the well-being of his country he lived not long but wholly.']—*Footnote added* 1925:] The actual wording of the inscription is:

> Saluti publicae vixit
> non diu sed totus.

The reason for my mistake in putting *'patriae'* for *'publicae'* has probably been rightly guessed by Wittels [1924, 86; Engl. trans. (1924), 100 f.]

I extracted from this inscription just enough to fit in with a hostile train of ideas among the dream-thoughts, just enough to imply that 'this fellow has no say in the matter—he isn't even alive.' And this reminded me that I had the dream only a few days after the unveiling of the memorial to Fleischl in the cloisters of the University.[1] At that time I had seen the Brücke memorial once again and must have reflected (unconsciously) with regret on the fact that the premature death of my brilliant friend P., whose whole life had been devoted to science, had robbed him of a well-merited claim to a memorial in these same precincts. Accordingly, I gave him this memorial in my dream; and, incidentally, as I remembered, his first name was Josef.[2]

By the rules of dream-interpretation I was even now not entitled to pass from the *Non vixit* derived from my recollection of the Kaiser Josef Memorial to the *Non vixit* required by the sense of the dream-thoughts. There must have been some other element in the dream-thoughts which would help to make the transition possible. It then struck me as noticeable that in the scene in the dream there was a convergence of a hostile and an affectionate current of feeling towards my friend P., the former being on the surface and the latter concealed, but both of them being represented in the single phrase *Non vixit*. As he had deserved well of science I built him a memorial; but as he was guilty of an evil wish[3] (which was expressed at the end of the dream) I annihilated him. I noticed that this last sentence had a quite special cadence, and I must have had some model in my mind. Where was an antithesis of this sort to be found, a juxtaposition like this of two opposite reactions towards a single person, both of them claiming to be completely justified and yet not incompatible? Only in one passage in literature—but a passage which makes a profound impression on the reader: in Brutus's speech of self-justification in Shakespeare's *Julius Caesar* [iii, 2], 'As Caesar loved me, I weep for him; as he was fortunate, I rejoice at it; as he was valiant, I honour him; but, as he was ambitious, I slew him.' Were not the formal structure of these sentences and their antitheti-

---

[1] [This ceremony took place on October 16, 1898.]

[2] I may add as an example of overdetermination that my excuse for arriving too late at the laboratory lay in the fact that after working far into the night I had in the morning to cover the long distance between the *Kaiser Josef* Strasse and the Währinger Strasse.

[3] [This detail is further explained below, on p. 490.]

cal meaning precisely the same as in the dream-thought I had uncovered? Thus I had been playing the part of Brutus in the dream. If only I could find one other piece of evidence in the content of the dream to confirm this surprising collateral connecting link! A possible one occurred to me. *'My friend Fl. came to Vienna in July.'* There was no basis in reality for this detail of the dream. So far as I knew, my friend Fl. had never been in Vienna in July. But the month of July was named after Julius Caesar and might therefore very well represent the allusion I wanted to the intermediate thought of my playing the part of Brutus.[1]

Strange to say, I really did once play the part of Brutus. I once acted in the scene between Brutus and Caesar from Schiller[2] before an audience of children. I was fourteen years old at the time and was acting with a nephew who was a year my senior. He had come to us on a visit from England; and he, too, was a *revenant*, for it was the playmate of my earliest years who had returned in him. Until the end of my third year we had been inseparable. We had loved each other and fought with each other; and this childhood relationship, as I have already hinted above [pp. 219 and 251], had a determining influence on all my subsequent relations with contemporaries. Since that time my nephew John has had many reincarnations which revived now one side and now another of his personality, unalterably fixed as it was in my unconscious memory. There must have been times when he treated me very badly and I must have shown courage in the face of my tyrant; for in my later years I have often been told of a short speech made by me in my own defence when my father, who was at the same time John's grandfather, had said to me accusingly: 'Why are you hitting John?' My reply—I was not yet two years old at the time—was 'I hit him 'cos he hit me.' It must have been this scene from my childhood which diverted *'Non vivit'* into *'Non vixit,'* for in the language of later childhood the word for to hit is *'wichsen'* [pronounced like the English 'vixen']. The dream-work is not ashamed to make use of links such as this one. There was little basis in reality for my hostility to my friend P., who was very greatly my superior and for that reason was well fitted to appear as a new edition of my early playmate. This hostility must

---

[1] There was the further connection between 'Caesar' and 'Kaiser.'
[2] [This is in fact a lyric in dialogue form recited by Karl Moor in Act IV, Scene 5, of the earlier version of Schiller's play *Die Räuber.*]

therefore certainly have gone back to my complicated childhood relations
to John. [See further pp. 488.][1]

As I have said, I shall return to this dream later.

(G)

ABSURD DREAMS—INTELLECTUAL
ACTIVITY IN DREAMS[2]

In the course of our dream-interpretations we have so often come
across the element of absurdity that we cannot postpone any longer the
moment of investigating its source and significance, if it has any. For it
will be remembered that the absurdity of dreams has provided those who
deny the value of dreams with one of their principal arguments in favour
of regarding them as the meaningless product of a reduced and fragmentary mental activity [see pp. 84 ff.].

I shall begin by giving a few examples in which the absurdity is only
an apparent one and disappears as soon as the meaning of the dream is
more closely examined. Here are two or three dreams which deal (by
chance, as it may seem at first sight) with the dreamer's dead father.

I

This is the dream of a patient who had lost his father six years earlier.
His father had met with a grave calamity. He had been travelling by the night
train, which had been derailed. The carriage seats were forced together and

---

[1] [Freud discusses his relations with his nephew John in a letter to Fliess of October 3, 1897. (Freud, 1950a, Letter 70.) A further, somewhat disguised account
of an early episode, in which John and his younger sister Pauline (referred to below on p. 491) figured, is no doubt to be seen in the latter part of Freud's paper
on 'Screen Memories' (1899a).—The subject of speeches in dreams is also mentioned on pp. 207, 321, 329 and 471.]

[2] [Henceforward, until the end of the book, it is to be assumed once more that the
whole of the matter appeared in the first (1900) edition, except for passages to
which a later date is specifically assigned.]

*his head was compressed from side to side. The dreamer then saw him lying
in bed with a wound over his left eyebrow which ran in a vertical direction.
He was surprised at his father's having met with a calamity (since he was already dead,* as he added in telling me the dream). *How clear his eyes were!*

According to the ruling theory of dreams we should have to explain the
content of this dream as follows. To begin with, we should suppose, while
the dreamer was imagining the accident, he must have forgotten that his
father had been in his grave for several years; but, as the dream proceeded,
the recollection must have emerged, and led to his astonishment at his
own dream while he was still asleep. Analysis teaches us, however, that it is
eminently useless to look for explanations of this kind. The dreamer had
commissioned a bust of his father from a sculptor and had seen it for the
first time two days before the dream. It was this that he had thought of as
a calamity. The sculptor had never seen his father and had worked from
photographs. On the day immediately before the dream the dreamer, in
his filial piety, had sent an old family servant to the studio to see whether
he would form the same opinion of the marble head, namely, that it was
too narrow from side to side at the temples. He now proceeded to recall
from his memory the material which had gone to the construction of the
dream. Whenever his father was tormented by business worries or family
difficulties, he had been in the habit of pressing his hands to the sides of
his forehead, as though he felt that his head was too wide and wanted to
compress it.—When the patient was four years old he had been present
when a pistol, which had been accidentally loaded, had been discharged
and had blackened his father's eyes. (*'How clear his eyes were!'*)—At the
spot on his forehead at which the dream located his father's injury, a deep
furrow showed during his lifetime whenever he was thoughtful or sad. The
fact that this furrow was replaced in the dream by a wound led back to the
second exciting cause of the dream. The dreamer had taken a photograph
of his little daughter. The plate had slipped through his fingers, and when
he picked it up showed a crack which ran perpendicularly down the little
girl's forehead as far as her eyebrow. He could not help feeling superstitious about this, since a few days before his mother's death he had broken
a photographic plate with her portrait on it.

The absurdity of this dream was thus no more than the result of a piece
of carelessness in verbal expression which failed to distinguish the bust and
the photograph from the actual person. We might any of us say [looking
at a picture]: 'There's something wrong with Father, don't you think?' The
appearance of absurdity in the dream could easily have been avoided; and

if we were to judge from this single example, we should be inclined to
think that the apparent absurdity had been permitted or even designed.

II

Here is another, almost exactly similar, example from a dream of my
own. (I lost my father in 1896.) *After his death my father played a political
part among the Magyars and brought them together politically.* Here I saw a
small and indistinct picture: *a crowd of men as though they were in the Reichstag; someone standing on one or two chairs, with other people round him.
I remembered how like Garibaldi he had looked on his death-bed, and felt
glad that that promise had come true.*

What could be more absurd than this? It was dreamt at a time at
which the Hungarians had been driven by parliamentary *obstruction* into
a state of lawlessness and were plunged into the crisis from which they
were rescued by Koloman Széll.[1] The trivial detail of the scene in the
dream appearing in pictures of such a small size was not without rele-
vance to its interpretation. Our dream-thoughts are usually represented
in visual pictures which appear to be more or less life-size. The picture
which I saw in my dream, however, was a reproduction of a woodcut inserted in an illustrated history of Austria, which showed Maria Theresa at
the Reichstag [Diet] of Pressburg in the famous episode of '*Moriamur pro
rege nostro.*'[2] Like Maria Theresa in the picture, so my father stood in the
dream surrounded by the crowd. But he was *standing on one or two chairs*
['chair' = '*Stuhl*']. He had *brought them together*, and was thus a presiding
judge ['*Stuhlrichter,*' literally 'chair-judge']. (A connecting link was provided by the common [German] phrase 'we shall need no judge.')—

---

[1] [An acute political crisis in Hungary in 1898–9 had been solved by the formation of a coalition government under Széll.]

[2] ['We will die for our king!' The response of the Hungarian nobles to Maria
Theresa's plea for support, after her accession in 1740, in the War of the Austrian Succession.]—I cannot remember where I read an account of a dream
which was filled with unusually small figures, and the source of which turned
out to be one of Jacques Callot's etchings seen by the dreamer during the day.
These etchings do in fact contain a large number of very small figures. One series
of them depicts the horrors of the Thirty Years' War.

Those of us who were standing round had in fact remarked how like Garibaldi my father looked on his death-bed. He had had a *post mortem* rise of temperature, his cheeks had been flushed more and more deeply red. . . . As I recalled this, my thoughts involuntarily ran on:

Und hinter ihm in wesenlosem Scheine
Lag, was uns alle bändigt, das Gemeine.[1]

These elevated thoughts prepared the way [in the analysis] for the appearance of something that was common [*'gemein'*] in another sense. My father's *post mortem* rise of temperature corresponded to the words 'after his death' in the dream. His most severe suffering had been caused by a complete paralysis (*obstruction*) of the intestines during his last weeks. Disrespectful thoughts of all kinds followed from this. One of my contemporaries who lost his father while he was still at his secondary school—on that occasion I myself had been deeply moved and had offered to be his friend—once told me scornfully of how one of his female relatives had had a painful experience. Her father had fallen dead in the street and had been brought home; when his body was undressed it was found that at the moment of death, or *post mortem,* he had passed a stool [*'Stuhl'*]. His daughter had been so unhappy about this that she could not prevent this ugly detail from disturbing her memory of her father. Here we have reached the wish that was embodied in this dream. 'To stand before one's children's eyes, after one's death, great and unsullied'—who would not desire this? What has become of the absurdity of the dream? Its apparent absurdity is due only to the fact that it gave a literal picture of a figure of speech which is itself perfectly legitimate and in which we habitually overlook any absurdity involved in the contradiction between its parts. In this instance, once again, it is impossible to escape an impression that the apparent absurdity is intentional and has been deliberately produced.[2]

---

[1] [These lines are from the Epilogue to Schiller's 'Lied von der Glocke' written by Goethe a few months after his friend's death. He speaks of Schiller's spirit moving forward into the eternity of truth, goodness and beauty, while 'behind him, a shadowy illusion, lay what holds us all in bondage—the things that are common.']

[2] [This dream is further discussed on pp. 455.]

The frequency with which dead people appear in dreams[1] and act and associate with us as though they were alive has caused unnecessary surprise and has produced some remarkable explanations which throw our lack of understanding of dreams into strong relief. Yet the explanation of these dreams is a very obvious one. It often happens that we find ourselves thinking: 'If my father were alive, what would he say to this?' Dreams are unable to express an 'if' of this kind except by representing the person concerned as present in some particular situation. Thus, for instance, a young man who had been left a large legacy by his grandfather, dreamt, at a time when he was feeling self-reproaches for having spent a considerable sum of money, that his grandfather was alive again and calling him to account. And when, from our better knowledge, we protest that after all the person in question is dead, what we look upon as a criticism of the dream is in reality either a consoling thought that the dead person has not lived to witness the event, or a feeling of satisfaction that he can no longer interfere in it.

There is another kind of absurdity, which occurs in dreams of dead relatives but which does not express ridicule and derision.[2] It indicates an extreme degree of repudiation, and so makes it possible to represent a repressed thought which the dreamer would prefer to regard as utterly unthinkable. It seems impossible to elucidate dreams of this kind unless one bears in mind the fact that dreams do not differentiate between what is wished and what is real. For instance, a man who had nursed his father during his last illness and had been deeply grieved by his death, had the following senseless dream some time afterwards. *His father was alive once more and was talking to him in his usual way, but* (the remarkable thing was that) *he had really died, only he did not know it.* This dream only becomes intelligible if, after the words 'but he had really died' we insert 'in consequence of the dreamer's wish,' and if we explain that what 'he did

---

[1] [This paragraph was added as a footnote in 1909 and included in the text in 1930.]

[2] [This paragraph was added as a footnote in 1911 and included in the text in 1930. The first sentence of the paragraph implies that Freud has already explained absurdity in dreams as being due to the presence of 'ridicule and derision' in the dream-thoughts. Actually he has not yet done so, and this conclusion is only explicitly stated in the paragraph below (on p. 452) in which he sums up his theory of absurd dreams. It seems possible that the present paragraph, in its original footnote form, may by some oversight have been introduced here instead of at the later point.]

not know' was that the dreamer had had this wish. While he was nursing his father he had repeatedly wished his father were dead; that is to say, he had had what was actually a merciful thought that death might put an end to his sufferings. During his mourning, after his father's death, even this sympathetic wish became a subject of unconscious self-reproach, as though by means of it he had really helped to shorten the sick man's life. A stirring up of the dreamer's earliest infantile impulses against his father made it possible for this self-reproach to find expression as a dream; but the fact that the instigator of the dream and the daytime thoughts were such worlds apart was precisely what necessitated the dream's absurdity.[1]

It is true that dreams of dead people whom the dreamer has loved raise difficult problems in dream-interpretation and that these cannot always be satisfactorily solved. The reason for this is to be found in the particularly strongly marked emotional ambivalence which dominates the dreamer's relation to the dead person. It very commonly happens that in dreams of this kind the dead person is treated to begin with as though he were alive, that he then suddenly turns out to be dead and that in a subsequent part of the dream he is alive once more. This has a confusing effect. It eventually occurred to me that this alternation between death and life is intended to represent *indifference* on the part of the dreamer. ('It's all the same to me whether he's alive or dead.') This indifference is, of course, not real but merely desired; it is intended to help the dreamer to repudiate his very intense and often contradictory emotional attitudes and it thus becomes a dream-representation of his *ambivalence*.—In other dreams in which the dreamer associates with dead people, the following rule often helps to give us our bearings. If there is no mention in the dream of the fact that the dead man is dead, the dreamer is equating himself with him: he is dreaming of his own death. If, in the course of the dream, the dreamer suddenly says to himself in astonishment, 'why, he died ever so long ago,' he is repudiating this equation and is denying that the dream signifies his own death.[2]—But I willingly confess to a feeling that dream-interpretation is far from having revealed all the secrets of dreams of this character.

---

[1] [*Footnote* 1911:] Cf. my paper on the two principles of mental functioning (1911*b*) [at the end of which this same dream is discussed.—A very similar dream is analysed as No. 3 in the twelfth of Freud's *Introductory Lectures* (1916–17).— The next paragraph was added as a footnote in 1919 and included in the text in 1930.]

[2] [This point was first made in Freud (1913*h*).]

III

In the example which I shall next bring forward I have been able to catch the dream-work in the very act of intentionally fabricating an absurdity for which there was absolutely no occasion in the material. It is taken from the dream which arose from my meeting with Count Thun as I was starting for my holidays. [See pp. 229 ff.] *I was driving in a cab and ordered the driver to drive me to a station. 'Of course I can't drive with you along the railway line itself,' I said, after he had raised some objection, as though I had overtired him. It was as if I had already driven with him for some of the distance one normally travels by train.* The analysis produced the following explanations of this confused and senseless story. The day before, I had hired a cab to take me to an out-of-the-way street in Dornbach.[1] The driver, however, had not known where the street was and, as these excellent people are apt to do, had driven on and on until at last I had noticed what was happening and had told him the right way, adding a few sarcastic comments. A train of thought, to which I was later in the analysis to return, led from this cab-driver to aristocrats. For the moment it was merely the passing notion that what strikes us bourgeois plebs about the aristocracy is the preference they have for taking the driver's seat. Count Thun, indeed, was the driver of the State Coach of Austria. The next sentence in the dream, however, referred to my brother, whom I was thus identifying with the cab-driver. That year I had called off a trip I was going to make with him to Italy. ('*I can't drive with you along the railway line itself.*') And this cancellation had been a kind of punishment for the complaints he used to make that I was in the habit of over-tiring him on such trips (this appeared in the dream unaltered) by insisting upon moving too rapidly from place to place and seeing too many beautiful things in a single day. On the evening of the dream my brother had accompanied me to the station; but he had jumped out shortly before we got there, at the suburban railway station adjoining the main line terminus, in order to travel to Purkersdorf[2] by the suburban line. I had remarked to him that he might have stayed with me a little longer by travelling to Purkersdorf by the main line instead of the suburban one. This led to the passage in the dream in which I drove in the cab *for some of the distance one normally travels by train.* This was an

---

[1] [On the outskirts of Vienna.]
[2] [Seven or eight miles outside Vienna.]

inversion of what had happened in reality—a kind of '*tu quoque*' argument What I had said to my brother was: 'you can travel on the main line in my company for the distance you would travel by the suburban line.' I brought about the whole confusion in the dream by putting 'cab' instead of 'suburban line' (which, incidentally, was of great help in bringing together the figures of the cab-driver and my brother). In this way I succeeded in producing something senseless in the dream, which it seems scarcely possible to disentangle and which was almost a direct contradiction of an earlier remark of mine in the dream ('*I can't drive with you along the railway line itself*'). Since, however, there was no necessity whatever for me to confuse the suburban railway and a cab, I must have arranged the whole of this enigmatic business in the dream on purpose.

But for *what* purpose? We are now to discover the significance of absurdity in dreams and the motives which lead to its being admitted or even created. The solution of the mystery in the present dream was as follows. It was necessary for me that there should be something absurd and unintelligible in this dream in connection with the word '*fahren*'[1] because the dream-thoughts included a particular judgement which called for representation. One evening, while I was at the house of the hospitable and witty lady who appeared as the 'housekeeper' in one of the other scenes in the same dream, I had heard two riddles which I had been unable to solve. Since they were familiar to the rest of the company, I cut a rather ludicrous figure in my vain attempts to find the answers. They depended upon puns on the words '*Nachkommen*' and '*Vorfahren*' and, I believe, ran as follows:

> Der Herr befiehlt's,
> Der Kutscher tut's.
> Ein jeder hat's,
> Im Grabe ruht's.

> [With the master's request
> The driver complies:
> By all men possessed
> In the graveyard it lies.]

---

[1] [The German word '*fahren*,' which has already been used repeatedly in the dream and the analysis, is used for the English 'drive' (in a cab) and 'travel' (in a train) and has had to be translated by both of those words in different contexts. See also p. 231 *n*.]

(Answer: *'Vorfahrer'* ['Drive up' and 'Ancestry'; more literally 'go in front' and 'predecessors'].)

It was particularly confusing that the first half of the second riddle was identical with that of the first:

> Der Herr befiehlt's,
> Der Kutscher tut's.
> Nicht jeder hat's,
> In der Wiege ruht's.

> [With the master's request
> The driver complies:
> Not by all men possessed
> In the cradle it lies.]

(Answer: *'Nachkommen'* ['Follow after' and 'Progeny'; more literally 'come after' and 'successors'].)

When I saw Count Thun *drive up* so impressively and when I thereupon fell into the mood of Figaro, with his remarks on the goodness of great gentlemen in having taken the trouble to be born (to become *progeny*), these two riddles were adopted by the dream-work as intermediate thoughts. Since aristocrats could easily be confused with drivers and since there was a time in our part of the world when a driver was spoken of as *'Schwager'* ['coachman' and 'brother-in-law'], the work of condensation was able to introduce my brother into the same picture. The dream-thought, however, which was operating behind all this ran as follows: 'It is absurd to be proud of one's ancestry; it is better to be an ancestor one-self.' This judgement, that something 'is absurd,' was what produced the absurdity in the dream. And this also clears up the remaining enigma in this obscure region of the dream, namely why it was that I thought I had already driven with the driver *before* [*vorhergefahren* ('driven before')— *vorgefahren* ('driven up')— *'Vorfahren'* ('ancestry')].

A dream is made absurd, then, if a judgement that something 'is absurd' is among the elements included in the dream-thoughts—that is to say, if any one of the dreamer's unconscious trains of thought has criticism or ridicule as its motive. Absurdity is accordingly one of the methods by which the dream-work represents a contradiction—alongside such other methods as the reversal in the dream-content of some material relation in the dream-thoughts [pp. 341 f.], or the exploitation of the sensation of motor inhibition [pp. 351 f.]. Absurdity in a dream, however, is not to be translated by a simple 'no'; it is intended to reproduce the *mood* of the dream-thoughts, which combines derision or laughter with the contradiction. It is only with such an aim in view that the dream-work produces anything ridiculous. Here once again *it is giving a manifest form to a portion of the latent content.*[1]

Actually we have already come across a convincing example of an absurd dream with this kind of meaning: the dream—I interpreted it without any analysis—of the performance of a Wagner opera which lasted till a quarter to eight in the morning and in which the orchestra was conducted from a tower, and so on (see pp. 356 f.). It evidently meant to say: 'This is a *topsy-turvy* world and a *crazy* society; the person who deserves something doesn't get it, and the person who doesn't care about something *does* get it'—and there the dreamer was comparing her fate with her cousin's.—Nor is it by any means a matter of chance that our first examples of absurdity in dreams related to a dead father. In such cases, the conditions for creating absurd dreams are found together in characteristic fashion. The authority wielded by a father provokes criticism from his children at an early age, and the severity of the demands he makes upon them leads them, for their own relief, to keep their eyes open to any weakness of their father's; but the filial piety called up in our minds by the figure of a father, particularly after his death, tightens the censorship which prohibits any such criticism from being consciously expressed.

---

[1] The dream-work is thus parodying the thought that has been presented to it as something ridiculous, by the method of creating something ridiculous in connection with that thought. Heine adopted the same line when he wanted to ridicule some wretched verses written by the King of Bavaria. He did so in still more wretched ones:

> Herr Ludwig ist ein grosser Poet,
> Und singt er, so stürzt Apollo
> Vor ihm auf die Kniee und bittet und fleht,
> 'Halt ein! ich werde sonst toll, o!'

> [Sir Ludwig is a magnificent bard
> And, as soon as he utters, Apollo
> Goes down on his knees and begs him: 'Hold hard!
> Or I'll shortly become a clod-poll oh!'
> *Lobgesänge auf König Ludwig,* I.]

IV

Here is another absurd dream about a dead father. *I received a communication from the town council of my birthplace concerning the fees due for someone's maintenance in the hospital in the year 1851, which had been necessitated by an attack he had had in my house. I was amused by this since, in the first place, I was not yet alive in 1851 and, in the second place, my father, to whom it might have related, was already dead. I went to him in the next room, where he was lying on his bed, and told him about it. To my surprise, he recollected that in 1851 he had once got drunk and had had to be locked up or detained. It was at a time at which he had been working for the firm of T———. 'So you used to drink as well?' I asked; 'did you get married soon after that?' I calculated that, of course, I was born in 1856, which seemed to be the year which immediately followed the year in question.*

We should conclude from the preceding discussion that the insistence with which this dream exhibited its absurdities could only be taken as indicating the presence in the dream-thoughts of a particularly embittered and passionate polemic. We shall therefore be all the more astonished to observe that in this dream the polemic was carried on in the open and that my father was the explicit object of the ridicule. Openness of this kind seems to contradict our assumptions as regards the working of the censorship in connection with the dream-work. The position will become clearer, however, when it is realized that in this instance my father was merely put forward as a show-figure, and that the dispute was really being carried on with someone else, who only appeared in the dream in a single allusion. Whereas normally a dream deals with rebellion against someone else, behind whom the dreamer's father is concealed, the opposite was true here. My father was made into a man of straw, in order to screen someone else; and the dream was allowed to handle in this undisguised way a figure who was as a rule treated as sacred, because at the same time I knew with certainty that it was not he who was really meant. That this was so was shown by the exciting cause of the dream. For it occurred after I had heard that a senior colleague of mine, whose judgement was regarded as beyond criticism, had given voice to disapproval and surprise at the fact that the psycho-analytic treatment of one of my patients had already entered its *fifth year.*[1] The first sentences of

---

[1] [This was the patient frequently referred to in Freud's letters to Fliess (Freud, 1950*a*) as 'E.' The present dream is referred to in Letter 126 (December 21, 1899)

the dream alluded under a transparent disguise to the fact that for some time this colleague had taken over the duties which my father could no longer fulfil ('*fees due*,' '*maintenance in the hospital*'), and that, when our relations began to be less friendly, I became involved in the same kind of emotional conflict which, when a misunderstanding arises between a father and son, is inevitably produced owing to the position occupied by the father and the assistance formerly given by him. The dream-thoughts protested bitterly against the reproach that I was *not getting on faster*—a reproach which, applying first to my treatment of the patient, extended later to other things. Did he know anyone, I thought, who could get on more quickly? Was he not aware that, apart from my methods of treatment, conditions of that kind are altogether incurable and last a lifetime? What were *four or five years* in comparison with a whole life-time, especially considering that the patient's existence had been so very much eased during the treatment?

A great part of the impression of absurdity in this dream was brought about by running together sentences from different parts of the dream-thoughts without any transition. Thus the sentence '*I went to him in the next room*,' etc., dropped the subject with which the preceding sentences had been dealing and correctly reproduced the circumstances in which I informed my father of my having become engaged to be married without consulting him. This sentence was therefore reminding me of the admirable unselfishness displayed by the old man on that occasion, and contrasting it with the behaviour of someone else—of yet another person. It is to be observed that the dream was allowed to ridicule my father because in the dream-thoughts he was held up in unqualified admiration as a model to other people. It lies in the very nature of every censorship that of forbidden things it allows those which are *untrue* to be said rather than those which are *true*. The next sentence, to the effect that he recollected '*having once got drunk and been locked up for it*' was no longer concerned with anything that related to my father in reality. Here the figure for whom he stood was no less a person than the great Meynert,[1] in whose footsteps I had trodden with such deep veneration and whose behaviour towards me, after a short period of favour, had turned to undisguised hostility. The dream reminded me that he himself had told me that at one

---

and the very satisfactory termination of the treatment is announced in Letter 133 (April 16, 1900).]

[1] [Theodor Meynert (1833–1892) had been Professor of Psychiatry at the Vienna University.]

time in his youth he had indulged in the habit of making himself *intoxicated with chloroform* and that on account of it he had had to go into a *home*. It also reminded me of another incident with him shortly before his death. I had carried on an embittered controversy with him in writing, on the subject of male hysteria, the existence of which he denied.[1] When I visited him during his fatal illness and asked after his condition, he spoke at some length about his state and ended with these words: 'You know, I was always one of the clearest cases of male hysteria.' He was thus admitting, to my satisfaction and astonishment, what he had for so long obstinately contested. But the reason why I was able in this scene of the dream to use my father as a screen for Meynert did not lie in any analogy that I had discovered between the two figures. The scene was a concise but entirely adequate representation of a conditional sentence in the dream-thoughts, which ran in full: 'If only I had been the second generation, the son of a professor or Hofrat, I should certainly have *got on faster.*' In the dream I made my father into a Hofrat and professor.—The most blatant and disturbing absurdity in the dream resides in its treatment of the date 1851, which seemed to me not to differ from 1856, *just as though a difference of five years was of no significance whatever.* But this last was precisely what the dream-thoughts sought to express. *Four or five years* was the length of time during which I enjoyed the support of the colleague whom I mentioned earlier in this analysis; but it was also the length of time during which I made my *fiancée* wait for our marriage; and it was also, by a chance coincidence which was eagerly exploited by the dream-thoughts, the length of time during which I made my patient of longest standing wait for a complete recovery. '*What are five years?*' asked the dream-thoughts; '*that's no time at all, so far as I'm concerned; it doesn't count.* I have time enough in front of me. And just as I succeeded in the end in *that,* though you would not believe it, so I shall achieve *this,* too.' Apart from this, however, the number 51 by itself, without the number of the century, was determined in another, and indeed, in an opposite sense; and this, too, is why it appeared in the dream several times. 51 is the age which seems to be a particularly dangerous one to men; I have known colleagues who have died suddenly at that age, and amongst them

---

[1] [This controversy is described in some detail in the first chapter of Freud's *Autobiographical Study* (1925*d*).]

one who, after long delays, had been appointed to a professorship only a few days before his death.[1]

V

Here is yet another absurd dream which plays about with numbers. *One of my acquaintances, Herr M., had been attacked in an essay with an un-justifiable degree of violence, as we all thought—by no less a person than Goethe. Herr M. was naturally crushed by the attack. He complained of it bit-terly to some company at table; his veneration for Goethe had not been affected, however, by this personal experience. I tried to throw a little light on the chronological data, which seemed to me improbable. Goethe died in 1832. Since his attack on Herr M. must naturally have been made earlier than that, Herr M. must have been quite a young man at the time. It seemed to be a plausible notion that he was eighteen. I was not quite sure, however, what year we were actually in, so that my whole calculation melted into obscurity. Inci-dentally, the attack was contained in Goethe's well-known essay on 'Nature.'*

We shall quickly find means of justifying the nonsense in this dream. Herr M., whom I had got to know among some *company at table,* had not long before asked me to examine his brother, who was showing signs of *general paralysis.* The suspicion was correct; on the occasion of this visit an awkward episode occurred, for in the course of his conversation the patient for no accountable reason gave his brother away by talking of his *youthful follies.* I had asked the patient the year of his birth and made him do sev-eral small sums so as to test the weakness of his memory—though, inci-dentally, he was still able to meet the tests quite well. I could already see that I myself behaved like a paralytic in the dream. (*I was not quite sure what year we were in.*) Another part of the material of the dream was de-rived from another recent source. The editor of a medical journal, with whom I was on friendly terms, had printed a highly unfavourable, a *'crush-ing'* criticism of my Berlin friend Fl.'s [Fliess's] last book. The criticism

---

[1] [This is no doubt a reference to Fliess's theory of periodicity. 51 = 28 + 23, the male and female periods respectively. Cf. Sections I and IV of Kris's introduction to Freud's correspondence with Fliess (Freud, 1950*a*). See also above, pp. 192 ff.— The fact that the number 51 occurs several times is referred to on p. 517. The analysis of the dream is continued below on pp. 457 ff.]

had been written by a very *youthful* reviewer who possessed small judgement. I thought I had a right to intervene and took the editor to task over it. He expressed lively regret at having published the criticism but would not undertake to offer any redress. I therefore severed my connection with the journal, but in my letter of resignation expressed a hope that *our personal relations would not be affected by the event.* The third source of the dream was an account I had just heard from a woman patient of her brother's mental illness, and of how he had broken out in a frenzy with cries of *'Naturel Nature!'* The doctors believed that his exclamation came from his having read *Goethe's* striking essay on that subject and that it showed he had been overworking at his studies in natural philosophy. I myself preferred to think of the sexual sense in which the word is used even by the less educated people here. This idea of mine was at least not disproved by the fact that the unfortunate young man subsequently mutilated his own genitals. *He was eighteen* at the time of his outbreak.

I may add that my friend's book which had been so severely criticized ('one wonders whether it is the author or oneself who is crazy,' another reviewer had said) dealt with the *chronological data* of life and showed that the length of *Goethe's* life was a multiple of a number [of days] that has a significance in biology. So it is easy to see that in the dream I was putting myself in my friend's place. (*I tried to throw a little light on the chronological data.*) But I behaved like a paralytic, and the dream was a mass of absurdities. Thus the dream-thoughts were saying ironically: *'Naturally,* it's *he* [my friend F.] who is the crazy fool, and it's *you* [the critics] who are the men of genius and know better. Surely it can't by any chance be the reverse?' There were plenty of examples of this *reversal* in the dream. For instance, Goethe attacked the young man, which is absurd, whereas it is still easy for quite a young man to attack Goethe, who is immortal. And again, I calculated from the year of Goethe's *death*, whereas I had made the paralytic calculate from the year of his *birth*. [See p. 342, where this dream has already been mentioned.]

But I have also undertaken to show that no dream is prompted by motives other than egoistic ones. [See pp. 285 ff.] So I must explain away the fact that in the present dream I made my friend's cause my own and put myself in his place. The strength of my critical conviction in waking life is not enough to account for this. The story of the eighteen-year-old patient, however, and the different interpretations of his exclaiming *'Nature!'* were allusions to the opposition in which I found myself to most doctors on account of my belief in the sexual aetiology of the psychoneuroses. I could say to myself: 'The kind of criticism that has been applied to your friend will be applied to you—indeed, to some extent it already *has* been.' The 'he' in the dream can therefore be replaced by 'we': 'Yes, you're quite right, it's *we* who are the fools.' There was a very clear reminder in the dream that '*mea res agitur,*' in the allusion to Goethe's short but exquisitely written essay; for when at the end of my school-days I was hesitating in my choice of a career, it was hearing that essay read aloud at a public lecture that decided me to take up the study of natural science.[1]

VI

Earlier in this volume I undertook to show that another dream in which my own ego did not appear was nevertheless egoistic. On p. 286 I reported a short dream to the effect that Professor M. said: '*My son, the Myops...,*' and I explained that the dream was only an introductory one, preliminary to another in which I *did* play a part. Here is the missing main dream, which introduces an absurd and unintelligible verbal form which requires an explanation.

On account of certain events which had occurred in the city of Rome, it had become necessary to remove the children to safety, and this was done. The scene was then in front of a gateway, double doors in the ancient style (the 'Porta Romana' at Siena, as I was aware during the dream itself). I was sitting on the edge of a fountain and was greatly depressed and almost in tears. A female figure—an attendant or nun—brought two boys out and handed them over to their father, who was not myself. The elder of the two was clearly my eldest son; I did not see the other one's face. The woman who brought out the boy asked him to kiss her good-bye. She was noticeable for having a red nose. The boy refused to kiss her, but, holding out his hand in farewell, said 'Auf Geseres' to her, and then 'Auf Ungeseres' to the two of us (or to one of us). I had a notion that this last phrase denoted a preference.[2]

This dream was constructed on a tangle of thoughts provoked by a play which I had seen, called *Das neue Ghetto* [*The New Ghetto*]. The Jewish

---

[1] [This dream is further discussed on pp. 456 f.; it is also analysed at length, and with a few additional details, in Part VI of Freud's short study *On Dreams* (1901*a*), Standard Ed., **5,** 662—An English translation of Goethe's '*Fragment über die Natur*' will be found in Wittels, 1931, 31.]

[2] [The words '*Geseres*' and '*Ungeseres,*' neither of them German, are discussed below.]

problem, concern about the future of one's children, to whom one cannot give a country of their own, concern about educating them in such a way that they can move freely across frontiers—all of this was easily recognizable among the relevant dream-thoughts.

'By the waters of Babylon we sat down and wept.' Siena, like Rome, is famous for its beautiful fountains. If Rome occurred in one of my dreams, it was necessary for me to find a substitute for it from some locality known to me (see pp. 215 f.). Near the Porta Romana in Siena we had seen a large and brightly lighted building. We learned that it was the *Manicomio,* the insane asylum. Shortly before I had the dream I had heard that a man of the same religious persuasion as myself had been obliged to resign the position which he had painfully achieved in a State asylum.

Our interest is aroused by the phrase *'Auf Geseres'* (at a point at which the situation in the dream would have led one to expect *'Auf Wiedersehen'*) as well as its quite meaningless opposite *'Auf Ungeseres.'* According to information I have received from philologists, *'Geseres'* is a genuine Hebrew word derived from a verb *'goiser,'* and is best translated by 'imposed sufferings' or 'doom.' The use of the word in slang would incline one to suppose that it meant 'weeping and wailing.' *'Ungeseres'* was a private neologism of my own and was the first word to catch my attention, but to begin with I could make nothing of it. But the short remark at the end of the dream to the effect that *'Ungeseres'* denoted a preference over *'Geseres'* opened the door to associations and at the same time to an elucidation of the word. An analogous relationship occurs in the case of caviare; *unsalted* [*'ungesalzen'*] caviare is esteemed more highly than *salted* [*'gesalzen'*]. 'Caviare to the general,' aristocratic pretensions; behind this lay a joking allusion to a member of my household who, since she was younger than I, would, I hoped, look after my children in the future. This tallied with the fact that another member of my household, our excellent nurse, was recognizably portrayed in the female attendant or nun in the dream. There was still, however, no transitional idea between *'salted—unsalted'* and *'Geseres—Ungeseres.'* This was provided by *'leavened—unleavened'* [*'gesäuert—ungesäuert'*]. In their flight out of Egypt the Children of Israel had not time to allow their dough to rise and, in memory of this, they eat unleavened bread to this day at Easter. At this point I may insert a sudden association that occurred to me during this portion of the analysis. I remembered how, during the previous Easter, my Berlin friend and I had been walking through the streets of Breslau, a town in which we were strangers. A little girl asked me the way to a particular street, and I was obliged to confess that

I did not know; and I remarked to my friend: 'It is to be hoped that when she grows up that little girl will show more discrimination in her choice of the people whom she gets to direct her.' Shortly afterwards, I caught sight of a door-plate bearing the words 'Dr. Herodes. Consulting hours: . . .' 'Let us hope,' I remarked, 'that our colleague does not happen to be a children's doctor.' At this same time my friend had been telling me his views on the biological significance of *bilateral symmetry* and had begun a sentence with the words 'If we had an eye in the middle of our foreheads like a Cyclops . . .' This led to the Professor's remark in the introductory dream, *'My son, the Myops . . .'*[1] and I had now been led to the principal source of *'Geseres.'* Many years before, when this son of Professor M.'s, today an independent thinker, was still sitting at his school-desk, he was attacked by a disease of the eyes which, the doctor declared, gave cause for anxiety. He explained that so long as it remained *on one side* it was of no importance, but that if it passed over to the *other eye* it would be a serious matter. The affection cleared up completely in the one eye; but shortly afterwards signs in fact appeared of the other one being affected. The boy's mother, terrified, at once sent for the doctor to the remote spot in the country where they were staying. The doctor, however, now went over *to the other side.* 'Why are you making such a *"Geseres"?'* he shouted at the mother, 'if *one* side has got well, so will the *other.'* And he was right.

And now we must consider the relation of all this to me and my family. The school-desk at which Professor M.'s son took his first steps in knowledge was handed over by his mother as a gift to my eldest son, into whose mouth I put the farewell phrases in the dream. It is easy to guess one of the wishes to which this transference gave rise. But the construction of the desk was also intended to save the child from being *short-sighted* and *one-sided.* Hence the appearance in the dream of *'Myops'* (and, behind it, *'Cyclops'*) and the reference to *bilaterality.* My concern about one-sidedness had more than one meaning: it could refer not only to physical one-sidedness but also to one-sidedness of intellectual development. May it not even be that it was precisely this concern which, in its crazy way, the scene in the dream was contradicting? After the child had turned to *one side* to say farewell words, he turned to the *other side* to say the contrary, as though to restore the balance. *It was as though he was acting with due attention to bilateral symmetry!*

---

[1] [The German *'Myop'* is an *ad hoc* form constructed on the pattern of *'Zyklop.'*]

Dreams, then, are often most profound when they seem most crazy. In every epoch of history those who have had something to say but could not say it without peril have eagerly assumed a fool's cap. The audience at whom their forbidden speech was aimed tolerated it more easily if they could at the same time laugh and flatter themselves with the reflection that the unwelcome words were clearly nonsensical. The Prince in the play, who had to disguise himself as a madman, was behaving just as dreams do in reality; so that we can say of dreams what Hamlet said of himself, concealing the true circumstances under a cloak of wit and unintelligibility: 'I am but mad north-north-west: when the wind is southerly, I know a hawk from a hand-saw!'[1]

Thus I have solved the problem of absurdity in dreams by showing that the dream-thoughts are never absurd—never, at all events, in the dreams of sane people—and that the dream-work produces absurd dreams and dreams containing individual absurd elements if it is faced with the necessity of representing any criticism, ridicule or derision which may be present in the dream-thoughts.[2]

My next task is to show that the dream-work consists in nothing more than a combination of the three factors I have mentioned[3]—and of a fourth which I have still to mention [see p. 493]; that it carries out no other function than the translation of dream-thoughts in accordance with the four conditions to which it is subject; and that the question whether the mind operates in dreams with all its intellectual faculties or with only a part of them is wrongly framed and disregards the facts. Since, however,

---

[1] [*Hamlet*, II, 2.] This dream also provides a good example of the generally valid truth that dreams which occur during the same night, even though they are recollected as separate, spring from the ground-work of the same thoughts. [See above, pp. 348 f.] Incidentally, the situation in the dream of my removing my children to safety from the City of Rome was distorted by being related back to an analogous event that occurred in my own childhood: I was envying some relatives who, many years earlier, had had an opportunity of removing their children to another country.

[2] [The subject of absurdity in dreams is also discussed in the course of Chapter VI of Freud's book on jokes (1905c).—Towards the end of Section I of the case history of the 'Rat Man' (1909d), Freud remarks in a footnote that the same mechanism is used in obsessional neuroses.]

[3] [Viz. condensation, displacement and consideration for representability.]

there are plenty of dreams in whose content judgements are passed, criticisms made, and appreciations expressed, in which surprise is felt at some particular element of the dream, in which explanations are attempted and argumentations embarked upon, I must now proceed to meet the objections arising from facts of this kind by producing some chosen examples.

My reply [put briefly] is as follows: *Everything that appears in dreams as the ostensible activity of the function of judgement is to be regarded not as an intellectual achievement of the dream-work but as belonging to the material of the dream-thoughts and as having been lifted from them into the manifest content of the dream as a ready-made structure.* I can even carry this assertion further. Even the judgements made *after waking* upon a dream that has been remembered, and the feelings called up in us by the reproduction of such a dream, form part, to a great extent, of the latent content of the dream and are to be included in its interpretation.

I

I have already quoted a striking example of this [p. 347 f.][1] A woman patient refused to tell me a dream of hers because 'it was not clear enough.' She had seen someone in the dream but did not know whether it was her husband or her father. There then followed a second piece of dream in which a dust-bin [*Misttrügerl*] appeared, and this gave rise to the following recollection. When she had first set up house she had jokingly remarked on one occasion in the presence of a young relative who was visiting in the house that her next job was to get hold of a new dust-bin. The next morning one arrived for her, but it was filled with lilies of the valley. This piece of the dream served to represent a common [German] phrase 'not grown on my own manure.'[2] When the analysis was completed, it turned out that the dream-thoughts were concerned with the after-effects of a story, which the dreamer had heard when she was young, of how a girl had had a baby and of how it was *not clear who the father really was*. Here, then, the dream-representation had overflowed

---

[1] [Another example was also quoted in the same passage, p. 347.]

[2] [*'Nicht auf meinem eigenen Mist gewachsen'*—meaning 'I am not responsible for that,' or 'It's not my baby.' The German word *'Mist,'* properly meaning manure, is used in slang for 'rubbish' and occurs in this sense in the Viennese term for a dust-bin: *'Misttrügerl.'*]

into the waking thoughts: one of the elements of the dream-thoughts had found representation in a waking judgement passed upon the dream as a whole.

II

Here is a similar case. One of my patients had a dream which struck him as interesting, for immediately after waking he said to himself: 'I *must tell the doctor that.*' The dream was analysed and produced the clearest allusions to a *liaison* which he had started during the treatment and which he had decided to himself *not to tell me about.*[1]

III

Here is a third example, one from my own experience. *I was going to the hospital with P. through a district in which there were houses and gardens. At the same time I had a notion that I had often seen this district before in dreams. I did not know my way about very well. He showed me a road that led round the corner to a restaurant (indoors, not a garden). There I asked for Frau Doni and was told that she lived at the back in a small room with three children. I went towards it, but before I got there met an indistinct figure with my two little girls; I took them with me after I had stood with them for a little while. Some sort of reproach against my wife, for having left them there.*

When I woke up I had a feeling of great *satisfaction,* the reason for which I explained to myself as being that I was going to discover from this analysis the meaning of 'I've dreamt of that before.'[1] In fact, however, the analysis taught me nothing of the kind; what it did show me was that the satisfaction belonged to the latent content of the dream and not to any judgement upon it. My satisfaction was with the fact that my marriage had brought me children. P. was a person whose course in life lay for some time

---

[1] [See above, pp. 353 f.] A protracted discussion on this subject has run through recent volumes of the *Revue Philosophique* [1896–98] under the title of 'Paramnesia in Dreams'.—[This dream is referred to again on pp. 483 f.]

alongside mine, who then outdistanced me both socially and materially, but whose marriage was childless. The two events which occasioned the dream will serve, instead of a complete analysis, to indicate its meaning. The day before, I had read in a newspaper the announcement of the death of Frau Dona A——y (which I turned into 'Doni' in the dream), who had died in childbirth. My wife told me that the dead woman had been looked after by the same midwife who had attended her at the birth of our two youngest children. The name 'Dona' had struck me because I had met it for the first time a short while before in an English novel. The second occasion for the dream was provided by the date on which it occurred. It was on the night before the birthday of my eldest boy—who seems to have some poetic gifts.

IV

I was left with the same feeling of satisfaction when I woke from the absurd dream of my father having played a political part among the Magyars after his death; and the reason I gave myself for this feeling was that it was a continuation of the feeling that accompanied the last piece of the dream. [See p. 436.] *I remembered how like Garibaldi he had looked on his death-bed and felt glad that it had come true.... (There was a continuation which I had forgotten).* The analysis enabled me to fill in this gap in the dream. It was a mention of my second son, to whom I had given the first name of a great historical figure [Cromwell] who had powerfully attracted me in my boyhood, especially since my visit to England. During the year before the child's birth I had made up my mind to use this name if it were a son and I greeted the new-born baby with it with a feeling of high *satisfaction.* (It is easy to see how the suppressed megalomania of fathers is transferred in their thoughts on to their children, and it seems quite probable that this is one of the ways in which the suppression of that feeling, which becomes necessary in actual life, is carried out.) The little boy's right to appear in the context of this dream was derived from the fact that he had just had the same misadventure—easily forgivable both in a child and in a dying man—of soiling his bedclothes. Compare in this connection *Stuhlrichter* ['presiding judge,' literally 'chair-' or 'stool-judge'] and the wish expressed in the dream to stand before one's children's eyes *great* and *unsullied.* [See below, p. 483.]

V

I now turn to consider expressions of judgement passed in the dream itself but not continued into waking life or transposed into it. In looking for examples of these, my task will be greatly assisted if I may make use of dreams which I have already recorded with other aims in view. The dream of Goethe's attack on Herr M. [pp. 447 ff.] appears to contain a whole number of acts of judgement. '*I tried to throw a little light on the chronological data, which seemed to me improbable.*' This has every appearance of being a criticism of the absurd idea that Goethe should have made a literary attack on a young man of my acquaintance. '*It seemed to be a plausible notion that he was eighteen.*' This, again, sounds exactly like the outcome of a calculation, though, it is true, of a feeble-minded one. Lastly, '*I was not quite sure what year we were in*' seems like an instance of uncertainty or doubt in a dream.

Thus all of these seemed to be acts of judgement made for the first time in the dream. But analysis showed that their wording can be taken in another way, in the light of which they become indispensable for the dream's interpretation, while at the same time every trace of absurdity is removed. The sentence '*I tried to throw a little light on the chronological data*' put me in the place of my friend [Fliess] who was in fact seeking to throw light on the chronological data of life. This deprives the sentence of its significance as a judgement protesting against the absurdity of the preceding sentences. The interpolated phrase, '*which seemed to me improbable,*' belonged with the subsequent one, '*It seemed to be a plausible notion.*' I had used almost these precise words to the lady who had told her brother's case-history. '*It seems to me an improbable notion* that his cries of "Nature! Nature!" had anything to do with Goethe; *it seems to me far more plausible* that the words had the sexual meaning you are familiar with.*' It is true that here a judgement was passed—not in the dream, however, but in reality, and on an occasion which was recollected and exploited by the dream-thoughts. The content of the dream took over this judgement just like any other fragment of the dream-thoughts. The number '18' to which the judgement in the dream was senselessly attached, retains a trace of the real context from which the judgement was torn. Lastly, '*I was not quite sure what year we were in*' was intended merely to carry further my identification with the paralytic patient in my examination of whom this point had really arisen.

The resolution of what are ostensibly acts of judgement in dreams may serve to remind us of the rules laid down at the beginning of this book [pp. 129 f.] for carrying out the work of interpretation: namely, that we should disregard the apparent coherence between a dream's constituents as an unessential illusion, and that we should trace back the origin of each of its elements on its own account. A dream is a conglomerate which, for purposes of investigation, must be broken up once more into fragments. [Cf. p. 428 f.] On the other hand, however, it will be observed that a psychical force is at work in dreams which creates this apparent connectedness, which, that is to say, submits the material produced by the dream-work to a 'secondary revision.' This brings us face to face with the manifestations of a force whose importance we shall later [pp. 493 ff.] assess as the fourth of the factors concerned in the construction of dreams.

VI

Here is a further instance of a process of judgement at work in a dream that I have already recorded. In the absurd dream of the communication from the town council [pp. 447 ff.] I asked: *'Did you get married soon after that?' I calculated that, of course, I was born in 1856, which seemed to be the year which immediately followed the year in question.* All of this was clothed in the form of a set of logical conclusions. My father had married in 1851, immediately after his attack; I, of course, was the eldest of the family and had been born in 1856; Q.E.D. As we know, this false conclusion was drawn in the interests of wish-fulfilment; and the predominant dream-thought ran: *'Four or five years, that's no time at all; it doesn't count.'* Every step in this set of logical conclusions, however alike in their content and their form, could be explained in another way as having been determined by the dream-thoughts. It was the *patient,* of whose long analysis my colleague had fallen foul, who had decided to get married immediately the treatment was finished. The manner of my interview with my father in the dream was like an interrogation or examination, and reminded me too of a teacher at the University who used to take down exhaustive particulars from the students who were enrolling themselves for his lectures: 'Date of birth?'—'1856.'—'*Patre?*' In reply to this one gave one's father's first name with a Latin termination; and we students assumed that the Hofrat *drew conclusions* from the first name of the father which could not always be drawn from that of the student himself. Thus the *drawing of the conclusion* in the dream was no more than a repetition of the *drawing of a conclusion* which appeared as a piece of the material of the dream-thoughts. Something new emerges from this. If a conclusion appears in the content of the dream there is no question that it is derived from the dream-thoughts; but it may either be present in these as a piece of recollected material or it may link a series of dream-thoughts together in a logical chain. In any case, however, a conclusion in a dream represents a conclusion in the dream-thoughts.[1]

At this point we may resume our analysis of the dream. The interrogation by the professor led to a recollection of the register of University Students (which in my time was drawn up in Latin). It led further to thoughts upon the course of my academic studies. The *five years* which are prescribed for medical studies were once again too few for me. I quietly went on with my work for several more years; and in my circle of acquaintances I was regarded as an idler and it was doubted whether I should ever get through. Thereupon I *quickly* decided to take my examinations and I got through them *in spite of the delay*. Here was a fresh reinforcement of the dream-thoughts with which I was defiantly confronting my critics: 'Even though you won't believe it because I've taken my time, I *shall* get through; I *shall* bring my medical training to a *conclusion*. Things have often turned out like that before.'

This same dream in its opening passage contained some sentences which could hardly be refused the name of an argument. This argument was not even absurd; it might just as well have occurred in waking thought: *I was amused in the dream at the communication from the town council since, in the first place, I was not yet in the world in* 1851 *and, in the second place, my father, to whom it might have related, was already dead.* Both of these statements were not only correct in themselves but agreed precisely with the real arguments that I should bring up if I were actually to receive a communication of that kind. My earlier analysis of the dream showed that it grew out of deeply embittered and derisive dream-thoughts. If we may also assume that there were strong reasons present for the activity of the censorship, we shall understand that the dream-work had every motive for producing, *a perfectly valid refutation of an absurd suggestion* on the model contained in the dream-thoughts. The analysis showed, however, that the dream-work

---

[1] These findings are in some respects a correction of what I have said above (p. 328 f.) on the representation of logical relations in dreams. This earlier passage describes the general behaviour of the dream-work but takes no account of the finer and more precise details of its functioning.

did not have a free hand in framing this parallel but was obliged, for that purpose, to use material from the dream-thoughts. It was just as though there were an algebraic equation containing (in addition to numerals) plus and minus signs, indices and radical signs, and as though someone were to copy out the equation without understanding it, taking over both the operational symbols and the numerals into his copy but mixing them all up together. The two arguments [in the dream-content] could be traced back to the following material. It was distressing to me to think that some of the premises which underlay my psychological explanations of the psychoneuroses were bound to excite scepticism and laughter when they were first met with. For instance, I had been driven to assume that impressions from the second year of life, and sometimes even from the first, left a lasting trace on the emotional life of those who were later to fall ill, and that these impressions—though distorted and exaggerated in many ways by the memory—might constitute the first and deepest foundation for hysterical symptoms. Patients, to whom I explained this at some appropriate moment, used to parody this newly-gained knowledge by declaring that they were ready to look for recollections dating from a time *at which they were not yet alive.* My discovery of the unexpected part played by their *father* in the earliest sexual impulses of female patients might well be expected to meet with a similar reception (see the discussion on pp. 276). Nevertheless, it was my well-grounded conviction that both of these hypotheses were true. By way of confirmation I called to mind some instances in which the death of the father occurred while the child was at a very early age and in which later events, otherwise inexplicable, proved that the child had nevertheless retained unconsciously recollections of the figure which had disappeared so early in his life. I was aware that these two assertions of mine rested on *the drawing of conclusions* whose validity would be disputed. It was therefore an achievement of wish-fulfilment when the material of precisely *those conclusions which I was afraid would be contested* was employed by the dream-work for drawing *conclusions which it was impossible to contest.*

VII

At the beginning of a dream, which I have so far hardly touched upon [see p. 422], there was a clear expression of astonishment at the subject which had cropped up. *Old Brücke must have set me some task;* STRANGELY ENOUGH, *it related to a dissection of the lower part of my own body, my pelvis and legs, which I saw before me as though in the dissecting-room, but without noticing their absence in myself and also without a trace of any gruesome feeling. Louise N. was standing beside me and doing the work with me. The pelvis had been eviscerated, and it was visible now in its superior, now in its inferior, aspect, the two being mixed together. Thick flesh-coloured protuberances (which, in the dream itself, made me think of haemorrhoids) could be seen. Something which lay over it and was like crumpled silver-paper[1] had also to be carefully fished out. I was then once more in possession of my legs and was making my way through the town. But (being tired) I took a cab. To my astonishment the cab drove in through the door of a house, which opened and allowed it to pass along a passage which turned a corner at its end and finally led into the open air again.[2] Finally I was making a journey through a changing landscape with an Alpine guide who was carrying my belongings. Part of the way he carried me too, out of consideration for my tired legs. The ground was boggy; we went round the edge; people were sitting on the ground like Red Indians or gipsies—among them a girl. Before this I had been making my own way forward over the slippery ground with a constant feeling of surprise that I was able to do it so well after the dissection. At last we reached a small wooden house at the end of which was an open window. There the guide set me down and laid two wooden boards, which were standing ready, upon the window-sill, so as to bridge the chasm which had to be crossed over from the window. At that point I really became frightened about my legs, but instead of the expected crossing, I saw two grown-up men lying on wooden benches that were along the walls of the hut, and what seemed to be two children sleeping beside them. It was as though what was going to make the crossing possible was not the boards but the children. I awoke in a mental fright.*

Anyone who has formed even the slightest idea of the extent of condensation in dreams will easily imagine what a number of pages would be filled by a full analysis of this dream. Fortunately, however, in the present context I need only take up one point in it, which provides an example of astonishment in dreams, as exhibited in the interpolation ‘*strangely enough.*’ The following was the occasion of the dream. Louise N., the lady who was assisting me in my job in the dream, had been calling on me. ‘Lend me something to read,’ she had said. I offered her Rider Haggard’s *She*. ‘A *strange* book,

---

[1] Stanniol, which was an allusion to the book by Stannius on the nervous system of fishes. (Cf. loc. cit.)

[2] It was the place on the ground-floor of my block of flats where the tenants keep their perambulators; but it was overdetermined in several other ways.

but full of bidden meaning,' I began to explain to her; 'the eternal feminine, the immortality of our emotions . . .' Here she interrupted me: 'I
know it already. Have you nothing of your own?'—'No, my own immortal
works have not yet been written.'—'Well, when are we to expect these so-
called ultimate explanations of yours which you've promised even *we* shall
find readable?' she asked, with a touch of sarcasm. At that point I saw that
someone else was admonishing me through her mouth and I was silent. I
reflected on the amount of self-discipline it was costing me to offer the public even my book upon dreams—I should have to give away so much of my
own private character in it.

> Das Beste was du wissen kannst,
> Darfst du den Buben doch nicht sagen.[1]

The task which was imposed on me in the dream of carrying out a dissection *of my own body* was thus my *self-analysis*[2] which was linked up
with my giving an account of my dreams. Old Brücke came in here appropriately; even in the first years of my scientific work it happened that
I allowed a discovery of mine to lie fallow until an energetic remonstrance
on his part drove me into publishing it. The further thoughts which were
started up by my conversation with Louise N. went too deep to become
conscious. They were diverted in the direction of the material that had
been stirred up in me by the mention of Rider Haggard's *She*. The judgement *'strangely enough'* went back to that book and to another one, *Heart
of the World*, by the same author; and numerous elements of the dream
were derived from these two imaginative novels. The boggy ground over
which people had to be carried, and the chasm which they had to cross
by means of boards brought along with them, were taken from *She*; the
Red Indians, the girl and the wooden house were taken from *Heart of the
World*. In both novels the guide is a woman; both are concerned with per-
ilous journeys; while *She* describes an adventurous road that had scarcely
ever been trodden before, leading into an undiscovered region. The tired
feeling in my legs, according to a note which I find I made upon the
dream, had been a real sensation during the daytime. It probably went

---

[1] [*See* footnote, p. 166.]

[2] [Freud's self-analysis during the years before the publication of this book is one
of the themes of his correspondence with Fliess (Freud, 1950*a*). Cf. Part III of
Kris's introduction to the latter volume.]

along with a tired mood and a doubting thought: 'How much longer will my legs carry me?' The end of the adventure in *She* is that the guide, instead of finding immortality for herself and the others, perishes in the mysterious subterranean fire. A fear of that kind was unmistakably active in the dream-thoughts. The Vooden house' was also, no doubt, a coffin, that is to say, the grave. But the dream-work achieved a masterpiece in its representation of this most unwished-for of all thoughts by a wish-fulfilment. For I had already been in a grave once, but *it* was an excavated Etruscan grave near Orvieto, a narrow chamber with two stone benches along its walls, on which the skeletons of two grown-up men were lying. The inside of the wooden house in the dream looked exactly like it, except that the stone was replaced by wood. The dream seems to have been saying: 'If you must rest in a grave, let it be the Etruscan one.' And, by making this replacement, it transformed the gloomiest of expectations into one that was highly desirable.[1] Unluckily, as we are soon to hear [pp. 466 ff.], a dream can turn into its opposite the *idea* accompanying an affect but not always the affect itself. Accordingly, I woke up in a *'mental fright,'* even after the successful emergence of the idea that children may perhaps achieve what their father has failed to—a fresh allusion to the strange novel in which a person's identity is retained through a series of generations for over two thousand years.[2]

VIII

Included in yet another of my dreams there was an expression of surprise at something I had experienced in it; but the surprise was accompanied by such a striking, farfetched and almost brilliant attempt at an explanation that, if only on *its* account, I cannot resist submitting the whole dream to analysis, quite apart from the dream's possessing two other points to attract our interest. I was travelling along the *Südbahn* railway-line during the night of July 18–19th, and in my sleep I heard: *'Holl-thurn,*[3] *ten minutes' being called out.* I at once thought of holo-thurians [sea-slugs]—*of a natural history museum*—that this was the spot at which

---

[1] [This detail is used as an illustration in Chapter III of Freud's *Future of an Illusion* (1927c).]

[2] [This dream is further discussed below on pp. 483 f.]

[3] [Not the name of any real place.]

valiant men had fought in vain against the superior power of the ruler of their country—yes:, the Counter-Reformation in Austria—it was as though it were a place in Styria or the Tyrol. I then saw indistinctly a small museum, in which the relics or belongings of these men were preserved. I should have liked to get out, but hesitated to do so. There were women with fruit on the platform. They were crouching on the ground and holding up their baskets invitingly.—I hesitated because I was not sure whether there was time, but we were still not moving.—I was suddenly in another compartment, in which the upholstery and seats were so narrow that one's back pressed directly against the back of the carriage.[1] *I was surprised by this, but I reflected that* I MIGHT HAVE CHANGED CARRIAGES WHILE I WAS IN A SLEEPING STATE. *There were several people, including an English brother and sister; a row of books were distinctly visible on a shelf on the wall. I saw 'The Wealth of Nations' and 'Matter and Motion' (by Clerk-Maxwell), a thick volume and bound in brown cloth. The man asked his sister about a book by Schiller, whether she had forgotten it. It seemed as though the books were sometimes mine and sometimes theirs. I felt inclined at that point to intervene in the conversation in a confirmatory or substantiating sense. . . .* I woke up perspiring all over, because all the windows were shut. The train was drawn up at Marburg [in Styria].

While I was writing the dream down a new piece of it occurred to me, which my memory had tried to pass over. *I said* [in English] *to the brother and sister, referring to a particular work: 'It is from . . . ,' but corrected myself: 'It is by . . . ' 'Yes,' the man commented to his sister, 'he said that right.'*[2]

The dream opened with the name of the station, which must no doubt have partly woken me up. I replaced its name, *Marburg*, by *Hollthurn*. The fact that I heard 'Marburg' when it was first called out, or perhaps later, was proved by the mentioning in the dream of Schiller, who was born at Marburg, though not at the one in Styria.[3] I was making my

---

[1] This description was unintelligible even to myself; but I have followed the fundamental rule of reporting a dream in the words which occurred to me as I was writing it down. The wording chosen is itself part of what is represented by the dream. [Cf. p. 516.]

[2] [This piece of the dream is further considered on pp. 522 f.]

[3] [*Footnote added* 1909:] Schiller was not born at any Marburg, but at Marbach, as every German school-boy knows, and as I knew myself. This was one more of those mistakes (see above, p. 219 *n.*) which slip in as a substitute for an intentional falsification at some other point, and which I have tried to explain in my *Psycho-pathology of Everyday Life*, [1901*b*, Chapter X, No. 1.]

journey on that occasion, although I was travelling first class, under very uncomfortable conditions. The train was packed full, and in my compartment I had found a lady and gentleman who appeared to be very aristocratic and had not the civility, or did not think it worth the trouble, to make any disguise of their annoyance at my intrusion. My polite greeting met with no response. Although the man and his wife were sitting side by side (with their backs to the engine) the woman nevertheless made haste, under my very eyes, to engage the window-seat facing her by putting an umbrella on it. The door was shut immediately, and pointed remarks were exchanged between them on the subject of opening windows. They had probably seen at once that I was longing for some fresh air. It was a hot night and the atmosphere in the completely closed compartment soon became suffocating. My experiences of travelling have taught me that conduct of this ruthless and overbearing kind is a characteristic of people who are travelling on a free or half-price ticket. When the ticket-collector came and I showed him the ticket I had bought at such expense, there fell from the lady's mouth, in haughty and almost menacing tones, the words: 'My husband has a free pass.' She was an imposing figure with discontented features, of an age not far from the time of the decay of feminine beauty; the man uttered not a word but sat there motionless. I attempted to sleep. In my dream I took fearful vengeance on my disagreeable companions; no one could suspect what insults and humiliations lay concealed behind the broken fragments of the first half of the dream. When this need had been satisfied a second wish made itself felt—to change compartments. The scene is changed so often in dreams, and without the slightest objection being raised, that it would not have been in the least surprising if I had promptly replaced my travelling companions by more agreeable ones derived from my memory. But here was a case in which something resented the change of scene and thought it necessary to explain it. How did I suddenly come to be in another compartment? I had no recollection of having changed. There could be only one explanation: *I must have left the carriage while I was in a sleeping state*—a rare event, of which, however, examples are to be found in the experience of a neuropathologist. We know of people who have gone upon railway journeys in a twilight state, without betraying their abnormal condition by any signs, till at some point in the journey they have suddenly come to themselves completely and been amazed at the gap in their memory. In the dream itself, accordingly, I was declaring myself to be one of these cases of *'automatisme ambulatoire.'*

Analysis made it possible to find another solution. The attempt at an explanation, which seemed so striking when I was obliged to ascribe it to the dream-work, was not an original one of my own, but was copied from the neurosis of one of my patients. I have already spoken elsewhere [pp. 277 f.] of a highly educated and, in real life, softhearted man who, shortly after the death of his parents, began to reproach himself with having murderous inclinations, and then fell a victim to the precautionary measures which he was obliged to adopt as a safeguard. It was a case of severe obsessions accompanied by complete insight. To begin with, walking through the streets was made a burden to him by a compulsion to make certain where every single person he met disappeared to; if anyone suddenly escaped his watchful eye, he was left with a distressing feeling and the idea that he might possibly have got rid of him. What lay behind this was, among other things, a 'Cain' phantasy—for 'all men are brothers.' Owing to the impossibility of carrying out this task, he gave up going for walks and spent his life incarcerated between his own four walls. But reports of murders which had been committed outside were constantly being brought into his room by the newspapers, and his conscience suggested to him, in the form of a doubt, that he might be the wanted murderer. The certainty that he had in fact not left his house for weeks protected him from these charges for a while, till one day the possibility came into his head that *he might have left his house while he was in an unconscious state* and have thus been able to commit the murder without knowing anything about it. From that time onwards he locked the front door of the house and gave the key to his old housekeeper with strict instructions never to let it fall into his hands even if he asked for it.

This, then, was the origin of my attempted explanation to the effect that I had changed carriages while I was in an unconscious state; it had been carried over ready-made into the dream from the material of the dream-thoughts, and was evidently intended in the dream to serve the purpose of identifying me with the figure of this patient. My recollection of him had been aroused by an easy association. My last night-journey, a few weeks earlier, had been made in the company of this very man. He was cured, and was travelling with me into the provinces to visit his relatives, who had sent for me. We had a compartment to ourselves; we left all the windows open all through the night and had a most entertaining time for as long as I stayed awake. I knew that the root of his illness had been hostile impulses against his father, dating from his childhood and involving a sexual situation. In so far, therefore, as I was identifying myself with him, I was seeking to confess to something analogous. And in fact the second scene of the dream ended in a somewhat extravagant phantasy that my two elderly travelling companions had treated me in such a stand-offish way because my arrival had prevented the affectionate exchanges which they had planned for the night. This phantasy went back, however, to a scene of early childhood in which the child, probably driven by sexual curiosity, had forced his way into his parents' bedroom and been turned out of it by his father's orders.

It is unnecessary, I think, to accumulate further examples. They would merely serve to confirm what we have gathered from those I have already quoted—that an act of judgement in a dream is only a repetition of some prototype in the dream-thoughts. As a rule, the repetition is ill-applied and interpolated into an inappropriate context, but occasionally, as in our last instances, it is so neatly employed that to begin with it may give the impression of independent intellectual activity in the dream. From this point we might turn our attention to the psychical activity which, though it does not appear to accompany the construction of dreams invariably, yet, whenever it does so, is concerned to fuse together elements in a dream which are of a disparate origin into a whole which shall make sense and be without contradiction. Before approaching that subject, however, we are under an urgent necessity to consider the expressions of affect which occur in dreams and to compare them with the affects which analysis uncovers in the dream-thoughts.

(H)

AFFECTS IN DREAMS

A shrewd observation made by Strieker [1879, 51] has drawn our attention to the fact that the expression of affect in dreams cannot be dealt with in the same contemptuous fashion in which, after waking, we are accustomed to dismiss their *content*. 'If I am afraid of robbers in a dream, the robbers, it is true, are imaginary—but the fear is real.' [Cf. p. 101.] And this is equally true if I feel *glad* in a dream. Our feeling tells us that an affect experienced in a dream is in no way inferior to one of equal intensity experienced in waking life; and dreams insist with greater energy upon their right to be included among our real mental experiences in respect to their affective than in respect to their ideational content. In our waking state, however, we cannot in fact include them in this way, because we cannot make any psychical assessment of an affect unless it is linked to a piece of ideational material. If the affect and the idea are incompatible in their character and intensity, our waking judgement is at a loss.

It has always been a matter for surprise that in dreams the ideational content is not accompanied by the affective consequences that we should regard as inevitable in waking thought. Strümpel [1877, 27 f.] declared that in dreams ideas are denuded of their psychical values [cf. pp. 82 f.]. But there is no lack in dreams of instances of a contrary kind, where an intense expression of affect appears in connection with subject-matter which seems to provide no occasion for any such expression. In a dream I may be in a horrible, dangerous and disgusting situation without feeling any fear or repulsion; while another time, on the contrary, I may be terrified at something harmless and delighted at something childish.

This particular enigma of dream-life vanishes more suddenly, perhaps, and more completely than any other, as soon as we pass over from the manifest to the latent content of the dream. We need not bother about the enigma, since it no longer exists. Analysis shows us that *the ideational material has undergone displacements and substitutions, whereas the affects have remained unaltered.* It is small wonder that the ideational material, which has been changed by dream-distortion, should no longer be compatible with the affect, which is retained unmodified; nor is there anything left to be surprised at after analysis has put the right material back into its former position.[1]

---

[1] [*Footnote added* 1919:] If I am not greatly mistaken, the first dream that I was able to pick up from my grandson, at the age of one year and eight months, revealed a state of affairs in which the dream-work had succeeded in transforming the *material* of the dream-thoughts into a wish-fulfilment, whereas the *affect* belonging to them persisted unchanged during the state of sleep. On the night before the day on which his father was due to leave for the front, the child cried out, sobbing violently: 'Daddy! Daddy!—baby!' This can only have meant that Daddy and baby were remaining together; whereas the tears recognized the approaching farewell. At that time the child was already quite well able to express the concept of separation. '*Fort*' ['gone'] (replaced by a long-drawn-out and peculiarly stressed 'o—o—o') had been one of his first words, and several months before this first dream he had played at 'gone' with all his toys. This game went back to a successful piece of self-discipline which he had achieved at an early age in allowing his mother to leave him and be 'gone.' [Cf. Chapter II of *Beyond the Pleasure Principle* (Freud, 1920*g*).]

In the case of a psychical complex which has come under the influence of the censorship imposed by resistance, the *affects* are the constituent which is least influenced and which alone can give us a pointer as to how we should fill in the missing thoughts. This is seen even more clearly in the psychoneuroses than in dreams. Their affects are always appropriate, at least in their *quality*, though we must allow for their intensity being increased owing to displacements of neurotic attention. If a hysteric is surprised at having to be so frightened of something trivial or if a man suffering from obsessions is surprised at such distressing self-reproaches arising out of a mere nothing, they have both gone astray, because they regard the ideational content—the triviality or the mere nothing—as what is essential; and they put up an unsuccessful fight because they take this ideational content as the starting-point of their thought-activity. Psycho-analysis can put them upon the right path by recognizing the affect as being, on the contrary, justified and by seeking out the idea which belongs to it but has been repressed and replaced by a substitute. A necessary premise to all this is that the release of affect and the ideational content do not constitute the indissoluble organic unity as which we are in the habit of treating them, but that these two separate entities may be merely *soldered* together and can thus be detached from each other by analysis. Dream-interpretation shows that this is in fact the case.

I shall begin by giving an example in which analysis explained the apparent absence of affect in a case where the ideational content should have necessitated its release.

I

She saw three lions in a desert, one of which was laughing; but she was not afraid of them. Afterwards, however, she must have run away from them, for she was trying to climb up a tree; but she found that her cousin, who was a French mistress, was up there already, etc.

The analysis brought up the following material. The indifferent precipitating cause of the dream was a sentence in her English composition: 'The mane is the ornament of the lion.' Her father wore a beard which framed his face like a mane. Her English mistress was called Miss Lyons. An acquaintance had sent her the ballads of Loewe [the German word for 'lion']. These, then, were the three lions; why should she be afraid of them?—She had read a story in which a negro, who had stirred up his companions to revolt, was hunted with blood-hounds and climbed up a tree to save himself. She went on, in the highest spirits, to produce a number of fragmentary recollections, such as the advice on how to catch lions from *Fliegende Blätter*: 'Take a desert and put it through a sieve and the lions will be left over.' And again, the highly amusing but not very proper anecdote of an official who was asked why he did not take more trouble to ingratiate himself with the head of his department and replied that he had tried to make his way in, but his superior *was up there already.* The whole material became intelligible when it turned out that the lady had had a visit on the dream-day from her husband's superior. He had been very polite to her and had kissed her hand and *she had not been in the least afraid of him,* although he was a very 'big hug' [in German, *'grosses Tier'* = 'big animal'], and played the part of a 'social *lion*' in the capital of the country she came from. So this lion was like the lion in *A Midsummer Night's Dream* that concealed the figure of Snug the joiner; and the same is true of all dream-lions of which the dreamer is not afraid.

II

As my second example I may quote the dream of the young girl who saw her sister's little son lying dead in his coffin [pp. 176 ff. and 267], but who, as I may now add, felt neither pain nor grief. We know from the analysis why this was. The dream merely disguised her wish to see the man she was in love with once more; and her affect had to be in tune with her wish and not with its disguise. There was thus no occasion for grief.

In some dreams the affect does at least remain in contact with the ideational material which has replaced that to which the affect was originally attached. In others, the dissolution of the complex has gone further. The affect makes its appearance completely detached from the idea which belongs to it and is introduced at some other point in the dream, where it fits in with the new arrangement of the dream-elements. The situation is then similar to the one we have found in the case of acts of judgement in dreams [pp. 452 ff.]. If an important conclusion is drawn in the dream-thoughts, the dream also contains one; but the conclusion in the dream may be displaced on to quite different material. Such a displacement not infrequently follows the principle of antithesis.

This last possibility is exemplified in the following dream, which I have submitted to a most exhaustive analysis.

III

A castle by the sea; later it was no longer immediately on the sea, but on a narrow canal leading to the sea. The Governor was a Herr P. I was standing with him in a big reception room—with three windows in front of which there rose buttresses with what looked like crenellations. I had been attached to the garrison as something in the nature of a volunteer naval officer. We feared the arrival of enemy warships, since we were in a state of war. Herr P. intended to leave, and gave me instructions as to what was to be done if the event that we feared took place. His invalid wife was with their children in the threatened castle. If the bombardment began, the great hall was to be evacuated. He breathed heavily and turned to go; I held him back and asked him how I was to communicate with him in case of necessity. He added something in reply, but immediately fell down dead. No doubt I had put an unnecessary strain upon him with my questions. After his death, which made no further impression on me, I wondered whether his widow would remain in the castle, whether I should report his death to the Higher Command and whether I should take over command of the castle as being next in order of rank. I was standing at the window, and observing the ships as they went past. They were merchant vessels rushing past rapidly through the dark water, some of them with several funnels and others with bulging decks (just like the station buildings in the introductory dream—not reported here). *Then my brother was standing beside me and we were both looking out of the window at the canal. At the sight of one ship we were frightened and cried out: 'Here comes the warship!' But it turned out that it was only the same ships that I already knew returning. There now came a small ship, cut off short, in a comic fashion, in the middle. On its deck some curious cup-shaped or box-shaped objects were visible. We called out with one voice: 'That's the breakfast-ship!'*

The rapid movements of the ships, the deep dark blue of the water and the brown smoke from the funnels—all of this combined to create a tense and sinister impression.

The localities in the dream were brought together from several trips of mine to the Adriatic (to Miramare, Duino, Venice and Aquileia). A short but enjoyable Easter trip which I had made to Aquileia with my brother a few weeks before the dream was still fresh in my memory.[1] The dream also contained allusions to the *maritime war* between America and Spain and to anxieties to which it had given rise about the fate of my relatives in America. At two points in the dream affects were in question. At one point an affect that was to be anticipated was absent: attention was expressly drawn to the fact that the Governor's death made no impression on me. At another point, when I thought I saw the warship, I was *frightened* and felt all the sensations of fright in my sleep. In this well-constructed dream the affects were distributed in such a way that any striking contradiction was avoided. There was no reason why I should be frightened at the death of the Governor and it was quite reasonable that as Commandant of the Castle I should be frightened at the sight of the warship. The analysis showed, however, that Herr P. was only a substitute for my own self. (In the dream *I* was the substitute for *him*.) *I* was the Governor who suddenly died. The dream-thoughts dealt with the future of my family after my premature death. This was the only distressing one among the dream-thoughts; and it must have been from it that the fright was detached and brought into connection in the dream with the sight of the warship. On the other hand, the analysis showed that the region of the dream-thoughts from which the warship was taken was filled with the most cheerful recollections. It was a year earlier, in Venice, and we were standing one magically beautiful day at the windows of our room on the Riva degli Schiavoni and were looking across the blue lagoon on which that day there was more movement than usual. English ships were expected and were to be given a ceremonial reception. Suddenly my wife cried out gaily as a child: '*Here comes the English warship!*' In the dream I was frightened at these same words. (We see once again that speeches in a dream are derived from speeches in real life [cf. pp. 427 ff.]; I shall show shortly that the element 'English' in my wife's exclamation did not elude the dream-work either.) Here, then, in the process of changing the dream-thoughts into the manifest dream-content, I have transformed cheerfulness into fear, and I need only hint that this transformation was itself giving expression to a portion of the latent dream-content. This example proves, however, that the dream-work is at liberty to

---

[1] [This trip was described at length by Freud in a letter to Fliess of April 14, 1898 (Freud, 1950*a*, Letter 88). Aquileia, a few miles inland, is connected by a small canal with the lagoon, on one of whose islands Grado is situated. These places, at the northern end of the Adriatic, formed part of Austria before 1918.]

detach an affect from its connections in the dream-thoughts and introduce it at any other point it chooses in the manifest dream.

I take this opportunity of making a somewhat detailed analysis of the 'breakfast-ship,' the appearance of which in the dream brought such a nonsensical conclusion to a situation which had up to then been kept at a rational level. When subsequently I called the dream-object more precisely to mind, it struck me that it was black and that, owing to the fact that it was cut off short where it was broadest in the middle, it bore a great resemblance at that end to a class of objects which had attracted our interest in the museums in the Etruscan towns. These were rectangular trays of black pottery, with two handles, on which there stood things like coffee- or tea-cups, not altogether unlike one of our modern *breakfast-sets*. In response to our enquiries we learned that this was the *'toilette'* [toilet-set] of an Etruscan lady, with receptacles for cosmetics and powder on it, and we had jokingly remarked that it would be a good idea to take one home with us for the lady of the house. The object in the dream meant, accordingly, a black 'toilette,' i.e. mourning dress, and made a direct reference to a death. The other end of the dream-object reminded me of the funeral boats[1] in which in early times dead bodies were placed and committed to the sea for burial. This led on to the point which explained why the ships *returned* in the dream:

Still, auf gerettetem Boot, treibt in den Hafen der Greis.[2]

It was the return after a shipwreck [*'Schiffbruch,'* literally 'ship-break']—the breakfast-ship was broken off short in the middle. But what was the origin of the name 'breakfast'-ship? It was here that the word 'English' came in, which was left over from the warships. The English word 'breakfast' means 'breaking fast.' The 'breaking' related once more to the shipwreck ['ship-break'] and the fasting was connected with the black dress or *toilette.*

But it was only the *name* of the breakfast-ship that was newly constructed by the dream. The *thing* had existed and reminded me of one of

---

[1] *'Nachen'* [in German], a word which is derived, as a philological friend tells me, from the root 'νέχυς' [corpse].

[2] [Safe on his ship, the old man quietly sails into port.
(Part of an allegory of life and death.)
Schiller, *Nachträge zu den Xenien,*
'Erwartung und Erfüllung.']

the most enjoyable parts of my last trip. Mistrusting the food that would be provided at Aquileia, we had brought provisions with us from Gorizia and had bought a bottle of excellent Istrian wine at Aquileia. And while the little mail steamer made its way slowly through the *'Canale delle Mee'* across the empty lagoon to Grado we, who were the only passengers, ate our breakfast on deck in the highest spirits, and we had rarely tasted a better one. This, then, was the 'breakfast-ship,' and it was precisely behind this memory of the most cheerful *joie de vivre* that the dream concealed the gloomiest thoughts of an unknown and uncanny future.[1]

The detachment of affects from the ideational material which generated them is the most striking thing which occurs to them during the formation of dreams; but it is neither the only nor the most essential alteration undergone by them on their path from the dream-thoughts to the manifest dream. If we compare the affects of the dream-thoughts with those in the dream, one thing at once becomes clear. Whenever there is an affect in the dream, it is also to be found in the dream-thoughts. But the reverse is not true. A dream is in general poorer in affect than the psychical material from the manipulation of which it has proceeded. When I have reconstructed the dream-thoughts, I habitually find the most intense psychical impulses in them striving to make themselves felt and struggling as a rule against others that are sharply opposed to them. If I then turn back to the dream, it not infrequently appears colourless, and without emotional tone of any great intensity. The dream-work has reduced to a level of indifference not only the content but often the emotional tone of my thoughts as well. It might be said that the dream-work brings about a *suppression of affects*. Let us, for instance, take the dream of the botanical monograph [pp. 193 ff.]. The thoughts corresponding to it consisted of a passionately agitated plea on behalf of my liberty to act as I chose to act and to govern my life as seemed right to me and me alone. The dream that arose from them has an indifferent ring about it: 'I had written a monograph; it lay before me; it contained coloured plates; dried plants accompanied each copy.' This reminds one of the peace that has descended upon a battlefield strewn with corpses; no trace is left of the struggle which raged over it.

Things can be otherwise: lively manifestations of affect can make their way into the dream itself. For the moment, however, I will dwell upon the

---

[1] [This dream is mentioned again on p. 548.]

incontestable fact that large numbers of dreams appear to be indifferent, whereas it is never possible to enter into the dream-thoughts without being deeply moved.

No complete theoretical explanation can here be given of this suppression of affect in the course of the dream-work. It would require to be preceded by a most painstaking investigation of the theory of affects and of the mechanism of repression. [Cf. pp. 600 ff.] I will only permit myself a reference to two points. I am compelled—for other reasons—to picture the release of affects as a centrifugal process directed towards the interior of the body and analogous to the processes of motor and secretory innervation.[1] Now just as in the state of sleep the sending out of motor impulses towards the external world appears to be suspended, so it may be that the centrifugal calling-up of affects by unconscious thinking may become more difficult during sleep. In that case the affective impulses occurring during the course of the dream-thoughts would from their very nature be weak impulses, and consequently those which found their way into the dream would be no less weak. On this view, then, the 'suppression of affect' would not in any way be the consequence of the dream-work but would result from the state of sleep. This may be true, but it cannot be the whole truth. We must also bear in mind that any relatively complex dream turns out to be a compromise produced by a conflict between psychical forces. For one thing, the thoughts constructing the wish are obliged to struggle against the opposition of a censoring agency; and for another thing, we have often seen that in unconscious thinking itself every train of thought is yoked with its contradictory opposite. Since all of these trains of thought are capable of carrying an affect, we shall by and large scarcely be wrong if we regard the suppression of affect as a consequence of the inhibition which these contraries exercise upon each other and which the censorship exercises upon the impulsions suppressed by it. *The inhibition of affect, accordingly, must be considered as the second consequence of the censorship of dreams, just as dream-distortion is its first consequence.*

---

[1] [The release of affects is described as 'centrifugal' (though directed towards the interior of the body) from the point of view of the mental apparatus. The theory of the release of affects implicit in this passage is explained at some length in Section 12 ('The Experience of Pain') of Part I of Freud's 'Project for a Scientific Psychology' (in Freud, 1950a). See also p. 580 below.—For Freud's use of the term 'innervation' see footnote, p. 539.]

I will here give as an instance a dream in which the indifferent feeling-tone of the content of the dream can be explained by the antithesis between the dream-thoughts. It is a short dream, which will fill every reader with disgust.

IV

A hill, on which there was something like an open-air closet: a very long seat with a large hole at the end of it. Its back edge was thickly covered with small heaps of faeces of all sizes and degrees of freshness. There were bushes behind the seat. I micturated on the seat; a long stream of urine washed everything clean; the lumps of faeces came away easily and fell into the opening. It was as though at the end there was still some left.

Why did I feel no disgust during this dream?

Because, as the analysis showed, the most agreeable and satisfying thoughts contributed to bringing the dream about. What at once occurred to me in the analysis were the Augean stables which were cleansed by Hercules. This Hercules was I. The hill and bushes came from Aussee, where my children were stopping at the time. I had discovered the infantile aetiology of the neuroses and had thus saved my own children from falling ill. The seat (except, of course, for the hole) was an exact copy of a piece of furniture which had been given to me as a present by a grateful woman patient. It thus reminded me of how much my patients honoured me. Indeed, even the museum of human excrement could be given an interpretation to rejoice my heart. However much I might be disgusted by it in reality, in the dream it was a reminiscence of the fair land of Italy where, as we all know, the W.C.s in the small towns are furnished in precisely this way. The stream of urine which washed everything clean was an unmistakable sign of greatness. It was in that way that Gulliver extinguished the great fire in Lilliput—though incidentally this brought him into disfavour with its tiny queen. But Gargantua, too, Rabelais' superman, revenged himself in the same way on the Parisians by sitting astride on Notre Dame and turning his stream of urine upon the city. It was only on the previous evening before going to sleep that I had been turning over Garnier's illustrations to Rabelais. And, strangely enough, here was another piece of evidence that I was the superman. The platform of Notre Dame was my favourite resort in Paris; every free afternoon I used to clamber about there on the towers of the church between the monsters and the devils. The fact that all the faeces disappeared so quickly under the stream recalled the motto: '*Afflavit et dissipati sunt,*' which I intended one day to put at the head of a chapter upon the therapy of hysteria.[1]

And now for the true exciting cause of the dream. It had been a hot summer afternoon; and during the evening I had delivered my lecture on the connection between hysteria and the perversions, and everything I had had to say displeased me intensely and seemed to me completely devoid of any value. I was tired and felt no trace of enjoyment in my difficult work; I longed to be away from all this grubbing about in human dirt and to be able to join my children and afterwards visit the beauties of Italy. In this mood I went from the lecture room to a café, where I had a modest snack in the open air, since I had no appetite for food. One of my audience, however, went with me and he begged leave to sit by me while I drank my coffee and choked over my cresent roll. He began to flatter me: telling me how much he had learnt from me, how he looked at, everything now with fresh eyes, how I had cleansed the *Augean stables* of errors and prejudices in my theory of the neuroses. He told me, in short, that I was a very great man. My mood fitted ill with this paean of praise; I fought against my feeling of disgust, went home early to escape from him, and before going to sleep turned over the pages of Rabelais and read one of Conrad Ferdinand Meyer's short stories, '*Die Leiden eines Knaben*' ['A Boy's Sorrows'].

Such was the material out of which the dream emerged. Meyer's short story brought up in addition a recollection of scenes from my childhood. (Cf. the last episode in the dream about Count Thun [pp. 235 f.].) The daytime mood of revulsion and disgust persisted into the dream in so far as it was able to provide almost the entire material of its manifest content. But during the night a contrary mood of powerful and even exaggerated self-assertiveness arose and displaced the former one. The content of the dream had to find a form which would enable it to express both the delusions of inferiority and the megalomania in the same material. The compromise between them produced an ambiguous dream-content; but it also resulted in an indifferent feeling-tone owing to the mutual inhibition of these contrary impulses.

---

[1] [*Footnote in 1925 edition only:*] For a correction of this quotation see above, p. 235 *n.* 2.

According to the theory of wish-fulfilment, this dream would not have become possible if the antithetical megalomanic train of thought (which, it is true, was suppressed, but had a pleasurable tone) had not emerged in addition to the feeling of disgust. For what is distressing may not be represented in a dream; nothing in our dream-thoughts which is distressing can force an entry into a dream unless it at the same time lends a disguise to the fulfilment of a wish. [Cf. pp. 557 f.]

There is yet another alternative way in which the dream-work can deal with affects in the dream-thoughts, in addition to allowing them through or reducing them to nothing. It can *turn them into their opposite*. We have already become acquainted with the interpretative rule according to which every element in a dream can, for purposes of interpretation, stand for its opposite just as easily as for itself. [See p. 334.] We can never tell beforehand whether it stands for the one or for the other; only the context can decide. A suspicion of this truth has evidently found its way into popular consciousness: 'dream-books' very often adopt the principle of contraries in their interpretation of dreams. This turning of a thing into its opposite is made possible by the intimate associative chain which links the idea of a thing with its opposite in our thoughts. Like any other kind of displacement it can serve the ends of the censorship; but it is also frequently a product of wish-fulfilment, for wish-fulfilment consists in nothing else than a replacement of a disagreeable thing by its opposite. Just as ideas of things can make their appearance in dreams turned into their opposite, so too can the *affects* attaching to dream-thoughts; and it seems likely that this reversal of affect is brought about as a rule by the dream-censorship. In social life, which has provided us with our familiar analogy with the dream-censorship, we also make use of the suppression and reversal of affect, principally for purposes of dissimulation. If I am talking to someone whom I am obliged to treat with consideration while wishing to say something hostile to him, it is almost more important that I should conceal any expression of my *affect* from him than that I should mitigate the verbal form of my thoughts. If I were to address him in words that were not impolite, but accompanied them with a look or gesture of hatred and contempt, the effect which I should produce on him would not be very different from what it would have been if I had thrown my contempt openly in his face. Accordingly, the censorship bids me above all suppress my affects; and, if I am a master of dissimulation, I shall assume the *opposite* affect—smile when I am angry and seem affectionate when I wish to destroy.

We have already come across an excellent example of a reversal of affect of this kind carried out in a dream on behalf of the dream-censorship. In the dream of 'my uncle with the yellow beard' [pp. 163 ff.] I felt the greatest affection for my friend R., whereas and because the dream-thoughts called him a simpleton. It was from this example of reversal of affect that we derived our first hint of the existence of a dream-censorship. Nor is it necessary to assume, in such cases either, that the dream-work *creates* contrary affects of this kind out of nothing; it finds them as a rule lying ready to hand in the material of the dream-thoughts, and merely intensifies them with the psychical force arising from a motive of defence, till they can predominate for the purposes of dream-formation. In the dream of my uncle which I have just mentioned, the antithetical, affectionate affect probably arose from an infantile source (as was suggested by the later part of the dream), for the uncle-nephew relationship, owing to the peculiar nature of the earliest experiences of my childhood (cf. the analysis on pp. 433 f. [and below, pp. 488]) had become the source of all my friendships and all my hatreds.

An excellent example of a reversal of affect of this kind[1] will be found in a dream recorded by Ferenczi (1916): 'An elderly gentleman was awakened one night by his wife, who had become alarmed because he was laughing so loudly and unrestrainedly in his sleep. Subsequently the man reported that he had had the following dream: *I was lying in bed and a gentleman who was known to me entered the room; I tried to turn on the light but was unable to: I tried over and over again, but in vain. Thereupon my wife got out of bed to help me, but she could not manage it either. But as she felt awkward in front of the gentleman owing to being 'en négligé,' she finally gave it up and went back to bed. All of this was so funny that I couldn't help roaring with laughter at it. My wife said, 'Why are you laughing? why are you laughing?' but I only went on laughing till I woke up.*—Next day the gentleman was very depressed and had a headache: so much laughing had upset him, he thought.

'The dream seems less amusing when it is considered analytically. The "gentleman known to him" who entered the room was, in the latent dream-thoughts, the picture of Death as the "great Unknown"—a picture which had been called up in his mind during the previous day. The old gentleman,

---

[1] [This paragraph and the next were added in 1919.]

who suffered from arterio-sclerosis, had had good reason the day before for thinking of dying. The unrestrained laughter took the place of sobbing and weeping at the idea that he must die. It was the light of life that he could no longer turn on. This gloomy thought may have been connected with attempts at copulation which he had made shortly before but which had failed even with the help of his wife *en négligé*. He realized that he was already going down hill. The dream-work succeeded in transforming the gloomy idea of impotence and death into a comic scene, and his sobs into laughter.'

There is one class of dreams which have a particular claim to be described as 'hypocritical' and which offer a hard test to the theory of wish-fulfilment.[1] My attention was drawn to them when Frau Dr. M. Hilferding brought up the following record of a dream of Peter Rosegger's for discussion by the Vienna Psycho-Analytical Society.

Rosegger writes in his story *'Fremd gemacht!'*[2] 'As a rule I am a sound sleeper but many a night I have lost my rest—for, along with my modest career as a student and man of letters, I have for many years dragged around with me, like a ghost from which I could not set myself free, the shadow of a tailor's life.

'It is not as though in the daytime I had reflected very often or very intensely on my past. One who had cast off the skin of a Philistine and was seeking to conquer Earth and Heaven had other things to do. Nor would I, when I was a dashing young fellow, have given more than a thought to my nightly dreams. Only later, when the habit had come to me of reflecting upon everything, or when the Philistine within me began to stir a trifle, did I ask myself why it should be that, if I dreamt at all, I was always a journeyman tailor and that I spent so long a time as such with my master and worked without pay in his workshop. I knew well enough, as I sat like that beside him, sewing and ironing, that my right place was no longer there and that as a townsman I had other things to occupy me. But I was always on vacation, I was always having holidays, and so it was that I sat beside my master as his assistant. It often irked me and I felt sad at the loss of time in which I might well have found better and more useful things to do. Now and then, when something went awry, I had to put up with a

---

[1] [This paragraph and the following quotation from Rosegger, together with the discussion of it, were added in 1911. Rosegger (1843–1918) was a well-known Austrian writer who reached celebrity from very humble, peasant beginnings.]

[2] ['Dismissed!'] In the second volume of *Waldheimat*, p. 303.

scolding from my master, though there was never any talk of wages. Often, as I sat there with bent back in the dark workshop, I thought of giving notice and taking my leave. Once I even did so; but my master paid no heed and I was soon sitting beside him again and sewing.

'After such tedious hours, what a joy it was to wake! And I determined that if this persistent dream should come again I would throw it from me with energy and call aloud: "This is mere hocus-pocus, I am lying in bed and want to sleep. . . ." But next night I was once more sitting in the tailor's workshop.

'And so it went on for years with uncanny regularity. Now it happened once that my master and I were working at Alphelhofer's (the peasant in whose house I had worked when I was first apprenticed) and my master showed himself quite especially dissatisfied with my work. "I'd like to know where you're wool-gathering," he said, and looked at me darkly. The most reasonable thing to do, I thought, would be to stand up and tell him that I was only with him to please him and then go off. But I did not do so. I made no objection when my master took on an apprentice and ordered me to make room for him on the bench. I moved into the corner and sewed. The same day another journeyman was taken on as well, a canting hypocrite—he was a Bohemian—who had worked at our place nineteen years before, and had fallen into the brook once on his way back from the inn. When he looked for a seat there was no more room. I turned to my master questioningly, and he said to me: "You've no gift for tailoring, you can go! you're dismissed!" My fright at this was so overpowering that I awoke.

'The grey light of morning was glimmering through the uncurtained windows into my familiar home. Works of art surrounded me; there in my handsome bookcase stood the eternal Homer, the gigantic Dante, the incomparable Shakespeare, the glorious Goethe—all the magnificent immortals. From the next room rang out the clear young voices of the awakening children joking with their mother. I felt as though I had found afresh this idyllically sweet, this peaceful, poetic, spiritual life in which I had so often and so deeply felt a meditative human happiness. Yet it vexed me that I had not been beforehand with my master in giving him notice, but had been dismissed by him.

'And how astonished I was! From the night on which my master dismissed me, I enjoyed peace; I dreamt no more of the tailoring days which lay so far back in my past—days which had been so cheerfully unassuming but had thrown such a long shadow over my later years.'

In this series of dreams dreamt by an author who had been a journey-man tailor in his youth, it is hard to recognize the dominance of wish-fulfilment. All the dreamer's enjoyment lay in his daytime existence, whereas in his dreams he was still haunted by the shadow of an unhappy life from which he had at last escaped. Some dreams of my own of a simi-lar kind have enabled me to throw a little light on the subject. As a young doctor I worked for a long time at the Chemical Institute without ever be-coming proficient in the skills which that science demands; and for that reason in my waking life I have never liked thinking of this barren and in-deed humiliating episode in my apprenticeship. On the other hand I have a regularly recurring dream of working in the laboratory, of carrying out analyses and of having various experiences there. These dreams are dis-agreeable in the same way as examinations dreams and they are never very distinct. While I was interpreting one of them, my attention was eventu-ally attracted by the word *'analysis,'* which gave me a key to their under-standing. Since those days I have become an 'analyst,' and I now carry out analyses which are very highly spoken of, though it is true that they are *'psycho-analyses.'* It was now clear to me: if I have grown proud of carrying out analyses of that kind in my daytime life and feel inclined to boast to myself of how successful I have become, my dreams remind me during the night of those other, unsuccessful analyses of which I have no reason to feel proud. They are the punishment dreams of a *parvenu,* like the dreams of the journeyman tailor who had grown into a famous author. But how does it become possible for a dream, in the conflict between a *parvenu's* pride and his self-criticism, to side with the latter, and choose as its content a sensible warning instead of an unlawful wish-fulfilment? As I have already said, the answer to this question raises difficulties. We may conclude that the foundation of the dream was formed in the first instance by an exag-geratedly ambitious phantasy, but that humiliating thoughts that poured cold water on the phantasy found their way into the dream instead. It may be remembered that there are masochistic impulses in the mind, which may be responsible for a reversal such as this. I should have no objection to this class of dreams being distinguished from 'wish-fulfilment dreams' under the name of 'punishment dreams.' I should not regard this as im-plying any qualification of the theory of dreams which I have hitherto put forward; it would be no more than a linguistic expedient for meeting the difficulties of those who find it strange that opposites should converge.[1]

---

[1] [The last two sentences were added in 1919.]

But a closer examination of some of these dreams brings something more to light. In an indistinct part of the background of one of my laboratory dreams I was of an age which placed me precisely in the gloomiest and most unsuccessful year of my medical career. I was still without a post and had no idea how I could earn my living; but at the same time I suddenly discovered that I had a choice open to me between several women whom I might marry! So I was once more young, and, more than everything, *she* was once more young—the woman who had shared all these difficult years with me. The unconscious instigator of the dream was thus revealed as one of the constantly gnawing wishes of a man who is growing older. The conflict raging in other levels of the mind between vanity and self-criticism had, it is true, determined the content of the dream; but it was only the more deeply-rooted wish for youth that had made it possible for that conflict to appear as a dream. Even when we are awake we sometimes say to ourselves: Things are going very well today and times were hard in the old days; all the same, it was lovely then—I was still young.'[1]

Another group of dreams,[2] which I have often come across in myself and recognized as hypocritical, have as their content a reconciliation with people with whom friendly relations have long since ceased. In such cases analysis habitually reveals some occasion which might urge me to abandon the last remnant of consideration for these former friends and to treat them as strangers or enemies. The dream, however, prefers to depict the opposite relationship. [Cf. p. 169 *n*.]

In forming any judgement upon dreams recorded by an imaginative writer it is reasonable to suppose that he may have omitted from his account details in the content of the dream which he regards as unessential or distracting. His dreams will in that case raise problems which would be quickly solved if their content were reported in full.

---

[1] [*Footnote added* 1930:] Since psycho-analysis has divided the personality into an ego and super-ego (Freud, 1921*c* [and 1923*b*]), it has become easy to recognize in these punishment dreams fulfillments of the wishes of the super-ego. [See below, pp. 557 ff.—The Rosegger dreams are also discussed in Section IX of Freud, 1923*c*.]

[2] [This paragraph was added in 1919, and seems to have been wrongly interpolated at this point. It should probably have come *after* the two next paragraphs. These date from 1911, like the preceding Rosegger discussion, to which they are clearly related. What follows them goes back once more to 1900.—Some further remarks on hypocritical dreams will be found near the end of Section III of Freud's paper on a case of female homosexuality (1920*a*.)]

Otto Rank has pointed out to me that the Grimms' fairy tale of 'The Little Tailor, or Seven at a Blow' contains an exactly similar dream of a *parvenu*. The tailor, who has become a hero and the son-in-law of the King, dreams one night of his former handicraft, as he lies beside his wife, the Princess. She, becoming suspicious, posts armed guards the next night to listen to the dreamer's words and to arrest him. But the little tailor is warned, and sees to it that his dream is corrected.

The complicated process of elimination, diminution and reversal, by means of which the affects in the dream-thoughts are eventually turned into those in the dream, can be satisfactorily followed in suitable syntheses of dreams that have been completely analysed. I will quote a few more examples of affects in dreams where some of the possibilities I have enumerated will be found realized.

v

If we turn back to the dream about the strange task set me by old Brücke of making a dissection of my own pelvis [p. 459 f.], it will be recalled that in the dream itself I missed the gruesome feeling ['*Grauen*'] appropriate to it. Now this was a wish-fulfilment in more than one sense. The dissection meant the self-analysis which I was carrying out, as it were, in the publication of this present book about dreams—a process which had been so distressing to me in reality that I had postponed the printing of the finished manuscript for more than a year. A wish then arose that I might get over this feeling of distaste; hence it was that I had no gruesome feeling ['*Grauen*'] in the dream. But I should also have been very glad to miss growing grey—'*Grauen*' in the other sense of the word. I was already growing quite grey, and the grey of my hair was another reminder that I must not delay any longer. And, as we have seen, the thought that I should have to leave it to my children to reach the goal of my difficult journey forced its way through to representation at the end of the dream.

Let us next consider the two dreams in which an expression of satisfaction was transposed to the moment after waking. In the one case the reason given for the satisfaction was an expectation that I should now discover what was meant by 'I've dreamt of that before,' while the satisfaction really referred to the birth of my first children [pp. 454 f.]. In the other case the ostensible reason was my conviction that something that had been 'prognosticated' was now coming true, while the real reference was similar to that in the former dream: it was the satisfaction with which I greeted the birth of my second son [pp. 455 f.] Here the affects which dominated the dream-thoughts persisted in the dreams; but it is safe to say that in *no* dream can things be as simple as all that. If we go a little more deeply into the two analyses we find that this satisfaction which had escaped censorship had received an accession from another source. This other source had grounds for fearing the censorship, and its affect would undoubtedly have aroused opposition if it had not covered itself by the similar, legitimate affect of satisfaction, arising from the permissible source, and slipped in, as it were, under its wing.

Unfortunately, I cannot demonstrate this in the actual case of these dreams, but an instance taken from another department of life will make my meaning clear. Let us suppose the following case. There is a person of my acquaintance whom I hate, so that I have a lively inclination to feel glad if anything goes wrong with him. But the moral side of my nature will not give way to this impulse. I do not dare to express a wish that he should be unlucky, and if he meets with some undeserved misfortune, I suppress my satisfaction at it and force myself to manifestations and thoughts of regret. Everyone must have found himself in this situation at some time or other. What now happens, however, is that the hated person, by a piece of misconduct of his own, involves himself in some well-deserved unpleasantness; when that happens, I may give free rein to my satisfaction that he has met with a just punishment and in this I find myself in agreement with many other people who are impartial. I may observe, however, that my satisfaction seems more intense than that of these other people; it has received an accession from the source of my hatred, which till then has been prevented from producing its affect, but in the altered circumstances is no longer hindered from doing so. In social life this occurs in general wherever antipathetic people or members of an unpopular minority put themselves in the wrong. Their punishment does not as a rule correspond to their wrong-doing but to their wrong-doing *plus* the ill-feeling directed against them which has previously been without any consequences. It is no doubt true that those who inflict the punishment are committing an injustice in this; but they are prevented from perceiving it by the satisfaction resulting from the removal of a suppression which has long been maintained within them. In cases such as this the affect is justified in its *quality* but not in its *amount;* and self-criticism which is set at rest on the one point is only too apt to neglect examination of the second one. When once a door has been opened, it is easy for more people to push their way through it than there had originally been any intention of letting in.

A striking feature in neurotic characters—the fact that a cause capable of releasing an affect is apt to produce in them a result which is qualitatively justified but quantitatively excessive—is to be explained along these same lines, in so far as it admits of any psychological explanation at all. The excess arises from sources of affect which had previously remained unconscious and suppressed. These sources have succeeded in setting up an associative link with the *real* releasing cause, and the desired path from the release of their own affect has been opened by the *other* source of affect, which is unobjectionable and legitimate. Our attention is thus drawn to the fact that in considering the suppressed and suppressing agencies, we must not regard their relation as being exclusively one of mutual inhibition. Just as much regard must be paid to cases in which the two agencies bring about a pathological effect by working side by side and by intensifying each other.

Let us now apply these hints upon psychical mechanisms to an understanding of the expressions of affect in *dreams*. A satisfaction which is exhibited in a dream and can, of course, be immediately referred to its proper place in the dream-thoughts is not always completely elucidated by this reference alone. It is as a rule necessary to look for *another* source of it in the dream-thoughts, a source which is under the pressure of the censorship. As a result of that pressure, this source would normally have produced, not satisfaction, but the contrary affect. Owing to the presence of the first source of affect, however, the second source is enabled to withdraw its affect of satisfaction from repression and allow it to act as an intensification of the satisfaction from the first source. Thus it appears that affects in dreams are fed from a confluence of several sources and are overdetermined in their reference to the material of the dream-thoughts. *During the dream-work, sources of affect which are capable of producing the same affect come together in generating it.*[1]

We can gain a little insight into these complications from the analysis of that fine specimen of a dream of which the words '*Non vixit*' formed

---

[1] [*Footnote added* 1909:] I have given an analogous explanation of the extraordinarily powerful pleasurable effect of tendentious jokes [Freud, 1905*c*, towards the end of Chapter IV.]

the centre-point. (See pp. 430 ff.) In that dream manifestations of affect of various qualities were brought together at two points in its manifest content. Hostile and distressing feelings—'overcome by strange emotions' were the words used in the dream itself—were piled up at the point at which I annihilated my opponent and friend with two words. And again, at the end of the dream, I was highly delighted, and I went on to approve the possibility, which in waking life I knew was absurd, of there being *revenants* who could be eliminated by a mere wish.

I have not yet related the exciting cause of the dream. It was of great importance and led deep into an understanding of the dream. I had heard from my friend in Berlin, whom I have referred to as 'Fl.' [i.e. Fliess], that he was about to undergo an operation and that I should get further news of his condition from some of his relatives in Vienna. The first reports I received after the operation were not reassuring and made me feel anxious. I should have much preferred to go to him myself, but just at that time I was the victim of a painful complaint which made movement of any kind a torture to me. The dream-thoughts now informed me that I feared for my friend's life. His only sister, whom I had never known, had, as I was aware, died in early youth after a very brief illness. (In the dream *Fl. spoke about his sister and said that in three quarters of an hour she was dead.*) I must have imagined that his constitution was not much more resistant than his sister's and that, after getting some much worse news of him, I should make the journey after all—and arrive *too late,* for which I might never cease to reproach myself.[1] This reproach for coming too late became the central point of the dream but was represented by a scene in which Brücke, the honoured teacher of my student years, levelled this reproach at me with a terrible look from his blue eyes. It will soon appear what it was that caused the situation [in regard to Fl.] to be switched on to these lines. The scene [with Brücke] itself could not be reproduced by the dream in the form in which I experienced it. The other figure in the dream was allowed to keep the blue eyes, but the annihilating role was allotted to me—a reversal which was obviously the work of wish-fulfilment. My anxiety about my friend's recovery, my self-reproaches for not going to see him, the shame I felt about this—*he had come to Vienna* (to see

---

[1] It was this phantasy, forming part of the unconscious dream-thoughts, which so insistently demanded '*Non vivit*' instead of '*Non vixit*': 'You have come too late, he is no longer alive.' I have already explained on pp. 430–1 that '*Non vivit*' was also required by the *manifest* situation in the dream.

me) *'unobtrusively'*—the need I felt to consider that I was excused by my illness—all of this combined to produce the emotional storm which was clearly perceived in my sleep and which raged in this region of the dream-thoughts.

But there was something else in the exciting cause of the dream, which had a quite opposite effect upon me. Along with the unfavourable reports during the first few days after the operation, I was given a warning not to discuss the matter with anyone. I had felt offended by this because it implied an unnecessary distrust of my discretion. I was quite aware that these instructions had not emanated from my friend but were due to tactlessness or over-anxiety on the part of the intermediary, but I was very disagreeably affected by the veiled reproach because it was—not wholly without justification. As we all know, it is only reproaches which have something in them that 'stick'; it is only they that upset us. What I have in mind does not relate, it is true, to this friend, but to a much earlier period of my life. On that occasion I caused trouble between two friends (both of whom had chosen to honour me, too, with that name) by quite unnecessarily telling one of them, in the course of conversation, what the other had said about him. At that time, too, reproaches had been levelled at me, and they were still in my memory. One of the two friends concerned was Professor Fleischl; I may describe the other by his first name of 'Josef'—which was also that of P., my friend and opponent in the dream.[1]

The reproach of being unable to keep anything to myself was attested in the dream by the element 'unobtrusive' and by Fl.'s question as to *how much I had told P. about his affairs.* But it was the intervention of this memory (of my early indiscretion and its consequences) that transported the reproach against me for coming too late from the present time to the period at which I had worked in Brucke's laboratory. And, by turning the

---

[1] [What follows will be made more intelligible by some facts derived from a paper by Bernfeld (1944). Freud worked at the Vienna Physiological Institute ('Brücke's laboratory') from 1876 to 1882. Ernst Brücke (1819–92) was at its head; his two assistants in Freud's time were Sigmund Exner (1846–1925) and Ernst Fleischl von Marxow (1846–91), both some ten years older than Freud. Fleischl suffered from a very severe physical affliction during the later years of his life. It was at the Physiological Institute that Freud met Josef Breuer (1842–1925), his greatly senior collaborator in *Studies on Hysteria* (1895d) and the second Josef in the present analysis. The first Josef—Freud's early deceased 'friend and opponent P.'—was Josef Paneth (1857–90) who succeeded to Freud's position at the Institute.—See also the first volume of Ernest Jones's Freud biography.]

second person in the scene of annihilation in the dream into a Josef, I made the scene represent not only the reproach against me for coming too late but also the far more strongly repressed reproach that I was unable to keep a secret. Here the processes of condensation and displacement at work in the dream, as well as the reasons for them, are strikingly visible.

My present-day anger, which was only slight, over the warning I had been given not to give anything away [about Fl.'s illness] received reinforcements from sources in the depth of my mind and thus swelled into a current of hostile feelings against persons of whom I was in reality fond. The source of this reinforcement flowed from my childhood. I have already shown [pp. 433 f.] how my warm friendships as well as my enmities with contemporaries went back to my relations in childhood with a nephew who was a year my senior; how he was my superior, how I early learned to defend myself against him, how we were inseparable friends, and how, according to the testimony of our elders, we sometimes fought with each other and—made complaints to them about each other. All my friends have in a certain sense been re-incarnations of this first figure who 'früh sich einst dem truben Blick gezeigt'[1]: they have been *revenants*. My nephew himself re-appeared in my boyhood, and at that time we acted the parts of Caesar and Brutus together. My emotional life has always insisted that I should have an intimate friend and a hated enemy. I have always been able to provide myself afresh with both, and it has not infrequently happened that the ideal situation of childhood has been so completely reproduced that friend and enemy have come together in a single individual—though not, of course, both at once or with constant oscillations, as may have been the case in my early childhood.

I do not propose at this point to discuss how it is that in such circumstances as these a recent occasion for the generation of an affect can hark back to an infantile situation and be replaced by that situation as far as the production of affect is concerned. [See p. 547.] This question forms part of the psychology of unconscious thinking, and would find its proper place in a psychological elucidation of the neuroses. For the purposes of dream-interpretation let us assume that a childhood memory arose, or was constructed in phantasy, with some such content as the following. The two children had a dispute about some object. (What the object was may

---

[1] ['. . . long since appeared before my troubled gaze' (Goethe, *Faust*, Dedication).]

be left an open question, though the memory or pseudo-memory had a quite specific one in view.) Each of them claimed to have *got there before the other* and therefore to have a better right to it. They came to blows and might prevailed over right. On the evidence of the dream, I may myself have been aware that I was in the wrong (*'I myself noticed the mistake'*). However, this time I was the stronger and remained in possession of the field. The vanquished party hurried to his grandfather—my father—and complained about me, and I defended myself in the words which I know from my father's account: 'I hit him 'cos he hit me.' This memory, or more probably phantasy, which came into my mind while I was analysing the dream—without further evidence I myself could not tell how[1]—constituted an intermediate element in the dream-thoughts, which gathered up the emotions raging in them as a well collects the water that flows into it. From this point the dream-thoughts proceeded along some such lines as these: 'It serves you right if you had to make way for me. Why did you try to push *me* out of the way? I don't need you, I can easily find someone else to play with,' and so on. These thoughts now entered upon the paths which led to their representation in the dream. There had been a time when I had had to reproach my friend Josef [P.] for an attitude of this same kind: '*Ôte-toi que je m'y mette!*' He had followed in my footsteps as demonstrator in Brücke's laboratory, but promotion there was slow and tedious. Neither of Brücke's two assistants was inclined to budge from his place, and youth was impatient. My friend, who knew that he could not expect to live long, and whom no bonds of intimacy attached to his immediate superior, sometimes gave loud expression to his impatience, and, since this superior [Fleischl] was seriously ill, P.'s wish to have him out of the way might have an uglier meaning than the mere hope for the man's promotion. Not unnaturally, a few years earlier, I myself had nourished a still livelier wish to fill a vacancy. Wherever there is rank and promotion the way lies open for wishes that call for suppression. Shakespeare's Prince Hal could not, even at his father's sick-bed, resist the temptation of trying on the crown. But, as was to be expected, the dream punished my friend, and not me, for this callous wish.[2]

---

[1] [This point is discussed below on p. 517.]

[2] It will be noticed that the name Josef plays a great part in my dreams (cf. the dream about my uncle [pp. 163 ff.]). My own ego finds it very easy to hide itself behind people of that name, since Joseph was the name of a man famous in the Bible as an interpreter of dreams.

'As he was ambitious, I slew him.' As he could not wait for the removal of another man, he was himself removed. These had been my thoughts immediately after I attended the unveiling at the University of the memorial—not to him but to the other man. Thus a part of the satisfaction I felt in the dream was to be interpreted: 'A just punishment! It serves you right.'

At my friend's [P.'s] funeral, a young man had made what seemed to be an inopportune remark to the effect that the speaker who had delivered the funeral oration had implied that without this one man the world would come to an end. He was expressing the honest feelings of someone whose pain was being interfered with by an exaggeration. But this remark of his was the starting-point of the following dream-thoughts: 'It's quite true that no one's irreplaceable. How many people I've followed to the grave already! But I'm still alive. I've survived them all; I'm left in possession of the field.' A thought of this kind, occurring to me at a moment at which I was afraid I might not find my friend [Fl.] alive if I made the journey to him, could only be construed as meaning that I was delighted because I had once more survived someone, because it was *he* and not I who had died, because I was left in possession of the field, as I had been in the phantasied scene from my childhood. This satisfaction, infantile in origin, at being in possession of the field constituted the major part of the affect that appeared in the dream. I was delighted to survive, and I gave expression to my delight with all the naïve egoism shown in the anecdote of the married couple one of whom said to the other: 'If one of us dies, I shall move to Paris.' So obvious was it to me that I should not be the one to die.

It cannot be denied that to interpret and report one's dreams demands a high degree of self-discipline. One is bound to emerge as the only villain among the crowd of noble characters who share one's life. Thus it seemed to me quite natural that the *revenants* should only exist for just so long as one likes and should be removable at a wish. We have seen what my friend Josef was punished for. But the *revenants* were a series of reincarnations of the friend of my childhood. It was therefore also a source of satisfaction to me that I had always been able to find successive substitutes for that figure; and I felt I should be able to find a substitute for the friend whom I was now on the point of losing: no one was irreplaceable.

But what had become of the dream-censorship? Why had it not raised the most energetic objections against this blatantly egoistic train of thought?

And why had it not transformed the satisfaction attached to that train of thought into severe unpleasure? The explanation was, I think, that other, unobjectionable trains of thought in connection with the same people found simultaneous satisfaction and screened with *their* affect the affect which arose from the forbidden infantile source. In another stratum of my thoughts, during the ceremonial unveiling of the memorial, I had reflected thus: 'What a number of valued friends I have lost, some through death, some through a breach of our friendship! How fortunate that I have found a substitute for them and that I have gained one who means more to me than ever the others could, and that, at a time of life when new friendships cannot easily be formed, I shall never lose his!' My satisfaction at having found a substitute for these lost friends could be allowed to enter the dream without interference; but there slipped in, along with it, the hostile satisfaction derived from the infantile source. It is no doubt true that infantile affection served to reinforce my contemporary and justified affection. But infantile hatred, too, succeeded in getting itself represented.

In addition to this, however, the dream contained a clear allusion to another train of thought which could legitimately lead to satisfaction. A short time before, after long expectation, a daughter had been born to my friend [Fl.]. I was aware of how deeply he had mourned the sister he had so early lost and I wrote and told him I was sure he would transfer the love he felt for her on to the child, and that the baby girl would allow him at last to forget his irreparable loss.

Thus this group of thoughts was connected once again with the intermediate thought in the latent content of the dream [cf. pp. 488–9] from which the associative paths diverged in contrary directions: 'No one is irreplaceable!' 'There are nothing but *revenants:* all those we have lost come back!' And now the associative links between the contradictory components of the dream-thoughts were drawn closer by the chance fact that my friend's baby daughter had the same name as the little girl I used to play with as a child, who was of my age and the sister of my earliest friend and opponent. [See p. 434 *n.*] It gave me great *satisfaction* when I heard that the baby was to be called 'Pauline.' And as an allusion to this coincidence, I had replaced one Josef by another in the dream and found it impossible to suppress the similarity between the opening letters of the names 'Fleischl' and 'Fl.' From here my thoughts went on to the subject of the names of my own children. I had insisted on their names being chosen, not according to the fashion of the moment, but in memory of people I have been fond of.

Their names made the children into *revenants*. And after all, I reflected, was not having children our only path to immortality?

I have only a few more remarks to add on the subject of affect in dreams from another point of view. A dominating element in a sleeper's mind may be constituted by what we call a 'mood'—or *tendency* to some affect—and this may then have a determining influence upon his dreams. A mood of this kind may arise from his experiences or thoughts during the preceding day, or its sources may be somatic. [Cf. pp. 257 f.] In either case it will be accompanied by the trains of thought appropriate to it. From the point of view of dream-construction it is a matter of indifference whether, as sometimes happens, these ideational contents of the dream-thoughts determine the mood in a primary fashion, or whether they are themselves aroused secondarily by the dreamer's emotional disposition which is in its turn to be explained on a somatic basis. In any case the construction of dreams is subject to the condition that it can only represent something which is the fulfilment of a wish and that it is only from wishes that it can derive its psychical motive force. A currently active mood is treated in the same way as a sensation arising and becoming currently active during sleep (cf. p. 254 f.), which can be either disregarded or given a fresh interpretation in the sense of a wish-fulfilment. Distressing moods during sleep can become the motive force of a dream by arousing energetic wishes which the dream is supposed to fulfil. The material to which moods are attached is worked over until it can be used to express the fulfilment of a wish. The more intense and dominating a part is played in the dream-thoughts by the distressing mood, the more certain it becomes that the most strongly suppressed wishful impulses will make use of the opportunity in order to achieve representation. For, since the unpleasure which they would otherwise necessarily produce themselves is already present, they find the harder part of their task—the task of forcing their way through to representation—already accomplished for them. Here once more we are brought up against the problem of anxiety-dreams; and these, as we shall find, form a marginal case in the function of dreaming. [Cf. pp. 579 ff.]

(I)

SECONDARY REVISION[1]

And now at last we can turn to the fourth of the factors concerned in the construction of dreams. If we pursue our investigation of the content of dreams in the manner in which we have begun it—that is, by comparing conspicuous events in the dream-content with their sources in the dream-thoughts, we shall come upon elements the explanation of which calls for an entirely new assumption. What I have in mind are cases in which the dreamer is surprised, annoyed or repelled in the dream, and, moreover, by a piece of the dream-content itself. As I have shown in a number of instances (in the last section), the majority of these critical feelings in dreams are not in fact directed against the content of the dream, but turn out to be portions of the dream-thoughts which have been taken over and used to an appropriate end. But some material of this kind does not lend itself to this explanation; its correlate in the material of the dream-thoughts is nowhere to be found. What, for instance, is the meaning of a critical remark found so often in dreams: 'This is only a dream'? [See p. 353.] Here we have a genuine piece of criticism of the dream, such as might be made in waking life. Quite frequently, too, it is actually a prelude to waking up; and still more frequently it has been preceded by some distressing feeling which is set at rest by the recognition that the state is one of dreaming. When the thought 'this is only a dream' occurs during a dream, it has the same purpose in view as when the words are pronounced on the stage by *la belle Hélène* in Offenbach's comic opera of that name:[2] it is aimed at reducing the importance of what has just been experienced and at making it possible to tolerate what is to follow. It serves to lull a particular agency to sleep which would have every reason at that moment to bestir itself and forbid the continuance of the

---

[1] ['*Sekundäre Bearbeitung.*' This term has previously been given the somewhat misleading English rendering of 'secondary elaboration.']

[2] [In the love duet between Paris and Helen in the second act, at the end of which they are surprised by Menelaus.]

dream—or the scene in the opera. It is more comfortable, however, to go on sleeping and tolerate the dream, because, after all, 'it is only a dream.' In my view the contemptuous critical judgement, 'it's only a dream,' appears in a dream when the censorship, which is never quite asleep, feels that it has been taken unawares by a dream which has already been allowed through. It is too late to suppress it, and accordingly the censorship uses these words to meet the anxiety of the distressing feeling aroused by it. The phrase is an example of *esprit d'escalier* on the part of the psychical censorship.

This instance, however, provides us with convincing evidence that not everything contained in a dream is derived from the dream-thoughts, but that contributions to its content may be made by a psychical function which is indistinguishable from our waking thoughts. The question now arises whether this only occurs in exceptional cases, or whether the psychical agency which otherwise operates only as a censorship plays a *habitual* part in the construction of dreams.

We can have no hesitation in deciding in favour of the second alternative. There can be no doubt that the censoring agency, whose influence we have so far only recognized in limitations and omissions in the dream-content, is also responsible for interpolations and additions in it. The interpolations are easy to recognize. They are often reported with hesitation, and introduced by an 'as though'; they are not in themselves particularly vivid and are always introduced at points at which they can serve as links between two portions of the dream-content or to bridge a gap between two parts of the dream. They are less easily retained in the memory than genuine derivatives of the material of the dream-thoughts; if the dream is to be forgotten they are the first part of it to disappear, and I have a strong suspicion that the common complaint of having dreamt a lot, but of having forgotten most of it and of having only retained fragments [p. 297], is based upon the rapid disappearance precisely of these connecting thoughts. In a complete analysis these interpolations are sometimes betrayed by the fact that no material connected with them is to be found in the dream-thoughts. But careful examination leads me to regard this as the less frequent case; as a rule the connecting thoughts lead back nevertheless to material in the dream-thoughts, but to material which could have no claim to acceptance in the dream either on its own account or owing to its being overdetermined. Only in extreme cases, it seems, does the psychical function in dream-formation which we are now considering proceed to make new creations. So long as possible, it employs anything appropriate that it can find in the material of the dream-thoughts.

The thing that distinguishes and at the same time reveals this part of the dream-work[1] is its *purpose*. This function behaves in the manner which the poet maliciously ascribes to philosophers: it fills up the gaps in the dream-structure with shreds and patches.[2] As a result of its efforts, the dream loses its appearance of absurdity and disconnectedness and approximates to the model of an intelligible experience. But its efforts are not always crowned with success. Dreams occur which, at a superficial view, may seem faultlessly logical and reasonable; they start from a possible situation, carry it on through a chain of consistent modifications and—though far less frequently—bring it to a conclusion which causes no surprise. Dreams which are of such a kind have been subjected to a far-reaching revision by this psychical function that is akin to waking thought; they appear to have a meaning, but that meaning is as far removed as possible from their true significance. If we analyse them, we can convince ourselves that it is in these dreams that the secondary revision has played about with the material the most freely, and has retained the relations present in that material to the least extent. They are dreams which might be said to have been already interpreted once, before being submitted to waking interpretation.[3] In other dreams this tendentious revision has only partly succeeded; coherence seems to rule for a certain distance, but the dream then becomes senseless or confused, while perhaps later on in its course it may for a second time present an appearance of rationality. In yet other dreams the revision has failed altogether; we find ourselves helplessly face to face with a meaningless heap of fragmentary material.

I do not wish to deny categorically that this fourth power in dream-construction—which we shall soon recognize as an old acquaintance, since in fact it is the only one of the four with which we are familiar in other connections—I do not wish to deny that this fourth factor has the capacity

---

[1] [Elsewhere Freud remarks that, strictly speaking, 'secondary revision' is *not* a part of the dream-work. Cf. his article on 'Psycho-Analysis' in Marcuse's *Handwörterbuch* (Freud, 1923*a*, end of paragraph on 'The Interpretation of Dreams.') This same point is also mentioned towards the end of Freud (1913*a*).]

[2] [An allusion to some lines in Heine's 'Die Heimkehr' (LVIII). The whole passage is quoted by Freud near the beginning of the last of his *New Introductory Lectures* (1933*a*).]

[3] [See, for instance, the dreams recorded on pp. 598 f. and 581.]

to create new contributions to dreams. It is certain, however, that, like the others, it exerts its influence principally by its preferences and selections from psychical material in the dream-thoughts that has already been formed. Now there is one case in which it is to a great extent spared the labour of, as it were, building up a façade for the dream—the case, namely, in which a formation of that kind already exists, available for use in the material of the dream-thoughts. I am in the habit of describing the element in the dream-thoughts which I have in mind as a 'phantasy.'[1] I shall perhaps avoid misunderstanding if I mention the 'day-dream' as something analogous to it in waking life.[2] The part played in our mental life by these structures has not yet been fully recognized and elucidated by psychiatrists, though M. Benedikt has made what seems to me a very promising start in that direction.[3] The importance of day-dreams has not escaped the unerring vision of imaginative writers; there is, for instance, a well-known account by Alphonse Daudet in Le Nabab of the day-dreams of one of the minor characters in that story. [Cf. p. 536 f.] The study of the psychoneuroses leads to the surprising discovery that these phantasies or daydreams are the immediate fore-runners of hysterical symptoms, or at least of a whole number of them. Hysterical symptoms are not attached to actual memories, but to phantasies erected on the basis of memories.[4] The frequent occurrence of conscious daytime phantasies brings these structures to our knowledge; but just as there are phantasies of this kind which are conscious, so, too, there are unconscious ones in great numbers, which have to remain unconscious on account of their content and of their origin from repressed material. Closer investigation of the characteristics of these daytime phantasies shows us how right it is that these formations should bear the same name as we give to the products of our thought during the night—the

---

[1] ['Phantasie.' This German word was earlier used only to mean 'imagination'; 'Phantasiebildung' ('imaginative formation') would have been used here.]

[2] 'Rêve,' 'petit roman,'—day-dream,' '[continuous] story.' [These last words are in English in the original. The term 'Tagtraum,' used in the text above, was unfamiliar to German readers and called for elucidation.]

[3] [Freud himself later devoted two papers to the subject of daydreams: 1908a and 1908e. In 1921 The Psychology of Day-Dreams was published by J. Varendonck, to which Freud provided an introduction (Freud, 1921b).]

[4] [This was expressed by Freud more trenchantly in a memorandum accompanying his letter to Fliess of May 2, 1897 (Freud, 1950a, Draft L): 'Phantasies are psychical façades constructed in order to bar the way to these memories [of primal scenes].']

name, that is, of 'dreams.' They share a large number of their properties with night-dreams, and their investigation might, in fact, have served as the shortest and best approach to an understanding of night-dreams.

Like dreams, they are wish-fulfillments; like dreams, they are based to a great extent on impressions of infantile experiences; like dreams, they benefit by a certain degree of relaxation of censorship. If we examine their structure, we shall perceive the way in which the wishful purpose that is at work in their production has mixed up the material of which they are built, has re-arranged it and has formed it into a new whole. They stand in much the same relation to the childhood memories from which they are derived as do some of the Baroque palaces of Rome to the ancient ruins whose pavements and columns have provided the material for the more recent structures.

The function of 'secondary revision,' which we have attributed to the fourth of the factors concerned in shaping the content of dreams, shows us in operation once more the activity which is able to find free vent in the creation of day-dreams without being inhibited by any other influences. We might put it simply by saying that this fourth factor of ours seeks to mould the material offered to it into something like a day-dream. If, however, a day-dream of this kind has already been formed within the nexus of the dream-thoughts, this fourth factor in the dream-work will prefer to take possession of the ready-made day-dream and seek to introduce it into the content of the dream. There are some dreams which consist merely in the repetition of a daytime phantasy which may perhaps have remained unconscious:[1] such, for instance, as the boy's dream of driving in a war-chariot with the heroes of the Trojan War [p. 154]. In my 'Autodidasker' dream [pp. 316 ff.] the second part at all events was a faithful reproduction of a daytime phantasy, innocent in itself, of a conversation with Professor N. In view of the complicated conditions which a dream has to satisfy when it comes into existence, it happens more frequently that the ready-made phantasy forms only a *portion* of the dream, or that only a portion of the phantasy forces its way into the dream. Thereafter, the phantasy is treated in general like any other portion of the latent material, though it often remains recognizable as an entity in the dream. There are often parts of my dreams which stand out as producing

---

[1] [Cf. the long footnote to the section on 'The Barrier against Incest' near the end of the third of Freud's *Three Essays on the Theory of Sexuality* (1905d). This footnote was added in the Fourth Edition of that book (1920).]

a different impression from the rest. They strike me as being, as it were, more fluent, more connected and at the same time more fleeting than other parts of the same dream. These, I know, are unconscious phantasies which have found their way into the fabric of the dream, but I have never succeeded in pinning down a phantasy of this kind. Apart from this, these phantasies, like any other component of the dream-thoughts, are compressed, condensed, superimposed on one another, and so on. There are, however, transitional cases, between the case in which they constitute the content (or at least the façade) of the dream unaltered and the extreme opposite, in which they are represented in the content of the dream only by *one* of their elements or by a distant allusion. What happens to phantasies present in the dream-thoughts is evidently also determined by any advantages they may have to offer the requirements of the censorship and of the urge towards condensation.

In selecting examples of dream-interpretation I have so far as possible avoided dreams in which unconscious phantasies play any considerable part, because the introduction of this particular psychical element would have necessitated lengthy discussions on the psychology of unconscious thinking. Nevertheless, I cannot completely escape a consideration of phantasies in this connection, since they often make their way complete into dreams and since still more often clear glimpses of them can be seen behind the dream. I will therefore quote one more dream, which seems to be composed of two different and opposing phantasies which coincide with each other at a few points and of which one is superficial while the second is, as it were, an interpretation of the first. [See above p. 495].[1]

The dream—it is the only one of which I possess no careful notes—ran roughly as follows. The dreamer, a young unmarried man, was sitting

---

[1] [*Footnote added* 1909:] In my 'Fragment of an Analysis of a Case of Hysteria' (1905*e* [Part II]), I have analysed a good specimen of a dream of this sort, made up of a number of superimposed phantasies. Incidentally, I underestimated the importance of the part played by these phantasies in the formation of dreams so long as I was principally working on my own dreams, which are usually based on discussions and conflicts of thought and comparatively rarely on day-dreams. In the case of other people it is often much easier to demonstrate the complete analogy between night-dreams and day-dreams. With hysterical patients, a hysterical attack can often be replaced by a dream; and it is then easy to convince oneself that the immediate forerunner of *both* these psychical structures was a day-dream phantasy.

in the restaurant at which he usually ate and which was presented realis-
tically in the dream. Several people then appeared, in order to fetch him
away, and one of them wanted to arrest him. He said to his companions
at table: 'I'll pay later; I'll come back.' But they exclaimed with derisive
smiles: 'We know all about that; that's what they all say!' One of the
guests called out after him: 'There goes another one!' He was then led
into a narrow room in which he found a female figure carrying a child.
One of the people accompanying him said: 'This is Herr Müller.' A police inspector, or some such official, was turning over a bundle of cards or
papers and as he did so repeated 'Müller, Müller, Müller.' Finally he asked
the dreamer a question, which he answered with an 'I will.' He then
turned round to look at the female figure and observed that she was now
wearing a big beard.

Here there is no difficulty in separating the two components. The superficial one was a *phantasy of arrest* which appears as though it had been
freshly constructed by the dream-work. But behind it some material is visible which had been only slightly re-shaped by the dream-work: *a phantasy
of marriage*. Those features which were common to both phantasies emerge
with special clarity, in the same way as in one of Galton's composite photographs. The promise made by the young man (who up till then had been
a bachelor) that he would come back and join his fellow-diners, at their
table, the scepticism of his boon-companions (whom experience had taught
better), the exclamation 'there goes another one [to get married]'—all of
these features fitted in easily with the alternative interpretation. So, too, did
the 'I will' with which he replied to the official's question. The turning over
the bundle of papers, with the constant repetition of the same name corresponded to a less important but recognizable feature of wedding festivities,
namely the reading out of a bundle of telegrams of congratulation, all of
them with addresses bearing the same names. The phantasy of marriage actually scored a victory over the covering phantasy of arrest in the fact of the
bride's making a personal appearance in the dream. I was able to discover
from an enquiry—the dream was not analysed—why it was that at the end
of it the bride wore a beard. On the previous day the dreamer had been
walking in the street with a friend who was as shy of marrying as he was
himself, and he had drawn his friend's attention to a darkhaired beauty who
had passed them. 'Yes,' his friend had remarked, 'if only women like that
didn't grow beards like their fathers' in a few years' time.' This dream did
not, of course, lack elements in which dream-distortion had been carried
deeper. It may well be, for instance, that the words 'I'll pay later' referred to

what he feared might be his father-in-law's attitude on the subject of a dowry. In fact, all kinds of qualms were evidently preventing the dreamer from throwing himself into the phantasy of marriage with any enjoyment. One of these qualms, a fear that marriage might cost him his freedom, was embodied in the transformation into a scene of arrest.

If we return for a moment to the point that the dream-work is glad to make use of a ready-made phantasy instead of putting one together out of the material of the dream-thoughts, we may perhaps find ourselves in a position to solve one of the most interesting puzzles connected with dreams. On pp. 58 f. I told the well-known anecdote of how Maury, having been struck in his sleep on the back of his neck by a piece of wood, woke up from a long dream which was like a full-length story set in the days of the French Revolution. Since the dream, as reported, was a coherent one and was planned entirely with an eye to providing an explanation of the stimulus which woke him and whose occurrence he could not have anticipated, the only possible hypothesis seems to be that the whole elaborate dream must have been composed and must have taken place during the short period of time between the contact of the board with Maury's cervical vertebrae and his consequent awakening. We should never dare to attribute such rapidity to thought-activity in waking life, and we should therefore be driven to conclude that the dream-work possesses the advantage of accelerating our thought-processes to a remarkable degree. Strong objections have been raised to what quickly became a popular conclusion by some more recent writers (Le Lorrain, 1894 and 1895, Egger, 1895, and others). On the one hand they throw doubts upon the accuracy of Maury's account of his dream; and on the other hand they attempt to show that the rapidity of the operations of our waking thoughts is no less than in this dream when exaggerations have been discounted. The discussion raised questions of principle which do not seem to me immediately soluble. But I must confess that the arguments brought forward (by Egger, for instance), particularly against Maury's guillotine dream, leave me unconvinced. I myself would propose the following explanation of this dream. Is it so highly improbable that Maury's dream represents a phantasy which had been stored up ready-made in his memory for many years and which was aroused—or I would rather say 'alluded to'—at the moment at which he became aware of the stimulus which woke him? If this were so, we should have escaped the whole difficulty of understanding how such a long story with all its details could have been composed in the extremely short period of time which was at the dreamer's disposal—for the story would have been composed already. If the piece of wood had struck the back of Maury's neck while he was awake, there would have been an opportunity for some such thought as: 'That's just like being guillotined.' But since it was in his sleep that he was struck by the board, the dream-work made use of the impinging stimulus in order rapidly to produce a wish-fulfilment; it was *as though* it thought (this is to be taken purely figuratively) : 'Here's a good opportunity of realizing a wishful phantasy which was formed at such and such a time in the course of reading.' It can hardly be disputed, I think, that the dream-story was precisely of a sort likely to be constructed by a young man under the influence of powerfully exciting impressions. Who—least of all what Frenchman or student of the history of civilization—could fail to be gripped by narratives of the Reign of Terror, when the men and women of the aristocracy, the flower of the nation, showed that they could die with a cheerful mind and could retain the liveliness of their wit and the elegance of their manners till the very moment of the fatal summons? How tempting for a young man to plunge into all this in his imagination—to picture himself bidding a lady farewell—kissing her hand and mounting the scaffold unafraid! Or, if ambition were the prime motive of the phantasy, how tempting for him to take the place of one of those formidable figures who, by the power alone of their thoughts and flaming eloquence, ruled the city in which the heart of humanity beat convulsively in those days—who were led by their convictions to send thousands of men to their death and who prepared the way for the transformation of Europe, while all the time their own heads were insecure and destined to fall one day beneath the knife of the guillotine—how tempting to picture himself as one of the Girondists, perhaps, or as the heroic Danton! There is one feature in Maury's recollection of the dream, his being 'led to the place of execution, surrounded by an immense mob,' which seems to suggest that his phantasy was in fact of this ambitious type.

Nor is it necessary that this long-prepared phantasy should have been gone through during sleep; it would have been sufficient for it to be merely touched on. What I mean is this. If a few bars of music are played and someone comments that it is from Mozart's *Figaro* (as happens in *Don Giovanni*) a number of recollections are roused in me all at once, none of which can enter my consciousness singly at the first moment. The key-phrase serves as a port of entry through which the whole network is simultaneously put in a state of excitation. It may well be the same in the case of unconscious thinking. The rousing stimulus excites the psychical port of entry which allows access to the whole guillotine phantasy. But the phantasy is not gone through during sleep but only in the recollection of the sleeper after his awakening. After waking he remembers in all its details the phantasy which was stirred up as a whole in his dream. One has no means of assuring oneself in such a case that one is really remembering something one has dreamt This same explanation—that it is a question of ready-made phantasies which are brought into excitation as a whole by the rousing stimulus—can be applied to other dreams which are focused upon a rousing stimulus, such, for instance, as Napoleon's battle dream before the explosion of the infernal machine [pp. 58 and 252 f.].

Among the dreams[1] collected by Justine Tobowolska in her dissertation on the apparent passage of time in dreams, the most informative seems to me to be the one reported by Macario (1857, 46) as having been dreamt by a dramatic author, Casimir Bonjour. One evening Bonjour wanted to attend the first performance of one of his pieces; but he was so fatigued that as he was sitting behind the scenes he dozed off just at the moment the curtain went up. During his sleep he went through the whole five acts of the play, and observed all the various signs of emotion shown by the audience during the different scenes. At the end of the performance he was delighted to hear his name being shouted with the liveliest demonstrations of applause. Suddenly he woke up. He could not believe either his eyes or his ears, for the performance had not gone beyond the first few lines of the first scene; he could not have been asleep for longer than two minutes. It is surely not too rash to suppose in the case of this dream that the dreamer's going through all five acts of the play and observing the attitude of the public to different passages in it need not have arisen from any fresh production of material during his sleep, but may have reproduced a piece of phantasy-activity (in the sense I have described) which had already been completed. Tobowolska, like other writers, emphasizes the fact that dreams with an accelerated passage of ideas have the common characteristic of seeming specially coherent, quite unlike other dreams, and that the recollection of them is summary far more than detailed. This would indeed be a characteristic which ready-made phantasies of this kind, touched upon by the dream-work, would be bound to possess, though this is a conclusion which the writers

---

[1] [This paragraph was added in 1914 with the exception of the last sentence, which appeared in the original edition.]

in question fail to draw. I do not assert, however, that *all* arousal dreams admit of this explanation, or that the problem of the accelerated passage of ideas in dreams can be entirely dismissed in this fashion.

At this point it is impossible to avoid considering the relation between this secondary revision of the content of dreams and the remaining factors of the dream-work. Are we to suppose that what happens is that in the first instance the dream-constructing factors—the tendency towards condensation, the necessity for evading the censorship, and considerations of representability by the psychical means open to dreams—put together a provisional dream-content out of the material provided, and that this content is subsequently re-cast so as to conform so far as possible to the demands of a second agency? This is scarcely probable. We must assume rather that from the very first the demands of this second factor constitute one of the conditions which the dream must satisfy and that this condition, like those laid down by condensation, the censorship imposed by resistance, and representability, operates simultaneously in a conducive and selective sense upon the mass of material present in the dream-thoughts. In any case, however, of the four conditions for the formation of dreams, the one we have come to know last is the one whose demands appear to have the least cogent influence on dreams.

The following consideration makes it highly probable that the psychical function which carries out what we have described as the secondary revision of the content of dreams is to be identified with the activity of our waking thought. Our waking (preconscious[1]) thinking behaves towards any perceptual material with which it meets in just the same way in which the function we are considering behaves towards the content of dreams. It is the nature of our waking thought to establish order in material of that kind, to set up relations in it and to make it conform to our expectations of an intelligible whole. [Cf. pp. 60 f. and 76.] In fact, we go too far in that direction. An adept in sleight of hand can trick us by relying upon this intellectual habit of ours. In our efforts at making an intelligible pattern of the sense-impressions that are offered to us, we often fall into the strangest errors or even falsify the truth about the material before us.

---

[1] [Freud's first published use of the term seems to occur on p. 352; it is explained below on pp. 542 f. It appears as early as December 6, 1896, in his correspondence with Fliess (Freud, 1950*a*, Letter 52).]

The evidences of this are too universally known for there to be any need to insist upon them further. In our reading we pass over misprints which destroy the sense, and have the illusion that what we are reading is correct. The editor of a popular French periodical is said to have made a bet that he would have the words 'in front' or 'behind' inserted by the printer in every sentence of a long article without a single one of his readers noticing it. He won his bet. Many years ago I read in a newspaper a comic instance of a false connection. On one occasion during a sitting of the French Chamber a bomb thrown by an anarchist exploded in the Chamber itself and Dupuy subdued the consequent panic with the courageous words: *'La séance continue.'* The visitors in the gallery were asked to give their impressions as witnesses of the outrage. Among them were two men from the provinces. One of these said that it was true that he had heard a detonation at the close of one of the speeches but had assumed that it was a parliamentary usage to fire a shot each time a speaker sat down. The second one, who had probably already heard *several* speeches, had come to the same conclusion, except that he supposed that a shot was only fired as a tribute to a particularly successful speech.

There is no doubt, then, that it is our normal thinking that is the psychical agency which approaches the content of dreams with a demand that it must be intelligible, which subjects it to a first interpretation and which consequently produces a complete misunderstanding of it. [See p. 495.] For the purposes of *our* interpretation it remains an essential rule invariably to leave out of account the ostensible continuity of a dream as being of suspect origin, and to follow the same path back to the material of the dream-thoughts, no matter whether the dream itself is clear or confused.

We now perceive, incidentally, on what it is that the range in the quality of dreams between confusion and clarity which was discussed on p. 346 depends. Those parts of a dream on which the secondary revision has been able to produce some effect are clear, while those parts on which its efforts have failed are confused. Since the confused parts of a dream are so often at the same time the less vivid parts, we may conclude that the secondary dream-work is also to be held responsible for a contribution to the plastic intensity of the different dream-elements.

If I look around for something with which to compare the final form assumed by a dream as it appears after normal thought has made its contribution, I can think of nothing better than the enigmatic inscriptions with which *Fliegende Blätter* has for so long entertained its readers. They are intended to make the reader believe that a certain sentence—for the sake of contrast, a sentence in dialect and as scurrilous as possible—is a Latin inscription. For this purpose the letters contained in the words are torn out of their combination into syllables and arranged in a new order. Here and there a genuine Latin word appears; at other points we seem to see abbreviations of Latin words before us; and at still other points in the inscription we may allow ourselves to be deceived into overlooking the senselessness of isolated letters by parts of the inscription seeming to be defaced or showing lacunae. If we are to avoid being taken in by the joke, we must disregard everything that makes it seem like an inscription, look firmly at the letters, pay no attention to their ostensible arrangement, and so combine them into words belonging to our own mother tongue.[1]

Secondary revision[2] is the one factor in the dream-work which has been observed by the majority of writers on the subject and of which the significance has been appreciated. Havelock Ellis (1911, 10–11) has given an amusing account of its functioning: 'Sleeping consciousness we may even imagine as saying to itself in effect: "Here comes our master, Waking Consciousness, who attaches such mighty importance to reason and logic and so forth. Quick! gather things up, put them in order—any order will do—before he enters to take possession."'

The identity of its method of working with that of waking thought has been stated with particular clarity by Delacroix (1904, 926): 'Cette fonction d'interprétation n'est pas particulière au rêve; c'est le même travail de coordination logique que nous faisons sur nos sensations pendant la veille.'[3] James Sully [1893, 355–6] is of the same opinion. So, too, is Tobowolska (1900, 93): 'Sur ces successions incohérentes d'hallucinations, l'esprit s'efforce de faire le même travail de coordination logique qu'il fait

---

[1] [An instance of the operation of the process of secondary revision in the case of a fairy-tale is given on p. 261 f. and in the case of *Oedipus Rex* on p. 282. Its application to obsessions and phobias is mentioned on p. 262, and to paranoia in Lecture XXIV of Freud's *Introductory Lectures* (1916–17). An example of secondary revision in a telegraphic error is recorded in Chapter VI (No. 19) of *The Psychopathology of Everyday Life* (1901*b*). The analogy between the secondary revision of dreams and the formation of 'systems' of thought is discussed at some length in Chapter III, Section 4, of *Totem and Taboo* (1912–13).]

[2] [The remainder of this chapter, with the exception of the last paragraph, which was in the original edition, was added in 1914.]

[3] ['This interpretative function is not peculiar to dreams. It is the same work of logical co-ordination which we carry out upon our sensations while we are awake.']

pendant la veille sur les sensations. Il relie entre elles par un lien imaginaire toutes ces images décousues et bouche les écarts trop grands qui se trouvaient entre elles.'[1]

According to some writers, this process of arranging and interpreting begins during the dream itself and is continued after waking. Thus Paulhan (1894, 546): 'Cependant j'ai souvent pensé qu'il pouvait y avoir une certaine déformation, ou plutôt reformation, du rêve dans le souvenir. . . . La tendence systématisante de l'imagination pourrait fort bien achever après le réveil ce qu'elle a ébauché pendant le sommeil. De la sorte, la rapidité réelle de la pensée serait augmentée en apparence par les perfectionnements dus à l'imagination éveillée.'[2] Bernard-Leroy and Tobowolska (1901, 592): 'Dans le rêve, au contraire, l'interprétation et la coordination se font non seulement à l'aide des données du rêve, mais encore à l'aide de celles de la veille. . . .'[3]

Inevitably, therefore, this one recognized factor in the formation of dreams has had its importance overestimated, so that it has been credited with the whole achievement of the creation of dreams. This act of creation, as Goblot (1896, 288 f.) and still more Foucault (1906) suppose, is performed at the moment of waking; for these two writers attribute to waking thought an ability to construct a dream out of the thoughts that emerge during sleep. Bernard-Leroy and Tobowolska (1901) comment on this view: 'On a cru pouvoir placer le rêve au moment du réveil, et ils ont attribué à la pensée de la veille la fonction de construire le rêve avec les images présentes dans la pensée du sommeil.'[4]

---

[1] ['The mind endeavours to carry out upon these incoherent trains of hallucinations the same work of logical co-ordination that it carries out upon sensations during the daytime. It connects up all these detached images by an imaginary link and stops up any excessively wide gaps between them.']

[2] ['I have often thought, however, that dreams may be to some extent misshaped, or rather reshaped, in memory. . . . The tendency of the imagination towards systematization might very well complete after waking what it had started upon in sleep. In that way the real speed of thought would be given an apparent increase by the improvements due to the waking imagination.']

[3] ['In a dream, on the contrary, interpretation and co-ordination are carried out by the help not only of the data presented in the dream, but of the data available in waking life. . . .']

[4] ['It has been thought possible to locate dreams at the moment of waking, and [these authors] have ascribed to waking thought the function of constructing dreams out of the images present in sleeping thought.']

From this discussion of secondary revision I will go on to consider a further factor in the dream-work which has recently been brought to light by some finely perceptive observations carried out by Herbert Silberer. As I have mentioned earlier (pp. 358 ff.), Silberer has, as it were, caught in the very act the process of transforming thoughts into images, by forcing himself into intellectual activity while he was in a state of fatigue and drowsiness. At such moments the thought with which he was dealing vanished and was replaced by a vision which turned out to be a substitute for what were as a rule abstract thoughts. (Cf. the examples in the passage just referred to.) Now it happened during these experiments that the image which arose, and which might be compared to an element of a dream, sometimes represented something other than the thought that was being dealt with—namely, the fatigue itself, the difficulty and unpleasure involved in the work. It represented, that is to say, the subjective state and mode of functioning of the person making the effort instead of the object of his efforts. Silberer described occurrences of this kind, which were very frequent in his case, as a 'functional phenomenon' in contrast to the 'material phenomenon' which would have been expected.

For instance: 'One afternoon I was lying on my sofa feeling extremely sleepy; nevertheless I forced myself to think over a philosophical problem. I wanted to compare the views of Kant and Schopenhauer upon Time. As a result of my drowsiness I was unable to keep the arguments of both of them before my mind at once, which was necessary in order to make the comparison. After a number of vain attempts, I once more impressed Kant's deductions upon my mind with all the strength of my will, so that I might apply them to Schopenhauer's statement of the problem. I then directed my attention to the latter; but when I tried to turn back again to Kant, I found that his argument had once more escaped me and I tried vainly to pick it up once more. This vain effort at recovering the Kant *dossier* which was stored away somewhere in my head was suddenly represented before my closed eyes as a concrete and plastic symbol, as though it were a dream-picture: *I was asking for information from a disobliging secretary who was bent over his writing-table and refused to put himself out at my insistent demand. He half straightened himself and gave me a disagreeable and uncomplying look.*' (Silberer, 1909, 513 f. [Freud's italics.])

Here are some other instances, which relate to the oscillation between sleeping and waking:

'Example No. 2.—Circumstances: In the morning, at waking. While I was at a certain depth of sleep (a twilight state) and reflecting over a previous dream and in a sort of way continuing to dream it, I felt myself approaching nearer to waking consciousness but wanted to remain in the twilight state.

'Scene: *I was stepping across a brook with one foot but drew it back again at once with the intention of remaining on this side.*' (Silberer, 1911, 625.)

'Example No. 6—Conditions as in example No. 4' (in which he had wanted to lie in bed a little longer, though without oversleeping). 'I wanted to give way to sleep for a little longer.

'Scene: *I was saying good-bye to someone and was arranging with him (or her) to meet him (or her) again soon.*' (Ibid., 627.)

The 'functional' phenomenon, 'the representation of a state instead of an object,' was observed by Silberer principally in the two conditions of falling asleep and waking up. It is obvious that dream-interpretation is only concerned with the latter case. Silberer has given examples which show convincingly that in many dreams the last pieces of the manifest content, which are immediately followed by waking, represent nothing more nor less than an intention to wake or the process of waking. The representation may be in terms of such images as crossing a threshold ('threshold symbolism'), leaving one room and entering another, departure, home-coming, parting with a companion, diving into water, etc. I cannot, however, refrain from remarking that I have come across dream-elements which can be related to threshold symbolism, whether in my own dreams or in those of subjects whom I have analysed, far less frequently than Silberer's communications would have led one to expect.

It is by no means inconceivable or improbable that this threshold symbolism might throw light upon some elements in the middle of the texture of dreams—in places, for instance, where there is a question of oscillations in the depth of sleep and of an inclination to break off the dream. Convincing instances of this, however, have not been produced.[1] What seem to occur more frequently are cases of overdetermination, in which a part of a dream which has derived its material content from the nexus of dream-thoughts is employed to represent *in addition* some state of mental activity.

This very interesting functional phenomenon of Silberer's has, through no fault of its discoverer's, led to many abuses; for it has been regarded as lending support to the old inclination to give abstract and symbolic interpretations to dreams. The preference for the 'functional category' is carried so far by some people that they speak of the functional phenomenon

---

[1] [See, however, a subsequent remark by Freud on p. 559 below.]

wherever intellectual activities or emotional processes occur in the dream-thoughts, although such material has neither more nor less right than any other kind to find its way into a dream as residues of the previous day. [Cf. pp. 236 *n*. 3, and 421 *n*.]

We are ready to recognize the fact that Silberer's phenomena constitute a second contribution on the part of waking thought to the construction of dreams; though it is less regularly present and less significant than the first one, which has already been introduced under the name of 'secondary revision.' It has been shown that a part of the attention which operates during the day continues to be directed towards dreams during the state of sleep, that it keeps a check on them and criticizes them and reserves the power to interrupt them. It has seemed plausible to recognize in the mental agency which thus remains awake the censor[1] to whom we have had to attribute such a powerful restricting influence upon the form taken by dreams. What Silberer's observations have added to this is the fact that in certain circumstances a species of self-observation plays a part in this and makes a contribution to the content of the dream. The probable relations of this self-observing agency, which may be particularly prominent in philosophical minds, to endopsychic perception, to delusions of observation, to conscience and to the censor of dreams can be more appropriately treated elsewhere.[2]

I will now try to sum up this lengthy disquisition on the dream-work. We were faced by the question whether the mind employs the whole of its faculties without reserve in constructing dreams or only a functionally restricted fragment of them. Our investigations led us to reject entirely the form in which the question was framed as being inadequate to the circumstances. If, however, we had to reply to the question on the basis of the terms in which it was stated, we should be obliged to reply in the affirmative to *both* the alternatives, mutually exclusive though they appear to be. Two separate functions may be distinguished in mental activity during the

---

[1] [Freud almost always uses the German word '*Zensur*' ('censorship'); but here and a few lines lower down he uses the personal form '*Zensor*' ('censor'). Other instances of this very rare occurrence will be found in Section III of the paper on 'Narcissism' (Freud, 1914*c*) and in Lecture XXIX of the *New Introductory Lectures* (Freud, 1933*a*).]

[2] [*Footnote added* 1914:] 'On Narcissism' (Freud, 1914*c* [Section III]).—The next paragraph appeared in the first edition.

construction of a dream: the production of the dream-thoughts, and their transformation into the content of the dream. The dream-thoughts are entirely rational and are constructed with an expenditure of all the psychical energy of which we are capable. They have their place among thought-processes that have not become conscious—processes from which, after some modification, our conscious thoughts, too, arise. However many interesting and puzzling questions the dream-thoughts may involve, such questions have, after all, no special relation to dreams and do not call for treatment among the problems of dreams.[1] On the other hand, the second function of mental activity during dream-construction, the transformation of the unconscious thoughts into the content of the dream, is peculiar to dream-life and characteristic of it. This dream-work proper diverges further from our picture of waking thought than has been supposed even by the most determined depredator of psychical functioning during the formation of dreams. The dream-work is not simply more careless, more irrational, more forgetful and more incomplete than waking thought; it is completely different from it qualitatively and for that reason not immediately comparable with it. It does not think, calculate or judge in any way at all; it restricts itself to giving things a new form. It is exhaustively described by an enumeration of the conditions which it has to satisfy in producing its result. That product, the dream, has above all to evade the censorship, and

---

[1] [*Footnote added* 1925:] I used at one time to find it extraordinarily difficult to accustom readers to the distinction between the manifest content of dreams and the latent dream-thoughts. Again and again arguments and objections would be brought up based upon some uninterpreted dream in the form in which it had been retained in the memory, and the need to interpret it would be ignored. But now that analysts at least have become reconciled to replacing the manifest dream by the meaning revealed by its interpretation, many of them have become guilty of falling into another confusion which they cling to with equal obstinacy. They seek to find the essence of dreams in their latent content and in so doing they overlook the distinction between the latent dream-thoughts and the dream-work. At bottom, dreams are nothing other than a particular *form* of thinking, made possible by the conditions of the state of sleep. It is the *dream-work* which creates that form, and it alone is the essence of dreaming—the explanation of its peculiar nature. I say this in order to make it possible to assess the value of the notorious 'prospective purpose' of dreams. [See below, p. 577 *n.*] The fact that dreams concern themselves with attempts at solving the problems by which our mental life is faced is no more strange than that our conscious waking life should do so; beyond this it merely tells us that that activity can also be carried on in the preconscious—and this we already knew.

with that end in view the dream-work makes use of a *displacement of psychical intensities* to the point of a transvaluation of all psychical values. The thoughts have to be reproduced exclusively or predominantly in the material of visual and acoustic memory-traces, and this necessity imposes upon the dream-work *considerations of representability* which it meets by carrying out fresh displacements. Greater intensities have probably to be produced than are available in the dream-thoughts at night, and this purpose is served by the extensive *condensation* which is carried out with the constituents of the dream-thoughts. Little attention is paid to the logical relations between the thoughts; those relations are ultimately given a disguised representation in certain *formal* characteristics of dreams. Any affect attached to the dream-thoughts undergoes less modification than their ideational content. Such affects are as a rule suppressed; when they are retained, they are detached from the ideas that properly belong to them, affects of a similar character being brought together. Only a single portion of the dream-work and one which operates to an irregular degree, the working over of the material by partly aroused waking thought, tallies to some extent with the view which other writers have sought to apply to the entire activity of dream-construction.[1]

---

[1] [At this point there followed in the fourth, fifth, sixth and seventh editions (from 1914 to 1922) two self-contained essays by Otto Rank, bearing the titles 'Dreams and Creative Writing' and 'Dreams and Myths.' These were omitted from the *Gesammelte Schriften,* 1924, with a comment by Freud (**3,** 150) that they were 'naturally not included in a collected edition of my works.' They were, however, not re-inserted in the subsequent (eighth) edition of 1930. See the Editor's Introduction, p. xxi.]

CHAPTER VII

THE PSYCHOLOGY OF THE
DREAM-PROCESSES[1]

AMONG the dreams which have been reported to me by other people, there is one which has special claims upon our attention at this point. It was told to me by a woman patient who had herself heard it in a lecture on dreams: its actual source is still unknown to me. Its content made an impression on the lady, however, and she proceeded to 're-dream' it, that is, to repeat some of its elements in a dream of her own, so that, by taking it over in this way, she might express her agreement with it on one particular point.

The preliminaries to this model dream were as follows. A father had been watching beside his child's sick-bed for days and nights on end. After the child had died, he went into the next room to lie down, but left the door open so that he could see from his bedroom into the room in which his child's body was laid out, with tall candles standing round it. An old man had been engaged to keep watch over it, and sat beside the body murmuring prayers. After a few hours' sleep, the father had a dream that *his child was standing beside his bed, caught him by the arm and whispered to him reproachfully: 'Father, don't you see I'm burning?'* He woke up, noticed a bright glare of light from the next room, hurried into it and found that the old watchman had dropped off to sleep and that the wrappings and

---

[1] [Some light has been thrown on the difficulties presented in the later sections of this chapter by Freud's early correspondence with Wilhelm Fliess (Freud, 1950a). Cf. the Editor's Introduction (p. xv ff.).]

one of the arms of his beloved child's dead body had been burned by a lighted candle that had fallen on them.

The explanation of this moving dream is simple enough and, so my patient told me, was correctly given by the lecturer. The glare of light shone through the open door into the sleeping man's eyes and led him to the conclusion which he would have arrived at if he had been awake, namely that a candle had fallen over and set something alight in the neighbourhood of the body. It is even possible that he had felt some concern when he went to sleep as to whether the old man might not be incompetent to carry out his task.

Nor have I any changes to suggest in this interpretation except to add that the content of the dream must have been overdetermined and that the words spoken by the child must have been made up of words which he had actually spoken in his lifetime and which were connected with important events in the father's mind. For instance, '*I'm burning*' may have been spoken during the fever of the child's last illness, and '*Father, don't you see?*' may have been derived from some other highly emotional situation of which we are in ignorance.

But, having recognized that the dream was a process with a meaning, and that it can be inserted into the chain of the dreamer's psychical experiences, we may still wonder why it was that a dream occurred at all in such circumstances, when the most rapid possible awakening was called for. And here we shall observe that this dream, too, contained the fulfilment of a wish. The dead child behaved in the dream like a living one: he himself warned his father, came to his bed, and caught him by the arm, just as he had probably done on the occasion from the memory of which the first part of the child's words in the dream were derived. For the sake of the fulfilment of this wish the father prolonged his sleep by one moment. The dream was preferred to a waking reflection because it was able to show the child as once more alive. If the father had woken up first and then made the inference that led him to go into the next room, he would, as it were, have shortened his child's life by that moment of time.

There can be no doubt what the peculiar feature is which attracts our interest to this brief dream. Hitherto we have been principally concerned with the secret meaning of dreams and the method of discovering it and with the means employed by the dream-work for concealing it. The problems of dream-interpretation have hitherto occupied the centre of the picture. And now we come upon a dream which raises no problem of interpretation and the meaning of which is obvious, but which, as we see, nevertheless retains the essential characteristics that differentiate dreams so strikingly from waking life and consequently call for explanation. It is only after we have disposed of everything that has to do with the work of interpretation that we can begin to realize the incompleteness of our psychology of dreams.

But before starting off along this new path, it will be well to pause and look around, to see whether in the course of our journey up to this point we have overlooked anything of importance. For it must be clearly understood that the easy and agreeable portion of our journey lies behind us. Hitherto, unless I am greatly mistaken, all the paths along which we have travelled have led us towards the light—towards elucidation and fuller understanding. But as soon as we endeavour to penetrate more deeply into the mental process involved in dreaming, every path will end in darkness. There is no possibility of *explaining* dreams as a psychical process, since to explain a thing means to trace it back to something already known, and there is at the present time no established psychological knowledge under which we could subsume what the psychological examination of dreams enables us to infer as a basis for their explanation. On the contrary, we shall be obliged to set up a number of fresh hypotheses which touch tentatively upon the structure of the apparatus of the mind and upon the play of forces operating in it. We must be careful, however, not to pursue these hypotheses too far beyond their first logical links, or their value will be lost in uncertainties. Even if we make no false inferences and take all the logical possibilities into account, the probable incompleteness of our premises threatens to bring our calculation to a complete miscarriage. No conclusions upon the construction and working methods of the mental instrument can be arrived at or at least fully proved from even the most painstaking investigation of dreams or of any other mental function taken *in isolation*. To achieve this result, it will be necessary to correlate all the established implications derived from a comparative study of a whole series of such functions. Thus the psychological hypotheses to which we are led by an analysis of the processes of dreaming must be left, as it were, in suspense, until they can be related to the findings of other enquiries which seek to approach the kernel of the same problem from another angle.

(A)

THE FORGETTING OF DREAMS

I suggest, therefore, that we should first turn to a topic that raises a difficulty which we have not hitherto considered but which is nevertheless capable of cutting the ground from under all our efforts at interpreting dreams. It has been objected on more than one occasion that we have in fact no knowledge of the dreams that we set out to interpret, or, speaking more correctly, that we have no guarantee that we know them as they actually occurred. (See pp. 76 f.)

In the first place, what we remember of a dream and what we exercise our interpretative arts upon has been mutilated by the untrustworthiness of our memory, which seems quite especially incapable of retaining a dream and may well have lost precisely the most important parts of its content. It quite frequently happens that when we seek to turn our attention to one of our dreams we find ourselves regretting the fact that, though we dreamt far more, we can remember nothing but a single fragment which is itself recollected with peculiar uncertainty.

Secondly, there is every reason to suspect that our memory of dreams is not only fragmentary but positively inaccurate and falsified. On the one hand it may be doubted whether what we dreamt was really as disconnected and hazy as our recollection of it; and on the other hand it may also be doubted whether a dream was really as connected as it is in the account we give of it, whether in attempting to reproduce it we do not fill in what was never there, or what has been forgotten, with new and arbitrarily selected material, whether we do not add embellishments and trimmings and round it off so that there is no possibility of deciding what its original content may have been. Indeed one author, Spitta (1882, [338]),[1] goes to the point of suggesting that in so far as a dream shows any kind of order or coherence, these qualities are only introduced into it when we try to recall it to mind. [Cf. p. 77.] Thus there seems to be a danger that the very

---

[1] [Added in text in 1914 and transferred to footnote in 1930:] So too Foucault [1906, 141 f.] and Tannery [1898].

thing whose value we have undertaken to assess may slip completely through our fingers.

Hitherto in interpreting dreams we have disregarded such warnings. On the contrary, we have accepted it as being just as important to interpret the smallest, least conspicuous and most uncertain constituents of the content of dreams as those that are most clearly and certainly preserved. The dream of Irma's injection contained the phrase 'I *at once* called in Dr. M.' [p. 136]; and we assumed that even this detail would not have found its way into the dream unless it had had some particular origin. It was thus that we came upon the story of the unfortunate patient to whose bedside I had 'at once' called in my senior colleague. In the apparently absurd dream which treated the difference between 51 and 56 as a negligible quantity, the number 51 was mentioned several times. [See p. 443.] Instead of regarding this as a matter of course or as something indifferent, we inferred from it that there was a *second* line of thought in the latent content of the dream leading to the number 51; and along this track we arrived at my fears of 51 years being the limit of my life, in glaring contrast to the dream's dominant train of thought which was lavish in its boasts of a long life. In the *'Non vixit'* dream [pp. 430 ff.] there was an inconspicuous interpolation which I overlooked at first: *'As P. failed to understand him, Fl. asked me,'* etc. When the interpretation was held up, I went back to these words and it was they that led me on to the childhood phantasy which turned out to be an intermediate nodal point in the dream-thoughts. [See pp. 488 f.] This was arrived at by way of the lines:

> Selten habt ihr mich *verstanden,*
> Selten auch verstand ich Euch,
> Nur wenn wir im *Kot* uns fanden,
> So verstanden wir uns gleich.[1]

Examples could be found in every analysis to show that precisely the most trivial elements of a dream are indispensable to its interpretation and that the work in hand is held up if attention is not paid to these elements until too late. We have attached no less importance in interpreting dreams to every shade of the form of words in which they were laid before us. And even when it happened that the text of the dream as we had it was meaningless or

---

[1] [Literally: 'Rarely have you *understood* me, and rarely too have I understood you. Not until we both found ourselves in the *mud* did we promptly understand each other.' Heine, *Buch der Lieder,* 'Die Heimkehr,' LXXVIII.]

inadequate—as though the effort to give a correct account of it had been unsuccessful—we have taken this defect into account as well. In short, we have treated as Holy Writ what previous writers have regarded as an arbitrary improvisation, hurriedly patched together in the embarrassment of the moment. This contradiction stands in need of an explanation.

The explanation is in our favour, though without putting the other writers in the wrong. In the light of our newly-won understanding of the origin of dreams the contradiction disappears completely. It is true that we distort dreams in attempting to reproduce them; here we find at work once more the process which we have described as the secondary (and often ill conceived) revision of the dream by the agency which carries out normal thinking [pp. 493 ff.]. But this distortion is itself no more than a part of the revision to which the dream-thoughts are regularly subjected as a result of the dream-censorship. The other writers have at this point noticed or suspected the part of dream-distortion which operates manifestly; *we* are less interested, since we know that a much more far-reaching process of distortion, though a less obvious one, has already developed the dream out of the hidden dream-thoughts. The only mistake made by previous writers has been in supposing that the modification of the dream in the course of being remembered and put into words is an *arbitrary* one and cannot be further resolved and that it is therefore calculated to give us a misleading picture of the dream.[1] They have underestimated the extent to which psychical events are determined. There is nothing arbitrary about them. It can be shown quite generally that if an element is left undetermined by one train of thought, its determination is immediately effected by a second one. For instance, I may try to think of a number arbitrarily. But this is impossible: the number that occurs to me will be unambiguously and necessarily determined by thoughts of mine, though they may be remote from my immediate intention.[2] The modifications

---

[1] [A misunderstanding in a contrary direction of the importance of the text of dreams is discussed towards the end of Freud's paper on the technical uses of dream-interpretation in therapeutic analyses (1911*e*).]

[2] [*Footnote added* 1909:] See my *Psychopathology of Everyday Life* [1901*b*, Chapter XII(A), Nos. 2 to 7.—No. 2 relates to a letter written by Freud to Fliess on August 27, 1899 (Freud, 1950*a*, Letter 116), while he was correcting the proofs of the present volume, in which he prophesied that the book would contain 2,467 misprints. (See below, p. 534 *n*. 2.)].

to which dreams are submitted under the editorship of waking life are just as little arbitrary. They are associatively linked to the material which they replace, and serve to show us the way to that material, which may in its turn be a substitute for something else.

In analysing the dreams of my patients I sometimes put this assertion to the following test, which has never failed me. If the first account given me by a patient of a dream is too hard to follow I ask him to repeat it. In doing so he rarely uses the same words. But the parts of the dream which he describes in different terms are by that fact revealed to me as the weak spot in the dream's disguise: they serve my purpose just as Hagen's was served by the embroidered mark on Siegfried's cloak.[1] That is the point at which the interpretation of the dream can be started. My request to the patient to repeat his account of the dream has warned him that I was proposing to take special pains in solving it; under pressure of the resistance, therefore, he hastily covers the weak spots in the dream's disguise by replacing any expressions that threaten to betray its meaning by other less revealing ones. In this way he draws my attention to the expression which he has dropped out. The trouble taken by the dreamer in preventing the solution of the dream gives me a basis for estimating the care with which its cloak has been woven.

Previous writers have had less justification in devoting so much space to the *doubt* with which our judgement receives accounts of dreams. For this doubt has no intellectual warrant. There is in general no guarantee of the correctness of our memory; and yet we yield to the compulsion to attach belief to its data far more often than is objectively justified. Doubt whether a dream or certain of its details have been correctly reported is once more a derivative of the dream-censorship, of resistance to the penetration of the dream-thoughts into consciousness.[2] This resistance has not been exhausted even by the displacements and substitutions it has brought about; it persists in the form of doubt attaching to the material which has been allowed through. We are especially inclined to misunderstand this

---

[1] [There was only one spot on Siegfried's body where he could be wounded. By a trick, Hagen persuaded Kriemhild, who alone knew where the spot was, to embroider a small cross on Siegfried's cloak at the vital point. It was there that Hagen later stabbed him. (*Nibelungenlied*, XV and XVL.)]

[2] [For the same mechanism of doubt in cases of hysteria see a passage near the beginning of Part I of the case history of 'Dora' (1905*e*).]

doubt since it is careful never to attack the more intense elements of a dream but only the weak and indistinct ones. As we already know, however, a complete reversal of all psychical values takes place between the dream-thoughts and the dream [p. 345]. Distortion is only made possible by a withdrawal of psychical value; it habitually expresses itself by that means and is occasionally content to require nothing more. If, then, an indistinct element of a dream's content is in addition attacked by doubt, we have a sure indication that we are dealing with a comparatively direct derivative of one of the proscribed dream-thoughts. The state of things is what it was after some sweeping revolution in one of the republics of antiquity or the Renaissance. The noble and powerful families which had previously dominated the scene were sent into exile and all the high offices were filled by newcomers. Only the most impoverished and powerless members of the vanquished families, or their remote dependents, were allowed to remain in the city; and even so they did not enjoy full civic rights and were viewed with distrust. The distrust in this analogy corresponds to the doubt in the case we are considering. That is why in analysing a dream I insist that the whole scale of estimates of certainty shall be abandoned and that the faintest possibility that something of this or that sort may have occurred in the dream shall be treated as complete certainty. In tracing any element of a dream it will be found that unless this attitude is firmly adopted the analysis will come to a standstill. If any doubt is thrown upon the value of the element in question, the psychical result in the patient is that none of the involuntary ideas underlying that element comes into his head. This result is not a self-evident one. It would not make nonsense if someone were to say: 'I don't know for certain whether such and such a thing came into the dream, but here is what occurs to me in connection with it.' But in fact no one ever does say this; and it is precisely the fact that doubt produces this interrupting effect upon an analysis that reveals it as a derivative and tool of psychical resistance. Psycho-analysis is justly suspicious. One of its rules is that *whatever interrupts the progress of analytic work is a resistance.*[1]

---

[1] [*Footnote added* 1925:] The proposition laid down in these peremptory terms— 'whatever interrupts the progress of analytic work is a resistance'—is easily open to misunderstanding. It is of course only to be taken as a technical rule, as a warning to analysts. It cannot be disputed that in the course of an analysis various events may occur the responsibility for which cannot be laid upon the patient's intentions. His father may die without his having murdered him; or a war

The *forgetting* of dreams, too, remains inexplicable unless the power of the psychical censorship is taken into account. In a number of cases the feeling of having dreamt a great deal during the night and of only having retained a little of it may in fact have some other meaning, such as that the dream-work has been perceptibly proceeding all through the night but has only left a short dream behind. [Cf. pp. 297, 494, and 574 f.] It is no doubt true that we forget dreams more and more as time passes after waking; we often forget them in spite of the most painstaking efforts to recall them. But I am of opinion that the extent of this forgetting is as a rule overestimated; and there is a similar overestimation of the extent to which the gaps in a dream limit our knowledge of it. It is often possible by means of analysis to restore all that has been lost by the forgetting of the dream's content; at least, in quite a number of cases one can reconstruct from a single remaining fragment not, it is true, the dream—which is in any case a matter of no importance—but all the dream-thoughts. This demands a certain amount of attention and self-discipline in carrying out the analysis; that is all—but it shows that there was no lack of a hostile (i.e. resistant) purpose at work in the forgetting of the dream.[1]

---

may break out which brings the analysis to an end. But behind its obvious exaggeration the proposition is asserting something both true and new. Even if the interrupting event is a real one and independent of the patient, it often depends on him how great an interruption it causes; and resistance shows itself unmistakably in the readiness with which he accepts an occurrence of this kind or the exaggerated use which he makes of it.

[1] [*Footnote added* 1919:] I may quote the following dream from my *Introductory Lectures* [Freud, 1916–17, Lecture VII] as an example of the meaning of doubt and uncertainty in a dream and of its content being at the same time shrunk down to a single element; in spite of this the dream was successfully analysed after a short delay:

'A sceptical woman patient had a longish dream in the course of which some people told her about my book on jokes and praised it highly. Something came in then about a *"channel," perhaps it was another book that mentioned a channel, or something else about a channel . . . she didn't know . . . it was all so indistinct.*

'No doubt you will be inclined to expect that the element "channel," since it was so indistinct, would be inaccessible to interpretation. You are right in suspecting a difficulty; but the difficulty did not arise from the indistinctness: both the difficulty and the indistinctness arose from another cause. Nothing occurred to the dreamer in connection with "channel," and *I* could of course throw no light on it. A little later—it was the next day, in point of fact—she told me that she had thought of something that *might* have something to do with it. It was a joke, too—a joke she

Convincing evidence of the fact that the forgetting of dreams is tendentious and serves the purpose of resistance[1] is afforded when it is possible to observe in analyses a preliminary stage of forgetting. It not
infrequently happens that in the middle of the work of interpretation an
omitted portion of the dream comes to light and is described as having
been forgotten till that moment. Now a part of a dream that has been rescued from oblivion in this way is invariably the most important part; it
always lies on the shortest road to the dream's solution and has for that
reason been exposed to resistance more than any other part. Among the
specimen dreams scattered through this volume, there is one in which a
part of its content was added like this as an after-thought.[2] It is the travel
dream in which I revenged myself on two disagreeable fellow-travellers
and which I had to leave almost uninterpreted on account of its gross in-
decency. [See pp. 462 ff.] The omitted portion ran as follows: 'I *said* [in
English], *referring to one of Schiller's works: "It is from . . ."* but, *noticing
the mistake, I corrected myself: "It is by . . ." "Yes," the man commented to his
sister, "he said that right."*'[3]

---

had heard. On the steamer between Dover and Calais a well-known author fell into
conversation with an Englishman. The latter had occasion to quote the phrase:
"Du sublime au ridicule il n'y a qu'un pas. [It is only a step from the sublime to
the ridiculous.]" Yes, replied the author, *"le Pas de Calais"*—meaning that he
thought France sublime and England ridiculous. But the *Pas de Calais* is a channel—the English Channel. You will ask whether I think this had anything to do
with the dream. Certainly I think so; and it provides the solution of the puzzling
element of the dream. Can you doubt that this joke was already present before the
dream occurred, as the unconscious thought behind the element "channel"? Can
you suppose that it was introduced as a subsequent invention? The association betrayed the scepticism which lay concealed behind the patient's ostensible admiration; and her resistance against revealing this was no doubt the common cause both
of her delay in producing the association and of the indistinctness of the dream-
element concerned. Consider the relation of the dream-element to its unconscious
background: it was, as it were, a fragment of that background, an allusion to it, but
it was made quite incomprehensible by being isolated.'

[1] On the purposes of forgetting in general see my short paper on the psychical mechanism of forgetting (Freud, 1898*b*). [*Added* 1909:] Later included [with modifica-
tions] as the first chapter in my *Psychopathology of Everyday Life* (Freud, 1901*b*).

[2] [Another instance will be found on p. 178 *n*. Yet another occurs in the analysis
of Dora's second dream (Freud, 1905*e*, Section III).]

[3] [*Footnote added* 1914:] Corrections such as this in the usages of foreign languages are not infrequent in dreams but are more often attributed to other

Self-corrections in dreams, which seem so marvellous to some writers, need not occupy our attention. I will indicate instead the recollection which served as the model for my verbal error in this dream. When I was nineteen years old I visited England for the first time and spent a whole day on the shore of the Irish Sea. I naturally revelled in the opportunity of collecting the marine animals left behind by the tide and I was occupied with a starfish—the words '*Hollthurn*' and '*holothurians* [sea-slugs]' occurred at the beginning of the dream—when a charming little girl came up to me and said: 'Is it a starfish? Is it alive?' 'Yes,' I replied, 'he is alive,' and at once, embarrassed at my mistake, repeated the sentence correctly. The dream replaced the verbal error which I then made by another into which a German is equally liable to fall. '*Das Buch ist von Schiller*' should be translated not with a 'from' but with a 'by.' After all that we have heard of the purposes of the dream-work and its reckless choice of methods for attaining them, we shall not be surprised to hear that it effected this replacement because of the magnificent piece of condensation that was made possible by the identity of sound of the English 'from' and the German adjective '*fromm*' ['pious']. But how did my blameless memory of the sea-shore come to be in the dream? It served as the most innocent possible example of my using a word indicating gender or sex in the wrong place—of my bringing in sex (the word 'he') where it did not belong. This, incidentally, was one of the keys to the solution of the dream. No one who has heard, furthermore, the origin attributed to the title of Clerk-Maxwell's 'Matter and Motion [mentioned in the dream, p. 463] will have any difficulty in filling in the gaps: Molière's 'Le Malade Imaginaire'—'La matière est-elle laudable?'[1]—A motion of the bowels.

Moreover I am in a position to offer an ocular demonstration of the fact that the forgetting of dreams is to a great extent a product of resistance. One of my patients will tell me he has had a dream but has forgotten every trace of it: it is therefore just as though it had never happened. We proceed with our work. I come up against a resistance; I therefore explain something to the patient and help him by encouragement and pressure to come to

---

people. Maury (1878, 143) once dreamt, at a time when he was learning English, that, in telling someone that he had visited him the day before, he used the words 'I called for you yesterday.' Whereupon the other answered correctly: 'You should have said "I called *on* you yesterday."'

[1] ['Is the matter laudable?'—Old medical terminology for 'Is the excretion healthy?'—The next phrase is in English in the original.]

terms with some disagreeable thought. Hardly have I succeeded in this than he exclaims: 'Now I remember what it was I dreamt.' The same resistance which interfered with our work that day also made him forget the dream. By overcoming this resistance I have recalled the dream to his memory.

In just the same way, when a patient reaches some particular point in his work, he may be able to remember a dream which he had dreamt three or four or even more days before and which had hitherto remained forgotten.[1]

Psycho-analytic experience[2] has provided us with yet another proof that the forgetting of dreams depends far more upon resistance than upon the fact, stressed by the authorities, that the waking and sleeping states are alien to each other [p. 75]. It not infrequently happens to me, as well as to other analysts and to patients under treatment, that, having been woken up, as one might say, by a dream, I immediately afterwards, and in full possession of my intellectual powers, set about interpreting it. In such cases I have often refused to rest till I have arrived at a complete understanding of the dream; yet it has sometimes been my experience that after finally waking up in the morning I have entirely forgotten both my interpretative activity and the content of the dream, though knowing that I have had a dream and interpreted it.[3] It happens far more often that the dream draws the findings of my interpretative activity back with it into oblivion than that my intellectual activity succeeds in preserving the dream in my memory. Yet there is no such psychical gulf between my interpretative activity and my waking thoughts as the authorities suppose to account for the forgetting of dreams.

Morton Prince (1910 [141]) has objected to my explanation of the forgetting of dreams on the ground that that forgetting is only a special case of the amnesia attaching to dissociated mental states, that it is impossible to extend my explanation of this special amnesia to other types and that my explanation is consequently devoid of value even for its immediate purpose. His readers are thus reminded that in the course of all his descriptions of these dissociated states he has never attempted to discover a dynamic explanation of such phenomena. If he had, he would in-

---

[1] [*Footnote added* 1914:] Ernest Jones has described [1912b] an analogous case which often occurs: while a dream is being analysed the patient may recollect a second one which was dreamt during the same night but whose very existence had not been suspected.

[2] [This paragraph and the next were added in 1911.]

[3] [Cf. Postscript to the 'Analysis of a Phobia in a Five-Year-Old Boy' (Freud, 1922c).]

evitably have found that repression (or, more precisely, the resistance created by it) is the cause both of the dissociations and of the amnesia attaching to their psychical content.

An observation which I have been able to make in the course of preparing this manuscript has shown me that dreams are no more forgotten than other mental acts and can be compared, by no means to their disadvantage, with other mental functions in respect of their retention in the memory. I had kept records of a large number of my own dreams which for one reason or another I had not been able to interpret completely at the time or had left entirely uninterpreted. And now, between one and two years later, I have attempted to interpret some of them for the purpose of obtaining more material in illustration of my views. These attempts have been successful in every instance; indeed the interpretation may be said to have proceeded more easily after this long interval than it did at the time when the dream was a recent experience. A possible explanation of this is that in the meantime I have overcome some of the internal resistances which previously obstructed me. When making these subsequent interpretations I have compared the dream-thoughts that I elicited at the time of the dream with the present, usually far more copious, yield, and I have always found that the old ones are included among the new. My astonishment at this was quickly halted by the reflection that I had long been in the habit of getting my patients, who sometimes tell me dreams dating from earlier years, to interpret them—by the same procedure and with the same success—as though they had dreamt them the night before. When I come to discuss anxiety-dreams I shall give two examples of postponed interpretations like these. [See pp. 581 ff.] I was led into making my first experiment of this kind by the justifiable expectation that in this as in other respects dreams would behave like neurotic symptoms. When I treat a psychoneurotic—a hysteric, let us say—by psycho-analysis, I am obliged to arrive at an explanation for the earliest and long since vanished symptoms of his illness no less than for the contemporary ones which brought him to me for treatment; and I actually find the earlier problem easier to solve than the immediate one. As long ago as in 1895 I was able to give an explanation in *Studies on Hysteria* [Breuer and Freud, 1895, Case History V (Frau Cäcilie M.)] of the first hysterical attack which a woman of over forty had had in her fifteenth year.[1]

---

[1] [Added in the text in 1919 and transferred to a footnote in 1930:] Dreams which occur in the earliest years of childhood and are retained in the memory for dozens of years, often with complete sensory vividness, are almost always of

And here I will mention a number of further, somewhat disconnected, points on the subject of interpreting dreams, which may perhaps help to give readers their bearings should they feel inclined to check my statements by subsequent work upon their own dreams.

No one should expect that an interpretation of his dreams will fall into his lap like manna from the skies. Practice is needed even for perceiving endoptic phenomena or other sensations from which our attention is normally withheld; and this is so even though there is no psychical motive fighting against such perceptions. It is decidedly more difficult to get hold of 'involuntary ideas.' Anyone who seeks to do so must familiarize himself with the expectations raised in the present volume and must, in accordance with the rules laid down in it, endeavour during the work to refrain from any criticism, any *parti pris,* and any emotional or intellectual bias. He must bear in mind Claude Bernard's[1] advice to experimenters in a physiological laboratory: 'travailler comme une bête'—he must work, that is, with as much persistence as an animal and with as much disregard of the result. If this advice is followed, the task will no longer be a hard one.

The interpretation of a dream cannot always be accomplished at a single sitting. When we have followed a chain of associations, it not infrequently happens that we feel our capacity exhausted; nothing more is to be learnt from the dream that day. The wisest plan then is to break off and resume our work another day: another part of the dream's content may then attract our attention and give us access to another stratum of dream-thoughts. This procedure might be described as 'fractional' dream-interpretation.

It is only with the greatest difficulty that the beginner in the business of interpreting dreams can be persuaded that his task is not at an end when he has a complete interpretation in his hands—an interpretation which makes sense, is coherent and throws light upon every element of the dream's content. For the same dream may perhaps have another interpretation as well, an 'over-interpretation', which has escaped him. It is, indeed, not easy to form any conception of the abundance of the unconscious trains of thought, all striving to find expression, which are active in our minds. Nor is it easy

---

great importance in enabling us to understand the history of the subject's mental development and of his neurosis. Analysis of such dreams protects the physician from errors and uncertainties which may lead, among other things, to theoretical confusion. [The example of the 'Wolf Man's' dream was no doubt especially in Freud's mind (1918*b*).]

[1] [The French physiologist (1813–78).]

to credit the skill shown by the dream-work in always hitting upon forms of expression that can bear several meanings—like the Little Tailor in the fairy story who hit seven flies at a blow. My readers will always be inclined to accuse me of introducing an unnecessary amount of ingenuity into my interpretations; but actual experience would teach them better. [See p. 315 *n*.]

On the other hand,[1] I cannot confirm the opinion, first stated by Silberer [e.g. 1914, Part II, Section 5], that all dreams (or many dreams, or certain classes of dreams) require two different interpretations, which are even stated to bear a fixed relation to each other. One of these interpretations, which Silberer calls the 'psycho-analytic' one, is said to give the dream some meaning or other, usually of an infantile-sexual kind; the other and more important interpretation, to which he gives the name of 'anagogic,' is said to reveal the more serious thoughts, often of profound import, which the dream-work has taken as its material. Silberer has not given evidence in support of this opinion by reporting a series of dreams analysed in the two directions. And I must object that the alleged fact is nonexistent. In spite of what he says, the majority of dreams require no 'overinterpretation' and, more particularly, are insusceptible to an anagogic interpretation. As in the case of many other theories put forward in recent years, it is impossible to overlook the fact that Silberer's views are influenced to some extent by a purpose which seeks to disguise the fundamental circumstances in which dreams are formed and to divert interest from their instinctual roots. In a certain number of cases I have been able to confirm Silberer's statements. Analysis showed that in such cases the dream-work found itself faced with the problem of transforming into a dream a series of highly abstract thoughts from waking life which were incapable of being given any direct representation. It endeavoured to solve the problem by getting hold of another group of intellectual material, somewhat loosely related (often in a manner which might be described as 'allegorical') to the abstract thoughts, and at the same time capable of being represented with fewer difficulties. The *abstract* interpretation of a dream that has arisen in this way is given by the dreamer without any difficulty; the *correct* interpretation of the material that has been interpolated must be looked for by the technical methods which are now familiar to us.[2]

---

[1] [This paragraph was added in 1919.]

[2] [Freud also discussed this point in a long footnote in his paper 'A Metapsychological Supplement to the Theory of Dreams' (1917*d*) and towards the end of his 'Dreams and Telepathy' (1922*a*).]

The question whether it is possible to interpret *every* dream must be answered in the negative.[1] It must not be forgotten that in interpreting a dream we are opposed by the psychical forces which were responsible for its distortion. It is thus a question of relative strength whether our intellectual interest, our capacity for self-discipline, our psychological knowledge and our practice in interpreting dreams enable us to master our internal resistances. It is always possible to go *some* distance: far enough, at all events, to convince ourselves that the dream is a structure with a meaning, and as a rule far enough to get a glimpse of what that meaning is. Quite often an immediately succeeding dream allows us to confirm and carry further the interpretation we have tentatively adopted for its predecessor. A whole series of dreams, continuing over a period of weeks or months, is often based upon common ground and must accordingly be interpreted in connection with one another. [Cf. pp. 215 and 375 f.] In the case of two consecutive dreams it can often be observed that one takes as its central point something that is only on the periphery of the other and *vice versa,* so that their interpretations too are mutually complementary. I have already given instances which show that different dreams dreamt on the same night are, as a quite general rule, to be treated in their interpretation as a single whole. [See pp. 348 f.]

There is often a passage in even the most thoroughly interpreted dream which has to be left obscure; this is because we become aware during the work of interpretation that at that point there is a tangle of dream-thoughts which cannot be unravelled and which moreover adds nothing to our knowledge of the content of the dream. This is the dream's navel, the spot where it reaches down into the unknown. [Cf. p. 135 *n.*] The dream-thoughts to which we are led by interpretation cannot, from the nature of things, have any definite endings; they are bound to branch out in every direction into the intricate network of our world of thought. It is at some point where this meshwork is particularly close that the dream-wish grows up, like a mushroom out of its mycelium.

But we must return to the facts concerning the forgetting of dreams, for we have failed to draw one important conclusion from them. We have seen that waking life shows an unmistakable inclination to forget any dream that has been formed in the course of the night—whether as a whole directly after waking, or bit by bit in the course of the day; and we

---

[1] [This question is considered at greater length in Freud, 1925*i*, Section A.]

have recognized that the agent chiefly responsible for this forgetting is the mental resistance to the dream which has already done what it could against it during the night. But if all this is so, the question arises how it comes about that a dream can be formed at all in the face of this resistance. Let us take the most extreme case, in which waking life has got rid of a dream as though it had never occurred. A consideration of the interplay of psychical forces in this case must lead us to infer that the dream would in fact not have occurred at all if the resistance had been as strong during the night as during the day. We must conclude that during the night the resistance loses some of its power, though we know it does not lose the whole of it, since we have shown the part it plays in the formation of dreams as a distorting agent. But we are driven to suppose that its power may be diminished at night and that this makes the formation of dreams possible. This makes it easy to understand how, having regained its full strength at the moment of waking, it at once proceeds to get rid of what it was obliged to permit while it was weak. Descriptive psychology tells us that the principal *sine qua non* for the formation of dreams is that the mind shall be in a state of sleep; and we are now able to explain this fact: *the state of sleep makes the formation of dreams possible because it reduces the power of the endopsychic censorship.*

It is no doubt tempting to regard this as the only possible inference that can be drawn from the facts of the forgetting of dreams, and to make it the basis for further conclusions as to the conditions of energy prevailing during sleeping and waking. For the moment, however, we will stop at this point. When we have entered a little more deeply into the psychology of dreams we shall find that the factors making possible the formation of dreams can be viewed in another way as well. It may be that the resistance against the dream-thoughts becoming conscious can be evaded without any reduction having taken place in its power. And it seems a plausible idea that *both* of the two factors favouring the formation of dreams—the reduction and the evasion of the resistance—are simultaneously made possible by the state of sleep. I will break off here, though I shall pick up the argument again presently. [Cf. pp. 572 f.]

There is another set of objections to our method of interpreting dreams with which we must now deal. Our procedure consists in abandoning all those purposive ideas which normally govern our reflections, in focussing our attention on a single element of the dream and in then taking note of whatever involuntary thoughts may occur to us in connection with it. We then take the next portion of the dream and repeat the process with *it*. We allow ourselves to be led on by our thoughts regardless of the direction in which they carry us and drift on in this way from one thing to another. But we cherish a confident belief that in the end, without any active intervention on our part, we shall arrive at the dream-thoughts from which the dream originated.

Our critics argue against this along the following lines. There is nothing wonderful in the fact that a single element of the dream should lead us *somewhere;* every idea can be associated with *something.* What *is* remarkable is that such an aimless and arbitrary train of thought should happen to bring us to the dream-thoughts. The probability is that we are deceiving ourselves. We follow a chain of associations from one element, till, for one reason or another, it seems to break off. If we then take up a second element, it is only to be expected that the originally unrestricted character of our associations will be narrowed. For we still have the earlier chain of thoughts in our memory, and for that reason, in analysing the second dream-idea, we are more likely to hit upon associations which have something in common with associations from the first chain. We then delude ourselves into thinking that we have discovered a thought which is a connecting point between two elements of the dream. Since we give ourselves complete liberty to connect thoughts as we please and since in fact the only transitions from one idea to another which we exclude are those which operate in normal thinking, we shall find no difficulty in the long run in concocting out of a number of 'intermediate thoughts' something which we describe as the dream-thoughts and which—though without any guarantee, since we have no other knowledge of what the dream-thoughts are—we allege to *be* the psychical substitute for the dream. But the whole thing is completely arbitrary; we are merely exploiting chance connections in a manner which gives an effect of ingenuity. In this way anyone who cares to take such useless pains can worry out any interpretation he pleases from any dream.

If we were in fact met by objections such as these, we might defend ourselves by appealing to the impression made by our interpretations, to the surprising connections with other elements of the dream which emerge in the course of our pursuing a single one of its ideas, and to the improbability that anything which gives such an exhaustive account of the dream could have been arrived at except by following up psychical connections which had already been laid down. We might also point out in our defence that our procedure in interpreting dreams is identical with the procedure by which we resolve hysterical symptoms; and there the correctness of our method is warranted by the coincident emergence and disappearance of the symptoms, or, to use a simile, the assertions made in the text are borne out by the accompanying illustrations. But we have no reason for evading the problem of how it is possible to reach a pre-existing goal by following the drift of an arbitrary and purposeless chain of thoughts; since, though we may not be able to solve the problem, we can completely cut the ground from under it.

For it is demonstrably untrue that we are being carried along a purposeless stream of ideas when, in the process of interpreting a dream, we abandon reflection and allow involuntary ideas to emerge. It can be shown that all that we can ever get rid of are purposive ideas that are *known* to us; as soon as we have done this, *unknown*—or, as we inaccurately say, 'unconscious'—purposive ideas take charge and thereafter determine the course of the involuntary ideas. No influence that we can bring to bear upon our mental processes can ever enable us to think without purposive ideas; nor am I aware of any states of psychical confusion which can do so.[1] Psychiatrists have been far too ready in this respect to abandon their belief in the connectedness of psychical processes. I know for a fact that trains of thought without

---

[1] [*Footnote added* 1914:] It was not until later that my attention was drawn to the fact that Eduard von Hartmann takes the same view on this important matter of psychology: 'In discussing the part played by the unconscious in artistic creation, Eduard von Hartmann (1890, **1**, Section **B**, Chapter V) made a clear statement of the law in accordance with which the association of ideas is governed by unconscious purposive ideas, though he was unaware of the scope of the law. He set out to prove that "every combination of sensuous presentations, when it is not left purely to chance, but is led to a definite end, requires the help of the Unconscious" [ibid., **1**, 245; English translation, 1884, **1**, 283], and that the part played by conscious interest is to stimulate the unconscious to select the most appropriate idea among the countless possible ones. It is the unconscious which makes the appropriate selection of a purpose for the interest and this "holds good of the association of ideas in abstract thinking as well as in sensuous imagining and artistic combination" and in the production of jokes [ibid., **1**, 247; English translation, **1**, 285 f.]. For this reason a limitation of the association of ideas to an exciting idea and an excited idea (in the sense of a pure association psychology) cannot be upheld. Such a limitation could be justified "only if there are conditions in human life in which man is free not only from every conscious purpose, but also from the sway or co-operation of every unconscious interest, every passing mood. This is, however, a condition hardly ever occurring, for even if one in appearance completely abandons his train of thought to accident,

purposive ideas no more occur in hysteria and paranoia than they do in the formation or resolution of dreams. It may be that they do not occur in any of the endogenous psychical disorders. Even the deliria of confusional states may have a meaning, if we are to accept Leuret's brilliant suggestion [1834, 131] that they are only unintelligible to us owing to the gaps in them. I myself have formed the same opinion when I have had the opportunity of observing them. Deliria are the work of a censorship which no longer takes the trouble to conceal its operation; instead of collaborating in producing a new version that shall be unobjectionable, it ruthlessly deletes whatever it disapproves of, so that what remains becomes quite disconnected. This censorship acts exactly like the censorship of newspapers at the Russian frontier, which allows foreign journals to fall into the hands of the readers whom it is its business to protect only after a quantity of passages have been blacked out.

It may be that free play of ideas with a fortuitous chain of associations is to be found in destructive organic cerebral processes; what is regarded as such in the psychoneuroses can always be explained as an effect of the censorship's influence upon a train of thought which has been pushed into the foreground by purposive ideas that have remained hidden.[1] It has been regarded as an unfailing sign of an association being uninfluenced by purposive ideas if the associations (or images) in question seem to be interrelated, in what is described as a 'superficial' manner—by assonance, verbal ambiguity, temporal coincidence without connection in meaning,

---

or if one abandons oneself entirely to the involuntary dreams of fancy, yet always other leading interests, dominant feelings and moods prevail at one time rather than at another, and these will always exert an influence on the association of ideas." [Ibid., 1, 246; English translation, 1, 284.] "In semi-conscious dreams always only such ideas as correspond to the main [unconscious] interest of the moment occur." [Loc. cit.] The emphasis thus laid upon the influence of feelings and moods on the free sequence of thoughts makes it possible to justify the methodological procedure of psycho-analysis completely from the standpoint of Hartmann's psychology.' (Pohorilles, 1913.)—Du Prel (1885, 107) refers to the fact that after we have vainly tried to recall a name, it often comes into our heads again suddenly and without any warning. He concludes from this that unconscious but none the less purposeful thinking has taken place and that its result has suddenly entered consciousness.

[1] [*Footnote added* 1909:] This assertion has received striking confirmation from C. G. Jung's analyses in cases of dementia praecox. (Jung, 1907.)

or by any association of the kind that we allow in jokes or in play upon words. This characteristic is present in the chains of thought which lead from the elements of a dream to the intermediate thoughts and from these to the dream-thoughts proper; we have seen instances of this—not without astonishment—in many dream analyses. No connection was too loose, no joke too bad, to serve as a bridge from one thought to another. But the true explanation of this easy-going state of things is soon found. *Whenever one psychical element is linked with another by an objectionable or superficial association, there is also a legitimate and deeper link between them which is subjected to the resistance of the censorship.*[1]

The real reason for the prevalence of superficial associations is not the abandonment of purposive ideas but the pressure of the censorship. Superficial associations replace deep ones if the censorship makes the normal connecting paths impassable. We may picture, by way of analogy, a mountain region, where some general interruption of traffic (owing to floods, for instance) has blocked the main, major roads, but where communications are still maintained over inconvenient and steep footpaths normally used only by the hunter.

Two cases may here be distinguished, though in essence they are the same. In the first of these, the censorship is directed only against the *connection* between two thoughts, which are unobjectionable separately. If so, the two thoughts will enter consciousness in succession; the connection between them will remain concealed, but, instead, a superficial link between them will occur to us, of which we should otherwise never have thought. This link is usually attached to some part of the complex of ideas quite other than that on which the suppressed and essential connection is based. The second case is where the two thoughts are in themselves subject to censorship on account of their content. If so, neither of them appears in its true shape but only in a modified one which replaces it; and the two replacing thoughts are chosen in such a way that they have a superficial association that repeats the essential connection which relates the two thoughts that have been replaced. *In both these cases the pressure of the censorship has resulted in a displacement from a normal and serious association to a superficial and apparently absurd one.*

---

[1] [Everywhere else in this work Freud speaks of 'the censorship of the resistance.' A later clarification of the relation between the concepts of 'resistance' and 'censorship' will be found in Lecture XXIX of the *New Introductory Lectures* (1933a).]

Since we are aware that displacements of this kind occur, we have no hesitation when we are interpreting dreams in relying upon superficial associations as much as upon others.[1]

In the psycho-analysis of neuroses the fullest use is made of these two theorems—that, when conscious purposive ideas are abandoned, concealed purposive ideas assume control of the current of ideas, and that superficial associations are only substitutes by displacement for suppressed deeper ones. Indeed, these theorems have become basic pillars of psycho-analytic technique. When I instruct a patient to abandon reflection of any kind and to tell me whatever comes into his head, I am relying firmly on the presumption that he will not be able to abandon the purposive ideas inherent in the treatment and I feel justified in inferring that what seem to be the most innocent and arbitrary things which he tells me are in fact related to his illness. There is another purposive idea of which the patient has no suspicion—one relating to myself. The full estimate of the importance of these two theorems, as well as more detailed information about them, fall within the province of an account of the technique of psycho-analysis. Here, then, we have reached one of the frontier posts at which, in accordance with our programme, we must drop the subject of dream-interpretation.[2]

There is one true conclusion that we may glean from these objections, namely that we need not suppose that every association that occurs dur-

---

[1] The same considerations apply equally, of course, to cases in which the superficial associations appear openly in the content of the dream, as, for instance, in the two dreams of Maury's quoted above on pp. 87–8. (*Pélerinage—Pelletier—pelle; kilomètre—kilogramme—Gilolo—Lobelia—Lopez—lotto.*) My work with neurotic patients has taught me the nature of the memories of which this is a favourite method of representation. They are occasions on which the subject has turned over the pages of encyclopaedias or dictionaries in order (like most people at the inquisitive age of puberty) to satisfy their craving for an answer to the riddle of sex.—[An example of this will be found in the analysis of 'Dora's' second dream (Freud, 1905*e*, Section III).]

[2] [*Footnote added* 1909:] These two theorems, which sounded most unplausible at the time they were made, have since been experimentally employed and confirmed by Jung and his pupils in their studies in word-association. [Jung, 1906.—A most interesting argument on the allied topic of the validity of chains of association starting from numbers selected 'by chance' (see above, pp. 518 f.) is developed by Freud in the long footnote added in 1920 to Chapter XII (A, No. 7) of *The Psychopathology of Everyday Life* (1901*b*).]

ing the work of interpretation had a place in the dream-work during the night. [Cf. pp. 298 and 327] It is true that in carrying out the interpretation in the waking state we follow a path which leads back from the elements of the dream to the dream-thoughts and that the dream-work followed one in the contrary direction. But it is highly improbable that these paths are passable both ways. It appears, rather, that in the daytime we drive shafts which follow along fresh chains of thought and that these shafts make contact with the intermediate thoughts and the dream-thoughts now at one point and now at another. We can see how in this manner fresh daytime material inserts itself into the interpretative chains. It is probable, too, that the increase in resistance that has set in since the night makes new and more devious detours necessary. The number and nature of the collaterals [see p. 298 *n.* 1] that we spin in this way during the day is of no psychological importance whatever, so long as they lead us to the dream-thoughts of which we are in search.

(B)

REGRESSION

Having now repelled the objections that have been raised against us, or having at least indicated where our defensive weapons lie, we must no longer postpone the task of setting about the psychological investigations for which we have so long been arming ourselves. Let us summarize the principal findings of our enquiry so far as it has gone. Dreams are psychical acts of as much significance as any others; their motive force is in every instance a wish seeking fulfilment; the fact of their not being recognizable as wishes and their many peculiarities and absurdities are due to the influence of the psychical censorship to which they have been subjected during the process of their formation: apart from the necessity of evading this censorship, other factors which have contributed to their formation are a necessity for the condensation of their psychical material, a regard for the possibility of its being represented in sensory images and—though not invariably—a demand that the structure of the dream shall have a rational and intelligible exterior. Each of these propositions opens a way to fresh psychological postulates and speculations; the mutual relation between the wish which is the dream's motive force and the four conditions to which the dream's formation is subject, as well as the inter-relations between the latter, require to be investigated; and the place of dreams in the nexus of mental life has to be assigned.

It was with a view to reminding us of the problems which have still to be solved that I opened the present chapter with an account of a dream. There was no difficulty in interpreting that dream—the dream of the burning child—even though its interpretation was not given fully in our sense. I raised the question of why the dreamer dreamt it at all instead of waking up, and recognized that one of his motives was a wish to represent his child as still alive. Our further discussions will show us that yet another wish also played a part. [See below, p. 570.] Thus it was in the first instance for the sake of fulfilling a wish that the process of thought during sleep was transformed into a dream.

If we eliminate the wish-fulfilment, we shall see that only one feature is left to distinguish the two forms of psychical event. The dream-thought would have run: 'I see a glare coming from the room where the dead body is lying. Perhaps a candle has fallen over and my child may be burning.' The dream repeated these reflections unaltered, but it represented them in a situation which was actually present and which could be perceived through the senses like a waking experience. Here we have the most general and the most striking psychological characteristic of the process of dreaming: a thought, and as a rule a thought of something that is wished, is objectified in the dream, is represented as a scene, or, as it seems to us, is experienced.

How, then, are we to explain this characteristic peculiarity of the dream-work, or, to put the question more modestly, how are we to find a place for it in the nexus of psychical processes?

If we look into the matter more closely we shall observe that two almost independent features stand out as characteristic of the form taken by this dream. One is the fact that the thought is represented as an immediate situation with the 'perhaps' omitted, and the other is the fact that the thought is transformed into visual images and speech.

In this particular dream the change made in the thoughts by the conversion of the expectation expressed by them into the present tense may not seem particularly striking. This is because of what can only be described as the unusually subordinate part played in this dream by wish-fulfilment. Consider instead another one, in which the dream-wish was not detached from the waking thoughts that were carried over into sleep—for instance, the dream of Irma's injection [pp. 131 ff.]. There the dream-thought that was represented was in the optative: 'If only Otto were responsible for Irma's illness!' The dream repressed the optative and replaced it by a straightforward present: 'Yes, Otto is responsible for Irma's illness.' This, then, is the first of the transformations which is brought about in the dream-thoughts even by a distortionless dream. We need not linger long over this first peculiarity of dreams. We can deal with it by drawing attention to conscious phantasies—to day-dreams—which treat their ideational content in just the same manner. While Daudet's Monsieur Joyeuse[1] was wandering, out of work, through the streets of Paris (though his daughters believed that he had a job and was sitting in an office), he was dreaming of developments that might bring him influential help and lead to his finding employment—and he was dreaming in the present tense. Thus dreams make use of the present tense in the same manner and by the same right as day-dreams. The present tense is the one in which wishes are represented as fulfilled.

But dreams differ from day-dreams in their second characteristic: namely, in the fact of their ideational content being transformed from thoughts into sensory images, to which belief is attached and which appear to be experienced. I must add at once that not every dream exhibits this transformation from idea into sensory image. There are dreams which consist only of thoughts but which cannot on that account be denied the essential nature of dreams. My 'Autodidasker' dream [pp. 315 ff.] was of that kind; it included scarcely more sensory elements than if I had thought its content in the daytime. And in every dream of any considerable length there are elements which have not, like the rest, been given a sensory form, but which are simply thought or known, in the kind of way in which we are accustomed to think or know things in waking life. It should also be remembered here that it is not only in dreams that such transformations of ideas into sensory images occur: they are also found in hallucinations and visions, which may appear as independent entities, so to say, in health or as symptoms in the psychoneuroses. In short, the relation which we are examining now is not in any respect an exclusive one. Nevertheless it remains true that this characteristic of dreams, when it is present, strikes us as being their most notable one; so that it would be impossible for us to imagine the

---

[1] [In *Le Nabab* (cf. p. 496). A slip made by Freud over this name in his first draft of this sentence is discussed by him in his *Psychopathology of Everyday Life* (1901*b*), Chapter VII, towards the end of Section A.]

dream-world without it. But in order to arrive at an understanding of it we must embark upon a discussion that will take us far afield.

As the starting point for our enquiry, I should like to pick out one from among many remarks made upon the theory of dreaming by those who have written on the subject. In the course of a short discussion on the topic of dreams, the great Fechner (1889, **2,** 520–1) puts forward the idea that *the scene of action of dreams is different from that of waking ideational life.* [Cf. above, p. 78.] This is the only hypothesis that makes the special peculiarities of dream-life intelligible.[1]

What is presented to us in these words is the idea of *psychical locality.* I shall entirely disregard the fact that the mental apparatus with which we are here concerned is also known to us in the form of an anatomical preparation, and I shall carefully avoid the temptation to determine psychical locality in any anatomical fashion. I shall remain upon psychological ground, and I propose simply to follow the suggestion that we should picture the instrument which carries out our mental functions as resembling a compound microscope or a photographic apparatus, or something of the kind. On that basis, psychical locality will correspond to a point inside the apparatus at which one of the preliminary stages of an image comes into being. In the microscope and telescope, as we know, these occur in part at ideal points, regions in which no tangible component of the apparatus is situated. I see no necessity to apologize for the imperfections of this or of any similar imagery. Analogies of this kind are only intended to assist us in our attempt to make the complications of mental functioning intelligible by dissecting the function and assigning its different constituents to different component parts of the apparatus. So far as I know, the experiment has not hitherto been made of using this method of dissection in order to investigate the way in which the mental instrument is put together, and I can see no harm in it. We are justified, in my view, in giving free rein to our speculations so long as we retain the coolness of our judgement and do not mistake the scaffolding for the building. And since at our first approach to something unknown all that we need is the assistance of provisional ideas, I shall give preference in the first instance to hypotheses of the crudest and most concrete description.

---

[1] [In a letter to Fliess of February 9, 1898 (Freud, 1950*a*, Letter 83), Freud writes that this passage in Fechner is the only sensible remark he has found in the literature on dreams.]

Accordingly, we will picture the mental apparatus as a compound instrument, to the components of which we will give the name of 'agencies,'[1] or (for the sake of greater clarity) 'systems.' It is to be anticipated, in the next place, that these systems may perhaps stand in a regular spatial relation to one another, in the same kind of way in which the various systems of lenses in a telescope are arranged behind one another. Strictly speaking, there is no need for the hypothesis that the psychical systems are actually arranged in a *spatial* order. It would be sufficient if a fixed order were established by the fact that in a given psychical process the excitation passes through the systems in a particular *temporal* sequence. In other processes the sequence may perhaps be a different one; that is a possibility that we shall leave open. For the sake of brevity we will in future speak of the components of the apparatus as 'ψ-systems.'

The first thing that strikes us is that this apparatus, compounded of ψ-systems, has a sense or direction. All our psychical activity starts from stimuli (whether internal or external) and ends in innervations.[2] Accordingly, we shall ascribe a sensory and a motor end to the apparatus. At the sensory end there lies a system which receives perceptions; at the motor end there lies another, which opens the gateway to motor activity. Psychical processes advance in general from the perceptual end to the motor end. Thus the most general schematic picture of the psychical apparatus may be represented thus (Fig. 1):

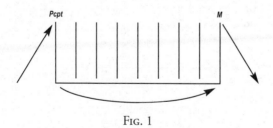

Fig. 1

---

[1] [*'Instanzen,'* literally 'instances,' in a sense similar to that in which the word occurs in the phrase 'a Court of First Instance.']

[2] ['Innervation' is a highly ambiguous term. It is very frequently used in a structural sense, to mean the anatomical distribution of nerves in some organism or bodily region. Freud uses it more often (though not invariably) to mean the transmission of energy into a system of nerves, or (as in the present instance) specifically into an *efferent* system—to indicate, that is to say, a process tending towards discharge.]

This, however, does no more than fulfil a requirement with which we have long been familiar, namely that the psychical apparatus must be constructed like a reflex apparatus. Reflex processes remain the model of every psychical function.

Next, we have grounds for introducing a first differentiation at the sensory end. A trace is left in our psychical apparatus of the perceptions which impinge upon it. This we may describe as a 'memory-trace'; and to the function relating to it we give the name of 'memory.' If we are in earnest over our plan of attaching psychical processes to systems, memory-traces can only consist in permanent modifications of the elements of the systems. But, as has already been pointed out elsewhere,[1] there are obvious difficulties involved in supposing that one and the same system can accurately retain modifications of its elements and yet remain perpetually open to the reception of fresh occasions for modification. In accordance, therefore, with the principle which governs our experiment, we shall distribute these two functions on to different systems. We shall suppose that a system in the very front of the apparatus receives the perceptual stimuli but retains no trace of them and thus has no memory, while behind it there lies a second system which transforms the momentary excitations of the first system into permanent traces. The schematic picture of our psychical apparatus would then be as follows (Fig. 2):

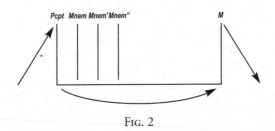

Pcpt   Mnem Mnem'Mnem"   M

Fig. 2

It is a familiar fact that we retain permanently something more than the mere *content* of the perceptions which impinge upon the system *Pcpt.* Our perceptions are linked with one another in our memory—first and

---

[1] [By Breuer in a footnote to Section I of his theoretical contribution to Breuer and Freud, 1895, where, among other things, he writes: 'The mirror of a reflecting telescope cannot at the same time be a photographic plate.']

foremost according to simultaneity of occurrence. We speak of this fact as 'association.' It is clear, then, that, if the *Pcpt.* system has no memory whatever, it cannot retain any associative traces; the separate *Pcpt.* elements would be intolerably obstructed in performing their function if the remnant of an earlier connection were to exercise an influence upon a fresh perception. We must therefore assume the basis of association lies in the mnemic systems. Association would thus consist in the fact that, as a result of a diminution in resistances and of the laying down of facilitating paths, an excitation is transmitted from a given *Mnem.* element more readily to one *Mnem.* element than to another.

Closer consideration will show the necessity for supposing the existence not of one but of several such *Mnem.* elements, in which one and the same excitation, transmitted by the *Pcpt.* elements, leaves a variety of different permanent records. The first of these *Mnem.* systems will naturally contain the record of association in respect to *simultaneity in time;* while the same perceptual material will be arranged in the later systems in respect to other kinds of coincidence, so that one of these later systems, for instance, will record relations of similarity, and so on with the others. It would of course be a waste of time to try to put the psychical significance of a system of this kind into words. Its character would lie in the intimate details of its relations to the different elements of the raw material of memory, that is—if we may hint at a theory of a more radical kind—in the degrees of conductive resistance which it offered to the passage of excitation from those elements.

At this point I will interpolate a remark of a general nature which may perhaps have important implications. It is the *Pcpt.* system, which is without the capacity to retain modifications and is thus without memory, that provides our consciousness with the whole multiplicity of sensory qualities. On the other hand, our memories—not excepting those which are most deeply stamped on our minds—are in themselves unconscious. They can be made conscious; but there can be no doubt that they can produce all their effects while in an unconscious condition. What we describe as our 'character' is based on the memory-traces of our impressions; and, moreover, the impressions which have had the greatest effect on us—those of our earliest youth—are precisely the ones which scarcely ever become conscious. But if memories become conscious once more, they exhibit no sensory quality or a very slight one in comparison with perceptions. A most promising light would be thrown on the conditions governing the excitation of neurones if it could be confirmed that *in the* ψ-*systems memory and the quality that characterizes consciousness are mutually exclusive.*[1]

The assumptions we have so far put forward as to the construction of the psychical apparatus at its sensory end have been made without reference to dreams or to the psychological information that we have been able to infer from them. Evidence afforded by dreams will, however, help us towards understanding another portion of the apparatus. We have seen [see pp. 168 ff.] that we were only able to explain the formation of dreams by venturing upon the hypothesis of there being two psychical agencies, one of which submitted the activity of the other to a criticism which involved its exclusion from consciousness. The critical agency, we concluded, stands in a closer relation to consciousness than the agency criticized: it stands like a screen between the latter and consciousness. Further, we found reasons [p. 494] for identifying the critical agency with the agency which directs our waking life and determines our voluntary, conscious actions. If, in accordance with our assumptions, we replace these agencies by systems, then our last conclusion must lead us to locate the critical system at the motor end of the apparatus. We will now introduce the two systems into our schematic picture and give them names to express their relation to consciousness (Fig. 3).

We will describe the last of the systems at the motor end as 'the preconscious,' to indicate that the excitatory processes occurring in it can enter consciousness without further impediment provided that certain other conditions are fulfilled: for instance, that they reach a certain degree of intensity, that the function which can only be described as 'attention' is dis-

---

[1] [*Footnote added* 1925:] I have since suggested that consciousness actually arises *instead of* the memory-trace. See my 'Note upon the "Mystic Writing-Pad"' (1925*a*). [Cf. also Chapter IV of *Beyond the Pleasure Principle* (1920*g*), where the same point is made.—The whole of the present discussion on memory will be made more intelligible by a study of these two passages from Freud's later writings. But still more light is thrown on it by some of his earlier reflections on the subject revealed in the Fliess correspondence (Freud, 1950*a*). See, for instance, Section 3 of Part I of the 'Project for a Scientific Psychology' (written in the autumn of 1895) and Letter 52 (written on December 6, 1896). This letter, incidentally, contains what is evidently an early version of the 'schematic picture' represented above as well as the first appearance of the abbreviations by which the various systems are here distinguished. The equivalent English symbols are self-explanatory: '*Cs.*' for the 'conscious' system, '*Pcs.*' for the 'preconscious,' '*Ucs.*' for the 'unconscious,' '*Pcpt.*' for the 'perceptual' and '*Mnem.*' for the 'mnemic' systems.]

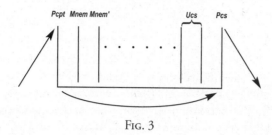

Fig. 3

tributed in a particular way [see p. 590], and so on. This is at the same time the system which holds the key to voluntary movement. We will describe the system that lies behind it as 'the unconscious,' because it has no access to consciousness *except via the preconscious,* in passing through which its excitatory process is obliged to submit to modifications.[1]

In which of these systems, then, are we to locate the impetus to the construction of dreams? For simplicity's sake, in the system *Ucs.* It is true that in the course of our future discussion we shall learn that this is not entirely accurate, and that the process of forming dreams is obliged to attach itself to dream-thoughts belonging to the preconscious system [p. 562]. But when we consider the dream-wish, we shall find that the motive force for producing dreams is supplied by the *Ucs.* [p. 561]; and owing to this latter factor we shall take the unconscious system as the starting-point of dream-formation. Like all other thought-structures, this dream-instigator will make an effort to advance into the *Pcs.* and from there to obtain access to consciousness.

Experience shows us that this path leading through the preconscious to consciousness is barred to the dream-thoughts during the daytime by the censorship imposed by resistance. During the night they are able to obtain access to consciousness; but the question arises as to how they do

---

[1] [*Footnote added* 1919:] If we attempted to proceed further with this schematic picture, in which the systems are set out in linear succession, we should have to reckon with the fact that the system next beyond the *Pcs.* is the one to which consciousness must be ascribed—in other words, that *Pcpt.* = *Cs.* [See below, pp. 609 ff. For a fuller discussion of this see Freud, 1917*d*.—Freud's later 'schematic picture' of the mind, first given in *The Ego and the Id* (1923*b*), Chapter II, and repeated (with some modifications) in the *New Introductory Lectures* (1933*a*), Lecture XXXI, lays more stress on structure than on function.]

so and thanks to what modification. If what enabled the dream-thoughts to achieve this were the fact that at night there is a lowering of the resistance which guards the frontier between the unconscious and the preconscious, we should have dreams which were in the nature of ideas and which were without the hallucinatory quality in which we are at the moment interested. Thus the lowering of the censorship between the two systems *Ucs.* and *Pcs.* can only explain dreams formed like 'Autodidasker' and not dreams like that of the burning child which we took as the starting-point of our investigations.

The only way in which we can describe what happens in hallucinatory dreams is by saying that the excitation moves in a *backward* direction. Instead of being transmitted towards the *motor* end of the apparatus it moves towards the *sensory* end and finally reaches the perceptual system. If we describe as 'progressive' the direction taken by psychical processes arising from the unconscious during waking life, then we may speak of dreams as having a 'regressive' character.[1]

This regression, then, is undoubtedly one of the psychological characteristics of the process of dreaming; but we must remember that it does not occur only in dreams. Intentional recollection and other constituent processes of our normal thinking involve a retrogressive movement in the psychical apparatus from a complex ideational act back to the raw material of the memory-traces underlying it. In the waking state, however, this backward movement never extends beyond the mnemic images; it does not succeed in producing a hallucinatory revival of the *perceptual* images. Why is it otherwise in dreams? When we were considering the work of condensation in dreams we were driven to suppose that the intensities attaching to ideas can be completely transferred by the dream-work from one idea to another [p. 345]. It is probably this alteration in the normal

---

[1] [*Footnote added* 1914:] The first hint at the factor of regression is to be found as far back as in Albertus Magnus [the thirteenth century Scholastic writer]. The '*imaginatio,*' he tells us, constructs dreams out of the stored-up images of sensory objects; and the process is carried out in a reverse direction to that in waking life. (Quoted by Diepgen, 1912, 14.)—Hobbes writes in the *Leviathan* (1651, Pt. I, Chapter 2): 'In sum, our dreams are the reverse of our waking imaginations, the motion, when we are awake, beginning at one end, and when we dream at another.' (Quoted by Havelock Ellis, 1911, 109.)—[Breuer, in Section I of Chapter III of Breuer and Freud, 1895, speaks (in connection with hallucinations) of 'a "regressive" excitation, emanating from the organ of memory, and acting upon the perceptual apparatus by means of ideas.']

psychical procedure which makes possible the cathexis of the system *Pcpt.* in the reverse direction, starting from thoughts, to the pitch of complete sensory vividness.

We must not delude ourselves into exaggerating the importance of these considerations. We have done no more than *give* a name to an inexplicable phenomenon. We call it 'regression' when in a dream an idea is turned back into the sensory image from which it was originally derived. But even this step requires justification. What is the point of this nomenclature if it teaches us nothing new? I believe the name 'regression' is of help to us in so far as it connects a fact that was already known to us with our schematic picture, in which the mental apparatus was given a sense or direction. And it is at this point that that picture begins to repay us for having constructed it. For an examination of it, without any further reflection, reveals a further characteristic of dream-formation. If we regard the process of dreaming as a regression occurring in our hypothetical mental apparatus, we at once arrive at the explanation of the empirically established fact that all the logical relations belonging to the dream-thoughts disappear during the dream-activity or can only find expression with difficulty [p. 328]. According to our schematic picture, these relations are contained not in the *first Mnem.* systems but in *later* ones; and in case of regression they would necessarily lose any means of expression except in perceptual images. *In regression the fabric of the dream-thoughts is resolved into its raw material.*

What modification is it that renders possible a regression which cannot occur in daytime? We must be content with some conjectures on this point. No doubt it is a question of changes in the cathexes of energy attaching to the different systems, changes which increase or diminish the facility with which those systems can be passed through by the excitatory process. But in any apparatus of this kind the same results upon the passage of excitations might be produced in more than one way. Our first thoughts will of course be of the state of sleep and the changes in cathexis which it brings about at the sensory end of the apparatus. During the day there is a continuous current from the *Pcpt.* system flowing in the direction of motor activity; but this current ceases at night and could no longer form an obstacle to a current of excitation flowing in the opposite sense. Here we seem to have the 'shutting-out of the external world,' which some authorities regard as the theoretical explanation of the psychological characteristics of dreams. (See pp. 80.)

In explaining regression in dreams, however, we must bear in mind the regressions which also occur in pathological waking states; and here the explanation just given leaves us in the lurch. For in those cases regression occurs in spite of a sensory current flowing without interruption in a forward direction. My explanation of hallucinations in hysteria and paranoia and of visions in mentally normal subjects is that they are in fact regressions—that is, thoughts transformed into images—but that the only thoughts that undergo this transformation are those which are intimately linked with memories that have been suppressed or have remained unconscious.

For instance, one of my youngest hysterical patients, a twelve-year-old boy, was prevented from falling asleep by *'green faces with red eyes'* which terrified him. The source of this phenomenon was a suppressed, though at one time conscious, memory of a boy whom he had often seen four years earlier. This boy had presented him with an alarming picture of the consequences of bad habits in children, including masturbation—a habit with which my patient was now reproaching himself in retrospect. His mother had pointed out at the time that the ill-behaved boy had a *greenish face* and *red* (i.e. red-rimmed) *eyes.* Here was the origin of his bogey, whose only purpose, incidentally, was to remind him of another of his mother's predictions—that boys of that sort grow into idiots, can learn nothing at school and die young. My little patient had fulfilled one part of the prophecy, for he was making no progress at his school, and, as was shown from his account of the involuntary thoughts that occurred to him, he was terrified of the other part. I may add that after a short time the treatment resulted in his being able to sleep, in his nervousness disappearing and his being awarded a mark of distinction at the end of his school-year.

In the same connection I will give the explanation of a vision that was described to me by another hysterical patient (a woman of forty) as having happened before she fell ill. One morning she opened her eyes and saw her brother in the room, though, as she knew, he was in fact in an insane asylum. Her small son was sleeping in the bed beside her. To save the child from having a *fright* and *falling into convulsions* when he saw his *uncle,* she pulled the *sheet* over his face, whereupon the apparition vanished. This vision was a modified version of a memory from the lady's childhood; and, though it was conscious, it was intimately related to all the unconscious material in her mind. Her nurse had told her that her mother (who had died very young, when my patient was only eighteen months old) had suffered from epileptic or hysterical *convulsions,* which went back to a *fright* caused by her brother (my patient's *uncle*) appearing to her disguised as a ghost with a *sheet* over his head. Thus the vision contained the same elements as the memory: the brother's appearance, the sheet, the fright and its results. But the elements had been arranged in a different context and transferred on to other figures. The obvious motive of the vision, or of the thoughts which it replaced, was her concern lest her little boy might follow in the footsteps of his uncle, whom he greatly resembled physically.

The two instances that I have quoted are neither of them entirely devoid of connection with the state of sleep and for that reason are perhaps not well chosen for what I want them to prove. I will therefore refer the reader to my analysis of a woman suffering from hallucinatory paranoia (Freud, 1896b [Part III]) as well as to the findings in my still unpublished studies on the psychology of the psychoneuroses,[1] for evidence that in such instances of the regressive transformation of thoughts we must not overlook the influence of memories, most from childhood, which have been suppressed or have remained unconscious. The thoughts which are connected with a memory of this kind and which are forbidden expression by the censorship are, as it were, attracted by the memory into regression as being the form of representation in which the memory itself is couched. I may also recall that one of the facts arrived at in the *Studies on Hysteria* [Breuer and Freud, 1895—e.g. in Breuer's first case history] was that when it was possible to bring infantile scenes (whether they were memories or phantasies) into consciousness, they were seen like hallucinations and lost that characteristic only in the process of being reported. It is moreover a familiar observation that, even in those whose memory is not normally of a visual type, the earliest recollections of childhood retain far into life the quality of sensory vividness.

If we now bear in mind how great a part is played in the dream-thoughts by infantile experiences or by phantasies based upon them, how frequently portions of them re-emerge in the dream-content and how often the dream-wishes themselves are derived from them, we cannot dismiss the probability that in dreams too the transformation of thoughts into visual images may be in part the result of the attraction which memories couched in visual form and eager for revival bring to bear upon thoughts cut off from consciousness and struggling to find expression. On this view a dream might be described as *a substitute for an infantile scene modified by being transferred on to a recent experience.* The infantile scene is unable to bring about its own revival and has to be content with returning as a dream.

---

[1] [Never published under any such title.]

This indication of the way in which infantile scenes (or their reproductions as phantasies) function in a sense as models for the content of
dreams, removes the necessity for one of the hypotheses put forward by
Scherner and his followers in regard to internal sources of stimulation.
Scherner [1861] supposes that, when dreams exhibit particularly vivid or
particularly copious visual elements, there is present a state of 'visual stimulation,' that is, of internal excitation in the organ of vision [cf. p. 247].
We need not dispute this hypothesis, but can content ourselves with assuming that this state of excitation applies merely to the *psychical* perceptual system of the visual organ; we may, however, further point out that
the state of excitation has been set up by a *memory*, that it is a *revival* of a
visual excitation which was originally an immediate one. I cannot produce any good example from my own experience of an *infantile* memory
producing this kind of result. My dreams are in general less rich in sensory elements than I am led to suppose is the case in other people. But in
the case of my most vivid and beautiful dream of the last few years I was
easily able to trace back the hallucinatory clarity of the dream's content
to the sensory qualities of recent or fairly recent impressions. On pp. 470
ff. I recorded a dream in which the deep blue colour of the water, the
brown of the smoke coming from the ship's funnels, and the dark brown
and red of the buildings left behind a profound impression on me. This
dream, if any, should be traceable to a visual stimulus. What was it that
had brought my visual organ into this state of stimulation? A recent impression, which attached itself to a number of earlier ones. The colours
which I saw were in the first instance those of a box of toy bricks with
which, on the day before the dream, my children had put up a fine building and shown it off for my admiration. The big bricks were of the same
dark red and the small ones were of the same blue and brown. This was
associated with colour impressions from my last travels in Italy: the beautiful blue of the Isonzo and the lagoons and the brown of the Carso.[1] The
beauty of the colours in the dream was only a repetition of something
seen in my memory.

Let us bring together what we have found out about the peculiar
propensity of dreams to recast their ideational content into sensory images.
We have not explained this feature of the dream-work, we have not traced

---

[1] [The limestone plateau behind Trieste.]

it back to any known psychological laws; but we have rather picked it out as something that suggests unknown implications and we have characterized it with the word 'regressive.' We have put forward the view that in all probability this regression, wherever it may occur, is an effect of a resistance opposing the progress of a thought into consciousness along the normal path, and of a simultaneous attraction exercised upon the thought by the presence of memories possessing great sensory force.[1] In the case of dreams, regression may perhaps be further facilitated by the cessation of the progressive current which streams in during the daytime from the sense organs; in other forms of regression, the absence of this accessory factor must be made up for by a greater intensity of the other motives for regression. Nor must we forget to observe that in these pathological cases of regression as well as in dreams the process of transference of energy must differ from what it is in regressions occurring in normal mental life, since in the former cases that process makes possible a complete hallucinatory cathexis of the perceptual systems. What we have described, in our analysis of the dream-work, as 'regard for representability' might be brought into connection with the *selective attraction* exercised by the visually recollected scenes touched upon by the dream-thoughts.

It is further to be remarked[2] that regression plays a no less important part in the theory of the formation of neurotic symptoms than it does in that of dreams. Three kinds of regression are thus to be distinguished: (*a*) *topographical* regression, in the sense of the schematic picture of the ψ-*systems* which we have explained above; (*b*) *temporal* regression, in so far as what is in question is a harking back to older psychical structures; and (*c*) *formal* regression, where primitive methods of expression and representation take the place of the usual ones. All these three kinds of regression are, however, one at bottom and occur together as a rule; for what is older in time is more primitive in form and in psychical topography lies nearer to the perceptual end. [Cf. Freud, 1917*d*.]

---

[1] [*Footnote added* 1914:] In any account of the theory of repression it would have to be laid down that a thought becomes repressed as a result of the combined influence upon it of *two* factors. It is pushed from the one side (by the censorship of the *Cs.*) and pulled from the other (by the *Ucs.*), in the same kind of way in which people are conveyed to the top of the Great Pyramid. [*Added* 1919:] Cf. [the opening pages of] my paper on repression (Freud, 1915*d*).

[2] [This paragraph was added in 1914.]

Nor can we leave the subject of regression in dreams[1] without setting down in words a notion by which we have already repeatedly been struck and which will recur with fresh intensity when we have entered more deeply into the study of the psychoneuroses: namely that dreaming is on the whole an example of regression to the dreamer's earliest condition, a revival of his childhood, of the instinctual impulses which dominated it and of the methods of expression which were then available to him. Behind this childhood of the individual we are promised a picture of a phylogenetic childhood—a picture of the development of the human race, of which the individual's development is in fact an abbreviated recapitulation influenced by the chance circumstances of life. We can guess how much to the point is Nietzsche's assertion that in dreams 'some primaeval relic of humanity is at work which we can now scarcely reach any longer by a direct path'; and we may expect that the analysis of dreams will lead us to a knowledge of man's archaic heritage, of what is psychically innate in him. Dreams and neuroses seem to have preserved more mental antiquities than we could have imagined possible; so that psycho-analysis may claim a high place among the sciences which are concerned with the reconstruction of the earliest and most obscure periods of the beginnings of the human race.

It may well be that this first portion of our psychological study of dreams will leave us with a sense of dissatisfaction. But we can console ourselves with the thought that we have been obliged to build our way out into the dark. If we are not wholly in error, other lines of approach are bound to lead us into much the same region and the time may then come when we shall find ourselves more at home in it.

(C)

WISH-FULFILMENT

The dream of the burning child at the beginning of this chapter gives us a welcome opportunity of considering the difficulties with which the theory of wish-fulfilment is faced. It will no doubt have surprised all of us to be told that dreams are nothing other than fulfilments of wishes, and

---

[1] [This paragraph was added in 1919.]

not only on account of the contradiction offered by anxiety-dreams. When analysis first revealed to us that a meaning and a psychical value lay concealed behind dreams, we were no doubt quite unprepared to find that that meaning was of such a uniform character. According to Aristotle's accurate but bald definition, a dream is thinking that persists (in so far as we are asleep) in the state of sleep. [Cf. p. 37.] Since, then, our daytime thinking produces psychical acts of such various sorts—judgements, inferences, denials, expectations, intentions, and so on—why should it be obliged during the night to restrict itself to the production of wishes alone? Are there not, on the contrary, numerous dreams which show us psychical acts of other kinds—worries, for instance—transformed into dream-shape? And was not the dream with which we began this chapter (a quite particularly transparent one) precisely a dream of this sort? When the glare of light fell on the eyes of the sleeping father, he drew the worrying conclusion that a candle had fallen over and might have set the dead body on fire. He turned this conclusion into a dream by clothing it in a sensory situation and in the present tense. What part was played in this by wish-fulfilment? Can we fail to see in it the predominating influence of a thought persisting from waking life or stimulated by a new sense-impression? All this is quite true and compels us to enter more closely into the part played by wish-fulfilment in dreams and into the importance of waking thoughts which persist into sleep.

We have already been led by wish-fulfilment itself to divide dreams into two groups. We have found some dreams which appeared openly as wish-fulfilments, and others in which the wish-fulfilment was unrecognizable and often disguised by every possible means. In the latter we have perceived the dream-censorship at work. We found the undistorted wishful dreams principally in children; though *short*, frankly wishful dreams *seemed* (and I lay emphasis upon this qualification) to occur in adults as well.

We may next ask where the wishes that come true in dreams originate. What contrasting possibilities or what alternatives have we in mind in raising this question? It is the contrast, I think, between the consciously perceived life of daytime and a psychical activity which has remained unconscious and of which we can only become aware at night. I can distinguish three possible origins for such a wish. (1) It may have been aroused during the day and for external reasons may not have been satisfied; in that case an acknowledged wish which has not been dealt with is left over for the night. (2) It may have arisen during the day but been repudiated; in that case what is left over is a wish which has not been dealt with but has been suppressed. (3) It may have no connection with daytime life and be one of those wishes which only emerge from the suppressed part of the mind and become active in us at night. If we turn again to our schematic picture of the psychical apparatus, we shall localize wishes of the first kind in the system *Pcs.*; we shall suppose that wishes of the second kind have been driven out of the system *Pcs.* into the *Ucs.*, where, if at all, they continue to exist; and we shall conclude that wishful impulses of the third kind are altogether incapable of passing beyond the system *Ucs.* The question then arises whether wishes derived from these different sources are of equal importance for dreams and have equal power to instigate them.

If we cast our minds over the dreams that are at our disposal for answering this question, we shall at once be reminded that we must add a fourth source of dream-wishes, namely the current wishful impulses that arise during the night (e.g. those stimulated by thirst or sexual needs). In the next place, we shall form the opinion that the place of origin of a dream-wish probably has no influence on its capacity for instigating dreams. I may recall the little girl's dream which prolonged a trip on the lake that had been interrupted during the day and the other children's dreams which I have recorded. [See pp. 152 ff.] They were explained as being due to unfulfilled, but unsuppressed, wishes from the previous day. Instances of a wish that has been suppressed in the daytime finding its way out in a dream are exceedingly numerous. I will add a further very simple example of this class. The dreamer was a lady who was rather fond of making fun of people and one of whose friends, a woman younger than herself, had just become engaged. All day long she had been asked by her acquaintances whether she knew the young man and what she thought of him. She had replied with nothing but praises, with which she had silenced her real judgement; for she would have liked to tell the truth—that he was a *'Dutzendmensch'* [literally a 'dozen man,' a very commonplace sort of person—people like him are turned out by the *dozen*]. She dreamt that night that she was asked the same question, and replied with the formula: *'In the case of repeat orders it is sufficient to quote the number.'* We have learnt, lastly, from numerous analyses that wherever a dream has undergone distortion the wish has arisen from the unconscious and was one which could not be perceived during the day. Thus it seems at a first glance as though all wishes are of equal importance and equal power in dreams.

I cannot offer any proof here that the truth is nevertheless otherwise; but I may say that I am strongly inclined to suppose that dream-wishes are more strictly determined. It is true that children's dreams prove beyond a doubt that a wish that has not been dealt with during the day can act as a dream-instigator. But it must not be forgotten that it is a *child's* wish, a wishful impulse of the strength proper to children. I think it is highly doubtful whether in the case of an adult a wish that has not been fulfilled during the day would be strong enough to produce a dream. It seems to me, on the contrary, that, with the progressive control exercised upon our instinctual life by our thought-activity, we are more and more inclined to renounce as unprofitable the formation or retention of such intense wishes as children know. It is possible that there are individual differences in this respect, and that some people retain an infantile type of mental process longer than others, just as there are similar differences in regard to the diminution of visual imagery, which is so vivid in early years. But in general, I think, a wish that has been left over unfulfilled from the previous day is insufficient to produce a dream in the case of an adult. I readily admit that a wishful impulse originating in the conscious will *contribute* to the instigation of a dream, but it will probably not do more than that. The dream would not materialize if the preconscious wish did not succeed in finding reinforcement from elsewhere.

From the unconscious, in fact. *My supposition is that a conscious wish can only become a dream-instigator if it succeeds in awakening an unconscious wish with the same tenor and in obtaining reinforcement from it.* From indications derived from the psycho-analysis of the neuroses, I consider that these unconscious wishes are always on the alert, ready at any time to find their way to expression when an opportunity arises for allying themselves with an impulse from the conscious and for transferring their own great intensity on to the latter's lesser one.[1] It will then *appear* as though the conscious wish alone had been realized in the dream; only some small

---

[1] They share this character of indestructibility with all other mental acts which are truly unconscious, i.e. which belong to the system *Ucs.* only. These are paths which have been laid down once and for all, which never fall into disuse and which, whenever an unconscious excitation re-cathects them, are always ready to conduct the excitatory process to discharge. If I may use a simile, they are only capable of annihilation in the same sense as the ghosts in the underworld of the Odyssey—ghosts which awoke to new life as soon as they tasted blood. Processes which are dependent on the preconscious system are destructible in quite another sense. The psychotherapy of the neuroses is based on this distinction. [See below, p. 576.]

peculiarity in the dream's configuration will serve as a finger-post to put us on the track of the powerful ally from the unconscious. These wishes in our unconscious, ever on the alert and, so to say, immortal, remind one of the legendary Titans, weighed down since primaeval ages by the massive bulk of the mountains which were once hurled upon them by the victorious gods and which are still shaken from time to time by the convulsion of their limbs. But these wishes, held under repression, are themselves of infantile origin, as we are taught by psychological research into the neuroses. I would propose, therefore, to set aside the assertion made just now [p. 552], that the place of origin of dream-wishes is a matter of indifference and replace it by another one to the following effect: *a wish which is represented in a dream must be an infantile one.* In the case of adults it originates from the *Ucs.,* in the case of children, where there is as yet no division or censorship between the *Pcs.* and the *Ucs.,* or where that division is only gradually being set up, it is an unfulfilled, unrepressed wish from waking life. I am aware that this assertion cannot be proved to hold universally; but it can be proved to hold frequently, even in unsuspected cases, and it cannot be *contradicted* as a general proposition.

In my view, therefore, wishful impulses left over from conscious waking life must be relegated to a secondary position in respect to the formation of dreams. I cannot allow that, as contributors to the content of dreams, they play any other part than is played, for instance, by the material of sensations which become currently active during sleep. [See p. 248.] I shall follow the same line of thought in now turning to consider those psychical instigations to dreaming, left over from waking life, which are *other* than wishes. When we decide to go to sleep, we may succeed in temporarily bringing to an end the cathexes of energy attaching to our waking thoughts. Anyone who can do this easily is a good sleeper; the first Napoleon seems to have been a model of this class. But we do not always succeed in doing so, nor do we always succeed completely. Unsolved problems, tormenting worries, overwhelming impressions—all these carry thought-activity over into sleep and sustain mental processes in the system that we have named the preconscious. If we wish to classify the thought-impulses which persist in sleep, we may divide them into the following groups: (1) what has not been carried to a conclusion during the day owing to some chance hindrance; (2) what has not been dealt with owing to the insufficiency of our intellectual power—what is unsolved; (3) what has been rejected and suppressed during the daytime. To these we must add (4) a powerful group consisting of what has been set in action in our *Ucs.* by the activity of the preconscious in the course of the day; and finally (5) the group of daytime impressions which are indifferent and have for that reason not been dealt with.

There is no need to underestimate the importance of the psychical intensities which are introduced into the state of sleep by these residues of daytime life, and particularly of those in the group of unsolved problems. It is certain that these excitations continue to struggle for expression during the night; and we may assume with equal certainty that the state of sleep makes it impossible for the excitatory process to be pursued in the habitual manner in the preconscious and brought to an end by becoming conscious. In so far as our thought-processes are able to become conscious in the normal way at night, we are simply not asleep. I am unable to say what modification in the system *Pcs.* is brought about by the state of sleep;[1] but there can be no doubt that the psychological characteristics of sleep are to be looked for essentially in modifications in the cathexis of this particular system—a system that is also in control of access to the power of movement, which is paralysed during sleep. On the other hand, nothing in the psychology of dreams gives me reason to suppose that sleep produces any modifications other than secondary ones in the state of things prevailing in the *Ucs.* No other course, then, lies open to excitations occurring at night in the *Pcs.* than that followed by wishful excitations arising from the *Ucs.;* the preconscious excitations must find reinforcement from the *Ucs.* and must accompany the unconscious excitations along their circuitous paths. But what is the relation of the preconscious residues of the previous day to *dreams?* There is no doubt that they find their way into dreams in great quantity, and that they make use of the content of dreams in order to penetrate into consciousness even during the night. Indeed they occasionally dominate the content of a dream and force it to carry on the activity of daytime. It is certain, too, that the day's residues may be of any other character just as easily as wishes; but it is highly instructive in this connection, and of positively decisive importance for the theory of wish-fulfilment, to observe the condition to which they must submit in order to be received into a dream.

---

[1] [*Footnote added* 1919:] I have tried to penetrate further into an understanding of the state of things prevailing during sleep and of the determining conditions of hallucination in a paper entitled 'A Metapsychological Supplement to the Theory of Dreams' [Freud, 1917*d*].

Let us take one of the dreams I have already recorded—for instance, the one in which my friend Otto appeared with the signs of Graves' disease. (See pp. 286 ff.) I had been worried during the previous day by Otto's looks; and, like everything else concerned with him, this worry affected me closely. And it pursued me, as I may assume, into my sleep. I was probably anxious to discover what could be wrong with him. This worry found expression during the night in the dream I have described, the content of which was in the first place nonsensical and in the second place was in no respect the fulfilment of a wish. I then began to investigate the origin of this inappropriate expression of the worry I had felt during the day, and by means of analysis I found a connection through the fact of my having identified my friend with a certain Baron L. and myself with Professor R. There was only one explanation of my having been obliged to choose this particular substitute for my daytime thought. I must have been prepared at all times in my *Ucs.* to identify myself with Professor R., since by means of that identification one of the immortal wishes of childhood—the megalomaniac wish—was fulfilled. Ugly thoughts hostile to my friend, which were certain to be repudiated during the day, had seized the opportunity of slipping through with the wish and getting themselves represented in the dream; but my daytime worry had also found some sort of expression in the content of the dream by means of a substitute. [Cf. p. 284.] The daytime thought, which was not in itself a wish but on the contrary a worry, was obliged to find a connection in some way or other with an infantile wish which was now unconscious and suppressed, and which would enable it—suitably decocted, it is true—to 'originate' in consciousness. The more dominating was the worry, the more far-fetched a link could be established; there was no necessity for there being any connection whatever between the content of the wish and that of the worry, and in fact no such connection existed in our example.

It may perhaps be useful[1] to continue our examination of the same question by considering how a dream behaves when the dream-thoughts present it with material which is the complete reverse of a wish-fulfilment—well-justified worries, painful reflections, distressing realizations. The many possible outcomes can be classed under the two following groups. (A) The dream-work may succeed in replacing all the distressing ideas by contrary ones and in suppressing the unpleasurable affects attaching to them. The re-

---

[1] [This paragraph and the two following ones were added in 1919.]

sult will be a straightforward dream of satisfaction, a palpable 'wish-fulfilment,' about which there seems no more to be said. (B) The distressing ideas may make their way, more or less modified but none the less quite recognizable, into the manifest content of the dream. This is the case which raises doubts as to the validity of the wish theory of dreams and needs further investigation. Dreams of this sort with a distressing content may either be experienced with indifference, or they may be accompanied by the whole of the distressing affect which their ideational content seems to justify, or they may even lead to the development of anxiety and to awakening.

Analysis is able to demonstrate that these unpleasurable dreams are wish-fulfilments no less than the rest. An unconscious and repressed wish, whose fulfilment the dreamer's ego could not fail to experience as something distressing, has seized the opportunity offered to it by the persisting cathexis of the distressing residues of the previous day; it has lent them its support and by that means rendered them capable of entering a dream. But whereas in Group A the unconscious wish coincided with the conscious one, in Group B the gulf between the unconscious and the conscious (between the repressed and the ego) is revealed and the situation in the fairy tale of the three wishes which were granted by the fairy to the husband and wife is realized. (See below, p. 579 *n.*) The satisfaction at the fulfilment of the repressed wish may turn out to be so great that it counterbalances the distressing feelings attaching to the day's residues [cf. p. 508]; in that cass the feeling-tone of the dream is indifferent, in spite of its being on the one hand the fulfilment of a wish and on the other the fulfilment of a fear. Or it may happen that the sleeping ego takes a still larger share in the constructing of the dream, that it reacts to the satisfying of the repressed wish with violent indignation and itself puts an end to the dream with an outburst of anxiety. Thus there is no difficulty in seeing that unpleasurable dreams and anxiety-dreams are just as much wish-fulfilments in the sense of our theory as are straightforward dreams of satisfaction.

Unpleasurable dreams may also be 'punishment-dreams.' [See pp. 479 ff.] It must be admitted that their recognition means in a certain sense a new addition to the theory of dreams. What is fulfilled in them is equally an unconscious wish, namely a wish that the dreamer may be punished for a repressed and forbidden wishful impulse. To that extent dreams of this kind fall in with the condition that has been laid down here that the motive force for constructing a dream must be provided by a wish belonging to the unconscious. A closer psychological analysis, however, shows how they differ from other wishful dreams. In the cases forming Group B the dream-constructing wish is an unconscious one and belongs to the repressed, while in punishment-dreams, though it is equally an unconscious one, it must be reckoned as belonging not to the repressed but to the 'ego.' Thus punishment-dreams indicate the possibility that the ego may have a greater share than was supposed in the construction of dreams. The mechanism of dream-formation would in general be greatly clarified if instead of the opposition between 'conscious' and 'unconscious' we were to speak of that between the 'ego' and the 'repressed.' This cannot be done, however, without taking account of the processes underlying the psychoneuroses, and for that reason it has not been carried out in the present work. I will only add that punishment-dreams are not in general subject to the condition that the day's residues shall be of a distressing kind. On the contrary, they occur most easily where the opposite is the case—where the day's residues are thoughts of a satisfying nature but the satisfaction which they express is a forbidden one. The only trace of these thoughts that appears in the manifest dream is their diametric opposite, just as in the case of dreams belonging to Group A. The essential characteristic of punishment-dreams would thus be that in their case the dream-constructing wish is not an unconscious wish derived from the repressed (from the system *Ucs.*), but a punitive one reacting against it and belonging to the ego, though at the same time an unconscious (that is to say, preconscious) one.[1]

I will report a dream of my own[2] in order to illustrate what I have just said, and in particular the way in which the dream-work deals with a residue of distressing anticipations from the previous day.

'Indistinct beginning. *I said to my wife that I had a piece of news for her, something quite special. She was alarmed and refused to listen. I assured her that on the contrary it was something that she would be very glad to hear, and began to tell her that our son's officer's mess had sent a sum of money (5000*

---

[1] [*Footnote added* 1930:] This would be the appropriate point for a reference to the 'super-ego,' one of the later findings of psychoanalysis. [Cf. p. 482, *n.*—A class of dreams which are an exception to the 'wish-theory' (those which occur in traumatic neuroses) is discussed in Chapter II of *Beyond the Pleasure Principle* (1920*g*) and in the last pages of Lecture XXIX in the *New Introductory Lectures* (1933*a*).]

[2] [This paragraph and the two following ones were added as a footnote in 1919, and incorporated in the text in 1930.]

Kronen?) . . . *something about distinction* . . . *distribution.* . . . *Meanwhile I had gone with her into a small room, like a storeroom, to look for something. Suddenly I saw my son appear. He was not in uniform but in tight-fitting sports clothes (like a seal?), with a little cap. He climbed up on to a basket that was standing beside a cupboard, as though he wanted to put something on the cupboard. I called out to him: no reply. It seemed to me that his face or forehead was bandaged. He was adjusting something in his mouth, pushing something into it. And his hair was flecked with grey. I thought: "Could he be as exhausted as all that? And has he got false teeth?"* Before I could call out again I woke up, feeling no anxiety but with my heart beating rapidly. My bedside clock showed that it was two thirty.'

Once again it is impossible for me to present a complete analysis. I must restrict myself to bringing out a few salient points. Distressing anticipations from the previous day were what gave rise to the dream: we had once more been without news of our son at the front for over a week. It is easy to see that the content of the dream expressed a conviction that he had been wounded or killed. Energetic efforts were clearly being made at the beginning of the dream to replace the distressing thoughts by their contrary. I had some highly agreeable news to communicate—something about money being sent . . . distinction . . . distribution. (The sum of money was derived from an agreeable occurrence in my medical practice; it was an attempt at a complete diversion from the topic.) But these efforts failed. My wife suspected something dreadful and refused to listen to me. The disguises were too thin and references to what it was sought to repress pierced through them everywhere. If my son had been killed, his fellow-officers would send back his belongings and I should have to distribute what he left among his brothers and sisters and other people. A 'distinction' is often awarded to an officer who has fallen in battle. Thus the dream set about giving direct expression to what it had first sought to deny, though the inclination towards wish-fulfilment was still shown at work in the distortions. (The change of locality during the dream is no doubt to be understood as what Silberer [1912] has described as 'threshold symbolism.' [Cf. above, pp. 508.]) We cannot tell, it is true, what it was that provided the dream with the motive force for thus giving expression to my distressing thoughts. My son did not appear as someone 'falling' but as someone 'climbing.' He had in fact been a keen mountaineer. He was not in uniform but in sports clothes; this meant that the place of the accident that I *now* feared had been taken by an *earlier*, sporting one; for he had had a fall during a skiing expedition and broken his thigh. The way in which he was dressed, on the other hand, which made him look like a seal, at once recalled someone younger—our funny little grandson; while the grey hair reminded me of the latter's father, our son-in-law, who had been hard hit by the war. What could this mean? . . . but I have said enough of it.—The locality in a store-closet and the cupboard from which he wanted to take something ('on which he wanted to put something' in the dream)—these allusions reminded me unmistakably of an accident of my own which I had brought on myself when I was between two and three years old.[1] I had climbed up on to a stool in the store-closet to get something nice that was lying on a cupboard or table. The stool had tipped over and its corner had struck me behind my lower jaw; I might easily, I reflected, have knocked out all my teeth. The recollection was accompanied by an admonitory thought: 'that serves you right'; and this seemed as though it was a hostile impulse aimed at the gallant soldier. Deeper analysis at last enabled me to discover what the concealed impulse was which might have found satisfaction in the dreaded accident to my son: it was the envy which is felt for the young by those who have grown old, but which they believe they have completely stifled. And there can be no question that it was precisely the *strength* of the painful emotion which would have arisen if such a misfortune had really happened that caused that emotion to seek out a repressed wish-fulfilment of this kind in order to find some consolation.[2]

I am now in a position to give a precise account of the part played in dreams by the unconscious wish. I am ready to admit that there is a whole class of dreams the *instigation* to which arises principally or even exclusively from the residues of daytime life; and I think that even my wish that I might at long last become a Professor Extraordinarius might have allowed me to sleep through the night in peace if my worry over my friend's health had not still persisted from the previous day (p. 207). But the worry alone could not have made a dream. The *motive force* which the dream required had to be provided by a wish; it was the business of the worry to get hold of a wish to act as the motive force of the dream.

The position may be explained by an analogy. A daytime thought may very well play the part of *entrepreneur* for a dream; but the *entrepreneur,*

---

[1] [Cf. p. 50, footnote.]
[2] [This dream is discussed briefly in its possible telepathic aspect at the beginning of Freud's paper on 'Dreams and Telepathy' (1922*a*).]

who, as people say, has the idea and the initiative to carry it out, can do nothing without capital; he needs a *capitalist* who can afford the outlay, and the capitalist who provides the psychical outlay for the dream is invariably and indisputably, whatever may be the thoughts of the previous day, *a wish from the unconscious.*[1]

Sometimes the capitalist is himself the *entrepreneur*, and indeed in the case of dreams this is the commoner event: an unconscious wish is stirred up by daytime activity and proceeds to construct a dream. So, too, the other possible variations in the economic situation that I have taken as an analogy have their parallel in dream-processes. The *entrepreneur* may himself make a small contribution to the capital; several *entrepreneurs* may apply to the same capitalist; several capitalists may combine to put up what is necessary for the *entrepreneur*. In the same way, we come across dreams that are supported by more than one dream-wish; and so too with other similar variations, which could easily be run through, but which would be of no further interest to us. We must reserve until later what remains to be said of the dream-wish.

The *tertium comparationis* [third element of comparison] in the analogy that I have just used—the quantity[2] put at the disposal of the *entrepreneur* in an appropriate amount—is capable of being applied in still greater detail to the purpose of elucidating the structure of dreams. In most dreams it is possible to detect a central point which is marked by peculiar sensory intensity, as I have shown on pp. 322 [and 345 f.]. This central point is as a rule the direct representation of the wish-fulfilment, for, if we undo the displacements brought about by the dream-work, we find that the *psychical* intensity of the elements in the dream-thoughts has been replaced by the *sensory* intensity of the elements in the content of the actual dream. The elements in the *neighbourhood* of the wish-fulfilment often have nothing to do with its meaning, but turn out to be derivatives of distressing thoughts that run contrary to the wish. But owing to their being in what is often an artificially established connection with the central element, they have acquired enough intensity to become capable of being represented in the dream. Thus the wish-fulfilment's power of bringing about representation

---

[1] [These last two paragraphs are quoted in full by Freud at the end of his analysis of Dora's first dream (1905*e*, Part II), which, he comments, is a complete confirmation of their correctness.]

[2] [Of capital in the case of the analogy, and of psychical energy in the case of a dream.]

is diffused over a certain sphere surrounding it, within which all the elements—including even those possessing no means of their own—become empowered to obtain representation. In the case of dreams that are actuated by *several* wishes, it is easy to delimit the spheres of the different wish-fulfilments, and gaps in the dream may often be understood as frontier zones between those spheres.[1]

Though the preceding considerations have reduced the importance of the part played by the day's residues in dreams, it is worth while devoting a little more attention to them. It must be that they are essential ingredients in the formation of dreams, since experience has revealed the surprising fact that in the content of every dream some link with a recent daytime impression—often of the most insignificant sort—is to be detected. We have not hitherto been able to explain the necessity for this addition to the mixture that constitutes a dream (see p. 203 f.). And it is only possible to do so if we bear firmly in mind the part played by the unconscious wish and then seek for information from the psychology of the neuroses. We learn from the latter that an unconscious idea is as such quite incapable of entering the preconscious and that it can only exercise any effect there by establishing a connection with an idea which already belongs to the preconscious, by transferring its intensity on to it and by getting itself 'covered' by it. Here we have the fact of 'transference,'[2] which provides an explanation of so many striking phenomena in the mental life of neurotics. The preconscious idea, which thus acquires an undeserved degree of intensity, may either be left unaltered by the transference, or it may have a modification forced upon it, derived from the content of the idea which effects the transference. I hope I may be forgiven for drawing analogies

---

[1] [A particularly clear summary of the part played by the 'day's residues' in the construction of dreams will be found in the course of Freud's short paper, 1913*a*.]

[2] [In his later writings Freud regularly used this same word 'transference' (*'Übertragung'*) to describe a somewhat different, though not unrelated, psychological process, first discovered by him as occurring in the course of psycho-analytic treatment—namely, the process of 'transferring' on to a contemporary object feelings which originally applied, and still unconsciously apply, to an infantile object. (See, e.g., Freud, 1905*e*, Section IV; and Freud, 1915*a*.) The word occurs also in this other sense in the present volume—e.g. on pp. 207 and 221—and had already been so used by Freud in the last pages of Chapter IV of *Studies on Hysteria* (Breuer and Freud, 1895).]

from everyday life, but I am tempted to say that the position of a repressed idea resembles that of an American dentist in this country: he is not allowed to set up in practice unless he can make use of a legally qualified medical practitioner to serve as a stalking-horse and to act as a 'cover' in the eyes of the law. And just as it is not exactly the physicians with the largest practices who form alliances of this kind with dentists, so in the same way preconscious or conscious ideas which have already attracted a sufficient amount of the attention that is operating in the preconscious will not be the ones to be chosen to act as covers for a repressed idea. The unconscious prefers to weave its connections round preconscious impressions and ideas which are either indifferent and have thus had no attention paid to them, or have been rejected and have thus had attention promptly withdrawn from them. It is a familiar article in the doctrine of associations, and one that is entirely confirmed by experience, that an idea which is bound by a very intimate tie in one direction, tends, as it were, to repel whole groups of new ties. I once attempted to base a theory of hysterical paralyses on this proposition.[1]

If we assume that the same need for transference on the part of repressed ideas which we have discovered in analysing the neuroses is also at work in dreams, two of the riddles of the dream are solved at a blow: the fact, namely, that every analysis of a dream shows some recent impression woven into its texture and that this recent element is often of the most trivial kind [p. 203]. I may add that (as we have already found elsewhere [p. 200]) the reason why these recent and indifferent elements so frequently find their way into dreams as substitutes for the most ancient of all the dream-thoughts is that they have least to fear from the censorship imposed by resistance. But while the fact that *trivial* elements are preferred is explained by their freedom from censorship, the fact that *recent* elements occur with such regularity points to the existence of a need for transference. Both groups of impressions satisfy the demand of the repressed for material that is still clear of associations—the indifferent ones because they have given no occasion for the formation of many ties, and the recent ones because they have not yet had time to form them.

It will be seen, then, that the day's residues, among which we may now class the indifferent impressions, not only *borrow* something from the *Ucs.* when they succeed in taking a share in the formation of a dream—namely

---

[1] [See Section IV of Freud, 1893c.]

the instinctual force which is at the disposal of the repressed wish—but that they also *offer* the unconscious something indispensable—namely the necessary point of attachment for a transference. If we wished to penetrate more deeply at this point into the processes of the mind, we should have to throw more light upon the interplay of excitations between the preconscious and the unconscious—a subject towards which the study of the psychoneuroses draws us, but upon which, as it happens, dreams have no help to offer.

I have only one thing more to add about the day's residues. There can be no doubt that it is they that are the true disturbers of sleep and not dreams, which, on the contrary are concerned to guard it. I shall return to this point later. [See pp. 576 ff.]

We have so far been studying dream-wishes: we have traced them from their origin in the region of the *Ucs.* and have analysed their relations to the day's residues, which in their turn may either be wishes or psychical impulses of some other kind or simply recent impressions. In this way we have allowed room for every claim that may be raised by any of the multifarious waking thought-activities on behalf of the importance of the part played by them in the process of constructing dreams. It is not impossible, even, that our account may have provided an explanation of the extreme cases in which a dream, pursuing the activities of daytime, arrives at a happy solution of some unsolved problem of waking life.[1] All we need is an example of this kind, so that we might analyse it and trace the source of the infantile or repressed wishes whose help has been enlisted and has reinforced the efforts of preconscious activity with such success. But all this has not brought us a step nearer to solving the riddle of why it is that the unconscious has nothing else to offer during sleep but the motive forces for the fulfilment of a *wish*. The answer to this question must throw light upon the psychical nature of wishes, and I propose to give the answer by reference to our schematic picture of the psychical apparatus.

There can be no doubt that that apparatus has only reached its present perfection after a long period of development. Let us attempt to carry it back to an earlier stage of its functioning capacity. Hypotheses, whose justification must be looked for in other directions, tell us that at first the apparatus's efforts were directed towards keeping itself so far as possible free

---

[1] [See above, pp. 93 f. An instance of this is mentioned in a footnote at the end of Section II of *The Ego and the Id* (Freud, 1923*b*).]

from stimuli;[1] consequently its first structure followed the plan of a reflex apparatus, so that any sensory excitation impinging on it could be promptly discharged along a motor path. But the exigencies of life interfere with this simple function, and it is to them, too, that the apparatus owes the impetus to further development. The exigencies of life confront it first in the form of the major somatic needs. The excitations produced by internal needs seek discharge in movement, which may be described as an 'internal change' or an 'expression of emotion.' A hungry baby screams or kicks helplessly. But the situation remains unaltered, for the excitation arising from an internal need is not due to a force producing a *momentary* impact but to one which is in continuous operation. A change can only come about if in some way or other (in the case of the baby, through outside help) an 'experience of satisfaction' can be achieved which puts an end to the internal stimulus. An essential component of this experience of satisfaction is a particular perception (that of nourishment, in our example) the mnemic image of which remains associated thenceforward with the memory trace of the excitation produced by the need. As a result of the link that has thus been established, next time this need arises a psychical impulse will at once emerge which will seek to re-cathect the mnemic image of the perception and to re-evoke the perception itself, that is to say, to re-establish the situation of the original satisfaction. An impulse of this kind is what we call a wish; the reappearance of the perception is the fulfilment of the wish; and the shortest path to the fulfilment of the wish is a path leading direct from the excitation produced by the need to a complete cathexis of the perception. Nothing prevents us from assuming that there was a primitive state of the psychical apparatus in which this path was actually traversed, that is, in which wishing ended in hallucinating. Thus the aim of this first psychical activity was to produce a 'perceptual identity'[2]—a repetition of the perception which was linked with the satisfaction of the need.

---

[1] [This is the so-called 'Principle of Constancy' which is discussed in the opening pages of *Beyond the Pleasure Principle* (1920*g*). But it was already a fundamental assumption in some of Freud's earliest psychological writings, e.g. in his posthumously published 'Letter to Josef Breuer' of June 29, 1892 (Freud, 1941*a*). The whole gist of the present paragraph is already stated in Sections 1, 2, 11 and 16 of Part I of his 'Project for a Scientific Psychology' written in the autumn of 1895 (Freud, 1950*a*). Cf. Editor's Introduction, pp. xiv ff.]

[2] [I.e. something perceptually identical with the 'experience of satisfaction.']

The bitter experience of life must have changed this primitive thought-activity into a more expedient secondary one. The establishment of a perceptual identity along the short path of regression within the apparatus does not have the same result elsewhere in the mind as does the cathexis of the same perception from without. Satisfaction does not follow; the need persists. An internal cathexis could only have the same value as an external one if it were maintained unceasingly, as in fact occurs in hallucinatory psychoses and hunger phantasies, which exhaust their whole psychical activity in clinging to the object of their wish. In order to arrive at a more efficient expenditure of psychical force, it is necessary to bring the regression to a halt before it becomes complete, so that it does not proceed beyond the mnemic image, and is able to seek out other paths which lead eventually to the desired perceptual identity being established from the direction of the external world.[1] This inhibition of the regression and the subsequent division of the excitation become the business of a second system, which is in control of voluntary movement—which for the first time, that is, makes use of movement for purposes remembered in advance. But all the complicated thought-activity which is spun out from the mnemic image to the moment at which the perceptual identity is established by the external world—all this activity of thought merely constitutes a roundabout path to wish-fulfilment which has been made necessary by experience.[2] Thought is after all nothing but a substitute for a hallucinatory wish; and it is self-evident that dreams must be wish-fulfilments, since nothing but a wish can set our mental apparatus at work. Dreams, which fulfil their wishes along the short path of regression, have merely preserved for us in that respect a sample of the psychical apparatus's primary method of working, a method which was abandoned as being inefficient. What once dominated waking life, while the mind was still young and incompetent, seems now to have been banished into the night—just as the primitive weapons, the bows and arrows, that have been abandoned by adult men, turn up once more in the nursery. *Dreaming is a piece of infantile*

---

[1] [*Footnote added* 1919:] In other words, it becomes evident that there must be a means of 'reality-testing' [i.e. of testing things to see whether they are real or not].

[2] The wish-fulfilling activity of dreams is justly extolled by Le Lorrain, who speaks of it as 'sans fatigue sérieuse, sans être obligé de recourir à cette lutte opiniâtre et longue qui use et corrode les jouissances poursuivies [incurring no serious fatigue and not being obliged to embark upon the long and obstinate struggle that wears away and spoils enjoyments that have to be pursued.']

mental life that has been superseded. These methods of working on the part of the psychical apparatus, which are normally suppressed in waking hours, become current once more in psychosis and then reveal their incapacity for satisfying our needs in relation to the external world.[1]

The unconscious wishful impulses clearly try to make themselves effective in daytime as well, and the fact of transference, as well as the psychoses, show us that they endeavour to force their way by way of the preconscious system into consciousness and to obtain control of the power of movement. Thus the censorship between the *Ucs.* and the *Pcs.,* the assumption of whose existence is positively forced upon us by dreams, deserves to be recognized and respected as the watchman of our mental health. Must we not regard it, however, as an act of carelessness on the part of that watchman that it relaxes its activities during the night, allows the suppressed impulses in the *Ucs.* to find expression, and makes it possible for hallucinatory regression to occur once more? I think not. For even though this critical watchman goes to rest—and we have proof that its slumbers are not deep—it also shuts the door upon the power of movement.—No matter what impulses from the normally inhibited *Ucs.* may prance upon the stage, we need feel no concern; they remain harmless, since they are unable to set in motion the motor apparatus by which alone they might modify the external world. The state of sleep guarantees the security of the citadel that must be guarded. The position is less harmless when what brings about the displacement of forces is not the nightly relaxation in the critical censorship's output of force, but a pathological reduction in that force or a pathological intensification of the unconscious excitations while the preconscious is still cathected and the gateway to the power of movement stands open. When this is so, the watchman is overpowered, the unconscious excitations overwhelm the *Pcs.,* and thence obtain control over our speech and actions; or they forcibly bring about hallucinatory regression and direct the course of the apparatus (which was not designed for their use) by virtue of the attraction exercised by perceptions on the distribution of our psychical energy. To this state of things we give the name of psychosis.

---

[1] [*Footnote added* 1914:] I have elsewhere carried this train of thought further in a paper on the two principles of mental functioning (Freud, 1911*b*)—the pleasure principle and the reality principle, as I have proposed calling them. [The argument is in fact developed further below, on pp. 594 ff.]

We are now well on the way to proceeding further with the erection of the psychological scaffolding, which we stopped at the point at which we introduced the two systems *Ucs.* and *Pcs.* But there are reasons for continuing a little with our consideration of wishes as the sole psychical motive force for the construction of dreams. We have accepted the idea that the reason why dreams are invariably wish-fulfilments is that they are products of the system *Ucs.*, whose activity knows no other aim than the fulfilment of wishes and which has at its command no other forces than wishful impulses. If we insist, for even a moment longer, upon our right to base such far-reaching psychological speculations upon the interpretation of dreams, we are in duty bound to prove that those speculations have enabled us to insert dreams into a nexus which can include other psychical structures as well. If such a thing as a system *Ucs.* exists (or something analogous to it for the purposes of our discussion), dreams cannot be its only manifestation; every dream may be a wish-fulfilment, but apart from dreams there must be other forms of abnormal wish-fulfilments. And it is a fact that the theory governing all psychoneurotic symptoms culminates in a single proposition, which asserts that *they too are to be regarded as fulfilments of unconscious wishes.*[1] Our explanation makes the dream only the first member of a class which is of the greatest significance to psychiatrists and an understanding of which implies the solution of the purely psychological side of the problem of psychiatry.[2]

The other members of this class of wish-fulfilments—hysterical symptoms, for instance—possess one essential characteristic, however, which I cannot discover in dreams. I have learnt from the researches which I have mentioned so often in the course of this work that in order to bring about the formation of a hysterical symptom *both* currents of our mind must converge. A symptom is not merely the expression of a realized unconscious wish; a wish from the preconscious which is fulfilled by the same symptom must also be present. So that the symptom will have *at least* two determinants, one arising from each of the systems involved in the conflict. As in the case of dreams, there are no limits to the further determi-

---

[1] [*Footnote added* 1914:] Or more correctly, one portion of the symptom corresponds to the unconscious wish-fulfilment and another portion to the mental structure reacting against the wish.

[2] [*Footnote added* 1914:] As Hughlings Jackson said: 'Find out all about dreams and you will have found out all about insanity.' [Quoted by Ernest Jones (1911), who had heard it at first hand from Hughlings Jackson.]

nants that may be present—to the 'overdetermination' of the symptoms.[1] The determinant which does not arise from the *Ucs.* is invariably, so far as I know, a train of thought reacting against the unconscious wish—a self-punishment, for instance. I can therefore make the quite general assertion that *a hysterical symptom develops only where the fulfilments of two opposing wishes, arising each from a different psychical system, are able to converge in a single expression.* (Compare in this connection my most recent formulations on the origin of hysterical symptoms in my paper on hysterical phantasies and their relation to bisexuality. [Freud, 1908*a*.][2]) Examples would serve very little purpose here, since nothing but an exhaustive elucidation of the complications involved could carry conviction. I will therefore leave my assertion to stand for itself and only quote an example in order to make the point clear, and not to carry conviction. In one of my women patients, then, hysterical vomiting turned out to be on the one hand the fulfilment of an unconscious phantasy dating from her puberty—of a wish, that is, that she might be continuously pregnant and have innumerable children, with a further wish, added later, that she might have them by as many men as possible. A powerful defensive impulse had sprung up against this unbridled wish. And, since the patient might lose her figure and her good looks as a result of her vomiting, and so might cease to be attractive to anyone, the symptom was acceptable to the punitive train of thought as well; and since it was permitted by both sides it could become a reality. This was the same method of treating a wish-fulfilment as was adopted by the Parthian queen towards the Roman triumvir Crassus. Believing that he had embarked on his expedition out of love of gold, she ordered molten gold to be poured down his throat when he was dead: 'Now,' she said, 'you have what you wanted.' But all that we so far know about dreams is that they express the fulfilment of a wish from the unconscious; it seems as though the dominant, preconscious system acquiesces in this after insisting upon a certain number of distortions. Nor is it possible as a general rule to find a train of thought opposed to the dream-wish and, like its counterpart, realized in the dream. Only here and there in dream analyses do we come upon signs of reactive creations, like, for instance, my affectionate feelings for my friend R. in the dream of my uncle [with the yellow beard] (cf. pp. 174 ff.). But

---

[1] [Cf. Freud in Breuer and Freud, 1895, Chapter IV, Section 1, Observation 3.]
[2] [This sentence was added in 1909.]

we can find the missing ingredients from the preconscious elsewhere. Whereas the wish from the *Ucs.* is able to find expression in the dream after undergoing distortions of every kind, the dominant system withdraws into a *wish to sleep,* realizes that wish by bringing about the modifications which it is able to produce in the cathexes within the psychical apparatus, and persists in that wish throughout the whole duration of sleep.[1]

This determined wish on the part of the preconscious to sleep exercises a generally facilitating effect on the formation of dreams. Let me recall the dream dreamt by the man who was led to infer from the glare of light coming out of the next room that his child's body might be on fire [pp. 513 ff.]. The father drew this inference in a dream instead of allowing himself to be woken up by the glare; and we have suggested that one of the psychical forces responsible for this result was a wish which prolonged by that one moment the life of the child whom he pictured in the dream. Other wishes, originating from the repressed, probably escape us, since we are unable to analyse the dream. But we may assume that a further motive force in the production of the dream was the father's need to sleep; his sleep, like the child's life, was prolonged by one moment by the dream. 'Let the dream go on'—such was his motive—'or I shall have to wake up.' In every other dream, just as in this one, the wish to sleep lends its support to the unconscious wish. On pp. 150 f. I described some dreams which appeared openly as dreams of convenience. But in fact all dreams can claim a right to the same description. The operation of the wish to continue sleeping is most easily to be seen in arousal dreams, which modify external sensory stimuli in such a way as to make them compatible with a continuance of sleep; they weave them into a dream in order to deprive them of any possibility of acting as reminders of the external world. That same wish must, however, play an equal part in allowing the occurrence of all other dreams, though it may only be from *within* that they threaten to shake the subject out of his sleep. In some cases, when a dream carries things too far, the *Pcs.* says to consciousness: 'Never mind! go on sleeping! after all it's only a dream!' [See pp. 493 f.] But this describes in general the attitude of our dominant mental activity towards dreams, though it may not be openly expressed. I am driven to conclude that *throughout our whole sleeping state we*

---

[1] I have borrowed this idea from the theory of sleep put forward by Liébeault (1889), to whom is due the revival in modern times of research into hypnotism.

know just as certainly that we are dreaming as we know that we are sleeping. We must not pay too much attention to the counter-argument that our consciousness is never brought to bear on the latter piece of knowledge and that it is only brought to bear on the former on particular occasions when the censorship feels that it has, as it were, been taken off its guard.

On the other hand,[1] there are some people who are quite clearly aware during the night that they are asleep and dreaming and who thus seem to possess the faculty of consciously directing their dreams. If, for instance, a dreamer of this kind is dissatisfied with the turn taken by a dream, he can break it off without waking up and start it again in another direction— just as a popular dramatist may under pressure give his play a happier ending. Or another time, if his dream has led him into a sexually exciting situation, he can think to himself: 'I won't go on with this dream any further and exhaust myself with an emission; I'll hold it back for a real situation instead.'

The Marquis d'Hervey de Saint-Denys [1867, 268 ff.],[2] quoted by Vaschide (1911, 139), claimed to have acquired the power of accelerating the course of his dreams just as he pleased, and of giving them any direction he chose. It seems as though in his case the wish to sleep had given place to another preconscious wish, namely to observe his dreams and enjoy them. Sleep is just as compatible with a wish of this sort as it is with a mental reservation to wake up if some particular condition is fulfilled (e.g. in the case of a nursing mother or wet-nurse) [p. 244]. Moreover, it is a familiar fact that anyone who takes an interest in dreams remembers a considerably greater number of them after waking.

Ferenczi (1911),[3] in the course of a discussion of some other observations upon the directing of dreams, remarks: 'Dreams work over the thoughts which are occupying the mind at the moment from every angle; they will drop a dream-image if it threatens the success of a wish-fulfilment and will experiment with a fresh solution, till at last they succeed in constructing a wish-fulfilment which satisfies both agencies of the mind as a compromise.'

---

[1] [This paragraph was added in 1909.]

[2] [This paragraph was added in 1914.]

[3] [This paragraph was added as a footnote in 1914 and included in the text in 1930.]

(D)

AROUSAL BY DREAMS—THE FUNCTION OF
DREAMS—ANXIETY-DREAMS

Now that we know that all through the night the preconscious is concentrated upon the wish to sleep, we are in a position to carry our understanding of the process of dreaming a stage further. But first let us summarize what we have learnt so far.

The situation is this. Either residues of the previous day have been left over from the activity of waking life and it has not been possible to withdraw the whole cathexis of energy from them; or the activity of waking life during the course of the day has led to the stirring up of an unconscious wish; or these two events have happened to coincide. (We have already discussed the various possibilities in this connection.) The unconscious wish links itself up with the day's residues and effects a transference on to them; this may happen either in the course of the day or not until a state of sleep has been established. A wish now arises which has been transferred on to the recent material; or a recent wish, having been suppressed, gains fresh life by being reinforced from the unconscious. This wish seeks to force its way along the normal path taken by thought-processes, through the *Pcs.* (to which, indeed, it in part belongs) to consciousness. But it comes up against the censorship, which is still functioning and to the influence of which it now submits. At this point it takes on the distortion for which the way has already been paved by the transference of the wish on to the recent material. So far it is on the way to becoming an obsessive idea or a delusion or something of the kind—that is, *a thought* which has been intensified by transference and distorted in its expression by censorship. Its further advance is halted, however, by the sleeping state of the preconscious. (The probability is that that system has protected itself against the invasion by diminishing its own excitations.) The dream-process consequently enters on a regressive path, which lies open to it precisely owing to the peculiar nature of the state of sleep, and it is led along that path by the attraction exercised on it by groups of memories; some of these memories themselves exist only in the form of visual cathexes and not as translations into the terminology of the later systems. [Cf. p. 547.] In the course of its regressive path the dream-process acquires the attribute of representability. (I shall deal later with the question of compression [p. 592].) It has now completed the second portion of its zigzag journey. The first portion was a progressive one, leading from the unconscious scenes or phantasies to the preconscious; the second portion led from the frontier of the censorship back again to perceptions. But when the content of the dream-process has become perceptual, by that fact it has, as it were, found a way of evading the obstacle put in its way by the censorship and the state of sleep in the *Pcs.* [Cf. p. 529.] It succeeds in drawing attention to itself and in being noticed by consciousness.

For consciousness, which we look upon in the light of a sense organ for the apprehension of psychical qualities, is capable in waking life of receiving excitations from two directions. In the first place, it can receive excitations from the periphery of the whole apparatus, the perceptual system; and in addition to this, it can receive excitations of pleasure and unpleasure, which prove to be almost the only psychical quality attaching to transposition of energy in the inside of the apparatus. All other processes in the ψ-systems, including the *Pcs.*, are lacking in any psychical quality and so cannot be objects of consciousness, except in so far as they bring pleasure or unpleasure to perception. We are thus driven to conclude that *these releases of pleasure and unpleasure automatically regulate the course of cathectic processes.* But, in order to make more delicately adjusted performances possible, it later became necessary to make the course of ideas less dependent upon the presence or absence of unpleasure. For this purpose the *Pcs.* system needed to have qualities of its own which could attract consciousness; and it seems highly probably that it obtained them by linking the preconscious processes with the mnemic system of linguistic symbols, a system which was not without quality. [See p. 612.] By means of the qualities of that system, consciousness, which had hitherto been a sense organ for perceptions alone, also became a sense organ for a portion of our thought-processes. Now, therefore, there are, as it were, *two* sensory surfaces, one directed towards perception and the other towards the preconscious thought-processes.

I must assume that the state of sleep makes the sensory surface of consciousness which is directed towards the *Pcs.* far more insusceptible to excitation than the surface directed towards the *Pcpt.* systems. Moreover, this abandonment of interest in thought-processes during the night has a purpose: thinking is to come to a standstill, for the *Pcs.* requires sleep. Once, however, a dream has become a *perception,* it is in a position to excite consciousness, by means of the qualities it has now acquired. This sensory excitation proceeds to perform what is its essential function: it directs a part of the available cathectic energy in the *Pcs.* into attention to what is causing the excitation. [See p. 590.] It must therefore be admitted that every dream has an *arousing* effect, that it sets a part of the quiescent force of the *Pcs.* in action. The dream is then submitted by this force to the influence which we have described as secondary revision with an eye to consecutiveness and intelligibility. That is to say, the dream is treated by it just like any other perceptual content; it is met by the same anticipatory ideas, in so far as its subject-matter allows [p. 503]. So far as this third portion of the dream-process has any direction it is once again a progressive one.

To avoid misunderstandings, a word about the chronological relations of these dream-processes will not be out of place. A very attractive conjecture has been put forward by Goblot [1896, 289 f.], suggested, no doubt, by the riddle of Maury's guillotine dream [p. 58 f.]. He seeks to show that a dream occupies no more than the transition period between sleeping and waking. The process of awakening takes a certain amount of time, and during that time the dream occurs. We imagine that the final dream-image was so powerful that it compelled us to wake; whereas in fact it was only so powerful because at that moment we were already on the point of waking. 'Un rêve c'est un réveil qui commence.'[1]

It has already been pointed out by Dugas [1879*b*] that Goblot would have to disregard many facts before he could assert his thesis generally. Dreams occur from which we do not awaken—for instance, some in which we dream that we are dreaming. With our knowledge of the dream-work, we could not possibly agree that it only covers the period of awakening. It seems probable, on the contrary, that the first portion of the dream-work has already begun during the day, under the control of the preconscious. Its second portion—the modification imposed by the censorship, the attraction exercised by unconscious scenes, and the forcing of its way to perception—no doubt proceeds all through the night; and in this respect we may perhaps always be right when we express a feeling of having been dreaming all night long, though we cannot say what. [See p. 521.]

But it seems to me unnecessary to suppose that dream-processes really maintain, up to the moment of becoming conscious, the chronological order in which I have described them: that the first thing to appear is the transferred dream-wish, that distortion by the censorship follows, then the

---

[1] ['A dream is an awakening that is beginning.']

regressive change in direction, and so on. I have been obliged to adopt this order in my description; but what happens in reality is no doubt a simultaneous exploring of one path and another, a swinging of the excitation now this way and now that, until at last it accumulates in the direction that is most opportune and one particular grouping becomes the permanent one. Certain personal experiences of my own lead me to suspect that the dream-work often requires more than a day and a night in order to achieve its result; and if this is so, we need no longer feel any amazement at the extraordinary ingenuity shown in the construction of the dream. In my opinion even the demand for the dream to be made intelligible as a perceptual event may be put into effect before the dream attracts consciousness to itself. From then onwards, however, the pace is accelerated, for at that point a dream is treated in the same fashion as anything else that is perceived. It is like a firework, which takes hours to prepare but goes off in a moment.

The dream-process has by now either acquired sufficient intensity through the dream-work to attract consciousness to itself and arouse the preconscious, irrespectively of the time and depth of sleep; or its intensity is insufficient to achieve this and it must remain in a state of readiness until, just before waking, attention becomes more mobile and comes to meet it. The majority of dreams appear to operate with comparatively low psychical intensities, for they mostly wait until the moment of waking. But this also explains the fact that, if we are suddenly woken from deep sleep, we usually perceive something that we have dreamt. In such cases, just as when we wake of our own accord, the first thing we see is the perceptual content that has been constructed by the dream-work and immediately afterwards we see the perceptual content that is offered to us from outside ourselves.

Greater theoretical interest, however, attaches to the dreams which have the power to rouse us in the middle of our sleep. Bearing in mind the expediency which is everywhere else the rule, we may ask why a dream, that is, an unconscious wish, is given the power to interfere with sleep, that is, with the fulfilment of the preconscious wish. The explanation no doubt lies in relations of energy of which we have no knowledge. If we possessed such knowledge, we should probably find that allowing the dream to take its course and expending a certain amount of more or less detached attention on it is an economy of energy compared with holding the unconscious as tightly under control at night as in the daytime. [Cf. p. 576.] Experience shows that dreaming is compatible with sleeping, even if it interrupts sleep several times during the night. One wakes up for an instant and then falls asleep again at once. It is like brushing away a fly in one's sleep: a case of *ad hoc* awakening. If one falls asleep again, the interruption has been disposed of. As is shown by such familiar examples as the sleep of a nursing mother or wet-nurse [p. 244], the fulfilment of the wish to sleep is quite compatible with maintaining a certain expenditure of attention in some particular direction.

At this point an objection arises, which is based on a better knowledge of unconscious processes. I myself have asserted that unconscious wishes are always active. But in spite of this they seem not to be strong enough to make themselves perceptible during the day. If, however, while a state of sleep prevails, an unconscious wish has shown itself strong enough to construct a dream and arouse the preconscious with it, why should this strength fail after the dream has been brought to knowledge? Should not the dream continue to recur perpetually, precisely as the vexatious fly keeps on coming back after it has been driven away? What right have we to assert that dreams get rid of the disturbance of sleep?

It is perfectly true that unconscious wishes always remain active. They represent paths which can always be traversed, whenever a quantity of excitation makes use of them. [Cf. p. 592 *n.*] Indeed it is a prominent feature of unconscious processes that they are indestructible. In the unconscious nothing can be brought to an end, nothing is past or forgotten. This is brought most vividly home to one in studying the neuroses, and especially hysteria. The unconscious path of thoughts, which leads to discharge in a hysterical attack, immediately becomes traversable once more, when sufficient excitation has accumulated. A humiliation that was experienced thirty years ago acts exactly like a fresh one throughout the thirty years, as soon as it has obtained access to the unconscious sources of emotion. As soon as the memory of it is touched, it springs into life again and shows itself cathected with excitation which finds a motor discharge in an attack. This is precisely the point at which psychotherapy has to intervene. Its task is to make it possible for the unconscious processes to be dealt with finally and be forgotten. For the fading of memories and the emotional weakness of impressions which are no longer recent, which we are inclined to regard as self-evident and to explain as a primary effect of time upon mental memory-traces, are in reality secondary modifications which are only brought about by laborious work. What performs this work is the preconscious, and *psychotherapy can pursue no other course than to bring the Ucs. under the domination of the Pcs.*[1]

---

[1] [The last clause of this sentence was printed in spaced type only from 1919 onwards. Cf. p. 553 n.]

Thus there are two possible outcomes for any particular unconscious excitatory process. Either it may be left to itself, in which case it eventually forces its way through at some point and on this single occasion finds discharge for its excitation in movement; or it may come under the influence of the preconscious, and its excitation, instead of being *discharged,* may be *bound* by the preconscious. *This second alternative is the one which occurs in the process of dreaming.* [See p. 597 n.] The cathexis from the *Pcs.* which goes halfway to meet the dream after it has become perceptual, having been directed on to it by the excitation in consciousness, binds the dream's unconscious excitation and makes it powerless to act as a disturbance. If it is true that the dreamer wakes for an instant, yet he really *has* brushed away the fly that was threatening to disturb his sleep, it begins to dawn on us that it actually *is* more expedient and economical to allow the unconscious wish to take its course, to leave the path to regression open to it so that it can construct a dream, and then to bind the dream and dispose of it with a small expenditure of pre-conscious work—rather than to continue keeping a tight rein on the unconscious throughout the whole period of sleep. [Cf. p. 575.] It was indeed to be expected that dreaming, even though it may originally have been a process without a useful purpose, would have procured itself some function in the interplay of mental forces. And we can now see what that function is. Dreaming has taken on the task of bringing back under control of the preconscious the excitation in the *Ucs.* which has been left free; in so doing, it discharges the *Ucs.* excitation, serves it as a safety valve and at the same time preserves the sleep of the preconscious in return for a small expenditure of waking activity. Thus, like all the other psychical structures in the series of which it is a member, it constitutes a compromise; it is in the service of both of the two systems, since it fulfils the two wishes in so far as they are compatible with each other. If we turn back to the 'excretion theory' of dreams put forward by Robert [1886], which I explained on pp. 105 ff., we shall see at a glance that in its essence we must accept his account of the *function* of dreams, though differing from him in his premises and in his view of the dream-process itself. [See pp. 201 f.][1]

---

[1] [*Footnote added* 1914:] Is this the only function that can be assigned to dreams? I know of no other. It is true that Maeder [1912] has attempted to show that dreams have other, 'secondary,' functions. He started out from the correct observation that some dreams contain attempts at solving conflicts, attempts which are later carried out in reality and which thus behave as though they were trial

The qualification 'in so far as the two wishes are compatible with each other' implies a hint at the possible case in which the function of dreaming may come to grief. The dream-process is allowed to begin as a fulfilment of an unconscious wish; but if this attempted wish-fulfilment jars upon the preconscious so violently that it is unable to continue sleeping, then the dream has made a breach in the compromise and has failed to carry out the second half of its task. In that case the dream is immediately broken off and replaced by a state of complete waking. Here again it is not really the fault of the dream if it has now to appear in the role of a *disturber* of sleep instead of in its normal one of a *guardian* of sleep; and this fact need not prejudice us against its having a useful purpose. This is not the only instance in the organism of a contrivance which is normally useful becoming useless and disturbing as soon as the conditions that give rise to it are somewhat modified; and the disturbance at least serves the new purpose of drawing attention to the modification and of setting the organism's regulative machinery in motion against it. What I have in mind is of course the case of anxiety-dreams, and in order that I may not be thought to be

---

practices for waking actions. He therefore drew a parallel between dreams and the play of animals and children, which may be regarded as practice in the operation of innate instincts and as preparation for serious activity later on, and put forward the hypothesis that dreams have a *'fonction ludique'* ['play function']. Shortly before Maeder, Alfred Adler [1911, 215 *n*.], too, had insisted that dreams possessed a function of 'thinking ahead.' (In an analysis which I published in 1905 ['Fragment of an Analysis of a Case of Hysteria,' Part II (1905*e*)], a dream, which could only be regarded as expressing an intention, was repeated every night until it was carried out. [Cf. above, p. 211 f.])

A little reflection will convince us, however, that this 'secondary' function of dreams has no claim to be considered as a part of the subject of dream-interpretation. Thinking ahead, forming intentions, framing attempted solutions which may perhaps be realized later in waking life, all these, and many other similar things, are products of the unconscious and preconscious activity of the mind; they may persist in the state of sleep as 'the day's residues' and combine with an unconscious wish (cf. pp. 550 ff.) in forming a dream. Thus the dream's function of 'thinking ahead' is rather a function of preconscious waking thought, the products of which may be revealed to us by the analysis of dreams or of other phenomena. It has long been the habit to regard dreams as identical with their manifest content; but we must now beware equally of the mistake of confusing dreams with latent dream-thoughts. [Cf. p. 510 *n*. above and a passage at the end of the discussion of Case I in Freud's paper on 'Dream and Telepathy' (1922*a*).]

evading this evidence against the theory of wish-fulfilment whenever I come across it, I will at all events give some hints of their explanation.

There is no longer anything contradictory to us in the notion that a psychical process which develops anxiety can nevertheless be the fulfilment of a wish. We know that it can be explained by the fact that the wish belongs to one system, the *Ucs.*, while it has been repudiated and suppressed by the other system, the *Pcs.*[1] Even where psychical health is perfect, the subjugation of the *Ucs.* by the *Pcs.* is not complete; the measure of suppression indicates the degree of our psychical normality. Neurotic symptoms show that the two systems are in conflict with each other; they are the products of a compromise which brings the conflict to an end for the time being. On the one hand, they allow the *Ucs.* an outlet for the discharge of its excitation, and provide it with a kind of sally-port,

---

[1] [*Footnote added* 1919:] 'A second factor, which is much more important and far-reaching, but which is equally overlooked by laymen is the following. No doubt a wish-fulfilment must bring pleasure; but the question then arises "To whom?" To the person who has the wish, of course. But, as we know, a dreamer's relation to his wishes is a quite peculiar one. He repudiates them and censors them—he has no liking for them, in short. So that their fulfilment will give him no pleasure, but just the opposite; and experience shows that this opposite appears in the form of anxiety, a fact which has still to be explained. Thus a dreamer in his relation to his dream-wishes can only be compared to an amalgamation of two separate people who are linked by some important common element. Instead of enlarging on this, I will remind you of a familiar fairy tale [referred to above on p. 557] in which you will find the same situation repeated. A good fairy promised a poor married couple to grant them the fulfilment of their first three wishes. They were delighted, and made up their minds to choose their three wishes carefully. But a smell of sausages being fried in the cottage next door tempted the woman to wish for a couple of them. They were there in a flash; and this was the first wish-fulfilment. But the man was furious, and in his rage wished that the sausages were hanging on his wife's nose. This happened too; and the sausages were not to be dislodged from their new position. This was the second wish-fulfilment; but the wish was the man's, and its fulfilment was most disagreeable for his wife. You know the rest of the story. Since after all they were in fact one—man and wife—the third wish was bound to be that the sausages should come away from the woman's nose. This fairy tale might be used in many other connections; but here it serves only to illustrate the possibility that if two people are not at one with each other the fulfilment of a wish of one of them may bring nothing but unpleasure to the other.' (*Introductory Lectures on Psycho-Analysis* [Freud, 1916–17], Lecture XIV.)

while, on the other hand, they make it possible for the *Pcs.* to control the *Ucs.* to some extent. It is instructive to consider, for instance, the significance of a hysterical phobia or an agoraphobia. Let us suppose that a neurotic patient is unable to cross the street alone—a condition which we rightly regard as a 'symptom.' If we remove this symptom by compelling him to carry out the act of which he believes himself incapable, the consequence will be an attack of anxiety; and indeed the occurrence of an anxiety-attack in the street is often the precipitating cause of the onset of an agoraphobia. We see, therefore, that the symptom has been constructed in order to avoid an outbreak of anxiety; the phobia is erected like a frontier fortification against the anxiety.

Our discussion cannot be carried any further without examining the part played by the affects in these processes; but we can only do so imperfectly in the present connection. Let us assume, then, that the suppression of the *Ucs.* is necessary above all because, if the course of ideas in the *Ucs.* were left to itself, it would generate an affect which was originally of a pleasurable nature, but became unpleasurable after the process of 'repression' occurred. The purpose, and the result too, of suppression is to prevent this release of unpleasure. The suppression extends over the ideational content of the *Ucs.,* since the release of unpleasure might start from that content. This presupposes a quite specific assumption as to the nature of the generation of affect.[1] It is viewed as a motor or secretory function, the key to whose innervation lies in the ideas in the *Ucs.* Owing to the domination established by the *Pcs.* these ideas are, as it were, throttled, and inhibited from sending out impulses which would generate affect. If, therefore, the cathexis from the *Pcs.* ceases, the danger is that the unconscious excitations may release affect of a kind which (as a result of the repression which has already occurred) can only be experienced as unpleasure, as anxiety.

This danger materializes if the dream-process is allowed to take its course. The conditions which determine its realization are that repressions must have occurred and that the suppressed wishful impulses shall be able to grow sufficiently strong. These determinants are thus quite outside the psychological framework of dream-formation. If it were not for the fact that our topic is connected with the subject of the generation of anxiety by the single factor of the liberation of the *Ucs.* during sleep, I should be able to omit any discussion of anxiety-dreams and avoid the necessity for entering in these pages into all the obscurities surrounding them.

---

[1] [For this assumption cf. p. 474 and footnote.]

The theory of anxiety-dreams, as I have already repeatedly declared, forms part of the psychology of the neuroses.[1] We have nothing more to do with it when once we have indicated its point of contact with the topic of the dream-process. There is only one thing more that I can do. Since I have asserted that neurotic anxiety arises from sexual sources, I can submit some anxiety-dreams to analysis in order to show the sexual material present in their dream-thoughts.[2]

I have good reasons for leaving on one side in the present discussion the copious examples afforded by my neurotic patients, and for preferring to quote some anxiety-dreams dreamt by young people.

It is dozens of years since I myself had a true anxiety-dream. But I remember one from my seventh or eighth year, which I submitted to interpretation some thirty years later. It was a very vivid one, and in it I saw *my beloved mother, with a peculiarly peaceful, sleeping expression on her features, being carried into the room by two (or three) people with birds' beaks and laid upon the bed.* I awoke in tears and screaming, and interrupted my parents' sleep. The strangely draped and unnaturally tall figures with birds' beaks were derived from the illustrations to Philippson's Bible.[3] I fancy they must have been gods with falcons' heads from an ancient Egyptian funerary relief. Besides this, the analysis brought to mind an ill-mannered boy, a son of a *concierge,* who used to play with us on the grass in front of the house when we were children, and who I am inclined to think was called Philipp. It seems to me that it was from this boy that I first heard the vulgar term for sexual intercourse, instead of which educated people always use a Latin word, 'to copulate,' and which was clearly enough indicated by the choice of the falcons' heads.[4] I must have guessed the sexual significance of the word from the face of my young instructor, who was well acquainted with the facts of life. The expression on my mother's features in

---

[1] [The following sentence was added at this point in 1911, but omitted again in 1925 and subsequently: 'Anxiety in dreams, I should like to insist, is an anxiety problem and not a dream problem.']

[2] [Some of the comments in what follows would require revision in the light of Freud's later views on anxiety. See also pp. 194 ff., 256 and 352.]

[3] [*Die israelitische Bibel,* an edition of the Old Testament in Hebrew and German, Leipzig, 1839–54 (Second ed. 1858). A footnote to the fourth chapter of Deuteronomy shows a number of woodcuts of Egyptian gods, several with birds' heads.]

[4] [The German slang term referred to is *'vögeln,'* from *'Vogel'* the ordinary word for 'bird.']

the dream was copied from the view I had had of my grandfather a few days before his death as he lay snoring in a coma. The interpretation carried out in the dream by the 'secondary revision' [p. 495] must therefore have been that my mother was dying; the funerary relief fitted in with this. I awoke in anxiety, which did not cease till I had woken my parents up. I remember that I suddenly grew calm when I saw my mother's face, as though I had needed to be reassured that she was not dead. But this 'secondary' interpretation of the dream had already been made under the influence of the anxiety which had developed. I was not anxious because I had dreamt that my mother was dying; but I interpreted the dream in that sense in my preconscious revision of it because I was already under the influence of the anxiety. The anxiety can be traced back, when repression is taken into account, to an obscure and evidently sexual craving that had found appropriate expression in the visual content of the dream.

A twenty-seven-year-old man, who had been seriously ill for a year, reported that when he was between eleven and thirteen he had repeatedly dreamt (to the accompaniment of severe anxiety) that *a man with a hatchet was pursuing him; he tried to run away, but seemed to be paralysed and could not move from the spot.* This is a good example of a very common sort of anxiety-dream, which would never be suspected of being sexual. In analysis, the dreamer first came upon a story (dating from a time later than the dream) told him by his uncle, of how he had been attacked in the street one night by a suspicious-looking individual; the dreamer himself concluded from this association that he may have heard of some similar episode at the time of the dream. In connection with the hatchet, he remembered that at about that time he had once injured his hand with a hatchet while he was chopping up wood. He then passed immediately to his relations with his younger brother. He used to ill-treat this brother and knock him down; and he particularly remembered an occasion when he had kicked him on the head with his boot and had drawn blood, and how his mother had said: 'I'm afraid he'll be the death of him one day.' While he still seemed to be occupied with the subject of violence, a recollection from his ninth year suddenly occurred to him. His parents had come home late and had gone to bed while he pretended to be asleep; soon he had heard sounds of panting and other noises which had seemed to him uncanny, and he had also been able to make out their position in the bed. Further thoughts showed that he had drawn an analogy between this relation between his parents and his own relation to his younger brother. He had subsumed what happened between his parents under the concept of violence and struggling; and he had found evidence in favour of this view in the fact that he had often noticed blood in his mother's bed.

It is, I may say, a matter of daily experience that sexual intercourse between adults strikes any children who may observe it as something uncanny and that it arouses anxiety in them. I have explained this anxiety by arguing that what we are dealing with is a sexual excitation with which their understanding is unable to cope and which they also, no doubt, repudiate because their parents are involved in it, and which is therefore transformed into anxiety. At a still earlier period of life sexual excitations directed towards a parent of the opposite sex have not yet met with repression and, as we have seen, are freely expressed. (See pp. 274 ff.)

I should have no hesitation in giving the same explanation of the attacks of night terrors accompanied by hallucinations (*pavor nocturnus*) which are so frequent in children. In this case too it can only be a question of sexual impulses which have not been understood and which have been repudiated. Investigation would probably show a periodicity in the occurrence of the attacks, since an increase in sexual libido can be brought about not only by accidental exciting impressions but also by successive waves of spontaneous developmental processes.

I lack a sufficiency of material based upon observation to enable me to confirm this explanation.[1]

Paediatricians, on the other hand, seem to lack the only line of approach which can make this whole class of phenomena intelligible, whether from the somatic or from the psychical aspect. I cannot resist quoting an amusing instance of the way in which the blinkers of medical mythology can cause an observer to miss an understanding of such cases by a narrow margin. My instance is taken from a thesis on *pavor nocturnus* by Debacker (1881, 66):

A thirteen-year-old boy in delicate health began to be apprehensive and dreamy. His sleep became disturbed and was interrupted almost once a week by severe attacks of anxiety accompanied by hallucinations. He always retained a very clear recollection of these dreams. He said that the Devil had shouted at him: 'Now we've got you, now we've got you!' There was then a smell of pitch and brimstone and his skin was burnt by flames. He woke up from the dream in terror, and at first could not cry

---

[1] [*Footnote added* 1919:] Since I wrote this a great quantity of such material has been brought forward in psycho-analytic literature.

out. When he had found his voice he was clearly heard to say: 'No, no, not me; I've not done anything!' or 'Please not! I won't do it again!' or sometimes: 'Albert never did that!' Later, he refused to undress 'because the flames only caught him when he was undressed.' While he was still having these devil-dreams, which were a threat to his health, he was sent into the country. There he recovered in the course of eighteen months, and once, when he was fifteen, he confessed: 'Je n'osais pas l'avouer, mais j'éprouvais continuellement des picotements et des surexcitations aux *parties*[1]; à la fin, cela m'énervait tant que plusieurs fois j'ai pensé me jeter par la fenêtre du dortoir.'[2]

There is really very little difficulty in inferring: (1) that the boy had masturbated when he was younger, that he had probably denied it, and that he had been threatened with severe punishment for his bad habit (cf. his admission: 'Je ne le ferais plus,' and his denial: 'Albert n'a jamais fait ça'); (2) that with the onset of puberty the temptation to masturbate had revived with the tickling in his genitals; but (3) that a struggle for repression had broken out in him, which had suppressed his libido and transformed it into anxiety, and that the anxiety had taken over the punishments with which he had been threatened earlier.

And now let us see the inferences drawn by our author (ibid., 69): 'The following conclusions can be drawn from this observation:

'(1) The influence of puberty upon a boy in delicate health can lead to a condition of great weakness and can result in a considerable degree of *cerebral anaemia*.[3]

'(2) This cerebral anaemia produces character changes, demonomanic hallucinations and very violent nocturnal (and perhaps also diurnal) anxiety-states.

'(3) The boy's demonomania and self-reproaches go back to the influences of his religious education, which affected him as a child.

'(4) All the symptoms disappeared in the course of a somewhat protracted visit to the country, as the result of physical exercise and the regaining of strength with the passage of puberty.

---

[1] I have italicized this word, but it is impossible to misunderstand it.

[2] ['I didn't dare admit it; but I was continually having prickly feelings and overexcitement in my parts; in the end it got on my nerves so much that I often thought of jumping out of the dormitory window.']

[3] The italics are mine.

'(5) A predisposing influence upon the origin of the child's brain condition may perhaps be attributed to heredity and to a past syphilitic infection in his father.'

And here is the final conclusion: 'Nous avons fait entrer cette observation dans le cadre des délires apyrétiques d'inanition, car c'est à l'ischémie cérébrale que nous rattachons cet état particulier.'[1]

(E)

THE PRIMARY AND SECONDARY PROCESSES— REPRESSION

In venturing on an attempt to penetrate more deeply into the psychology of dream-processes, I have set myself a hard task, and one to which my powers of exposition are scarcely equal. Elements in this complicated whole which are in fact simultaneous can only be represented successively in my description of them, while, in putting forward each point, I must avoid appearing to anticipate the grounds on which it is based: difficulties such as these it is beyond my strength to master. In all this I am paying the penalty for the fact that in my account of dream-psychology I have been unable to follow the historical development of my own views. Though my own line of approach to the subject of dreams was determined by my previous work on the psychology of the neuroses, I had not intended to make use of the latter as a basis of reference in the present work. Nevertheless I am constantly being driven to do so, instead of proceeding, as I should have wished, in the contrary direction and using dreams as a means of approach to the psychology of the neuroses. I am conscious of all the trouble in which my readers are thus involved, but I can see no means of avoiding it. [See p. 129 n.]

In my dissatisfaction at this state of things, I am glad to pause for a little over another consideration which seems to put a higher value on my efforts. I found myself faced by a topic on which, as has been shown in my

---

[1] ['We have classified this case among the apyretic deliria of inanition, for we attribute this particular state to cerebral ischaemia.']

first chapter, the opinions of the authorities were characterized by the sharpest contradictions. My treatment of the problems of dreams has found room for the majority of these contradictory views. I have only found it necessary to give a categorical denial of two of them—the view that dreaming is a meaningless process [pp. 83 ff.] and the view that it is a somatic one [pp. 104 f.]. Apart from this, I have been able to find a justification for all these mutually contradictory opinions at one point or other of my complicated thesis and to show that they had lighted upon some portion of the truth.

The view that dreams carry on the occupations and interests of waking life [pp. 41 f.] has been entirely confirmed by the discovery of the concealed *dream-thoughts*. These are only concerned with what seems important to us and interests us greatly. Dreams are never occupied with minor details. But we have also found reason for accepting the contrary view, that dreams pick up indifferent refuse left over from the previous day [pp. 51 ff.] and that they cannot get control of any major daytime interest until it has been to some extent withdrawn from waking activity [p. 51]. We have found that this holds good of the dream's *content*, which gives expression to the dream-thoughts in a form modified by distortion. For reasons connected with the mechanism of association, as we have seen, the dream-process finds it easier to get control of recent or indifferent ideational material which has not yet been requisitioned by waking thought-activity; and for reasons of censorship it transfers psychical intensity from what is important but objectionable on to what is indifferent.

The fact that dreams are hypermnesic [pp. 44 ff.] and have access to material from childhood [pp. 48 ff.] has become one of the cornerstones of our teaching. Our theory of dreams regards wishes originating in infancy as the indispensable motive force for the formation of dreams.

It has naturally not occurred to us to throw any doubt on the significance, which has been experimentally demonstrated, of external sensory stimuli during sleep [pp. 55 ff.]; but we have shown that such material stands in the same relation to the dream-wish as do the residues of thought left over from daytime activity. Nor have we seen any reason to dispute the view that dreams interpret objective sensory stimuli just as illusions do [pp. 60 f.]; but we have found the motive which provides the reason for that interpretation, a reason which has been left unspecified by other writers. Interpretation is carried out in such a way that the object perceived shall not interrupt sleep and shall be usable for purposes of wish-fulfilment. As regards subjective states of excitation in the sense organs during sleep, the occurrence of which seems to have been proved by Trumbull Ladd [1892; see above, pp. 64 f.], it is true that we have not accepted them as a particular source of dreams; but we have been able to explain them as resulting from the regressive revival of memories that are in operation behind the dream.

Internal organic sensations, which have commonly been taken as a cardinal point in explanations of dreaming [pp. 65 ff.], have retained a place, though a humbler one, in our theory. Such sensations—sensations of falling, for instance, or floating, or being inhibited—provide a material which is accessible at any time and of which the dream-work makes use, whenever it has need of it, for expressing the dream-thoughts.

The view that the dream-process is a rapid or instantaneous one [p. 92 f.] is in our opinion correct as regards the perception by consciousness of the preconstructed dream-content; it seems probable that the preceding portions of the dream-process run a slow and fluctuating course. We have been able to contribute towards the solution of the riddle of dreams which contain a great amount of material compressed into the briefest moment of time; we have suggested that it is a question in such cases of getting hold of ready-made structures already present in the mind.

The fact that dreams are distorted and mutilated by memory [pp. 76 f.] is accepted by us but in our opinion constitutes no obstacle; for it is no more than the last and manifest portion of a distorting activity which has been in operation from the very start of the dream's formation.

As regards the embittered and apparently irreconcilable dispute as to whether the mind sleeps at night [p. 83 f.] or is as much in command of all its faculties as it is by day [pp. 89 f.], we have found that both parties are right but that neither is wholly right. We have found evidence in the dream-thoughts of a highly complex intellectual function, operating with almost the whole resources of the mental apparatus. Nevertheless it cannot be disputed that these dream-thoughts originated during the day, and it is imperative to assume that there is such a thing as a sleeping state of the mind. Thus even the theory of partial sleep [p. 103 f.] has shown its value, though we have found that what characterizes the state of sleep is not the disintegration of mental bonds but the concentration of the psychical system which is in command during the day upon the wish to sleep. The factor of withdrawal from the external world [pp. 41 f.] retains its significance in our scheme; it helps, though not as the sole determinant, to make possible the regressive character of representation in dreams. The renunciation of voluntary direction of the flow of ideas [pp. 78 f.] cannot be disputed;

but this does not deprive mental life of all purpose, for we have seen how, after voluntary purposive ideas have been abandoned, involuntary ones assume command. We have not merely accepted the fact of the looseness of associative connections in dreams [p. 87], but we have shown that it extends far further than had been suspected; we have found, however, that these loose connections are merely obligatory substitutes for others which are valid and significant. It is quite true that we have described dreams as absurd; but examples have taught us how sensible a dream can be even when it appears to be absurd.

We have no difference of opinion over the functions that are to be assigned to dreams. The view that dreams act as a safety-valve to the mind [p. 105 f.] and that, in the words of Robert [1886, 10 f.], all kinds of harmful things are made harmless by being presented in a dream—not only does this view coincide exactly with our theory of the double wish-fulfilment brought about by dreams, but the way in which it is phrased is more intelligible to us than to Robert himself. The view that the mind has free play in its functioning in dreams [p. 109] is represented in our theory by the fact of the preconscious activity allowing dreams to take their course. Such phrases as 'the return of the mind in dreams to an embryonic point of view' or the words used by Havelock Ellis [1899, 721] to describe dreams—'an archaic world of vast emotions and imperfect thoughts' [p. 88]—strike us as happy anticipations of our own assertions that primitive modes of activity which are suppressed during the day are concerned in the construction of dreams. We have been able to accept entirely as our own what Sully [1893, 362] has written: 'Our dreams are a means of conserving these [earlier] successive personalities. When asleep we go back to the old ways of looking at things and of feeling about them, to impulses and activities which long ago dominated us' [p. 89].[1] For us no less than for Delage [1891] what has been 'suppressed' [p. 107 f.] has become 'the motive force of dreams.'

We have fully appreciated the importance of the part ascribed by Scherner [1861] to 'dream-imagination,' as well as Scherner's own interpretations [pp. 109 ff.], but we have been obliged to transport them, as it were, to a different position in the problem. The point is not that dreams create the imagination, but rather that the unconscious activity of the imagination has a large share in the construction of the dream-thoughts.

---

[1] [This sentence was added in 1914.]

We remain in Schemer's debt for having indicated the source of the dream-thoughts; but nearly everything that he ascribes to the dream-work is really attributable to the activity of the unconscious during daytime, which is the instigating agent of dreams no less than of neurotic symptoms. We have been obliged to distinguish the 'dream-work' as something quite different and with a much narrower connotation.

Finally, we have by no means abandoned the relation between dreams and mental disorders [pp. 114 ff.], but have established it more firmly on fresh ground.

We have thus been able to find a place in our structure for the most various and contradictory findings of earlier writers, thanks to the novelty of our theory of dreams, which combines them, as it were, into a higher unity. Some of those findings we have put to other uses, but we have wholly rejected only a few. Nevertheless our edifice is still uncompleted. Apart from the many perplexing questions in which we have become involved in making our way into the obscurities of psychology, we seem to be troubled by a fresh contradiction. On the one hand we have supposed that the dream-thoughts arise through entirely normal mental activity; but on the other hand we have discovered a number of quite abnormal processes of thought among the dream-thoughts, which extend into the dream-content, and which we then repeat in the course of our dream-interpretation. Everything that we have described as the 'dream-work' seems to depart so widely from what we recognize as rational thought-processes that the most severe strictures passed by earlier writers on the low level of psychical functioning in dreams must appear fully justified.

It may be that we shall only find enlightenment and assistance in this difficulty by carrying our investigation still further. And I will begin by picking out for closer examination one of the conjunctures which may lead to the formation of a dream.

A dream, as we have discovered, takes the place of a number of thoughts which are derived from our daily life and which form a completely logical sequence. We cannot doubt, then, that these thoughts originate from our normal mental life. All the attributes which we value highly in our train of thought, and which characterize them as complex achievements of a high order, are to be found once more in dream-thoughts. There is no need to assume, however, that this activity of thought is performed during sleep— a possibility which would gravely confuse what has hitherto been our settled picture of the psychical state of sleep. On the contrary, these thoughts may very well have originated from the previous day, they may have proceeded unobserved by our consciousness from their start, and may already have been completed at the onset of sleep. The most that we can conclude from this is that it proves that *the most complicated achievements of thought are possible without the assistance of consciousness*—a fact which we could not fail to learn in any case from every psycho-analysis of a patient suffering from hysteria or from obsessional ideas. These dream-thoughts are certainly not in themselves inadmissible to consciousness; there may have been a number of reasons for their not having become conscious to us during the day. Becoming conscious is connected with the application of a particular psychical function [p. 542], that of attention—a function which, as it seems, is only available in a specific quantity, and this may have been diverted from the train of thought in question on to some other purpose.[1] There is another way, too, in which trains of thought of this kind may be withheld from consciousness. The course of our conscious reflections shows us that we follow a particular path in our application of attention. If, as we follow this path, we come upon an idea which will not bear criticism, we break off: we drop the cathexis of attention. Now it seems that the train of thought which has thus been initiated and dropped can continue to spin itself out without attention being turned to it again, unless at some point or other it reaches a specially high degree of intensity which forces attention to it. Thus, if a train of thought is initially rejected (consciously, perhaps) by a judgement that it is wrong or that it is useless for the immediate intellectual purposes in view, the result may be that this train of thought will proceed, unobserved by consciousness, until the onset of sleep.

To sum up—we describe a train of thought such as this as 'preconscious'; we regard it as completely rational and believe that it may either have been simply neglected or broken off and suppressed. Let us add a frank account of how we picture the occurrence of a train of ideas. We believe that, starting from a purposive idea, a given amount of excitation, which we term 'cathectic energy,' is displaced along the associative paths selected by that purposive idea. A train of thought which is 'neglected' is one which has *not received* this cathexis; a train of thought which is 'suppressed' or 'repudiated' is one from which this cathexis has been *with-*

---

[1] [The concept of 'attention' plays a very small part in Freud's later writings. It figures prominently, on the other hand, in his 'Project for a Scientific Psychology' (Freud, 1950*a*), e.g. in the opening section of Part III. Cf. also pp. 573 f. and 608.]

drawn. In both cases they are left to their own excitations. Under certain conditions a train of thought with a purposive cathexis is capable of attracting the attention of consciousness to itself and in that event, through the agency of consciousness, receives a 'hyper-cathexis.' We shall be obliged presently to explain our view of the nature and function of consciousness. [See pp. 610 ff.]

A train of thought that has been set going like this in the preconscious may either cease spontaneously or persist. We picture the first of these outcomes as implying that the energy attaching to the train of thought is diffused along all the associative paths that radiate from it; this energy sets the whole network of thoughts in a state of excitation which lasts for a certain time and then dies away as the excitation in search of discharge becomes transformed into a quiescent cathexis. If this first outcome supervenes, the process is of no further significance so far as dream-formation is concerned. Lurking in our preconscious, however, there are other purposive ideas, which are derived from sources in our unconscious and from wishes which are always on the alert. These may take control of the excitation attaching to the group of thoughts which has been left to its own devices, they may establish a connection between it and an unconscious wish, and they may 'transfer' to it the energy belonging to the unconscious wish. Thenceforward the neglected or suppressed train of thought is in a position to persist, though the reinforcement it has received gives it no right of entry into consciousness. We may express this by saying that what has hitherto been a preconscious train of thought has now been 'drawn into the unconscious.'

There are other conjunctures which may lead to the formation of a dream. The preconscious train of thought may have been linked to the unconscious wish from the first and may for that reason have been repudiated by the dominant purposive cathexis; or an unconscious wish may become active for other reasons (from somatic causes, perhaps) and may seek to effect a transference on to the psychical residues that are uncathected by the *Pcs.* without their coming halfway to meet it. But all three cases have the same final outcome: a train of thought comes into being in the preconscious which is without a preconscious cathexis but has received a cathexis from an unconscious wish.

From this point onwards the train of thought undergoes a series of transformations which we can no longer recognize as normal psychical processes and which lead to a result that bewilders us—a psychopathological structure. I will enumerate these processes and classify them.

(1) The intensities of the individual ideas become capable of discharge *en bloc* and pass over from one idea to another, so that certain ideas are formed which are endowed with great intensity. [Cf. pp. 345 f.] And since this process is repeated several times, the intensity of a whole train of thought may eventually be concentrated in a single ideational element. Here we have the fact of 'compression' or 'condensation,' which has become familiar in the dream-work. It is this that is mainly responsible for the bewildering impression made on us by dreams, for nothing at all analogous to it is known to us in mental life that is normal and accessible to consciousness. In normal mental life, too, we find ideas which, being the nodal points or end-results of whole chains of thought, possess a high degree of psychical significance; but their significance is not expressed by any feature that is obvious in a *sensory* manner to internal perception; their perceptual presentation is not in any respect more intense on account of their psychical significance. In the process of condensation, on the other hand, every psychical interconnection is transformed into an *intensification* of its ideational content. The case is the same as when, in preparing a book for the press, I have some word which is of special importance for understanding the text printed in spaced or heavy type; or in speech I should pronounce the same word loudly and slowly and with special emphasis. The first of these two analogies reminds us at once of an example provided by the dream-work itself: the word '*trimethylamin*' in the dream of Irma's injection [p. 132]. Art historians have drawn our attention to the fact that the earliest historical sculptures obey a similar principle: they express the rank of the persons represented by their size. A king is represented twice or three times as large as his attendants or as his defeated enemies. A sculpture of Roman date would make use of subtler means for producing the same result. The figure of the Emperor would be placed in the middle, standing erect, and would be modelled with especial care, while his enemies would be prostrate at his feet; but he would no longer be a giant among dwarfs. The bows with which inferiors greet their superiors among ourselves today are an echo of the same ancient principle of representation.

The direction in which condensations in dreams proceed is determined on the one hand by the rational preconscious relations of the dream-thoughts, and on the other by the attraction exercised by visual memories in the unconscious. The outcome of the activity of condensation is the achievement of the intensities required for forcing a way through into the perceptual systems.

(2) Owing, once more, to the freedom with which the intensities can be transferred, 'intermediate ideas,' resembling compromises, are constructed under the sway of condensation. (Cf. the numerous instances I have given of this [e.g. pp. 310 ff.].) This is again something unheard-of in normal chains of ideas, where the main stress is laid on the selection and retention of the 'right' ideational element. On the other hand, composite structures and compromises occur with remarkable frequency when we try to express preconscious thoughts in speech. They are then regarded as species of 'slips of the tongue.'

(3) The ideas which transfer their intensities to each other stand in the loosest mutual relations. They are linked by associations of a kind that is scorned by our normal thinking and relegated to the use of jokes. In particular, we find associations based on homonyms and verbal similarities treated as equal in value to the rest.

(4) Thoughts which are mutually contradictory make no attempt to do away with each other, but persist side by side. They often combine to form condensations, just as though there were no contradiction between them, or arrive at compromises such as our conscious thoughts would never tolerate but such as are often admitted in our actions.

These are some of the most striking of the abnormal processes to which the dream-thoughts, previously constructed on rational lines, are subjected in the course of the dream-work. It will be seen that the chief characteristic of these processes is that the whole stress is laid upon making the cathecting energy mobile and capable of discharge; the content and the proper meaning of the psychical elements to which the cathexes are attached are treated as of little consequence. It might have been supposed that condensation and the formation of compromises is only carried out for the sake of facilitating regression, that is, when it is a question of tranforming thoughts into images. But the analysis—and still more the synthesis—of dreams which include no such regression to images, e.g. the dream of 'Autodidasker' [pp. 316 ff.], exhibits the same processes of displacement and condensation as the rest.

Thus we are driven to conclude that two fundamentally different kinds of psychical process are concerned in the formation of dreams. One of these produces perfectly rational dream-thoughts, of no less validity than normal thinking; while the other treats these thoughts in a manner which is in the highest degree bewildering and irrational. We have already in Chapter VI segregated this second psychical process as being the dream-work proper. What light have we now to throw upon its origin?

It would not be possible for us to answer this question if we had not made some headway in the study of the psychology of the neuroses, and particularly of hysteria. We have found from this that the same irrational psychical processes, and others that we have not specified, dominate the production of hysterical symptoms. In hysteria, too, we come across a series of perfectly rational thoughts, equal in validity to our conscious thoughts; but to begin with we know nothing of their existence in this form and we can only reconstruct them subsequently. If they force themselves upon our notice at any point, we discover by analysing the symptom which has been produced that these normal thoughts have been submitted to abnormal treatment: *they have been transformed into the symptom by means of condensation and the formation of compromises, by way of superficial associations and in disregard of contradictions, and also, it may be, along the path of regression.* In view of the complete identity between the characteristic features of the dream-work and those of the psychical activity which issues in psychoneurotic symptoms, we feel justified in carrying over to dreams the conclusions we have been led to by hysteria.

We accordingly borrow the following thesis from the theory of hysteria: *a normal train of thought is only submitted to abnormal psychical treatment of the sort we have been describing if an unconscious wish, derived from infancy and in a state of repression, has been transferred on to it.* In accordance with this thesis we have constructed our theory of dreams on the assumption that the dream-wish which provides the motive power invariably originates from the unconscious—an assumption which, as I myself am ready to admit, cannot be proved to hold generally, though neither can it be disproved. But in order to explain what is meant by 'repression,' a term with which we have already made play so many times, it is necessary to proceed a stage further with our psychological scaffolding.

We have already [pp. 564 ff.] explored the fiction of a primitive psychical apparatus whose activities are regulated by an effort to avoid an accumulation of excitation and to maintain itself so far as possible without excitation. For that reason it is built upon the plan of a reflex apparatus. The power of movement, which is in the first instance a means of bringing about internal alterations in its body, is at its disposal as the path to discharge. We went on to discuss the psychical consequences of an 'experience of satisfaction'; and in that connection we were already able to add a second hypothesis, to the effect that the accumulation of excitation (brought about in various ways that need not concern us) is felt as unpleasure and that it sets the apparatus in action with a view to repeating the experience of satisfaction, which involved a diminution of excitation and was felt as pleasure. A current of this kind in the apparatus, starting from unpleasure and aiming at pleasure, we have termed a 'wish'; and we have asserted that only a wish is able to set the apparatus in motion and that the course of the excitation in it is automatically regulated by feelings of pleasure and unpleasure. The first wishing seems to have been a hallucinatory cathecting of the memory of satisfaction. Such hallucinations, however, if they were not to be maintained to the point of exhaustion, proved to be inadequate to bring about the cessation of the need or, accordingly, the pleasure attaching to satisfaction.

A second activity—or, as we put it, the activity of a second system—became necessary, which would not allow the mnemic cathexis to proceed as far as perception and from there to bind the psychical forces; instead, it diverted the excitation arising from the need along a roundabout path which ultimately, by means of voluntary movement, altered the external world in such a way that it became possible to arrive at a real perception of the object of satisfaction. We have already outlined our schematic picture of the psychical apparatus up to this point; the two systems are the germ of what, in the fully developed apparatus, we have described as the *Ucs.* and *Pcs.*

In order to be able to employ the power of movement to make alterations in the external world that shall be effective, it is necessary to accumulate a great number of experiences in the mnemic systems and a multiplicity of permanent records of the associations called up in this mnemic material by different purposive ideas. [Cf. p. 541.] We can now carry our hypotheses a step further. The activity of this second system, constantly feeling its way, and alternately sending out and withdrawing cathexes, needs on the one hand to have the whole of the material of memory freely at its command; but on the other hand it would be an unnecessary expenditure of energy if it sent out large quantities of cathexis along the various paths of thought and thus caused them to dream away to no useful purpose and diminish the quantity available for altering the external world. I therefore postulate that for the sake of efficiency the second system succeeds in retaining the major part of its cathexes of energy in a state of quiescence and in employing only a small part on displacement. The mechanics of these processes are quite unknown to me; anyone who wished to take these ideas seriously would have to look for physical analogies to them and find a means of picturing the movements that accompany excitation of neurones. All that I insist upon is the idea that the activity of the *first ψ-system* is directed towards securing the *free discharge* of the quantities of excitation, while the *second* system, by means of the cathexes emanating from it, succeeds in *inhibiting* this discharge and in transforming the cathexis into a quiescent one, no doubt with a simultaneous raising of its potential. I presume, therefore, that under the dominion of the second system the discharge of excitation is governed by quite different mechanical conditions from those in force under the dominion of the first system. When once the second system has concluded its exploratory thought-activity, it releases the inhibition and damming-up of the excitations and allows them to discharge themselves in movement.

Some interesting reflections follow if we consider the relations between this inhibition upon discharge exercised by the second system and the regulation effected by the unpleasure principle.[1] Let us examine the antithesis to the primary experience of satisfaction—namely, the experience of an external fright. Let us suppose that the primitive apparatus is impinged upon by a perceptual stimulus which is a source of painful excitation. Unco-ordinated motor manifestations will follow until one of them withdraws the apparatus from the perception and at the same time from the pain. If the perception re-appears, the movement will at once be repeated (a movement of flight, it may be) till the perception has disappeared once more. In this case, no inclination will remain to recathect the perception of the source of pain, either hallucinatorily or in any other way. On the contrary, there will be an inclination in the primitive apparatus to drop the distressing memory-picture immediately, if anything happens to revive it, for the very reason that if its excitation were to overflow into perception it would provoke unpleasure (or, more precisely, would *begin* to provoke it). The avoidance of the memory, which is no more than a repetition of the previous flight from the perception, is also facilitated by the fact that the memory, unlike the perception, does not possess enough quality to excite consciousness and thus to attract fresh cathexis to itself. This effortless and regular avoidance by the psychical process of the memory of anything that had once been distressing affords us the prototype and first example of *psychical repression*. It is a familiar fact that much of this avoidance of what is distressing—this ostrich policy—is still to be seen in the normal mental life of adults.

---

[1] [In his later works Freud speaks of it as the 'pleasure principle.']

As a result of the unpleasure principle, then, the first ψ-system is totally incapable of bringing anything disagreeable into the context of its thought. It is unable to do anything but wish. If things remained at that point, the thought-activity of the second system would be obstructed, since it requires free access to *all* the memories laid down by experience. Two possibilities now present themselves. Either the activity of the second system might set itself entirely free from the unpleasure principle and proceed without troubling about the unpleasure of memories; or it might find a method of cathecting unpleasurable memories which would enable it to avoid releasing the unpleasure. We may dismiss the first of these possibilities, for the unpleasure principle clearly regulates the course of excitation in the second system as much as in the first. We are consequently left with the remaining possibility that the second system cathects memories in such a way that there is an inhibition of their discharge, including, therefore, an inhibition of discharge (comparable to that of a motor innervation) in the direction of the development of unpleasure. We have therefore been led from two directions to the hypothesis that cathexis by the second system implies a simultaneous inhibition of the discharge of excitations: we have been led to it by regard for the unpleasure principle and also [as was shown in the last paragraph but one] by the principle of the least expenditure of innervation. Let us bear this firmly in mind, for it is the key to the whole theory of repression: *the second system can only cathect an idea if it is in a position to inhibit any development of unpleasure that may proceed from it.* Anything that could evade that inhibition would be inaccessible to the second system as well as to the first; for it would promptly be dropped in obedience to the unpleasure principle. The inhibition of unpleasure need not, however, be a complete one: a beginning of it must be allowed, since that is what informs the second system of the nature of the memory concerned and of its possible unsuitability for the purpose which the thought-process has in view.

I propose to describe the psychical process of which the first system alone admits the 'primary process,' and the process which results from the inhibition imposed by the second system as the 'secondary process.'[1]

---

[1] [The distinction between the primary and secondary systems, and the hypothesis that psychical functioning operates differently in them, are among the most fundamental of Freud's concepts. They are associated with the theory (indicated on pp. 595 f. and at the opening of the next Section) that psychical energy occurs in two forms: 'free' or 'mobile' (as it occurs in the system *Ucs.*) and 'bound' or 'quiescent' (as it occurs in the system *Pcs.*). Where Freud discusses this subject

There is yet another reason for which, as I can show, the second system is obliged to correct the primary process. The primary process endeavours to bring about a discharge of excitation in order that, with the help of the amount of excitation thus accumulated, it may establish a 'perceptual identity' [with the experience of satisfaction (see pp. 564–5)]. The secondary process, however, has abandoned this intention and taken on another in its place—the establishment of a *'thought* identity' [with that experience]. All thinking is no more than a circuitous path from the memory of a satisfaction (a memory which has been adopted as a purposive idea) to an identical cathexis of the same memory which it is hoped to attain once more through an intermediate stage of motor experiences. Thinking must concern itself with the connecting paths between ideas, without being led astray by the *intensities* of those ideas. But it is obvious that condensations of ideas, as well as intermediate and compromise structures, must obstruct the attainment of the identity aimed at. Since they substitute one idea for another, they cause a deviation from the path which would have led on from the first idea. Processes of this kind are therefore scrupulously avoided in secondary thinking. It is easy to see, too, that the unpleasure principle, which in other respects supplies the thought-process with its most important signposts, puts difficulties in its path towards establishing 'thought identity.' Accordingly, thinking must aim at freeing itself more and more from exclusive regulation by the unpleasure principle and at restricting the development of affect in thought-activity to the minimum required for acting as a signal.[1] The achievement

---

in his later writings (e.g. in his paper on 'The Unconscious,' 1915*e*, end of Section V, and in *Beyond the Pleasure Principle,* 1920*g*, Chapter IV) he attributes this latter distinction to some statement of Breuer's in their joint *Studies on Hysteria* (1895). There is some difficulty in identifying any such statement in Brevier's contribution to that work (Chapter III). The nearest approach to it is a footnote near the beginning of Section 2, in which Breuer distinguishes *three* forms of nervous energy: 'a potential energy which rests in the chemical substance of the cell,' 'a kinetic energy which is discharged when the fibres are in a state of excitation' and 'yet another quiescent state of nervous excitation: tonic excitation or nervous tension.' On the other hand, the question of 'bound' energy is discussed at some length towards the end of the first section of Part III of Freud's 'Project' (1950*a*), written only a few months after the publication of the *Studies on Hysteria*.]

[1] [This idea of a small amount of unpleasure acting as a 'signal' to prevent the occurrence of a much larger amount was taken up by Freud many years later and applied to the problem of anxiety. See Freud, 1926*d*, Chapter XI, Section A(*b*).]

of this greater delicacy in functioning is aimed at by means of a further hypercathexis, brought about by consciousness. [See below, pp. 610 ff.] As we well know, however, that aim is seldom attained completely, even in normal mental life, and our thinking always remains exposed to falsification by interference from the unpleasure principle.

This, however, is not the gap in the functional efficiency of our mental apparatus which makes it possible for thoughts, which represent themselves as products of the secondary thought-activity, to become subject to the primary psychical process—for such is the formula in which we can now describe the activity which leads to dreams and to hysterical symptoms. Inefficiency arises from the convergence of two factors derived from our developmental history. One of these factors devolves entirely upon the mental apparatus and has had a decisive influence on the relation between the two systems, while the other makes itself felt to a variable degree and introduces instinctual forces of organic origin into mental life. Both of them originate in childhood and are a precipitate of the modifications undergone by our mental and somatic organism since our infancy.

When I described one of the psychical processes occurring in the mental apparatus as the 'primary' one, what I had in mind was not merely considerations of relative importance and efficiency; I intended also to choose a name which would give an indication of its chronological priority. It is true that, so far as we know, no psychical apparatus exists which possesses a primary process only and that such an apparatus is to that extent a theoretical fiction. But this much is a fact: the primary processes are present in the mental apparatus from the first, while it is only during the course of life that the secondary processes unfold, and come to inhibit and overlay the primary ones; it may even be that their complete domination is not attained until the prime of life. In consequence of the belated appearance of the secondary processes, the core of our being, consisting of unconscious wishful impulses, remains inaccessible to the understanding and inhibition of the preconscious; the part played by the latter is restricted once and for all to directing along the most expedient paths the wishful impulses that arise from the unconscious. These unconscious wishes exercise a compelling force upon all later mental trends, a force which those trends are obliged to fall in with or which they may perhaps endeavour to divert and direct to higher aims. A further result of the belated appearance of the secondary process is that a wide sphere of mnemic material is inaccessible to preconscious cathexis.

Among these wishful impulses derived from infancy, which can neither be destroyed nor inhibited, there are some whose fulfilment would be a contradiction of the purposive ideas of secondary thinking. The fulfilment of these wishes would no longer generate an affect of pleasure but of unpleasure; and *it is precisely this transformation of affect which constitutes the essence of what we term 'repression.'* The problem of repression lies in the question of how it is and owing to what motive forces that this transformation occurs; but it is a problem that we need only touch upon here.[1] It is enough for us to be clear that a transformation of this kind does occur in the course of development—we have only to recall the way in which disgust emerges in childhood after having been absent to begin with—and that it is related to the activity of the secondary system. The memories on the basis of which the unconscious wish brings about the release of affect were never accessible to the *Pcs.*, and consequently the release of the affect attaching to those memories cannot be inhibited either. It is for the very reason of this generation of affect that these ideas are now inaccessible even by way of the preconscious thoughts on to which they have transferred their wishful force. On the contrary, the unpleasure principle takes control and causes the *Pcs.* to turn away from the transference thought. They are left to themselves—'repressed'—and thus it is that the presence of a store of infantile memories, which has from the first been held back from the *Pcs.*, becomes a *sine qua non* of repression.

In the most favourable cases the generation of unpleasure ceases along with the withdrawal of cathexis from the transference thoughts in the *Pcs.;* and this outcome signifies that the intervention of the unpleasure principle has served a useful purpose. But it is another matter when the repressed unconscious wish receives an organic reinforcement, which it passes on to its transference thoughts; in that way it may place them in a position to make an attempt at forcing their way through with their excitation, even if they have lost their cathexis from the *Pcs.* There then follows a defensive struggle—for the *Pcs.* in turn reinforces its opposition to the repressed thoughts (i.e. produces an 'anticathexis')—and thereafter the transference thoughts, which are the vehicles of the unconscious wish, force their way through in some form of compromise which is reached by the production of a symptom. But from the moment at which the repressed thoughts are

---

[1] [The subject was afterwards dealt with by Freud at much greater length in his paper on 'Repression' (1915*d*); his later views on the subject are given in Lecture XXXII of his *New Introductory Lectures* (1933*a*).]

strongly cathected by the unconscious wishful impulse and, on the other hand, abandoned by the preconscious cathexis, they become subject to the primary psychical process and their one aim is motor discharge or, if the path is open, hallucinatory revival of the desired perceptual identity. We have already found empirically that the irrational processes we have described are only carried out with thoughts that are under repression. We can now see our way a little further into the whole position. The irrational processes which occur in the psychical apparatus are the *primary* ones. They appear wherever ideas are abandoned by the preconscious cathexis, are left to themselves and can become charged with the uninhibited energy from the unconscious which is striving to find an outlet. Some other observations lend support to the view that these processes which are described as irrational are not in fact falsifications of normal processes—intellectual errors—but are modes of activity of the psychical apparatus that have been freed from an inhibition. Thus we find that the transition from preconscious excitation to movement is governed by the same processes, and that the linking of preconscious ideas to words may easily exhibit the same displacements and confusions, which are then attributed to inattention. Evidence, finally, of the increase in activity which becomes necessary when these primary modes of functioning are inhibited is to be found in the fact that we produce a *comic* effect, that is, a surplus of energy which has to be discharged in *laughter, if we allow these modes of thinking to force their way through into consciousness.*[1]

The theory of the psychoneuroses asserts as an indisputable and invariable fact that only sexual wishful impulses from infancy, which have undergone repression (i.e. a transformation of their affect) during the developmental period of childhood, are capable of being revived during *later* developmental periods (whether as a result of the subject's sexual constitution, which is derived from an initial bisexuality, or as a result of unfavourable influences acting upon the course of his sexual life) and are thus able to furnish the motive force for the formation of psychoneurotic symptoms of every kind.[2] It is only by reference to these sexual forces that we can close the gaps that are still patent in the theory of repression. I will

---

[1] [This topic was dealt with by Freud at greater length in Chapter V of his book on jokes (1905*c*). The question of intellectual errors was discussed more fully in the closing pages of the 'Project' (1950*a*).]

[2] The theme of this sentence was elaborated by Freud in his *Three Essays on the Theory of Sexuality* (1905*d*).]

leave it an open question whether these sexual and infantile factors are equally required in the theory of dreams : I will leave that theory incomplete at this point, since I have already gone a step beyond what can be demonstrated in assuming that dream-wishes are invariably derived from the unconscious.[1] Nor do I propose to enquire further into the nature of the distinction between the play of psychical forces in the formation of dreams and in that of hysterical symptoms: we are still without a sufficiently accurate knowledge of one of the two objects of the comparison.

There is, however, another point to which I attach importance; and I must confess that it is solely on its account that I have embarked here

---

[1] Here and elsewhere I have intentionally left gaps in the treatment of my theme because to fill them would on the one hand require too great an effort and on the other would involve my basing myself on material that is alien to the subject of dreams. For instance, I have omitted to state whether I attribute different meanings to the words 'suppressed' and 'repressed.' It should have been clear, however, that the latter lays more stress than the former upon the fact of attachment to the unconscious. Nor have I entered into the obvious problem of why the dream-thoughts are subjected to distortion by the censorship even in cases where they have abandoned the progressive path towards consciousness and have chosen the regressive one. And there are many similar omissions. What I was above all anxious to do was to create an impression of the problems to which a further analysis of the dream-work must lead and to give a hint of the other topics with which that further analysis would come into contact. It has not always been easy for me to decide the point at which to break off my pursuit of this line of exposition.—There are special reasons, which may not be what my readers expect, why I have not given any exhaustive treatment to the part played in dreams by the world of sexual ideas and why I have avoided analysing dreams of obviously sexual content. Nothing could be further from my own views or from the theoretical opinions which I hold in neuropathology than to regard sexual life as something shameful, with which neither a physician nor a scientific research worker has any concern. Moreover, the moral indignation by which the translator of the *Oneirocritica* of Artemidorus of Daldis allowed himself to be led into withholding the chapter on sexual dreams from the knowledge of his readers strikes me as laughable. What governed my decision was simply my seeing that an explanation of sexual dreams would involve me deeply in the still unsolved problems of perversion and bisexuality; and I accordingly reserved this material for another occasion. [It should perhaps be added that the translator of *Oneirocritica*, F. S. Krauss, himself subsequently published the omitted chapter in his periodical *Anthropophyteia*, from which Freud has quoted above (p. 368 *n.*) and of which he speaks so highly elsewhere (1910*f* and 1913*k*).]

upon all these discussions of the two psychical systems and their modes of activity and of repression. It is not now a question of whether I have formed an approximately correct opinion of the psychological factors with which we are concerned, or whether, which is quite possible in such difficult matters, my picture of them is distorted and incomplete. However many changes may be made in our reading of the psychical censorship and of the rational and abnormal revisions made of the dream-content, it remains true that processes of this sort are at work in the formation of dreams and that they show the closest analogy in their essentials to the processes observable in the formation of hysterical symptoms. A dream, however, is no pathological phenomenon; it presupposes no disturbance of psychical equilibrium; it leaves behind it no loss of efficiency. The suggestion may be made that no conclusions as to the dreams of normal people can be drawn from my dreams or those of my patients; but this, I think, is an objection which can be safely disregarded. If, then, we may argue back from the phenomena to their motive forces, we must recognize that the psychical mechanism employed by neuroses is not created by the impact of a pathological disturbance upon the mind but is present already in the normal structure of the mental apparatus. The two psychical systems, the censorship upon the passage from one of them to the other, the inhibition and overlaying of one activity by the other, the relations of both of them to consciousness—or whatever more correct interpretations of the observed facts may take their place—all of these form part of the normal structure of our mental instrument, and dreams show us one of the paths leading to an understanding of its structure. If we restrict ourselves to the minimum of new knowledge which has been established with certainty, we can still say this of dreams: they have proved that *what is suppressed continues to exist in normal people as well as abnormal, arid remains capable of psychical functioning.* Dreams themselves are among the manifestations of this suppressed material; this is so theoretically in every case, and it can be observed empirically in a great number of cases at least, and precisely in cases which exhibit most clearly the striking peculiarities of dream-life. In waking life the suppressed material in the mind is prevented from finding expression and is cut off from internal perception owing to the fact that the contradictions present in it are eliminated—one side being disposed of in favour of the other; but during the night, under the sway of an impetus towards the construction of compromises, this suppressed material finds methods and means of forcing its way into consciousness.

Flectere si nequeo superos, Acheronta movebo.[1]

The interpretation of dreams is the royal road to a knowledge of the unconscious activities of the mind.

By analysing dreams we can take a step forward in our understanding of the composition of that most marvellous and most mysterious of all instruments. Only a small step, no doubt; but a beginning. And this beginning will enable us to proceed further with its analysis, on the basis of other structures which must be termed pathological. For illnesses—those, at least, which are rightly named 'functional'—do not presuppose the disintegration of the apparatus or the production of fresh splits in its interior. They are to be explained on a *dynamic* basis—by the strengthening and weakening of the various components in the interplay of forces, so many of whose effects are hidden from view while functions are normal. I hope to be able to show elsewhere how the compounding of the apparatus out of two agencies makes it possible for the normal mind too to function with greater delicacy than would be possible with only one of them.[2]

---

[1] ['If I cannot bend the Higher Powers, I will move the Infernal Regions.' Freud remarks in a note in *Ges. Schr.,* **3** (1925), 169, that this line of Virgil [*Aeneid,* VII, 312] is intended to picture the efforts of the repressed instinctual impulses.' He has used the same line as the motto for the whole volume. In a letter to Fliess of December 4, 1896 (Freud, 1950*a,* Letter 51) he proposed using it as a motto for a chapter on 'Symptom Formation' in some projected but unrealized work.—The next sentence was added in 1909. It was included in the same year in the third of his lectures at Clark University (Freud, 1910*a*).]

[2] Dreams are not the only phenomena which allow us to find a basis for psychopathology in psychology. In a short series of papers (1898*b* and 1899*a*) which is not yet completed, I have attempted to interpret a number of phenomena of daily life as evidence in favour of the same conclusions. [*Added* 1909:] These, together with some further papers on forgetting, slips of the tongue, bungled actions, etc., have since been collected under the title of *The Psychopathology of Everyday Life* (Freud, 1901*b*).

(F)

THE UNCONSCIOUS AND CONSCIOUSNESS—
REALITY

It will be seen on closer consideration that what the psychological discussion in the preceding sections invites us to assume is not the existence of two *systems* near the motor end of the apparatus but the existence of two kinds of *processes of excitation* or *modes of its discharge*. It is all one to us, for we must always be prepared to drop our conceptual scaffolding if we feel that we are in a position to replace it by something that approximates more closely to the unknown reality. So let us try to correct some conceptions which might be misleading so long as we looked upon the two systems in the most literal and crudest sense as two localities in the mental apparatus—conceptions which have left their traces in the expressions 'to repress' and 'to force a way through.' Thus, we may speak of an unconscious thought seeking to convey itself into the preconscious so as to be able then to force its way through into consciousness. What we have in mind here is not the forming of a second thought situated in a new place, like a transcription which continues to exist alongside the original; and the notion of forcing a way through into consciousness must be kept carefully free from any idea of a change of locality. Again, we may speak of a preconscious thought being repressed or driven out and then taken over by the unconscious. These images, derived from a set of ideas relating to a struggle for a piece of ground, may tempt us to suppose that it is literally true that a mental grouping in one locality has been brought to an end and replaced by a fresh one in another locality. Let us replace these metaphors by something that seems to correspond better to the real state of affairs, and let us say instead that some particular mental grouping has had a cathexis of energy attached to it or withdrawn from it, so that the structure in question has come under the sway of a particular agency or been withdrawn from it. What we are doing here is once again to replace a topographical way of representing things by a dynamic one. What we regard as mobile is not the psychical structure itself but its innervation.[1]

---

[1] [*Footnote added* 1925:] It became necessary to elaborate and modify this view after it was recognized that the essential feature of a preconscious idea was the fact

Nevertheless, I consider it expedient and justifiable to continue to make use of the figurative image of the two systems. We can avoid any possible abuse of this method of representation by recollecting that ideas, thoughts and psychical structures in general must never be regarded as localized in organic elements of the nervous system but rather, as one might say, *between* them, where resistances and facilitations [*Bahnungen*] provide the corresponding correlates. Everything that can be an object of our internal perception is *virtual*, like the image produced in a telescope by the passage of light-rays. But we are justified in assuming the existence of the systems (which are not in any way psychical entities themselves and can never be accessible to our psychical perception) like the lenses of the telescope, which cast the image. And, if we pursue this analogy, we may compare the censorship between two systems to the refraction which takes place when a ray of light passes into a new medium.

So far we have been psychologizing on our own account. It is time now to consider the theoretical views which govern present-day psychology and to examine their relation to our hypotheses. The problem of the unconscious in psychology is, in the forcible words of Lipps (1897), less *a* psychological problem than *the* problem of psychology. So long as psychology dealt with this problem by a verbal explanation to the effect that 'psychical' *meant* 'conscious' and that to speak of 'unconscious psychical processes' was palpable nonsense, any psychological evaluation of the observations made by physicians upon abnormal mental states was out of the question. The physician and the philosopher can only come together if they both recognize that the term 'unconscious psychical processes' is 'the appropriate and justified expression of a solidly established fact.' The physician can only shrug his shoulders when he is assured that 'consciousness is an indispensable characteristic of what is psychical,' and perhaps, if he still feels enough respect for the utterances of philosophers, he may presume that they have not been dealing with the same thing or working at the same science. For even a single understanding observation of a neurotic's mental life or a single analysis of a dream must leave him with an unshakable conviction that the most complicated and most rational thought-processes,

---

of its being connected with the residues of verbal presentations. Cf. 'The Unconscious' (1915*e*, [Section VII]). [As is there pointed out, however, this was already indicated in the first edition of the present work. (See pp. 573 and 612.)—For the use of the word 'innervation' cf. p. 539 *n*.]

which can surely not be denied the name of psychical processes, can occur without exciting the subject's consciousness.[1] It is true that the physician cannot learn of these unconscious processes until they have produced some effect upon consciousness which can be communicated or observed. But this conscious effect may exhibit a psychical character quite different from that of the unconscious process, so that internal perception cannot possibly regard the one as a substitute for the other. The physician must feel at liberty to proceed by *inference* from the conscious effect to the unconscious psychical process. He thus learns that the conscious effect is only a remote psychical result of the unconscious process and that the latter has not become conscious as such; and moreover that the latter was present and operative even without betraying its existence in any way to consciousness.

It is essential to abandon the overvaluation of the property of being conscious before it becomes possible to form any correct view of the origin of what is mental. In Lipps's words [1897, 146 f.], the unconscious must be assumed to be the general basis of psychical life. The unconscious is the larger sphere, which includes within it the smaller sphere of the conscious. Everything conscious has an unconscious preliminary stage; whereas what is unconscious may remain at that stage and nevertheless claim to be regarded as having the full value of a psychical process. The unconscious is the true psychical reality; *in its innermost nature it is as much unknown to us as the reality of the external world, and it is as incompletely presented by the data of consciousness as is the external world by the communications of our sense organs.*

Now that the old antithesis between conscious life and dream-life has been reduced to its proper proportions by the establishment of unconscious psychical reality, a number of dream-problems with which earlier writers were deeply concerned have lost their significance. Thus some of the activities whose successful performance in dreams excited astonishment are now no longer to be attributed to dreams but to unconscious thinking,

---

[1] [*Footnote added* 1914:] I am happy to be able to point to an author who has drawn from the study of dreams the same conclusions as I have on the relation between conscious and unconscious activity. Du Prel (1885, 47) writes: 'The problem of the nature of the mind evidently calls for a preliminary investigation as to whether consciousness and mind are identical. This preliminary question is answered in the negative by dreams, which show that the concept of the mind is a wider one than that of consciousness, in the same kind of way in which the gravitational force of a heavenly body extends beyond its range of luminosity.' And again (ibid., 306 [quoting Maudsley, 1868, 15]): 'It is a truth which cannot be too distinctly borne in mind that consciousness is not co-extensive with mind.'

which is active during the day no less than at night. If, as Schemer [1861, 114 f.] has said, dreams appear to engage in making symbolic representations of the body [p. 111], we now know that those representations are the product of certain unconscious phantasies (deriving, probably, from sexual impulses) which find expression not only in dreams but also in hysterical phobias and other symptoms. If a dream carries on the activities of the day and completes them and even brings valuable fresh ideas to light, all we need do is to strip it of the dream disguise, which is the product of dream-work and the mark of assistance rendered by obscure forces from the depths of the mind (cf. the Devil in Tartini's sonata dream);[1] the intellectual achievement is due to the same mental forces which produce every similar result during the daytime. We are probably inclined greatly to over-estimate the conscious character of intellectual and artistic production as well. Accounts given us by some of the most highly productive men, such as Goethe and Helmholtz, show rather that what is essential and new in their creations came to them without premeditation and as an almost ready-made whole. There is nothing strange if in other cases, where a con-centration of every intellectual faculty was needed, conscious activity also contributed its share. But it is the much-abused privilege of conscious ac-tivity, wherever it plays a part, to conceal every other activity from our eyes.

It would scarcely repay the trouble if we were to treat the historical significance of dreams as a separate topic. A dream may have impelled some chieftain to embark upon a bold enterprise the success of which has changed history. But this only raises a fresh problem so long as a dream is regarded as an alien power in contrast to the other more familiar forces of the mind; no such problem remains if a dream is recognized as a *form of expression* of impulses which are under the pressure of resistance during the day but which have been able to find reinforcement during the night from deep-lying sources of excitation.[2] The respect paid to dreams in antiquity is, however, based upon correct psychological insight and is the homage

---

[1] [Tartini, the composer and violinist (1692–1770), is said to have dreamt that he sold his soul to the devil, who thereupon seized a violin and played a sonata of exquisite beauty upon it with consummate skill. When the composer awoke he at once wrote down what he could recollect of it, and the result was his famous 'Trillo del Diavolo.']

[2] [*Footnote added* 1911:] Cf. in this connection Alexander the Great's dream during his siege of Tyre (σά-τυρος). [See p. 131 n. 2.]

paid to the uncontrolled and indestructible forces in the human mind, to
the 'daemonic' power which produces the dream-wish and which we find
at work in our unconscious.

It is not without intention that I speak of 'our' unconscious. For what I
thus describe is not the same as the unconscious of the philosophers or even
the unconscious of Lipps. By them the term is used merely to indicate a contrast with the conscious: the thesis which they dispute with so much heat
and defend with so much energy is the thesis that apart from conscious there
are also unconscious psychical processes. Lipps carries things further with his
assertion that the whole of what is psychical exists unconsciously and that a
part of it also exists consciously. But it is not in order to establish *this* thesis
that we have summoned up the phenomena of dreams and of the formation
of hysterical symptoms; the observation of normal waking life would by itself suffice to prove it beyond any doubt. The new discovery that we have
been taught by the analysis of psychopathological structures and of the first
member of that class—the dream—lies in the fact that the unconscious (that
is, the psychical) is found as a function of two separate systems and that this
is the case in normal as well as in pathological life. Thus there are two kinds
of unconscious, which have not yet been distinguished by psychologists.
Both of them are unconscious in the sense used by psychology; but in our
sense one of them, which we term the *Ucs.,* is also *inadmissible to conscious-*
ness, while we term the other the *Pcs.* because its excitations—after observing
certain rules, it is true, and perhaps only after passing a fresh censorship,
though nonetheless without regard to the *Ucs.*—are able to reach consciousness. The fact that excitations in order to reach consciousness must pass
through a fixed series or hierarchy of agencies (which is revealed to us by the
modifications made in them by censorship) has enabled us to construct a
spatial analogy. We have described the relations of the two systems to each
other and to consciousness by saying that the system *Pcs.* stands like a screen
between the system *Ucs.* and consciousness. The system *Pcs.* not merely bars
access to consciousness, it also controls access to the power of voluntary
movement and has at its disposal for distribution a mobile cathectic energy,
a part of which is familiar to us in the form of attention.[1] [See p. 598.]

---

[1] [*Footnote added* 1914:] Cf. my 'Remarks on the Concept of the Unconscious in
Psycho-Analysis' (Freud, 1912*g*), first published in English in the *Proceedings* of
the Society for Psychical Research, **26** [312], in which I have distinguished the
descriptive, dynamic and systematic meanings of the highly ambiguous word
'unconscious.' [The whole topic is discussed in the light of Freud's later views in
Chapter II of *The Ego and the Id* (1923*b*).]

We must avoid, too, the distinction between 'supraconscious' and 'subconscious,' which has become so popular in the more recent literature of the psychoneuroses, for such a distinction seems precisely calculated to stress the equivalence of what is psychical to what is conscious.

But what part is there left to be played in our scheme by consciousness, which was once so omnipotent and hid all else from view? *Only that of a sense-organ for the preception of psychical qualities.*[1] In accordance with the ideas underlying our attempt at a schematic picture, we can only regard conscious perception as the function proper to a particular system; and for this the abbreviation *Cs.* seems appropriate. In its mechanical properties we regard this system as resembling the perceptual systems *Pcpt.:* as being susceptible to excitation by qualities but incapable of retaining traces of alterations—that is to say, as having no memory. The psychical apparatus, which is turned towards the external world with its sense-organ of the *Pcpt.* systems, is itself the external world in relation to the sense-organ of the *Cs.,* whose teleological justification resides in this circumstance. Here we once more meet the principle of the hierarchy of agencies, which seems to govern the structure of the apparatus. Excitatory material flows in to the *Cs.* sense-organ from two directions: from the *Pcpt.* system, whose excitation, determined by qualities, is probably submitted to a fresh revision before it becomes a conscious sensation, and from the interior of the apparatus itself, whose quantitative processes are felt qualitatively in the pleasure-unpleasure series when, subject to certain modifications, they make their way to consciousness.

Those philosophers who have become aware that rational and highly complex thought-structures are possible without consciousness playing any part in them have found difficulty in assigning any function to consciousness; it has seemed to them that it can be no more than a superfluous reflected picture of the completed psychical process. We, on the other hand, are rescued from this embarrassment by the analogy between our *Cs.* system and the perceptual systems. We know that perception by our sense-organs has the result of directing a cathexis of attention to the paths along which the in-coming sensory excitation is spreading: the qualitative excitation of the *Pcpt.* system acts as a regulator of the discharge of the mobile

---

[1] [Freud's use of the terms 'quantity' and 'quality' is fully explained in Part I of his 'Project' (1950a).]

quantity in the psychical apparatus. We can attribute the same function to the overlying sense-organ of the *Cs.* system. By perceiving new qualities, it makes a new contribution to directing the mobile quantities of cathexis and distributing them in an expedient fashion. By the help of its perception of pleasure and unpleasure it influences the discharge of the cathexes within what is otherwise an unconscious apparatus operating by means of the displacement of quantities. It seems probable that in the first instance the unpleasure principle regulates the displacement of cathexes automatically. But it is quite possible that consciousness of these qualities may introduce in addition a second and more discriminating regulation, which is even able to oppose the former one, and which perfects the efficiency of the apparatus by enabling it, in contradiction to its original plan, to cathect and work over what is associated with the release of unpleasure. We learn from the psychology of the neuroses that these processes of regulation carried out by the qualitative excitation of the sense organs play a great part in the functional activity of the apparatus. The automatic domination of the primary unpleasure principle and the consequent restriction imposed upon efficiency are interrupted by the processes of sensory regulation, which are themselves in turn automatic in action. We find that repression (which, though it served a useful purpose to begin with, leads ultimately to a damaging loss of inhibition and mental control) affects memories so much more easily than perceptions because the former can receive no extra cathexis from the excitation of the psychical sense organs. It is true on the one hand that a thought which has to be warded off cannot become conscious, because it has undergone repression; but on the other hand it sometimes happens that a thought of this kind is only repressed because for other reasons it has been withdrawn from conscious perception. Here are some hints of which we take advantage in our therapeutic procedure in order to undo repressions which have already been effected.

The value of the hypercathexis which is set up in the mobile quantities by the regulating influence of the sense organ of the *Cs.* cannot be better illustrated in its teleological aspect than by the fact of its creation of a new series of qualities and consequently of a new process of regulation which constitutes the superiority of men over animals. Thought-processes are in themselves without quality, except for the pleasurable and unpleasurable excitations which accompany them, and which, in view of their possible disturbing effect upon thinking, must be kept within bounds. In order that thought-processes may acquire quality, they are associated in human beings with verbal memories, whose residues of quality are sufficient to draw the attention of consciousness to them and to endow the process of thinking with a new mobile cathexis from consciousness. [Cf. pp. 573 and 605 *n*.]

The whole multiplicity of the problems of consciousness can only be grasped by an analysis of the thought-processes in hysteria. These give one the impression that the transition from a preconscious to a conscious cathexis is marked by a censorship similar to that between the *Ucs.* and the *Pcs.*[1] This censorship, too, only comes into force above a certain quantitative limit, so that thought-structures of low intensity escape it. Examples of every possible variety of how a thought can be withheld from consciousness or can force its way into consciousness under certain limitations are to be found included within the framework of psychoneurotic phenomena; and they all point to the intimate and reciprocal relations between censorship and consciousness. I will bring these psychological reflections to an end with a report of two such examples.

I was called in to a consultation last year to examine an intelligent and unembarrassed-looking girl. She was most surprisingly dressed. For though as a rule a woman's clothes are carefully considered down to the last detail, she was wearing one of her stockings hanging down and two of the buttons on her blouse were undone. She complained of having pains in her leg and, without being asked, exposed her calf. But what she principally complained of was, to use her own words, that she had a feeling in her body as though there was something 'stuck into it' which was 'moving backwards and forwards' and was 'shaking' her through and through: sometimes it made her whole body feel 'stiff.' My medical colleague, who was present at the examination, looked at me; he found no difficulty in understanding the meaning of her complaint. But what struck both of us as extraordinary was the fact that it meant nothing to the patient's mother—though she must often have found herself in the situation which her child was describing. The girl herself had no notion of the bearing of her remarks; for if she had, she would never have given voice to them. In this case it had been possible to hoodwink the censorship into allowing a phantasy which would normally have been kept in the preconscious to emerge into consciousness under the innocent disguise of making a complaint.

---

[1] [The censorship between the *Pcs.* and the *Cs.* appears only rarely in Freud's later writings. It is, however, discussed at length in Section VI of his paper on 'The Unconscious' (1915*e*).]

Here is another example. A fourteen-year-old boy came to me for psycho-analytic treatment suffering from *tic convulsif,* hysterical vomiting, headaches, etc. I began the treatment by assuring him that if he shut his eyes he would see pictures or have ideas, which he was then to communicate to me. He replied in pictures. His last impression before coming to me was revived visually in his memory. He had been playing at draughts with his uncle and saw the board in front of him. He thought of various positions, favourable or unfavourable, and of moves that one must not make. He then saw a dagger lying on the board—an object that belonged to his father but which his imagination placed on the board. Then there was a sickle lying on the board and next a scythe. And there now appeared a picture of an old peasant mowing the grass in front of the patient's distant home with a scythe. After a few days I discovered the meaning of this series of pictures. The boy had been upset by an unhappy family situation. He had a father who was a hard man, liable to fits of rage, who had been unhappily married to the patient's mother, and whose educational methods had consisted of threats. His father had been divorced from his mother, a tender and affectionate woman, had married again and had one day brought a young woman home with him who was to be the boy's new mother. It was during the first few days after this that the fourteen-year-old boy's illness had come on. His suppressed rage against his father was what had constructed this series of pictures with their understandable allusions. The material for them was provided by a recollection from mythology. The sickle was the one with which Zeus castrated his father; the scythe and the picture of the old peasant represented Kronos, the violent old man who devoured his children and on whom Zeus took such unfilial vengeance. [See p. 274.] His father's marriage gave the boy an opportunity of repaying the reproaches and threats which he had heard from his father long before because he had played with his genitals. (Cf. the playing at draughts; the forbidden moves; the dagger which could be used to kill.) In this case long-repressed memories and derivatives from them which had remained unconscious slipped into consciousness by a roundabout path in the form of apparently meaningless pictures.

Thus I would look for the *theoretical* value of the study of dreams in the contributions it makes to psychological knowledge and in the preliminary light it throws on the problems of the psychoneuroses. Who can guess the importance of the results which might be obtained from a thorough understanding of the structure and functions of the mental apparatus, since even the present state of our knowledge allows us to exert a favourable therapeutic influence on the curable forms of psychoneurosis? But what of the *practical* value of this study—I hear the question raised—as a means towards an understanding of the mind, towards a revelation of the hidden characteristics of individual men? Have not the unconscious impulses brought out by dreams the importance of real forces in mental life? Is the ethical significance of suppressed wishes to be made light of—wishes which, just as they lead to dreams, may some day lead to other things?

I do not feel justified in answering these questions. I have not considered this side of the problem of dreams further. I think, however, that the Roman emperor was in the wrong when he had one of his subjects executed because he had dreamt of murdering the emperor. [See above, p. 94 f.] He should have begun by trying to find out what the dream meant; most probably its meaning was not what it appeared to be. And even if a dream with another content had had this act of *lèse majesté* as its meaning, would it not be right to bear in mind Plato's dictum that the virtuous man is content to *dream* what a wicked man really *does* [p. 94 f.]? I think it is best, therefore, to acquit dreams. Whether we are to attribute *reality* to unconscious wishes, I cannot say. It must be denied, of course, to any transitional or intermediate thoughts. If we look at unconscious wishes reduced to their most fundamental and truest shape, we shall have to conclude, no doubt, that *psychical* reality is a particular form of existence not to be confused with *material* reality.[1] Thus there seems to be no justification for people's reluctance in accepting responsibility for the immorality of their dreams. When the mode of functioning of the mental apparatus is rightly appreciated and the relation between the conscious and the unconscious understood, the greater part of what is ethically objectionable in our dream and phantasy lives will be found to disappear. In the words of Hanns Sachs [1912, 569]: 'If we look in our consciousness at something

---

[1] [This sentence does not appear in the first edition. In 1909 it appeared in the following form: 'If we look at unconscious wishes reduced to their most fundamental and truest shape, we shall have to remember, no doubt, that psychical reality too has more than one form of existence.' In 1914 the sentence first appeared as printed in the text, except that the last word but one was 'factual' and not 'material.' 'Material' was substituted in 1919.—The remainder of this paragraph was added in 1914.—Freud had already drawn a distinction between 'thought reality' and 'external reality' in the second section of Part III of his 'Project' (1950a).]

that has been told us by a dream about a contemporary (real) situation, we ought not to be surprised to find that the monster which we saw under the magnifying glass of analysis turns out to be a tiny infusorian.'

Actions and consciously expressed opinions are as a rule enough for practical purposes in judging men's characters. Actions deserve to be considered first and foremost; for many impulses which force their way through to consciousness are even then brought to nothing by the real forces of mental life before they can mature into deeds. In fact, such impulses often meet with no psychical obstacles to their progress, for the very reason that the unconscious is certain that they will be stopped at some other stage. It is in any case instructive to get to know the much trampled soil from which our virtues proudly spring. Very rarely does the complexity of a human character, driven hither and thither by dynamic forces, submit to a choice between simple alternatives, as our antiquated morality would have us believe.[1]

And the value of dreams for giving us knowledge of the future? There is of course no question of that.[2] [Cf. p. 39 n.] It would be truer to say instead that they give us knowledge of the past. For dreams are derived from the past in every sense. Nevertheless the ancient belief that dreams foretell the future is not wholly devoid of truth. By picturing our wishes as fulfilled, dreams are after all leading us into the future. But this future, which the dreamer pictures as the present, has been moulded by his indestructible wish into a perfect likeness of the past.

---

[1] [This subject is further discussed in Freud, 1925*i* (Section B).]

[2] [In the 1911 edition only, the following footnote appeared at this point: 'Professor Ernst Oppenheim of Vienna has shown me, from the evidence of folklore, that there is a class of dreams in which the prophetic meaning has been dropped even in popular belief and which are perfectly correctly traced back to wishes and needs emerging during sleep. He will shortly be giving a detailed account of these dreams, which are as a rule narrated in the form of comic stories.']

APPENDIX A

A PREMONITORY DREAM FULFILLED[1]

FRAU B., an estimable woman who moreover possesses a critical sense, told me in another connection and without the slightest *arrière pensée* that once some years ago she dreamt she had met Dr. K., a friend and former family doctor of hers, in the Kärntnerstrasse[2] in front of Hiess's shop. The next morning, while she was walking along the same street, she in fact met the person in question at the very spot she had dreamt of. So much for my theme. I will only add that no subsequent event proved the importance of this miraculous coincidence, which cannot therefore be accounted for by what lay in the future.

Analysis of the dream was helped by questioning, which established the fact that there was no evidence of her having had any recollection at all of the dream on the morning after she dreamt it, until after her walk— evidence such as her having written the dream down or told it to someone

---

[1] [The manuscript of this paper is dated November 10, 1899—six days after the publication of *The Interpretation of Dreams*. In the same letter to Fliess in which Freud announced that event (Freud, 1950a, Letter 123, of November 5, 1899) he remarked that he had just discovered the origin and meaning of premonitory dreams. The paper was first published posthumously in *Ges. Werke,* **17** (1941), 21. The present English translation (by James Strachey) first appeared in *Coll. Papers,* **5** (1950), 70.—The same incident was reported by Freud very much more briefly in his *Psychopathology of Everyday Life* (1901b), Chapter XII, Section D.—The topic of premonitory dreams is touched upon in *The Interpretation of Dreams* on pp. 97 and 659.]

[2] [The principal shopping-street in the centre of Vienna.]

before it was fulfilled. On the contrary, she was obliged to accept the following account of what happened, which seems to me more plausible, without raising any objection to it. She was walking along the Kärntnerstrasse one morning and met her old family doctor in front of Hiess's shop. On seeing him she felt convinced that she had dreamt the night before of having this very meeting at that precise spot. According to the rules that apply to the interpretation of neurotic symptoms, her conviction must have been justified; its content may, however, require to be re-interpreted.

The following is an episode with which Dr. K. is connected from Frau B.'s earlier life. When she was young she was married, without her wholehearted consent, to an elderly but wealthy man. A few years later he lost his money, fell ill of tuberculosis and died. For many years the young woman supported herself and her sick husband by giving music lessons. Among her friends in misfortune was her family doctor, Dr. K., who devoted himself to looking after her husband and helped her in finding her first pupils. Another friend was a barrister, also a Dr. K., who put the chaotic affairs of the ruined merchant in order, while at the same time he made love to the young woman and—for the first and last time—set her passion aflame. This love affair brought her no real happiness, for the scruples created by her upbringing and her cast of mind interfered with her complete surrender while she was married and later when she was a widow. In the same connection in which she told me the dream, she also told me of a real occurrence dating from this unhappy period of her life, an occurrence which in her opinion was a remarkable coincidence. She was in her room, kneeling on the floor with her head buried in a chair and sobbing in passionate longing for her friend and helper the barrister, when at that very moment the door opened and in he came to visit her. We shall find nothing at all remarkable in this coincidence when we consider how often she thought of him and how often he probably visited her. Moreover, accidents which seem preconcerted like this are to be found in every love story. Nevertheless this coincidence was probably the true content of her dream and the sole basis of her conviction that it had come true.

Between the scene in which her wish had been fulfilled and the time of the dream more than twenty-five years elapsed. In the meantime Frau B. had become the widow of a second husband who left her with a child and a fortune. The old lady's affection was still centred on Dr. K., who was now her adviser and the administrator of her estate and whom she saw frequently. Let us suppose that during the few days before the dream she had been expecting a visit from him, but that this had not taken place—he was no longer so pressing as he used to be. She may then have quite well had a nostalgic dream one night which took her back to the old days. Her dream was probably of a *rendez-vous* at the time of her love affair, and the chain of her dream-thoughts carried her back to the occasion when, without any pre-arrangement, he had come in at the very moment at which she had been longing for him. She probably had dreams of this kind quite often now; they were a part of the belated punishment with which a woman pays for her youthful cruelty. But such dreams—derivatives of a suppressed current of thought, filled with memories of *rendez-vous* of which, since her second marriage, she no longer liked to think—such dreams were put aside on waking. And that was what happened to our ostensibly prophetic dream. She then went out, and in the Kärntnerstrasse, at a spot which was in itself indifferent, she met her old family doctor, Dr. K. It was a very long time since she had seen him. He was intimately associated with the excitements of that happy-unhappy time. He too had been a helper, and we may suppose that he had been used in her thoughts, and perhaps in her dreams as well, as a screen figure behind which she concealed the better-loved figure of the other Dr. K. This meeting now revived her recollection of the dream. She must have thought: 'Yes, I had a dream last night of my *rendez-vous* with Dr. K.' But this recollection had to undergo the distortion which the dream escaped only because it had been completely forgotten. She inserted the indifferent K. (who had reminded her of the dream) in place of the beloved K. The content of the dream—the *rendez-vous*—was transferred to a belief that she had dreamt of that particular spot, for a *rendez-vous* consists in two people coming to the same spot at the same time. And if she then had an impression that a dream had been fulfilled, she was only giving effect in that way to her memory of the scene in which she had longed in her misery for him to come and her longing had at once been fulfilled.

Thus the creation of a dream after the event, which alone makes prophetic dreams possible, is nothing other than a form of censoring, thanks to which the dream is able to make its way through into consciousness.

10 *Nov.* 99

APPENDIX B

LIST OF WRITINGS BY FREUD DEALING PREDOMINANTLY OR LARGELY WITH DREAMS

[*It would scarcely be an exaggeration to say that dreams are alluded to in the majority of Freud's writings. The following list of works (of greatly varying importance) may however be of some practical use. The date at the beginning of each entry is that of the year during which the work in question was written. The date at the end is that of publication; and under that date fuller particulars of the work will be found in the General Bibliography. The items in square brackets were published posthumously.*]

[1895   'Project for a Scientific Psychology' (Sections 19, 20 and 21 of
         Part I). (1950*a*.)]
1899   *The Interpretation of Dreams*. (1900*a*.)
[1899   'A Premonitory Dream Fulfilled.' (1941*c*.)]
1901   *On Dreams*. (1901*a*.)
1901   'Fragment of an Analysis of a Case of Hysteria.' [Original title:
         'Dreams and Hysteria.'] (1905*e*.)
1905   *Jokes and Their Relation to the Unconscious* Chapter VI). (1905*c*.)
1907   *Delusions and Dreams in Jensen's 'Gradiva.'* (1907*a*.)
1910   'A Typical Example of a Disguised Oedipus Dream.' (1910*l*.)
1911   'Additions to the Interpretation of Dreams.' (1911*a*.)
1911   'The Handling of Dream-Interpretation in Psycho-Analysis.'
         (1911*e*.)
1913   'An Evidential Dream.' (1913*a*.)

1913   'The Occurrence in Dreams of Material from Fairy Tales.'
       (1913*d*.)
1913   'Observations and Examples from Analytic Practice.' (1913*h*.)
1914   'The Representation in a Dream of a "Great Achievement."'
       (1914*e*.)
1916   *Introductory Lectures on Psycho-Analysis* (Part II). (1916–1917.)
1917   'A Metapsychological Supplement to the Theory of Dreams.'
       (1917*d*.)
1918   'From the History of an Infantile Neurosis' (Section IV). (1918*b*.)
1920   'Supplements to the Theory of Dreams.' (1920*b*.)
1922   'Dreams and Telepathy.' (1922*a*.)
1923   'Remarks upon the Theory and Practice of Dream-Interpretation.'
       (1923*c*.)
1923   'Josef Popper-Lynkeus and the Theory of Dreams.' (1923*f*.)
1925   'Some Additional Notes on Dream-Interpretation as a Whole.'
       (1925*i*.)
1929   'A Letter to Maxime Leroy on a Dream of Descartes.' (1929*b*.)
1932   'My Contact with Josef Popper-Lynkeus.' (1932*c*.)
1932   *New Introductory Lectures on Psycho-Analysis* (Lectures XXIX and
       XXX). (1933*a*.)
[1938 *An Outline of Psycho-Analysis* (Chapter V). (1940*a*.)]

N.B.—An unauthorized concoction of portions of *The Interpretation of
Dreams* and *On Dreams* has appeared in two editions in America under the
title of *Dream Psychology: Psychoanalysis for Beginners* (with an introduction
by André Tridon). New York: McCann, 1920 and 1921. Pp. xi + 237.

ADDITIONAL NOTES

194, line 25. *'Festschrift.'* This *Festschrift* was in honour of Professor Strieker, Director of the Institute of Pathological Anatomy, at which Dr. Gärtner was Assistant, and where Freud had worked in his student days.

447, line 26. The journal in question was the *Wiener klinische Rundschau.*

523, line 4. 'Nineteen.' In the first edition only (but not in the 1925 reprint of it) this read 'seventeen.' See Jones (1953), 35–6.

636, line 35. 'Freud (1950a). *Aus den Anfängen der Psychoanalyse.'* An English translation of this work under the title of *The Origins of Psycho-Analysis* appeared in 1954 (London: Imago Publishing Co.). This includes the 'Project for a Scientific Psychology' written by Freud in 1895.

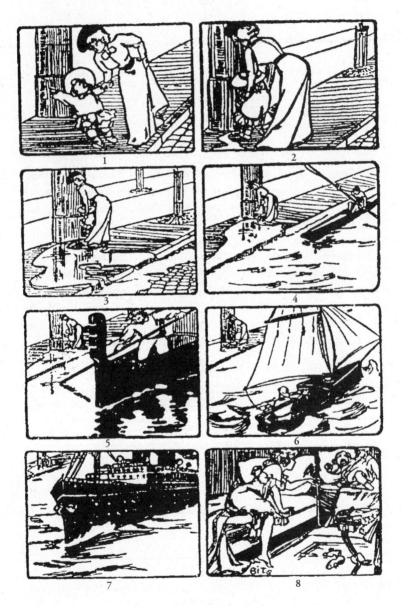

A French Nurse's Dream

BIBLIOGRAPHY

[Titles of books and periodicals are in italics; titles of papers are in inverted commas. Abbreviations are in accordance with the *World List of Scientific Periodicals* (Oxford, 1950). Numerals in thick type refer to volumes; ordinary numerals refer to pages. *G.S.* = Freud, *Gesammelte Schriften* (12 vols.), Vienna, 1924–34. *G.W.* = Freud, *Gesammelte Werke* (18 vols.), London, from 1940. *C.P.* = Freud, *Collected Papers* (5 vols.), London, 1924–50. *Standard Ed.*—Freud, *Standard Edition* (24 vols.), London, from 1953. Entries marked with an asterisk have not been verified for the present edition. See Translator's Introduction, p. xx. For non-technical authors, and for technical authors where no specific work is mentioned, see the *General Index*.].

A

AUTHOR INDEX AND LIST OF WORKS REFERRED TO IN THE TEXT

[The figures in round brackets at the end of each entry indicate the page or pages of this volume on which the work in question is mentioned. In the case of the Freud entries, the letters attached to the dates of publication are in accordance with the corresponding entries in the complete bibliography of Freud's writings to be included in the last volume of the *Standard Edition*.]

ABEL, K. (1884) *Der Gegensinn der Urworte,* Leipzig. (353, *n.* 3)

ABRAHAM, K. (1909) *Traum und Mythus,* Vienna. (386, *n.* 2, 437)

ADLER, A. (1910) 'Der psychische Hermaphroditismus im Leben und in der Neurose', *Fortschr. Med.,* **28,** 486. (432)

(1911) 'Beitrag zur Lehre vom Widerstand', *Zbl. Psychoanal.,* **1,** 214. (618 *n.*)

ALLISON, A. (1868) 'Nocturnal Insanity' *Méd. Times & Gaz.*, **947**, 210. (121)

ALMOLI, S. See Salomon Almoli.

AMRAM, N. (1901) 'Sepher pithrôn chalômôth, Jerusalem' (38, *n.* 2)

ARISTOTLE *De somniis* and *De divinatione per somnum.* (36–7, 67, 130, *n.* 1, 355 *n.*, 588–9)
  [*Trans.* by W. S. Hett (in volume 'On the Soul', Loeb Classical Library), London & New York, 1935.]

ARTEMIDORUS OF DALDIS *Oneirocritica.* (37–8, 130, 131, *n.* 2, 389 *n.*, 645, *n.* 2)
  [*German trans.: Symbolik der Träume* by F. S. Krauss, Vienna, 1881, and 'Erotische Träume und ihre Symbolik', *Anthropophyteia,* **9,** 316, by Hans Licht.
  Engl. trans, (abridged): *The Interpretation of Dreams,* by R. Wood, London, 1644.]

ARTIGUES, R. (1884) *Essai sur la valeur séméiologique du rêve,* (Thesis) Paris. (68)

BENINI, V. (1898) 'La memoria e la durata dei sogni', *Riv. ital. Filos.,* 13*a*, 149. (78, 103)

BERNARD-LEROY and TOBOWOLSKA, J. (1901) 'Mécanisme intellectuel du rêve', *Rev. phil.,* **51,** 570. (540–1)

BERNFELD, S. (1944) 'Freud's Earliest Theories and the School of Helmholtz', *Psychoanal. Quart.,* **13,** 341. (xvi *n.*, 520 *n.*)

BERNSTEIN, I., and SEGEL, B. W. (1908) *Jüdische Sprichwürter und Redensarten,* Warsaw. (165, *n.* 1)

BETLHEIM, S., AND HARTMANN, H. (1924) 'Über Fehlreaktionen des Gedächtnisses bei Korsakoffschen Psychose', *Arch. Psychiat. Nervenkr.,* **72,** 278. (419)

BIANCHIERI, F. (1912) 'I sogni dei bambini di cinque anni', *Riv. Psicol.,* **8,** 325. (164 *n.*)
  See also DOGLIA and BIANCHIERI.

BINZ, C. (1878) *Über den Traum,* Bonn. (53, 89, 109, 119)

BLEULER, E. (1910) 'Die Psychoanalyse Freuds', *Jb. Psychoanal. psychopath. Forsch.,* **2,** 623. (386, *n.* 2)

BONATELLI, F. (1880) 'Del sogno', *La filosofia delle scuole italiane,* Feb. 16. (78)

BÖRNER, J. (1855) *Das Alpdrücken, seine Begründung und Verhütung,* Würzburg. (68)

BÖTTINGER (1795) In C. P. J. SPRENGEL: *Beiträge zur Geschichte der Medizin,* **2.** (67 *n.*)

BOUCHÉ-LECLERCQ, A. (1879–82) *Histoire de la divination dans l'antiquité,* Paris. (67 *n.*)

Breuer, J., and Freud, S. (1895) see Freud, S. (1895*d*)

(1940 [1892]) see Freud, S. (1940*d*)

Büchsenschütz, B. (1868) *Traum und Traumdeutung im Altertum,* Berlin. (36 *n.* 2, 130, *n.* 1, 165, *n.* 2)

Burdach, K. F. (1838) *Die Physiologie als Erfahrungswis-senschaft,* Vol. 3 of 2nd ed., 1832–40 (1st ed. 1826–32). (41, 83, 85, 110, 114, 257)

Busemann, A. (1909) 'Traumleben der Schulkinder', *Z. päd. Psychol.,* **10,** 294. (164 *n.*)

(1910) 'Psychologie der kindlichen Traumerlebnisse', *Z. päd. Psychol.,* **11,** 320. (164 *n.*)

Cabanis, P. J. G. (1802) *Rapports du physique et du moral de l'homme,* Paris. (121)

Calkins, M. W. (1893) 'Statistics of Dreams', *Amer. J. Psychol.,* **5,** 311. (53, 55, 77, 254–5)

Carena, Caesar (1641) *Tractatus de Officio Sanctissimae Inquisitionis,* Cremona. (102, *n.* 1)

Chabaneix, P. (1897) *Physiologie cérébrale: le subconscient chez les artistes, les savants, et les écrivains,* Paris. (77, *n.,* 97)

Cicero: *De divinatione.* (43, 88)

[*Trans.* by W. A. Falconer (Loeb Classical Library), London & New York, 1922.]

Claparède, E. (1905) 'Esquisse d'une théorie biologique du sommeil', *Arch. psychol.,* **4,** 245. (85, *n.* 2)

Clerk-Maxwell, J. (1876) *Matter and Motion,* London. (493, 558)

Corlat, I. H. (1913) 'Zwei sexual-symbolische Beispiele von Zahnarzt-Träumen', *Zbl. Psychoanal. Psychother.,* **3,** 440. (422, *n.* 1)

Dattner, B. (1913) 'Gold und Kot', *Int. Z. Psychoanal.,* **1,** 495. (439)

Davidson, Wolf (1799) *Versuch über den Schlaf,* Berlin. 2nd ed. (1st ed., 1795). (94)

Debacker, F. (1881) *Des hallucinations et terreurs nocturnes chez les enfants,* (Thesis) Paris. (168, *n.* 1, 625–6)

Delacroix, H. (1904) 'Sur la structure logique du rêve', *Rev. Métaphys.,* **12,** 921. (540)

Delage, Y. (1891) 'Essai sur la théorie du rêve', *Rev. industr.,* **2,** 40. (52, 112–4, 212 *n.,* 630)

Delbœuf, I. (1885) *Le sommeil et les rêves,* Paris. (45–6, *54–5,* 84, 90, 93, 137–8, 212 *n.,* 217, *n.* 1)

Diepgen, P. (1912) *Traum und Traumdeutung als mediz. naturwissenschaftl. Problem im Mittelatler,* Berlin. (38, *n.* 2, 581 *n.*)

Doglia, S. and Bianchieri, F. (1910–11) 'I sogni dei bambini di tre anni', *Contrib. psicol.,* **1,** 9. (164 *n.*)

DÖLLINGER, J. (1857) *Heidenthum und Judenthum*, Regensburg. (67 *n.*)

DREXL, F. X. (1909) *Achmets Traumbuch: Einleitung und Probe eines kritischen Textes*, (Thesis) Munich. (38, *n.* 2)

DUGAS, L. (1897*a*) 'Le sommeil et la cérébration inconsciente durant le sommeil', *Rev. phil.*, **43**, 410. (88, 92)

(1897*b*) 'Le souvenir du rêve', *Rev. phil*, **44**, 220. (614)

DU PREL, C. (1885) *Die Philosophie der Mystik*, Leipzig. (96, *n.* 2, 164 *n.*, 167 *n.*, 314, *n.* 1, 567 *n.*, 650 *n.*)

EDER, M. D. (1913) 'Augenträume', *Int. Z. Psychoanal.*, **1**, 157. (433 *n.*)

EGGER, V. (1895) 'La durée apparente des rêves', *Rev. phil.*, **40**, 41. (60, 97, 534)

(1898) 'Le souvenir dans le rêve', *Rev. phil.*, **46**, 154. (79)

ELLIS, HAVELOCK (1899) 'The Stuff that Dreams are made of', *Popular Science Monthly*, **54**, 721. (53, 92, 630)

(1911) *The World of Dreams*, London. (97, *n.* 2, 201, 215 *n.*, 388, 408, 438, 539, 581)

ERDMANN, J. E. (1852) *Psychologische Briefe* (Brief VI), Leipzig (103)

FECHNER, G. T. (1860) *Elemente der Psychophysik*, Leipzig. (81, 88, 574)

FEDERN, P. (1914) 'Über zwei typische Traumsensationen', *Jb. Psychoanal.*, **6**, 89. (430)

FÉRÉ, C. (1886) 'Note sur un cas de paralysie hystérique consécutive à un rêve', *Soc. biolog.*, **41** (Nov. 20). (120)

(1887) 'A Contribution to the Pathology of Dreams and of Hysterical Paralysis', *Brain*, **9**, 488. (120, *n.* 1)

FERENCZI, S. (1910) 'Die Psychoanalyse der Träume', *Psychiat.-neurol. Wschr.*, **12**, Nos. 11–13. (131, *n.* 2, 165, *n.* 1, 278, *n.* 2, 361)

[*Trans.:* 'The Psychological Analysis of Dreams', Chap. III of *Contributions to Psychoanalysis*, Boston, 1916.]

(1911) 'Über lenkbare Träume', *Zbl. Psychoanal.*, **2**, 31. (611)

(1912) 'Symbolische Darstellung des Lust-und Realitätsprinzips im Ödipus-Mythos', *Imago*, **1**, 276. (297, *n.* 1)

[*Trans.:* 'The Symbolic Representation of the Pleasure and Reality Principles in the Oedipus Myth', Chap. X, Part I of *Contributions to Psycho-Analysis*, Boston, 1916.]

(1913) 'Zur Augensymbolik', *Int. Z. Psychoanal.*, **1**, 161. (433 *n.*)

[*Trans.:* 'On Eye Symbolism', Chap. X, Pt. II of *Contributions to Psycho-Analysis*, Boston, 1916.]

(1916) 'Affektvertauschung im Träume', *Int. Z. Psychoanal.*, **4**, 112. (510)

[*Trans.:* 'Interchange of Affect in Dreams', No. LV in *Further Contributions*, London, 1926.]

(1917) 'Träume der Ahnungslosen', *Int. Z. Psychoanal.*, **4**, 208. (412)

[*Trans.*: 'Dreams of the Unsuspecting', No. LVI of *Further Contributions*, London, 1926.]

FICHTE, I. H. (1864) *Psychologie: die Lehre vom bewussten Geiste des Menschen*, (2 vols.), Leipzig. (41, 96, 103)

FISCHER, K. P. (1850) *Grundzüge des Systems der Anthropologie*, Erlangen. (Pt. I, Vol. 2, in *Grundzüge des Systems der Philosophie*.) (98)

FLIESS, W. (1906) *Der Ablauf des Lebens*, Vienna. (126, 199, *n.* 2)

FÖRSTER, M. (1910) 'Das lateinisch-altenglische pseudo-Danielsche Traumbuch in Tiberius A. III', *Archiv Stud. neueren Sprachen und Literaturen*, **125**, 39. (38, *n.* 2)

(1911) 'Ein mittelenglisches Vers-Traumbuch des 13 Jahrhunderts', *Archiv Stud, neueren Sprachen und Literaturen*, **127**, 31. (38, *n.* 2)

FOUCAULT, M. (1906) *Le rêve: études et observations*, Paris. (541, 551 *n.*)

FREUD, S. (1877*a*) 'Über den Ursprung der hinteren Nerven-wurzeln im Rückerunark von Ammocoetes (Petromyzon Planeri)', *Sitzungsber. k. Akad. Wiss.*, III Abt, Bd. 75, January. (448–9)

(1884*e*) 'Über Coca', *Centralbl. ges. Therap.*, **2**, 289. (203)
[*Trans.*: (abbreviated) 'Coca', *Saint Louis Med. Surg. J.*, **47** (1884), 502.]

(1893*c*) 'Quelques considérations pour une étude comparative des paralysies motrices organiques et hystériques', *G.S.*, **1**, 30; *G.W.*, **1**, 37. (601 *n.*)
[*Trans.*: 'Some Points for a Comparative Study of Organic and Hysterical Motor Paralyses', *C.P.*, **1**, 42; *Standard Ed.*, **1**.]

(1894*a*) 'Die Abwehr-Neuropsychosen', *G.S.*, **1**, 290; *G.W.*, **1**, 57. (xvi, 264 *n.*)
[*Trans.*: 'The Neuro-Psychoses of Defence', *C.P.*, **1**, 59; *Standard Ed.*, **3**.]

(1895*b*) 'Über die Berechtigung, von der Neurasthenie einen bestimmten Symptomenkomplex als "Angstneurose" abzutrennen', *G.S.*, **1**, 306; *G.W.*, **1**, 313. (190, 195)
[*Trans.*: 'On the Grounds for Detaching a Particular Syndrome from Neurasthenia under the Description "Anxiety Neurosis"', *C.P.*, **1**, 76; *Standard Ed.*, **3**.]

(1895*d*) With Breuer, J., *Studien über Hysterie*, Vienna. (*G.S.*, **1**, *G.W.*, **1**, 75. Omitting Breuer's contributions.) (xiv–xvii, 112, *n.* 1, 132, 139, *n.* 1, 176, *n.* 1, 212 *n.*, 520 *n.*, 560, 576, *n.* 2, 581 *n.*, 585, 608, *n.* 3, 640 *n.*)
[*Trans.*: *Studies on Hysteria, Standard Ed.*, **2**.]

(1896*b*) 'Weitere Bemerkungen über die Abwehr-Neuropsychosen', *G.S.*, **1**, 363; *G.W.*, **1**, 377. (176 *n.* 1, 264 *n.*, 584)
[*Trans.*: 'Further Remarks on the Neuro-Psychoses of Defence', *C.P.*, **1**, 155; *Standard Ed.*, **3**.]

Freud, S. *(cont.)*

(1898*b*) 'Zum psychischen Mechanismus der Vergesslichkeit', *G.W.*, **1**, 517. (202, *n.* 1, 557, *n.* 1, 648 *n.*)

    [*Trans.*: 'The Psychical Mechanism of Forgetting', *Standard Ed.*, **3**.]

(1899*a*) 'Über Deckerinnerungen', *GJS.*, **1**, 465; *G.W.*, **1**. (51 *n.*, 205, *n.* 2, 279 *n.*, 323, *n.* 2, 383, *n.* 9, 461, *n.* 1, 648 *n.*)

    [*Trans.*: 'Screen Memories', *C.P.*, **5**, 47; Standard Ed., **3**.]

(1900*a*) *Die Traumdeutung*, Vienna. (*G.S.*, **2–3**; *G.W.*, **2–3**.)

    [*Trans.*: *The Interpretation of Dreams*, London, 1954; Standard Ed., **4–5**.] (297, *n.* 1, 425, 427, 432)

(1901*a*) *Über den Traum*, Wiesbaden. (*G.S.*, **3**, 189; *G. W.*, **2–3**, 643.) (166 *n.*, 187, *n.* 1, 217, *n.* 1, 452 *n.*, 477 *n.*)

    [*Trans.*: *On Dreams*, London, 1951; *Standard Ed.*, **5**, 629.]

(1901*b*) *Zur Psychopathologie des Alltagslebens*, Berlin. (*G.S.*, **4**; *G.W.*, **4**.) (151, *n.* 1, 202 *n.*, 230, *n.* 1, 244, *n.* 2, 281 *n.*, 290, *n.* 1, 330, *n.* 2, 435, *n.* **1**, 493, *n.* 3, 539, *n.* 1, 553, *n.* 1, 557 *n.*, 570, *n.* 2, 573 *n.*, 648 *n.*)

    [*Trans.*: *The Psychopathology of Everyday Life*, *Standard Ed.*, **6**.]

(1904*a*) 'Die Freud'sche psychoanalytische Methode', *G.S.*, **6**, 3; *G.W.*, **5**, 3. (133 *n.*)

    [*Trans.*: 'Freud's Psycho-Analytic Method', *C.P.*, **1**, 264; *Standard Ed.* 7.]

(1905*c*) *Der Witz und seine Beziehung zum Unbewussten*, Vienna. (*G.S.*, **9**; *G. W.*, **6**.) (153 *n.*, 227, *n.* 2, 301, *n.* 2, 332 *n.*, 338, *n.* 1, 376, *n.* 1, 391, *n.* 2, 481, *n.* 2, 518 *n.*, 644 *n.*)

    [*Trans.*: *Jokes and their Relation to the Unconscious*, *Standard Ed.*, **8**.]

(1905*d*) *Drei Abhandlungen zur Sexualtheorie*, Vienna. (*G.S.*, **5**, 3; *G.W.*, **5**, 29.) (xii, 163, *n.* 2, 278, *n.* 1, 306, *n.* 2, 390, *n.* 1, 432, 531 *n.*, 645, *n.* 1)

    [*Trans.*: *Three Essays on the Theory of Sexuality*, London, 1949; *Standard Ed.*, **7**.]

(1905*e*) 'Bruchstück einer Hysterie-Analyse', *G.S.*, **8**, 3; *G. W.*, **5**, 163. (xiv, 223, *n.* 1, 345 *n.*, 376, *n.* 1, 389, 422, *n.* 2, 430, 532 *n.*, 554 *n.*, 557, *n.* 2, 570, *n.* 1, 600, *n.* 1, 601, *n.* 2, 618 *n.*)

    [*Trans.*: 'Fragment of an Analysis of a Case of Hysteria', *C.P.*, **3**, 13; *Standard Ed.*, 7.]

(1907*a*) *Der Wahn und die Träume in W. Jensens 'Gradiva'*, Vienna. (*G.S.*, **9**, 273; *G.W.*, 7, 31.) (129 *n.*, 407 *n.*)

    [*Trans.*: *Delusion and Dreams in Jensen's 'Gradiva'*, *Standard Ed.*, **9**.]

(1908*a*) 'Hysterische Phantasien und ihre Beziehung zur Bisexualität', *G.S.*, **5**, 246; *G.W.*, 7, 191. (529, *n.* 3, 608)

    [*Trans.*: 'Hysterical Phantasies and their Relation to Bisexuality', *C.P.*, **2**, 51; *Standard Ed.*, **9**.]

(1908*b*) 'Charakter und Analerotik', *G.S.,* **5,** 261; *G.W.,* **7,** 203. (250, *n.* 1, 439)

[Trans.: 'Character and Anal Erotism', *C.P.,* **2,** 45; Standard Ed., **9.**]

(1908*c*) 'Über infantile Sexualtheorien', *G.S.,* **5,** 168; *G.W.,* **7,** 171. (283 *n.*)

[*Trans.:* 'On the Sexual Theories of Children', *C.P.,* **2,** 59; *Standard Ed.,* **9.**]

(1908*e*) 'Der Dichter und das Phantasieren', *G.S.,* **10,** 229; *G.W.,* **7,** 213. (529, *n.* 3)

[*Trans.:* 'Creative Writers and Day-Dreaming', *C.P.,* **4,** 173; *Standard Ed.,* **9.**]

(1909*b*) 'Analyse der Phobie eines fünfjährigen Knaben', *G.S.,* **8,** 129; *G.W.,* **7,** 243. (164 *n.,* 283 *n.,* 284 *n.,* 286 *n.*)

[*Trans.:* 'Analysis of a Phobia in a Five-Year-Old Boy', *C.P.,* **3,** 149; *Standard Ed.,* **10.**]

(1909*d*) 'Bemerkungen über einen Fall von Zwangsneurose', *G.S.,* **8,** 269; *G.W.,* **7,** 381. (339 *n.,* 376, *n.* 1, 481, *n.* 2)

[*Trans.:* 'Notes upon a Case of Obsessional Neurosis', C.P., **3,** 293; *Standard Ed.,* **10.**]

(1910*a*) *Über Psychoanalyse,* Vienna. (*G.S.,* **4,** 349; *G.W.,* **8,** 3.) (647 *n.*)

[*Trans.: Five Lectures on Psycho-Analysis, Standard Ed.,* **11.**]

(1910*d*) 'Die zukünftigen Chancen der psychoanalytischen Therapie', *G.S.,* **6,** 25; *G.W.,* **8,** 104. (390, *n.* 2, 401, 405, 439, *n.* 2)

[*Trans.:* 'The Future Prospects of Psycho-Analytic Therapy', *C.P.,* **2,** 285; *Standard Ed.,* **11.**]

(1910*e*) '"Über den Gegensinn der Urworte"', *G.S.,* **10,** 221; *G.W.,* **8,** 214. (353, *n.* 3)

[*Trans.:* '"The Antithetical Sense of Primal Words"', *C.P.,* **4,** 184; *Standard Ed.,* **11.**]

(1910*f*) 'Brief an Dr. Friedrich S. Krauss über die *Anthro-pophyteia',* G.S., **11,** 242; *G.W.,* **8,** 224. (645, *n.* 2)

[*Trans.:* 'Letter to Dr. Friedrich S. Krauss on *Anthro-pophyteia', Standard Ed.,* **11.**]

(1910*h*) 'Über einen besonderen Typus der Objektwahl beim Manne' (Beiträge zur Psychologie des Liebeslebens' **I**), *G.S.,* **5,** 186; *G.W.,* **8,** 66. (297, *n.* 1, 439, *n.* 2)

[*Trans.:* 'A Special Type of Choice of Object made by Men' ('Contributions to the Psychology of Love' **I**), *C.P.,* **4,** 192; *Standard Ed.,* 11.]

(1910*l*) 'Typisches Beispiel eines verkappten Ödipustraumes', *Zentralbl. Psychoanal.,* **1,** 45; reprinted in *Die Traum-deutung, G.S.,* **3,** 118, *n.;* *G.W.,* **2–3,** 404 *n.* (178 *n.,* 433 *n.*)

[*Trans.:* 'A Typical Example of a Disguised Oedipus Dream'; included in *The Interpretation of Dreams, Standard Ed.,* **5,** 398 *n.*]

FREUD, S. (cont.)

(1911*a*) 'Nachträge zur Traumdeutung', *Zentralbl. Psycho-anal,* **1,** 187. (Partly reprinted *G.S.,* **3,** 77 ff. and 126 f.; *G.W.,* **2–3,** 365 ff. and 412 f.) (395 *n.,* 401, *n.* 1, 443 *n.*)
[*Trans.:* 'Additions to the Interpretation of Dreams', (wholly incorporated in *The Interpretation of Dreams, Standard Ed.,* **5,** 360 ff. and 408 f.)]

(1911*b*) 'Formulierungen über die zwei Prinzipien des psychischen Geschehens', *G.S.,* **5,** 409; *G.W.,* **8,** 230. (466 *n.,* 606, *n.* **2**)
[*Trans.:* 'Formulations on the Two Principles of Mental Functioning', *C.P.,* **4,** 13; *Standard Ed.,* **12.**]

(1911*e*) 'Die Handhabung der Traumdeutung in der Psycho-analyse', *G.S.,* **6,** 45; *G.W.,* **8,** 350. (136 *n.,* 553, *n.* 1)
[*Trans.:* 'The Handling of Dream-Interpretation in Psycho-Analysis', *C.P.,* **2,** 305; *Standard Ed.,* **12.**]

(1912*g*) 'Einige Bernerkungen über den Begriff des Unbe-wussten in der Psychoanalyse', *G.W.,* **8,** 360. (653 *n.*)
[*Trans.:* 'Some Remarks on the Concept of the Unconscious as used in Psycho-Analysis', *C.P.,* **4,** 22; *Standard Ed.,* **12.**]

(1912–13) *Totem und Tabu,* Vienna. (*G.S.,* **10; G.W.,* **9.**) (289, *n.* 1, 290 *n.,* 297, *n.* 1, 445 *n.,* 539, *n.* 1)
[*Trans.: Totem and Taboo,* London, 1950; *Standard Ed.,* **13.**]

(1913*a*) 'Ein Traum als Beweismittel', *G.S.,* **3,** 267; *G.W.,* **10,** 12. (386, *n.* 1, 528, *n.* 1, 601, *n.* 1)
[*Trans.:* 'An Evidential Dream', *C.P.,* **2,** 133; *Standard Ed.,* **13.**]

(1913*d*) 'Märchenstoffe in Träumen', *G.S.,* **3,** 259; *G.W.,* **10,** 2. (Appendix B, 666)
[*Trans.:* 'The Occurrence in Dreams of Material from Fairy Tales', *C.P.,* **4,** 236; *Standard Ed.,* **13.**]

(1913*f*) 'Das Motiv der Kästchenwahl', *G.S.,* **10,** 243–56; *G.W.,* **10,** 24–37.
[*Trans.:* 'The Theme of the Three Caskets', *C.P.,* **4,** 244–56; *Standard Ed.,* **12.**]

(1913*h*) 'Erfahrungen und Beispiele aus der analytischen Praxis', *Int. Z. Psychoanal.,* **1,** 377. (Partly reprinted *G.S.,* **11,** 301; *G.W.,* **10,** 40. Partly included in *Traumdeutung, G.S.,* **3,** 41, 71 f., 127 and 135; *G.W.,* **2–3,** 238, 359 ff., 413 f. and 433.) (265, *n.* 2, 444, *n.* 2, 467, *n.* 1)
[*Trans.:* 'Observations and Examples from Analytic Practice', *Standard Ed.,* **13** (in full). Also partly incorporated in *The Interpretation of Dreams, Standard Ed.,* **4,** 232 and **5,** 409 f.]

(1913*k*) 'Geleitwort zu Bourke's *Der Unrat in Sitte, Brauch, Glauben und Gewohnheitsrecht der Vöjker*', *G.S.,* **11,** 249; *G.W.,* **10,** 453. (645, *n.* 2)

[Trans.: 'Preface to Bourke, *Scatalogic Rites of All Nations*', C.P., **5**, 88; *Standard Ed.*, **12.**]

(1914*a*) 'Über fausse reconnaissance ("déjà raconté") während der psychoanalytischen Arbeit', *G.S.*, **6**, 76; *G.W.*, **10**, 116. (435, *n*. 1)
  [*Trans.:* 'Fausse reconnaissance ("déjà raconté") in Psycho-Analytic Treatment', C.P., **2**, 334; *Standard Ed.*, **14.**]

(1914*c*) 'Zur Einführung des Narzissmus', *G.S.*, **6**, 155; *G.W.*, **10**, 138 (543, *n*. 2)
  [*Trans.:* 'On Narcissism: an Introduction', *Cf.*, **4**, 30; *Standard Ed.*, **14.**]

(1914*d*) 'Zur Geschichte der psychoanalytischen Bewegung', *G.S.*, **4**, 411; *G.W.*, **10**, 44. (xii, xiv, 384, *n*. 3)
  [*Trans.:* 'On the History of the Psycho-Analytic Movement', C.P., **1**, 287; *Standard Ed.*, **14.**]

(1914*e*) 'Darstellungen der "grossen Leistung" im Traume', *Int. Z. Psychoanal.*, **2**, 384; reprinted in *Die Traumdeutung, G.S.*, **3**, 130; *G.W.*, **2–3**, 416. (448, *n*. 1)
  [*Trans.:* 'The Representation in a Dream of a "Great Achievement"'; included in *The Interpretation of Dreams, Standard Ed.*, **5**, 412.]

(1915*a*) 'Weitere Ratschläge zur Technik der Psychoanalyse III: Bemerkungen über die Übertragungsliebe', *G.S.*, **6**, 120; *G.W.*, **10**, 306. (601, *n*. 2)
  [*Trans.:* 'Observations on Transference-Love (Further Recommendations on the Technique of Psycho-Analysis, III)', C.P., **2**, 377; *Standard Ed.*, **12.**]

(1915*b*) 'Zeitgemässes über Krieg und Tod', *G.S.*, **10**, 315–46; *G.W.*, **10**, 324–55. (289, *n*. 1)
  [*Trans.:* 'Thoughts for the Times on War and Death', C.P., **4**, 288–317; *Standard Ed.*, **14.**]

(1915*d*) 'Die Verdrängung', *G.S.*, **5**, 466; *G.W.*, **10**, 248. (586, *n*. 2, 643 *n*.)
  [*Trans.:* 'Repression', C.P., **4**, 84; *Standard Ed.*, **14.**]

(1915*e*) 'Das Unbewusste', *G.S.*, **5**, 480; *G.W.*, **10**, 264. (640 *n*., 649 *n*., 656 *n*.)
  [*Trans.:* 'The Unconscious', C.P., **4**, 98; *Standard Ed.*, **14.**]

(1916*c*) 'Eine Beziehung zwischen einem Symbol und einem Symptom', *G.S.*, **5**, 310; *G.W.*, **10**, 394. (397 *n*.)
  [*Trans.:* 'A Connection between a Symbol and a Symptom', C.P., **2**, 162; *Standard Ed.*, **14.**]

(1916*d*) 'Einige Charaktertypen aus der psychoanalytischen Arbeit', *G.S.*, **10**, 287; *G.W.*, **10**, 364. (300 *n*.)
  [*Trans.:* 'Some Character-Types Met with in Psycho-Analytic Work', C.P., **4**, 318; *Standard Ed.*, 14.]

FREUD, S. *(cont.)*

(1916–17) *Vorlesungen zur Einführung in die Psychoanalyse,* Vienna. (*G.S.,* 7; *G.W.,* **11.**) (xxix, 51 *n.,* 166 *n.,* 176, *n.* 2, 188 *n.* 1, 265 *n.* 2, 311 *n.,* 332 *n.,* 395, 399, *n.* 1, 440 *n.,* 444, *n.* 1, 449, *n.* 1, 452 *n.,* 466, *n.* 1, 556 *n.,* 620 *n.*)
[*Trans.:* *Introductory Lectures on Psycho-Analysis,* revised ed. London, 1929; *Standard Ed.,* **15** and **16.**]

(1917*d*) 'Metapsychologische Ergänzung zur Traumlehre', *G.S.,* **5,** 520; *G.W.,* **10,** 412. (67 *n.,* 563, *n.* 1, 580 *n.,* 587, 593 *n.*)
[*Trans.:* 'A Metapsychological Supplement to the Theory of Dreams', *C.P.,* **4,** 137; *Standard Ed.,* **14.**]

(1918*b*) 'Aus der Geschichte einer infantilen Neurose', *G.S.,* **8,** 439; *G.W.,* **12,** 29. (217, *n.* 2, 345 *n.,* 407 *n.,* 561, *n.* 1)
[*Trans.:* 'From the History of an Infantile Neurosis', *C.P.,* **3,** 473; *Standard Ed.,* **17.**]

(1919*h*) 'Das Unheimliche', *G.S.,* **10,** 369; *G.W.,* **12,** 229. (392 *n.,* 449, *n.* 3)
[*Trans.:* '"The Uncanny"', *C.P.,* **4,** 368; *Standard Ed.,* **17.**]

(1920*a*) 'Über die Psychogenese eines Falles von weiblicher Homosexualität', *G.S.,* **5,** 312; *G.W.,* **12,** 271. (514, *n.* 2)
[*Trans.:* 'The Psychogenesis of a Case of Female Homosexuality', *C.P.,* **2,** 202; *Standard Ed.,* **18.**]

(1920*f*) 'Ergänzungen zur Traumlehre' (Author's Abstract of Congress Address), *Int. Z. Psychoanal.,* **6,** 397. (Appendix B, 666)
[*Trans.:* 'Supplements to the Theory of Dreams', *Int. J. Psycho-Anal.,* **1,** 354; *Standard Ed.,* **18.**]

(1920*g*) *Jenseits des Lustprinzips,* Vienna. (*G.S.,* **6,** 191; *G.W.,* **13,** 3.) (278, *n.* 2, 301, *n.* 2, 498 *n.,* 578 *n.,* 597, *n.* 1, 604 *n.,* 640 *n.*)
[*Trans.:* *Beyond the Pleasure Principle,* London, 1950; *Standard Ed.,* **18.**]

(1921*b*) Introduction [in English] to Varendonck, *The Psychology of Day-Dreams,* London. (*G.W.,* **13,** 439; *Standard Ed.,* **18.**) (529, *n.* 3)

(1921*c*) Massenpsychologie und Ich-Analyse, Vienna. (*G.S.,* **6,** 261; *G.W.,* **13,** 73.) (184 *n.,* 514, *n.* 1)
[*Trans.:* *Group Psychology and the Analysis of the Ego,* London, 1922; *Standard Ed.,* **18.**]

(1922*a*) 'Traum und Telepathie', *G.S.,* **3,** 278; *G.W.,* **13,** 165. (39 *n.,* 195, *n.* 1, 366, *n.,* 439, *n.* 2, 563, *n.* 1, 599, *n. 2,* 618, *n.*)
[*Trans.:* 'Dreams and Telepathy', *C.P.,* **4,** 408; *Standard Ed.,* **18.**]

(1922*b*) 'Über einige neurotische Mechanismen bei Eifer-sucht, Paranoia und Homosexualität', *G.S.,* **5.** 387; *G.W.,* **13,** 195. (121 *n.*)
[*Trans.:* 'Some Neurotic Mechanisms in Jealousy, Paranoia and Homosexuality', *C.P.,* **2,** 232; *Standard Ed.,* **18.**]

(1922c) 'Nachschrift zur Analyse des kleinen Hans', *G.S.*, **8**, 264; *G.W.*, **13**, 431. (559, *n.* 3)

[*Trans.*: 'Postscript to the "Analysis of a Phobia in a Five-Year-Old-Boy"', *C.P.*, **3**, 288; *Standard Ed.*, **10.**]

(1923a [1922]) '"Psychoanalyse" und "Libido Theorie"', *G.S.*, **11**, 201; *G.W.*, **13**, 211. (528, *n.* 1)

[*Trans.*: Two Encyclopædia Articles', *C.P.*, **5**, 107; *Standard Ed.*, **18.**]

(1923b) *Das Ich und das Es*, Vienna. (*G.S.*, **6**, 353; *G.W.*, **13**, 237.) (194 *n.*, 514, *n.* 1, 580 *n.*, 603 *n.*, 653 *n.*)

[*Trans.*: *The Ego and the Id*, London, 1927; *Standard Ed.*, **19.**]

(1923c) 'Bemerkungen zur Theorie und Praxis der Traumdeutung', *G.S.*, **3**, 305; *G.W.*, **13**, 301. (136 *n.*, 197 *n.*, 358, *n.* 3, 514, *n.* 1)

[*Trans.*: 'Remarks on the Theory and Practice of Dream-Interpretation', *C.P.*, **5**, 136; *Standard Ed.*, **19.**]

(*1923d*) 'Eine Teufelsneurose im siebzehnten Jahrhundert', *G.S.*, **10**, 409; *G.W.*, **13**, 317. (393, *n.* 3)

[*Trans.*: 'A Seventeenth Century Demonological Neurosis', *C.P.*, **4**, 436; *Standard Ed.*, **19.**]

(1923f) 'Josef Popper-Lynkeus und die Theorie des Traumes', *G.S.*, **11**, 295; *G.W.*, **13**, 357. (126, *n.* 3, 343, *n.* 2)

[*Trans.*: 'Josef Popper-Lynkeus and the Theory of Dreams', *Standard Ed.*, **19.**]

(1924–34) *Gesammelte Schriften*, Vienna, (xii, xxxi, 37, *n.* 1, 55, *n.* 1, 160, *n.* 1, 223, *n.* 2, 346 *n.*, 546 *n.*)

(1924c) 'Das ökonomische Problem des Masochismus', *G.S.*, **5**, 374; *G.W.*, **13**, 371. (192, *n.* 3)

[*Trans.*: 'The Economic Problem of Masochism', *C.P.*, **2**, 255; *Standard Ed.*, **19.**]

(1925a) 'Notiz über den Wunderblock', *G.S.*, **6**, 415; *G.W.*, **14**, 3. (578 *n.*)

[*Trans.*: 'A Note on the "Mystic Writing-Pad"', *C.P.*, **5**, 175; *Standard Ed.*, **20.**]

(1925d) *'Selbstdarstellung'*, *G.S.*, **11**, 119; *G.W.*, **14**, 33. (474 *n.*)

[*Trans.*: *An Autobiographical Study*, London, 1935; *Standard Ed.*, **20.**]

(1925i) 'Einige Nachträge zum Ganzen der Traumdeutung', *G.S.*, **3**, 172; *G.W.*, **1**, 559. (39 *n.*, 106, *n.* 2, 563, *n.* 2, 659, *n.* 2)

[*Trans.*: 'Some Additional Notes upon Dream-Interpretation as a Whole', *C.P.*, **5**, 150; *Standard Ed.*, **20.**]

(1925j) 'Einige psychische Folgen des anatomischen Geschlechtsunterschieds', *G.S.*, **11**, 8; *G.W.*, **14**, 19. (291 *n.*)

[*Trans.*: 'Some Psychological Consequences of the Anatomical Distinction between the Sexes', *C.P.*, **5**, 186; *Standard Ed.*, **19.**]

FREUD, S. *(cont.)*

(1926*d*) *Hemmung, Symptom und Angst,* Vienna. (*G.S.,* **11,** 23; *G.W.,* **13,** 113.) (195, *n.* 2, 373, *n.* 1, 436, *n.* 2, 643 *n.*)

[*Trans.: Inhibitions, Symptoms and Anxiety,* London, 1936; *The Problem of Anxiety,* New York, 1936; *Standard Ed.,* **20.**]

(1927*c*) *Die Zukunft einer Illusion,* Vienna. (*G.S.,* **11,** 411; *G.W.,* **14,** 325.) (492, *n.* 1)

[*Trans.: The Future of an Illusion,* London, 1928; *Standard Ed.,* **21.**]

(1929*b*) 'Brief an Maxime Leroy über einen Traum des Cartesius', *G.S.,* **12,** 403; *G.W.,* **14,** 558. (Appendix B, 666)

[*Trans.:* 'A Letter to Maxime Leroy on a Dream of Descartes', *Standard Ed.,* **21.**]

(1930*a*) *Das Unbehagen in der Kultur,* Vienna. (*G.S.,* **12,** 29; *G.W.,* **14,** 421). (109 *n.*)

[*Trans.: Civilization and its Discontents,* London, 1930; *Standard Ed.,* **21.**]

(1930*e*) 'Goethe-Preis 1930', *G.S.,* **12,** 406; *G.W.,* **14,** 545. (175 *n.,* 300 *n.*)

[*Trans.:* 'The Goethe Prize for 1930', *Standard Ed.,* **21.**]

(1931*b*) 'Über die weibliche Sexualität', *G.S.,* **12,** 120; *G.W.,* **14,** 517. (291 *n.*)

[*Trans.:* 'Female Sexuality', *C.P.,* **5,** 252; *Standard Ed.,* **21.**]

(1932*c*) 'Meine Berührung mit Josef Popper-Lynkeus', *G.S.,* **12,** 415; *G.W.,* **16,** 261. (xii, 126, *n.* 3, 343, *n.* 2)

[*Trans.:* 'My Contact with Josef Popper-Lynkeus', *C.P.,* **5,** 295; *Standard Ed.,* **22.**]

(1933*a*) *Neue Folge der Vorlesungzur Einführung in die Psychoanalyse,* Vienna. (*G.S.,* **12,** 151; *G.W.,* **15.**) (39 *n.,* 124 *n.,* 369 *n.,* 528, *n.* 2, 543, *n.* 2, 569 *n.,* 580 *n.,* 597, *n.* 1, 643 *n.*)

[*Trans.: New Introductory Lectures on Psycho-Analysis,* London, 1933; *Standard Ed.,* **22.**]

(1940*a* [1938]) *Abriss der Psychoanalyse,* (*G.W.,* **17,** 67.) (Appendix B, 666)

[*Trans.: An Outline of Psycho-Analysis,* London and New York, 1949; *Standard Ed.,* **23.**]

(1940*c* [1922]) 'Das Medusenhaupt', *G.W.,* **17,** 47. (392 *n.*)

[*Trans.:* 'Medusa's Head', *C.P.,* **5,** 105; *Standard Ed.,* **18.**]

(1940*d* [1892]) With Breuer, J., 'Zur Theorie des hysterischen Anf alls', *G.W.,* **17,** 9. (xvii)

[*Trans.:* 'On the Theory of Hysterical Attacks', *C.P.,* **5,** 27; *Standard Ed.,* **1.**]

(1941*a* [1892]) 'Brief an Josef Breuer', *G.W.,* **17,** 5. (604 *n.*)

[*Trans.:* 'A Letter to Josef Breuer', *C.P.,* **5,** 25; *Standard Ed.,* **1.**]

(1941*c* [1899]) 'Eine erfüllte Traumahnung', *G.W.*, **17**, 21. (39 *n.*, 97, *n.* 3, 661–4)

[*Trans.:* 'A Premonitory Dream Fulfilled', *C.P.*, **5**, 70; *Standard Ed.*, **5**, 623.

(1950*a* [1887–1902]) *Aus den Anfängen der Psychoanalyse*, London, (xii, xiv-xx, xxvi, 51 *n.*, 126, *n.* 1, 145, *n.* 1, 149, *n.* 2, 150 *n.*, 151, *n.* 1, 154 *n.*, 155 *n.*, 158 *n.*, 163 *n.*, 170 *n.*, 175 *n.*, 178 *n.*, 184 *n.*, 190, *n.* 2, 195, *n.* 1, 205, *n.* 1, 226, *n.* 1, 226, *n.* 2, 227, *n.* 2, 228, *n.* 2, 233 *n.*, 238, *nn.* 1 and 2, 247 *n.*, 265 *n.*, 274 *n.*, 277, *n.* 1, 281 *n.*, 297, *n.* 1, 301, *n.* 2, 332 *n.*, 352 *n.*, 353, *n.* 1, 422, *n.* 2, 461, *n.* 1, 472 *n.*, 475 *n.*, 491, *n.* 2, 501 *n.*, 505 *n.*, 530 *n.*, 537 *n.*, 547 *n.*, 553, *n.* 2, 574 *n.*, 578 *n.*, 604 *n.*, 632 *n.*, 640 *n.*, 644 *n.*, 647 *n.*, 654 *n.*, 659, *n.* 1, 661, *n.* 1, 667) [In part in *Standard Ed.*, **1**.]

FUCHS, E. (1909–12) *Illustrierte Sittengeschichte* (Ergänzungs bande), Munich. (382 *n.*)

GALTON, F. (1907) *Inquiries into Human Faculty and its Development*, 2nd ed., Everyman's Edition, London (1st ed., 1883.) (172, 328, 532–3)

GARNEER, A. (1872) *Traité des facultés de Pâme, contenant l'histoire des principales théories psychologiques*, (3 vols.), Paris. (1st ed., 1852.) (**60**, 266–7)

GIESSLER, C. M. (1888) *Beiträge zur Phänomenologie des Traumlebens*, Halle. (120, n. 1)

(1890) *Aus den Tiefen des Traumlebens*, Halle. (120, n. 1)

(1896) *Die physiologischen Beziehungen der Traumvor-gänge*, Halle. (120, n. 1)

GIROU DE BOUZAREINGES, C. and GIROU DE BOUZAREINGES, L. (1848) *Physiologie: essai sur le mécanisme des sensations, des idées et des sentiments*, Paris. (58)

GOBLOT, E. (1896) 'Sur le souvenir des rêves', *Rev. phil.*, **42**, 288. (540, 614)

GOMPERZ, T. (1866) *Traumdeutung und Zauberei*, Vienna. (130, *n.* 2)

GOTTHARDT, O. (1912) *Die Traumbcher des Mittelalters*, Eisleben. (38, *n.* 2)

GRŒSINGER, W. (1845) *Pathologie und Therapie der psychischen Krankheiten*, Stuttgart. (167)

(1861) do., 2nd ed. (quoted by Radestock). (123, 264 *n.*)

GRUPPE, O. (1906) *Griechische Mythologie und Religions-geschichte*, Munich. (In Müller, *Handbuch der klassischen Altertums-Wissenschaft*, **5**, 2.) (37–8)

GUISLAIN, J. (1833) *Leçons orales sur les phrénopathies* (3 vols.), Brussels. (121) [Quotation in text is from *German trans.: Abhandlungen über die Phrenopathien*, Nuremberg, 1838.]

HAFFNER, P. (1887) 'Schlafen und Träumerf, *Sammlung zeitgemässer Broschüren*, 226, Frankfurt. (39, 84 *n.*, 96, *n.* 1, 99–101)

HAGEN, F. W. (1846) 'Psychologie und Psychiatrie', *Wagner's Handwörterbuch der Physiologie,* **2,** 692, Brunswick. (122)

HALLAM, F. and WEED, S. (1896) 'A Study of Dream Consciousness', *Amer. J. Psychol.,* **7,** 405. (52, 168, 197)

HARTMANN, E. VON (1890) *Philosophie des Unbewussten,* 10th ed., Leipzig. (1st ed., 1869.) (167, 567 *n.*)
[*Trans.: Philosophy of the Unconscious,* by W. C. Coup-land, London, 1884.]

HARTMANN, H., See BETLHEIM and HARTMANN.

HENNINGS, J. C. (1784) *Von den Träumen und Nachtwandlern,* Weimar. (47, 58)

HENZEN, W. (1890) *Über die Träume in der altnordischen Sagaliteratur,* (Thesis) Leipzig. (442–3)

HERBERT, J. F. (1892) *Psychologie als Wissenschaft neu gegrundet auf Erfahrung, Metaphysik und Mathematik.* (*Zweiter, analytischer Teil*); Vol. 6 in *Herbart's Sämtliche Werke* (ed. K. Kehrbach), Langensalza. (1st ed., Königsberg, 1825.) (108)

HERMANN, K. F. (1858) *Lehrbuch der gottesdienstlichen Alterthümer der Griechen,* 2nd ed., Heidelberg. (Pt. II of *Lehrbuch der griechischen Antiquitäten.*) (67 *n.*)
(1882) *Lehrbuch der griechischen Privatalterthümer,* 3rd ed., Freiburg. (Pt. IV of *Lehrbuch der griechischen Antiquitäten*). (67 *n.*)

HERODOTUS *History.* (433 *n.*)
- [*Trans,* by A. D. Godley, Vol. III (Loeb Classical Library), London and New York, 1922.]

HERVEY DE SAINT-DENYS, MARQUIS D', (1867) *Les rêves et les moyens de les diriger,* Paris. (Published anonymously.) (47, 59, 93–4, 611)

HILDEBRANDT, F. W. (1875) *Der Traum und seine Verwer-thung für's Leben,* Leipzig. (43–4, 49, 52–4, 59–61, 88, 95–7, 99–104)

HIPPOCRATES *Ancient Medicine* and *Regimen.* (37, *n.* 3, 67 *n.*, 438)
[*Trans,* by W. H. S. Jones, Vols. I and IV (Loeb Classical Library), London and New York, 1923 and 1931.]

HITSCHMANN, E. (1913) 'Goethe als Vatersymbol', *Int. Z. Psychoanal.,* **1,** 569. (389) Hobbes, T. (1651) *Leviathan,* London. (581 *n.*)

HOFFBAUER, J. C. (1796) *Naturlehre der Seele,* Halle. (58)

HOHNBAUM (1830) In C. F. Nasse: *Jb. Anthrop.,* **1** (120)

HUG-HELLMUTH, H. VON (1911) 'Analyse eines Traumes eines 5½ jährigen Knaben', *Zbl. Psychoanal.,* **2,** 122. (164 *n.*)
(1913) 'Kindertraume', *Int. Z. Psychoanal.,* **1,** 470. (164 *n.*)
(1915) 'Ein Traum der sich selbst deutet', *Int. Z. Psycho-anal.,* **3,** 33. (176, *n.* 2)

*IDELER, K. W. (1862) 'Die Enstehung des Wahnsinns aus den Traumen', *Charité Annalen,* **3,** Berlin. (120, *n.* 1)

*IWAYA, S. (1902) 'Traumdeutung in Japan', *Ostasien,* 302. (38, *n.* 2)

JEKELS, L. (1917) 'Shakespeare's Macbeth', *Imago, S,* 170. (300 *n.*)

JESSEN, P. (1855) *Versuch einer wissenschaftlichen Begründung der Psychologie,* Berlin. (42, 47, 57, 79, 98, 104)

JODL, F. (1896) *Lehrbuch der Psychologie,* Stuttgart. (89)

JONES, E. (1910*a*) 'The Oedipus Complex as an Explanation of Hamlet's Mystery', *Amer. J. Psychol.,* **21,** 72. (300 *n.*)

(1910*b*) 'Freud's Theory of Dreams', *Amer. J. PsychoL,* **21,** 283. (436–7)

(1911) 'The Relationship between Dreams and Psycho-neurotic Symptoms', *Am. J. Insanity,* **68,** 57. (608, *n.* 2)

(1912*a*) 'Unbewusste Zahlenbehandlung', *Zbl. Psychoanal.,* **2,** 241. (453, *n.* 2)

(1912*b*) 'A Forgotten Dream', *J. Abnorm. PsychoL,* **7,** 5. (559, *n.* 2)

(1914*a*) 'Frau und Zimmer', *Int. Z. Psychoanal.,* **2,** 380. (389 *n.*)

(1914*b*) 'Zahnziehen und Geburt', *Int. Z. Psychoanal.,* **2,** 380. (423, *n.* 1)

(1916) 'The Theory of Symbolism', *Brit. J. PsychoL,* **9,** 181. (386, *n.* 2)

(1949) *Hamlet and Oedipus,* London. (300 *n.*)

(1953) *Sigmund Freud: Life and Work,* 1, London, (xxii, 144, *n.* 1, 203 *n.,* 667)

JOSEPHUS, FLAVIUS *Antiquitates Judaicae.* (369)

  [*Trans.: Ancient History of the Jews* by W. Whiston, London, 1874.]

JUNG, C. G. (ed.) (1906) *Diagnostische Assoziationsstudien* (2 vols.), Leipzig. (570, *n.* 2)

  [*Trans.: Studies in Word-Association,* London.]

(1907) Über die Psychologie der Dementia præcox, Halle. (568 *n.*)

  [*Trans.:* The Psychology of Dementia Præcox, New York, 1909.]

(1910*a*) 'Über Konflikte der kindlichen Seele', *Jb. psycho-anal, psychopath. Forsch.,* **2,** 33. (164 *n.*)

(1910*b*) 'Ein Beitrag zur Psychologie des Gerüchtes', *Zbl. Psychoanal.,* **1,** 81. (370)

(1911) 'Ein Beitrag zur Kenntnis des Zahlentraumes', *Zbl. PsychoanaL,* **1,** 567. (453, *n.* 2)

KANT, I. (1764) *Versuch über die Krankheiten des Kopjes.* (121–2)

(1798) *Anthropologie in pragmatischer Hinsichi.* (103–4)

KARPINSKA, L. VON (1914) 'Ein Beitrag zur Analyse "sinnloser" Worte in Traume', *Int. Z. Psychoanal.,* **2,** 164. (339)

KAZOWSKY, A. D. (1901) 'Zur Frage nach dem Zusammenhange von Träumen und Wahnvorstellungen', *Neurol. Zbl.,* 440 and 508. (120, *n.* 1)

KERCHGRABER, F. (1912) 'Der Hut als Symbol des Genitales', *Zbl. Psychoanal. Psychother.*, **3**, 95. (397 *n.*)

KLEINPAUL, R. (1898) *Die Lebendigen und die Toten in Volksglauben, Religion und Sage,* Leipzig. (386, *n.* 2)

KRAUSS, A. (1858–59) 'Der Sinn im Wahnsinn', *Allg. Z. Psychol.*, **15**, 617 and **16**, 222. (70–1, 120–2, 123)

KRAUSS, F. S. See Artemidorus. (391, *n.* 1)

LADD, G. T. (1892) 'Contribution to the Psychology of Visual Dreams', *Mind,* (New Series) **1**, 299. (66–7, 628)

LANDAUER, K. (1918) 'Handlungen des Schlafenden', *Z. ges. Neur. Psychiat.*, 39, 329. (258 *n.*)

*LASÈGUE, C. (1881) 'Le délire alcoolique n'est pas un délire, mais un rêve', *Arch. gén. Méd.* (120, *n.* 1)

LAUER, C. (1913) 'Das Wesen des Traumes in der Beurteilung der talmudischen und rabbinischen Literatur', *Int. Z. Psychoanal.*, **1**, 459. (38, *n.* 2)

LEHMANN, A. (1908) *Aberglaube und Zauberei von den ältesten Zeiten bis in die Gegenwart* (German trans, by Petersen), Stuttgart. (67 *n.*)

LE LORRAIN, J. (1894) 'La durée du temps dans les rêves', *Rev. phil.*, **38**, 275. (60, 97, 534) (1895) 'Le rêve', *Rev. phil,* **40**, 59. (534, 606, *n.* 1)

LÉLUT. (1852) 'Mémoire sur les sommeil, les songes et le sonnambulisme', *Ann. méd.-psychol.*, **4**, 331. (121)

LEMOINE, A. (1855) *Du sommeil au point de vue physiologique et psychologique,* Paris. (87)

Leroy. See Bernard-Leroy.

LEURET, F. (1834) *Fragments psychologiques sur la folie,* Paris. (568)

LIÉBEAULT, A. A. (1889) *Le sommeil provoqué et les états analogues,* Paris. (609 *n.*)

LIPPS, T. (1883) *Grundtatsachen des Seelenlebens,* Bonn. (257) (1897) 'Der Begriff des Unbewussten in der Psychologie', *Records of the Third Internat. Congr. Psychol.*, Munich. (650–51, 652)

*LLOYD, W. (1877) *Magnetism and Mesmerism in Antiquity,* London (67 *n.*)

LÖWINGER. (1908) 'Der Traum in der jüdischen Literatur', *Mitt. jüd. Volksk.*, **10**. (38, *n.* 2)

LUCRETIUS *De rerum natura.* (42) [*Trans,* by W. H. D. Rouse (Loeb Classical Library), London and New York, 1924.]

'LYNKEUS' (J. Popper) (1899) *Phantasien eines Realisten,* Dresden. (126, 343, *n.* 2)

MAASS, J. G. E. (1805) *Versuch über die Leidenschaften,* Halle. (42)

MACARIO, M. M. A. (1847) 'Des rêves, considérés sous le rapport physiologique et pathologique', Pt. II, *Ann. médpsychol.*, **9**, 27. (121)

(1857) *Du sommeil, des rêves et du sonnambulisme dans l'état de santé et de maladie*, Paris-Lyons. (536)

MACNTSH, R. (1830) *Philosophy of Sleep*, Glasgow. (58)
[*German trans.: Der Schlaf in alien seinen Gestalten*, Leipzig, 1835.]

MAEDER, A. (1908) 'Die Symbolik in den Legenden, Märchen, Gebrauchen, und Träumen', *Psychiat.-neurol. Wschr.*, **10**, 55. (386, *n.* 2)

(1912) 'Über die Funktion des Traumes', *Jb. psychoanal. psychopath. Forsch.*, **4**, 692. (618 *n.*)

MAINE DE BIRAN, M. F. P. (1834) *Nouvelles considérations sur les rapports du physique et du moral de l'homme*, (ed. by V. Cousin), Paris. (121)

MARCINOWSKI, J. (1911) 'Eine kleine Mitteilung', *Zbl. Psycho-anal*, **1**, 575. (337–8)

(1912*a*) 'Gezeichnete Träume', *Zbl. Psychoanal.*, **2**, 490 (391)

(1912*b*) 'Drei Romane in Zahlen', *Zbl. Psychoanal.*, **2**, 619. (453, *n.* 2)

MAUDSLEY, H. (1868) *Psychology and Pathology of the Mind*, London. (1st ed., 1867.) (650 *n.*)

MAURY, L. F. A. (1853) 'Nouvelles observations sur les analogies des phénomènes du rêve et de l'aliénation mentale', Pt. II, *Ann. méd-psychol*, **5**, 404. (61, 121, 533–5)

(1878) *Le sommeil et les rêves*, Paris. (1st ed., 1861.) (42, 46, 50, 58–61, 65–6, 68–9, 87–9, 91–4, 97, 104–6, 109, 120, 121, 124, 222, 562 *n.*, 570, *n.* 1, 614)

*MEIER, G. F. (1758) *Versuch einer Erkdärung des Nachtwandelns*, Halle. (57–8)

MEYNERT, T. (1892) *Sammlung von populärwissenschaftlichen Vorträgen über den Bau und die Leistungen des Gehirns*, Vienna. (256, 284)

MIURA, K. (1906) 'Über japanische Traumdeutere', *Mitt. dtsch. Ges. Naturk. Ostasiens*, **10**, 291. (38, *n.* 2)

MOREAU, J. (1855) 'De l'identité de l'état de rêve et de folie', *Ann. méd.-psychol.*, **1**, 361. (121)

MÜLLER, J. (1826) *Vber die phantastischen Gesichtserscheinungen*, Coblenz. (65–6)

MYERS, F. W. H. (1892) 'Hypermnesic Dreams', *Proc. Soc. Psych. Res.*, **8**, 362. (47)

NÄCKE, P. (1903) 'Über sexuelle Träume', *Arch. Kriminalanthropol*, 307. (431)

(1905) 'Der Traum als feinstes Reagens f. d. Art d. sexuellen Empfindens', *Monatschr. f. Krim.-Psychol.*, **2**, 500. (431)

(1907) 'Kontrastträume und spez. sexuelle Kontrastträume', *Arch. Kriminalanthropol.*, **24**, 1. (431)

NÄCKE, P. *(cont.)*

(1908) 'Beiträge zu den sexuellen Träumen', *Arch. Kriminalanthropol.*, **29,** 363. (431)

(1911) 'Die diagnostische und prognostische Brauchbarkeit der sex. Träume', *Ärztl. Sachv.-Ztg.*, 2. (431)

NEGELEIN, J. VON (1912) 'Der Traumschlüssel des Jaggadeva', *Relig. Gesch. Vers.*, **11,** 4. (38, *n.* 2)

NELSON, J. (1888) 'A Study of Dreams', *Amer. J. Psychol.*, **1,** 367. (51)

NORDENSKJÖLD, O. *et al* (1904) *Antarctic. Zwei Jahre in Schnee und Eis am Südpol*, (2 vols.), Berlin. (164 *n.*)

[*English trans*, (abr.) : *Antarctica*, London, 1905.]

PACHANTONI, D. (1909) 'Der Traum als Urschprung von Wahnideen bei Alkoholdelirianten', *Zbl. Nervenheilk.*, **32,** 796. (120, *n.* 1)

PAULHAN, F. (1894) 'À propos de l'activité de l'esprit dans le rêve'; under 'Correspondence' in *Rev. phil*, **38,** 546. (540)

PEISSE, L. (1857) *La médecine et les médecins*, Paris. (124)

PFAFF, E. R. (1868) *Das Traumleben und seine Deutung nach den Prinzipien der Araber, Perser, Griechen, Inder und Ägypter*, Leipzig. (99)

PFISTER, O. (1909) 'Ein Fall von psychoanalytischer Seelsorge und Seelenheilung', *Evangelische Freiheit*, Tubingen. (439, *n.* 2)

(1911–12) 'Die psychologische Enträtselung der religiösen Glossolalie und der automatischen Kryptographie', *Jb. psychoanal, psychopath. Forsch.*, **3,** 427 and 730. (392)

(1913) 'Kryptolalie, Kryptographie und unbewusstes Vexierbild bei Normalen', *Jb. psychoanal, und psychopath. Eorsch.*, **5,** 115. (392)

PICHON, A. E. (1896) *Contribution à l'étude des délires oniriques ou délires de rêve*, Bordeaux. (120, *n.* 1)

PILCZ, A. (1899) 'Über eine gewisse Gesetzmässigkeit in den Träumen', Author's Abstract, *Mschr. Psychiat. Neurol.*, **5,** 231, Berlin. (54)

PLATO *Republic.* (99, 658)

[*Trans*, by B. Jowett (Dialogues, Vol. II), Oxford, 1871.]

POHORILLES, N. E. (1913) 'Eduard von Hartmanns Gesetz der von unbewussten Zielvorstellungen geleiteten Assoziationen', *Int. Z. Psychoanal.*, **1,** 605. (567 *n.*)

PÖTZL, O. (1917) 'Experimentell erregte Traumbilder in ihren Beziehungen zum indirekten Sehen', *Z, ges. Neurol. Psychiat.*, **37,** 278. (214, *n.* 2)

PRINCE, MORTON (1910) 'The Mechanism and Interpretation of Dreams', *J. abnorm. Psychol.*, **5,** 139. (559)

PURKINJE, J. E. (1846) 'Wachen, Schlaf, Traum und verwandte Zustände', *R. Wagner's Handwörterbuch der Physiologie*, **3,** 412, Brunswick. (115, 167)

PUTNAM, J. J. (1912) 'Ein charakteristischer Kindertraum', *Zbl. Psychoanal.,* **2,** 328. (164 *n.*)

*RAALTE, F. VAN (1912) 'Kinderdroomen', *Het Kind,* Jan. (164 *n.*)

RADESTOCK, P. (1879) *Schlaf und Traum,* Leipzig. (42, 68, 77–8, 88–9, 98, 103, 120–3, 167)

RANK, O. (1909) *Der Mythus von der Geburt des Helden,* Leipzig and Vienna. (290 *n.*, 436, *n.* 1.)

[*Trans.: Myth of the Birth of the Hero,* New York, 1913]

(1910) 'Ein Traum der sich selbst deutet', *Jb. Psychoanal. psychopath. Forsch.,* **2,** 465. (194 *n.*, 271, *n.* 2, 345 *n.*, 370, 384, *n.* 3, 433 *n.*, 441)

(1911*a*) 'Beispiel eines verkappten Ödipustraumes', *Zbl. Psychoanal.,* **1,** 167. (433 *n.*)

(1911*b*) 'Belege zur Rettungsphantasie', *Zbl. Psychoanal.,* **1,** 331. (439, *n.* 2)

(1911*c*) 'Zum Thema der Zahnreizträume', *Zbl. Psychoanal.,* **1,** 408. (423–27)

(1912*a*) 'Die Symbolschichtung im Wecktraum und ihre Wiederkehr im mythischen Denken', *Jb. psychoanal. psychopath. Forsch.,* **4,** 51. (253 *n.*, 271, *n.* 2, 387, *n.* 2, 402, 437–39)

(1912*b*) 'Aktuelle Sexualregungen als Traumanlässe', *Zbl. Psychoanal.,* **2,** 596. (271, *n.* 2)

(1912*c*) *Das Inzest-Motiv in Dichtung und Sage,* Leipzig and Vienna. (290 *n.*)

(1913) 'Eine noch nicht beschriebene Form des Ödipus-Traumes', *Int. Z. Psychoanal.,* **1,** 151. (433 *n.*)

(1914) 'Die "Geburts-Rettungsphantasie" in Traum und Dichtung', *Int. Z. Psychoanal.,* **2,** 43. (439, *n.* 2)

RANK, O., and SACHS, H. (1913) *Die Bedeutung der Psychoanalyse für die Geisteswissenschaften,* Wiesbaden. (386, *n.* 2)

[*Trans.: The Significance of Psychoanalysis for the Mental Sciences,* New York, 1915.]

RÉGIS, E. (1894) 'Les hallucinations oniriques ou du sommeil des dégénérés mystiques', *Compte rendu Congrès Méd. Alién.,* 260, Paris, 1895. (120, *n.* 1)

REIK, T. (1911) 'Zur Rettungssymbolik', *Zbl. Psychoanal.,* **1,** 499. (439, *n.* 2)

(1915) 'Gold und Kot', *Int. Z. Psychoanal,* **3.,** 183. (439)

REITLER, R. (1913*a*) 'Zur Augensymbolik', *Int. Z. Psychoanal.,* **1,** 159. (433 *n.*)

(1913*b*) 'Zur Genital-und Sekret-Symbolik', *Int. Z. Psychoanal,* **1,** 492. (394)

ROBERT, W. (1886) *Der Traum als Naturnotwendigkeit erklärt,* Hamburg. (51, 110–3, 197, 210–1, 221, 618, 630)

ROBITSEK, A. (1912) 'Zur Frage der Symbolik in dem Träumen Gesunder', *Zbl. Psychoanal.,* **2.,** 340. (408–11)

ROFFENSTEIN, G. (1923) 'Experimentelle Symbolträume', Z. ges. Neurol. Psychiat., **87**, 362. (419)

R[ORSCHACH], H. (1912) 'Zur Symbolik der Schlange und der Kravatte', Zbl. Psychoanal., **2**, 675. (391, n. 1)

SACHS, H. (1911) 'Zur Darstellungs-Technik des Traumes', Zbl. Psychoanal., **1**, 413. (445–46)

—— (1912) 'Traumdeutung und Menschenkenntnis', Jb. Psychoanal, psychopath. Forsch., **3**, 568. (659)

—— (1913) 'Ein Traum Bismarcks', Int. Z. Psychoanal., **1**, 80. (413–16)

—— (1914) 'Das Zimmer als Traumdarstellung des Weibes', Int. Z. Psychoanal., **2**, 35. (390) See also Rank and Sachs.

SALOMON, ALMOLI BEN JACOB (1637) Pithrôn Chalômôth, Amsterdam. (38, n. 2)

SANCTIS, SANTE DE (1896) I sogni e il sonno nell' islerismo e nella epilepsia, Rome. (120)

—— (1897a) 'Les maladies mentales et les rêves', extrait des Ann. Soc. Méd. de Gand, **76**, 177. (120)

*(1897b) 'Sui rapporti d'identità, di somiglianza, di analogia e di equivalenza fra sogno e pazzia', Riv. quindicinale Psicol. Psichiàt. Neuropatol., Nov. 15. (120)

—— (1898a) 'Psychoses et rêves', Rapport au Congrès de neurol. et d'hypnologie de Bruxelles 1897; Comptes rendus, **1**, 137. (120)

—— (1898b) 'I sogni dei neuropatici e dei pazzi', Arch, psichiat. antrop. crim., **19**, 342. (120) (1899) I sogni, Turin. (121, 125)

[German transi, by O. Schmidt, Halle, 1901.]

SCHERNER, K. A. (1861) Das Leben des Traumes, Berlin. (70–1, 115–19, 165 n., 258–61, 370, 381, 388, 394 n., 438, 585, 630, 651)

SCHLEIERMACHER, F. (1862) Psychologie, (Vol. 6, Sec. 3 in Collected Works, ed. L. George), Berlin. (82, 103, 134)

SCHOLZ, F. (1887) Schlaf und Traum, Leipzig. (54, 90, 99, 168)

[Trans.: Sleep and Dreams by H. M. Jewett, New York, 1893.]

SCHOPENHAUER, A. (1862) 'Versuch über das Geistersehen und was damit zusammenhängt', Parerga und Paralipomena (Essay V), **1**, 213, 2nd ed., Berlin. (1st ed. 1851.) (70, 98, 122)

SCHRÖTTER, K. (1912) 'Experimentelle Träume', Zbl. Psychoanal., **2**, 638. (419)

SCHUBERT, G. H. VON (1814) Die Symbolik des Traumes, Bamberg. (96, 387)

SCHWARZ, F. (1913) 'Traum und Traumdeutung nach "Abdalgan an-Nabulusi"', Z. deutsch. morgenl. Ges., **67**, 473. (38, n. 2)

SECKER, F. (1909–10) 'Chinesische Ansichten über den Traum', Neue metaph. Rndschr., **17**, 101. (38, n. 2)

SIEBECK, H. (1877) 'Das Traumleben der Seele', Sammlung gemeinverständlicher Vorträge, Berlin. (90)

SILBERER, H. (1909) 'Bericht über eine Methode, gewisse symbolische Halluzinations-Erscheinungen hervorzurufen und zu beobachten', *Jb. psychoanal, psychopath. Forsch., 1,* 513. (82, *n.* 1, 134, *n.* 2, 379–80, 413, 448 *n.*, 541–3)

  (1910) 'Phantasie und Mythos', *Jb. psychoanal, psychopath. Forsch.,* **2,** 541. (134, *n.* 2, 248, *n.* 3)

  (1912) 'Symbolik des Erwachens und Schwellensymbolik überhaupt', *Jb. psychoanal, psychopath. Forsch.,* **3,** 621. (134, *n.* 2,541–3, 598)

  (1914) *Probleme der Mystik und Hirer Symbolik,* Vienna and Leipzig. (562)

SIMON, P. M. (1888) *Le monde des rêves,* Paris. (63, 67–8, 72, 167)

*SPERBER, H. (1912) 'Über den Einfluss sexueller Momente auf Entstehung und Entwicklung der Sprache', *Imago,* **1,** 405. (387 *n.*)

SPIELREIN, S. (1913) 'Traum von "Pater Freudenreich"', *Int. Z. Psychoanal.,* **1,** 484. (164 *n.*)

SPITTA, K. (1882) *Die Schlaf-und Traumzustände der mensch-lichen Seele,* Tubingen. (1st ed., 1878.) (68, 80, 83, 88, 89–92, 96, *n.* 1, 98–9, 102, 104, 120, 122, 255, 551)

SPITTELER, C. (1914) *Meine frühesten Erlebnisse,* Jena. (194 *n.*, 285, *n.* 2)

STANNIUS, H. (1849) *Das peripherische Nervensystem der Fische, anatomisch und physiologisch untersucht,* Rostock. (448, 489, *n.* 1)

STÄRCKE, A. (1911) 'Ein Traum der das Gegenteil einer Wunscherfullung zu verwirklichen schien', *Zbl. Psychoanal.,* **2,** 86. (192)

STÄRCKE, J. (1913) 'Neue Traumexperimente in Zusammenhang mit älteren und neueren Traumtheorien', *Jb. psychoanal, psychopath. Forsch.,* **5,** 233. (94, 165, *n.* 2)

STEKEL, W. (1909) 'Beiträge zur Traumdeutung', *Jb. psycho-anal, psychopath. Forsch.,* **1,** 458. (310, 373, 384, *n.* 3, 392–4, 397 *n.*, 398 *n.*, 415)

  (1911) *Die Sprache des Traumes,* Wiesbaden. (385, 392–4, 420, *n.* 1, 432, 446)

STRICKER, S. (1879) *Studien fiber das Bewusstsein,* Vienna. (90, 106, 497)

STRÜMPELL, A. VON (1883–84) *Lehrbuch der speciellen Pathologie und Therapie der inneren Krankheiten,* Leipzig. (56)

  [*Trans.: Text-book of Medicine,* (2 vols.), 4th Amer. Ed., New York, 1912.]

STRÜMPELL, L. (1877) *Die Natur und Enstehung der Träume,* Leipzig. (41, 49, 52, 54–5, 62–3, 67, 71–2, 76–9, 83, 86–7, 89–91, 110, 215, 255–6, 260, 268, 497)

STUMPF, E. J. G. (1899) *Der Traum und seine Deutung,* Leipzig. (132, *n.* 1)

SULLY, J. (1893) 'The Dream as a Revelation', *Fortnightly Rev.,* **53,** 354. (93, 168, *n.* 2, 540, 630)

SWOBODA, H. (1904) *Die Perioden des Menschlichen Organis-mus,* Vienna. (126, 199, 419)

TANNERY, M. P. (1898) 'Sur la mémoire dans le rêve', *Rev. phil.,* **45,** 637. (551 *n.*)

TAUSK, V. (1913) 'Zur Psychologie der Kindersexualitäf, *Int. Z. Psychoanal.*, **1**, 444. (164 *n.*, 339]

(1914) 'Kleider und Farben im Dienste der Traumdarstel-lung', *Int. Z. Psychoanal.*, **2**, 464. (446)

TFINKDJI, J. (1913) 'Essai sur les songes et l'art de les interpréter (onirocritie) en Mésopotomie', *Anthropos*, **8**, 505. (38, *n.* 2, 139, *n.* 2)

THOMAYER, S. and SIMERKA (1897) 'Sur la signification de quelques rêves', *Rev. neurol.*, **5**, 98. (121)

TISSIÉ, P. (1898) *Les rêves, physiologie et pathologie*, Paris. (1st ed., 1870.) (68, 69–70, 7–5, 78, 120–1, 167)

TOBOWOLSKA, J. (1900) *Etude sur les illusions de temps dans les rêves du sommeil normal*, (Thesis) Paris. (97, *n.* 1, 536, 540–1)

See also Bernard-Leroy and Tobowolska.

VARENDONCK, J. (1912) The Psychology of Day-Dreams, London. (529, *n.* 3)

VASCHIDE, N. (1911) *Le sommeil et les rêves*, Paris. (45 *n.*, 47, 94, 611)

VESPA, B. (1897) 'Il sonno e i sogni nei neuro-e psicopatici', *Boll. Soc. Lancisiana Osp.*, **17**, 193. (120, *n.* 1)

VOLD, J. MOURLY (1896) 'Expériences sur les rêves et en particulier sur ceux d'origine musculaire et optique' (review), *Rev. phil.*, **42**, 542. (72)

(1910–12) *Vber den Traum* (2 vols.) (*German transl*, by O. Klemm), Leipzig. (73 *n.*, 256, *n.* 2, 430)

VOLKELT, J. (1875) *Die traum-Phantasie*, Stuttgart. (50, 70, 74, 88, 91–2, 98, 103, 115–18, 168, 258–60, 381)

WEED, S. See Hallam and Weed.

WEYGANDT, W. (1893) *Entstehung der Träume*, Leipzig. (42, 59, 69, 75, 91, 157 *n.*)

WHITON CALKINS. See CALKINS, WHITON.

WIGGAM, A. (1909) 'A Contribution to the Data of Dream Psychology', *Ped. Sem. J. Genet. Psychol.*, **16**, 250. (164 *n.*)

WINTERSTEIN, A. VON (1912) 'Zwei Belege fur die Wunscher-füllung im Traume', *Zbl. Psychoanal.*, **2**, 292. (42)

WITTELS, F. (1924) *Sigmund Freud: der Mann, die Lehre, die Schule*, Vienna. (247, *n.* 3, 458 *n.*)

[*Trans.: Sigmund Freud: his Personality, his Teaching and his School*, by Eden and Cedar Paul, London, 1924.]

(1931) *Freud and his Time* (trans, by Louise Brink), New York. (477 *n.*)

WUNDT, W. (1874) *Grundzüge der physiologischen Psychologie*, Leipzig. (62, 64, 74–5, 90–1, 122, 256–7, 268)

ZELLER, A. (1818) 'Irre', *Ersch and Gruber: Allgemeine Encyclopedie der Wissenschaften*, **24**, 120. (102)}

B

LIST OF OTHER WORKS ON DREAMS PUBLISHED BEFORE THE YEAR 1900

[*These are works included in Freud's Bibliographies but not referred to in the text.*]

AHMAD IBN SIRIN, *Achmetis f. Seirim Oneirocriticae,* ed. N. Rigaltius, Paris, 1603.

*ALBERTI, MICHAEL (1744) *Diss. de insomniorum influxi in sanitatem et morbos.* Resp. Titius Halae M

ALIX (1883) 'Les rêves', *Rev. Sci. Industr.* 3rd series, **6**, 554.

*ANON (1890) 'Rêves et l'hypnotisme', *Le Monde,* Aug. 25.

*(1890) 'Science of Dreams', *The Lyceum,* p. 28, Dublin.

(1893) 'The Utility of Dreams', J. *Comp. Neurol,* **3**, 17, Granville.

BACCI, DOMENICO (1857) *Sui sogni e sul sonnambulismo, pensiero fisiologico-metafisici,* Venice.

BALL, B. (1885) *La morphinomanie, les rêves prolongés,* Paris.

BENEZÉ, EMIL (1897) 'Das Traummotiv in der mittelhoch-deutschen Dichtung bis 1250 und in alten deutschen Volksliedern', Benezé: *Sageng. und lit.-hist. Unters,* 1, *Das Traummotiv,* Halle.

*BENINI, V. (1898) 'Nel moneto dei sogni', *Il Pensiero nuovo,* Apr.

*BIRKMAIER, HIERON (1715) *Licht im Finsterniss der nächt-lichen Gesichte und Träume,* Nuremberg.

BISLAND, E. (1896) 'Dreams and their Mysteries', *N. Am. Rev.* **162**, 716.

BRADLEY, F. H. (1894) 'On the Failure of Movement in Dream', *Mind,* (new series), **3**, 373, London.

BRANDER, R. (1884) *Der Schlaf und das Traumleben,* Leipzig.

Bremer, L. (1893) 'Traum und Krankheit', *New York med. Monatschr.,* **5**, 281.

*BUSSOLA, SERAFINO (1834) *De somnüs,* (Thesis) Ticini Reg.

*CAETANI-LOVATELLI (1889) 'I sogni e l'ipnotismo nel mondo antico', *Nuova AnloL,* Dec. 1.

CANE, FRANCES E. (1889) 'The Physiology of Dreams', *The Lancet,* **67 II**, 1330 (Dec. 28)

CARDANO, GIROLAMO (1562) *Somiorum synesiorum, omnis generis insomnia explicantes libri IV,* Bale. (2nd ed. in *Opera omnia Cardani,* **5**, 593, Lyons, 1663.)

CARIERO, ALESSANDRO (1575) *De somnüs deque divinatione per somnia*, Padua.

CARPENTER (1849–52) 'Dreaming' (under 'Sleep'), *Cyclop, of Anat. and Physiol.*, **4,** 687, London.

CLAVIÈRE (1897) La rapidité de la pensée dans le rêve, Rev. *phil.*, **43,** 507.

COUTTS, G. A. (1896) 'Night-terrors', *Amer. J. med. Sc.* D. L. (1895) 'A propos de l'appréciation du temps dans le rêve, *Rev. phil.*, **40,** 69.

DAGONET, H. (1889) 'Du rêve et du délire alcoolique', *Ann. méd.-psychol.*, Series 7, **10,** 193.

DANDOLO, G. (1889) *La conscienza nel sogno*, Padua.

DECHAMBRE, A. (1880) 'Cauchemar', *Dict, encycl. sc. méd.*, **2,** 48.

*DIETRICH, J. D. (1726) *An ea, quae hominibus in somno et somnio accidunt, üsdem possint imputari?* resp. Gava, Wittemberg.

*DOCHMASA, A. M. (1890) *Dreams and their Significance as Forebodings of Disease*, Kazan.

DREHER, E. (1890) 'Sinneswahrnehmung und Traumbild', *Reichs-med. Anzeiger*, **15,** Nos. 20, 21, 22, 23, 24; **16,** Nos. 3, 8, Leipzig.

DUCOSTÉ, M. (1899) 'Les songes d'attaques des épileptiques', *Journ. Méd. Bordeaux*, Nov. 26 and Dec. 3.

*DU PREL, C. (1869) 'Oneirokritikon: der Traum vom Stand-punkte des transcend. Idealismus', *Deutsche Vierteljahr-schrift*, **2,** Stuttgart.

   (1880) Psychologie der Lyrik, Leipzig.

   *(1889) 'Künstliche Träume', Sphinx, July.

EGGER, V. (1888) 'Le sommeil et la certitude, le sommeil et la mémoire', *Critique philos.*, **1,** 341, Paris.

ELUS, HAVELOCK (1895) 'On Dreaming of the Dead', *Psychol. Rev.* **2,** 458.

   (1897) 'A Note on hypnagogic Paramnesia', *Mind*, **6,** 283.

ERDMANN, J. E. (1855) 'Das Träumen', *Ernste Spiele*, Chap. 12, Berlin.

ERK, VINZ. VON (1874) *Über den Unterschied von Traum und Wachen*, Prague.

*ESCANDE DE MESSIÈRES (1895) 'Les rêves chez les hystériques', (Thesis) Bordeaux.

FAURE (1876) 'Études sur les rêves morbides. Rêves persistants', *Arch, génér. Méd.*, 6th ser., **27,** 550.

*ENIZIA (1896) 'L'azione suggestiva delie cause esterne nei sogni', *Arch, per l'Antrop.*, **26.**

*FÉRÉ, C. (1897) 'Les rêves d'accès chez les épileptiques', *Méd. mod.* Dec. 8.

*FISCHER, JOH. (1899) *Ad artis veterum onirocriticae historiam symbole*, (Thesis) Jena.

*FLORENTIN, V. (1899) 'Das Traumleben: Plauderei', *Die alte und die neue Welt*, **33,** 725.

FORNASCHON, H. (1897) 'Die Geschichte eines Traumes als Beitrag der Transcendentalpsychologie', *Psychische Studien*, **24**, 274.

FRENSBERG. (1885) 'Schlaf und Traum', *Sammlung gemein-verst. wiss. Vortr.*, Virchow-Holtzendorf, Ser. 20, 466.

FRERICHS, J. H. (1866) *Der Mensch: Traum, Herz, Verstand*, Norden.

GALEN. *De praecognitione, ad Epigenem*, Lyons, 1540.

*GIRGENSOHN, L. (1845) *Der Traum: psychol.-physiol. Versuch.*

*GLEICHEN-RUSSWURM, A. VON (1899) 'Traum in der Dich-tung', *Nat. Z.*, Nos. 553–559.

*GLEY, E. (1898) 'Appréciation du temps pendant le sommeil', *L'intermédiaire des Biologistes*, **10**, 228.

GORTON, D. A. (1896) 'Psychology of the Unconscious', *Amer. Med. Times*, **24**, 33, 37.

GOULD, G. M. (1889) 'Dreams, Sleep, and Consciousness', *The Open Court* (Chicago), **2**, 1433–6 and 1444–7.

*GRABENER, G. C. (1710) *Ex antiquitate judaica de menûdim bachalôm siv excommunicatis per insomnia exerc. resp. Klebius*, Wittemberg.

GRAFFUNDER, P. C. (1894) 'Traum und Traumdeutung,' *Samml. gemeinv. wiss. Vorträge*, **197**.

GREENWOOD, F. (1894) *Imaginations in Dreams and their Study*, London.

*GROT, N. (1878) *Dreams, a Subject of Scientific Analysis* (in Russian), Kiev.

GUARDIA, J. M. (1892) 'La personnalité dans les rêves', *Rev. Phil*, **34**, 225.

GUTFELDT, I. (1899) 'Ein Traum', *Psychol. Studien*, **26**, 491.

*HAMPE, T. (1896) 'Uber Hans Sachsen Traumgedichte', *Z. deutsch. Unterricht*, **10**, 616.

HEERWAGEN (1889) 'Statist Untersuch. über Träumme u. Schlaf', *Philos. Stud.*, **5**, 301.

HILLER, G. (1899) 'Traum, Ein Kapitel zu den zwölf Nächten', *Leipz. Tagbl. und Anz.*, No. 657, Suppl. 1.

HTTSCHMANN, F. (1894) 'Über das Traumleben der Blinden*, *Z. PsychoL*, **7**, 387.

JASTROW, J. (1888) 'The Dreams of the Blind', New *Princeton* Rev., **5**, 18.

JENSEN, J. (1871) 'Träumen und Denken', *Samml. gemeinv. wiss. Vortr.*, Virchow-Holtzendorff, Ser. 6, 134.

KINGSFORD, A. (1888) *Dreams and Dream-Stories*, (ed. E. Maitland), London. (2nd ed.)

KLOEPFEL, F. (1899) 'Träumerei and Traum: Allerlei aus unserem Traumleben', *Universum*, **15**, 2469 and 2607.

*KRAMAR, OLDRICH (1882) *O spànku a snu*, *Prager Akad. Gymn.*

KRASNICKI, E. VON (1897) 'Karls IV Wahrtraum', *Psych Stud.*, **24**, 697.

KUCERA, E. (1895) 'Aus dem Traumleben', *Mähr-Weisskirchen, Gymn.*

LAISTNER, L. (1889) *Das Rätsel der Sphinx*, (2 vols.), Berlin.

*LANDAU, M. (1892) 'Aus dem Traumleben', *Münchner Neueste Nachrichten*, Jan. 9.

LAUPTS. (1895) 'Le fonctionnement cérébral pendant le rêve et pendant le sommeil hypnotique', *Ann. méd.-psychol.*, Ser. 8, 2, 354.

*LEIDESDORF, M. (1880) 'Das Traumleben', *Sammlung der 'Aima Mater'*, Vienna.

*LERCH, M. F. (1883–84) 'Das Traumleben und sein Bedeu-tung', *Gymn. Progr.*, Komotau.

*LIBERALI, FRANCESCO (1834) *Dei sogni*, (Thesis) Padua.

LIÉBEAULT, A. (1893) 'A travers les états passifs, le sommeil et les rêves', *Rev. hypnot.*, **8,** 41, 65, 106.

LUKSCH, L. (1894) *Wunderbare Traumerfüllung als Inhalt des wirklichen Lebens*, Leipzig.

MACARIO, M. M. A. (1846) 'Des rêves, considérés sous le rapport physiologique et pathologique', Pt. I, *Ann. méd-psychol.*, **8,** 170.

(1889) 'Des rêves morbides', *Gaz. méd. de Paris*, **8,** 1, 85, 97, 109, 121.

MACFARLANE, A. W. (1890) 'Dreaming', *Edinb. med. J.*, **36,** 499.

MAINE DE BIRAN, M. F. P. (1792) 'Nouvelles Considérations sur le sommeil, les songes, et le sonnambulisme', *Œuvres Philosophiques*, 209 (Ed. V. Cousin), Paris, 1841.

MAURY, L. F. A. (1857) 'De certains faits observés dans les rêves', *Ann. méd.-psychol.*, Ser. 3, **3,** 157.

*MEISEL (pseud.) (1783) *Natürlich-göitliche und teuflische Träume*, Seighartstein.

MELINAND, M. C. (1898) 'Dream and Reality," *Pop. Sc. Mo.*, **54, 96.**

MELZENTIN, C. (1899) 'Über wissenschaftliche Traumdeu-tung', *Gegenwart*, **50,** Leipzig.

MENTZ, R. (1888) *Die Träume in den altfranzösischen Karls-und Artusepen*, Marburg.

MONROE, W. S. (1899) 'A study of taste-dreams', *Am. I. Psychol.*, **10,** 326.

MOREAU DE LA SARTHE, J. L. (1820) 'Rêve', *Dict. sc. méd.*, **48,** 245.

MOTET (1829–36) 'Cauchemar', *Dict, méd, chir. pratiques*, Paris.

MURRAY, J. C. (1894) 'Do we ever dream of tasting?' *Proc. Am. psychol. Ass.*, 20.

*NAGELE, A. (1889) 'Der Traum in der epischen Dichtung', *Programm der Realschule*, Marburg.

NEWBOLD, W. R. (1896) 'Sub-conscious Reasoning', *Proc. Soc. psychic. Res.*, **12,** 11, London.

PASSAVANTI, J. (1891) *Libro dei sogni*, Rome.

PAULHAN, F. (1894) 'A propos de l'activité de l'esprit dans le rêve', *Rev. phil,* **38,** 546.

PICK, A. (1896) 'Über pathologische Träumerei und ihre Bezie-hungen zur Hysterie', *Jb. Psychiat.,* **14,** 280.

*RAMM, K. (1889) *Diss. pertractans somnia,* Vienna.

*RÉGIS, E. (1890) 'Les rêves Bordeaux', *La Gironde* (Variétés), May 31.

RICHARD, JEROME (1766) *La théorie des songes,* Paris.

RICHARDSON, B. W. (1892) 'The Physiology of Dreams', *Asclep.,* **9,** 129.

RICHIER, E. (1816) *Onéirologie ou dissertation sur les songes, considérés dans l'état de maladie,* (Thesis) Paris.

*RICHTER, J. P. (Jean Paul) (1813) 'Blicke in die Traum-welf, *Museum,* **2,** (also in *Werke,* ed. Hempel, **44,** 128.)

*'ÜBER WAHL-UND HALBTRÄUME', *Werke,* **44,** 142.

(1826–33) *Wahrheit aus Jean Pauls Leben.*

ROBINSON, L. (1893) 'What Dreams are made of, *N. Am. Rev.,* **157,** 687.

ROUSSET, C. (1876) *Contribution à l'étude du cauchemar,* (Thesis) Paris.

ROUX, J. (1898) 'Le rêve et les délires onitiques', *Province méd. Lyons,* **12,** 212.

*RYFF, W. H. (1554) *Traumbüchlein,* Strassburg.

*SANTEL, A. (1874) 'Poskus raz kladbe nekterih pomentjivih prokazni spanja in sanj', *Progr. Gymn.,* Görz.

SARLO, F. DE (1887) *I sogni. Saggio psicologico,* Naples.

SCH. FR. (1897) 'Etwas über Träume', *Psych. Studien,* **24,** 686.

SCHLEICH, K. L. (1899) 'Schlaf und Traum', *Zukunjt,* **29,** 14, 54.

SCHWARTZKOPFF, P. (1887) *Das Leben im Traum: eine Studie,* Leipzig.

STEVENSON, R. L. (1892) 'A Chapter on Dreams', *Across the Plain.*

STRYK, M. VON (1899) 'Der Traum und die Wirklichkeit', (after C. Méli-nand), *Baltische Mschr.,* 189, Riga.

SULLY, J. (1881) *Illusions, a Psychological Study,* London.

(1882) 'Etudes sur les rêves', *Rev. scientif.,* Ser. 3, **3,** 385.

(1892) *The Human Mind,* (2 vols.), London.

(1875–89) 'Dreams', *Enc. Brit.,* 9th ed.

SUMMERS, T. O. (1895) 'The Physiology of Dreaming', *St. Louis Clin.,* **8,** 401.

SURBLED, G. (1895) 'Origine des rêves', *Rev. quest, scient.* (1898) *Le rêve,* Paris.

SYNESIUS OF SYRENE *Liber de insomnüs.*

[*German trans.: Oneiromantik* by Krauss, Vienna, 1888.]

TANNERY, M. P. (1894) "Sur l'activité de l'esprit dans le rêve', *Rev. phil.,* **38,** 630.

(1898) 'Sur la paramnésie dans les rêves', *Rev. phil.,* **46,** 420.

652   BIBLIOGRAPHY

THIÉRY, A. (1896) 'Aristote et la psychologie physiologique du rêve', *Rev. neo-scol.*, **3**, 260.

*THOMAYER, S. (1887) 'Contributions to the Pathology of Dreams' (in Czech), *Policlinic of the Czech University,* Prague.

TISSIÉ, P. (1896) 'Les rêves; rêves pathogènes et thérapeutiques; rêves photographiés', *Journ. méd. Bordeaux,* **36**, 293, 308, 320.

TITCHENER, E. B. (1895) 'Taste Dreams', *Am. J. Psychol.,* **6**, 505.

TONNINI, S. (1887) 'Suggestione e sogni', *Arch, psichiatr. antrop. crim.,* **8**, 264

*TONSOR, J. H. (1627) *Disp. de vigilia, somno et somniis, prop.* Lucas, Marburg.

TUKE, D. H. (1892) 'Dreaming', *Dict, of Psychol. Med.* (ed. Tuke), London.

ULLRICH, M. W. (1896) *Der Schlaf und das Traumleben, Geisteskraft und Geistesschwäche,* (3rd ed.), Berlin.

UNGER, F. (1898) *'Die Magie des Traumes als Unsterblich-keitsbeweis. Nebst e. Vorwort: Okkultismus und Sozial-ismus von C. du Prel,* (2nd ed.), Münster.

VIGNOLI, T. (1879) *Mito e scienza: Saggio,* Milan.

[*Trans.: Myth and Science: An Essay,* London, 1882 (Chap. VIII).]

*VISCHER, F. T. (1876) 'Studien über den Traum', *Beilage allg. Z.,* 105.

VOLD, J. MOURLY (1897) 'Einige Expérimente über Gesichts-bilder im Traume', *Report of 3rd. Psych. Congr.,* Munich, and *Z. Psychol. Physiol. Sinnerorgane,* **13**, 66.

*VYKOUKAL, F. V. (1898) *On Dreams and Dream-interpretations,* (in Czech) Prague.

WEDEL, R. (1899) 'Untersuchungen auslandischer Gelehrter über gew. Traumphanomene', *Beitr. zur Grenzwissenschaft,* p. 24.

*WEHR, H. (1887) 'Das Unbewusste im menschlichen Denken', *Programm der Oberrealschule,* Klagenfurt.

WEILL, A. (1872) *Qu'est-ce que le rêve?* Paris.

*WENDT, K. (1858) *Kriemhilds Traum,* (Thesis) Rostock.

WILKS, S. (1893–94) 'On the Nature of Dreams', *Med. Mag.,* **2**, 597, London.

WILLIAMS, H. S. (1891–92) 'The Dream State and its Psychic Correlatives, *Amer. J. Insanity,* **48**, 445.

WOODWORTH, R. S. (1897) 'Note on the Rapidity of Dreams', *Psychol. Rev.,* **4**, 524.

*(1886) 'Ce qu'on peut rêver en cinq secondes', *Rev. sc,* 3rd. ser., **11**, 572.

ZUCCARELLI (1894–95) 'Polluzioni notturne ed epilepsia', *L'anomalo,* **1, 2, 3**.

INDEX OF DREAMS

A

FREUD'S OWN DREAMS

B

OTHER PEOPLE'S DREAMS

GENERAL INDEX